THE
MEDIATOR

THE
MEDIATOR

A STUDY OF THE CENTRAL DOCTRINE
OF THE CHRISTIAN FAITH

EMIL BRUNNER

Professor of Theology in Zürich

TRANSLATED BY OLIVE WYON

*"Jesus Christ, in His infinite love, has
become what we are, in order that He
may make us entirely what He is."*
IRENAEUS
*"Nostra assumsit, ut conferret nobis
sua."*
LUTHER

Philadelphia
THE WESTMINSTER PRESS

PRINTED IN THE UNITED STATES OF AMERICA

In Memory
of My Godfather
FRIEDRICH ZÜNDEL
(1827–1891)

CONTENTS

BOOK ONE
PRELIMINARY CONSIDERATIONS

BOOK TWO
THE PERSON OF THE MEDIATOR

BOOK THREE

THE WORK OF THE MEDIATOR

SECTION 1—THE REVELATION

SECTION 2—RECONCILIATION

SECTION 3—THE DOMINION OF GOD

FOREWORD

TWENTY-FIVE years ago Dr. P. T. Forsyth, in the preface to his greatest book, *The Person and Place of Jesus Christ*, called attention to the loss involved in the almost uniform character of the theological works that were translated into English. These, he pointed out, were rarely the work of scholars who, while recognizing the rights of criticism, yet preserved the positive Gospel. The situation has changed in many ways since 1909. The older theological Liberalism has largely passed away; the most arresting and influential doctrinal movement in Continental Protestantism is that which takes its name from Karl Barth; and British students of theology are no longer likely to imagine that every theologian of the first rank in Europe outside the Roman Catholic Church will most probably have given up the doctrines of the Trinity, the Incarnation, and the Atonement. Any such idea will seem truly extravagant to a reader of the English translation of Dr. Emil Brunner's book, *Der Mittler*. For the sureness of its grasp and the lucidity and adequacy of its exposition of the Gospel of our Lord's Person and Work there will be deep gratitude among all those who see no future for any Christianity except that which rests upon faith in Jesus Christ as the true and only Son of God, incarnate and atoning. I am the more glad to pay this tribute to Professor Brunner's book, since there are certain points of importance in it, especially in respect of some of its negative judgments, where I cannot follow him. But such disagreement is in no way incompatible with a profound sense of the debt that all who revere the great names "Evangelical" and "Catholic" owe to Dr. Brunner. For the Christ of whom he writes is the Christ of the apostolic Gospel and of the historic Faith.

J. K. MOZLEY

FOREWORD

IT is well that Professor Emil Brunner's great book on the Person of Christ has now been rendered into English. The service it has already done to theology and to the Church will thus, one may hope, be widely extended. While differing from his views at certain important points, I should find it hard to name any recent major work in its field which is comparable with *The Mediator* in direct relevance and power. Emphatically it is a book for the times. Alike for critical acumen and for reverent believing insight into the being and work of our Lord, as the Person in whom God is revealed, finally and decisively, it stands out conspicuously. The reader comes to feel that the Bible is behind this man's argument.

Besides, the book is intensely interesting. Even those—and they will no doubt be many—who disagree with some of its main conclusions will find it hard to lay it down. They will be laid hold of by its manifest knowledge, sincerity, and glowing faith. The fact that Professor Brunner has for a number of years been a close but wholly independent theological associate of Professor Karl Barth will not, we may be sure, lessen the importance of his work in the eyes of all who wish to keep in touch with the most living theological movement of our time.

H. R. MACKINTOSH

NEW COLLEGE, EDINBURGH

TRANSLATOR'S NOTE

THE first edition of *Der Mittler* appeared in 1927; the second edition (unaltered) was published in 1932. The present translation has been made from the text of the second edition. The author has read the typescript and has made several valuable criticisms. In a few instances, at his suggestion, some slight alterations and corrections have been introduced into the text. The note on page 276 has been abbreviated.

Words which have become technical terms in the theology of Barth and Brunner can usually be understood from their context. The word "existential" (*existenziell*), however, which occurs frequently in the present work, is an exception. The term has been coined recently to describe a mode of thought which appeals not merely to the intellect but to the whole personality of the man who accepts it. "Existential thinking" means thinking in a way which involves one's whole life. It means the attitude of one who is at every moment involved in the question at issue, that is, of one who is no mere spectator. "Existentiality" is the very opposite of all that is academic, abstract, or theoretical. We think "existentially" when we are conscious that for us matters of life and death are at stake.

In conclusion, the translator desires to express her gratitude to several friends who have rendered invaluable assistance in this work. She would offer her cordial thanks to Mrs. Margrieta Beer, M.A., Edwyn Bevan, Esq., D.Litt., LL.D.; and also to Professor H. R. Mackintosh, M.A., D.D., Ph.D., for his detailed care in reading the proofs, and for much generous help and criticism. The translator would also express her special thanks to Dr. Brunner himself for the courtesy and promptness with which he has answered the various questions sent to him in the course of this work. A final word of thanks is due to the clerical staff of the Lutterworth Press.

OLIVE WYON

"GOD alone matters": this is the one question which concerns humanity supremely. For it is this which gives meaning and significance to all other questions. For every human being, yesterday, to-day and for ever, this is the decisive question. It is of course true that if "religion" means the desire for God, and the feeling for and "awareness" of something divine and Eternal, then, in spite of much that seems superficial in the modern world, there is more religion to-day than there has been at other periods of world history. But the thing that matters supremely is not whether man is "aware" of, or has a "feeling" for "something divine," but whether he knows God as the One who challenges him to decision. The question of God—in the form of decision—is the question of Christ. Religion, and an incipient "awareness" of the Divine, exists indeed in every part of the world, but there is only one "place" at which God challenges man to decision, because He Himself confronts man: Jesus Christ.

Possibly to-day few are willing to listen to this truth; perhaps, however, there are more than we in our desponding moods are inclined to believe. But it may be that the majority have never yet heard of *this* Christ at all. In any case, one who knows this truth has no right to hold his peace because he feels unworthy to speak.

It is the one task of the Church to proclaim this Name aloud to the world. The Church exists, through Christ, for this end. Whenever she forgets this, and forgets it to such an extent that instead of summoning men to decision (through this Name) she simply argues about Him, then she has ceased to be the Church; she has become like salt which has lost its savour and is only fit to be thrown away and trodden under foot of men. It is of course possible for a Church in this con-dition to accomplish an amazing amount of activity; but it *achieves* nothing; nothing *happens*. The Church is the salt of the earth wherever, and to the extent in which, she really knows this Name and makes it known to the world. Without this Name, inevitably the world will rot, and no social reform, no

Church activity, however well-intentioned, can arrest the process of disintegration. There is only *one* element which can unconditionally oppose and arrest this process of corruption and preserve the Church from it: the divine seriousness of faith in Christ.

It is one thing to proclaim Christ to the world as this decisive factor; it is quite another thing to remind the Church of the paramount importance of this duty and to urge her to fulfil it. Whatever else may be the task of theology, this is certainly its primary duty. Hence, in spite of a sense of inadequacy, it is this which I am trying to express in the present work. I would have had no right to venture on this task were it not a mere restatement of old and well-known truth. I have nothing new to say; on the contrary, my main concern is to make clear that what is said here has been the faith of the Christian Church from the very earliest days. But I would not have had the courage to undertake this work did I not clearly perceive that this reminder is urgently necessary. Not only among the rank and file of the Christian Church, but also among the ecclesiastical leaders, this ancient and familiar truth is in danger either of sinking into oblivion, or of being weakened to such an extent that it is impossible to distinguish it from something different and wholly impotent. The fundamental reason for the impotence of the Church is her ignorance of the power of Christ. For she possesses and needs no other power than this knowledge. But the intellectual reminder, theological reflection on what the Gospel means and what it does *not* mean, is not itself this power. It is just as dangerous to underestimate the importance of this reminder as it is to attach to it extravagant expectations. The present work is predominantly intellectual; it is not intended to produce faith, but to make faith conscious, and to help it to steer clear of error. The work of theology is like that of those whose business it is to test food-values. It is the duty of the theologian to examine the spiritual "food-values" of the faith which the Church offers to the world in her proclamation of the truth—to distinguish the true from the false. The theologian is unable to do this if he does not know the taste of the genuine spiritual food; theology without faith is impossible. But the function of theology is to criticize and eliminate; it is not positively creative. It therefore requires a mass of intellectual activity which, when its subject matter is taken into account, may often seem like the profanation of a holy thing. Yet the reproach of profanation should be levelled not at the theologians but at those who make this work necessary, because they confuse the language of faith; those who—more or less deliberately—offer other "substances" in the guise of scriptural truth. Theological critical work is therefore not intended for edification, but, if it is done in the right way, it is most necessary and valuable. The Church needs to use theology as a check, in order to protect herself against "food-poisoning," and against the acceptance of worthless and deceptive "food substitutes." Theology cannot herself create the Divine Food of Life, but she can render yeoman service to the Church, and to the cause of God on earth, by exposing the poverty-stricken condition of Christendom.

The whole purpose of a reminder is to render itself superfluous. It is my sincere desire that as soon as possible this book will no longer be necessary; indeed, that people will hardly be able to understand why it was necessary to take so much trouble to say what every Christian knows; that the Church, as she proclaims the Name of Christ to the world, will do so with such mighty fervour, clarity, and conviction that she will convince the world. This clear reverberating sound, as of a trumpet call, does not echo through this book, but this should not be expected in a work of this character. For it is not itself a proclamation of the truth; it simply deals intellectually with the question of the content of the true message. This book does not set out to be "prophetic." I would feel amply rewarded if it could be said that this is an honest theological book. This is, however, almost more than I dare to expect. For though there may be many honest books to-day, written by those who bear the name of theologians, can it be said that their works are really theological books?

Nor does this book claim to be a "doctrine of Christ." In my opinion, the time is not yet ripe for this; in any case, I am not equal to such a task. I do not venture to offer more than an introduction to the subject. My friend Barth was certainly right when in his criticism of my book on Schleier-macher he reminded me that it is easier to see the mistakes of others than it is to lead forward oneself along the right path. And yet I believe that destructive work is not unnecessary, all the more because it would itself be impossible without at least some—however inadequate—knowledge of the new truth. So far as that particular book is concerned I retract none of my criticism of modern theology, although I admit that I regret a certain asperity of tone which often arises when a conviction is being gradually formed. Meanwhile the opposition has become so much deeper that this external asperity falls away of itself. The present book has grown out of that conflict with modern theology, and still more out of reflection on the message of the Bible, which is just as much the life-work of the preacher as it is of the academic teacher of theology. This book has come into being at the same time as another,[1] which for external reasons was published first. The observation that "prolegomena"—with which the other work deals—cannot be rightly understood without at least some specimen of actual theological work, has induced me to bring out this second book on the heels of the first, although a delay of several years for further study and reflection would have been of great advantage to the present work.

This book is not intended to be a scholarly work in the actual sense of the word, and I would beg my readers to regard the few notes and quotations merely as elucidations and suggestions of the connection of the subject-matter of this book with the doctrines of the Early Church and of the Reformers; even in this sketchy form this work has grown much larger than I intended it to be. On the other hand, I hope that the intelligent reader will realize that what may strike him at first as constant repetition is the necessary spiral movement by which true theological work is carried out, since it has to show that there are not many "articles of faith," but only *one*.

In conclusion there remains only the pleasant duty of thanking my fellow workers, above all my honoured friend and colleague, Gottlob Schrenk, for the unselfish and obliging manner in which he has always placed at my disposal his

[1] *Religionsphilosophie* (Oldenbourg, Munich).

stores of knowledge and his valuable counsel; I would also express my gratitude to the faithful friends who once again have shared in the toilsome labour of correcting the proofs.

E. B.

ZÜRICH

PREFACE TO THE ENGLISH EDITION

POSITIVELY I have only one thing to add to the Preface to the German Edition which was written seven years ago: that to-day I am more convinced than ever that the world needs nothing so much as the message of the Christ, and that the Church needs nothing so urgently as meditation upon this message. This translation is based upon the unaltered text of the first German edition; hence it contains no allusions to publications which have appeared since 1927. My last word must be one of grateful thanks to the translator, Miss Olive Wyon, whose skill and devotion I sincerely admire.

E. B.

ZÜRICH

BOOK ONE
PRELIMINARY CONSIDERATIONS

CHAPTER I

THE DISTINCTION BETWEEN GENERAL AND SPECIAL REVELATION

THROUGH God alone can God be known. This is not a specifically Christian principle; on the contrary, it is the principle which is common to all religion and indeed, to the philosophy of religion as a whole. There is no religion which does not believe itself to be based upon divine revelation in one way or another. There is no religion worth the name which does not claim to be "revealed religion." Further, there is no speculative philosophy of religion which does not endeavour to base its statements about God and divine Truth upon a self-disclosure of the divine ground in the spirit of Man. The issue is clear: either religion is based upon Divine revelation, or it is simply the product of the phantasy of the mind which desires it. The statement: "Through God alone can God be known" might be made equally well by a Christian, a Neo-Platonist religious philosopher, a Parsee, or a Hindu. For many of our contemporaries this is sufficient reason to declare that the general principle of relativity applies also to the sphere of religion. I do not intend to enter into any discussion of this problem of apologetics; the question with which we are here concerned is a preliminary question, and indeed it is one which, if it were answered in a satisfactory way, might even make all apologetic superfluous. The preliminary question is this: wherever the appeal is made to revelation, is the word "revelation" used in the same sense?

This question at once makes us aware of a striking difference. All living popular religions[1] appeal to revelations; they feel it

---

[1] By living popular religions I mean those which may also be called historical religions, that is, all religions which are not essentially individualistic—like genuine mysticism and "spiritual religion" of a philosophical character—but which are essentially social. In them the one thing that matters is the cultus and the "myth"; the individual can only be religious at all in so far as he shares in the worship and life of the

essential to be able to produce a large number of revelations, theophanies and divine oracles, miraculous incidents of all kinds, in which the divine and personal character of the supersensible world manifests itself in this temporal world. The whole cultus with its conceptions and its ritual action, in fact, its life as a religion, is based upon manifestations of this kind. The religious man believes that the reality of the object of his faith is guaranteed by the concrete character of such revelations. Through them he "knows" that his god, or his gods, are beings which have a personal relation with him and with his world.

The philosophy of religion, religious speculation, and the mysticism which is connected with this school of thought, have a different conception of the nature of revelation. In their origin, indeed, they might actually be regarded as a conscious corrective to the "primitive," "falsely realistic," "revealed" character of the popular religions. To this type of thought "revelation" does not possess this solid character of historic fact which, in the majority of cases, is nothing more than an illusion based on an overstimulated imagination, due to lack of rational knowledge of the world and primitive psychology. In the "higher" relation to God of speculation and mysticism, in the "religion of educated people," revelation means rather the emergence of the eternal basis of all phenomena into consciousness, the perception of something which was always true, the growing consciousness of a Divine Presence, which might have been perceived before, since it was there all the time. Hence in this connection both revelation and religion are spoken of in the singular. Revelation as the objective element, and religion as the subjective element, are fundamentally everywhere one and the same; this is the "essence of religion," and its basis, even when it cannot be recognized as such by man owing to the hampering limitations of his sense-environment. Fundamentally, indeed, there is only one religion, and the differences between the various religions are due simply to the precise individual form of that which is ever

community; on the other hand, mysticism and philosophically speculative religion—the "religion of the educated man"—equally definitely flees from social religious life and seeks solitude.

the same, a non-essential modification of the "essence" of religion itself. Revelation of every kind means that the eternal Divine Presence behind all phenomena shines through the phenomena; religion means—however dimly and imperfectly— the realization of this divine reality. Religion, however, is not fully developed until it is freed from the trammels of these accidental elements, that is, from all that is historical and contingent. Thus the idea of revelation as "primitive" man conceives it, in the sense of a characteristic divine and objective event, a fact which has actually taken place in the world of time and space, has here become transformed into knowledge, vision, the sense of a Divine Being which, although in itself it is active and creative, is yet at the same time in absolute repose; the manifestation of this Being is not based upon any actual historical self-manifestation in particular, but simply upon the fact that certain hindrances within the individual have disappeared; hence this "revelation" is based upon a subjective process—like throwing back the shutters and opening he windows that the light of morning may stream into a darkened room—upon the unfolding of the soul to the Divine Light, upon the attainment of the right degree of "recollection," or "introversion," or "solitude," or "sinking into the Divine Ground," or some other expression which is characteristic of religion of this type.

Thus, while it belongs to the very essence of the living popular religions that they should be based upon "special revelations," it is of the very essence of religious speculation, religious idealism, and mysticism, to be independent of all special "external" revelations and, indeed, to regard them as merely subjectively determined forms of something different, namely, of the one fundamental revelation which is always and everywhere the same, a process freed from all the "accidents" of an historical process in time and space. The distinction is clear: on the one side are many revelations in the sense of actual incidents; on the other, a revelation which does not take place at all but simply "is"; on the one hand the idea of revelation is connected with definite events, on the other it means the consciousness of freedom from all that is actual in the sense of bondage to the world of time and space, from all

23

external, "sense-bound" events; on the one hand revelation is "special"; on the other it is "general."

The Christian religion[1] belongs neither to the first nor to the second group. It is opposed to both and yet connected with both. In common with the popular religions it points to an actual divine reality, which has been made known in a definite particular way through an act of revelation. It is based wholly upon something which has actually happened, within this world of time and space, and indeed, to put it still more plainly, it is based upon something which has taken place once for all. By its very nature it is absolutely opposed to that saying of Fichte's (which is an amazingly plain statement of the speculative and mystical idea of a divine "ground"): "It is the metaphysical element alone, and not the historical, which saves us." In the Christian religion "salvation" is always indissolubly connected with an historical fact: with the fact of the Incarnation of the Divine Word, with the fact of Atonement by Jesus Christ. Although the time and space element, that is, the element of historical contingency, does not, in itself,

---

[1] I am afraid lest the following observations may once more arouse the displeasure of Haitjema, who accuses me (in Karl Barth: *Kritische Theologie*, p. 109) "of beginning to operate with Faith, Revelation, the Word, as though they were impersonal entities," in the spirit of a mere spectator. I am fully sensible of the force of this accusation, for as soon as we use comparisons in speaking of the Christian religion it is impossible to avoid "operating" in a certain sense with "fixed" conceptions. This danger can be avoided, of course, by renouncing this work of comparison altogether. Until now this has been Barth's attitude—and with good reason—whereas I see clearly that this cannot be done if we wish to avoid the danger of gradually falling a prey to a kind of spiritual conservatism which may lead to obscurantism. Discussion with the thought of the day, with philosophy and religion is—it is true—certainly not the primary and most important task of theology; but we have no right, on that account, to neglect this duty altogether or to leave it to the next generation. Within this task, however—which Haitjema does not seem to understand at all— it is inevitable that we should employ certain fixed fundamental conceptions of Christianity. This does not mean that we regard the actual theological labour as already finished, but it does mean that this second duty cannot be discharged in any other way. From the second and third sections of this book, if not from the first part, it ought to become quite clear that I do not really regard those conceptions as "fixed," and that it is unjust to reproach me as a mere spectator.

constitute a revelation, yet the revelation upon which the Christian faith is based is founded upon this fact alone, and apart from it Christianity itself could not exist.

On the other hand, the Christian religion is equally opposed to all forms of popular religion, since it is not based upon a series of events, but upon one single event; moreover, it is fully conscious that this one fact of revelation, this event which took place once for all, is unique.[1] 'Εφ' ἅπαξ, once for all, this is the category to which the Christian revelation belongs. The Scriptures bear witness to this unique character of the Christian revelation—a revelation which can never be repeated. There is nothing accidental about the unique and unrepeatable character of revelation in the Christian religion; it is an integral element, or rather, it is not one element alone, but constitutes its very essence. The whole meaning of this revelation would be destroyed if it could be severed from this unique event which took place once for all. This means, however, that this idea of revelation, since it is of its very nature that it should be unique, is, essentially, entirely different from the conception of revelation in other forms of religion. The fact that this revelation[2] has taken place once for all does not constitute an arithmetical difference, but a positive difference, a difference in quality. In its essence a revelation which, by its very nature, can only take place once, differs absolutely from a revelation which, also by its very nature, can necessarily be repeated an indefinite number of times.

[1] *Einmaligkeit* (lit. *onceness*) is the word used by Brunner to express the exclusiveness of the Christian faith as a special revelation. "Uniqueness" is the nearest word in English, but it does not fully express the author's meaning. "*Einmaligkeit*" means occupying a *unique* moment in *time*. "Unrepeatableness" is the real meaning. This sense I have endeavoured to give in paraphrase form, since the word *Einmaligkeit* occurs frequently in this chapter, and at intervals throughout the book. Where a noun was necessary I have employed "uniqueness," usually suggesting that the real meaning is that of something which happened "once for all."—TR.

[2] The relation of this unique revelation to the wealth and variety of the revelations in Nature and in Holy Scripture will only become clear in the course of this whole inquiry. The Christian view of this relation is this: that that which took place once for all in Jesus Christ constitutes the truth of all other forms of revelation. The whole Bible witnesses to this Christ, and indeed this JESUS Christ, the Crucified and Risen One, to Whom the apostolic ἐφ' ἅπαξ was applied.

In order to see this more clearly let us return to the conception of "special revelations."

The fact that special revelations—as, for example, theophanies and incarnations—are said to have happened several times really means that nothing happened at all. The element which was repeated in each of these events was not final. A final event *can* only happen once. A final decision is made once, or it is not made at all. The serious nature of the decision can be gauged by the fact that inevitably the decisive event takes place once for all, and once only. A factor which recurs constantly belongs to the cyclic rhythm of Nature. Hence the mythological element—that is, the revelation which is frequently repeated—belongs to the realm of Nature. The essential rhythm of Nature is reflected in the recurrent type of revelation; the revelation-myth belongs to the sphere of natural religion. The myths of the Saviour-God who dies and then returns to life are typical of this kind of religion.

The distinction between the historical and the natural element lies in the fact that the historical event can only happen once; it cannot be repeated. But in history, as we know it, this absolute historical element does not exist; all that it possesses is the tendency towards that which cannot be repeated (*Einmaligkeit*). Just as Nature is not wholly without the tendency towards that which cannot be repeated, so also History contains some elements which recur. The distinction between History and Nature consists in the tendency to non-repetition. The distinction is, however, not absolute; therefore History has an aspect of natural law, and Nature has an historical aspect. If some historical event could be proved to have taken place once for all, it would be an absolutely decisive event. Such an event, however, cannot be discovered within history; for if such an event could be discovered, it would be the end of all history, the" fullness of time." It is precisely an event of this kind which the Christian religion regards as revelation. Revelation means the unique historical event which, *by its very nature*, must either take place once or not at all. And it is *only* revelation in this Christian sense which contains this element of absolute and never-recurring actuality. Here the word "uniqueness" (*Einmaligkeit*) has its full and absolute meaning; the relative element which is implied when we speak of something which only happened once has been eliminated. Hence by revelation we mean that historical event which is at the same time the end of history, that is, an event which, if it really did take place, by its very force shattered the framework of history; in other words, that in fulfilling the purpose of history it ends it. Here, however, we can only speak of a special revelation in the strict sense of the word. For where the opposite takes place, that is to say, where revelations are frequent, there can be no valid revelation in the ultimate sense of the word. In each of these revelations what was said to have happened did not take place; for if it had actually taken place it could not have happened repeatedly. This point of view is supported by the fact that these "revelations" on which certain religions are based are not actual events. They are not *Individual*[1] but *General*. They are myths which, in the strict sense of the word, can lay no serious claim to historicity. The mythical element eliminates historical reality from the actual event, and also prevents us from regarding the "revelation" as a serious decisive element; in both instances for the same reason.

Hence, in the last resort, the so-called "special" revelations of the various religions come to the same thing as the speculative assertions of the philosophy of religion and mysticism: namely, that revelation is merely an individual concrete instance of a general truth, or, in other words, the accidental incarnation of that Essence which reigns supreme beyond the confines of time and space, in the realm of eternal Being. The important

---

[1] If, however, in contradistinction to this, Buddha or Zoroaster were held up as examples of religious personalities who were themselves revealers, the answer might be made that whenever Buddha or Zoroaster is cited as a historical personality and, therefore, as strictly unique, in each instance he is not regarded as a revelation, but only as the bearer of a word of revelation, or even of a merely philosophical doctrine. There is no $\dot{\epsilon}\phi'\ddot{a}\pi a\xi$ either in Zoroastrianism or in Buddhism. On the other hand, in the history of universal religion, incarnations always occur more than once, and are thus essentially mythical, non-historical. We can state, therefore, with absolute certainty that only within the sphere of Christianity can historical criticism become a decisive problem for faith; this is the distinctive feature of the Christian belief in revelation which distinguishes it from all other religions.

distinction, therefore, is not that which exists between the Christian revelation and these mythological religions, with their recurring revelations, but the distinction between the Christian belief in the revelation which has taken place once for all, and this general kind of religion, with its conception of a general diffused type of revelation, and its non-historical outlook, since, in point of fact, the primitive type of religion tends either to be absorbed into this diffused type of religion, or into the Christian religion itself. More and more the distinction centres round one point, and the issue is clear: either the mystical, idealistic, ethical, general kind of religion (in all its various forms), which lays no claim to "revelation" in the concrete sense of the word, but which rejects such a conception of religion as "crude," "unspiritual," "sense-bound," "external," or the Christian belief in the unique revelation of Jesus Christ. Stated in this way, however, we can see that it is not correct to say that one claim to revelation is opposed to the other. A claim to revelation in the Christian, concrete, and at the same time absolutely serious sense is made only by the Christian religion. This may be regarded as settled without in the least anticipating any further conclusions. There is, however, a very sharp contrast between these two conceptions: the religion of general revelation, and the Christian belief in the unique and final revelation in the fact of Jesus Christ, a contrast which cannot be removed by any attempts at compromise. Attempts at reconciliation have been made, it is true; we shall be dealing with them in the next chapter; our first endeavour, however, must be to look steadily at the distinction itself, and then to keep it, as clearly as possible, before our minds

When the mystic, the idealist,[1] or the Neo-Platonist speaks of revelation he means that contact between the Divine and

[1] We use the word "Idealism" (and Idealist) always—save where a special modification of the term is clearly intended—in the sense of "religious Idealism," that is, in the sense of an independent interpretation of life and of God, and thus *not*—as for instance like Heinrich Barth—in the formal sense of philosophical reflection, which, in the perception of the crisis of reason, points to Revelation (in a Christian sense) and thus precisely does not construct a systematic independent structure of thought, but leaves it open.

the soul of man, that union between the infinite and the finite, between the Creator and the creature in the highest act of knowledge, in contemplation, intuition, in mystical experience, which by its very nature can take place anywhere and at any time; a "revelation" which, so far as it does take place, is independent of all the "accidents of history." But the "Aristotelian" also who finds proofs of the existence of God in Nature, the adherent of a religion based on ethics and on reason, who bases his faith upon the moral order of the world or upon the moral law—all these also, in spite of other forms of difference, unite with the mystic and the idealist in affirming Fichte's statement that "Man is saved by the metaphysical element alone, and not by the historical." All have this in common: they present a united front against the conception of a revelation which claims to be final and unique, and thus, since they also base their faith upon "revelation," they are one in the assertion that revelation is timeless and universal. It is of course true that the form of illumination or experience which they regard as a revelation of the Divine is not immediate, but that it is mediated to them through Nature and through history; nevertheless, so far as the content of the revelation is concerned, it is wholly detached from the time process; it is an act of direct contact with the Divine, with the eternal "ground of the soul." For a revelation of this kind all "mediation through history" is regarded merely as an accidental element, as the "vehicle" of the revelation, as a stimulus, or a symbol. It is like the scaffolding which can be removed as soon as the building itself has been completed. It is like the teacher whom everyone needs, but whose usefulness is over as soon as the required knowledge has been gained. Hence it may even be regarded as necessary from the psychological point of view— since apart from it an experience of this kind cannot be attained; but by its very nature this knowledge, and the revelation upon which it is based, can easily be detached from the historical element. For it is "the metaphysical element alone and not the historical which saves." To this category belong the contemplation of the Neo-Platonist, the knowledge of the "Ideas" of the idealist, the thought of the metaphysician who has arrived at the conclusion of his proofs for the existence of God, the moral postulate of the Kantian who grasps the Absolute in the moral imperative, as well as the faith of the simple adherent of the philosophy of the Enlightenment who bases his religion on "God in Nature and in the Moral Law"; moreover, to it also belong the vision and experience of the mystic who "released from images of every kind" sinks down into the depths of being, or the vision of the religious artist to whom the Infinite and the Eternal is revealed through his artistic inspiration, as, for instance, in the famous saying of Beethoven, "Music is a higher revelation than all wisdom and all philosophy." This is why I summarize all these varieties of religion under the concept of "universal religion": because the revelation upon which it is based is regarded as something universal in character, independent of the particular event, or a fact which has taken place once for all.

Christianity, and Christianity alone, is the absolute opposite of this form of religion. For the very existence of the Christian religion depends on vital connection with an "accidental" fact of history, with a real event in time and space, which, so it affirms, is the unique, final revelation, for time and for eternity, and for the whole world. In principle, therefore, its relation with God is not immediate but is mediated. Between the soul and God, between humanity and God, between the world and God, there stands a third element, or rather a third Person, who, although He unites man with God, yet equally maintains the absolute distinction between them; through Him alone that reconciliation takes place through which God reveals Himself: the Mediator. In the one form of religion it is claimed as fundamental that God reveals Himself directly to the human soul, in the other as fundamental that God reveals Himself through the Mediator. This is the fundamental distinction.

But this distinction is not simple. It is of course true that the "religion of universal revelation" excludes this faith. This, however, is not done explicitly and deliberately; rather in its own characteristic way, by its inclusiveness; that is, it regards the connection between the Christian faith and the Mediator—its insistence on the historical event which took place once for all in time—as a feature which, by its very nature, is merely a non-essential variety of the universal essence of religion or of revelation.[1] In the Christian religion, so it is said, the universal religion, the "essence of religion" is specialized in such a way that in it the historical phenomenon of Jesus plays a certain part. But however well disposed this religion without a Mediator may be towards this faith with a Mediator, and however ready it may be to join forces with it, the fact still remains that the Christian religion feels that it is bound to protest against this misinterpretation. For here it can see nothing but two opposing points of view. For it is evident that there can be no connection between these two assertions: everything depends upon the fact—and "at bottom" everything does *not* depend upon the fact—that religion has a Mediator or it has not. For each side—if they listen to each other properly —only one of these statements can be true.

This does not mean, however, that the Christian faith altogether denies this idea of "universal revelation." Over and over again a great deal of misunderstanding has arisen, even in the most recent theological discussion, through mistaking the first distinction for this second one.[2] Certainly the Christian faith stakes everything on the fact of the distinction between it, as the faith in that fact of revelation, in the Mediator, and the religion of idealism and of mysticism which, in principle,

[1] Recently this has come out most clearly in the religious philosophy of Scholz. His idea of religion is entirely mystical. But he also makes room for Christianity (always only in the form of Christ-*mysticism*, not of *faith* in Christ!) as a certain independent entity alongside of mysticism, which, however, he is only able to establish as a psychological variant. He says there are some people who feel a great need for authority and dependence,. and they need the mystical mediator, Christ.

[2] It is a striking fact, how many opponents of the so-called "Dialectical Theology" have facilitated their criticism by insinuating that we reject every form of general revelation in natural history and in the spirit of man. Thus they have not understood that the dialectic of faith in particular is based upon the fact that man bears within himself traces of the Divine Image, though they are disfigured, it is true; these traces witness to the fact that originally the Creation was good, and thus reveals God. The question is not *whether* there is any general revelation or not, for if there were none no one would search after God at all, but *in what sense*, whether it is direct or indirect, thus whether the Christian revelation constitutes the highest point in this general revelation or whether it is something quite different—namely—*the* actual revelation itself.

31

does not see any necessity for a Mediator at all. But this does not mean that it is unable to discern traces of truth in all forms of religion and traces of God in all existence and in all thought. In point of fact the Christian religion does admit this.

It is impossible to believe in a Christian way in the unique revelation, in the Mediator, without believing also in a universal revelation of God in creation, in history, and especially in the human conscience. But, on the other hand, a believer in the universal revelation who is a Christian and believes in the Mediator, can no longer be an idealist or a mystic. This twofold point of view is based on the fact that the Christian believer regards "general" revelation as an indirect (*gebrochen*) form of revelation. In so far as the idealist and the mystic are aware of its existence they have the truth. But in so far as they do not recognize that it is merely an indirect (*gebrochen*) revelation and think that in it they have an authentic knowledge of God they are not in the truth. The recognition of the indirect (*gebrochen*) general revelation is the presupposition of the Christian religion of revelation, with its unique character.

Therefore the question is not *whether* from the standpoint of faith in the Christian Mediator it is possible to recognize a general revelation in nature, history, and in the soul of man, but *how*, that is, what revelation may here be taken to mean, and what it is not. From the outset, however, it ought to be quite evident that on this point there can be no question of a supplementary revelation. The relation between general and special revelation can never be complementary: as, for instance, that of a "basic revelation" or a "revelation of truth" (Tillich) as the foundation, and above that, like the second story in a building, the "revelation of salvation." This certainly very closely resembles an existing definition of the relation between general and special revelation: that of the Catholic Church. The *Lex naturae*, natural life, natural ordinances, natural knowledge, natural theology, as the foundation; then, over-arching the whole, the Kingdom of Grace, the Church, with its "revealed" truth. This graded scheme of a special revelation erected on a basis of general revelation destroys the significance of the fact of Christ and distorts the image of the "natural man." If it is true that the decisive fact lies there, then it can be there and there only, and it cannot be divided into two stages. This division is, however, of the very essence of the Catholic conception, in which the structure of the Church is based upon the natural life of man, whereas theology is built up on the natural (metaphysical) knowledge of God; the good in man is completed by grace, and God and Man co-operate in the work of redemption.

If it is an actual fact that this event is unique, then its relation to a natural or general revelation can only be partial. Neither an absolute denial nor an absolute affirmation, but both at the same time, the Christian conception of a general revelation is in principle "dialectic." What the "natural man" knows apart from Christ is not half the truth but distorted truth. No religion in the world, not even the most primitive, is without some elements of truth. No religion is without its profound error, an error which is of its very essence; no religion—not even in its "highest" form—is free from this perversion of the truth. So also there is no philosophy which is without truth—not even materialism—but also there is none without a sinful distortion of the truth—even in its most religious and ethical form. Neither the magnificent development of the philosophy of religion in German Idealism nor the extraordinary increase of our knowledge of the non-Christian religions makes it in any way necessary for Christians to go beyond what the Reformers say about the relation between the "natural" and the Christian knowledge of God, that *quandam sui numinis intelligentiam universis Deus ipse indidit . . . insculptum esse divinitatis sensum. . . .* But: *eandem notitiam partim inscitia partim malitia . . . corrumpi.* The heathen know nothing distinct, stable or certain, but *confusis principiis esse affixos ut Deum incognitum adorent* (Calvin).[1]

The relation between Christianity and religion without a Mediator is therefore characterized by this, that the Christian

[1] *Institutio* I, from Chapters III, IV, and V. Cf. the excellent work by Vossberg, *Luther's Kritik aller Religionen,* from which we can see clearly with what genius Luther dealt also with the problem of Comparative Religion. The main lines of his criticism of religion, his comparison between the Christian faith and other religions are still valid for us to-day, in spite of our great advance in detailed knowledge of the religions of the world.

faith, to which revelation is a unique, absolute, decisive fact, includes "general revelation" and "universal religion" as distorted truth within itself, as its own presupposition. Religion without a Mediator, however, tries to incorporate the Christian faith into itself, by the assertion that what the Christian regards as essential, that is, relation to a unique historical event, is a non-essential psychological and educational aid to faith which can be discarded when we have reached maturity. At this point the two views confront each other in opposite camps; here there can be no reconciliation. Only one of these views can be true. It is, however, beyond a doubt that the Christian faith in revelation, in this decided sense, that is, as faith in a Mediator, has almost disappeared from the consciousness of our contemporaries. The Christian Church must bear some of the blame for this situation, not only on account of the weakening of its idea of revelation in the Catholic system (as has already been mentioned above), but scarcely less through its false interpretation in the orthodox emphasis on the Bible among Protestant Christians. Orthodoxy had placed the Bible itself, as a book, in the place which should have been reserved for the fact of revelation. It confused the fact of revelation with the witness to the fact. It was necessary that both should be connected, but orthodoxy made them identical. All the passionate interest which belonged to the unique event, to the Mediator and His act, was thus diverted from its true object and directed towards the scriptural testimony to it. Hence the destruction of the dogma of Verbal Inspiration,[1] with its emphasis upon an Infallible Book, by the modern process of research in natural and historical science inevitably carried away with it the whole Christian faith in revelation, the faith in the Mediator. For in traditional Christian doctrine these two great forces, the infallibility of the Bible and the revelation of God in Christ, had been coupled together too closely. The fall of the one led inevitably to the fall of the other. This was caused by the Enlightenment.

At the period of the Enlightenment the religious sense, if it escaped the dangers of atheism and sensualism, driven out of

[1] For the relation between the Bible and Revelation, see my *Religions philosophie*, especially pp. 76–80.

its shattered fortress by loss of confidence in the Bible, found a refuge in the metaphysical, moral, and rational knowledge of God. Revelation—so long as the word was still used at all— became the self-manifestation of God in the *notiones communes*, in the ultimate axiomatic statements of metaphysics and ethics, out of which men tried to build up a rational doctrine of God. The influence of Kant—from the theological and not the philosophical point of view—only caused a slight change of emphasis, namely, the step from the metaphysical theology of reason in the Aristotelian sense, which included that of St. Thomas Aquinas and the philosophy of Christian Wolff, to an ethical theology of reason and a deepening of the *a priori* knowledge of God through reflection on the theory of knowledge. In the speculative Idealism of the post-Kantian philosophy, in the classical "German Idealism," there arose that magnificent new formulation of the conception of revelation which reaches its highest and its culminating point in the religious philosophy of Hegel.

Two currents of thought here flowed into one: Revelation is the self-manifestation of the Divine in the depths of the human spirit. The old Platonic and Neo-Platonic thought of God, which had already dominated medieval mysticism, here reappeared, more vigorous than ever, reshaped and enriched by the "interior" spirit of Christianity, and by all the intellectual labour of later philosophy from the time of Descartes. With this, however, there was combined a second factor, springing directly from Christianity: the historical element. The "ideas" are not innate, in the sense of something already existing and "given," as the thinkers of the Enlightenment regarded them, but they are *becoming*; the spirit is *becoming*, and the law of its growth is this: the self-manifestation of the Divine. *The history of the Spirit is the history of revelation.* Since, however, the Spirit only truly understands Himself, in His growth, in His history, this knowledge of the historical element as a growing revelation of God belongs to the divine revelation itself. The religious philosophy of history, combined with the historical philosophy of religion, constitutes the ultimate height or depth of knowledge, in which the consciousness of the Divine and the Divine's consciousness become one.

35

It is not difficult to understand that for a time this dazzling new idea of the philosophy of religion could be confused with that which the Christian religion means by revelation. Do not both use the same terms; the incarnation of God in perfect humanity; the Eternal entering into time, in order that time may become eternal? Here it seemed as though at last the contradiction between general and special (historical) revelation had been overcome by the knowledge of the Idea translated into history. Philosophy and faith seemed at last to have found each other. But this unity was an illusion; again this can only be proved at the decisive point: uniqueness. Through the philosophy of Hegel history itself became a "universal." All that was contingent or accidental in the necessity of the Idea was removed; even the *apparently irrational* element in history, the element of contradiction, was interpreted as an illusory contradiction through the genius of dialectic.[1] A contradiction which can be mastered by thought is not a real contradiction, but only seems to be one. The irrational is only an element in the rationality of history, contingency, the accidental is only a factor within necessity and both are proved by the fact that the mind is able to think out rationally the course of history by means of the dialectical logic of history. Therefore, the connection with history is more apparent than real. The mind which comprehends the stages of history as necessary elements in development is by this fact of comprehension master of history, independent of the historical and particular. To him history is merely a picture-book, whose text he knows without the aid of the pictures; to him it means the Idea made concrete, hence there is nothing decisive about it. In its absolute and serious sense, there is no room here for the category of uniqueness. Here also the statement of Fichte that the metaphysical alone saves and not the historical, may be applied very

[1] Thus the fact that recently Hegel has been acclaimed as the greatest "irrationalist" among modern philosophers is not absolutely false, though it is very misleading. Certainly in his dialectic he made room for the irrational element; the zig-zag line of his system is determined by the irrational element which he recognizes. But the Irrational is still finally mastered by Reason—by the system—dialectic is the means he uses, through thought to master even the Irrational.

aptly. The new element in the Neo-Platonism of Hegel is this, that it was able, or seemed to be able, to absorb history into thought as Plotinus and Schelling did with Nature. It is the victory of the universal in the realm of history, where hitherto thought had always been opposed by her adversary.

Thus we may say of the whole of the newer intellectual movement that, in so far as it had any religious depth at all, it varied the theme of a universal revelation in many ways, but it never strayed outside this realm of ideas. In Goethe's Nature-Pantheism (or "Entheismus," or whatever we may like to call it) there is a very evident revival of the ancient Hellenic idea of movement in harmony and balance. In Lessing's *Education of the Human Race (Erziehung des Menschengeschlechts)*, however, it seems as though a compromise had been effected between the Enlightenment and the Christian religion; in truth, Reason the Universal, is supreme. For in whatever way we are to understand more closely this divine "education," in any case it is not more than a speeding up of the process by which the reason itself, even though somewhat more slowly, had attained by its own methods. But Herder's understanding of the history of humanity, in spite of all its wealth of historical insight and understanding of the world of the Bible, does not leave this general sphere of Idealism. For Herder also—as well as later on for Hegel—revelation means the making concrete of the divine universal idea, as it is applied to Nature and the spirit of man. In these idealistic philosophers of history—here Schleiermacher as a philosopher must be included—there is only one element which is, properly speaking, Christian, because it is unique, and that is the direction of history. This is the non-Greek, specific element in German Idealism, in absolute contrast to Greek and Indian Idealism and to all kinds of mysticism: history is hastening towards a goal. This idea of a world history which will attain fulfilment is the Christian strand in the web of thought woven by German Idealism and later by Positivism. This idea is neither necessary *a priori* as a speculative foundation, nor *a posteriori* as something which springs out of actuality. It is faith without a foundation, because it is detached from its foundation; hence it has become something quite different: it is the illusory

37

optimism of progress of the nineteenth century, the *secularized form of Christian eschatology*. Because it has thus been torn away from the moorings of its basis in faith and has entered into the sphere of Idealism, it has been doubly transformed. It has lost its decisive character—it expresses a necessary idea of becoming; and at the same time it has also lost its twofold character: the idea of judgment has disappeared; its place has been taken by a constant approximation of all to perfection. This is the twofold result of the fact that history has been interpreted in terms of the universal, has become an Idea.

The religion of our classical writers, that of the poets as well as of the philosophers, is, essentially, not Christianity but this religion of general revelation, religion without a Mediator. Obviously, however, it has exercised a very definite influence upon the intellectual life of the present day, both inside and outside the Christian Church; and it has left an indelible mark upon theology. When a modern man is religious, when he says that he "believes something," he means that he believes in general revelation. The idea of a special revelation, in the sense of an absolute connection with a unique event, is wholly unintelligible to him. In principle his religion has no Mediator. To him revelation means something timeless and general: the universal "miracle" of the natural order, the universal "miracle" of the moral law, of humanity, of morality, of thought and ideality; the general sense of the meaning of history as a picture-book to illustrate the text-book of ideas. To him the particular, in so far as he regards it as a revelation at all, is a symbol; that is, a universal element, timelessly true and shimmering through the veil of the particular. "The moral religious spirit is itself the great miracle, the divine in appearance" (Pfleiderer). Thus the modern man is a "believer" in this way, even when he thinks that he is a Christian.

Hence he may recognize differences in the revelational, or—and it comes to the same thing—symbolical value of Nature or History. Some symbols of Divine Eternal Truth are more transparent than others; there are certain peaks in the spiritual process of history at which the Divine can be more plainly discerned than at other times; there are personalities in whom the genuinely human element, and above all the religious element, possesses such power and such originality that in contrast to the general mass of mankind they stand out like the geniuses in the realm of art: heroes of religion, religious geniuses, whose experience can enkindle that of others; thus they serve others as "mediators" of religious knowledge and of religious experience.

But it would be a serious confusion of thought if we were to regard this idea as identical with that which we mean by a "Mediator" in the full Christian sense of the term. These stimulators of the religious life are, by their very nature, still only men. The "religious genius" is like genius in every other realm: he represents nothing more than humanity raised to its highest point—no less, but also no more. Therefore the significance of religious genius is not one of principle, nor is it decisive—that is, if we use the word "decisive" in a serious way. It does not matter whether we use the language of the Rationalistic period of the Enlightenment and speak of the "teacher" or "example" who mediates religious knowledge, or if we use the Romantic aesthetic terms of the nineteenth and the twentieth centuries, and speak of the "religious genius," the "hero," the "prophet," from whose "religious experience" or "personality" the piety of others, less strong and original, is "kindled"—measured by the standard we have set up this does not matter at all. In each instance their significance is this: the religious teacher or hero aims at leading men beyond himself, at making the "pupil" independent of the "teacher." By their very conception of their mission such men are not unique; they may constantly reappear in the course of history. One among them may perhaps be the greatest, the most dominating—if we can and desire to make comparisons at all. But this preferential position is relative—it is merely a maximum. Such a man is *primus inter pares*, and no intensification of the value of his qualities can make him anything else. He is, and he remains, separated as by a deep gulf from that which the Christian religion means by a Mediator. For he is and remains a man like other men; and this means that he is a sinner like other men. In the distinction between God and Man he stands as a man on the side of all

39

other men. In the procession of seekers after God he may
indeed be the leader; among those who pray earnestly, who
plead with God for forgiveness and redemption he may be the
noblest. the best, the most passionate and profound. But he is
no more than that. Even the greatest religious genius cannot
forgive sin, cannot reconcile man with God; but he himself has
need of forgiveness and reconciliation. Thus even the greatest
genius is essentially the same as the meanest mortal on earth,
therefore he can never be the mediator. Religious hero-worship
is still universal religion, the religion of general revelation, and
is therefore in opposition to the Christian faith, in exactly the
same way as every kind of idealism, mysticism, or system of
ethics.

In irreconcilable, unbridgeable, fatal opposition! For in
Christianity faith in the Mediator is not something optional,
not something about which, in the last resort, it is possible to
hold different opinions, if we are only united on the "main
point." For faith in the Mediator—in the event which took
place once for all, a revealed atonement—is the Christian
religion itself; it is the "main point"; it is not something
alongside of the centre, it is the substance and kernel, not the
husk; this is so true that we may even say: In distinction from
all other forms of religion the Christian religion is faith in the
one Mediator. There is no other form of belief which is, in
this sense, faith in the Mediator, because no other form of
faith knows and takes seriously the category of uniqueness
(once-for-all-ness). And there is no other possibility of being
a Christian than through faith in that which took place once
for all, revelation and atonement through the Mediator. It is,
of course, true that there are many respectable good pious
people who do not believe in the Mediator. I would say all
the good I can of them, but there is one thing which I cannot
and ought not to say about them: that they are Christians.
For to be a Christian means precisely to trust in the Mediator.
But in truth, when we say this, we may well ask ourselves:
Does anyone nowadays know what this means? What it means
practically? What we thereby confess regarding ourselves and
regarding God?

First of all, however, we must seek to secure this distinction against modern attempts to efface it; we must prove its existence, for everything in the Christian religion depends upon the clearness with which this is perceived, because only when this distinction stands out sharply and clearly is the significance of the Mediator taken seriously.

CHAPTER II

THE OBLITERATION OF THIS DISTINCTION
IN MODERN THEOLOGY

THIS is the stumbling-block in Christianity: that revelation, the divine manifestation—that is, eternal truth and everlasting salvation—has to be connected with a fact which took place once for all, or—it amounts to the same thing—that we can never approach God directly but only through the Mediator. This stumbling-block is not only a difficulty for the intellect—as Kierkegaard's teaching would suggest. It is true, of course, that to the Greeks the message of the Cross was foolishness. Pride of intellect revolts against the claim that truth lies outside the realm of reason. As reasonable people we are accustomed to see the criteria of truth within reason and to recognize its presence there alone. Reason is the universal arbiter to which we can and should appeal always and everywhere, in all men and in all circumstances. When witness is borne to revelation a doubt is raised as to the all-sufficiency of reason, and it raises it at this vital point by the assertion that God, the true and living God, cannot be known through the reason. It is not as though the reason, the ultimate court of appeal for our logical thinking, were not of divine origin. But for the very reason that it is of divine origin, it is not itself God and therefore cannot conceive God. How much less, then, can our clouded reason conceive God? Within reason the continuity of argument, the permanent logical order, is supreme. Even intuition which amounts to genius cannot be severed from this order, it merely carries it into regions which have hitherto been unexplored. But where this continuity of argument ceases, there reasonable thought ceases also, and a further step must be taken either into sentimentalism, or faith. It is true, of course, that we can speak of a "faith in reason," a faith, that is, which is based upon the possibility of thought itself, the belief that reason is valid. But this faith is, properly speaking, only another aspect of reason. Faith in revelation is absolutely different; it breaks through the intellectual process, and asserts that eternal truth is bound up with an event which took place in time. "Grace and truth came by Jesus Christ" (John i. 17)

Perhaps this statement would not give offence if it were intended merely as the expression of a complementary truth, which might be explained thus: beyond the truths known to reason there are others which cannot be attained by the reason; these, therefore, must be added by revelation. This is the Scholastic Catholic doctrine which has come to terms quite comfortably with philosophy of a certain kind. But the claim of Christian revelation goes further than this: through the revelation reason is placed in the wrong, namely, in all her attempts to comprehend and grasp the Divine which necessarily spring from reason. It is true, of course, that through revelation the reason, within its own limits, is at the same time confirmed. Faith is not that suicidal rigid *sacrificium intellectus* for which it is often mistaken; it does not imply the denial of the intellect as such, but only its limitation and control. But it is precisely this limitation which reason, or rather the rational man, does not like. Reason wishes to remain the supreme court of appeal. Reason does not wish to acknowledge the judgment passed on it by a unique fact. The will and the pride of reason rebel against faith.

Hence the real stumbling-block is not the theoretical paradox but the moral humiliation. The "Greek" scoffs at the Cross as "folly," but the resistance of the "Jew" is far more violent, for he rebels against it with all the religious and moral intensity of his nature. Hence, in this instance, the humiliation of moral and religious self-sufficiency is much greater, because it is far more personal. In objective thought the point at issue is the theory, the impersonal intellectual concept. Here, however, the whole personality is involved; the Cross challenges the centre of personality, that is, its moral disposition. The admission of the fact of revelation, of the Mediator, includes complete personal surrender to God. Not until man makes this admission does he really lay down his arms; this is why he finds it so difficult to take this final step. Here it is the innermost line of self-defence which must be surrendered; here—and here alone

—it is impossible to retreat any further. The Jews saw this very clearly; therefore they could not take the claim of Jesus to be the Christ as coolly as Pilate, the Hellenist. And wherever a man is earnest and serious in his striving after ethical purity and religious faith he also makes this discovery. This is why everything in Christianity pleases him save its central truth— belief in "justification through faith alone" and reconciliation through the Mediator. Against this challenge human pride of reason rises in indignant revolt.

It does not matter whether this opposition to revelation be direct or indirect. Direct opposition comes from the side of the Rationalists; they frankly reject the claim that reason can be limited by some other element; quite openly and honestly, from the standpoint of those who believe in general revelation, they protest against the idea of a special revelation. The indirect opposition comes from the side of the speculative idealists and mystics who, indeed, use the actual term "revelation" (whereas the Rationalist prefers to avoid this word and to speak of a "rational" knowledge of God and of religion)—they may even speak of "Christ," of "atonement" or "redemption," of the "Son of God," and indeed even of the "Mediator," but all along they do not mean this unique fact, the personal reality of Jesus Christ; they are thinking in general and abstract terms; they mean the "idea" or "principle" of Christ which can, if necessary, be detached from the fact of Christ. Or they mean that mystical "Christ-experience" which is wholly independent of the historical Mediator and is possible at any time, the unmediated immediacy of contact with God, which they call a "Christ" experience, because it is regarded as identical with that which the Christian experiences—who, however, is in "bondage" to his connection with history; his experience therefore is a *détour*, whereas the mystical idealist goes "straight" to God.

All these varieties of opposition are easy to recognize when our attention has once been directed to the essentially unique fact, the Mediator. There is, however, yet another possibility of concealing this opposition which is difficult to recognize: this is the point of view which claims that the general revelation, which here also is opposed to the unique fact, is concealed behind something historical, behind the historical fact of Jesus. It is this which has really determined the course of recent theology. This point therefore requires special attention.

So far as the ordinary Rationalism of the Enlightenment is concerned the situation is quite clear. "That which the dogmatic language of the supernaturalists calls Christology forms no integral part of my system, for this consists indeed of a religion which Jesus taught, but not of one of which He Himself could be the Object" (Röhr).[1] Behind the slogan "The Gospel of Jesus, not the Gospel concerning Jesus," there always lies this ordinary kind of Rationalism. For the Gospel of Jesus, detached from His Person is a universal idea, an ethical religious truth, which bears within itself its own guarantee. Of recent years a good deal of injustice has been done to the older theology of the Enlightenment by interpreting its use of the word "teaching" in a purely intellectual way, in order to be able to draw a clear line of demarcation between orthodoxy and rationalism. As a rule what the adherents of the school of thought of the Enlightenment mean by the "teaching" of Jesus does not differ essentially from that which Adolf von Harnack means by the summary of the "Gospel" in his book on the "Essence of Christianity" (*Wesen des Christentums*[2]): The Fatherhood of God, freedom—or the "infinite value of the Soul"—and immortality—or "eternal life."

Also we do an injustice to these older Rationalists if we think that they had no understanding of the significance of the Person of this Teacher. Only they were simple and straightforward in their conceptions, and when they meant "teacher" they said "teacher" plainly, and not "Son of God," or even "God," and when they meant "example" they said "example," and not "archetype" or "revelation."

They also, however, connected the Christian distinction between general and special revelation with the merely relative distinction between teacher and pupil, between the creative and receptive elements, between the exceptional genius and the ordinary man. But they did not attempt to conceal the

[1] *Briefe über den Rationalismus*, p. 36.
[2] Translated into English under the title, *What is Christianity?*—Tr.

fact that when they spoke of a "special revelation" they meant something quite different from the way in which the term is used by orthodox theologians of the old school, that is, they meant a mere modification of general revelation. "Since this is the position, the result is that only the natural revelation, or the manifestation of God, can be legitimately retained; this we can divide into two parts, a universal or general and a particular or special form of revelation. Our view of this particular form of revelation which, as such, is mediated differs widely from that of the older theologians; it is this:—it is that which is contained in the sum total of natural events, through which, by means of Divine Providence, some men above all others are awakened to the knowledge of the principles of true religion." Among these men Jesus is regarded as the foremost example of this type, as the one through whom the religious education of the human race has made the greatest progress (Wegscheider).[1]

Fifty years of theological discussion would have been unnecessary if the clear distinction made by this early Rationalist had been maintained. Almost inevitably, in attempting to describe the theological discussion which gathered round this question, we feel that it is represented by the truly symbolical names of the simple and restrained Wegscheider on the one hand, and that of his contemporary, Schleiermacher—who was far more gifted than Wegscheider, and, from the religious point of view, far more vital and alive—on the other. On this point, however, Wegscheider was quite clear: he knew that to speak of "mediators" in the plural, or of "a mediator" simply as the *primus inter pares*, meant something quite different from the Christian distinction between general and special revelation. Within the sphere of general revelation (which as a good Rationalist is the only kind he can accept) he rightly makes a distinction between the *a priori* knowledge of God which everyone possesses, and the historical knowledge which, in principle, it is true, everyone might have, but which in actual fact some individuals possess earlier than others; these more advanced souls, therefore, as those who have discovered this general truth, become their leaders, teachers, and prophets.

[1] *Institutiones theologicae*, p. 42. Translated from the Latin.

At the same time Wegscheider—and in this he is admirable—is quite clear in his own mind that the history of religion belongs to the realm of general "natural" revelation; for he knows that historical reputations are neither permanent nor based on principle, that even the greatest "teacher"—we would also add: the greatest "religious genius"—by the very urge of his interior life is always trying to make his hearers independent of himself, to point them away to the religious truth which he proclaims as that which is alone valid; hence that everything which at first appears new and mysterious, *ad origines naturales et cognitionis humanae veram indolem revocanda sunt.*[1] He does not confuse this relative distinction which occurs within history with that absolute Christian distinction between the "natural" and the "revealed" knowledge of God.

It is, however, not difficult to understand that when the narrow and limited intellectualism of Rationalism had been overcome by the magnificent development of post-Kantian Idealism, when, above all, its lack of the historical sense was conquered by the mighty vistas of historical perspective opened up by Herder and the Romantic Movement, the idea arose that this new view of history had also bridged the gulf between general and special revelation. We have already alluded to the philosophers. Their position is clear, to this extent at least: it is obvious that their whole attention is directed towards the general or universal element in history, to ideas and principles; for instance they regard "Christianity" or "dogma" as a system of thought, never as a personal relation. In spite of all their expressions of reverence and admiration for the Person of Jesus, actually, and in principle, they do not regard Him as significant. But the situation was soon entirely changed by a man who was himself one of the most famous leaders in that movement which taught a new philosophy of history; at the same time he regarded himself as a Christian, and he was a theologian and an ecclesiastic: I mean Schleiermacher. After Rationalism and speculative idealism in its theological form (as "liberal or free-thinking theology") had been driven off the field, it was Schleiermacher who blazed the trail for the theological thought of the nineteenth century.

[1] *Institutiones theologicae*, p. 42. Translated from the Latin.

47

One great mistake has been made in the estimate of Schleiermacher: his comparative hostility to the Rationalism of the Enlightenment has tended to conceal his actual affinity with it.

From the philosophical point of view, and from that of the general history of intellectual progress, the development from the Rationalism of the close of the eighteenth century, with its lack of the historical sense, to the Idealism of the nineteenth century, with its philosophy of history, means a great deal. But when it is measured by the Christian standard, with its distinction between reason and revelation, between a religion without a mediator or a faith with a mediator, its significance is nil. For it has no intention of turning from "general" to "special" revelation; its aim is merely to deepen "natural" religion, or the knowledge of God to be gained through mysticism and Neo-Platonic speculation, and, above all, to interpret history in terms of general ideas. The fundamental distinction remains; it is not altered in the very least.

This comes out very clearly in Schleiermacher's *Reden* (Speeches). Although in them the attack on the intellectualist and ethical form of the general religion of the Enlightenment is striking enough, still it remains true that Schleiermacher himself represents religion in general, the "religion within the religions." Only he seeks its origin not in intelligence and will but in feeling and intuition, in the uniting point of intelligence and will. Thus the new element in his thought is primarily only this new shade of emphasis in the conception of universal religion or of the "essence of religion."

This new conception of religion, however, certainly led to some important results. First came the establishment of the thesis that essentially religion is not *doctrine* but *life*; secondly, that all life, and all religion, is *individual* in character. From one point of view this Romantic definition of the essence of religion was, to some extent, an advance compared with the earlier Rationalistic conception of religion and revelation—though it could also be proved to be a reaction—but the fact remains that Schleiermacher never swerved from the fundamental main view of the Rationalism of the Enlightenment: that the "essence of religion," the "religion within religions,"

48

is something "general," and not "special," that therefore there does exist a common "essence of religion" in which all religions share, in which Christianity also has a share.

This applies equally, of course, to every system of theology which—with or without direct connection with Schleiermacher—seeks to interpret Christianity as a modification or individual form of the general "essence of religion"; this is true even when it is stated that Christianity occupies a preferential position, that in it this general form of religion finds its purest expression. This attitude produces a characteristic view of the problem of toleration. Because we believe in the underlying unity of all religions, including the Christian religion, because we distinguish the different religions from each other only as modifications, as grades and varieties of this one general religion, therefore, in principle, we are tolerant, that is, we hold a relative point of view. Each religion is recognized as being in principle equally true and equally valuable, only the truth and the essential element in each is differently shaped and expressed, and is present in each individual form to a different degree. There are different grades of development and differing phases, and different individual forms at the same stage of development.

This is precisely Schleiermacher's conception in his famous *Reden* (Speeches). At bottom the Christian religion is the same as any other religion, only it is more complete, and individually more definite and pronounced. This conception of religion does not suggest that there is any connection, in principle, with an historical event as a fact of revelation. From the point of view of practical psychology, however, the situation is different, that is, where we are not dealing with the actual essence of religion but with the means whereby it may be preserved and increased. For—and here a third idea is introduced—life can only be enkindled by life. This idea also is a general truth. It is true of all life, and therefore also of religion. Transferred to the religious sphere this is what it means: the individual needs religious stimulus from others. In religion—as well as in art and science—the richer can impart something to the poorer, and the less original mind is stimulated by the more creative mind. But the individual is not bound to a definite fact or to

49

a definite person; he is simply drawn for the time being to the person who happens to be able to impart this sense of general truth. In the *Reden* people of this kind, who have the power of imparting the sense of the truth of religion in a special time and way, are called "heroes" or "mediators." Naturally they exist in the plural, indeed there are an indefinite number of them, just like the "teachers" and "examples" of whom Rationalist theology used to speak. Correspondingly it is stated explicitly of Jesus that He never claimed to be "the only Mediator, the only One in whom the Idea is realized."[1] He is indeed "until now"[2] the most complete representative of the religious idea, but alongside of Him there are many others, and it is for each individual to find out from whom he gains most. Essentially Jesus represents not the Mediator, but the idea of mediation.

Secondly: just as there are several mediators, so also the service they render, like that of a teacher, is not permanent. For only those whose personal life is not sufficiently independent stand in any need of a mediator at all. In actual fact, however, the majority of human beings belong to the category of those who are thus dependent on others for religious stimulus; indeed, "every human being—with the exception of a few elect souls—certainly needs a mediator, a leader, one who will arouse him first of all from slumber and give him his first impulse in the right direction, but this stage of experience should not last very long, for every individual ought to learn to behold truth with his own eyes, and not through the eyes of another; he also ought to bring an offering to the general store of religion, otherwise he does not deserve a niche within the sphere of religion and, indeed, he will find that none is reserved for him."[3] Thus the connection with the "mediator"

---

[1] *Reden*[3], p. 432. In the first edition it is put still more plainly: "He never maintained that He was the sole object of the application of His idea, or that He was the only Mediator" (p. 304).

[2] Jesus is "the sublime author of all that is most glorious—up to the present—in religion." *Reden*,[1] p. 301.

[3] *Reden*[1], p. 121. "A genuinely religious man is not one who believes in a Sacred Book, but one who needs no Sacred Book at all, a man who might even compose his own Scriptures" (p. 122).

is psychological and educational, therefore it is relative, and is not based on principle; it is simply the stage for the beginner. In spite, therefore, of all Schleiermacher's understanding of the historical element in religion, and of the significance of mediators, the religious conception underlying the *Reden* is never that of Christianity but that of general religion, and that alone. The relation between general and special revelation is exactly the same as it is in the works of Wegscheider, that is, in the Rationalism of the Enlightenment.

Schleiermacher never actually swerved from this fundamental conception of religion, but in his later years it is possible to detect a certain change of emphasis; probably he himself was not altogether conscious of this change, but it is this which makes the *Glaubenslehre*, the work of his old age, so contradictory. Here also he takes as his starting-point religion in general, the "essence" of religion, which is also the essence of the Christian religion. There is no room in the religious conception of the *Glaubenslehre* for any idea of connection with an historical fact. For in this conception the central element is immediate "feeling"; now a conception of this kind cannot be intensified by the knowledge of some particular fact which has actually taken place; on the contrary, it would only lead to confusion. For here also it is true that "Religion is not knowledge." The "religion within religions" consists in feeling, or, to define it more precisely, in the "feeling of absolute dependence"; this is the "essence of religion," even of the Christian religion. The relation of this general "essence" of religion to the historical faiths is here also, as it is in the *Reden*, to be determined by two general conceptions (which indeed had not been clearly worked out until now) : (*a*) the conception of the stage of development, that is, through the degree of clearness or strength or purity of that "feeling" in which religion consists, and (*b*) the conception of the varied forms which this general "feeling" will take in different individuals in actual contact with life. There is only one religion, but this one religion passes through different stages of development, and it expresses itself—on the same plane of development—in various forms. Speaking of the religions on the highest plane of development, Schleiermacher says that here too the religion is the same, but it is differently "expressed."[1]

With this general definition of the essence of religion there is connected a third idea—also a general one—that life can only be enkindled by life, that is, the idea that religion, like everything else which is alive, is historical. And this idea again is connected with that of individuality. Each religion has its definite starting-point, which, at the same time, determines its individuality. This too is a general idea, which is true not only of every form of religion, but also of the moulding of life by the processes of history—Schleiermacher gives as a special illustration that of positive law. The individual element in all life is given with its historical genesis. That is the positive element in history, the original and undesirable element in every form of life. This positive historical element—which, as has been said, forms part not only of all religion but of all law—is now further described as "revelation," because in this newly emerging individuality a new element appears, something which cannot be explained simply from that which precedes it; because thus in it a new aspect of the universal life, and thus also a new window has been opened, disclosing further aspects of the Divine, the One. The individuality of each living religion is the same as its positive historical character, and this again is the same as its revealed character. Here therefore revelation is simply the mystery of the individualization of the universal, the mysterious entrance of the universal into existence, in the individual-universal element.

The Christian religion is no exception to this rule; it also is individual, that is, it is historically positive, and to this extent it is "revealed," like all other forms of religion with which it shares the common element of the essence of religion or "religion within the religions." In Christianity indeed, as in every positive form of religion, this essence is shaped in a particular way. But it arises out of the very nature of this conception of the essence of religion that what it brings forth is not this particular element, but the essence itself, that is, therefore, the element which Christianity possesses in common with all other forms of religion: the essence of religion itself.

[1] *Glaubenslehre*, col. v, 10, 2.

The particular aspect is the accidental element, although the Christian religion, like all other religions, only expresses this essence of religion in an individual and accidental form, in the positive aspect of history, and at the same time also within its limitations.

So far the line of thought has been clear and connected. None of the ideas which have been discussed go, in any way, beyond the framework of religion in general. The general conception of religion and revelation of the Rationalist school of thought has been replaced by that of the Romantic school. Even the element of historical positivism and individuality finds its place within it quite easily. At this point let us pause a moment to survey the general situation. The period of Rationalism with its lack of historical sense is over and the sense of the positive value of the historical element has been reawakened. But although on the one hand this new discovery is a fact of great significance for the intellectual progress of the world, on the other hand it must be stated quite emphatically that, measured by the standard of the distinction between religion in general and the Christian religion of revelation, it has no significance whatever. For this historical positivism itself is quite general in character, and has nothing whatever to do with the unique character of the fact of revelation. The Rationalistic conception of the importance of man as an individual has been replaced by the conception of man as an historical being, of humanity as a vast collective entity, extending in an unbroken line from generation to generation. The world of human life is now surveyed not only from the point of view of a mere cross-section, but from that of an extended line cutting through human history as a whole. It is this which constitutes the new element. From the Christian point of view, however, all that this means is that we are confronted with the spectacle of a humanity in need of redemption instead of an individual in need of redemption. From the Christian point of view even history itself is the object, and not the subject, of redemption. Neither humanity as an historical unity nor a solitary individual can produce revelation. In the last resort from the Christian point of view it makes little difference whether we speak of "history" or of "man." In both cases we are dealing with something which lies on the manward side of revelation. The point of view of absolute Idealism, however, with its emphasis on the philosophical value of history, is entirely different. For it history is not merely the object but also, and at the same time, the subject of the redeeming revelation. Thus man, conceived as historical humanity and not in terms of individualism, possesses the power of revelation and redemption within himself. From the point of view of the Christian religion, however, this is the meaning of "history": it shows us a number of souls, a whole succession of needy souls, who stand in need of redemption. Idealism regards history quite differently; to it this long succession of those who need redemption constitutes at the same time, and as such, as history, redemption. The history of those who need redemption and the history of redemption itself merge into one. This is possible because the redeeming revelation is not something which enters into humanity from without, but something which develops from within, and unfolds with its development. Because man possesses, potentially, the redeeming idea within himself, it is possible for the history of humanity as a whole to be both the history of revelation and of redemption.

Man as a human being is the "sphere" in which the Idea comes to be historical and real. The religious emphasis on the value of the positive historical element is thus not opposed to Idealism; it is simply the same thing in a special form. And the uniting factor is individuality. The idea individually realized: this is the Idealistic conception of history. Thus in so far as idea and revelation agree (see above page 22) the appearance of the individual element in history means the actualization of the "revelation." Since, however, the idea—that is, the essence of religion—is not connected with any individuality as such and is not fully represented in any individuality, the relation between the positive-historical element, that is, the individual representation of the Idea, and the Idea itself is symbolical. Revelation, therefore, is itself a symbol, that is, it is the universal expressed in a concrete and individual form.

Let us now return to Schleiermacher. So far his line of

thought in *Glaubenslehre* (*The Christian Faith*) is in entire accord with that of the *Reden* and of the general historical theory of absolute Idealism. But now—in a famous passage in the *Glaubenslehre* (paragraph xi)—a curious and radical change takes place which destroys the significance of all that he has said hitherto. Schleiermacher here says plainly that the distinctive element in the Christian religion is this: that the Christian believer knows that through redemption he is related to Jesus Christ, and, further, that it is this particular element which constitutes the essential element in his religion. This conclusion represents the result of a twofold process. First of all, the conception "religion" has absorbed into itself an element which, although it is only supposed to give an individual character to the Idea, in reality does away with it altogether. Let me explain what I mean: if religion is not knowledge, but feeling, then to *know* about Jesus Christ and the redemption which He has accomplished cannot be a particular modification of religion. Secondly, if the distinctive element in the Christian religion, its particular character—here the special manner in which it possesses the essential element of religion—is the knowledge of Jesus Christ, then this knowledge cannot be at the same time the essential element itself. One or the other must be true; but both cannot be true at the same time. Either religion—even the Christian religion—is feeling, and then it is not knowledge: then it is impossible that religion should consist in the knowledge of an historical personality and an historical event. Or, on the other hand: the relation to that historical fact is in point of fact the Christian faith: then it cannot be religion in the sense of religion as constituted by feeling. Further: either the relationship to Jesus Christ is the essential thing—and then it is certainly not an individual modification of a universal religion; or, on the other hand, the Christian religion is only a special variety of "religion" in general, an individual form of its essence, and then it is impossible for its individual or particular element to be at the same time the essential element. It is as essential to universal religion to be free from any connection with history as it is essential to the Christian religion to insist upon the fact that its basis and its life depend upon this unique historical event. Here again, one or the other must be true. Schleiermacher, however, turns this challenging question, with its demand for definite decision, into a compromise which includes both. The attempt to reconcile these two opposing ideas—this unedifying story of an impossible compromise which has nevertheless been fraught with such momentous significance —cannot here be dealt with in further detail. It led to the conception of Christ with which we shall be dealing in the following chapter.[1]

It is strange that Albert Ritschl, whose *Rechtfertigung und Versöhnung (Christian Doctrine of Justification and Reconciliation)* must be regarded as the second milestone in the theological history of the last century, although, quite rightly, he condemned Schleiermacher's dependence on the idea of a universal religion, conceived in the spirit of the Enlightenment, did not perceive that he had built his own theology upon a similar general conception of religion. According to Ritschl's view, this general conception of religion manifests itself most clearly in the Christian religion, but at the same time it is the ideal conception for all the non-Christian religions as well. But this is only possible because it does not contain any reference to an unique historical event. Here again, as in Schleiermacher's view, the distinction between a universal religion without a mediator and the Christian faith in the Mediator has been effaced. An acute theological critic of the Idealist and Liberal school once said of Ritschl, that he adorned a building constructed wholly in the Rationalistic style with a supernatural gateway.[2] If this statement is supposed to represent Ritschl's ultimate intention, it is undoubtedly false. Ritschl wished to break away from the idealistic speculative idea of universal religion and to return to the scriptural doctrine of a revealed religion. If we were estimating Ritschl's

[1] For further details, see my book: *Die Mystik und das Wort*, especially pp. 121 ff.

[2] The following passage from a letter of 1859, quoted by Otto Ritschl (Ritschl's *Leben*, I, 369) is of some interest: "I am now hunting out all the people of this type from Marcion to the present day; in so doing, however, I find few whom I can praise, apart from Faustus Socinus." Characteristically, this letter refers to the idea of the "Wrath of God."

theology from the historical and biographical point of view, we would lay great emphasis upon this intention. Here, however, we are dealing only with his actual completed and historical theological system; this being so, we can do no other than agree whole-heartedly with the severe remark which has just been quoted. The Ritschlian theology is a Rationalistic system clad in scriptural garments; indeed, it is a system which does all honour to the systematic ability of its builder, for it is an almost perfectly unified Rationalistic building of simple design.[1]

The reason why this was not generally realized throughout a whole generation (for only very acute and far-seeing opponents were able to perceive it clearly) is this: it was generally believed

---

[1] It is quite correct to say that in the third edition of his chief work Ritschl took pains to eliminate the most obvious expressions of his theological Rationalism. For instance, whereas in the first edition it is said (as a deliberately emphasized closing thesis): "The Idea of God, which is used as the means for the explanation of the co-existence of the ethical and the natural world . . ." (p. 284), the same passage in the third (and fourth) edition reads: "The thought of God, which is given in the revelation through Christ, etc. . . ." (p. 308). Further, it is true that the particularly illuminating statement is allowed to remain: "Thus this proves that the Idea of God and the religious view of life of Christianity is *the* method of solving the world-problem," but the word "proves" has disappeared— although even in the new edition the writer is dealing essentially with the same proof as in the first edition. But even though in this the *intention* of Ritschl to base faith solely upon Christ becomes visible, yet the whole structure of the Ritschlian system makes it impossible to give this idea its full value. We measure faith not by whether one *says* faith is based on Christ, but by whether this is actually *done* or not, that is, whether the categories which determine the conception of Revelation, permit this. This, however, is not the case. In this system neither is Revelation, in its content, anything other than the rational idea of Purpose, nor is it defined thus, as an authority; for the first Bearer and Shaper of an ethical rational idea is not by this necessarily the "Revealer" in the scriptural sense of the word. For this very reason, on the whole the first edition is more representative of Ritschl's *thought*, whereas in the third edition his *tendency* emerges more clearly, although this tendency is not theologically defined, but is only suggested by scriptural-sounding phrases. Hence the biographer may well take note of this, but not the theologian. In spite of this, according to the custom of scholars we quote everywhere from the fourth edition, save where some special circumstance requires the more pertinent expression of the first edition.

that historical positivism, as such, was a guarantee against any
suspicion of Rationalism. Historical positivism, however, is
itself a particular form of Rationalism; this has come out
plainly in our study of Schleiermacher, and we shall be able
to discern this still more clearly in Ritschl. In order to understand the Ritschlian conception of revelation, the main features
of the Ritschlian theology must be briefly indicated. The whole
system is dominated by the idea of the moral purpose of
humanity. Man needs religion, because he can only affirm
himself morally in the world on the presupposition of a world
order with a definite purpose. Hence the complete idea of God
is that which expresses this moral idea of purpose in the purest
manner. This idea, which is supposed to be the Christian
conception, is that of God as "Love," or perfect moral will
and purpose. This conception of God is the postulate[1]; only
on the presupposition of this conception can the world be
conceived in terms of a consistent whole.

This idea of God further betrays its rational origin in the
statement that "the Kingdom of God is the correlate of God's
love in so far as it is the association of men for reciprocal and
common action from the motive of love"; the "Kingdom" is
regarded as a perfect community based on reason, in which
the religious and ethical activities of man are combined. In
Ritschl's view to conceive of the will of God as the purpose
for which the world was created, and to think of the Kingdom
of moral perfection as this end, mean exactly the same. This
rational, one-sided view of the idea of God shows in the clearest
manner how far removed it is from the Christian conception,
in which the equal stress laid on the holiness, as well as on
the love, of God suggests the mystery of the Godhead.[2] The

---

[1] "Thus if God ought *necessarily* to be *thought* of as the guarantee of our
individual morality and our ethical fellowship, then the aim of the whole
world towards this purpose and God must also be admitted" (first edition,
p. 241). This very rational statement—which is absolutely fundamental—
has not been altered even in the third edition (III⁴, p. 267).

[2] Ritschl dismisses in one sentence the idea of the Holiness of God—
a conception which is equally fundamental to the Old and the New
Testament—saying simply that it does not "come into consideration,"
because "for various reasons it is not valid in its Old Testament sense, and
its use in the New Testament is equivocal" (III⁴, p. 260). To one who under-

Ritschlian God is not mysterious. Rigid adherence to the moral idea of purpose means that man already knows all there is to be known.

It is, of course, well known that Ritschl protested with great energy against the introduction of metaphysics into theology. In so doing, however, he was thinking only of the ontological speculations of the Hegelians; he had forgotten that there is also an ethical metaphysic, and he did not perceive that his whole theological system was simply a well-constructed system of ethical metaphysics developed along logical lines. Everything is deduced in the most rigid fashion from the idea of God as "Love," and from the idea of the "Kingdom of God." Revelation simply means the introduction of this idea of the Kingdom of God into history. Like every other discovery and introduction of an idea into history this also is something positive: a definite personal event. This personal event is the life of Jesus. The fact of revelation is held to consist in the life of Jesus, or even in Jesus Himself, in so far as in Him, on the one hand, the ethical idea of the Kingdom of God was founded, and, on the other, was personally exemplified.

"The ethical judgment of Christ, in the light of His vocation, leads inevitably to the religious judgment that He is the revelation of God": this is the characteristic title of a chapter in Ritschl's chief work. The claim of Jesus to be the Revealer of God is guaranteed by His moral fidelity to His vocation in relation to the divine purpose for the world. Therefore, He may be "judged as revelation"—whereas in the Christian conception of revelation the very possibility of judgment is excluded. In point of fact, however, it is not revelation at all with which we are here concerned but with something entirely different: namely, the historical introduction of the *a priori* idea, valid

stands, this is enough. For it is precisely this co-existence of two ideas which cannot be logically connected which constitutes the distinctive difference between the Christian idea of God and every other idea of God, above all it makes a clear distinction between it and all rational ideas of God; and this paradoxical co-existence is the secret of God, which cannot be attained by thought, but which must be revealed. From this point of view it is obvious that Ritschl—even if this were not explicitly stated—must speak about Revelation and Atonement in language which differs entirely from that of the Bible.

in itself, of the "Kingdom of God," in the Kantian sense.[1]
Ritschl's argument runs along the following lines: the purposive idea of the divine will ("Love") is regarded as identical
with the knowledge of God; therefore, since God cannot be
conceived as other than this purpose, the will which wholly
corresponds to this idea, namely, the will of Jesus, the historical person, is identical in intention with the divine will,
and it is therefore possible to use the expression, the "Deity"
of Christ. Historical Positivism and Phenomenalism, both
these characteristic features in the theology of Ritschl, spring
from the same root, that of ethical Rationalism.

In this conception of revelation the historical element has
a twofold significance. The first point is: Jesus was the first
to make this idea valid in history. The significant element in
the event of Jesus is this, "that historically this Idea first
received shape and form through Christ."[2] Obviously, this
has nothing whatever to do with revelation in the Christian
sense of the word. Every rational idea, and especially every
ethical rational idea, at some time or another, is expressed for
the first time. Indeed, to claim that Jesus was the first to give
shape and form to this idea within the realm of history is a
bold statement. For, firstly, this idea had been conceived long

[1] It should be recognized to-day that what is here meant by the Idea
of the Kingdom of God is a purely ethical rational idea and *not* the
scriptural eschatological conception which is described by the same name.
Nevertheless, particular attention ought to be paid to a passage which
the third edition omits, although in spite of the deleted expression the whole
line of thought, and to a large extent the language used, is the same as in
the first edition. It runs like this: "Whatever explanation may be offered
of the fact that the recognition of equal obligations towards all men found
so late an entrance among the nations, it is a fact of history that the idea of
the ethical unity of the human race only became universally effective in
the Christian conception of the Kingdom of God" (p. 242, omitted in
III[3], p. 260). Ritschl's pronouncements on the supernatural or supramun-
dane character of the Kingdom of God are merely negative—suggesting
that this Kingdom of God, since it is supernatural, would remain in existence
even if the present secular conditions of the spiritual life were to be changed
(*Unterricht in der christlichen Religion*, p. 6); thus, this means that the supernatural character of the Kingdom of God is identical with its ethical and
not with its eschatological character.
[2] *Rechtfertigung und Versöhnung*, III[4], p. 425.

before He appeared, and secondly, He in particular never actually put this idea into words; historical critics are quite clear about this at the present time. Here, however, this is not the point at issue; the point we are considering is the establishment of the category under which Ritschl thinks of the concept of revelation.

The second positive historical factor is that of the effective representation of the Idea in history. Through Jesus—according to Ritschl's theory—an historical movement arose, which was determined by that idea of the Kingdom of God, in which thus it attained historical reality. Both these ideas are summed up in the conception of the "Founder[1] of Christianity," or in somewhat more scriptural terms, the "Founder of the Kingdom of God."

From this standpoint some of the most striking features in the Ritschlian theology become intelligible. If the "establishment" of the Kingdom of God means an actual historical movement—a "collective life," as Schleiermacher calls it—that is, if the regulative idea of the significance of Christ consists in a causal scheme, then the historical impulse of the life of Christ is directly perpetuated in the movement which He called into being, and the way to share in this result is to participate historically in this great historical phenomenon, the Christian community. Ritschl himself, it is true, barely suggested the conclusion which must be drawn inevitably from these premisses, the conclusion, namely, that the predicate of Deity is transferred directly to the Christian community itself.[2] One of his early pupils, however, did say this quite boldly: "The Deity of Christ appears throughout only in connection with the deity of His community. It does not apply to Him as an

---

[1] This purely Rationalistic conception of the "Founder" (of Christianity) comes out most clearly in the following passage (*R. u. V.*, III⁴, p. 365): "For without any doubt Jesus had experienced a relation to God which had never before been known, and He affirmed this to His disciples, and it was His aim to lead His disciples into the same religious view of life and into the same self-judgment, and under these conditions into the universal task of the Kingdom of God which He knew devolved upon His disciples as well as upon Himself." The actual content of this statement is the same as that which was taught by a man like Wegscheider, only in other words.   [2] III¹, p. 352.

isolated personality; but as the starting-point of the new humanity" (Schulz).[1] This is why Ritschl lays such great emphasis upon the fact that the individual can only receive forgiveness within the Christian community, for he claims that the Christian community is the actual depository of the redeeming activity of Jesus.

From this point of view Ritschl's doctrine of "justification and reconciliation" also becomes intelligible in those very features which distinguish it so characteristically from the scriptural doctrine. Since God is "Love" alone, and it is impossible to speak either of His holiness or of His wrath, forgiveness, in the scriptural sense, cannot exist.[2] Forgiveness is only another term to express the application of the idea of the divine purpose. "Forgiveness" means the way in which God overlooks the disharmony which has been caused by the fact that mankind has not co-operated with Him in His work and purpose, in the realization of the "Kingdom of God." This disharmony consists in the fact that men do not know of that purposive will of God, and cannot therefore live in harmony with it. This disharmony is removed when men see that the divine will is a will of "Love" towards them, when the idea is banished from their minds that God could ever be anything else than "loving" will. Reconciliation with God is here a purely subjective process, based indeed upon the intellectual conviction that the wrong idea of God as Judge has been removed, and its place has been filled by the right idea that God is "Love." Atonement is therefore the same in the subjective sense as is the introduction of the idea in the objective sense: the making valid of the divine purposive will of "Love." When the individual is controlled by the right idea of God—that God is "Love"—instead of by the previous false idea that God is a Judge—then he is "reconciled" to God.

All this is logically conceived in rational ethical terms. The appearance of an agreement with the Christian religion arises from the introduction of the idea of historical positivism. That the idea is only historically effective from a definite point in time, and that it only reaches the individual through this historical medium, is indeed a quite general statement which

[1] *Gottheit Christi*, p. 439. [2] Cf. *R. u. V.*, III⁴, pp. 61 ff.

in no way transcends the framework of moral idealism; in contradistinction to abstract Rationalism, however, there is here certainly a connection with the fact of Christ as an actual event.

Yet the content of this historical element is nothing more than the rational and ethical idea of purpose, only here it is clothed in definite historical garb. It is not the bare rational and ethical idea, it is the same idea clothed in historical personal forms,[1] nevertheless it is no less rational and ethical; in principle it is not connected with history, but—like all ideas, as for instance those of science—it is only effective in connection with history; "effective," that is, in a double sense: the individual always draws his idea from history, that is, from the living connection of those who bear the idea; and in the individual it only becomes actual because it is at the same time historically effective, that is, because it is used in actual practice. This idea of the historical effectiveness of the moral idea has thus taken the place of the scriptural idea of revelation, and claims to be identical with it.

But this apparent agreement with the Christian Faith can only be maintained by adding something else to it. The (rational-ethical) "Idea," as we have heard, was "first formed historically through Christ." This is an historical statement, an assertion of priority, which not only has nothing to do with that which the Christian means by uniqueness, but is also in itself wholly untenable. Secondly, this idea is said to be perfectly represented by Christ in a unique way, and, it is claimed, this also guarantees the unique power of this historical impulse. But Ritschl himself is forced to admit that we are here concerned only with something gradual or quantitative; hence, as soon as his attention is drawn to the fact, he lays reiterated emphasis upon the element of priority, and the dependence on history which it involves. "If it could be proved that a second person had existed who was equal to Him in

[1] The Christian revelation consists in this: that through Christ the ethical Idea was first introduced and shaped in personal form, "whose vocational effect thus forms the material of the complete revelation of God present in Him, or in which the Word of God is a human personality" (III⁴, p. 426).

grace and fidelity . . . this person would still be historically dependent upon Christ, and would thus be formally unequal to Him."[1] Thus Jesus is only "the absolutely Unique Person" through His position of priority in history, as the "historical Founder of Christianity." The final result of this line of argument is this: revelation in the unique sense has practically disappeared; it amounts to little more than an assertion of historical dependence which may be compared with the actual historical dependence of every mathematician of the present day upon Euclid. Further, it is just as impossible to render historical priority absolute as it is to make a mere difference of degree absolute, and reflection upon this historical dependence and the fact of priority is something so foreign to the moral and religious life of the individual that both on scientific and on religious and practical grounds this artificial structure is untenable as a purely constructive force.

A Christ who is merely *primus inter pares* is not the Christ who can be preached; further, the statement that Jesus was the first in history to give shape and form to the ethico-rational purposive principle of the "Kingdom of God" or the "Love of God" is not tenable from the scientific point of view. Historical positivism is a dangerous ally of faith. Theology, led by Schleiermacher and Ritschl into this path, could not remain at the stage at which they asserted that the historical element as such was absolute. Either it had to proceed further along the path of historical positivism and glide into the historical relativism of the religious historical school (Troeltsch), or it was obliged to return to the older Rationalism, which in its own way was solid. A third possibility remained, and this may have been Ritschl's actual ultimate intention, the possibility of returning to genuine faith in Christianity as the revealed religion; in this connection, however, this possibility is not our concern; all that we have to do at this point is to lay bare the foundations of the theology which he actually worked out. The result of this theological system, which was constructed with so much acuteness and dialectical ability, and also with so much genuine Christian knowledge in points of detail, is this: that the historical Person

[1] *Rechtfertigung und Versöhnung*, III⁴, p. 438.

of Jesus, from the point of view of ethical and religious humanity, is to a certain extent regarded as the foundation and the centre of the religious life (faith we cannot call it); inevitably this procedure provoked opposition both from the idealist and mystical side and from the Christian side.

Adolf von Harnack was Ritschl's most influential disciple; in his teaching the spirit of Rationalism is far more evident than it is in that of Ritschl himself. To Harnack revelation simply means the Gospel of Jesus, the sum total of the moral and religious knowledge of the world and of life, conceived in terms of that which it contains which is "always valid," although the historical form may continually change.[1] It manifests itself therefore to everyone who "possesses an open mind and clear insight for that which is vital and alive, and a true feeling for that which is really great," in such a way that he can "detect it behind the veils of time and history."[2] Here also then "we are not concerned to ask: What was the new element?" but "Was the message itself powerful and pure?"[3] The Gospel—as Harnack himself testifies—is based upon these two elements: "God as Father, and the human soul, so ennobled that it is able to be united with Him, and is actually thus united."[4] "Not the Son, but the Father alone belongs to the Gospel as Jesus proclaimed it."[5]

This statement is not to be understood only as a fact of history, it also constitutes the reason for faith. "No alien element may intrude."[6] There is Christian faith without a "Christology"; and it is precisely in the lack of any relation

[1] *Wesen des Christentums*, 61–65 thousand, p. 9.   [2] Ibid.

[3] Loc. cit., p. 31.   [4] Loc. cit., p. 41.

[5] Loc. cit., p. 91. Although in a note in the later editions Harnack complains that his additional phrase: "As Jesus proclaimed it," has been overlooked, and that, as the real content, Jesus certainly does belong to the later Gospel of the Church, yet this historical affirmation alters nothing in the fact that for Harnack the norm is the Gospel of Jesus, from which point of view he criticizes the Gospel about Jesus Christ, as it was proclaimed by Paul and the other Apostles. It is quite clear what Harnack means here: It was not good to depart from this simplicity of the message of Jesus. We need not to deal with Harnack's further expressions, since the subject with which we are concerned is not Harnack, but the Rationalism of the Ritschlian theology, at the point at which it is most clearly expressed.

[6] Loc. cit., p. 90.

to the Person of Christ that the universal validity of the Gospel shines forth. It is universally valid because it does not include any confession of faith in an historical personality; hence "I cannot evade the issue by saying: 'I cannot reconcile myself to the claims of Christology.' "[1] Thus the Gospel is "simpler than the Churches want to make us believe, simpler and therefore also more universal and more serious."[2]

But this clear ethical religious Rationalism was supplemented and at the same time somewhat disturbed by another idea, that of historical positivism. Firstly, Jesus was the first to think these thoughts and to proclaim them in such purity. "Nothing can alter the fact that this has actually happened."[3] Though particular elements in the message of Jesus may not be new, the message itself is certainly new in its clarity and simplicity.[4] Because Jesus Himself knows that He occupies this unique position—that of priority in history, that of a discoverer—He calls Himself the Son of God. This favoured position in history, the fact that He is the first, becomes His Messianic consciousness.[5] This rationalistic idea of priority (cf. the quotation from Wegscheider on p. 46) is further connected with another idea which also belongs to the theology of the Enlightenment: the thought of Christ as an Example; He is more than a prophet, for He has proved that He "exemplifies His message in His own person."[6] This is why we may still call Him "the Son of God,"[7] for "He has not yielded His place to anyone else, and still to-day He gives meaning and a worthy end to the life of man." For "He has been the personal realization and the power of the Gospel, and again and again we find that He is so still."[8] In particular, in this connection, emphasis is laid on the fact of His sacrificial death, from the general point of view of the truth that "the great progressive movements in history owe their very existence, and their vitality, to those who have laid down their lives for a noble cause."[9]

What does all this mean—taken in conjunction with the previous denial, in principle, of any relation with the Person

---

[1] Loc. cit., p. 90. [2] Loc. cit., p. 90. [3] Loc. cit., p. 44.
[4] Loc. cit., p. 82. [5] Loc. cit., pp. 81, 87, 91.
[6] Loc. cit., p. 82. [7] Loc. cit., p. 82.
[8] Loc. cit., p. 92. [9] Loc. cit., p. 100.

of Jesus? Nothing more than this: that here there is a vague recollection of something which the New Testament calls revelation, namely, a decisive unique event in contradistinction to the doctrine of a universal religion. But this vague recollection is placed alongside of the actual ethical and religious "Gospel"; it has no inward connection with it at all. It is an historical reminiscence, an historical value-judgment, which has no connection, and is not intended to have any connection, with the relationship between man and God. It does not belong to the Gospel: for "No alien element may be introduced into it." The Gospel itself and the "faith" which corresponds to it have nothing whatever to do with this historical fact. The second element, however, the impressiveness of the ethical and religious example of Jesus, which supports the effectiveness of His teaching, and thus has become "the actualization and the power of the Gospel," is indeed an important psychological and historical fact, but, again, it has nothing to do with faith itself. If it were otherwise, Jesus Himself would again become the object of faith and the centre of the Christian message; once more "Christology" would have come into being, and the "alien element" would have once again "forced its way into Christianity." Thus here also the return to Rationalism is complete, though it is not frankly acknowledged; the element of uniqueness has been replaced by the general doctrine of the "value of the things and energies with which we have to do."[1]

The logical development of the historicism in the Ritschlian theology led to the rise of the religious-historical school. This school shows clearly that as an historical phenomenon Biblical history is not absolute, but that at the very most its preferential position is relative in character. Positive historical facts are therefore, as such, relative. Hence subjective religion also, "faith" in the general subjective sense, must inevitably, and in principle, be detached from historical facts. It draws its life from "revelation," it is true, but this "revelation" means the spirit of idealism and mysticism, a revelation which, at bottom and everywhere, is the same in all religions. It was therefore only natural that this school of thought should look back, beyond Ritschl, to Schleiermacher,

[1] Loc. cit., p. 92.

and indeed to the logical and historical relativism of the *Reden*. Thus Schleiermacher—the Schleiermacher of the earlier period —became the theological leader of the religious-historical school. The essence of religion is "the Holy," and this is an "*a priori* category" (Otto). Religion is once more conceived as a life which wells up from the depths of the human spirit manifesting itself in various forms. "Religion expresses itself historically in religions, which have much in common with each other, and yet are also as highly specialized and individual in character" as the physical forms of life. "Their generic uniformity, however, does not exclude (as in other aspects of the human mind) specific particular forms, but it includes them all."[1] Religion "is rooted"—so says the representative of the irrational theory of religion!—"in the instincts and depths of the reasonable mind itself." Therefore the claim of the Christian religion to be the universal religion, the only true religion, is an error.[2]

The definition of the "essence of religion" in the theology of this religious-historical school does not concern us here; it is enough to know that once more men are searching for such a definition. Whether we define it as the irrational experience of the Holy (Otto) or as the experience of the Divine Presence (Troeltsch), whether we use the expression "religious *a priori*" (Troeltsch, Otto) or reject it (Scholz): in each instance it is religion in general which is meant, and its "essence." This means that the idea of revelation is only used in the sense that it is the objective correlative of this general truth. "The whole of the world or God (*sic!*) can only manifest itself through itself, through the inward feeling and certainty of the whole and its being, which we call religious experience, and which we plainly feel as the presence of this whole within ourselves." "This interior experience is described in the language of religion as revelation." "This is the revelation as everyone can experience it and testify to it, which is peculiar to a real religious life." Thus Troeltsch,[3] the outstanding leader of this whole theological school, has formulated its essential common

[1] *Vishnu Naravana*, pp. 218, 220. [2] Loc. cit., pp. 219 ff.
[3] In the encyclopedia entitled: *Religion in Geschichte und Gegenwart*, vol. 4, ¶ 918 ff.

confession of faith. It is admirable in the frankness with which it expresses the renunciation of all that is specifically Christian, and in its recognition of general religion and revelation as the only form of religion.[1]

[1] It is a question to what extent Otto has departed from this point of view through the conclusion to his book *The Idea of the Holy*. If he really means what he says on the last page quite seriously, then all that is in the preceding two hundred pages is beside the mark. According to Otto, both the experience of "The Holy" itself, and also that of "divination" (i.e. the perception of the Holy in phenomena) are *a priori* categories. They describe the nature of religion as it is always and everywhere, wherever real religion exists. Here, therefore, the differences can only be differences of degree, not differences of nature, for the nature is the same in all. Actually, indeed, the difference between "productivity" and "receptivity" is not a difference of nature, but only of degree. Otto, however, after he has treated the subject of his book quite logically along Schleiermacher's line, suddenly, on the final half-page makes a fresh double assertion. The relative difference between the productive and the receptive suddenly becomes the difference of a "higher stage, not to be derived from the first stage of mere receptivity . . . the *prophet*." And, two lines further down, the conclusion of the book: "Yet the prophet does not represent the highest stage. We can think of a third, yet higher, beyond him, a stage of revelation as underivable from that of the prophet as was his from that of common men. We can look, beyond the prophet, to one in whom is found the Spirit in all its plenitude, and who at the same time in his person and in his performance is become most completely the object of divination, in whom Holiness is recognized apparent.

Such a one is more than Prophet. He is the Son" (*The Idea of the Holy*, English trans., p. 182, conclusion of the book).

Either this conclusion is meant seriously, or the book itself, or neither. For if it is true that even the prophet experiences the Holy in a measure which only becomes possible to the ordinary man *through him* (the prophet), and again that the difference which exists between the prophet and the Son is not merely one of degree but of principle, which makes the Son altogether the Only One, then the actual religious experience of those who are not the Son, must consist in their relation to Him. In that case, however, religion could not be a *mystical feeling*, with no relation to a person independent of every kind of event and especially wholly independent of something which has taken place once for all. Religion would then be no longer mysticism, but *faith*. But in reality—as the later works of Otto show plainly —this is *not* what is meant (*cf.* the above quotations from *Vishnu Narayana*). It cannot be the meaning. For the difference between productivity and receptivity is not a difference of essential character, but it is a relative difference, or one of degree. None are without a spark of genius, and no one is an absolute genius. The analogy of the difference between the

This clear statement of principle makes no difference at all to the secondary line of thought: concerning the part played by the historical mediators of this universal religion. We are already familiar with these ideas from the fifth *Speech* of Schleiermacher. Here modern thinkers return to his conception of the religious Hero or Genius, in order that they may thus maintain a certain connection with historical facts. In the same connection Troeltsch speaks of "intensified religious individuals," "prophetic individuals," whose "influence is of a supremely forceful kind."[1] At the same time, the defenders of this position are still more clearly conscious than Schleiermacher was himself of the relative character, variety, and impermanence of such mediators of religious experience. Finally they are all arranged in a series under the conception which plainly enough leads back to the Rationalism of the Enlightenment: "Our religious teachers," or, to meet the more aesthetic type of mind, the "classical representatives of religion," are presented in a long series which extends from Moses through Jesus and Paul down to Bismarck. The recognition of very varied high-water marks in religion, of which Christianity is one, makes it from the very outset impossible to assign to the concept of uniqueness, or indeed to the fact at all, any decisive position. On the contrary, it is clearly stated by such thinkers that the theology which is based on facts is based upon a misunderstanding, since true revelation is entirely independent of such accidental matters as events. In its essence this means the return—after the long *détour* by way of Ritschl—to the conception of the one "essence of religion," which always remains the same, and is present in one religion equally as much as in another, although some religions may express this in a purer way than others.

Thus after the impossible attempts at a compromise made by Schleiermacher in his later years, and by Ritschl, modern theological thinkers have returned to the conception of religion and revelation peculiar to Idealism; in this connection it is a matter of no importance whether this teaching is stamped with

receptive and the productive in the sphere of art (p. 193) really belongs to the sphere of immanence, to the conception of religion which dominates the *Reden* of Schleiermacher.   [1] Loc. cit., col. 920.

the imprint of Hegel, Kant, Fries, Schleiermacher, or Schelling. Along these lines theology has established a connection with the convictions of the European educated man—in so far as he is not without religion at all—and the effort is being made to regard theology as one branch of general religious science and thus of general intellectual culture.

One point alone has not yet been clearly perceived: it is not fully realized that it is impossible to combine the Christian Faith with this belief in a universal religion, with this relative conception of religion itself; men have not yet perceived that on this question there *can* be no compromise; we must choose one side or the other; there is no middle path. But this lack of clarity arises out of the very nature of the case. For the fact which the Christian regards as absolutely essential—the unique final fact, the Mediator—is, just as naturally, regarded as non-essential by the believer in "general revelation." Again, while the Christian regards "faith" as a relation to that unique event, the "fact of redemption," the event which constitutes the Christian revelation, the believer in "general revelation," on the other hand, regards this precisely as a misunderstanding; he thinks it means confusing the real religious element with "rigid dogma," and regards it as an over-intellectualization of religion itself. Thus he tends to explain this insistence on the central fact of Christianity either as a return to a forensic type of theology, or as a psychological symptom of the desire to depend on authority (Scholz). Thus here one faith confronts the other; the belief in "general" revelation, religion without a mediator, the faith of mysticism and Idealism, stands over against the religion with a Mediator, the faith of the Scriptures and of the Christian Church. The one thing this proves is that a theology which refuses to admit the existence of this contradiction is not Christian.

CHAPTER III

THE MODERN CONCEPTION OF CHRIST

"WE may certainly assert with confidence that at no period in the history of the Church has the significance and influence of Jesus Christ within the Christian community ever been greater than it is to-day. This is due in part to that increased emphasis on the cultivation of personality introduced by the German Renaissance of the eighteenth century and the Romantic movement; in part, however, it is also due to the intensive labour which the theology of the nineteenth century has expended upon research into the life and the self-consciousness of Jesus, the results of which have been imparted to the Christian community in general through teaching and preaching."[1] These words of a modern theologian, although not uttered for this purpose, could not express more plainly the change which has come over the religious situation. For that which he regards as the reason for the great significance of Jesus Christ within the Christian community might be considered, if it were measured by the standard of the fundamental opposition between the Christian religion and religion in general, as an argument leading to the opposite conclusion. For when we are concerned with the "cult of personality" in the Romantic sense, or with scientific "research into the life and the self-consciousness of Jesus"—when the main tendency runs along these lines, and there is an ardent interest in these questions—it is evident that, from the point of view of the Christian faith, Jesus Christ is regarded as of no importance.

The observation which is formulated in this quotation can scarcely be attacked, only we would draw from it exactly opposite conclusions. It is literally true that during the nine-teenth and twentieth centuries there has been an extraordinary activity in the study of Jesus Christ from the point of view of the "cult of personality," and of "scientific research into His

---

[1] *R.G.G.*[1], III, p. 411.

life and His self-consciousness." Interest in a Jesus of this kind is all that is left when Jesus Christ has no longer any decisive message to give us. A growing interest in this Christ "after the flesh" coincides with a decreasing understanding of the "Christ in the flesh."[1] When therefore we note an increase of this kind of interest within the Christian "community," that is, within the Church, this simply means a proportionate disintegration of the Church, if, that is, by the "Church," we mean the fellowship of those who believe in Christ.

In earlier days it was usual to make a distinction between believers in Christ and unbelievers. To-day, however, looking at our period as a whole, and not at the exceptions, we may say that the distinction is now simply between those who admire Jesus and those who despise Him—the indifferent belong to the latter group—or between those who are full of enthusiasm for Jesus and those who hate Him. This change of emphasis in the distinction is the point at issue, not the various possibilities of decision which may be adopted within the new formulation of the problem. The distinction between those who admire Jesus and those who despise Him, between those who are enthusiastic about Him and those who hate Him, is merely relative, for it is a distinction based on an estimate of a human being. An estimate of a human being—even if he were the most important personality in the history of the world—is, in principle, a matter of no importance. No personality in world history affects me personally. When Jesus is discussed from this modern point of view, the very fact that this point of view is adopted makes the question which used to be asked—Yes or No?—meaningless; it has been replaced by an endless multiplicity of varying conceptions. There can only be one conception of Jesus Christ: for apart from this He could not be the Christ at all. But the opinions which may be held about Jesus merely as a man are countless; they coincide with the various points of view from which a human life may be studied. This statement is borne out by the modern literature on the subject of Jesus. What an immense variety there lies between the Socialist picture of Jesus drawn by a writer like Kautzky and Oscar Wilde's representation of Jesus as the One

[1] See p. 157.

who has discovered and given shape and form to the beauty of suffering; between the humanistic picture of Jesus given us by the Liberal theologians and Schopenhauer's parallel between Jesus and the Buddha, between the reverent admiration of Goethe and Nietzsche's anti-Christian ravings, between the complacent *Lives of Jesus* produced about the middle of last century (which venture to give a description of a more or less flawless development of Jesus, and thus to explain Him in a human way) and the "Christ-myth" of a man like Drews, for whom the historical figure of Jesus recedes into the mists of mythology. There is scarcely one of the leading minds of the century which has not his own particular conception of Christ —for how could anyone be a leader in European thought without offering his own interpretation of the most important fact in the history of Europe?—and yet all these views, whether positive or negative in their conclusions, are only variations on one theme: these writers do not believe in Him. For it is as impossible to *believe* in a mere human being as it is to see a sound or to handle a thought. They all see the "Christ after the flesh," not the "Christ in the flesh."

In saying this I do not mean either to deny or to affirm that these modern interpretations have seen something historically real, or that they have even rediscovered it. We shall be dealing with this question in another connection. It may quite well be true that our historical knowledge of Jesus has thereby been essentially either increased or corrected; but this would not in the least alter the fact that we may still know less of Jesus Christ than ever. All the distinctions between these views within their own sphere of reference take place on this side of the boundary line between faith in Christ or unbelief. For they are all distinctions within the human sphere. It makes no difference whether we regard Him from the social-ethical or the individual-ethical point of view, whether we take as our criterion and highest point of view His attitude towards culture, towards art, towards life, towards fellowship and Nature, or His piety, His consciousness of God, His knowledge of God, His life of prayer: the boundary of humanity is never transcended, it is merely an exploration of possibilities within the human sphere.

The same may be said of the endeavour to comprehend the personality of Jesus. In our speech personality means two things: both the totality and the depth of human existence. We cannot deny that in the period in which we live, and indeed in this century as a whole, there has been an unprecedented attempt to understand and represent the personality of Jesus in both senses of the word: in the totality of His appearance in the contemporary world of history, and also in the innermost secrets of His nature, the growth and the being of His mental, moral, and religious personality. There is indeed a whole literature on the question of the self-consciousness of Jesus, the inmost point of human spiritual existence. It is, of course, obvious that in all this the main task and the chief point is the effort to understand the religious personality, in contradistinction to the interpretation of Jesus current at the period of the Enlightenment, when, as a rule, people were quite satisfied to regard Him as an ethical Teacher and a moral Example. Indeed, one eminent theologian of recent days has taken the interior life of Jesus as the proper object of the interest of Christian theology. But, whatever may be said about all these endeavours, with their countless shades of opinion, in any case, from the very outset, there is one thing which can be said without beating about the bush: all these endeavours have nothing at all to do with the Christian problem of Jesus Christ. They all ignore Him. The personality of Jesus, even when this is interpreted in a very interior and spiritual way, with all due regard for the moral and religious importance of this question, is, in this statement of the problem, always the "Christ after the flesh," who, as such, stands outside the sphere of faith and its interests.

Again, it is the same when we approach the problem from the point of view of historical interest in the personality of Jesus, or of the existence of Jesus, or of the Gospel of Jesus. "Whoever has a fresh and living power of grasping the reality of living things, and a true sense of that which is really great must see it"[1]—that is, the Gospel and the figure of Jesus, and "the question of the testimony of Jesus to Himself cannot be insoluble to anyone who will examine our Gospels with an

[1] Harnack. See above, p. 65.

open mind.''[1] This judgment corresponds to the general principle laid down by the same theologian: "What we are and what we possess—in the highest sense of the word—we have and possess through and in history, only in that, however, which has produced results within the historical sphere." In point of fact, the human sphere is historical, and the historical sphere is human. So far as we are human beings at all we are capable of understanding history. It is quite true that we only need "a living insight into all that is vitally alive," even in order to accept Jesus as an historical personality, even in order to understand the self-testimony of Jesus, in this general human sense. Only we must be quite clear in our own minds that when we speak of "seeing" or "meeting" Jesus in this way, we mean something entirely different from that which is implied in that mysterious scene in which, for the first time, a disciple made this confession: "Thou art the Son of the Living God!" and Jesus answered: "Blessed art thou, Simon Bar-Jonah, for flesh and blood hath not revealed it unto thee"; we mean a "seeing" and a "hearing" of a different kind from that suggested by the words: "he that hath ears to hear, let him hear; to you it is given to know the mysteries of the kingdom of heaven, but to them that are without all things are in parables."

In principle all that lies on the historical human plane is accessible to every human being. But, for this very reason, this historical interpretation of Jesus, however true and profound it may be, differs entirely from that of the witness of Christ in the New Testament, which, according to its own evidence, can only be gained through the special grace of vision which has been "illuminated by faith."

This "figure of Jesus" which forms the object of so many historical, biographical, psychological, humanitarian studies is on the same plane as that "personality" of Jesus (to which allusion has just been made). All these representations of Jesus are as far removed from the Jesus Christ of faith as the mystery of God is removed from the intellectual conception of God, as "general" revelation (which is really no revelation at all) is removed from "special" revelation, as the

[1] *Wesen des Christentums*, p. 79.

Word of God is distinct from moral and religious humanity. This interpretation of Jesus is an explanation in general terms; this does not mean that it is a universal empirical fact, but—as we have just heard from the lips of an excellent historian—that it is everywhere possible. This is precisely why it is not the interpretation offered by faith. Within humanity as such there is no faith, only the relation of immanence, the acceptance of another as essentially on the same plane as myself, an interpretation within that comprehensive whole, which is always and everywhere present, of reason, or Nature, or general revelation; essentially this is interpretation in terms of history.

Within this sphere there are of course heights and depths, peaks and depressions, masses and leaders, heroes and hero-worshippers, geniuses and average human beings, independent and dependent personalities. And just as in every chain of mountains there is always one peak which towers above the rest, so we must admit that even among the leaders of humanity there must be—at least from a certain point of view—one who stands out above all the rest. Hence in all this modern talk about Jesus discussion centres round this question: whether, and in what sense, properly speaking within what dimension and from what point of view Jesus may be regarded as the highest point attained by humanity. Within these possibilities there is, of course, a maximum; this is represented by the well-known testimony of Goethe in his old age (in his conversations with Eckermann), in which he says that in the Gospels we catch "the vital reflection of a certain majesty which radiated from the personality of Christ, an influence as divine as any manifestation of the Divine which ever has appeared upon earth. If I am asked whether I feel I can— whether it is in accordance with my nature—to offer Him reverent worship and homage, I reply: Certainly! I bow before Him as the divine revelation of the highest principle of morality."

Note that significant phrase: "whether it is in accordance with my nature." It indicates both the knowledge and the organ through which this knowledge is received: human nature, the nature of Goethe, understood wholly in the sense of the spiritual nature, of the deepest humanity. We must also note that the speaker goes on to say: "Does someone ask me whether it is in accordance with my nature to worship the sun, again I reply: Certainly! for the sun is likewise a revelation of the highest, and it is indeed the mightiest force which we children of men can perceive." This is not an irrelevant quotation, introduced at this point simply as an example of Goethe's "paganism." No, I quote it simply in order to show in what category Christ is placed, and regarded as a Revealer: it is the "natural light," the category of general revelation, explicitly defined as such both as to object and subject. Both the content and the recipient of the revelation are regarded in a general light, although of course the revelation is not manifested everywhere to so high a degree. Revelation is a symbol, Christ is the supporter, the representative, of a general principle, like many others, only more complete than many of them, perhaps the most complete of them all; these other men are, however, still "divine revelations of the highest principle" just as He is.

The preoccupation of the nineteenth century with Jesus, as has already been suggested, has also led to quite different results: it has been emphatically denied that Jesus is the One who has done most to shape and influence the general moral life of man. In spite of all the admiring homage which has been paid to this figure of Jesus, some have been offended by the picture of the "uncultivated Asiatic" (Naumann), or with Nietzsche they have made Him responsible for the slave revolt of the herd-man, for the ethic of retaliation. On the other hand, others, who were nearer to the Christian Church, have supplemented the testimony of Goethe on the religious side by laying special emphasis upon His leading position in the realm of religious knowledge; they point out that it is not only moral but, above all, religious force which radiates from Him towards us in incomparable majesty, and further, that He was the first to give us these standards which have now become our own, the first discoverer of the ultimate general truths, religious principles, and norms. But all these variants, however instructive and valuable they may be, however true—or untrue— have nothing to do with the faith in Christ of the Bible and of the Church. Even the most enthusiastic panegyric about

Jesus, the most ardent expression of homage, the recognition of Him as the highest of all religious revelations, does not necessarily imply that the speaker has the faintest spark of real faith in Christ. For all such expressions still belong to the sphere of general revelation, to the sphere of humanity, with its outstanding leaders in thought and life.

The names used to describe these outstanding personalities vary greatly; this is especially true of the highest of them all: the personality of Jesus. People speak of "heroes of religion," of "mediators," of "great souls," "elect souls," "prophets": or, if they wish to single out Jesus as the One above all others, they speak of His uniqueness, of His nature as One who is "more than prophet," as the Revealer. They use the name which the New Testament uses for its testimony to Him: He is the "Son of God," the "Redeemer," the "One who atones"; indeed, some even venture to go so far as to speak of the "Divinity" of Christ. Words are free, and we cannot forbid their use, but we must not allow ourselves to be misled by them. We must not allow the use of language to confuse the categories of our thought. Everything depends on whether these Christian expressions mean what they were coined to express, or whether they simply denote a description of the highest summit which can be attained within the sphere of humanity. If the latter supposition be true, then essentially—in spite of the use of the highest Christian terminology—the creed which these words imply differs no whit from that other point of view, where people do not use these expressions because they respect their meaning. On the whole, in this connection the "children of this world," for obvious reasons, use plainer language than the theologians. A great part of the theological history of the last century represents the labour of filling old wineskins with new wine, but the wine was offered as if it were old. When a man's real belief in Christ consists in regarding Him as leader, hero, the *primus inter pares*, the highest point in the history of religion, the loftiest peak in the moral and religious history of humanity, he would do better, for the sake of simplicity and truth, to renounce the use of the terms Christ, Son of God, Redeemer, Mediator, Reconciler, for all these terms mean something quite different.

Hoc est Christum cognoscere, beneficia ejus cognoscere. The way in which Christ is regarded comes out very plainly to-day in the way in which His "achievement" is considered. For obvious reasons on this point the modern conception is still more vague and more varied than it is in relation to His Person. For the modern "cult of personality" demands that first of all we should simply look at a great personality, seek to understand Him, and rejoice in the picture before us, without inquiring about any possible effect or influence He may have exercised; this means that the aesthetic factor is an important element in the modern conception of Christ. Thus Goethe uttered that amazingly clear and beautiful estimate of the Person of Jesus, but whether he would have returned an equally clear answer to the question: What is the *beneficium* of this Christ? what is the significance of this Christ? seems more than doubtful. That question is not asked. "Disinterested approval" (Kant) is an end in itself. If, however, this question is asked, then the answer which is given is that which corresponds to the conception of personality: the answer of history. Jesus Christ is one of those events which—to use Harnack's phrase—have really "produced results." Thus Jesus has initiated a new period in the history of the world, He is the Founder of the Christian religion. As we look back into the past[1] we can, to some extent, measure His influence, His achievement as a fixed and settled thing. This subject has received a great deal of attention, and has given rise to endless discussion. Whereas some thinkers, above all the great German Idealists, and the great historians of the Romantic School, regarded this movement inaugurated by Christ as an immense advance, indeed, as the decisive entrance into the final phase of spiritual development (Hegel), others came to the exactly opposite conclusion; in their opinion,

[1] Perhaps this might be expressed in the language Goethe uses about great "daemonic" human beings: "That creative energy, by means of which deeds are achieved which are able to manifest themselves in the presence of God and in Nature, and which, for this very reason, have effective and lasting results," where "often a single idea has influenced whole centuries, and as certain individuals, by means of the spirit which emanated from them, have impressed a certain character upon their own age which has been evident in later generations, and has exercised a beneficent influence upon them" (Weinel: *Jesus im 19 Jahrhundert*, p. 25).

Christianity was the plague-spot in the history of the world. Of late years the tendency has been to regard Christianity less as the cause of this historical epoch and more as its characteristic product, and Jesus Himself is more or less ignored.

Taking into account the infinite variety of possible positions which lie between these two extremes, I must confine myself to the statement that all these differences lie entirely outside the sphere with which Christianity is concerned. The Christian faith has just as little to do with the influence of Jesus on the history of the world as it has to do with His historical personality. It is not interested in the "Founder of Christianity," nor in His influence on history. For historical results are always capable of being interpreted in two different ways. The Christian believer, as such, has no "historical interest." For that which overcomes the world, the growth of the "Kingdom of God," with which he is concerned, is hid from the eyes of the world. Whoever cleaves to Christ from the historical point of view does not cleave to Him personally, but in an aesthetic manner, as a spectator, not as a participant. The *beneficia Christi* of which faith speaks are such as could not possibly be inserted into any historical reflection. That the Person of Christ has had an influence on the course of world history more beneficial and more enduring than any other fills the believer neither with elation nor with misgiving. All this lies entirely outside his formulation of the problem. Hence statements like the following have nothing to do with the Christian interest in Jesus: "Upon the path of the spiritualization of the ancient religion He was not the first, it is true, but He was the One who brought the process to completion" (Keim)[1]; "the redeeming word which guarantees true personality, enduring vital energy, and lasting peace, was pronounced first of all by

---

[1] Keim: *Geschichte Jesu*[3], p. 370. When Keim, at another point, speaks thus: "His religion, which He brought to the world, is unquestionably the most precious and abiding achievement of the human spirit" (p. 365) he implies, as indeed he himself always admitted, an interpretation of Christ which differs entirely from that of the New Testament and of the Church. But whereas a man like Keim does not seek to conceal this difference, and is not afraid of showing that it originates in the immanental habit of thought ("achievement of the human spirit"), during the last fifty years it has become customary to conceal this difference.

the Son of Joseph" (A. Meyer)[1]; "Jesus only brought to completion what the best men before Him had desired" (Weinel)[2]; "as the author of the perfect spiritual and ethical religion Jesus is above all other men" (Ritschl).[3] For all such opinions are historical estimates, the kind of remark made by a student of history, statements indeed which no one but a

[1] Arnold Meyer, in *Unsere religiösen Erzieher, Jesus*, p. 47.

[2] Weinel: *Neutestamentliche Theologie*, p. 226.

[3] Cf. Otto Ritschl, in his article on his father, in *P.R.E.*, p. 28. It is a remarkable fact that Weinel believes that Ritschl's view of Jesus differed from that of the Idealistic philosophers, who, "as we saw in the case of Fichte, Schleiermacher, and Hegel, could only understand and revere Jesus as the embodiment of an Idea" (*Jesus*, p. 268). They meant precisely the same as that which Weinel expressed in other forms: religion as something universal, the universal religious-ethical truths of God, love, forgiveness, etc., which are free from all relation to a Person. The Hegelian Biedermann meant the same when he spoke of his "Christ-principle," and, as we have just seen Keim means the same when he speaks about "spiritual religion." Indeed, we do the Idealists an injustice if we suppose that by an "Idea" they mean something purely logical, or coldly intellectual. If anyone doubts this, let him read once more Hegel's *Philosophy of Religion*, noting particularly what he describes as "cultus." The only difference is this: that the Idealists of those days knew what an "Idea" was, whereas modern theologians scarcely seem to know this at all. When it is said that Jesus possesses the true religion, "solutions for the deepest problems of life, which obviously have never been surpassed," solutions which give "release to our contemporaries just as effectively as to people of long ago" (Weinel, loc. cit., p. 66), there, essentially, what is meant is exactly that which the older Idealists meant by the word "idea" or "principle," and as it has been expressed still more clearly by a modern thinker: "As the Eternal Light of the Idea breaks out again and again in personal and historical conditions," so the aim of a *Life of Jesus* should be to illustrate this by a definite example (P. W. Schmidt: *Geschichte Jesu*, p. v). A similar point of view occurs in the older book by Bousset on *Jesus*. The connection with the "Hero" conception of Carlyle is evident, and this theory, which interprets Jesus as the highest example of religious humanity, is not destroyed by a statement of this kind: "To us also Jesus is more than one of a series, we cannot find any description which would fit Him and others, and yet would disclose the depths of His nature; He is beyond our reach." "We call Him the Son of the Heavenly Father" (p. 99). That also is only an historical estimate, which does not alter the fact that any one of us may be religious like Jesus, but not that only *through and in Him can we believe*. No bridge leads from the highest point in the realm of human personality to the Mediator.

student of history would venture to make at all, and which therefore are only of interest for those who are seeking historical knowledge. They are observations about historical priority, influence on history, and comparative originality; they may be perfectly correct, but so far as the central significance of Christ in the Christian religion is concerned, they are wholly irrelevant. The question "Who founded the Christian religion?" is one for the historian; it does not concern the Christian; indeed, it is only of interest for the historian. In the language of Christian faith this conception does not find a place. To confuse this historical interest and this historical point of view with the Christian point of view is a bad μετάβασις εἰς ἄλλο γένος, an intellectual confusion which a theological thinker ought not to allow himself to perpetrate.

Many modern thinkers, however, do not think of the influence of Christ in terms of world history. They mean a "personal" influence. We are not now thinking of the influence of the "Gospel of Jesus" as the modern man understands it, for this can be detached from the Person of Jesus. Nor do we mean, to use the words of Weinel,[1] that "Jesus was able to offer solutions to the ultimate questions of life which apparently have not yet been transcended . . . solutions which have a redemptive force for the people of the present day, just as they had for human beings many hundred years ago." The point with which we are here concerned is the statement of this same modern man, after he has detached the Gospel from the Person of Jesus as a general truth, about the *personal* influence and significance of Jesus. The first thing is the general statement that a universal moral and religious truth is only effective when it is presented in the actual life of an individual. That Jesus is the embodiment of His own teaching, that in Him the abstract Word took concrete form, that He "is the personal realization and energy of the Gospel, and is still felt and known to be such."[2] Such a view may even be described as a statement of the "Incarnation of the Word," but do not let us be misled, for this modern point of view has no connection with the Johannine doctrine of the "Word made flesh." For the Logos is the mystery of God, manifested only in His Incarnation.

[1] See above, p. 82.   [2] Harnack, see above, p. 66.

But the "Word" in this modernistic sense is a general truth, a "solution of ultimate questions," which is not necessarily connected with the Person of Jesus. Here the "Incarnation" belongs wholly to the sphere of human history; moreover, it is a process which, apart from Jesus, has always taken place, and is still taking place, wherever pure goodness and nobility of soul radiate from a human life. It is not as though this truth could not be known apart from the figure of Jesus, or were ineffective apart from Him; it simply means that nowhere else is it so clearly visible because nowhere else is it presented in such a concrete form, or manifested so perfectly in a human life.

This is what the modern man, so far as his attitude towards Jesus is one of respect and reverence, prizes in Him: this unique, or almost unique, congruence of life and teaching, this perfectly proportioned moral and religious humanity, as the most effective way of arousing a similar disposition in others. It is the contagious power of example, or—to use a rather less didactic expression—it is the personal "communication of life," which at this point alone in human life attains such purity, elevation, and matchless force. The validity of these moral and religious truths is indeed guaranteed by these ideas themselves; but for us feeble and imperfect human beings, who suffer from a thousand hindrances of one sort and another, something more is needed: we need someone, so to speak, to live out these ideas before our eyes. It is, of course, true, that this is not quite the way to put it. For how can a human being live out before others that God is Love, or that I ought to do good, to do the Will of God? But the proof by the analogy of human example is far more powerful than any reasons which may be adduced from the educational and psychological point of view. The moral reliability of a person increases to an infinite degree the credibility of his teaching. In itself His message can be detached from His Person. But, from the practical psychological point of view, His own life is a powerful factor, which also helps to increase its influence.

There is no need to labour this point any further. For in this realm of reverence for Jesus we are now in the purely relative sphere, with its educational and psychological point

of view. Here the central interest is the power of religious and
ethical stimulus. It amounts to no more than this, for truth
itself does not depend upon personal factors. This psychological
law of the relative co-operating factors does exist, however, in
which instruction through visible illustration is so much more
effective than abstract teaching in the moral and religious
sphere, as is the case in other spheres of knowledge. Here we
see the working of the principle that the idea which is clothed
in flesh and blood is, practically, vastly more effective than
the abstract idea, in spite of the fact that so far as the essence
of the matter is concerned the idea is exactly the same. This
law of psychological mediation determines the difference
between the Gospel as a doctrine and the Gospel as it is
formulated in the Person of Jesus; to those who "admire"
Jesus this difference constitutes the personal significance of
Jesus.

Thus so far what has been said does not really apply to
His Person but to His teaching. In principle it is only the
teaching, the truth itself, which is the redeeming element—
whatever this expression may mean; but, practically and
psychologically as well as historically, personality is a factor
which greatly strengthens the influence of the teaching, thus
it is itself "redeeming," it unites the soul with God, it acts as
a reconciling, mediating factor. This process is conceived in
such a way that the connection with the Person is not necessary
or unconditional, and the personal element declines in proportion to the strength of the interior life of the person
concerned. The distance between the productive and the
receptive elements is relative; there are degrees of approximation until complete assimilation has been attained.

Here the thought is the same as that expressed by Schleiermacher in his fifth *Speech*, where he says that religious heroes
in general are needed so long as we are not strong enough to
stand on our own feet. But even if we were to get as far as
this, the historical fact would still remain that we are historically
conditioned by Jesus, because He is the One who initiated this
historical-religious movement.

Further, it is only possible to compare the Christian religion
(that is, what in this sphere of general religion is regarded as

the Christian religion) with other religions on the basis of this specifically modern assumption. What Jesus is to the Christian, Buddha is—even if only approximately—to the Buddhist. What the Gospel is to the Christian that, approximately, the doctrine of the Bhagavadgita is to the Hindu. On the other hand, the modern conception of Jesus and of His significance makes a definite distinction between the Christian religion and the history of religion in general impossible, even when such an endeavour is made. Here Christ is not the decisive fact, in the absolute, serious sense. For His teaching is here regarded as a general truth towards which history has been moving, and is still moving, apart from His Person altogether. From the historical point of view no turning-points are absolute; they are all relative. If the truth which Jesus brought is not really new (and if the teaching of Jesus is regarded solely from the point of view of general truth it is not wholly new), if all that is new about it is its complete purity, power, and simplicity, then also it follows that its influence on the world cannot be regarded as the decisive event, but only as one very important event, perhaps, comparatively speaking, as the most important among other similar events. Lessing's idea of the education of the human race according to which the divine guidance of world history consists in the fact that the process of development has been speeded up and furthered by means of unusual personalities and events, and by the appearance of Jesus in particular, may be an intellectualistic and almost a pedagogical conception, but in principle the modern conception goes no further.

For an event to belong to the "wholly other," in principle, would be an event in "super-history"; it would belong to that kind of history whose end lies outside history altogether; it would be absolutely final and unique. The issue is clear: either this fact is unique and absolute, or it is only relative; either we are confronted with an absolutely incomparable new fact, or rather a new category which transcends history and is thus no longer history at all, the fulfilment of time in the midst of time; or it is something which is within the sphere of history, and which therefore can only be distinguished from the historical sphere in a purely relative sense. Between religious and moral humanity, and revelation in the Christian sense, there is no middle way. Even the highest stage of humanity is only another grade removed from that of the average man, and is only a relative distinction; it is therefore not the turning-point, the decisive point—not even if it is the highest—but only one point in the general line of development which is formed by all.

Further, this presupposes that what we call "redemption" is itself continuous with the need for redemption, that it is possible to step from the one to the other. This is actually the presupposition which underlies the German Idealistic philosophy of history. The whole of the historical process is the history of redemption, of the growing Kingdom of God. Just as when someone wakes in the morning, between the first moment of waking and the state of being fully awake there is an infinite series of continuous stages of becoming awake, so the whole of history is an awakening of humanity, within which Christ is the "moment" when humanity is fully awake. This "moment" is called redemption, the Kingdom of God. But within this process there is no real change, all flows on evenly and without interruption. The state of non-redemption merges naturally into that of being redeemed.

Thus the history of Christianity is embedded in the general history of thought and of religion. The truth that breaks forth in the Gospel of Jesus is not new truth which did not exist before that time, it was truth which had always existed, the immanent purpose of world history; but this purpose did not become clear and visible until Christ came. The differences between distinct and indistinct vision are, however, only relative. Hence the differences between the power of the distinct truth and that of the indistinct are also relative. If then Jesus exercises a redeeming influence as an historical personality, world history as a whole also exercises a redeeming influence. It is the stream which leads to the goal of redemption, even though there may be places where the stream flows more slowly on account of obstructions in its path, and others where it flows swiftly and unhindered.

If, however, the transition from the need of redemption to redemption itself is continuous, there can be no thought of a antithesis. For every historical "moment" contains already an admixture of redemption and that which needs redemption; then that which needs to be overcome and the force which overcomes it no longer stand in opposition to each other; they form a connected series, at the lower end of which stands the complete need of redemption, and at the upper end perfect redemption. This idea of continuity, characteristic of the Idealistic interpretation of history, is the presupposition which lies behind the modern view of the so-called "redemptive" influence of Jesus.

The same applies also to the individual. If Jesus is the most perfect incarnation of the moral and religious ideal, then His influence can only consist in the intensification of the movement which is already present towards the ideal. He is only taken into account as a dynamic, and therefore relative, factor. For all that is dynamic is relative. It strengthens, intensifies, furthers, brings the hour of decision nearer, but it is not itself the decisive factor. For if it were, I would be bound absolutely to it, I would have an attitude towards it which would be entirely different in principle from my attitude towards all other historical events, which can indeed never relieve me from the decision but can only bring the decision more or less near. All that is historical is a help to me for the time being, a means of stimulus, a means of education; it is never something decisive. The decisive step must be taken by me alone, and in order to do this I must look away from all that is historical. Then it comes to this: God and the soul, the soul and God. No one else can take my place. Thus an historical event may be a significant factor in the course of my development, so significant that in our loose way of speaking we may even call it "decisive," but in the ultimate sense of the word it is not. For this could only be the case if everything were to depend on the fact that this one thing has taken place, if my salvation and the salvation of everyone else were to depend on the fact that this has happened and *only* on this, the one absolutely decisive fact. No reasonable man, whether Christian or non-Christian, ever asserts anything of this kind of any historical event in the sense of universal humanity, or of religion in general, or of its highest achievements.

But this is exactly what the Christian religion does claim for Jesus Christ. It is precisely this that Christianity means by "uniqueness" and the Mediator, and it is on this account that it is impossible to fit these conceptions into the modern interpretation of Christ. To the modern man they seem arrogant, intolerant, and unworthy of free human beings. *This* is not the meaning of the modern talk about "uniqueness"; it also is intended in a relative sense. It is indeed admitted that Jesus is a Reconciler, but only in the sense that He helps me to be that which He is Himself. In principle He is on my side, determined that sooner or later I and all other men shall overtake Him. His significance for me consists solely in the fact that what I and all other men have, or should have, He possesses in fuller measure, and that He has it in the way in which we ought to have it. Therefore He can go on communicating His life to us until the difference between us has been effaced. The presupposition for the possibility of His influence consists in the fact that what He gives I already—even if in a very humble way—myself possess. His uniqueness is that of the *primus inter pares*, and for that very reason it is not absolute but relative, not the decision itself but a help towards a decision. In the end it comes to this: all that the modern man expects from Jesus is assistance. Hence, in principle, it is true he is independent of Him, but practically—and for the moment—he is dependent upon Him. Hence in principle Christ is on our side, and He can only so far be regarded as Redeemer to the extent in which all that is historical is at the same time redemption and in need of redemption.

It would not be necessary to give so much attention to this idea, in itself so simple, were it not for the fact that here too modern theology, in its fatal endeavour to be modern and Christian at the same time, has rendered the simple contrast infinitely complicated by its gift for producing a complicated tangle. It is quite clear that the modern conception of Christ, both of the Person and of the Work of the Redeemer, is no mere formulation of the ancient truth of the Scriptures and of the Church, but is something absolutely different; the difference is just as great as that which exists between general and special revelation. But modern theology, in so far as it is not "Liberal theology," which openly confessed its opposition to the faith of the Scriptures, has tried to conceal this fact by stating that it only desires to set aside certain undesirable formulations of ancient dogma, but that it does not touch the centre of the Christian faith itself. All that I now have to do is to show briefly that behind the language used by modern theology, which is modelled as far as possible on the language of the Bible, there lies simply this general modern conception of Christ, which is a contradiction of the Christian conception.

Once more, of course, it was Schleiermacher who was the most successful of these interpreters who have thus transformed the meaning of the leading ideas in Christian thought. At the same time we must admit, in all fairness to him, that in the depths of his heart, in his *Glaubenslehre* he really had the intention of directing the attention of his own romantic period away from religion in general to the Christian faith in particular. But he had not calculated the cost of this transformation. He did not go far enough; so, although he intended to go further, he remained on this side of the river he meant to cross. It is, of course, true that in his later work he no longer speaks (as in the *Reden*) of Jesus as one amongst many, as one of the "heroes of religion." On the other hand, he still maintains that Jesus can only be regarded as a subject of religion, as a religious personality. Thus he still retains the fundamental view of the Enlightenment and of Idealism, which regards Jesus merely as one of the representatives of piety, of religious humanity, even if one of the foremost, who thus in principle stands on our side, who is therefore not a new category but simply the highest point attainable by humanity.

In order, however, to describe Him as the Unique One, Schleiermacher invented a new expression to describe this maximum point, which at least appeared to suggest a new quality: the archetype. Jesus is the *archetype* of the religious man, through the absolute energy of His consciousness of God. In itself, indeed, it is quite possible to imagine that this expression does really imply a new category or a new quality, possibly that which Christian doctrine means by perfect humanity, which, as such, could belong only to the Son of God. But even this presupposition is lacking in Schleiermacher. This doctrine of the "archetype" in Christ is connected with his idea—an impossible one for the Christian faith—of a continual approximation of the historical to the ideal, which includes the possibility of an absolute maximum.

Within the Christian sphere of knowledge this possibility does not exist, because sin is not something which can continuously be set aside, nor is sinlessness the disappearance of a last relic of sin; it would be nothing less than the absolute miracle of a new creation. Therefore, from the Christian point of view, there can be no continuous approximation to that maximum, as is possible and even necessary in Schleiermacher's conception of sin and history. Hence for him the existence of a maximum of this kind, of the "archetype," does not imply the slightest break in the continuity of the history of humanity. It is produced simply by the intensification of the tendency which is itself placed within humanity, and consists in an ever more complete approximation to the goal. In other words, in the Christian religion the sinless human being means the miracle of an absolute new creation; but for Schleiermacher it means only the attainment of the final end of human development by a speeding-up process.[1]

[1] It is absolutely impossible to understand Schleiermacher's doctrine of Christ apart from its historical-philosophical presuppositions, as they are developed in his "Ethic." It is this optimistic monistic theory of development which determines not only his doctrine of Original Sin, but also his Christology and his doctrine of the New Birth. Read for instance paragraph 5 of the Introduction to the *Glaubenslehre* from this point of view, and it is evident that all is governed by the idea of continuity; nowhere is there a break, or a turning-point, everywhere suspicious comparatives are employed: "easier," "higher," "all the more pious" "gradually"—Christ is one "moment" in this unbroken stream of development, which before Him and apart from Him was already flowing in the same direction as after Him and through Him, and which is not concluded by Him—although it receives a powerful impulse from Him—but goes on further, from stage to stage, as it did before and alongside of Him, in the schema of "approximations." If the two fundamental factors in the thought of Schleiermacher are retained, namely, the optimistic idea of the development of civilization and the mystical idea of universal religion, which are both included in the *Glaubenslehre*, we know that this system *cannot* regard Christ as of final

The conception of the Work of Christ corresponds exactly with that of His Person. Here also in principle Schleiermacher cannot go further than the point which he reached in the *Reden*, where he spoke of "mediators" in the plural: they are stimulators, men who awaken the religious feeling in the hearts of others. Now in the very nature of the case an absolute stimulus is an impossibility. It contradicts the whole line of argument. For the greater the self-activity the less need there is for stimulus. Thus the one who stimulates others must, to the extent in which he is effective, make himself superfluous. This is what is said in the *Reden*, where the idea of stimulation is carried to its logical conclusion. In the *Glaubenslehre* (*The Christian Faith*), however, there arises the inconsistent conception of an absolute stimulation; for nothing less than this lies behind the much-discussed idea: "reception into the absolute potency of His God-consciousness." The nearer the Christian comes to this state the more unnecessary does Christ become to him. If he is really taken up into the absolutely potent God-consciousness, then he becomes an ideal (archetype) like Christ and needs Christ no longer.

Here the whole construction of Schleiermacher breaks down. On the one hand, in order to elevate the Work of Christ to the level of His Person, out of the sphere of the relative, he is obliged to speak of an absolute influence, thus of an absolute transference of religious power. This leads, however [because

significance, even though Schleiermacher takes great pains to *assert* that Christ does possess this kind of significance. Neither is the constant "strength of His God-consciousness" (p. 94) something by which Christ is in principle contrasted with the less pious person, for there is a continuous approximation to this constancy and strength; both are indeed only dynamic-relative conceptions—nor is the "absorption into the strength of His God-consciousness" (¶ 100) a turning-point in the life of humanity, or of the individual, since before and alongside of Christ there was and is a relatively strong God-consciousness, which indeed according to Schleiermacher himself (*Wesen der Religion*) does not differ essentially, but only in degree, from that which was achieved by Christ; and since even this communication of the powerful God-consciousness of Jesus only leads once more to an "approximation" to Perfection, as the religious life before and alongside of Christ consists precisely in this approximation. Where is there room in this scheme for any kind of decisive significance? In the dynamic idea there are only degrees, but no decision.

it is thought out directly, according to the causal law which here forms the framework], to the equivalence of cause and effect, so that the Christian himself becomes what Christ is. On the other hand, Schleiermacher certainly desires to preserve the union of the believer with Christ and the permanent pre-eminence of Christ. This he only succeeds in doing by a sudden leap from the causal relation of the stimulation to another: to the relation of faith, as dependent on the Word of God, which proclaims that in Christ God speaks forgiveness.

He cannot develop this idea, however, since to do so would destroy the whole edifice. His whole Christology is built up upon the causal *schema*, that is, upon the equivalence of cause and effect, by means of the famous statement: "we are all conscious that approximations to the state of blessedness which are present in the Christian life are based upon a new common life, brought into being by God, which works against the common life of sinfulness and the unhappiness which it produces"—this was the only possibility on the basis of Schleiermacher's conception of religion and of his theological method of regress. If redemption means having religion, then indeed we must strive to get as much religion as possible; then the significance of Christ can be no more than the imparting of this absolute amount of religion. But this gives rise to the contradictory statement: the historical-dynamic element is, by its very nature, relative, yet absoluteness is here predicated of it. If, however, this is predicated, then through this communication of energy the Christian becomes equal to Christ—and this is a conclusion which no Christian theology will tolerate for a moment.[1]

[1] Cf. on this point Brunner: *Die Mystik und das Wort*, pp. 247–67. The "turning-point" which Christ brings into the life of one who (apart from Him) is developing religiously is supposed to consist in this (¶ 106, 1) that through Him the "continuity of the old (life) ceased and that of the new began to grow." As though the development of anything in the spiritual life were not always a process of increasing stability, as though "becoming," growth—thus even the development of the religious consciousness apart from Christ—could be anything other than an ever-increasing stability of this element which is growing! And as though this beginning of becoming stable were a turning-point! Is it not plain to all who have eyes to see that the theologian who attempts the impossible task of trying to equate the principle of continuity of the Idealistic philosophy of history with its exact

93

The state of absolute redemption, in the sense of something which can be actually seen and handled in experience and corresponds to the absolute redeeming cause, contradicts both the facts of real experience and the Christian creed. This unhappy result can only be concealed to some extent by being broken off at either end, as is attempted by Schleiermacher's doctrine of the New Birth, by means of all sorts of distorted compromises. The basis of all these difficulties is this, that Schleiermacher is trying to combine the Christian doctrine of Christ with his idea of general religion inherited from the Enlightenment and the Romantic Movement. He desires to do this by using for the Person of Christ the general conception of "heroes of religion," and for His Work the general religious conception of "stimulation" or "communication of energy," but in order to connect both these ideas with Christian doctrine he tries to lift them up to the sphere of the Absolute. It is impossible, however, that this should succeed, since from the very outset both are relative magnitudes. This is the fundamental inconsistency in his doctrine of redemption through Christ.

So far as Ritschl is concerned the situation is not so very different. The difference between his view and that of Schleiermacher consists essentially in this: that he exchanges the formulae of Schleiermacher, which correspond with Schleiermacher's mystical conception of religion, for those which agree with his own rational and ethical conception of religion. For him also Christ is simply the ideal (archetype) of piety, the subject of religion. But he emphasizes more strongly than his predecessor that Jesus is the historical pioneer, the Founder; this can be done because from the outset the ethical idea has a closer connection with the life of history, with the community, and also a closer affinity with the Christian message than the mystical point of view. Thus the peculiar element in Jesus is this, that in Him the divine purposive will, the direction of the will towards the "Kingdom of God" is perfect, and this in a twofold sense: perfect in knowledge—and

opposite, the dualistic-eschatological idea, the philosophy of development with the uniqueness of revelation, becomes involved in an inextricable net of embarrassment!

thus in the word He proclaimed—and perfect in His life and will as an individual. Ritschl finds this expressed above all in His moral and religious fidelity to His vocation, in the fact that He finds "in the End of God His own personal realization as well,"[1] and that He realizes this practically in life. His death and His sufferings mean that in them we see most clearly expressed the perfect devotion of Jesus to His task, and His perfect power of overcoming the resistance of the world.

But this leads to a second point: Jesus, as the "Founder of the perfected spiritual and ethical religion," is definitely superior to all the rest of mankind.[2] "Since as the Founder of the Kingdom of God in the world, in other words, as the Bearer of God's ethical lordship over men, He occupies a unique position towards all who have received a like aim from Him, therefore He is that Being in the world, in whose self-end God makes effective and manifest after an original manner His own eternal self-end, whose whole activity therefore, in discharge of His vocation, forms the material of that complete revelation of God which is present in Him, in whom, in short, the Word of God is a human person."[3] Hence we can speak of the "Deity" of Christ.

The historical position of privilege, as the first, and the graduated position of privilege, as the most perfect representative of that which all men ought to be, are thus gathered up in the credal expression—borrowed from the usage of the Bible and the Church—of the Deity of Christ. It is not difficult to understand both that protests were made against this misuse of a word which in the language of the Bible and of the Church meant something entirely different, and also that Ritschl defended himself against these attacks. For, since to Ritschl the ethico-rational idea of purpose and the being of God mean one and the same thing, since all that can be said about God is in Ritschl's thinking abstract and not personal—a "value," not a "Being"—so it is entirely in line with the whole argument of his system to attribute to the first founder of this idea, from the historical and complete point of view, the predicate of "Deity." Then, however, the further

[1] *Rechtfertigung und Versöhnung*, III[4], p. 439.   [2] See above, p. 59.
[3] Loc. cit., p. 425,

logical inference could not fail to be drawn (see above, p. 62) that the predicate of Deity should be transferred from the first point of the historical series also to the next, that is, from Christ to the Christian Church. The "Deity" (and in this we see clearly the independence of the idea from all that is positively historical), once it is conceived in this way, is not dependent on the fact that it once took place at a certain point in time, nor on the perfection of its personal form. As the concrete form of the idea it is possible to be graduated, and in this graduated form it can be applied in an infinite number of ways to all that is historical. It is the "manifestation of the divine" of which Goethe used to speak.

That Ritschl believed that these ideas really did represent the meaning of the witness to Christ in the New Testament was certainly an error which could be proved, and in the endeavour to prove this both the adherents and the opponents of the New Testament faith were arrayed against him on the ground of scientific truth.

Ritschl's conception of the "Work" of Christ corresponds exactly with his conception of the Person of Christ. Indeed, scarcely anything need be added on this subject. For the Work of Christ—according to Ritschl—consists precisely in this, that He "formulated this idea within the sphere of history," "established" the Kingdom of God, "founded" Christianity, and in so doing, so far as individuals enter into the current of this historical movement, Christ "redeems" or "reconciles" them. Both simply mean this: that in them also the same idea is operative, since it leaves no room for other false ideas, and thus elbows out of the way all the purposes which are determined by these false ideas, and in so doing it draws them also as co-operative forces into the same historical movement. "The progressive incorporation of the world into this final purpose and aim,"[1] thus the moral and religious progress of the individual as of humanity as a whole, this is the work of Christ—even though the first impulse to this may be designated as *the* cause *par excellence*.

It is therefore intelligible why it was that of all the terms

[1] *Rechtfertigung und Versöhnung*, III², p. 351. The third (and fourth) edition does not contain this sentence.

used from time immemorial by the Christian Church to sum up the work of the Redeemer, Ritschl preferred to use that of the "royal Prophet," and entirely ignored that of the priestly Mediator. For whereas from the general presuppositions of the Ritschlian view as a whole there could certainly be no talk of Atonement through the work of a Mediator, the ideas of "revelation" and "dominion" seemed here to find at least a remote analogy. It was certainly very remote: for in the Christian faith we are not concerned—as in Ritschl's system—merely with the historical development of an historical impulse, but with the living presence of the heavenly King, Christ Jesus. Thus the doctrine of Jesus Christ in the system of Ritschl confirms what has already been said about his conception of revelation: in the garment of scriptural language it is the rational ethical philosophy of history, and here also Jesus Christ, in spite of Ritschl's use of scriptural language, is in the last resort no more than He is in the thought of the Idealist philosophers of history and the modern conception of Christ in general: the Bearer of a moral religious idea which in itself is valid. His relation to the Christian religion is, of course, causal and factual, but not positive and necessary. I must emphasize once again that this rational structure is clothed in much scriptural knowledge, and that this covering may often have been more effective than the inner structure itself. The further course of the history of theology, however, on the whole, and from the most comprehensive point of view, suggests the opposite. The elements of the Ritschlian theology which have been maintained belong essentially to the rational-historical structure, and not to the scriptural garb.[1]

---

[1] There is, of course, also a "Right wing" of Ritschlianism which on the whole strives to turn away from the ethical rationalism of Ritschl to the conception of Christ of the Reformers or of the Bible. But its hostility to the ecclesiastical Christological categories, which are in reality also those of the New Testament, a hostility due to the influence of Ritschl, has here led to as many forms of compromise as of theology, which indeed would be well worth while to explain in detail, but this would be impossible within the limits of this book. Above all, only the second and third part of this work, which is intended to make plain the meaning of the scriptural-ecclesiasticalcategories, will serve as abasis for a discussion with these theologians whose views are closer to those which we hold ourselves. It

97

Let me make this clear by a concrete example. This instance is peculiarly instructive for two reasons: firstly, because in it the main ideas of this whole tendency, and its connection with Schleiermacher and Ritschl, stand out extraordinarily clearly, and secondly, because here the characteristic self-deception about the supposed agreement between this conception and that of Christianity and the Bible is most ingenuously expressed. In the theological encyclopedia entitled *Religion in Geschichte und Gegenwart* (Religion in History and at the Present Day) the standard article entitled *Christology, dogmatic*, from the pen of an explicitly non-Liberal theologian (Rittelmeyer), deals with the subject along the following lines: *Question:* What tangible and definite changes have been introduced into the life of mankind under the influence of Jesus? *Answer:* A "confidence in Jesus which is wholly unparalleled in history, a sense of release which has never appeared in any other religion, not even in Buddhism." Then follows the characteristic inference: "Obviously, the first thing we can infer is this: that such extraordinary effects must be due to the influence of an extraordinary personality." Then the historical picture of Jesus is sketched and measured by a rational-ethical and universal religious standard: "He is a man of amazing moral energy." "Still more amazing is the religious uniqueness of Jesus," the strength of His religious intuition. "Such a unique individual cannot be matched anywhere in world history either before or since." So far all this is in the vein of Schleiermacher, with his conception of the "religious hero," but now for a moment this setting seems to be transcended by the admission that Jesus possessed the unique consciousness that He was "the decisive messenger of God to man, with whose appearance is connected weal or woe, not merely for His nation alone." But the "explanation" of this unique

is just as obvious that the conception of Christ of men like Kaftan, Loofs, Wilhelm Herrmann, or Hirsch is not simply the "modern" conception, which we have here been discussing, as it is on the other hand (as will become clear from our further observations) that a man like Schlatter, in his justifiable attack on the "Greek" element in Christianity, abandons, wrongly, important positions of the Reformation to modern thought. To discuss this, however, would take us far beyond the limits of our present task.

person which now follows allows the idea to glide back again into the previous rut, especially where the ecclesiastical doctrine —viewed from the standpoint of modern thought—is rejected at all characteristic points and is reformulated in connection with "several ideas inherent in German mysticism and German Idealism." "We regard the facts of the life of Jesus not as rigidly isolated miracles, but as the revelation of the natural laws of the supreme divine process. Wherever a human being gives himself as fully to God as Jesus did, there the voice of God becomes alive in him, there God appears in him, and appears to the world, revealing, judging, and saving . . . there also will his destiny be the sufferings of Christ, a suffering which we may indeed describe as a suffering of God for man, one also which will always have a healing, expiatory, and redeeming significance." (Compare the thought of Goethe: "pure humanity expiates all human faults and errors.") The Johannine phrase "God so loved the world" "simply gains an increased significance when we translate it into our own language: This is the mystery of the divine love as it broods over this world, that wherever the divine appears within it, everywhere, naturally and inevitably it will and must go to death for the salvation of this world."

Do not these "translations" remind us forcibly of Kant, in the sense in which he transfers the predicates of the doctrine of Christ to the ideal humanity? The only difference is that here the rational-ethical point of view has been transformed into a mystical point of view. Yet—according to Rittelmeyer— the "uniqueness" of the historical Jesus must not be denied. For "every time we look at history . . . we are instantly convinced that He was a wholly unique historical personality." Yet the scriptural and ecclesiastical doctrine which explains this uniqueness is once more rejected. "After we have carefully weighed all the evidence for the origin of Jesus, the only thing, and the ultimate thing we have to say is this: that on the one hand, Jesus must have brought with Him into the world a quite extraordinary endowment of religious and moral qualities, and on the other, that this endowment was confronted by a situation in world history which was also unique and would never occur again." And all this is supposed to represent the new formulation of the doctrines of the Incarnation and the Deity of Christ (the pre-existence of the Logos). The personal religious relation to Jesus does not lose through this at all; on the contrary, "it gains in vital historical relation and tender mystery and reverence, in religious concentration and vigorous moral impulse." "Through the historical facts of the personality of Jesus and His Life humanity has become aware, not by accident, but through the mysterious leading of the providential ordering of God, of the highest religious meaning of existence, and for all time this remains alive and vital, present with all the force of a concrete human life; in the personality of Jesus that wonderful interpenetration of the human spirit by the divine, to which we are called; in the life of Jesus that equally wonderful divine life of holiness and surrender of love, which makes itself known to us as the metaphysical background of all that happens in the world and draws us into communion with the life of God, which realizes in a vital historical manner that union of the human spirit with the divine." In other words, in Jesus the universal principle of human and ethical religion has taken shape in its most perfect, sublime, and historical form; it thus becomes finally manifest to us, and at the same time strengthens our own religious life. It must be admitted that the author of this article has done his very best to connect the general conception of religion with that of the Bible and of revelation. But all the more clearly do we perceive that the gulf between the two forms of faith remains as wide as ever; in principle it is exactly the same as the difference between revelation and the most sterile forms of the Rationalism of the Enlightenment. This Christ is the Christ we meet in Kant, Goethe, Herder, Lessing —but it is never the Christ of the Bible or the witness of the Reformers. For in principle this Christ is not different from the rest of us. He is the highest expression that can be imagined of a moral and religious human being, no less, but also no more.

It is to the credit of the Liberal theology in the narrower sense (which is in part the continuation of the old popular Rationalism, but far more a theology based on German speculative Idealism) that, in contrast to this theological view of history (*Historismus*), it has brought out clearly the difference between it and the scriptural and ecclesiastical doctrine of Christ. It has made no attempt to conceal the fact that when it speaks of Christ, it means the principle whose outstanding representative and most effective pioneer was Jesus of Nazareth. Hence it has quite openly and frankly rejected the "Pauline" or "Johannine" doctrine of the Mediator, and has set over against these doctrines the ethico-religious doctrine of the "Synoptic Jesus," conceived as a universal truth.[1]

To-day the word "idea" is rather avoided by the representatives of this school of thought; instead they are fond of using terms like "religious life," the "original religious principle," the "experience of the Holy," the "irrational element," "religious intuition," etc.; that is, there is a tendency to move away from Idealistic conceptions towards those which are mystical or aesthetic, and therefore their connection is rather with the Schleiermacher of the *Reden* than with Hegel. But whether Jesus be called a religious genius or a teacher, whether we speak of His "complete uniqueness" or of the greatness of the perfection of His moral character, makes no difference at all—measured by our standard. For in each case what is meant is the universal religious element that in Jesus has taken historical form in an outstanding, indeed, in an unsurpassable manner. But this does not mean that any of these thinkers would claim that Jesus is—in any sense of the word—the Mediator.

[1] For Biedermann, see my *Religionsphilosophie*, p. 17. In principle Pfleiderer and Lüdemann take the same position. The same also is intended when, for instance, a man like Jülicher (*Jesus and Paulus*) writes thus: "Jesus . . . brought a new piety, a new ideal, into the world. When He died, the power of His religion was already so great that among the best representatives of His people He was able to defy the terrible disillusion caused by this defeat: faith in Him and in the truth of His cause, found a way of representing His defeat as a victory. Ethical ideals only show their value to us human beings in this way" (p. 69): "Jesus was master of Himself before He gained the comparatively indifferent title of Messiah; He had created a new world within His own heart, before He found a name which reconciled the new with the old" (p. 60). The element which is supposed to be common to the religion of Jesus and of Paul—and to the Christian Church—alongside of which the whole Pauline theology appears only as "outworks," is held to consist of the "religious and ethical ideals" (p. 53), and the standard by which everything is measured is "the simple and sober piety of Jesus" (p. 21).

CHAPTER IV

THE REASON FOR THE DISTINCTION
THE ASSERTION OF UNBROKEN UNITY

IT becomes increasingly plain to us modern men that a profound gulf separates the "modern world" from the world of the Early Church and of the Middle Ages. Even the Neo-Romanticism which tries to reinterpret the medieval period through art and a certain mystical temper is in the last resort compelled to bear testimony to the existence of this gulf, which is far deeper than any division which could be bridged by that modern temper of longing for "inwardness," or for "wholeness of life." This division cuts through the whole of life, and in particular through the foundations; it separates us at the very point at which the modern man as such is constituted. It is therefore so profound that it could only be bridged at the cost of denying one's existence as a human being in the modern world.

It does not cut across—as Liberalism used to think—the point at which the Reformed faith and Catholicism parted company. Rather both of them stand on the further side of the gulf, over against the modern world. In their belief in the Christian revelation they are one, in spite of all the differences between them; they form the one Christian Church. On the other side, however—and this is the striking thing which upsets all our chronological calculations altogether—the modern man, in the consciousness of this difference feels himself, in the main, akin to and related to the ancient world of Graeco-Roman civilization. At least in the ancient world he does not find that which separates him from Christianity: the affirmation of the absolutely decisive divine revelation, which has taken place once for all. The great common element between the ancient and the modern world is the consciousness of one divine general truth, the truth of "general revelation," to which the concrete or "special" revelation is related as a symbol.

It is therefore quite natural that the transformation of the conception of revelation and of the conception of Christ of which we have been speaking is no isolated or accidental phenomenon. It is connected with, or rather it is the innermost tendency of, this whole vast intellectual upheaval which, as one of its results, has produced the modern mind. The new conception of revelation and of the fact of Christ is an absolutely characteristic expression of the modern mind. At the same time it is one of the fundamental causes of this change. When the modern mind gives an account of itself it also gives at the same time an explanation of the reason why it does not and cannot think about Christ as the believing Christian does—or did.[1] It will be necessary to ascertain the essential ideas underlying this account of the situation in so far as they stand in direct relation to our problem.

When we survey the history of the philosophical and theological thought which has been expended upon this subject, we can scarcely avoid the conclusion that these changes have taken place under great pressure. What was the nature of this pressure? We are tempted at first to lay the blame on the external changes in the Western way of life: the introduction of machinery, the permeation of life with rational science, the changed view of the universe, the rationalization of economic life, and other things of this kind. But ultimately, all these factors point to a deeper cause. In a word, they point to a

[1] Keim expresses his hostility to the orthodox view, and the reasons for this, characteristically and clearly. "It is quite plain that we must give up this Greek mythology—this idea of the Son of God, whom Alexandrine Jewish wisdom (to-day perhaps we would say Iranian Gnosticism) and the Greek Church have handed down to us, this idea of the God who came down from heaven, in order to become a human being, an infant, a crucified man, and then for the second time to become God. Our historical science is different; our way of thinking has become more sober" (*Geschichte Jesu*, p. 365). Similarly Weinel: *Jesus im 19 Jahrhundert*, p. 2: "The ancient dogma of the second Person in the Godhead broke down beneath the pressure of the increasing knowledge of Nature and of History. Then the question became all the more urgent: If He was not the Son of God and a Divine Being, who then was this man, Jesus?" The new answer to this question is the modern interpretation of Jesus, as it was expounded in the previous chapter. For the supposed conflict between modern science and "Greek mythology" in the scriptural and ecclesiastical witness to Christ, see the appendix to Chapter XIV (pp. 377 ff.).

new conception of truth; it is the new "knowledge." It is therefore—replies the modern man, like Dilthey or Troeltsch, with authoritative assurance—due to intellectual honesty, which has compelled religious philosophy and theological conceptions and views to adopt new forms. To-day man can no longer believe in Christ and in a divine revelation, in the old sense of the word, without cutting himself off from the knowledge and the best tendencies of the new age. Indeed, even Schleiermacher confessed that his work was an attempt to spare the modern man the trouble of making a choice between the new scientific culture and the Christian faith. Believing, in all good faith, that he had accomplished this task, he transformed the Christian faith to such an extent that in the ensuing structure of compromise it is scarcely possible to recognize the elements peculiar to Christianity at all. He had underestimated the extent of the antithesis. On the other hand, it is easy to understand his anxiety lest Christian theology and the Christian Church should fall a prey to scientific barbarism or dishonesty when we recall the attitude of some of the conservative defenders of the faith of the Primitive Church. He was compelled to watch the unfortunate spectacle presented by the fact that theology, supposedly on account of its faith, closed its mind to the new scientific views, so that too often the alternative feared by Schleiermacher appeared to be adopted at the expense of intellectual fearlessness and honesty.

There are three main groups of reasons which can be brought forward against the Christian faith in Christ from the side of modern thought. The first group is of a general scientific and philosophical character. It deals with principles. The second group has arisen particularly out of historical Biblical criticism and in connection with the Bible. The third is mainly opposed to the Christological dogma of the Church. The second group will be dealt with in one of the following chapters, and the third will be fully treated in the second and third main sections of this book. Hence at this point we need deal only with the first group, that is, with questions of principle.

For all three groups, however, the historical presupposition is the collapse of the orthodox system of doctrine, that is, the system based upon the doctrine of Verbal Inspiration. Whereas in Catholicism doctrine and Bible are part of the Church, and therefore the destruction of the Bible does not necessarily involve the destruction of the Church, in Protestantism everything was staked upon the Bible, and within orthodoxy upon the legal authority of the actual letter of Scripture. Hence when this foundation was destroyed, the whole building began to totter. But the shock led more and more to disaster. The orthodox doctrine of Verbal Inspiration has been finally destroyed. It is clear that there is no connection between it and scientific research and honesty: we are forced to make a decision for or against this view. But in spite of all the hot discussion which has raged round this point, and however much upon both sides the opinion prevailed that the Christian revelation had received a fatal blow, in the course of the struggle it became evident (as the most far-seeing had always known) that the doctrine of Verbal Inspiration was not the basic support of the classical Protestant witness. The Reformers had a quite different conception of the authority of the Bible. Thus the opposition to the Christian faith in revelation and in Christ Himself differs from that which is opposed to the doctrine of the infallible letter of Scripture. It is far more fundamental.

The fact is that Reason, which from the Renaissance onwards became increasingly self-conscious, has been, and still is, the fundamental root of this opposition. Here we must take reason to mean the sum total of all the intellectual faculties and powers of man himself, or, to put this in religious language, as the "Divine," the likeness of the Divine in man. At any rate, from the time of the Renaissance and the dawn of the Enlightenment all the emphasis has been laid upon this: all that over which man has control, all that is directly connected with his own activity and his own thought, whether it be Platonic Ideas which are founded on the basis of mental activity through methodical processes of thought, or the scientific spirit of inquiry with its causal principle, or the creative imagination, which discovers new territories or strata of thought by means of intuition, or the moral will, which causes a new being to arise out of its postulates and purposes, or the arid abstractions of Rationalistic logic, or the magnificent structure of dialectical speculation formed on the model of the growth of history, the theosophical profundity which in its deepest reaches merges into mysticism, or even becomes one with it: all this has a home in the "modern mind," however different and contradictory all these elements may seem within the common, inclusive whole.

In order to bring out the contrast more clearly, however, let us confine our attention, first of all, to the solid kernel of this somewhat incomprehensible whole: to Reason in the philosophical sense of the word. It is, of course, a recognized fact that there is very little justification for the attempt to assign a permanent and recognized content to the conception of Reason. But whatever separates the Realist from the Idealist, the Empiricist from those who hold *a priori* ideas, in any case Reason is the fundamental factor, which comes to its own conclusions in rigid sequence, in a continuity which can never be interrupted. In so far, then, as Reason takes into account a divine element at all—at present we are leaving atheism and agnosticism out of the picture—the divine element is simply the deepest basis of Reason, and can therefore only be found as such, as its ultimate presupposition. The divine truth is therefore both the deepest as well as the most general presupposition of thought which can be reached. It is that which is most opposed to the individual, to the accidental and factual. If all scientific knowledge consists in connecting the isolated *vérités de fait* with *vérités de raison*, in removing, as far as possible, their contingent character by means of law, and if philosophical knowledge consists in setting aside the remains of the accidental element which still clings to all merely scientific knowledge, by the discovery of ultimate principles, and finally of the ultimate principle, it is evident that the idea of God stands at the end of this whole movement. God, as the presupposition of all the Idea of ideas, the basis of all foundations, the end of all ends, is the absolute principle itself. The divine truth is therefore a principle, not a fact; it is the most important principle that exists, and therefore it is the one which is most opposed to the individual fact.

Therefore, to Reason there is no greater absurdity than to

assert that for us the divine truth is an isolated fact, that it is disclosed to us in one single event. So absurd does this idea seem to a reasonable intelligent man that at first he thinks that it must contain some misunderstanding, that its absurdity must be due to some awkward turn of expression: "You do not express yourself very well! You do not mean: *in* this *fact*, but perhaps that *through* this fact the meaning of divine truth is more clearly revealed than elsewhere? An individual fact may well serve as an illustration, as a symbol of the general truth, which, however, should not be made identical with the individual fact." But if the believing Christian sticks to his guns, and refuses to modify his statement, if he rejects this kindly and sensible interpretation, as the exact opposite of what he himself means, then there is nothing left for the philosopher to do but to turn away, shaking his head.

Let us try to understand this conflict a little more closely. The whole endeavour of Reason is directed towards uniting everything in an inclusive system. Even where this must be effected by means of antitheses, the antithesis is tolerated for the sake of the synthesis. In this synthetical process of Reason divine truth is simply the principle of the synthesis, the fundamental truth, in which all things cohere. This coherence and this "divine," this necessity, this idea of ideas, this whole behind the individual factor and the divine truth are one and the same. The continuity of thought is therefore simply a representation of the original relation. The divine is the original balance of being.

This fundamental presupposition of all thought is rendered problematic by the claim of revelation, in the Christian sense of the word. The divine truth is not the ultimate presupposition of all that exists, but is in conflict with it. It enters the arena as an alien force. The uniqueness of revelation, the Mediator, the fact of the Atonement, is the expression of the fact that the divine truth is not present, but—in contrast to that which is present—must be *given*. Hence this event is a disturbance of the "balance," because it breaks through all present and possible continuity. To believe in it means the denial of the presence of this "balance," of harmony in the world, thus it also means the denial of the possibility of finding truth from the point of view of cosmic reality.[1]

This is the real stumbling-block for the reason. Faith does not assert that the unique event, so far as it is "present," and is an empirical fact, is divine, but that in this unique event— and only in it—the divine truth is *given* to us. "Grace and truth came by Jesus Christ." It is against this that Reason rebels. For through this claim it has been attacked at its central point. If what the Christian faith says be true, then not only this or that system, but every system, as such, is false; indeed, any faith in a system which—even if only approximately —could be perfected, is false. Then it is false to conceive God as the hidden "balance," as the immanent presupposition of existence. In so doing not only is human reason robbed of the predicate of ultimate truth, but pure (theoretical) reason as well. The criterion of Reason as the ultimate judge of what is false and what is true is thus abandoned as useless; or—and it comes to the same in the end—the contrast between the true and the false, in the sense of reason, is not the conclusive argument in the question of reality.

Thus the stumbling-block of revelation is this: it denies that divine truth is a continuation of human thought, in line with existence as we can conceive it, and as it seems real to us. But our whole culture is built up upon this continuity, upon it is based our confidence in science, and —this is the root of the whole matter—upon it is based the *confidence of man in himself.* The strength of human self-confidence is based on the conviction that man himself is continuous with God. He believes that there is an unbroken connection between himself and God, or between himself and the Absolute. He believes that from himself there stretches a path up to the divine truth, from man to God. This confidence is shattered by the claim of revelation made by Christianity

[1] Hence there is perhaps nowhere a more sharp antithesis than that between the Christian interpretation of existence and that of Goethe, possibly because no modern thinker has ever grasped and affirmed more deeply than Goethe this deepest tendency of the modern mind—man's complete satisfaction with himself. And, indeed, Goethe has done more than any other thinker to influence the thought of modern educated people wherever German is spoken.

and—seriously—by it alone. For it alone makes this claim to be unique and final, which is the basis of the sharpness of this contrast. By this claim man is suddenly compelled to call a halt as he strides along his way full of self-confidence. Can it be possible that this method, which has proved so successful in secular matters—to think only of the rationality of science and of technical progress—will fail us when we are confronted by the ultimate and therefore most decisive question of all? Are we suddenly called to give up all our sense of security, to renounce all previous connections of every kind, and to surrender ourselves to something with which we are confronted which stands in opposition to everything else? The strongest reason for the hostility of the modern man to the Christian religion of revelation is this: he has gained such overweening confidence in his own reason, that is, in the unbroken character of his own existence.

Hitherto we have been arguing from the point of view of scientific philosophical reason. "But what has God to do with reason?" we hear the modern mystic protest. It is, of course, true that if he is also a thinker—like his revered Meister Eckhart and his Indian and Chinese prototypes—he will probably have no objection to offer to the argument that the most general principle there is, the "reason of all reasons" of ontological speculation, is, properly speaking, the intellectual reflection of that which he himself means by God; indeed, historically, in the East as well as in the West, in the Vedic period as well as in the Christian Middle Ages, ontological speculation and mysticism always went hand in hand. But in any case the mystic *means* something else by "God." To him God is not the end of a process of thought, but the All, the source of being, which is revealed in feeling or in contemplation, in ecstasy or in the depths of introversion, in complete "solitude" and "abstraction." The close relation between this God of the mystic and that of the speculative philosopher can be seen in the very fact of their common hostility to the Christian revelation. The mystic—like the speculative idealist—also seeks to reinterpret the Christian claim as an awkward expression, as a popular preparatory stage for his mystical truth, as the preliminary stage beyond which the mystic himself has passed.

The "Christ for us," the "Christ of the Bible" in whom we are told to believe, is not the true Christ; the "Christ in us," the timeless One, independent of all that is external, Him on whom one does not believe "externally" but whom one "inwardly experiences" or "contemplates," is the true God. In this attempt at reinterpretation, which is so often regarded by ingenuous souls as a sign of the affinity between mysticism and the Christian revelation, to one who has eyes to see there is evident the same complete opposition as in the system based on reason.

For here also, at the basis of the defence, lies the conviction that the divine, even if not in thought, yet in feeling or in "contemplation"—the neo-mystic would perhaps say, with Ricarda Huch, in the Unconscious—lies at the basis of our soul as the balance, as the inmost kernel of our being, as the centre of gravity of human and natural existence. It is certain that we must withdraw from the superficial levels of existence, but we must also likewise turn inwards, descend to the depths of our own being. For beneath all is—God. This path is therefore different from that of the philosopher; it does not pass through thought but through feeling and contemplation. But, all the same, it *is* a way. To the *via negationis*, that is—of abstraction—of the thinker, there corresponds to the practical *via negationis*, the meditative abstraction of the mystic, the process of dying to the world, the closing of the window towards the outer world, the establishment of the mental vacuum, which draws God to the soul as inevitably as the physical vacuum attracts the inrush of air. "The more man detaches himself from the creature the more does the Creator hasten towards him" (Eckhart).[1] In both instances it is the self-movement of man whose aim is God, whether it be through the soaring of thought or the introversion of the mystic. Both are in sharp contrast to the Christian faith,[2] where the movement is on

[1] Edition Büttner, I, p. 21.

[2] No modern theologian witnesses more clearly to this fundamental opposition between mysticism and the Christian faith than the one who most constantly denies it, namely, Otto. Can anyone read his most recent book: *Westöstliche Mystik*, without noticing that all his expert explanations prove exactly that which he is trying to explain away, namely, the essential relation between Eckhart and Sankara and the profound contrast between

the side of God, and the aim is man. Thus, whether in speculation or in mysticism, at bottom the confidence is the same: it is confidence in the continuity of the divine with man, in the unbroken character of the inmost connection. Therefore mysticism agrees very well with speculative philosophy—indeed, when it expresses itself it cannot do without it—but never with the Christian religion, unless a mutual misunderstanding can be described as an agreement.

The third path also leads to the same goal: that of the moral will. Behind all the self-confidence of the modern man stands the statement: man is good. Hence the moral aspect of the modern mind is that which is the most self-revealing. So long as the conviction that at heart man is good is undisturbed, the moral element is scarcely self-conscious at all. "Thou shalt" is, in its very nature, a slight disturbance of the balance, and for this reason it is detested by the aesthetic person. For it contains the implication that the divine is not yet really accessible, nor really visible, but that it still has to be realized, whereas mysticism and speculation assert that it

both and the Christian faith. Otto has now invented a new formula in order to get over this difficulty and explain away this contrast: the mysticism of Eckhart "overarches" "the simple foundation of faith" (p. 179) of the Christian faith of the Church. Likewise the mysticism of Sankara "overarches" the Theistic basis of the teaching of the Gita. The difference in the basis which is "overarched" determines their "special character" (p. 232). It is astonishing that one who can analyse religious systems so excellently can overlook the fact that it is precisely this "overarching" of mysticism over the basis of faith—in which both Eastern and Western mysticism are one, although their outlook is coloured by the difference in their basis of faith—which makes it incompatible with Christianity. For this "overarching" simply means this: that the Mediator is required by beginners, by simple believers, but that the mystic needs Him no longer. His mystical perception, his mystical immediacy leaves revealed religion behind, at a lower level, to such an extent, indeed, that the Western ("Christian") mystic, and the Eastern, Indian, non-Christian mystic not only give each other the right hand of fellowship—ignoring revealed religion altogether—but actually become one. When, also in this book, Otto again makes the impossible attempt to prove the close relationship which exists between Luther and Eckhart, he only "succeeds" in this effort by leaving out the decisive element in all Luther's statements, namely, the reference to Jesus Christ, the Mediator, that is, the reference in which Luther's faith *consists*. To such a degree can an outstanding scholar carry his prejudice in support of a favourite theory.

III

is—even though it may lie hid in the depths. Hence moral thought, the more clearly and purely the "Thou shalt" stands out in it, has a close affinity with Christianity. This affinity, however, is such that the closest proximity means at the same time the sharpest contrast. Nothing is nearer to faith than the highest form of legalism—and it is here that the opposition becomes most intense. The recognition of moral duty contains within itself a certain dualism: until the actual divine has been attained there is still a path to tread, and this path is not merely a way of thought, as though the alienation were merely a matter of wrong thinking, that is, an error, but it is a real way, that is, a way of action. Something must actually take place before the good can come into existence. But is not then the fact that we admit that this alienation exists, that we acknowledge the claim of duty, that we thus agree with the law, a proof that in the deepest depths we already stand where the goal gleams and attracts us, and not in the base reality, from which indeed we wish to escape? The fact that we desire to escape is a sign that we "really" are already outside. Thus the ideal will is the real will; this ideal will, the autonomous will of reason, is the centre of our personality, the deepest ground of the self. This ideal will, however, is identical with the divine willing and being. The intelligible ego, the subject of the ideal will, is the divine ego; only for this reason is it legislative, this alone is why we are autonomous.[1]

[1] The idea of autonomy is the centre of moral Idealism. It is at this point that the doctrine of the Intelligible Self arises; it is therefore also the real starting-point of the Idealistic philosophy of religion, and the point where Christianity and Idealism both meet, and are most sharply opposed. The point of contact is this: if the idea of autonomy is conceived in a purely formal way as the Idea of the good will, then it is just as Christian as it is Idealistic. Conflict, however, arises at this point: if this idea is held at the same time as a statement about the "true being" of the real man then it becomes opposed to the Christian knowledge of Evil. This statement is made when the ground of formal analysis has been abandoned for the ground of ethical metaphysics, that is, when it is maintained that the Intelligible Self is the true being of the real man. It is well known that Fichte in particular drew his "ethical mysticism" from this source. But even Kant followed this line, although with more circumspection and reserve. What was meant by this autonomy had to be decided in connection with the problem of Evil. On this point, see p. 128 (in this book). So far as the rest is concerned, cf. the explanations in my *Religionsphilosophie*, pp. 32 and 45.

Therefore the dualism which the moral task sets before us is not a serious one. Actually the step has already been taken; or, rather, this gulf does not exist at all. In the depths of personality the human will is one with the divine will. For the "true ego," the intelligible self, is indeed divinely good, its will identical with the will of God; indeed its will cannot be distinguished from the will of God. In so far as one does not engage in the moral struggle oneself, but simply reflects upon the moral will, one tends involuntarily to drift towards the theory of identity, or of mysticism, as we can perceive in Fichte. Then there appears the same opposition[1] to the Christian revelation as at the other points mentioned, only it is now intensified by the ethical sense of self-esteem. It is this which makes it most keen in self-defence against the attack on the ego which issues from the revelation of Christ. On the other hand, the opposition of revelation to the continuity of being is here aimed directly at the centre, at the moral will. It is directed against the self-sufficiency of moral energy, or—more deeply still—against the self-sufficiency of the loftiest dignity of the moral person, thus against the inmost heart of the moral personality. It is confidence in this which leads man to a definite rejection of the Christian revelation, as an infringement of the rights of our dignity as human beings. Man needs no mediator, he can redeem himself; for the divine energies of redemption are latent in the deepest foundation of being. Man is redeemed when he knows this, that he

---

[1] In German Idealism, however, this opposition is usually concealed behind what is supposed to be a "more spiritual" "exposition" of the Christian faith, above all, in connection with the Gospel of John. The most certain touchstone is therefore always the relation to Paul, where the contingent character of the idea of the Mediator and of revelation comes out most clearly. We would be on more solid ground, possibly, if the criterion were to consist in the relation to the Old Testament. For the Gospel is only completely protected against Idealistic alterations when it is interpreted from the point of view of the Old Testament, understood as it should be! The Divine Creator in the Old Testament and reconciliation through the Mediator in the New Testament are the two points at which the ever-present hostility between Idealism and Christianity breaks out openly and irrevocably. Only where the Christian faith has become unfaithful to itself at these points (as perhaps in Schleiermacher's *Glaubenslehre*) does it seem possible to effect an agreement with Idealism.

is in God. This is the fundamental idea of Fichte's "moral mysticism."

But the moral will does not always tend towards speculation of this kind. In Kant the process of thought which is characteristic and decisive is different. The overcoming of the dualism remains a real task, which cannot be resolved by any kind of mystical speculation. But man *can* actually perform this duty. "I ought, therefore I can."[1] The imperative duty is the guarantee, in spite of the appearance of dualism which arises within it, that this dualism can be overcome, it is the guarantee of the self-sufficiency of moral power. In spite of an incidental glance at the idea of radical evil (which follows logically from Idealism, and which the whole modern basis of Kantian thought would have torn to shreds), it retains that self-confidence which is so characteristic of the modern man. The idea of autonomy, the central idea of moral Idealism, conquers the idea of "radical evil" (see p. 128): the inmost heart of the moral personality is unspoilt.[2] It is true, of course, that man must actually take the step. Redemption does not exist, it becomes, the divine is not, it becomes; but its becoming is guaranteed by that which is in us. From the presence of the Categorical Imperative, that is, of the innermost moral will, we dare to make this optimistic prognosis, even if it were only in the shape of a postulate.

[1] This phrase does not occur literally in Kant's writings, but it is what he says in effect. "It is still his duty to improve himself, therefore he must also be able to do so" (*Religion innerhalb*, . . . p. 42, Ausg. Reclam). "This idea contains its reality on the practical side wholly within itself. For it lies in our ethical legislative reason. We *ought* (underlined by Kant) to live in accordance with it; hence we must also *be able* (underlined by Kant) to do so." Here also the point is visible (see above, p. 112, note) at which the transition from the purely formal principle of the Good becomes a statement about Reality. The transition is called, characteristically, *our* Reason! (loc. cit., p. 63).

[2] "The good and sincere disposition (which may be described as a good and ruling spirit), of which one is conscious, thus also lends confidence to its constancy and stability, although, it is true, only indirectly in itself" (loc. cit., p. 73), and the consciousness of such constancy "would be the same thing as knowing that one was already in possession of this Kingdom, for then the person who feels like this would naturally believe that all the rest (that which concerns physical well-being) would be his" (ibid., p. 69).

Hence because man believes in his inmost self that he is able to subdue what ought not to be, he does not wish to hear anything about an Atonement which had to take place in a special way, or of a Mediator. Here also the idea of the continuity of the personal life with the divine aim and reason bears upon the centre of the personality—the will.

Precisely because this is the case the rejection of the doctrine of the Atonement and of the Mediator is particularly decided. This message of Christianity is regarded not merely as an absurdity but as an offence. The will of the self-sufficient modern man reacts violently against this assistance which is only offered to those who have learned to despair of themselves. This is degrading to humanity; it is treating humanity as a minor and stripping it of all its rights; it is intolerable! In its most earnest form, in the form of personal moral dignity—or, as Christianity calls it, in the form of self-righteousness or a righteousness which is of works—reason here revolts against the claims of the Christian revelation.

This moral self-confidence is already to some extent weakened when this optimism is not attributed to the individual human being as such, but to humanity as a whole, as when it is suggested that the moral dualism between "ought" and "is" can be overcome not by the power of the individual, but by that of historical humanity. Hence it may even come to seem as though this historical faith, which expects redemption from history, were akin to the Christian belief in revelation.[1] In point of fact, however, this is simply another variety of the idea of continuity. Humanity as a whole is continuous with the

---

[1] Therefore it shows very little insight to say that Idealism, with its philosophy of history, simply because it assigns a great deal of value to history, has a greater affinity with Christianity than the non-historical ethical Individualism of Kant. The Kantian "Thou shalt" is far more serious than Hegelianism, to the extent in which it is less concerned with history, for in the Kantian philosophy at least the absolute Good becomes the challenge of the present moment to the individual, whereas in Hegelianism the individual, properly speaking, is relieved of any ethical burden: there is indeed plenty of time; the Good will only emerge at the close of the long process of development. To the same extent also the Kantian valuation of the individual personality is much more serious than in the philosophy of Hegel or even of Schleiermacher, whose philosophy of history is chiefly characterized by naturalistic traits.

divine; only as an individual one must not regard oneself as too important; the individual must be regarded simply as a member of the historical whole, and must look on his existence, which is limited by time, as a temporary stage in the great process of world history: then again we recognize that the divine absolute truth is that which gives direction to and constitutes the content of all history. Here the bold self-confidence of moral Idealism has broken down; at the same time, however, the seriousness of the "Thou shalt" has also been weakened. Spirit is assimilated to Nature. The individual stages of history are related to the divine basis of the world in the same way as the individual facts of the natural world. The unbroken process of growth from the most primitive to the highest forms of life, the law of progress as a world law, expresses more clearly than any other idea of modern man, the continuity of existence with its divine basis.

This has led us to a second main idea, which separates the consciousness of the modern man from the Christian religion of revelation: the idea of development. It is, however, a misunderstanding to state the contrast in some such way as this: Christianity posits an historical absolute, whereas for modern men the historical as such is relative. The statement would be more accurate if it were stated the other way round. It is of the essence of modern thought that it makes history absolute. This is the relative difference between ancient and modern thought, within their common opposition to the Christian belief: the Greek mind makes Nature the Absolute; essentially it deifies Nature, it is a static form of Pantheism; the modern mind makes the mind of man, history, the dynamic element, the Absolute. In each case, however, the continuity between human and divine existence is maintained. Nowhere does this come out more plainly than in the conception of history in German Idealism which culminates in Hegel's philosophy of history. History as such is the self-manifestation of God, that is, revelation. In history, or rather, through history, through the historical process as such, very gradually there takes place the overcoming of the relative opposition between existence and the divine. History therefore is itself the Mediator.

This implies two things. First, the relative character of each individual moment in history, and second, that history as a whole is made absolute. Both statements give each other mutual support. Historical relativism is not possible without reference to the Absolute, nor is it possible to make the whole absolute without rendering the individual factor relative. But both are only possible for a third reason, that is, by the knowledge of the absolute Idea, by the absolute divine truth as *terminus a quo* and *terminus ad quem* of the whole movement. Again this comes out most clearly in Hegel. His philosophy of history is not the whole of his philosophy, but his system of Absolute Idealism into which history itself is absorbed. Thus, however much the individual historical fact may be regarded as a relative phenomenon, behind this relativity there lies an Absolute with which the thinker in the act of contemplating his system is identical. For the system which he thinks is itself the absolute truth, the divine truth. The philosophy of history is thus itself only one ray of the light which shines from speculative Idealism, of which mention has already been made.

The reproach which is levelled at Christianity from this point of view is not so much that an historical fact is made absolute as that the idea of development is depreciated. In the philosophy of history all that is historical has a direct share in the absoluteness which belongs to history as a whole. History is the Absolute extended through time. This is the idea which underlies the famous saying of Hegel, that all that is real is rational. This means: all that is historical is the necessary point through which passes the self-manifestation of the absolute Idea. Every point in history is thus justified as such by the whole. Each stage of history is in its right place, it is what it is in virtue of its own right. From the Absolute there falls a ray of light which glorifies each part of the process of development.[1] Growth as such is divine; it is, properly speaking,

[1] The making absolute of development, which also underlies a system of the philosophy of history like that of Ernst Troeltsch, lies behind all those arguments advanced by the philosophy of history against the Christian religion of revelation. This idea has never been formulated more bluntly than in the well-known phrase of Strauss: "The Idea does not care to pour out all its wealth in one single example." Christ, an historical personality, cannot be the Absolute. Actually, however, the Christian faith in particular

a single long sentence in which the Divine Spirit expresses itself. The thesis of the Christian religion, however, is the very opposite: that no moment in historical existence is in its right place, nor can it be justified. It is against this desecration of history that the modern mind revolts when it turns against Christianity. It feels itself menaced and injured. Thus the idea of continuity in the philosophy of history is rooted in the same fundamental thought as the modern idea of continuity in general, that is, in the assertion that our given existence is continuous with the divine. The Idealism of the philosophy of history is only a variation on one of the themes of speculative Idealism.

The same is true, however, of every form of philosophy of history, whether it be the *évolution créatrice* of Bergson, or a combination of Hegel and Bergson (Croce), that is, of every conception of history through principles. Even the poorest of them all, the Positivist philosophy of history, is merely a weakened form of Hegelianism, which is not clearly conscious of its own principles. Here the *rôle* of the Absolute is represented by science. Science is the absolute standard by which everything is tested. Thus here the idea of divine truth has shrunk to a poverty-stricken conception of it as the sum total of scientific principles and knowledge; Positivism and every form of scientific Naturalism is an intellectualist, impoverished, absolu-

---

does not maintain that an historical phenomenon, as such, is the Absolute. For no Christian has ever asserted that the "Christ *after the flesh*" is, as such, the eternal Son of God. But the Christ "*in the flesh*"—who, as the Christ, is not an historical phenomenon at all—is the Son of God. But this misunderstanding is due to the fact that people are unwilling to allow this "more-than-history" to disturb history, because if this *is* allowed to happen history as a whole becomes uncertain, and its supposed balance is upset. Because it is believed that history is self-sufficient it is not desirable to limit it by revelation or to render its position insecure. Thinkers of the Enlightenment of the eighteenth century even openly made this protest against revelation in a religious interest (not, however, so much from the point of view of history as from that of the world-order); if such revelation as the New Testament asserts, exists, this would mean that God would have to improve His own work, the world, in a supplementary way. Yes, if the sinful world *were* His work! Whereas revelation is concerned precisely with the restoration of the world-order created by God, but hopelessly tangled by man!

tism of reason.[1] Hence the modern man, as a "scientific man," protests against the Christian faith because it casts a doubt upon the sufficiency of scientific knowledge and of the intellectualized existence which it produces. Again we find the sense of self-security being menaced, of that confidence in oneself which it rejects. This is all that matters; for the Christian faith has nothing to do with the results of scientific research.

The assertion of the continuity of human existence with the divine or with the Absolute—that is the deepest reason for the opposition between the modern mind and the Christian faith. Or, to put it more simply, it is the self-confidence of man. It is true, of course, that this confidence in oneself is never quite complete. Most emphatically is this true to-day. Not only is the day of the Hegelian absolutism of reason past, but also the great mystical period; not merely the period of "metaphysical" tendencies, but also the day of the absolutism of science. It looks as though humanity, having tested all the different forms of security, has now begun to doubt itself. It is true, of course, that even relativism and scepticism may be forms of the self-confidence of the spirit, in so far as this relativism and this scepticism are grounded on argument. And yet in these forms, which in spite of all metaphysical and mystical counter-currents have impressed their image on the intellectual life of the present day, there appear signs of the collapse of self-confidence. Man has become too much aware of the fragility of all existence, of all human opinion and endeavour, to be able to assert that continuity with the absolute conviction with which it used to be proclaimed by a Bruno or a Spinoza, by the great German Idealists, or even, on a smaller scale, in the shape of the supremacy of the intelligence—by the Liberalism, Positivism, and Materialism of the past century.

[1] This positivistic way of regarding scientific knowledge and scientific standards as absolute has penetrated so deeply into human thought during the last fifty years, and is so strongly entrenched at the present day, that any one who raises his voice against these idols must expect to be shouted down as an enemy of science and a supporter of barbarism. There are plenty even of Christian theologians for whom, in all questions of truth, the highest court of appeal is the standard of scientific thought, and who have thus entirely forgotten that it is impossible to combine this supremacy of science with Christianity.

The belief in absolute continuity (and this means faith in man himself) is at war with itself.

How is it possible to believe in one possible system of reason when there are so many systems, and each one claims to be "the" one *par excellence*? How, on the other hand, can man be so naïve as to believe in one form of science, in one causal connection, since it is precisely science itself which in perfecting itself breaks through the causal order by the process of thought? And among those who are coquetting with mysticism to-day, is there one who dares to be a real mystic, in dead earnest, in the serious fashion of the genuine mystics, who therefore, just because they were in earnest, also logically became saints and monks? Mysticism without asceticism is mere play-acting! And who seriously believes to-day in culture and progress as did the great Idealists?

No one doubts for a moment that the world, life, and culture are full of contradiction, for the fact is blatant enough. But the question is this: how *deep* do people think this disharmony is? Idealism believes that it is possible to master this contradiction through the system of rational thought. The Hegelian philosophy is perhaps the system which takes into account most seriously the irrational, the contradictory element in existence. It recognizes the contradiction by permitting the synthesis to be attained only after it has passed through one new antithesis after another. But, finally, the synthesis is attained. It presses through to the rationality of all being by means of dialectic. The contradiction is therefore only of the kind that can be resolved by thought. In the last resort it is only the semblance of contradiction. It is not real. It is the same with mysticism: it also recognizes the refractory and non-divine element in reality. But it believes in the possibility of transcending all contradiction by means of "inwardness," "sinking into the ground of being," and of finally reaching the harmonious One and All, there to find absolute stability and repose. Here also, finally, the contradiction of existence is not real. For the truth of all being is the divine; only so long as you are enmeshed in unreality—so thinks the mystic—do you feel the contradiction. There is a possibility of gradually overcoming this unreality, a practical method, a practical *via*, a practical system, that is, introversion. In this sense moralism is no system at all. For it recognizes that which ought not to be as existent, that is, as something which cannot be conquered by any dialectic, by any "sinking into the divine ground." The contradiction, because it exists, can only be overcome by action. But, through action (whether that of the individual or of humanity), it *can* be overcome. One can continually and progressively approach nearer to the goal, and that which separates from the goal need not frighten us; we only need to think optimistically about the final victory over all opposition. Therefore all these three "possibilities" are just so many forms of self-assurance. Beneath them all lies the assertion that the contradiction is not a serious obstacle, that in spite of it the continuity between existence and the divine is unbroken.

Scepticism and relativism no longer dare to make this assertion. They despair of the possibility of achieving an inner harmony. Is here also the contradiction recognized? No. It merely lurks behind their way of thinking, it menaces every solution,[1] but it is never honestly admitted. Man does not dare to look the actual fact of contradiction in the face. He evades it—scepticism is cowardice. It does not admit that there is a contradiction at all. All it does is to reject that assertive self-confident solution. But it does not dare to look more closely at the fact which moralism has perceived more keenly, the fact of that which ought not to be, the fact of evil. For this is the name of the contradiction. This is its depth It is round this point that the battle must be fought out whether the assertion of continuity, the self-assurance of the modern mind is true, or rather, why it is not true. Here lies the key to the understanding of the Christian faith and its opposition to the modern mind.

[1] Hence no one has seen so clearly as Pascal that the Christian religion has a close affinity with scepticism. It is not that *in spite* of the fact that he was such a sceptic, he was a Christian; but *because* he was a Christian, he was—in the sphere of philosophy—a sceptic. He saw the untenable character of every system, of Naturalism as well as of Idealism. But he did not, on that account, deny the propaedeutic-pedagogical value (taking these words in the broadest sense) of Idealism.

CHAPTER V

THE DEPTH OF THE DISTINCTION
THE INTERPRETATION OF THE PROBLEM OF EVIL

THE world, and man in particular, is in the depths of its being divine. This conviction colours the whole of the modern outlook, even in those forms which appear to reject this optimistic tenet of universal religion. It is all very well for a thinker like Schopenhauer to utter biting phrases about the wickedness of the world and all the utter stupidity of his fellow-men—he can do this because he is sure that he at least, and a few other wise men as well, know the truth; they are aware of the only path that an intelligent man can tread. In the last resort his pessimism is actually based upon an (aristocratic) religious metaphysic, that is, upon the general Idealist conception of Immanence. With prophetic wrath Nietzsche may condemn reason, and man as he now is: yet he believed that, through a certain inner faculty—"reason" in Christian terminology—it is possible for man to be trained for a higher development until he reaches the stature of the super-man; hence Nietzsche believes that humanity possesses the germ of development. Nietzsche's philosophy is perhaps the most daring form of human self-assertion, the most daring that has ever existed, daemonically bold, because, more deeply than many others, he was aware of the existence of the contradiction.

The modern spirit is the spirit of the self-assertion of man in face of the contradiction of existence; thus it means the denial of this contradiction, consequently above all it constitutes the denial of the existence of evil.

For the acknowledgment of the existence of evil would destroy this self-assurance. Even the intellectual philosophical self-assurance of the modern man is, from the very outset, an absolute moral fact, it is belief in the goodness of his own nature. It is therefore not surprising that the modern mind has always avoided the problem of evil with meticulous care; indeed, it has evaded this problem more sedulously than any

other—with the possible exception of the problem of death—
and has contributed practically nothing to its solution. To the
extent in which the modern mind has been concerned with
this question at all, it has been intent on the endeavour to
explain it away as far as possible. If the admission of the
irrational character of existence excludes any idea of a system—
since a system presupposes, if not rationality, at least the
possibility of being made rational, the ultimate possibility that
through thought the irrational may be overcome—so, only far
more, does the admission of the existence of evil as the primary
irrational element in life exclude any idea of system at all.
If we admit that evil exists, we must once for all renounce all
hope of conceiving life on systematic lines. For every system
in which evil would be acknowledged would automatically
transform evil into a concept, which would be to deny it,
because it would mean turning something which is anti-rational
into something which is less rational.[1] The great philosophical
systems of the modern period all end by denying evil. A
philosophical system, and the admission of the presence of evil
in the world, are mutually exclusive. Either we possess a
philosophical system, or we admit the existence of evil. It is
profoundly interesting to note that on the threshold of the
closing phase of the German Idealist movement, when the
Christian faith in revelation was once more considered as a
possibility, the reappearance of the problem of "evil" in the
later works of Schelling constituted the turning-point.
Schelling's treatise on freedom, his most brilliant piece of work,

[1] Certainly the Theosophical systems seem to constitute an exception.
In reality they have done great service by continually calling attention
to the problem of Evil, whereas systematic philosophy has ignored this
most weighty problem. All later German Theosophy from Boehme, via
St. Martin, down to Baader and Schelling, is characterized by penetrating
reflection on the problem of Evil. To the extent, however, in which this
Theosophy itself became a system, and the question of Evil was thus
absorbed into a connected whole, it once more became rationalized,
above all through being derived from the "Nature" of God. On the other
hand, not only for Schelling did attention to this problem and a closer
acquaintance with it, become a reason for a closer approach to the Christian
faith—but we ought never to forget that all the philosophers who are
more closely connected with Boehme are at the same time conscious that
they are building on a scriptural foundation.

which is really a dissertation on the problem of evil, heralds the decline of Idealism and the approach of Christian ideas. Twenty years earlier Idealism had approached this problem— only to glance off again in passing—when Kant in his *Religion within the Limits of Mere Reason* developed his doctrine of radical evil. If Kant, in the second part of this work, had not taken back what he said in the first part of the book (see p. 129), the break with Idealism, and hence the breakdown of modern thought in general, would have been inevitable.

The phenomenon of evil—let us call it this at present—has been the helpless victim of every kind of misrepresentation. Those who possess real vision can only protest very strongly against the forcible distortion of reality when an unspeakably shallow psychology, which calls itself "empirical," explains evil as the product of primitive thought, as the relic of an atavistic consciousness, as the result of a wrong system of education, etc. Even when it is pointed out that this naturalistic explanation of evil must destroy, at the very root, all power of moral judgment, this only produces a fresh misinterpretation. Here again the issue is clear: either we must admit that evil is natural, and then it does not exist as a moral fact at all; or we must admit that it is a moral factor, and then it must be confessed that it is inexplicable.

All attempts to explain evil end in explaining it away; they end by denying the fact of evil altogether. It is of the nature of evil, as it is of moral freedom, of responsible decision, that it should be inexplicable.

It is, of course, quite obvious that all speculative systems, in the narrower sense of the word—such as those of Spinoza, Leibniz, Fichte, Hegel, and Schopenhauer—throw no light on the problem of evil at all, and indeed they are incapable of doing so.[1] It is not that they do not see the fact which the

---

[1] Apart from materialistic and sense theories—which cannot even see that here any problem exists—naturally Pantheism goes furthest in denying the existence of Evil. To Spinoza Evil means privation of energy, and is only judged to be evil, that is, as something which ought not to be, by the finite, limited intelligence; thus Evil is not real at all. Evil is illusion. Leibniz sees somewhat further below the surface; but his concern with theodicy also prevents him from taking Evil seriously. To Fichte likewise Evil is something negative: laziness, lack of will. Hegel tackled the problem

moral sense calls "evil." But they all interpret it in a different sense. They cannot do otherwise. If they were to admit the reality of evil, all their systems would crumble into dust. The systematic philosopher is bound to assert that no contradiction in the world can be real; to those whose thought is not sufficiently profound even evil can only be a seeming contradiction. This contradiction can be removed by right thinking. Only on this assumption can a philosophical system exist. Evil is only an apparent contradiction, a mere illusion. That which men call evil cannot be denied, however, but we can deny that it constitutes an insuperable contradiction, that is, that in the last resort it is really evil at all. Rather, so they argue, so-called "evil" is a necessary stage of development, a stage in which the Spirit has not yet come fully into existence, it is the raw material of sense out of which Spirit has not yet developed, it is the raw material of nature, immediacy, instinct, which is still waiting to be worked up into something higher by Spirit.

Speaking generally, this represents the treatment of the problem of evil which, in very varying forms, we find in all speculative systems. It belongs to the very nature of speculative thought to interpret evil in this way. For such an interpretation alone makes speculative self-confidence possible. The position is rather different in the two other forms in which the modern spirit of self-assertion is expressed: in mysticism and in moralism. It would be going too far to say that the mystic absolutely denies the existence of evil. It is true that there are forms of mysticism where this happens quite obviously, where the moral struggle has been renounced both in theory and in practice, but such an attitude does not belong to the essence of mysticism. Mysticism admits the preliminary contradiction between God and the world of sense, between the state of union with God and that of being enmeshed in the toils of this earthly existence. At least it asserts that it does know this.

of Evil seriously, and his system nowhere contains so many inconsistencies as at this point. But essentially Hegel's view of Evil may be summed up thus: Evil is the Being-not-yet-Spirit of that which is destined to be Spirit, the raw immediacy of existence. On this point, cf. J. Müller, *Die Lehre von der Sünde*, I, pp. 371–573.

But in its fundamental conception it denies it: the fact that the relation between man and God is continuous excludes it; "at bottom" man is divine, indeed he is one with God. Thus here there is no real contradiction; here also the conception of evil simply means that man is still undeveloped. Here also evil means to be entangled in the things of sense, to be tied to the creature, to images, to illusions, to the "surface of existence," but it is not opposition to the will of God; it simply means that man stands outside the sphere ruled by the will of God. The belief in the mystic way is based upon the fact that ultimately the problem of evil is not taken seriously. Since evil is only "superficiality," it is possible, by sinking down into the depths of one's being, to reach the Divine Reality, and thus to become one with God.

Evil is therefore a lack of the divine, or separation from God. Hence a continuous approach is always possible; it means the same as the process of retreating from the surface of life. It is an emptiness; hence it contains the possibility of becoming increasingly "full" of the divine. Evil is not guilt and sin, it is not a hostile will, nor is it a break with the divine order. There is nothing "between" God and man save distance, and this man can overcome. Therefore there is a "Way," a continuous upward movement which leads finally to the goal, which is God Himself. For the mystical type of mind this process of approximation, which expresses itself in comparatives, is characteristic: the more you detach yourself from the world the nearer you come to God. Thus here also evil is only the lowest rung in a ladder; it is a passing phase, it is not a contradiction.

The question of evil receives by far the most serious attention where the moral will is regarded as the centre of the personality, and the fundamental fact in the interpretation of the world. The more purely the moral consciousness understands itself, that is, the more clearly "practical" reason is distinguished from "theoretical" reason, and the theoretical interpretation of the world, the clearer becomes the recognition of evil as a fact. In this respect the difference between Kant and Fichte is characteristic. To the extent in which Fichte is more speculative than Kant, to the extent in which he has a more fully developed system, he modifies the phenomenon of evil. Fichte regards evil as inertia, that is, as the border-line between a purely negative conception and a positive resistance. To him evil is essentially not an act of will, but a lack of will, an indeterminate middle point between mere sense-experience and a positive resistance of the personal will.

Kant, however, is the only one among the Idealistic thinkers, and indeed he is the only one among the great philosophers of modern days, who has recognized and admitted that evil is the positive resistance of the will to the law of good. Absolutely clearly he states his antitheses, which contradict the false conceptions of his own day : evil is not bondage to the experience of the sensible world, it is not inertia, it is not the raw material of nature, but it is a personal act, which takes place in the centre of personality, in the reason of man, it is the self-determination of the will in opposition to the law of God. From this point of view the doctrine of "radical evil"[1] is inevitable. For, since evil is the act of the personality, and this cannot be exhausted in a single element, the whole personality in each of its elements is responsible for evil, and is therefore never free from evil. This is the precise meaning of the conception of "radical evil."

[1] To the decisive definition of the Idea of the Good—that nothing save a good will may be called good—there corresponds that of Evil: it may only be conceived as a "determination of arbitrary caprice" (*Religion innerhalb*, . . . p. 28) ; it is said to consist in "divorcing the maxims from the Moral Law" (ibid.). "The ground of this Evil can . . . not be placed in the sense-life of man and the natural tendencies which arise out of this" (p. 35). It is not the tendencies or instincts which render the will evil—not the material utilized by the will—but "the subordination : . . . in which the will is held by the tendencies and instincts" (p. 37). Thus one single evil action already points to this wrong principle of the subordination of the Law to duty, hence there is "in man a natural inclination to evil," which, however, "must be sought in an arbitrary caprice." "This Evil is radical, because it corrupts the foundation of all maxims," it is a "perversion of the heart," and since this perversion is free, moral, and at the same time present from birth, it must be called "inherited guilt" (p. 38). Evil is "intelligible act" which "precedes all experience" (p. 40). "The rational origin . . . of this tendency to Evil, remains an impenetrable mystery . . . we can discover no comprehensible reason whence moral evil can first of all have entered into us" (p. 45).

Kant was quite aware that it is impossible to comprehend evil. He gazes at it as at some fearful abyss whose depth we do not fully know, to look down into which makes us giddy. He, the enemy of all muddled thinking, of all would-be clever profundity, the relentless logician, is forced by the very nature of the problem to come to the paradoxical conclusion of "inborn guilt." He reaches this conclusion simply because he sees what a moral will means, because he has understood the moral phenomenon better than other thinkers. If the moral will is that which Kant describes in the *Metaphysic of Ethics*, then he was forced to define evil as the paradox of "radical evil."

It is characteristic of the trend of modern thought that to this day this doctrine of Kant's has been practically suppressed by the great body of his followers. Still more characteristic is the protest which another, a far more "modern" great leader, raised against Kant. Goethe writes on June 7, 1793—that is, shortly after the publication of *Religion within the Limits of Mere Reason*—from the camp at Marienbronn to Herder: "On the other hand, however, even Kant, who, throughout a long life, has tried to cleanse his philosopher's cloak from various disfiguring prejudices, has now deliberately allowed it to be stained with the shameful idea of radical evil, in order that even Christians will be drawn to kiss the hem of his garment." This idea was so remote from Goethe's way of thinking that he could only explain it to himself by attributing it to some miserable personal motive on the part of Kant. But the power of the contradiction is seen in its most impressive form in Kant himself. He could not endure his own doctrine. For it would have shattered his Idealism, and it would have driven him—as Goethe maliciously suggests—towards Christianity. The doctrine of radical evil was a necessary consequence of the purity of his conception of morality. But as soon as it was admitted, it conflicted with the fundamental principles of Idealism as a whole: with the doctrine of autonomy, that is, with the assertion that the deepest basis in man as the producer of the moral law must be good, must be divine. If the inmost core of man—that "intelligible self" whose own will is the moral law—is not divinely good, how could man, by his own moral strength, overcome evil? This, however, he *must* be able to do; it *must* be possible to redirect the will by his own strength. Thus "in the deepest part of my nature" I am "actually" one with the Divine Lawgiver, that is, divine. It is the force of this fundamental conviction which forces Kant, clear thinker though he is, in the same work, in the first part of which he had so carefully developed his doctrine of radical evil, to deny it again in the second part; in the first part he had declared the will to be indissoluble, and therefore responsible for evil, yet in this second section he once more divides the will into a good part and a bad part, and ascribes to the good part, as the true self, the power to overcome the evil part.[1]

[1] The whole Kantian argument hangs on the slender thread of the postulate: "it is your duty, then you must be able to fulfil it" (see above, p. 114). This is the point at which the Christian faith and Idealism part company: the doctrine of the will as not free and yet responsible. Since Kant holds firmly to the postulate: "therefore he must be able to do it," he is further forced to maintain, in spite of the doctrine of Radical Evil, that "a germ of the good, in all its purity, has been left behind" (p. 47) from which "the revolution in the disposition of man" (p. 49), the "change of heart," must proceed. The inconsistency into which this leads the thinker, causing him to contradict his own idea of Evil, is simply swept away by the postulate: "when the moral Law *commands* us now to become better men, then it follows inevitably, that we *must* be able to achieve this" (p. 53). This assertion of a possibility which has been left to us, in spite of evil, is determined by the Idealistic idea of autonomy, by the idea of immanence, just as the contrary Christian assertion is determined by faith. The knowledge of duty which gives Kant sufficient reason to believe in the goodness of the human heart can only be regarded in this optimistic way by one who secretly turns duty into will, who thus recognizes in the mere fact of the Divine Imperative a divine-human will. If, however, the imperative is understood simply as an imperative and not as an act of volition—this means, however, as a divine command—then the fact that I *ought* to do so-and-so does not in any way mean that I *can* do it. The contradiction in which Kant entangles himself becomes still more evident as he proceeds to develop his thought about the change of heart. First of all, in order to make certain of the success of this change, we must be sure that this condition can be fulfilled, namely, that "a man can be quite sure of the unchangeable character of such a (good) disposition." In order to do this, however, the earlier idea of Evil as opposition to the Law must be given up, and for it there must be substituted the other Idealistic conception of "imperfection" (p. 65). As the basis for this he recurs—(as above (p. 124) we represented it as logically Idealistic)—to the difference between the

This whole process is very significant. At the very summit of Idealism the modern spirit very nearly came to a crisis in which it would have finally collapsed. But the will to self-affirmation was stronger than the desire for truth. The current of knowledge which menaced its existence was dammed up and the stream was held back. In spite of the admission of the problem of evil, the equation of the moral demand with the (intelligible) ego, that is, the principle of autonomy, was retained, and in so doing the knowledge of evil was again renounced. The deepest nature of man is still good—here also this is the ultimate conclusion. Evil is thus not a real contradiction. The real man is the intelligible man; what then is the non-intelligible man? An illusion?

If Kant had maintained his doctrine of radical evil, he would have been obliged to admit that this moral revolution of the will could not be, that the will which has been infected with evil cannot possibly cleanse itself from evil in its own strength. He would have been obliged to admit that the gulf between man and the Divine Will is one which man cannot bridge. Above all, he would have found it impossible to solve the problem of guilt by deducing divine forgiveness for the past from the fact that the will is for the most part good. The guilt account would have remained standing, and with it the "gaping world of human existence" (Kierkegaard).

The serious recognition of radical evil would have made it impossible to accept any immanent solution of the problem of human existence. For the recognition of evil as guilt and sin

Intelligible Perfect and the empirical imperfect (p. 68) and explicitly contrasts the good disposition with the imperfect action (p. 69). This, however, obviously renders the whole doctrine of Radical Evil very weak, for the purpose of this doctrine was precisely to prove that our *disposition*, and not merely the *appearance* of the same, is evil (intelligible act), and that therefore our action is really *evil* and not merely *imperfect*. Secondly, Kant is obliged to treat the problem of guilt and forgiveness in relation to God in a way which no one could do who really knows what guilt means; that is, from the fact of the good disposition the conclusion must be drawn that whatever is lacking in our behaviour God will overlook for the sake of our goodness of disposition (p. 69)! The only kind of person who cannot count on divine forgiveness is one who does not make steady progress, but is continaully falling back into evil (!) (pp. 70 ff.).

means such a contradiction within existence that nothing within the sphere of history is capable of dealing with it. If evil is actual separation from God—and that is what we mean when we speak of sin and guilt—then that continuity with the divine has been broken, and there is no way which leads back from man to God, there is no continuous process, not even that of mystical graces, to lead man back to his origin.

It would be possible to bring forward a kind of positive counter-proof from Schelling's later philosophy. It could be shown how for him the discovery of evil meant a break with the philosophy of Immanence, which he called henceforward the "negative philosophy," and made him open to an understanding of Christianity. The renunciation of Idealism—as a doctrine of God—meant for him the recognition of the break, of the Fall, of the fundamental contradiction in the world, and thus the recognition of the necessity for revelation as a contingent communication, as a fact. But Schelling also was not ready to pay the price of this new orientation. He held firmly to the possibility of a Christian *system*, or rather of a philosophical system, which produces the Christian truths from within itself. His "Philosophy of Revelation" presents us with the curious spectacle of a speculation which constructs in thought the happenings which it proves can only be discovered not by thought at all, but by something given, as a revelation. If Schelling had taken the idea of a contingent communication, which distinguishes his second period as a philosopher from his first, quite seriously, he would have had to cease being a philosopher, or at least he would have had to give up trying to express the ultimate truth in the name of philosophy; he would have had to be a believer and a personal witness. But this step was too costly; it was too much for his intellectual pride. "We reject revelation as a formal principle, *principium cognoscendi*, for all philosophy, thus also for the positive kind (for he who wishes to believe does not philosophize, and he who philosophizes makes it plain in so doing that for him faith alone is insufficient)." After Schelling himself had recognized that it was impossible to construct an *a priori* conception of God, but that all that man can do is "to follow after His ways," thus to seek after God's witness to Himself—which, however, means that at this point thought ceases and faith begins—he finally returned once more to the old path of speculation; henceforward, however, he speculated from the point of view of the knowledge of matters of faith, that is, he became a Gnostic. The consequence of this was that he again gave up the knowledge of evil as something incomprehensible, and conceived it as something which proceeds from the being of God Himself. The contingent element in revelation becomes illusory, an *a priori* cognizable theogonic process. Once again history is deified—this time not as a concept but as a myth. Thus even Schelling's positive philosophy is only a signal at the point at which the decision has to be made. The knowledge of evil decides concerning the relation of truth and history, revelation and Idea. Schelling saw plainly that this was the decisive point; and it was here that he raised the question. But his suggested solution is the old one, on immanental and *a priori* lines; for only along such lines is it possible to remain a philosopher. Hence in our further inquiry we must leave Schelling also out of account.

On the other hand, however, it is necessary to complete the foregoing survey with a glance at modern theology. If the interpretation which I have given in the preceding pages be correct, this means that the reinterpretation of the idea of revelation carries with it, as its presupposition, a corresponding reinterpretation of the Christian conception of sin. If evil be regarded as sin and guilt, in the Christian sense of the word, then a solution along the lines of modern theology is impossible. The interpretation of "revelation" in modern theology can only be regarded as a solution so long as evil is not regarded as sin, in the Christian sense of the word.

In this respect our task would be unduly simplified if we were to use Schleiermacher as our main illustration; for it is generally admitted that his conception of sin is quite extraordinarily superficial. Scarcely any other theologian has said as frankly as he that sin is purely negative, that in practice sin simply means bondage to the sense-life. Sin is the self-activity of the sense-life which has not yet been controlled by the spirit. His definition of sin as the "positive resistance of the flesh," which has a scriptural ring about it, must not be conceived in the Biblical sense. For in the Christian use of the language of the Bible the "flesh" means the whole man, as a personality made up of body and soul, in his whole attitude of hostility towards God; here, however, nothing more is meant than this: the independent life of the senses of the animal side of man. To this corresponds the other conception according to which sin is the self-activity of the "lower powers of the soul," in contradistinction to the "higher powers," thus the natural side in contrast to the side of reason. Hence sin, in relation to the good, is the "arrestation of our God-consciousness," or of the higher powers of the soul by the lower powers, the "independent activity of the flesh." One thing stands out very clearly in all these definitions: that sin is not the act of the spiritual personality itself, but it is the non-existence of this spiritual element, the "original non-consciousness of nature," the stifling and limitation of the spiritual life by the life of the senses. Sin means "that which is not yet spirit." "That moral perversion, in which the spiritual element is unable to control the instinctive impulses—is this anything else than that which we call *evil* and immoral?" Hence for Schleiermacher sin can be continuously overcome by ignoring the sense-life, which arrests the spiritual powers by its self-activity. Sin is a relative magnitude, a *quantum*; as shadow means the absence of light, so sin is the absence of the spiritual-good, non-being, not being. The "higher self-consciousness" as such is free from it. Evil is "an activity of nature and a passivity of reason."

His doctrine of Original Sin also corresponds to this conception. The only element which his doctrine has in common with the Christian doctrine is the word itself; in its nature it is the very opposite. For it teaches that sin arose out of the animal nature as a collective entity. Original Sin is thus thoroughly *explained*, and thus denied. It is simply the after-effect of our animal past, of the purely sense origin of man, which, as a collective fact, always also determines the condition of the individual. Original Sin is a phenomenon which should be explained purely from the biological point of view, it is a fact of nature. It is the collective form and way of working of the natural sense-element in the development of human life in the direction of spirit.

In no theological system is it usual to find the nature of evil misinterpreted so explicitly in the direction of weakening its force, as it is in that of Schleiermacher. Therefore here also where the gulf is ignored, the opposition is smoothed away almost entirely, a smooth unbroken line of evolutionary development is possible. There is here no trace of the mighty antithesis which always appears within Hegel's philosophy of history, which shows that the fact of opposition is realized. There is no doctrine of progress which is more directly single-minded and optimistic than that of Schleiermacher. It is purely dynamic and relative; the negative forces lose all the more significance the more the greater forces on the other side are introduced. The gradual disappearance of evil is identical with the gradual growth of the good; and this growth perfects itself by means of a natural process which is as universal and as self-evident as the natural process of evolution from the lower forms of life to the higher. It is obvious that in such a scheme there is no room for any turning-point at all.[1]

Ritschl's definition of evil is, essentially, far more profound. For here the starting-point is the Kantian doctrine of the moral will. Hence evil or sin is first of all conceived as opposition to the Divine Will. But in his perception of the contradiction the theologian remains far behind his philosophical authority. Whereas Kant—who at this point is close to the Gospel— confronts the individual human soul with the unconditional demand, and thus posits the moral challenge as a *hic et nunc*, as an unconditional demand of the absolute at the particular moment, in Ritschl the overwhelming gravity of this situation is modified in a very conventional way by pointing to historical development. For the Kantian central conception of "Law," by which is meant the absolute demand of the Divine Will, Ritschl substitutes the idea of "the calling," which sounds as though it came from the Bible and the Reformers, but which is really only meant in the very conventional sense of "a calling." The commandment of God demands from the individual nothing more than this, that he shall abide in the place where, in the process of history, he has been placed by

[1] For further details and the references to passages, see *Die Mystik und das Wort*, pp. 228 ff.

God, do his duty, and carry out his "calling" (as a citizen!),[1] as he is bound to do, at this particular point in the historical process. Thus the movement of history as such is in this way divinely legitimized. It is not, as in Christianity itself, determined by sin, as the rising of what is fallen, but it is regarded as a normal process. In the teaching of Ritschl, "Kingdom of God," history is not a "restoration," a *restitutio*, *regeneratio, recapitulatio*; he knows nothing of this "return" which is the main point in the Bible, all he knows is the Rationalistic ideal of "progress" in an ever-forward direction. This, however, means that redemption does not consist in the removal of a hindrance, of something which ought not to be there, but only in the building up of something which does not yet exist. It is sinful to arrest this forward movement, but the movement itself is not sinful. This theory of development shows very plainly that when Ritschl uses the term "sin" he means something which only faintly resembles what is meant by "sin" in the Christian religion.

From all this we can also understand the statement that there can be a "sinless life-development," which "neither *a priori* nor according to the conditions of experience can be controverted." Whereas Kant does not arrive at the knowledge of radical evil through "the summing up of all experience," but

[1] The Ritschlian idea of vocation is not that of the Bible and the Reformers, but that of Schleiermacher, indeed Ritschl explicitly appeals to Schleiermacher (*R. u. V.*, III⁴, p. 420). Its ruling idea is that of the purposive division of labour of the life of the citizen. It expresses particularly clearly the idea of the "building up" of that which Ritschl calls the "Kingdom of God." It arises out of Schleiermacher's conception of the Kingdom of God as that which is gradually achieved by human effort. The optimistic estimate of the moral possibilities of the individual life is based upon this optimistic estimate of the historical process. Nothing more is asked of man than that he should take his historical place in the ordinary life of the good citizen. In contrast with this, in the rigid idea of Law—also in the Kantian conception—there is expressed the absoluteness, the eschatological finality of the divine commandment, in which the question of what is historically possible does not arise at all. Where morality is understood in this sense, as it certainly is, not only in the Bible, but also by the Reformers, the possibility left open by Ritschl for a sinless human life seems utterly absurd. Fidelity to one's vocation as a citizen—why ever not? But to keep the divine commandments—No! Here we reach the point at which we confess: "You ought, but you *cannot*."

from the analysis of the Good Will, and of the conditions under which we now morally will, so that in order to attain this we do not have first of all to interrogate our experience,[1] here the world of experience and of human reality is regarded in such a way that in it a sinless life is absolutely possible. Therefore the doctrine of the "kingdom of sin" takes the place of the Christian doctrine of Original Sin; this is nothing more than the conceptual fixation of the fact of experience, that the individually evil is always also determined by a collective element, by the temptation to evil, as it appears to the individual in the sin of those with whom we live, and the circumstances which are created by them. The "kingdom of evil" is the sum total of all that which can provide an occasion for sin to the individual, but which does not necessarily lead to sin; it is simply the sum total of the temptations which arise out of our collective life.

Ritschl has entirely overlooked the Kantian doctrine of radical evil. To him, as to most of the moral Rationalists, evil as an act of the will is something separate, a moment which can be isolated; thus it is not a state of disharmony, or a contradiction at the basis of our present human existence, it is only a wrong attitude within the presuppositions of historical life, which are in themselves neutral. The Ritschlian doctrine of sin comes very close to that of Pelagius. It even goes further than the Pelagian doctrine in the stress it lays upon the element of ignorance in the fact of evil.[2] Certainly Ritschl does not say in so many words that sin is ignorance, but that "sin is judged by God as ignorance." Since, however, he is not here dealing with forgiveness—the gracious "covering" of sin of which the Bible speaks—but of the definition of the nature of

[1] Cf. *Religion innerhalb der blossen Vernunft*, p. 40, note.

[2] Otto Ritschl (Ritschl's *Leben*, II, p. 200) complains of the misunderstanding which asserts that Ritschl defined sin as ignorance. Certainly he can support this claim by appealing to many of Ritschl's statements. Of course, Ritschl desired to regard sin more seriously than (mere) ignorance. But in spite of this, it is no accident that he does use the actual expression, "ignorance"; thanks to his own presuppositions, he has no other choice than to define it thus, because he rejects the Law and the Primitive State as points of reference, and is indeed obliged to reject them, owing to his historical positivism.

sin, we must draw the conclusion from this statement that God judges sin to be what it is. The divine judgment of sin is also the valid right judgment. This then harmonizes with the whole argument: that, given Ritschl's whole conception of the human situation before Christ came, to him sin *cannot* be anything else than ignorance. Ultimately this agrees with his doctrine of Atonement, according to which the Atonement consists in the removal of a religious error, namely, that God is a Judge. All sin, with the exception of final hardening of heart against the divine proof of love, which does not take place in actual experience, is sin of ignorance; real knowledge of evil is only possible where the purposive will of God is known, which—according to Ritschl—is only possible through Christ.

Finally, sin as guilt is no hindrance to the purposive will of God. There is here no idea of divine punishment, of a divine righteousness manifested in punishment, of a divine wrath, of an opposition which, even from the side of God, is to be recognized as directed against Him, and of a divine reaction to this opposition. For that would be to return to the idea of God's holiness and righteousness rejected by Ritschl. The idea of punishment is rejected because it contains a forensic element mingled with the religious element, and the idea of the divine wrath is rejected as inconsistent with the Love of God. The conception of the heaven which overarches this earthly life is entirely serene, since it is not clouded by the phantasmagoria of men, with their illusions about a God of Wrath, the God who judges sinners, and the thought of a menacing Judgment to come. The Love of God radiates throughout human history with only one meaning to be attached to it. Historical development as such is the work of God, the building up of His Kingdom.

Thus we see that here also the idea of sin does not disturb the optimistic cheerful idea of progress in the Idealistic philosophy of history. The conception of sin is weakened to such an extent that it does not oppose this humanistic Monism at any point. History is a normal process. Outside the historical sphere of the influence of Christ, it is, it is true, imperfect, the purpose of history has not yet been fully recognized within it. But also it is not opposed to God. The only thing which Christ has to remove is, not any possible real opposition of sinful guilt, but our ignorance of the divine love, that is, of the divine will and purpose. There is no rent in the life of history as such which could not be healed by the historical process itself, but that which appears in Christ is connected with that which was before Him, and leads directly and positively towards His End. This optimistic view of history which Ritschl has taken over from the Idealistic philosophy of history through Schleiermacher does not permit a realistic serious knowledge of sin to appear at all. On the contrary, for the Ritschlian conception this optimism constitutes the presupposition for the doctrines of revelation and the Atonement. Because the rent has never been made, there is no need of a Mediator. Because there is nothing to overcome, because there is no hindrance to be removed, therefore it is sufficient to become acquainted with the divine will and purpose in its positive character in order to be able to judge present and future existence with joyful confidence.

But even where—as for instance in the writings of Troeltsch[1] —a definitely ethical judgment of sin prevails, the extent of the sphere of evil is not understood. The problem of sin is regarded as a purely subjective affair, as a mere question of the moral religious disposition, that is, in the spirit of Pietism. For those conceptions which regarded sin as contradiction at the basis of historical existence, the conception of the Fall and of Original Sin, have been thrown on the scrap-heap of discarded notions.[2] The thought of the present day—whether consciously or not—is thoroughly Pelagian. At bottom it thinks only of *sins*, not of *sin*, that is, of evil as isolated acts of the will, but

[1] Cf. Troeltsch's *Glaubenslehre*, pp. 300 ff.

[2] This individualistic moralism in the conception of sin can be perceived even amongst the most convinced of "positive" theologians. Even Adolf Schlatter comes very near to this, as he also explicitly gives up the central conceptions of the Christian idea of sin—the Fall and the doctrine of Original Sin (pp. 271–9). This explains why he evinces so little understanding of the significance of Christian Dualism and of the decisive influence of eschatology, in which he differs decidedly from Kähler, whose position is otherwise close to his own. His praiseworthy struggle against speculation and metaphysics in theology has led him, here as well as at other points, into an empiricism which is as unscriptural as speculation. This empiricism, however, is so penetrated with the scriptural outlook that there is no need to dispute it.

not as the corruption of human existence; only as disturbing elements, as accidental occurrences, within an existence which is otherwise neutral or good (for our present existence is regarded as identical with the Good Creation of God), not as something which is necessarily connected with the present bases of our existence. Hence it regards the contradiction as something merely subjective, which concerns man only, not as something which is objective, which concerns both sides. For the idea of the divine wrath is taboo. And, finally, it regards evil as in its essence only an individual thing; for in so far as a non-individual view is taken, it is not the solidarity of sin and guilt with which we are concerned, (this can only be recognized by faith), but the social environment which becomes to the individual the occasion for sinning. All this is included in the conception of Pelagianism, a conception which is of great importance in the history of dogma. It was this individualistic and moralistic conception of evil against which Augustine and the Reformers contended.

The Christian view of sin differs entirely from all those which have hitherto been mentioned; the difference is just as great at this point as it is on the question of general and special revelation. In fact, both ideas are indissolubly connected, in a relationship wh'ch· is mutually interdependent, as Calvin expresses it at the beginning of his *Institutes*: The knowledge of God and that of the self are *multis inter se vinculis connexae, utra tamen alteram praecedat et ex se pariat non facile est discernere.* For: *propriae infelicitatis conscientia unumquemque pungi necesse est, ut in aliquam saltem Dei notitiam veniat. . . . Rursum hominem in puram sui notitiam nunquam pervernire constat, nisi prius Dei faciem sit contemplatus.* The knowledge of sin and the knowledge of God mutually condition each other. Because here sin is *thus* recognized—as is done nowhere else—therefore we can speak of revelation only in *this* sense. Likewise, this knowledge of sin is possible only upon the basis of revelation.

The Christian conception of sin means the Fall and the doctrine of Original Sin. This does not mean a particular theory which *explains* the fact of sin.[1] We are not here dealing

[1] Unfortunately even Schlatter shares the erroneous view that in the doctrine of the Fall there is an attempt to explain the origin of Evil (loc.

with Jewish *theologumena* or Greek *philosophumena*, but with the fundamental Christian and scriptural conception of sin. It is this fundamental conception which is meant by the words "sin" and "original sin." A man's mind is closed to all understanding of the Christian view of the meaning of sin if he seeks to penetrate the mystery which lies behind these words and tries to find an explanation of the fact of evil, in the sense that man, whether from curiosity or from the needs of the scientific spirit, still seeks for a causal explanation of this mysterious phenomenon. On the contrary, both these conceptions are attempts to express the horror of sin, its terrible character—in a word, "the exceeding sinfulness of sin." These expressions do not aim at stating the cause of sin, but simply the fact of its existence. So long as we do not see what these two expressions are trying to tell us, the horrible character of sin is not recognized, sin is glossed over; it is treated lightly. It may be that the instinct to seek for a theoretical explanation may lead to theories which bear a certain resemblance to that which the Christian calls the Fall and Original Sin. A theory of this kind may, on that account, be easily confused with these two terms by anyone whose thought does not penetrate very far beneath the surface of life; however, we are not required to renounce these ideas themselves.

The two expressions, the Fall and Original Sin—which only have meaning when they are placed together—suggest first of all that sin is something far more powerful than moralism or Pietism, which use these words so much, would have us believe. Sin is not a merely moral phenomenon, and it is not a merely subjective process. That which bears the name of sin, in the moralist's sense and in the subjective sense, belongs indeed to sin as a whole, but it is not the whole. Sin, in the Christian sense, has quite as much to do with that which Greek tragedy calls Fate as with that which the moralist calls "sins." The term means quite as much a "cosmic potency" as a "moral" phenomenon. In reality neither of these expressions

cit., p. 277). He has confused the existential "whence?" with the causal-metaphysical "whence?"; this is all the more strange, since Schlatter sees clearly the meaning of the "whence?" of the Bible at another point—that is, in the doctrine of the pre-existence of Christ (pp. 356 ff.).

represents the whole truth; both simply represent isolated aspects of a view which includes both these partial truths within itself, apart from their errors.

Sin, interpreted in the Christian sense, is certainly not only a determination of the will—in the sense in which we use the word "will" nowadays. Sin is equally a determination of existence, of the being of humanity itself, as it now is, of human "nature." Pelagianism, which only recognizes the presence of sin in particular acts of the will, is no less false than Manichaeism, which regards sin as an evil substance which has been in existence from all eternity. The humanistic idea of the freedom of the will which dominates the ethical and religious thought of the present day is no less false than the ancient idea of guilt which broods over humanity like a fateful destiny. It is just as superficial to identify sin with the individual acts of our conscious will as it is to derive it from any kind of "nature" at all.

Sin, from the Christian point of view, is primarily something which affects the nature of man as a whole. At this point the Christian view of sin approaches the Kantian doctrine of radical evil. Evil has not been understood if we think: "Now, at this moment, I have done something wrong, but previously, before the actual decision, I was either good or neutral." Whoever takes a view of this kind is not merely lacking in the scientific impulse to try to explain the existence of evil, but he is lacking in moral earnestness. We take sin seriously when to some extent we become aware of the depth of its roots. For I need to see that evil has roots in the very depths of my nature in order to realize that "I" am really bad. Until I see this I regard evil as something accidental, like a splash of mud, not like something which belongs to "the essence of my nature."

To see how deeply rooted evil is, and to take sin seriously, are one and the same thing. Thus the question "Whence does it come?" does not arise out of the need for theoretical explanation. It is not an after-thought, a reflection upon the problem of evil, but this question suggests the dimension of evil, and in so doing its seriousness. A man who has not yet perceived that evil is entwined with the very roots of his personality is a superficial person; this means that where man is a unity, a whole, where the individual has the one foundation of his mental and spiritual life, evil is poisoning his existence. This is expressed—in harmony with the thought of the Bible—when we say: man does not only *do* wrong, he does not only commit sinful acts, but he *is* bad, he is a sinner. A sinner is not a human being who has sinned a certain number of times; he is a human being who sins whatever he is doing. So long as this is not perceived the gravity of sin is ignored, and the point of view remains superficial.

Kant, with his doctrine of radical evil, reached this point. It cannot be helped that many people regard this doctrine as a mere speculation. We can only deplore the fact that they are too superficial to realize that this is the truth about themselves. But the Kantian doctrine of radical evil is not the Christian doctrine. It is not our business here to inquire whether it is derived from the Christian doctrine or not; in any case, in vital seriousness it lags far behind the Christian doctrine, although it certainly attains far greater heights than all other philosophical theories of evil. The reason why the Kantian doctrine lags behind the Christian view is that it remains within the sphere of mere reason, and this means that it is not truly personal. For it measures man only by an impersonal law. Kant, therefore, rightly does not use the term "sin," but the impersonal conception of "evil," an expression which is never used of personal relationships. In his theory the point at issue is not the fact that the human will is contrary to the divine will, but that the human will does not agree with the law.

Kant knew very well why he did not go further. To go further would have meant leaving the rational standpoint of the philosopher behind and becoming a believer.

The Christian conception of radical evil is this: it is radical sin. As a sinner man is not confronted with an impersonal law of good, but with the will of the Creator. Sin is resistance to the will of the Creator and Lord. "Against Thee, Thee only, have I sinned." We can *sin* only against God. It is true, of course, that we live and move amongst men in the world of human life, and the person who is injured by sin is never God, but our fellow man. But this injury in itself is not the evil thing—why should I *not* injure my fellow man?—but disobedience to the will of God, who decrees that I should never injure my fellow man, who makes him "sacred." Sin means the non-recognition of the limitation of my own will by the divine will in the existence of my fellow men. Do we need to lay special emphasis upon the fact that to expose this root of evil is not due to curiosity but to a serious view of the question? That without this admission "Against Thee, Thee only, have I sinned" there is no real earnest recognition of the reality of sin?

This view, however, includes another point. If evil is measured by a law, then all that has to be estimated is the extent to which there has been lack of compliance with the law. "Contradiction" is too strong a word, unless we use the word in its weakened, purely logical sense. Sin, however, really means gainsaying, setting oneself *against*. Here, therefore, the movement is different, not that of not coming together but the actual movement of going away. "Evil" means: a certain difference is present. "Sin" means: man has torn himself away from his origin.

Only thus is evil seen to be no longer something negative, something which does "not yet exist," but something positive, and this positive character—this act of setting oneself *against* —is what we mean by the seriousness of evil. Sin is only understood in its full reality and gravity where it is regarded as insubordination, as the turning away of the creature from the Creator. Every other conception is superficial, because each regards evil as the absence of something—this is true even of the Kantian doctrine.

Yet we must take care that on no account do we lose from sight the Kantian idea of totality. Man *is* a sinner; he does not only commit sins. Insubordination towards God, the state of being alienated from God, is not the determination of certain moments; it is the character of man's existence, in spite of the fact that it is really insubordination, and thus neither a natural fact nor an element in creation, but a personal act. Kant, indeed, shook his head over his own admission: "The origin of evil . . . this propensity towards evil is an unfathomable mystery"; "for us thus there is no intelligible ground whence evil can first have entered into us," so still less can we understand that evil which, from the Christian point of view, we call sin. On the contrary, the more deeply we become aware of the reality of evil, the less can we explain it. Sin is something which we cannot explain, something which will not fit into any reasonable scheme at all. For it is the primal fact of non-reason. The more we try to explain evil, the more we deny its reality, and the more superficial we become. The more anyone knows what evil is, the more inexplicable does it become. The doctrine of the Fall is not a theory which is intended to explain the existence of evil; on the contrary, it is the idea in which the inexplicable character of evil finds its clearest expression.

But the Kantian conception of radical evil is not only an incomplete interpretation of the nature of evil, because it is impersonal, but also because it is wholly individualistic. Evil is a determination of the whole, as we have already seen. But this totality is not only related to the isolated acts of the individual but also to human life as a whole. A false abstraction is always introduced when we isolate the individual from the community to which he belongs. To do this is itself an act of falsity and lovelessness, a lack of solidarity and truth. We know already from experience to how great an extent we are affected by others even in evil. Thus experience itself tells us that it is wrong to be cut off from our fellows like this. Rationalism indeed cannot avoid it, if it does not wish to lower humanity to the rank of a mere species or "ζῷον." Its individualism, therefore, is a justifiable protest against all Naturalism and false determinism implied in theories of heredity and environment. Behind it there is the concern for responsibility.

Christianity, however, neither removes the individual out of solidarity with the community, nor does it make the individual merely part of a species. In the belief in creation the individual as an individual is always at the same time the representative of the species. Man is never a mere individual, but he is also at the same time humanity, and yet as an individual he is absolutely responsible. The image of our original parents (Adam and Eve) is only a vivid way of representing an abstract idea, namely, that we are indeed all responsible, but that our

144

guilt is always regarded collectively. For each human being is that particular human being who has been created in the image of God. Each of us has this origin, and upon this origin is based both our human unity as well as our solidarity. Whatever essentially concerns the one also concerns the other. Essentially we are one, in spite of the fact that as individuals we possess and express this essential element in different ways.

It is of the essence of our nature that we have been created by God. But it also belongs to the very essence of our nature that we are sinners. Sin is not something which has been superadded; it is something essential. It, as well as the fact that we have been created by God, affects the core of our personality. Hence we experience our human solidarity in sin, since we are essentially bound up in the bundle of life with our fellow men. It is simply loveless Pharisaism to try to separate my own sin from that of others, to regard sin as a private matter, referring to my own life alone. To take individualism as a matter of course is a specifically modern view. In the ancient world, and among pagan peoples to-day, this individualism is always kept within bounds, to some extent—even though in a sinful and erroneous way—by the ancient primitive tribal traditions, and by the idea which they incarnate that the tribe as a whole is responsible to the god or gods. The moral individualism of the man of the present day is a product of European Rationalism. We know scarcely anything to-day of that which every non-modern man knew in some way or another, namely, that he who stands before God as a sinner never stands there alone, but always as the representative of others. To deny the solidarity in sin is an egoistical perversion.

It is, however, true that this solidarity in sinfulness cannot be proved empirically. Experience merely throws out hints about it. Whoever intends to hold simply to that which experience shows him will oscillate between a sociological determinism and a humanistic individualism of freedom—and this is what is actually taking place at the present time. Both positions represent mutilated fragments of truth. Truth itself, however, lies deep down below the surface, beyond the reach of experience. Experience does not even show us radical evil itself. It is only when we reflect upon our experience that we gain this insight into truth. Experience never shows us that we are sinners. On the contrary, this is an article of faith. The extent of our conviction of sin depends upon the degree of our faith. The Christian religion defines sin as a whole, as a totality, both individual and general. We do nothing that is not sinful; and none of us is sinless. Both these truths are, however, summed up in the statement: "Man has fallen away from God." Not merely You or I or the other man, but "Man"; that is, sin belongs to the essential being of humanity.

This also implies that sin is no longer merely a matter of the will, but—although in its origin it is a personal act—it is at the same time a fact of nature. For man is a unity of body and soul. To conceive him dualistically is merely the concern of abstract reason. Belief in creation views him as a unity of body and soul, as it likewise views him as a community, and not merely as an individual. The knowledge of this character of man as a unity of body and soul, in distinction from the dualism of reason and the animal nature of man, arises at the same point as our knowledge of human solidarity in contradistinction to individualism; and that is, faith in Creation. The Christian religion, and it alone, takes faith in God as the Creator seriously. Hence it does not divide man into two parts, of which one is good and the other evil, but it claims that originally man as a whole was good, both in soul and body, and that the whole man has now been corrupted, both in soul and in body. Therefore even the new-born human being is not simply the being created by God. The good Creation lies beyond this visible world. The whole of history has been infected with the poison of sin. In the world of historical process there are no pure and sinless origins. It is not the empirical origin within time which is good, but Creation. The beginning within time, however, is for each individual an historical fact, and it is also connected with the whole of sinful history. This is the meaning of the doctrine of Original Sin.

Hence we say: sin, understood in the Christian sense, is the rent which cuts through the whole of existence. This is not the Manichaean view, which holds that existence, as such, is evil; nor is it a Pelagian conception, which holds that existence, as such, is an innocent and neutral condition; but our present historical existence is sinful owing to the Fall. We can understand this as little as we can understand what it means to say that we men and women who are born of human fathers and mothers have been created by God. Every statement of the faith is a riddle which will not be fully revealed until we reach the eternal world (1 Cor. xiii. 12). But since we know through faith that we have really been created by God in His image—although we cannot imagine what this means, and cannot incorporate it into our picture of experience —so also we know by faith that we have fallen away from God, collectively—although we cannot fit this either into our picture of experience.

This view is no mere religious speculation; it is, rather, the one and only serious interpretation of sin. All other theories estimate our freedom too highly and too light-heartedly, and underestimate the burden of sin; or else they undervalue freedom, in a dull and rigid way, and transform sin into Fate. In the Christian religion man knows that he has fallen away collectively from God, and that this Fall, as a sinful and guilty act, is perpetually and inevitably repeated. Neither the responsibility nor the necessity are denied; on the contrary, here alone is sin fully personal, and at the same time grasped in all its unavoidable force.

One further consideration, however, is still needed to give its full force to the Christian view of sin, and this is one in which alone its existential and personal significance is fully expressed. Sin is sin against God. It is the breaking of a personal relationship. Hence the most appalling thing about sin is this: that through it the original personal relation between the Creator and the creature has been distorted. Guilt now lies between man and God. God can no longer admit man to His Presence. Man has cast away the grace of God. "Guilt" is the term which expresses the broken fellowship. I am not speaking of "consciousness" of guilt. This consciousness of guilt is merely the subjective reflection of the guilt itself. Guilt is something objective, not something subjective, just as truly as the relation to God is objective and not merely subjective.

But guilt expressed in positive terms means the wrath of God. This is the new attitude of God towards man, that He is angry with him on account of his sin. That guilt is a real break, and indeed one which man can never mend, is expressed by the statement that "God is angry," "God will punish."

Thus this is the reality in which man lives. This gulf of separation between man and his Creator runs right through everything. This rent is the cause of all the other rents which become visible within existence. We cannot fit these elements into the picture of experience which we call the "world." They transcend it like the Creation, and sin itself. But they certainly manifest themselves in many ways in the reality which we can experience. The Christian religion certainly makes the claim to give a more intelligible and realistic account of that part of reality which we can experience than any other religion or any other world view. The Christian conception of sin does not need to fear the test of "facts." It is no accident that the greatest psychologists were Christians. For the Christian religion is as far removed from cynical realism as it is from ideological Idealism. It sees all the divinity of the Creation and of man, but it sees also its fallen state, its bondage, and yet its responsibility. It does not fit the "Ideal"—that is the Will of God—into reality, but also it does not say: "You ought, therefore you can"; but rather: "You ought, therefore you cannot." "For if you could, you would know nothing of duty, God's will would be to you no alien law but fatherly mercy." The law as a stern demand is already a sign of the great disturbance which has taken place, and is at the same time the means by which man pushes this disharmony to its utmost limit. For the law becomes to him the opportunity to attain that summit of sinful arrogance which is called autonomy, where the divine truth and its sinful perversion, separated from one another only by a hair's breadth, confront each other with the most absolute hostility.

Here again we have once more reached our starting-point. For this consciousness of autonomy, of self-determination, is indeed the most characteristic element in the modern outlook. "Modern," we say, although this spirit is really something quite general and timeless, because only the modern period with its rational emancipation has allowed this spirit to develop fully. Autonomy is another expression for that which we have already described as continuity between God and man. Autonomy means self-legislation. It is the arrogant opinion that man co-operates with God in the making of the divine law, that man too sits on the throne of God, that the Lord is alongside of and not above him; his own deepest foundation is indeed the Divine. "Existence is a continuous progress towards God" means that no serious breach has occurred; that it is possible to step from one sphere to the other, whether through profound thought, or through profound meditation or by mystical absorption, or by the deepest inwardness of desire. Man is not separated from God; it is only the surface which is separated from Him, but in the depths the rent has been healed. Hence it is possible to be united with God, to be one with Him. Sin, indeed, should not be denied altogether, but it does not affect the deepest root, the heart or essence of the personality and of the life. It does not mean corruption at the root, but only of the visible part of personality, not of the better self, not of the spirit in its depths. It does not need, therefore, to be taken too seriously. If we probe deeply enough beneath the surface, we find that the connection with God is still intact. Redemption is not necessary; rather, all that we need to do is to sink down into the depths of our own nature.

This is that opposition to the Christian faith which in its actual and most obvious form we call the "modern mind," although in point of fact it is simply the "natural man," the man of reason, the religious man, the ethical man. It is man apart from Christ. For now we see the connection between faith in revelation and the consciousness of sin in the Christian. The Christian view contains the knowledge of the fatal gulf, a gulf over which no bridge can ever be thrown, of the fatal wound which cannot be healed, that is, the wound which only a special act of God can heal, the gulf which God alone can bridge. The bridge over this abyss is the Mediator. Now, however, we must point out, on the other hand, that we are not of ourselves conscious of the greatness of this gulf, for if we were, it would not be so great. He who has lost innocence no longer knows what innocence is. He who has fallen away from God does not know what alienation from God means. If he were to know it, he would not really be so far away from God. To be in earnest about the knowledge of sin means that our knowledge can never be our own discovery, it must always be something which has been granted to us as a new gift and grace. To have a complete knowledge of the gulf would mean the knowledge that God has placed a bridge across this gulf. Perception of sin is not serious until we know that we can only be helped by the mediation which God Himself has provided. This, however, we only know when it happens. That this must happen first of all shows us where we are. Complete knowledge of sin is attained only in the Mediator.[1]

Knowledge of sin—genuine horror of sin—is the presupposition of faith in the Mediator. So long as we do not notice this, so long as we think that we have no need of a Mediator, so long are we embedded in the self-assurance of the pride of human reason. We still believe—however rent and seamed the surface of our life may be—that the underlying depths of our existence are untouched, that they are still united

---

[1] Then there is no real knowledge of sin in the non-Christian religions? In point of fact: no. Neither religious moralism—whether of the Stoics, or of original Zoroastrianism—nor mysticism, nor the ceremonial forms of religion have such a conception. It is, of course, true that religious moralism often has a great deal of insight into the nature of the Good, but how limited its view is, is shown precisely by its superficial statements about Evil; it lacks wholeness and the relation to God Himself. It is, of course, true that mysticism uses striking expressions to convey the sense of the soul's distance from God, but it has no sense of guilt. Ceremonial forms of religion, too, contain precisely in their sacrificial rites a truth which those "more spiritual" religions allow to slip from them: the consciousness, namely, that there is some obstacle between man and God, which must be removed: here, however, it is held that the cultus *does* remove the obstacle. This shows their limitations and their lack of seriousness. The Old Testament, however, adopts a special position. The view of sin in the Old Testament stands in the same relation to the Christian view of sin as Old Testament revelation. And it is common knowledge that the perception of sin in the prophetic message is precisely that which is most clearly connected with the consciousness of the covenant made with God. What would happen if a general history of religion were written from the point of view of sin, instead of from the point of view of myth, cultus, and experience of God? The parallelistic theories of comparative religion would be rent like a spider's web.

with God. So long as we do not see the need for the divine intervention we reject every assertion of such an intervention. For, rightly understood, the saying here also is true that only under stress of need do we learn to pray. Only when a man finds all ways of escape barred does he believe. Knowledge of sin, in this universal sense, is the presupposition of faith. This is the first point. The second point, however, is this: this presupposition is never produced by anyone save by faith, the divine revelation, the faith in the Mediator. "Repentance" and faith are inseparable. It is not merely that the one cannot happen without the other, but that the one grows within the other. Only the soul that despairs knows what it means to believe, and faith teaches to despair rightly. *Si deus vivificat, facit illud occidendo* (Luther).

One final word: to recall those who have gone astray is the revelation of Christ, a return to God which is made possible and right through divine intervention. Hence it is not an absolute new creation, but the new creation of that which God has created. The call of God comes to man who, it is true, is no longer with God, but who once *was* with Him. Only thus is it a call *back* to God, and this "Come back" is, in contra-distinction to the Rationalistic motto "Forwards," the characteristic word of the message of reconciliation. This means that this word is addressed to one who, although he no longer possesses the word, when the word is once more given to him is able to recognize it as the original word, the word of his state as a being created by God. Hence also his present sinful condition is not without God, nor without a revelation of God; but this revelation of God is the opposite of what some call revelation, and it has two aspects. It is God, and yet it is not God, in His Essence, who is here revealed. "The wrath of God has been revealed from heaven. . . ." Reason is not without a knowledge of God, but it is not the living God which it knows, and—as the history of rational "theology" shows plentifully enough—it is a confused and uncertain knowledge of God, a kind of twilight knowledge.

Thus mysticism also is not without some divine truth. How could it be otherwise! Its deepest longing after direct contact with God is truth, but the satisfaction of this longing is illusion.

The synthesis which it achieves is too cheap, like the synthesis attained by reason. Even the rational ethical conviction of the original good in man is not without some truth. It is the truth of the original, but it is distorted by an ethical optimism which does not see the breach between the original and the present state, and therefore fails to perceive either the original and the ultimate, or the way thither. This synthesis also is too cheap. It is, however, as we have already seen, the basis of all the others. Behind them all stands the self-confidence of the man who is alienated from God, in the strength which remains to him, in the possibilities which he still possesses, in the confidence which arises out of the fact that the rent is not perceived, that sin is neither confessed nor admitted. This is why he interprets the traces of divine truth in a way which seems direct, but which is really false, and is satisfied with it. For if his interpretation were correct, such a soul would realize that his condition was desperate. This is what the Reformers meant when they constantly affirmed that the knowledge of God through reason led only to the God of wrath, to the *merae tenebrae rationis*. From the psychological, empirical point of view this is not the case. A characteristic of people who live directly on the "natural" plane is quite as much frivolity as despair. But positively it is true; for the objective aspect of the divine which corresponds to the condition of man is the wrath of God. Hence a theology which uses the language of Christianity can be tested by its attitude towards the Biblical doctrine of the wrath of God, whether it means what the words of Scripture say. Where the idea of the wrath of God is ignored there also will there be no understanding of the central conception of the Gospel: the uniqueness of the revelation in the Mediator.

CHAPTER VI

THE CHRISTIAN FAITH AND HISTORICAL RESEARCH

I. FAITH AND HISTORICAL FACTS

It is of the very essence of the Christian faith that its relation to history should be entirely different from that of any other religion or philosophy. In the ordinary sense of the word it is not concerned with history at all. It is what it is through its relation to that unique event, which, although it is a fact of history, does not gain its unique character from its historical connection. It is this which determines the peculiar relation of the Christian faith to history in general. To the Christian faith revelation does not mean a reverent process of tracing the ways of God in history. Indeed, history as such is not a divine revelation; it merely represents humanity as a whole in its need of redemption. But precisely because something super-historical, unique, absolutely decisive has entered into human history, to faith history means something entirely different from its meaning for all other forms of thought. Our relation to history is determined by our relation to Jesus Christ, not vice versa. To regard the matter from the opposite point of view means thinking in terms of universal religion, of general revelation.

The peculiar fact about Christianity—and one which gives great offence—is this: it is absolutely concerned with an external historical fact. It is not the external fact itself with which it is concerned so deeply, but with the fact of the actuality of that upon which it depends; this too is intended in the absolutely literal sense of the word—in the sense of a fact which has actually taken place. All depends upon the fact that the Word did become flesh, and this means that the Eternal has entered into the sphere of external historical fact. To be "made flesh" means among other things an actual state of presence, sensible, external, non-spiritualized. Incarnation means entering into the realm of visible fact, being the object of police reports, a subject for the photographer, for the commonplace journalist, and other things of that kind. It is a state in which an individual can be touched, handled, or photographed; it is an isolated fact within time and space, the filling of a certain point within time and space which apart from this fact would have remained empty, and which can be filled in with this fact alone: all this belongs to the actuality of the Incarnation of the Word. In this sense the "Theology of Facts" cannot be interpreted too literally. For "flesh" means the brutal solidity of the facts of sensible existence.

Thus faith is passionately concerned with this actuality, in the most matter-of-fact sense of the word. Everything in the Christian faith depends upon the certainty that this event (and we mean *event* in the most matter-of-fact literal sense) actually happened. If it never did take place, then Christianity may be either a very foolish idea, or perhaps a very brilliant one, but it cannot be a religion.

It is precisely this connection with a "brute fact" which is the distinguishing mark of the Christian religion, contrasted with every other kind of religion and philosophy. Its concern with history in general is indirect. But it is directly and absolutely concerned with this historical fact, in a way in which the most earnest student of the history of the past can never be interested in an isolated fact. It is interested in this historical fact simply because it happened once for all; this very conception of uniqueness is unknown outside Christianity. In the strict sense of the word the "unique" can only mean *one* fact; there can be only one individual example of this species of uniqueness. This conception is wholly illustrated by this one example; indeed, this example exhausts the significance of the idea just because it is, in all seriousness, absolutely unique.

Thus our relation to Jesus is not a particular instance of our general attitude towards history, it does not form part of a reverent attitude towards history as such. Owing to this element of uniqueness, indeed, this particular instance is completely isolated. And the Christian faith *is* this special relation to this unique event, as to something absolutely unique, and thus to it alone.

Whether this connection with a fact, in this literal, realistic sense, leads to difficulties and conflicts of various kinds is a secondary question, which in principle should really belong to the sphere of ethics. This difficulty would then belong to the sphere of the "cross" which the Christian has to carry, that is, it would form part of the difficulties which arise in general out of the contrast between his faith and the spirit of the world and worldly connections. But there can never be any question of altering the Faith itself in such a way that these difficulties could be avoided. This temptation to evade the offence of the Cross besets us constantly. Universal religion, with its freedom from historical facts, avoids a host of difficulties. It is not surprising that this temptation should also assail faith,[1] especially at a time when intensive historical criticism tends to render the historical factual element uncertain. If Christianity yields to this temptation, it will perish. If, on account of the struggle it involves, Christianity were to withdraw from the sphere of conflict, from the realm of history, it would no longer be a living faith, but merely a general belief in religion, which has been confused with faith.

The desperate position in which faith is placed, from the point of view of the possibility of historical conflict, is caused by a misunderstanding of the believer about himself, that is, of his relation to history. If faith were dependent on history, in the scientific sense of the word, it would then be as remote from Christianity, in the Christian sense of the word, as it

---

[1] With his own peculiar decisiveness and outspokenness, Albert Schweitzer draws this inference, in connection with the discussion about the historicity of Jesus: it would have been far more impressive if theology, instead of being so anxious to prove the historicity of Jesus, had demonstrated, "that in the event of the failure to produce, in the personality of Jesus, the evidence required, much would be lost it is true, but by no means all, and Liberal Christianity would continue to live on the knowledge and energies of direct religion wholly independent of all historical foundation" (*Geschichte der Leben-Jesu-Forschung*, p. 511). In similar vein, but still more explicitly, P. W. Schmiedel: "My most intimate religious life would not be harmed even if to-day I were forced to acknowledge that Jesus never existed. . . . I would still know that I could not lose the degree of piety which I attained long ago, simply because I could no longer trace it back to Him" (*Die Person Jesu im Streit der Meinungen der Gegenwart*, Prot. Monh., 1906, p. 281).

would be if it were severed from the facts of history altogether.
For dependence on history as a science leads to a state of
hopeless uncertainty. Therefore, when a thoughtful person
refuses to build his relation to the eternal on anything so unsafe
as historical science, he is acting rightly; for such building is
indeed a glaring example of building one's house upon the
sand.

It is an equal misunderstanding to regard the object of the
Christian faith as a fact of history.[1] It is, of course, true that
it is essential to the Christian religion that the central object
of its faith can be perceived in no other mode of existence
than that of historical objectivity. The Word became flesh,
and only as the Incarnate Word do we know It, as that which
is concealed under the mode of existence of historical actuality
into which it has penetrated. But the exhortation not to deny
the "Christ who has come in the flesh" is paralleled by the
warning not to confuse the Christ who came "in the flesh"
with the "Christ after the flesh." Historical criticism has forced
us to perceive this, and for this we should be eternally grateful.
This distinction is only intelligible from the standpoint of
the Christian faith. Outside the Christian faith such an idea
could not even be entertained. Thus it is not a special instance
of a general law. The law applies to this case and to this alone,
that is, only Christ is "in the flesh" as the Word is "in the
flesh," Christ alone possesses this twofold relation to historical
objectivity: namely, that He can be known only "in the flesh"
but not "*after* the flesh."[2] This distinction is only another way

[1] Where faith is regarded empirically as a perception—as Schlatter,
and latterly his follower, Hirsch also, seems to do—a collision with historical
science is inevitable. For where the image which is perceived is the first
thing that matters to faith ("faith is enkindled by the image of Jesus Christ,"
Hirsch: *Jesus Christus der Herr*, p. 9) it is inevitably sucked into the whirlpool
of relativism, out of which even a man like Wilhelm Herrmann tried in
vain to work his way by means of his withdrawal to the "Inner Life" of
Jesus. For this too is an object of relativizing history.

[2] The distinction between the "Christ after the flesh" and the "Christ
in the flesh" can be based, verbally, only upon Rom. i. 3 and Rom. ix. 5.
Actually, it is connected indissolubly with faith in the Incarnation of the
Eternal Word of God, with His humiliation, and the "taking upon Him the
form of a servant." To me, it seems probable that in 2 Cor. v. 16, the
κατὰ σάρκα refers to γνῶναι and not to χριστόν. The point is knowledge

of expressing this unique fact, which, while it is really and truly historical, yet transcends all historical barriers. Historical actuality is the way in which the Eternal Divine Word, as the Eternal Son, touches the historical world. This actuality means a real entrance into the historical mode of existence, but so far as its significance is concerned this entrance merely touches the fringe of existence. Hence the possibility of making the distinction between the "Christ in the flesh" and the "Christ after the flesh." The "Christ in the flesh" offers a common point of interest both to the chronicler and to the believer. The believer believes in the Christ of whom the chronicler also must have something to report. But the Christ who is set forth by the chronicler, by the author of a report, or by the historian who is most profoundly prepared by all his previous training to understand the great and truly human in history, or by the man who in all reverence watches and listens for the voice of God within history, is the "Christ after the flesh." The believer alone sees more than the "Christ *after* the flesh" in the "Christ in the flesh."[1]

after the flesh in contrast to spiritual knowledge. Actually however, it amounts to the same thing in the end. For to knowledge there corresponds its object. That which is accessible to knowledge according to the flesh is precisely the $X\rho\iota\sigma\tau\acute{o}\varsigma$ $\kappa\alpha\tau\grave{\alpha}$ $\sigma\acute{\alpha}\rho\kappa\alpha$ and, to spiritual perception, the $X\rho\iota\sigma\tau\acute{o}\varsigma$ $\kappa\alpha\tau\grave{\alpha}$ $\pi\nu\varepsilon\tilde{\upsilon}\mu\alpha$.

[1] Bultmann's book on *Jesus*, which certainly constitutes an important event in theological-historical work, suffers from a remarkable discord, caused by the fact that Bultmann does not distinguish the personality of Jesus in the sense of an object of history from Jesus in the sense of faith. Hence at the same moment in which he is attacking Rationalism he is standing within the sphere of this very Rationalism, since he sets the *teaching* of Jesus as *the* important thing over against His Person, which is unimportant; he goes so far in this direction that he asserts his complete indifference to the question whether Jesus ever existed at all (p. 17). Bultmann certainly means this "teaching" to be conceived in a non-Rationalistic way, as a "Word" in a concrete situation. He is not successful in the use of this distinction, because the concreteness (which he means) of the prophetic Word in contrast to the rational idea, is connected precisely with the *Person* of the Bearer (of the Word), with the prophetic *commission* (see below, pp. 216 ff.). The distinction between an Idea and a "Word" consists precisely in this connection, and it is just this which constitutes subjectively (in faith) the difference between rational knowledge and obedient submission to a divine Word. That Bultmann really does mean

Thus Paul's point of view expressed in the words: "Yes, though we have known Christ after the flesh, yet now henceforth know we Him no more" (2 Cor. v. 16) can never lead to indifference towards the actual historical fact as such. The believer also knows Christ only as the One who has come in the flesh, as Him of whom the chronicler and the humanist historian must have something to say. But he knows this "Christ in the flesh" in a way of which they can know nothing; he knows Him therefore as someone quite different, and this is what matters. For the knowledge of others—of the chronicler and of the humanist historian—is not yet knowledge of Christ, of the "Word made flesh," but is itself "after the flesh." For according to the language of the Bible the whole world of history is summed up in the term "the flesh," including the finest flower of ethical and religious humanity. Even the most able historian as such only knows the "Christ after the flesh," that is, he only knows the ethico-religious, historical personality, unless he himself is a believer. But even the most ardent believer knows the "Christ after the spirit" only in the "Christ in the flesh," that is, in the historical personality. The knowledge of the brute facts of history, including the whole of humanity, is thus, it is true, a necessary presupposition, but it is never an adequate ground for the knowledge of Christ.

This makes it clear why we are bound to oppose the view that the Christian faith springs out of historical observation, out of the historical picture of Jesus of Nazareth. Christendom itself has always known otherwise. Christian faith springs only out of the witness to Christ of the preached message and the written word of the Scriptures. The historical picture is indeed included in the latter (how this is treated will come up again later); but this picture itself is not the basis of knowledge. If anyone were ever to become a Christian through the picture of the life of Jesus drawn by a non-believing historian, he would

this, becomes clearer towards the end of his book. Jesus matters to us "in so far as He has been *sent* by God, in so far as He is Bearer of the Word" (p. 198); "whether He has been *sent* by God—that is the decision which the hearer is forced to make, and Jesus' saying remains true: 'Blessed is he who is not offended in Me' " (p. 200). Here there emerges, still undefined, a new conception of "person," the Person of Christ, which is still more important than His teaching, because it is itself the Word.

be an apostle, and indeed more than this: he would be a super-apostle. For the apostles had experienced the resurrection of Jesus and the whole living reality of Jesus. No instance of this kind has ever been known; indeed, reasons of faith make it impossible. It is of the very essence of revelation and of faith that we should become Christians not through the historical picture of Jesus, but through the picture traced by the Gospels in the light of the Resurrection faith which has grown out of the testimony of the apostles, and has become the witness to Christ of the Christian Church.[1]

Faith justifies this attitude by pointing out that the revelation of Christ does not cease with the processes which the historian can verify—even when he has every possible kind of material at his disposal. Above all, the historian lacks knowledge of the Resurrection, the knowledge of which was granted only to the Apostles, and to those who believed through their word. He also lacks the knowledge of the significance of Christ, which, once again, is regarded by the Church as a special revelation of God to the Apostles. We might also add that he lacks the necessary understanding of the Old Testament, without which the picture of Jesus remains wholly unintelligible for the awakening of faith. All this the Church has held fast in its principle of the Scriptures. It is not the picture of Jesus isolated from the rest of Scripture (which indeed would not be the historical picture at all, but one already permeated with *Kerugma* or message), but the whole witness of the Scriptures to Christ is the adequate basis of the Christian faith. The isolation of, or even only the preference for, the picture of the so-called "historical Jesus" is based upon the failure to

---

[1] Hence, from the theological point of view the preference for the Synoptic Gospels evinced by theologians (not by historians) is always a sign of bondage to the historical point of view. In faith we are not concerned with the Jesus of History, as historical science sees Him, but with the Jesus Christ of personal testimony, who is the real Christ, and whom John shows us just as plainly—I could even say with Luther: still more clearly—as the Synoptists. Where liberal theologians base their arguments on the "Jesus of History," that is quite in order. They know only the Χριστός κατὰ σάρκά, which does not exclude a deep and keen historical insight. But when "positive" theologians do the same, it is a sign of their inner uncertainty.

distinguish between the Christ "in the flesh" and "after the flesh," upon a perversion of faith in the supposed interests of historicity. Faith never arises out of the observation of facts, but out of the Word of God. This Word of God, however, has certainly come "into the flesh," and is thus connected with observation.

It is therefore just as false to maintain that faith is born out of the historical picture of Jesus as it is to claim that it can arise apart from the picture of Jesus altogether. Rather faith arises out of the apostolic testimony to Jesus, or out of the witness of the Church, which always includes the picture of Jesus. The Jesus of the Gospels is always the One who was made flesh to whom the Church bears witness, the One who has entered into the realm of history, the Word "which we have seen with our eyes, which we have looked upon, which our hands have handled." But how much of this visible historical element is included in this Christian testimony, and how much ought to be included, is obviously a question which it is impossible to answer. The *bon mot* which suggests that most Christians have become so through the passages in the Bible which are printed in large letters[1] is just as justifiable as the opposite observation, that the Christian faith could not well have escaped serious perversion if it had been nourished on the Apostles' testimony alone, without the Gospels. This question will be studied, later on, in further detail.

2. FAITH AND HISTORICAL SCIENCE

The aim of history, of historical science, is primarily to fill in the spatio-temporal continuum of the imagination with representations which correspond to reality, and, secondly, to relate this spatio-temporal continuum to the "analogous continuum," that is, to that which we call the sum total of all the possibilities of nature and of history. Its aim, therefore, is to create, as far as possible, a complete "film picture of the past," and to interpret the pictures of reality which have thus been completely recaptured in the

[1] An allusion to the way in which important verses in the German Bible are printed in larger type than the rest.—TR.

light of previous happenings, and of that which is intelligible to humanity as a whole. The first of these two tasks is already impracticable in principle on account of the great variety of aspects of all events within time and space; this means that practically it can only be discharged in an approximate manner, and its results have therefore in each case only a relative certainty, that is, the certainty of probability.

The second task is still more impossible. The first is endless from the extensive point of view, the second from the intensive point of view. There can never be a full interpretation of historical reality, nor of any of its parts.

Above all, we must note that this second task (and therefore indirectly also the first) is dependent upon the means of interpretation, or the categories, which are at our disposal. Anyone who undertakes to interpret historical reality with the meagre categories of a materialist or a Positivist, is obviously in far worse case than an eminent scholar and humanist of the type of Ranke. The categories which are at the disposal of the historian or the historical student may be compared with the various retina of the eye with their varied sensitiveness to light and colour. According as one has or has not these faculties one is "blind" or "seeing" for certain forms of reality. The whole content of the means for knowledge which can be grasped by any one individual we might perhaps call the "humane eye"; at the same time we are bound to maintain that not every human being possesses this normal "humane eye," since, for example, certain general views or prejudices with regard to the world as a whole can dim this "humane eye," and even render it partially blind.

The Christian religion, however, asserts that the "humane eye" as such is diseased; it therefore asserts that it is not in a position to comprehend reality as a whole, but only a certain superficial aspect of reality. Its depths, the secret of God, are inaccessible to us as human beings; they can only be revealed to us through revelation, which cannot be perceived by the "humane eye," by everyone who has a "clear perception of all that is vitally alive and a true feeling for that which is genuinely great," but only by those whose inward sight has been illuminated by the Holy Spirit. This point of view opens

up a new category of historical interpretation, that which is
necessary for the interpretation of the history of revelation.
For the meaning of that history in which Christ manifested
Himself is only revealed to faith. Even the literary testimony
to this revelation can only be rightly understood by those who
believe, although the preparatory labours of the Humanist
historian should not be omitted or under-valued in this connection. For it is the "humane eye" enlightened by the Spirit
which is to see the meaning of this history.[1] Since, however,
this category, in contradistinction to all others, is in principle
not accessible to every man as such, educated humanity as a
whole is opposed to giving the name of history in the scientific
sense to that which works with this category. Judged from the
point of view of faith, however, it is precisely this knowledge
alone which should be accepted as the right way to grasp this
historical reality. Whether it should be called "scientific" or
not is merely a question of terminology. In any case, it shares
with science the character of strict positive necessity. Faith
alone is able to know rightly the historical reality of Jesus Christ.

[1] I agree heartily with E. von Dobschütz when he urges the pressing need
for a renewed study of the hermeneutic problem (*Vom Auslegen, insonderheit
des Neuen Testaments;* and *Die evangelische Theologie,* 2nd part, *Das Neue
Testament,* p. 38). For here, in the principles of Biblical exegesis is the decisive
point. Not in the technical rules—which are perhaps less fruitful—but in
the fundamental principles, as they are the subject of systematic theology.
The first step would be to abandon the idea, introduced by the thinkers
of the Enlightenment—and often regarded as an axiom—that the literature
which composes the Bible is on the same level as all other forms of literature.
It is this very question which is being debated by the theologians of the
present day. If every theologian to-day will admit that some "religious
affinity" is necessary for the understanding of the New Testament, then we
must ask the further question: "What kind of religious affinity?" Does
modern mysticism help us to understand the Gospel? But this raises the
most fundamental question of Christian theology: in the New Testament
are we dealing with general or with special revelation? If the New Testament contains a special revelation, then these writings can only be rightly
understood by one who is acquainted with this revelation, and no "affinity,"
in the sense of universal religion, is of any use to him. A different *organon*
is required, and the old exegetes are right when they insist that the Holy
Spirit alone, faith alone, can expound the Scriptures. Of course, it is taken
for granted that this principle also presupposes thorough scientific labour,
translation, in the fullest sense of the word.

In order to make the distinction between faith and history quite clear this seems to be the point at which to introduce the conception of pseudo-history. Owing to human imperfection all historical work is permeated with pseudo-scientific, and thus with pseudo-historical, elements. One of the characteristics of modern pseudo-history is the exaggeration of constructive interpretation—which ought always to be only a secondary means of assistance—over against the primary process of listening to evidence. This exaggerated interpretation is determined by the influence of the ideal of natural science. It is the duty of natural science to give explanations; it is the duty of history to record and interpret. In cases where the evidence is inadequate or unreliable it is, however, impossible to avoid the effort to make a constructive interpretation, but this always carries with it the danger of pseudo-historical construction.

In the realm of the New Testament pseudo-history is determined by the endeavour so to transform, by a process of "natural explanation," the statements of faith in the New Testament which have no place within the analogous continuum that, in spite of this, they may be incorporated into the analogous continuum after all. Thus here a general point of view about the world dictates to history its hypotheses, and the confusion of the modern world view with science leads to the result that these constructions or hypotheses, because they are in harmony with the general outlook of modern people, are regarded as more correct scientifically, from the historical point of view, than the evidence of the New Testament itself, which is not acceptable to the modern mind, even when the evidence[1] of the New Testament ought to be preferred on purely

[1] This difficulty is usually evaded by saying that the causal principle is the common sphere of science in general and of the modern world-view. But what does causality in history mean when we think of the way it is broken through by freedom of personality? Evidently it simply means the sum-total of all that is humanly possible. This means, however, that causality is derived from that which we called the Analogous Continuum. No science, however, can prove that only something analogous shall take place. The very conception of something unique causes embarrassment to the historian, yet he must take it into account. He is, however, entirely baffled by the assertion of uniqueness (lit. once-for-all-ness) in the strictly literal sense. Here no appeal to the principles of scientific research is of any avail, the only thing that counts is the decision of faith.

historical grounds. When the assertions of the New Testament are not understood by the modern man in their own light, then they are "explained" from a connection which is alien to their meaning. Thus, for example, the rise of faith in Christ as Lord (Kyrios) is explained as due to the influence of Hellenistic cults, the Pauline statements about the Spirit are "explained" by the use of analogies drawn from Hellenistic mysticism, etc., whereas in reality they are perfectly easy to understand without any external help of this kind at all— though, of course, only for him who has the power of understanding the matters which are there attested. An extreme instance of pseudo-history of this kind is the "explanation" of the whole story of Jesus as a myth. The border-line between pseudo-history and genuine history will always be defined at different points according to different points of view, even if a critical consideration of the difference between science and a world-view on the one hand, and of a statement of faith and a mere tradition on the other, would go a long way towards bringing about a closer understanding.

A conflict between faith and history is therefore possible, because faith is intensely concerned about a fact which is at the same time an object of historical research. The identity of this point for faith and history (for the moment we might say: the fact that Jesus ever actually existed) which is included in the Christian creed, with its belief in the Word made flesh, does not, however, claim that the way in which its certitude on this identical point is established[1] is itself identical. Rather the assertions of faith, even where they include an historical fact, are emphatically statements of *faith*, that is, they are

[1] To-day it is beginning once more to dawn on many minds that possibly in the last resort the way of rational scientific history may not be the only way to historical reality. (I am thinking more particularly of the problem of mythology as it is to-day being treated afresh, on the one hand by the school of Gundolf, and on the other from the standpoint of Bachofen and Schelling.) We will not enter into this general question, for it is impossible that faith in the event which took place once for all should be a special instance among these general possibilities. But those other possibilities ought to puzzle the historian, and prevent him from saying that "there is only one way to historical actuality, that of historical research." This statement is as false as is that of rationalistic natural philosophy: "there is no other way than that of physics to the reality of nature."

assertions which are attained in connection with faith, and not in connection with historical research. The identity of that point certainly includes this, that the statement of faith, in so far as it is concerned with a fact of history, ought not to contradict genuine historical research. The fact of the cross on Golgotha is both an historical fact, and thus an object for scientific research, and an object of faith, although to faith the cross means something quite different from that which it means to the purely scientific historian, and in spite of this faith knows of it in another way altogether than such verification through the labours of historical science. Thus the identity of the fact as such, for faith and for history, and the question of the verification of this fact, should be kept rigidly distinct.

The manner of verifying the external fact which is of moment for faith (for instance, that Jesus was crucified) differs for faith and for historical science. Faith becomes sure of this through the witness to Christ of the Church, that is, ultimately, on the word of the Apostles; the historian, on the contrary, seeks verification in the tradition which has been worked over critically and rationally. The external fact—the existence of Jesus, or the cross on Golgotha—becomes certain to everyone who believes in the interpretative proclamation of this fact, through the witness of the Church which includes both. Rather, it is one and the same, the Word made flesh. Therefore, too, the certainty of this fact—in so far as it is a fact of faith, that is, a fact standing in a necessary connection with faith—is the same as the certainty of its significance. Thus although the fact as in itself an external event, that is, within the natural relations of knowledge, only possesses in itself the certainty of probability, for the believer it carries the same absolute certainty as the content of the message itself, which includes this fact.[1] This relation to a fact of history, which has no

[1] It is only to be expected that this statement should arouse great hostility. The nerve of the counter-argument will be: In this manner any believer can "make" or postulate historical facts at will. The answer should be on these lines: the truth of faith will become evident in this—whether it is obliged to postulate facts which can be proved to be historically false, or whether it does not "need" such facts. Historical criticism has here a sacred office to exercise—as even the Reformers discovered in their fight

analogy, is based on the character of the Christian faith, which consists in its relation to this unique event. Since, however, it is a real fact, in the full sense of the word, with which faith has to deal, that statement of faith which is self-authenticated bears within itself the judgment that this fact can also be discovered and recognized—on the historical line—by the historian, or, in any case, that it cannot be denied with convincing scientific reasons; and this also means that it includes the willingness to examine this fact along the lines of scientific history. Faith, however, knows, for reasons which are not accessible to the historian as such, that this inquiry cannot yield a negative result. The absolute certainty of this conviction coincides with the certainty of faith. The one who believes must always defend himself by faith against the natural uncertainty arising out of unbelief, the unrest of historical relativism.

Of course, the historian as such must not in any way allow himself to be diverted from the path of strict historical research by the knowledge of the existence of this fundamental connection of faith, and the statements about facts which are based upon it. Whether he believes in the divine word of testimony or not, for this he is not responsible at the bar of science, but as a human being who stands in the presence of God. As an historian the utmost he can do is to accept the statements of faith on matters of fact as temporary hypotheses, which it is his duty to examine, as, for instance, he accepts the New Testament traditions, which are his most important sources, as temporary hypotheses. To him the absolute certainty

against Romish superstitition. The subjective conviction of a believer decides nothing about the objective truth of his faith. But the objective truth of faith is something entirely different from the power of producing rational proof. We ought not to forget that countless inconsistencies appeal to the evidence of reason! Just as little as reason is dependent on that which an individual may regard as reasonable, is faith dependent on that which an individual may regard as faith. If faith postulates as absolutely necessary certain historical facts which can be proved by historical science to be non-existent, then that faith is erroneous. This applies also to the Christian faith. This does not mean, however, that the truth and certainty of the Christian faith depends upon historical science. Faith is not afraid of the light of historical criticism; but what it sees, it does not see in this light.

of the believer about an historical fact, as something really unique, is wholly incomprehensible. As a modern man he may possibly interpret this phenomenon on psychological lines, but this is only a different way of showing that he is completely baffled. The believer, on the other hand, in so far as he also belongs to the ranks of those whose work lies in the realm of purely humanistic studies and science, never possesses a complete certitude, but only a certitude of the fact of faith which has to be gained over and over again; that is, here also, as everywhere else in the realm of faith, he is subject to that tension, in the perpetual overcoming of which faith consists.

One question which it is very hard to answer is that which inquires into the measure of the concern which faith has with the realm of fact at all, that is, the question concerning the delimitation of that "unique element" with which faith is concerned. In principle this question ought to be answered in the spirit of the Christian faith by pointing to the principle of Scripture. The Scriptures themselves constitute an historic fact, something quite concrete. But faith conceived in the purest sense—that is, not in the orthodox spirit, but in the spirit of the Reformers—does not identify the Scriptures directly with revelation. For the "fact" with which they are solely and infinitely concerned is Jesus Christ, the Christ, indeed, of whom the Prophets prophesied, and to whom the Apostles bear witness. To this Jesus Christ we may apply this saying: *Christus dominus et rex scripturae.* The two poles between which the concern of faith lies may possibly be described in the following way: the Christian religion is not disturbed by the fact that isolated verses in the Scriptures must be translated rather differently than had hitherto been thought necessary, or that isolated facts in the statements of Scripture must be corrected by science. But the Christian religion would be in a parlous condition if the Scriptures as a whole bore a different meaning from that which the Church had believed hitherto, and if whole groups of facts could be proved to be "unhistorical." But even if we admit this, it is not sufficient. For the statements about Jesus Christ in particular depend upon the actual historicity of individual facts (for example, the historical existence of Jesus, the fact of the Crucifixion, etc.)

even if and although with regard to these actual facts there is historically only a relative certainty, that is (from the historical point of view) a mere probability.

Thus even if we limit the formulation of our problem to the facts of the life of Jesus, here also, however, the general statement must be repeated: faith must neither be able to hold firmly to everything, nor could it surrender everything, without coming to an end of itself; that is, faith may indeed be combined with criticism of the Biblical tradition about the life of Jesus, perhaps even with a very radical form of criticism; but it is not possible to combine faith with *every* kind of criticism; for instance, it cannot be combined with the kind of criticism which denies the existence of Jesus altogether, or with that which represents Him as a psychopathic individual, or as a proletarian revolutionary. Indeed, in principle the question can only be answered thus: faith can be combined with all kinds of historical criticism which do not alter the historical image of the existence of Jesus to such an extent that—so far as faith is concerned—it would be impossible to understand the apostolic testimony to Christ. Thus in taking up this position faith does not set any limits to critical science; but these limits are actually set by the same reality which forms the foundation of faith; faith therefore lives in the certainty that every sort of criticism which goes beyond this standard will also prove itself to be spurious, or pseudo-historical, even when it is measured by scientific standards; for that very reason, however, faith is wholly undisturbed, even when purely scientific research and criticism lead to entirely negative "results." Criticism of this kind must run its course; faith knows that it can effect nothing against the truth; indeed, she is persuaded that of itself it will ultimately overthrow those purely negative "results." Of course, to the historian such confidence is incomprehensible; but he could only destroy it by producing actual proofs; until now such proofs have never been produced.

This brings us to our final question, concerning the results of previous historical criticism. Assured historical results, in the absolute sense of the word, do not exist, for the reasons which have already been given above, but there are always results which can be practically verified, in particular those which belong to the filling in of the continuum of time and space, that is, of a bare record of events. There are facts which may be described as "ascertained," just as there are traditional errors which have been "ascertained." There are also results of both kinds within the scientific historical criticism of the New Testament; I need only recall the establishment of the form of the text (in spite of countless uncertainties in points of detail), of the translation of this text, as well as a host of "ascertained" facts in the story of the life of Christ and of the Apostolic Age, etc., which are not usually noticed. Faith is only indirectly concerned with this process of the elaboration of established results of this kind. Faith makes full allowance for the relative character of the formation of opinion which is effected by the process of historical research. It is faith in particular which sees more clearly than the majority of the critics how very uncertain are all historical statements. It is precisely faith which does *not* take established results into account. Hence faith can also regard the formation of pseudo-historical "results" quite calmly, knowing very well that the scientific process will correct itself in its own good time. It cannot therefore be surprised at the uncertainty and continual fluctuations within the sphere of historical research. For this is of the very nature of historical reality, so far as actual knowledge is concerned. It knows that it believes in a Christ who, from the point of view of historical science, must always remain an unsolved problem, a Christ whose bare existence may even be called in question, for reasons which cannot entirely be disregarded. Faith knows that all this is involved in the fact of the Incarnation: in the "being found in fashion as a man," that it is of the very essence of the One who has come "in the flesh." But faith itself is not affected by these fluctuations, apart from the fact that faith in the believing soul is something which must be constantly growing. The believer, however, as one who belongs to both spheres, that of faith and that of science, remains to some extent in a state of tension, conditioned by this lack of established certainty in historical knowledge and tradition, since in faith he has to overcome this hindrance again and again, which is one aspect of the stumbling-block

169

of faith as a whole. He is always ready to compare his judgments of faith about the realm of fact with the results of science, but he knows beforehand that, in so far as he really does believe, science may indeed assault his faith, but can never really refute it.

This comparison therefore will be briefly attempted, less in order to prove the statement which has just been made than to make clearer both its meaning and also the meaning of all the previous arguments by means of concrete examples.

3. FAITH IN CHRIST AND THE RESULTS OF HISTORICAL RESEARCH

From what has already been said it will be quite evident that it is impossible to extract definite results from historical research, or even therefore as a systematic theologian to draw from historical research such a conclusion. Nowadays such a confident proceeding would be less justified than ever, since we are in no sense at the end of a period but rather at the beginning. All we intend to do here, therefore, is to examine once more the thesis which is so often debated: "that it is impossible to combine faith in Christ with the results of historical research"; this we will do at certain main points, using the expression "results" only in the hypothetical sense of a possibility.

We might lighten our task by playing off the various current contradictory "scientific views" and "results" against each other. We can indeed ask: is there a single positive important question in Biblical science which is not a matter of controversy? Thus there are no scientific results with which the Christian religion need be concerned. For some decades this has been the line taken by orthodox apologetic. We do not intend to evade the difficulty in any such easy way. We believe that in this question of scientific research it is not justifiable to adopt the attitude of a mere spectator. We take the conception of "scientific results" quite seriously (although we remember its relative character) within its own limits; we then inquire what a theologian of goodwill can really learn from scientific research, and to what conclusions these "results," which he regards at least as probable, lead us, even if they are only relatively certain so far as the Christian witness to the faith is concerned. We must certainly point out very plainly that it is not *we* who speak of such results, but those who think that the ancient faith of Christianity has been shaken by the scientific labours of the last century. Weinel's statement, which was quoted above, probably expresses the view of the majority of the theologians of the present day: "The ancient dogma of the second Person in the Godhead . . . broke down under the progressive pressure . . . of historical knowledge. Thus the question became all the more urgent: If He was not the Son of God and a Divine Being, who then was this Jesus?" Our previous theological thesis was this: If Jesus was not the Son of God, then the Christian faith itself is insecure; for there has never been nor can there be any other Christian faith than this. For apart from this the "Christian faith" is only another variety of religion in general, and stands therefore in irreconcilable opposition to the witness of the Bible and the Church. Secondly, therefore, we must examine this thesis of ours in the light of the "progressive historical knowledge" which is supposed to make it impossible; on the other hand, it behoves us to examine this counter-thesis of modern theology to see whether it is tenable.

It belongs to the very nature of the Christian religion that all its theological statements—and thus also those which concern the Person and Work of the Mediator—should be examined in the light of the Scriptures, and that without the authority of Scripture behind them they should be pronounced invalid, or at least not binding. Our own age, with its emphasis upon the meaning of history, has taken great offence at the way in which this proof from Scripture has been conducted; especially has it been offended by the way in which "proof texts" have been adduced from all parts of the Bible as though all were of equal inspiration and authority. It cannot be denied that this procedure led to forced interpretations and to exegesis which to-day we can no longer countenance. In spite of all this, however, in principle this method is the only right one; it is the only one which suits the nature of the Christian religion. For the Christian faith the Scriptures are a unity—at bottom the Old and the New Testament have only one Word of God to proclaim, and that is the message of Christ Himself. The Bible is the "crib in which Christ lies." If once the conviction is regained that the Christian faith does not arise out of the picture of the historical Jesus, but out of the testimony to Christ as such—this includes the witness of the prophets as well as that of the Apostles—and that it is based upon this testimony, then inevitably the preference for the Synoptic Gospels and for the actual words of Jesus, which was the usual position of the last generation, will disappear. This view springs from a conception of Jesus, and of our relation to Him, which cannot really be combined with the Christian faith in Christ.

It would therefore seem to be desirable to examine this fundamental assertion about the unity of the Scriptures, which underlies the Christian religion, in the light of the results of historical research. Here, however, for practical reasons this task must be confined to the New Testament; but this can be done all the more easily because the relation between the Old and New Testament has been treated elsewhere.[1] All I need to do here is to repeat the main lines of the view which is stated in that work. Historical criticism has indeed freed us for ever from the conception of that unity which was the fruit of the theory of the Verbal Inspiration of the Scriptures. It is not the letter of Scripture which is the same in the Old and the New Testament, but the Word, the Word of God, and indeed in a manner which differentiates the whole Bible, in principle and categorically, from all other forms of religious literature. The God who speaks to us in the Bible speaks to us nowhere else. The Christian religion does not only assert the unity, but the exclusive unity of the revelation contained in the Scriptures.[2] This Word of God is the Word of Jesus

---

[1] Cf. my *Religionsphilosophie*, pp. 82–4.

[2] Naturally this unity, and its exclusive character, will be questioned by every scholar who is not a Christian. But anyone who is a good historian will—without understanding it altogether—notice more of this than a pseudo-historian. The accuracy of "historical insight" will become evident precisely in this, that such an historian, without being a Christian, will feel this unity, and will have to attest it, even if his view is limited. He will then speak of the "unique character of the religion of Israel," of the "originality" and "independence" of the religious literature of the New

Christ in the Old Testament as well as in the New, the Word which is reality in Jesus Christ.

The first question within the compass of the statements of the New Testament about Christ is—to put it more exactly— the following: whether the New Testament witnesses at all to the Christ in whom the Church believes, quite apart from the question whether He only, that is uniformly, is attested therein. This first question was asked with the greatest vigour by the Fathers, especially in the great Christological controversies; at the period of the Reformation, too, it was examined again and again. The Church answered it in the affirmative, and this affirmative reply, so far as essentials were concerned, was not attacked by historical research until the time of Albert Ritschl. Even the critical theologians of the school of Baur did not merely admit the close connection between John and Christological dogma, but they laid particular emphasis upon it. Ritschl, however, was anxious to insert a wedge between the New Testament as a whole and the ecclesiastical doctrine as a whole, in order that as far as possible he might conceal his evident and explicit opposition to the doctrine of the Church, by the authority of the whole of the New Testament. In this endeavour certainly he had been preceded by Schleier-macher, but it was Ritschl alone who[1] tried to carry through the argument of the contrast between the Bible and the dogmas

Testament and of the Person of Jesus. This is the secular historical analogy to that which the believer calls the unity of Scripture.

[1] This does not mean that before Ritschl appeared upon the scene the differences between the Church Fathers on the one hand and the New Testament, or between the Church Fathers among themselves, on the other, had not been perceived and judged from the theological point of view. Luther's critical observations on the Platonism of certain Fathers of the Church are well known, and Pietism and Biblicism in particular have always been conscious of the difference between the teaching of the Church and the teaching of the Bible. But substantially their faith was that of the ecclesiastical dogma. The Enlightenment, it is true, was deliberately, entirely opposed to dogma, but it was no less hostile to the Christian faith of the New Testament. Even a man like Thiersch, whom Harnack (*Dogmengeschichte*, I, p. 40), properly speaking, reckons among the precursors of the Ritschl-Harnack point of view, never asserted the antithesis between the Christological dogma of the Church and the New Testament in the way in which Ritschl and Harnack do. Ritschl was indeed the first great

of the Church by means of particular works on the history of dogma and Biblical theology.

However much this thesis has fertilized research—this took place more in the realm of the history of doctrine than in that of Biblical theology—by the fact that it forced people to investigate the connection between the formation of dogma and extra-Biblical Hellenism and Greek thought as a whole, yet in essentials we may say it has proved untenable. The Christological dogma (to which we must also add the doctrine of the deity of the Son) may have been formulated under the influence of Greek philosophy, yet the connection with John at least is so clear, and the agreement in all that is essential so complete, that the trench which was dug by Ritschl became ever smaller and shallower. The fact that to-day it can scarcely be seen at all is due, above all, to a new tendency in historical work on the New Testament, which by this time had applied the Ritschlian argument of Hellenistic influence to the New Testament itself, which made it possible to perceive and admit the connection between dogma and the New Testament in a far more detached and objective manner.

Certainly in the New Testament the characteristic conceptions of dogma, the ὁμοούσιος and the doctrine of the two Natures in Christ are not explicitly stated, but in the very nature of the case it is impossible to detach them from the Gospel of John—and in this connection this is all that matters—to which the great teachers of those days specially appealed.

theologian who intended to be thoroughly "Scriptural," and yet actually was essentially of the type of the Enlightenment. Hence he felt obliged to seek to identify the antithesis between dogma and the New Testament with his own opposition to dogma, and this tendency dominates Harnack's conception of the History of Dogma and the point of view suggested by him. Hence the reaction was bound to come not from the side of the History of Dogma, but from that of New Testament research—I am thinking especially of Bousset—and, indeed, it came in full force; but at present the results are visible mainly in the sphere of New Testament criticism rather than in the sphere of the history of dogma. The future will see a return either to the fundamental conception of Baur, or to that of Thomasius, who both—even though from opposite points of view—taught the unity which exists between the New Testament testimony to Christ and ecclesiastical Christology.

The conception of the older historians of dogma, as they are represented by two men who are poles apart from one another, Baur and Thomasius, that is, the claim of the essential unity between the Johannine testimony to Christ and the doctrine of the Church, is in the main absolutely right as opposed to the teaching of the Ritschl-Harnack school, however much in detail it may need to be corrected by Ritschl's counter-thesis. In the Johannine writings Jesus Christ is "true God and true Man," in the sense of the ecclesiastical doctrine and the theology of the Reformation, thus in a sense which cannot be combined with the specific conception of Ritschl, or Harnack. (See above, p. 94.) In particular we must regard the attempt to separate the prologue to the Gospel of John, which already contains the leading idea of the dogma, the conception of the Logos, from the rest of the Johannine literature, as a failure. Thus not only the substance, but also the leading term of the ecclesiastical dogma of Christ, is scriptural through and through.

The second question also, the one which deals with the breadth of the New Testament basis for the Christian faith of the Church, is not difficult to answer to-day in the sense of the older view, to this extent at least, that the positive connection—we are not here concerned with the genetic connection—between Paul and John is accepted. There may still be a slight difference between the daring Christological assertions of Paul in the letters to the Colossians or the Philippians, and John—a certain reserve on the part of Paul, perhaps we might say—and although we cannot overlook the characteristic differences between this and the other apostolic statements about Christ, yet we would scarcely meet with any serious opposition if we were to formulate the present position of historical knowledge by saying that in any case, measured by the fundamental distinction which I have set in the forefront of the argument, the later apostolic witness as a whole is opposed to the modern view, that is, to a purely human conception of Christ.[1] It is the testimony to a Son of God,

[1] To give one example among many, Johannes Weiss says: "Since we have found the Logos Christology already in the teaching of Paul, the post-Pauline doctrine cannot add much that is new. . . . All this, as well

who, although He came to us in the form of a man, yet in His very nature was different from the rest of us, as different as the Creator is from the creature; thus it is not an ethical and evolutionary difference, but a difference in essence and in principle. In saying this we do not wish to deny the importance and the weight of the questions which are still to-day being discussed in this sphere. Two points, however, should not be overlooked: firstly, that we are here in the realm of interpretation, where the all-important point is to find the right category—the point of view—where, if we fail to find this, it means wandering about in a labyrinth of inconsistencies; above all, however, that these differences all lie on the further side of the great gulf which separates the modern conception of Christ from the apostolic witness of the Church to Christ.

The question of the relation between the so-called "mystical" element in Paul and John and the eschatological element, between the pneumatic and the legal elements, will be a subject of endless discussion, so long as it is not perceived that the unity of the present question lies far above these contrasts, and so long as men do not see that here we are dealing with important differences, which are not, however, opposed to each other, differences of emphasis, rather, which are determined by the intention and the position of the author in question. John is as little of a mystic as Paul, because he also is just as convinced as Paul that the supreme thing that matters is faith, faith in a personal Mediator of revelation and of salvation.[1] To him, as to Paul, salvation means something

as the important statements in the Prologue to John's Gospel, only furnish further proof that the doctrine of the Primitive Church was eager to absorb the Logos doctrine, in order to express the divine, absolute, universal character of the revelation of God in the Person of Christ" (*R.G.G.*[1], *Christologie*, I, 3). See also his *Urchristentum*, p. 371, in which he says "that the Logos conception is basic, as it was used by Philo." The latest attempts to interpret John from the point of view of the religious teaching of the Mandaeans, or that of popular Gnosticism, tend to bring Paul and John into closer relation with each other. Of course it is here impossible to enter upon a detailed discussion of the various difficult questions connected with this subject.

[1] The kindly criticism which Deissmann administers to me in the new edition of his book on Paul, is based upon this view, which dominates his whole conception of Paul, the view, namely, that this disjunction actually

which is both present and future at the same time: present in
the faith in the Son who is also the Logos, future as the
Resurrection and Exaltation, whose real foundation and basis
of knowledge is Christ, the fact of His Incarnation and His
atoning Death. In Paul as in "John" (including the book of
the Revelation), in "Peter" as in the Epistle to the Hebrews,
Jesus is the Lord who is worshipped, the Redeemer who was
appointed from all eternity and coming out of eternity, a
Divine Being, hence, in spite of His acceptance of our humanity,
different from us all, and a sharer in the divine authority. His
advent, His life, and His sufferings form the Divine Act, apart
from which God remains unknown and unreconciled, within
which there is deliverance from the αἰών οὗτος into the αἰών
μέλλων, from "death" to "life," in which we have our part
through faith alone.

The position is more confused when we come to the third
question: the one which concerns the relation between this

exists: either mystical or rational, either personal piety or a sterile dogmatic
belief. It seems to me that, from his own definition—which I accept as right
—mysticism is that form of religion in which the immediacy of the soul's
union with God is the constitutive element (p. 118), Deissmann ought to
be forced to the conviction that the faith of Paul is not mysticism at all.
For this faith is characterized by the most complete mediacy: the relation
to God *through the Mediator*. The opposite of mystical is not "rational"—
the mystics have always been on good terms with the philosophers—but
believing, namely, believing the Word of God, which most emphatically is
not "the deposit of mystical experiences" (p. 65), but—we need only remind
ourselves of the significance of the Word of God in the Old Testament to
Paul!—the incomprehensible but very definite and clear self-revelation of
God, which is not to be *experienced* mystically, but is to be *believed*, whereby
this faith is a far more personal relation and far more remote from that
which is merely rational, than mystical experience. In the Bible the definite
Word of God, and the definite statement about Christ, does not imply
—as Deissmann says it does—a process of "dogmatic vivisection" (p. 138),
a "petrification," a "doctrine" (p. 108), but a particularly great gift of
God. Otherwise why did Luther take such infinite pains to trace out the
exact meaning of the very words of Scripture? An "inward" faith is a right
faith; hence it is not mystical—although now and again it may be accompanied by mystical experiences. I am glad that Bultmann, at least as far
as John is concerned, definitely emphasizes this opposition to mysticism—
as I gather from a hitherto unpublished lecture he gave at Zürich; I believe
I am right in saying that he no longer accepts the idea of a Pauline
Christ-mysticism.

Pauline-Johannine faith in Christ and that of the Primitive Church. This, together with the fourth question, is at the present time the point towards which the most intensive form of research is being directed. Fifty years ago the assertion of a clear contrast between Paul and the earliest faith of the Church would have been regarded as a point which had been more or less verified and settled by research; the critical work which has taken place since then, and especially the critical work of the present day, on the contrary, tends more and more to bridge this gulf: Paul and the Primitive Church tend to come closer and closer together. Here, too, the effect of a hypothesis at first meant to be revolutionary was at least on this point conservative: the fact that traces of the "theology of the Church" have been discovered in the Synoptic Gospels has evidently done a great deal to make the difference between Paul and the pre-Pauline Church seem much less. Since, first of all, in order to conceive as clearly and pointedly as possible the contrast between the reality of Jesus and the theology of the Church (Wrede, Wellhausen) critics sought for the traces of a bold Christian faith in the most ancient tradition about Jesus; without intending it they made way for the conviction that the recognized contrast between Paul and the original Christian community was concerned with problems quite different from the central question of faith in Christ, and thus the critics came back to the old idea that the Christian creed of the Apostles at Jerusalem and that of the great Apostle to the Gentiles was essentially one and the same. Through the detailed researches of the "Formgeschichtliche Schule" we have reached this position—always with a good deal of reservation of opinion—of being able to verify directly two facts, which previously we could only gather from Paul.[1] First

[1] Already in the *Urchristentum* of Johannes Weiss and in the *Kyrios Christos* of Bousset, the gulf between Paul and pre-Pauline Christianity had been very largely obliterated. The works of the "Formgeschichtliche Schule" have carried the process further in this direction. Even the last wedge which Bousset tried to drive in between primitive and Hellenistic Christianity—the creative part played by the Christian community at Antioch—is wearing very thin: "essentially all that we can here discover is a change of emphasis" (K. L. Schmidt in *Die Stellung des Apostels Paulus im Urchristentum*, p. 10). Bertram's researches into the Passion Story were of great

of all, the assertion of Paul that his doctrine of Christ is, in its essential features, the tradition common to all the Churches, inclusive of the Primitive Church at Jerusalem, on whose judgment, in spite of all his controversies with it, he laid great emphasis;[1] and secondly, the fact that in the whole of the Pauline literature there is no trace of a Christological controversy, which, when we remember that Paul never evaded a difficulty where purity of doctrine was concerned, must certainly count for something. For this agreement there are to-day so many points of support in the Synoptic tradition and in the earliest sections of the Book of Acts that henceforth there can be no question of any difference at all.

This does not mean that definite differences do not exist; this cannot be denied. Indeed, we have no right to jump to the conclusion that the faith of the Church which is expressed in the Synoptic Gospels, or even in its two main sources, can be confused with the Christian faith of the *earliest* Christian community. But so much might be regarded as a result which has been to a very large extent established: to the Primitive Church in its earliest stage Jesus was already the Christ, the Messiah foretold by the prophets; thus He was not a prophet, but the One of whom the prophets had spoken; not merely One who proclaimed an authoritative message from God, but One who was Himself the ultimate, conclusive, divine authority,

---

importance, for they showed that it is possible to prove the existence of the worship of Jesus as "Lord" (*Kyrios*) in the earliest strata of the Gospel tradition. This, however, is the decisive element, and this is implied also in the faith in the Resurrection. Once the assertion has been made: "Christ is the exalted Lord," the Christology of the Church is present in the main features of the doctrine both of His Person and of His Work (cf. Johannes Weiss, *Urchristentum*, pp. 82 ff.). "The only alternative that remains is this: 'Jesus or the Hellenistic community'" (Schmidt, loc. cit.). For whether the belief in Jesus as "Lord" (*Kyrios*) was expressed in the Jewish eschatological formulae of "Messiah" or "Son of Man" (in the sense of the pre-existent One in Daniel), or in the Hellenistic mythological formulae of Paul and John, does indeed constitute a difference, but not one which is final or decisive. In both cases the "Kyrios" is the One who is worshipped, and the Judge at the Final Judgment, on the side of God, essentially over against mankind as a whole.

[1] Thus Jülicher in *Jesus und Paulus*: "We do not hear of any protest against the Pauline picture of Christ from other Christians" (p. 28).

the Son of God, who stands in a relation to the Father which is quite different from that of other men, and of all men everywhere. Not one who sought forgiveness, but One who was endowed with power on earth to forgive sins, not one who needed to be redeemed, but One who was Himself the Redeemer—the Redeemer of all who are to participate in the redemption according to the will of God, and who, through the decisive act of faith, become partakers of the divine nature; the One in whom the new age—not a new epoch in world history or a new religion, but the climax and end of all history—has appeared, and by whose return in power it shall be completed, the Risen One who even now is seated at the right hand of God, the future Judge of the world, who is worshipped along with God as the heavenly Lord, to whom the Church prays in these words: "Come, Lord Jesus."[1] On the question of the central significance of His Death, His sufferings, and His Resurrection an almost complete consensus of opinion between Paul and the Primitive Church seems to exist, since Paul, at this point in particular, with especial plainness of speech lays stress on the "tradition" which he simply took over just as it was, and which itself was derived directly from the Church in Jerusalem. The Supper of the Lord is the establishment of the New Covenant introduced by the Lord Himself[2]—whether rightly or wrongly this is everywhere admitted, and has become a settled custom, just as the application of the prophecy of the vicarious sufferings of

[1] In this connection the study of the forms of religious worship as historical phenomena has thrown a great deal of light upon the subject. Bertram, *Leidensgeschichte*, p. 96: "Behind them (the Synoptic passages) there stands already a complete picture of Christ, who in all these individual passages in the last resort confronts the Church as the Exalted Lord. Only in a group which believes in the Risen Lord is the Passion Story possible." With reference to the divine worship paid to Christ, "there exists no difference in principle between both types of the Gospel picture of Christ," *Joh. u Synoptiker* (loc. cit., p. 100).

[2] Cf. K. L. Schmidt's article: "Abendmahl," in *R.G.G.*[2]. Schmidt certainly comes to the conclusion, based on analyses of literary criticism, that "Jesus did not institute the Sacrament of the Lord's Supper with the formulas of administration to which we are accustomed." But "the word about the Cup in all the accounts of the institution of the Lord's Supper interprets the death of Jesus as a Covenant sacrifice."

the Servant of the Lord usually seems to have been transferred to Jesus in the earliest Church of all.

A settled doctrine about the origin of the divine personality of the Lord does not seem to have yet been formed; the overwhelming power of the event of Christ had evidently for the moment prevented such ideas from arising. This should be in general the leading idea to guide us in our attempt to understand the relative differences within the New Testament testimony to Christ: the customary explanation of these differences as due to the tendency to intensify the superhuman divine element in the picture of the "hero of the cultus," of the recognized head of the Church, is not the only possible solution. It only forms an unanswerable argument where the possibility is not taken into account that this apostolic doctrine about Christ may be *true*. The psychological and historical explanation of a statement is only invoked when the statement itself cannot be understood as it stands, that is, when its essential truth is not perceived. But now, supposing John and Paul were right after all? Is it a foregone conclusion that the latest witnesses *could* not have the deepest knowledge of the truth? Why should the complete knowledge have been present from the very beginning? Why should it be considered impossible and incompatible with the revealed character of the message of Christ, that the full truth of Christ should only be gradually revealed and become defined on all sides? Here we are possibly still suffering from the incubus of the old mechanical theory of inspiration, which left out of account the element of human and historical mediation in the process of revelation, whereas at this point even the Reformers, in the interest of the true divine humanity of the whole revelation, created sufficient room for this very element of gradual perception of the truth. Whereas in the struggle between orthodoxy and criticism it was regarded as axiomatic that it constituted an attack on the revealed character of the witness to Christ to doubt that from the very first moment, indeed in the proclamation of the Lord Himself, in a comprehensive and complete development, the whole truth was present, we have gradually learned to recognize that this axiom is quite arbitrary, and indeed that we may accustom ourselves to the idea that

Paul had a richer knowledge of Christ than the primitive
Apostles, and that it was reserved for the last of the Apostles,
"John," to understand fully what had taken place in Christ
and—with divine authority—to interpret this to others. If we
have once grasped the fact that the revelation of Christ was
not completed with the last words spoken by the Lord Himself,
because the most important events of all had not yet taken
place, His Death and His Resurrection, that thus the witness
to this completion itself brings the revelation to a close, then
it cannot offend our sensibilities also to admit this gradual
growth in perception, which indeed was regarded as perfectly
natural not only by Luther, Calvin, and Zwingli, but by
almost all the great teachers of the Church. The perception
that "John" alone taught the full doctrine of the deity of
Christ—if we assume that it is right—need not be conceived
in the sense in which it used to be understood, namely, that
Christian believers drifted further and further away from the
original truth, but it can—and from the point of view of faith
must—be interpreted in the contrary direction: namely, that
it was the task appointed to the Apostles by God, as witnesses
of the Resurrection and of the foundation of the Church, to
explain in an authoritative manner to the Church what had
really taken place in Christ, just as it was the God-given task
of the prophets to predict it—authoritatively, that is, in the
word of revelation.

All these questions which have been named are only preliminary questions. The crux of the problem, the one great
question which historical criticism put to the Christian faith
of the Bible and the Church, is this: the message of Jesus
Himself, and the message about Jesus Christ. The historical
question runs thus: how did the development take place which
we can trace between the message of Jesus Himself—a message
which, in spite of many difficulties, we can to some extent
reconstruct from the sources in the Synoptic Gospels—and the
message of the Christian Church, which from the days of the
original Apostles, in spite of all differences in detail, is in the
main one and the same? The theological question, however,
runs thus: how can we explain the difference between the
doctrine of Jesus and the doctrine of the Apostles from the

standpoint of the unity of the revelation contained in the Scriptures? This is the real problem which lies behind all these different expressions: Paul or Jesus, Jesus or Christianity, Jesus or the dogma of Christ. In the testimony of the Church, Christology, the witness to Jesus Christ, the Son of God, and the heavenly Redeemer of the world, is the one and only thing that matters; in the message of Jesus Himself there is no mention of all this, and history shows us a man, Jesus, not a God. It is this difference, or, as it is thought, contradiction, which lies behind the expression, the "Synoptic Jesus." Which is right? The doctrine of Jesus which contains no Christology, or the doctrine of the Apostles which is Christological through and through? Or can it be, perhaps, that this is a false antithesis?

The historical question, as such, does not concern us here. But it is quite possible that if the theological question could be answered rightly the historical problem itself would, in essentials, also be solved; thus it looks as though this problem can *only* be solved theologically, or, to put it still more clearly, through faith. For if the situation was such as the first apostolic community of believers itself conceived it, if it regarded Jesus of Nazareth as the Son of God, because this is what He *is*, and because He proved this by His Resurrection, there would then be no need to pursue our inquiries concerning the origin of this faith of the Primitive Church any further. This question, which has dominated the historical research of the last century, could then be regarded as illusory, as a question wrongly put, as a "problem" which only arises where the actual reality, the true causal connection has not been perceived, and an artificial connection has to be manufactured. That is why, ultimately, all the interest centres round this problem.

In this connection, however, we must anticipate at one point. For a time it was thought that this question was decided by the Johannine problem. The Christian faith, so it was thought, would vanish if the historical authenticity or reliability of the Johannine picture of Christ could be proved untrue. This was a misunderstanding. The writers of the Synoptic Gospels do not give us a biography of the human Jesus any more than

John. They also testify to the Jesus Christ who is the Son of God and the heavenly Lord.[1] There is no evidence at all for a purely human conception of Jesus within the literature of the New Testament. All the Christian literature which the Bible contains is dominated by a uniform witness to Christ, which may indeed stand out more clearly in the teaching of the later Apostles, and in the dogma of the Church, and intellectually it may be more clearly conceived, but in essentials the message is the same. Thus the problem is not the Synoptic Christ, or the Christ of Paul and John, but this: the testimony of the Church to Jesus, the Christ, or the merely human picture of the Jesus of history—this is how the problem ought to be stated, if it is a really honest question.

Before we enter into a detailed discussion there is one point of principle which needs to be established first of all: faith presupposes, as a matter of course, *a priori*, that the Jesus of history is not the same as the Christ of faith. This postulate is peculiar to the Christian faith, while the eye of the profane historian—and this means every historian who does not approach his task in the spirit of the Christian religion—can see in Christ no more than the human Jesus. Or, to put it differently, it is the presupposition of faith itself that He whom faith calls Christ can only be known as Christ through faith, whereas He must be regarded otherwise as a mere man—even if of a very remarkable kind. Thus to say that the mere historian can see in Jesus nothing more than a man is tautology, which really does not need to be proved, and a "result" from which the believer learns no more than he knew already.

This misrepresentation of the position is due not only to the rationalism of most critical theologians and historians, but also, and just as much, to false interpretation of the faith by their orthodox opponents. The orthodox apologists as well as their rationalist opponents argue from this assumption: either that Jesus spoke and was historically—in the sense of a fact which can be actually ascertained and verified in a scientific manner—in the way in which He is described in the Gospel of John, and not as the modern historians describe Him—

[1] On this point, see especially Bertram: *Die Leidensgeschichte.* See also the note on p. 180 (above).

or He is not the Christ at all. Thus the orthodox apologists, with their critics, have conceived the Johannine picture of Christ in a pragmatic historical manner, believing that a pragmatic story of this kind was a necessary presupposition of the Christian faith—or, rather, they have thus misconceived it. John does nôt draw a picture of the Christ which the historian would recognize—what does John care about historical knowledge?—but as He can be recognized only by faith, as the historic, and yet at the same time as the glorified Christ. His picture is not a "photograph"; it is a "portrait," painted by an artist. Certainly: this is the historical Christ, he seems to say; but this historical Christ can only really be perceived by faith. All the rest that is visible to the secular vision of any historian, however indifferent he may be towards Christ, is a matter of indifference for a writer like John. The orthodox have failed to understand the indirect character of the work of John, just as they have failed to understand the indirect connection between revelation and the word of Scripture; they have been as little able to present a true picture as their rationalistic opponents.

The moment this misunderstanding exists, however, the Johannine presentation is immediately regarded as erroneous. The statement of faith is confused with a fact which can be objectively established. The Christ who is proclaimed by His messengers becomes the pragmatic Christ, and as such He can be affected by pragmatic criticism. This actually means that the humanity of the Son of God is no longer taken seriously. Thus, if the Johannine evidence is confused with a biography, we must not categorically deny that Jesus in His visible historical form may have been quite different, perhaps far more human, than He appears to be. To use the language of Kierkegaard, the witness of faith becomes a direct communication. Interpreted, or rather misinterpreted, as a living picture, it is beyond doubt that the Synoptic picture is far nearer to objective actuality, that is, to what we usually call the historical element, much nearer than John, although it is quite clear that the Synoptists also intended their narrative to form part of the proclamation of Christ; hence the relative difference between the Synoptic and Johannine Christ. But both pictures of Christ have this in common: both mean something quite different from that which the modern historical picture of Jesus sets out to do. If this has once been understood, then it will be much easier to face the question: Which is the historical "photograph" of the life of Jesus? The historical picture is possibly even still more "human" than the picture given to us by the Synoptists. And why not? Let us put it in this way, in order to bring out the misunderstanding as clearly as possible: the Christ of faith, as an historical personality, is such that in Him the mere historian can see nothing more than a human being, unless history were to become for him the means by which he would enter into the realm of faith. The fact of the Incarnation, the "being found in the form of a servant," carries with it the possibilty of holding Jesus to be a mere human being, and the impossibility of seeing in Him anything more than a man, apart from the gift of faith. The question whether Jesus is the Christ is not a scientific question at all, it is a question which concerns faith alone.

But this does not mean that a conflict between faith and history is entirely ruled out. Such an assertion would amount absolutely to the denial of the humanity of Christ—and thus to Docetism. Rather, the Incarnation of Christ implies, *eo ipso*, the possibility of conflict between faith and history. On this point the main principles have already been laid down. Thus here the problem can be confined to the question: is the result of scientific research into the story of Jesus, which can be recognized as such, sufficient to produce overwhelming evidence against faith in Christ, so that we would be driven to say: either you must accept the results of historical research or you believe in the God-Man? Or, to put it in another way, whether the Jesus whom we see presented to us by the results of historical research corresponds to that which faith itself states about this Jesus of history—about the humanity of Christ. This question needs further to be divided into two parts: one which deals with the facts of history, and the other with the content of these facts.

The question whether Jesus ever existed will always hover upon the margin of history as a possibility, in spite of the protests of the theologians, and of the Liberal theologians in particular. Even the bare fact of the existence of Christ as an historical person is not assured.[1] It would be a good thing once for all to admit this consequence of (necessary) historical relativism. The question is only "solved" within the limits of historical evidence; this means, however, that the solution is not absolute. It belongs to the nature of the Christian religion to have such a Christ, whose historical existence can be doubted by non-believers, and even denied by them, without being able to offer any convincing proof of His historicity.

The situation would be entirely different if the existence of Jesus *had* to be denied. Then the conflict between faith and history would be unending. But the actual situation is the very opposite. It amounts to this: that even historians who have no particular interest in Jesus do not seriously deny His historical existence. It has already been made plain in the preceding pages that faith itself is not drawn into this business of weighing probabilities and reasons for and against belief in the historical existence of Jesus, although the believer, to the extent in which he is aware of the historical problems, can never quite escape from the tension caused by them.

Not only the actual existence of Jesus, but also the main facts of His external history must be regarded in the same light. On both sides the destructive effects of historical criticism have been greatly overestimated. On the whole the picture of Jesus which is sketched by the most extreme critics who verge on actual scepticism (like Bultmann, for instance) does not differ very greatly from the picture given by the Synoptic Gospels. Even when as much of the Synoptic tradition is rejected as is done by these radical historical critics (which most historical critics would not accept), we see that the final result is that what has been renounced does not amount to so very much after all.[2] Certainly there is no single historical

[1] That it is less certain historically, than that of Caesar, for instance, is in no wise accidental. It is only attested by those whom it actually concerns, and this means: the believers.

[2] Certainly there exists a great difference between the reliance on the Gospel of Mark of a man like Albert Schweitzer and the scepticism of a man like Bultmann (which has come through Strauss, Wellhausen, and Wrede). But does the historical picture of Jesus in Bultmann's book on *Jesus* really differ so greatly from that of Schweitzer? And, so far as the

fact, not even the famous "pillars," which can be defended absolutely against some still more radical doubt; but it is of the very nature of history ultimately to be defenceless. This is the contingency of *vérités de fait*, in contrast to the necessity of *vérités de raison*. But it is also of the very nature of history that in spite of this defencelessness it always succeeds in again establishing its worth and validity. Indeed, we may assert that even after the radical clearance effected by sceptical historians, the leading features of the public ministry of Jesus which are regarded as reliable seem to be those of the Synoptic tradition: the Rabbi from Nazareth, the Teacher of the Law (with intensified emphasis on its eschatological aspect), the One who proclaims the Kingdom of God, to which His Person has a special relationship, the One who strove against the Scribes and Pharisees, the Master who gathered disciples around Him as the germ-cell of the community of the Kingdom of God, the One who taught with authority and forgave with power, the Man who was conscious that He brought final decision and final revelation, the Healer and the Friend of sinners, who willingly accepts the death of the cross, because it is so ordered by God in working out His plan of redemption, whose central point He then knows Himself to be, even when His Work breaks down externally. He who was crucified under Pontius Pilate, whose resurrection is attested by believers, and about which unbelievers wrangle.

Only now can we put the second question: is the message and the personal attitude of Jesus in opposition to the faith in Christ proclaimed by the Church? The full weight of this question ought not to be weakened by pointing out that the only source the Christian community possesses, or indeed the historian, is the picture of the life of Jesus sketched by the community of Christian believers. For it was not necessary

historical picture is concerned, do they not meet each other in a sphere which has left the Liberal view behind? The Liberal-Christian picture of Jesus has been finally destroyed: this seems, if anything, to be the result precisely of the most radical criticism. The decisive question: whether the Jesus of History who again emerges as the result of all this re-ordering of the subject can be the Christ of faith? has nothing to do with the difference between the more conservative (Schweitzer) and the more sceptical (Bultmann) estimate of the Christian tradition.

that the Church should perceive the inconsistency between the report and its interpretation, as is the case, for instance, in the Buddhist tradition. Primarily, all we need grant to the historian is this: it is quite possible that, in its desire to honour Christ, the Church may have been mistaken in its witness. Purely historically, this possibility must be admitted. Here, however, we are not concerned with possibilities; but when one who really believes, on the instance of those who maintain that such a contradiction does exist on the basis of historical research, asks what is the actual historical truth which can be ascertained, we will anticipate the verdict and say frankly that a contradiction of this kind does not exist at all.

The apparent existence of a contradiction of this kind, which was for so long one of the firm bulwarks of Liberal theology, is based upon the following errors: primarily, and above all, upon the misunderstanding which has already been mentioned, of the possibility of a direct cognition of Christ; secondly, upon a misconception of the personal character of the message of Jesus; and thirdly (in closest connection with the foregoing), upon the misrepresentation of the eschatological Messianic character of the whole of His public ministry. The research into the life of Jesus of the Liberal theologians[1] of the last century unconsciously confused the rational-ethical and religious humanitarianism of their own ideal of religion with the thought and purpose of Jesus; the result was that this school of thought succeeded in representing Jesus as a teacher of general ethical and religious truths, a man who was distinguished from others by the fact that in his own life he exemplified these general ethical and religious truths in an unusual way. This picture is not that which we find in the actual history itself; but it is a fantasy picture conjured up

[1] "The Jesus of Nazareth who appeared as Messiah, proclaimed the ethic of the Kingdom of God, founded the Kingdom of Heaven upon earth, and died in order to consecrate His work, has never existed. This is a figure which was drawn by Rationalism, animated by Liberalism, and clothed in an historical garment by modern theology" (A. Schweitzer, loc. cit., p. 631). We would only add: because Schweitzer himself as a Rationalist does not understand the meaning of eschatology, he himself mingles alien elements with his picture of Jesus, which in other respects is very clear and compelling. Of this more will be said further on.

by the Liberal outlook of the last century. This Jesus never existed; further, the Gospel sources never give any occasion for this historical error to arise.

This misinterpretation—we have already spoken of the first point—arose out of the prejudices of the Enlightenment. The thinkers of the Enlightenment saw in Jesus a teacher of ethical and religious truths necessary to reason, timeless *vérités de raison*, which have been discovered apart from Him, and without Him would still be true. The Sermon on the Mount is transformed into a kind of moral code—as a parallel to the Kantian ethic—the message of the Kingdom of God becomes the idea of the perfect ethical social order, and God, the forgiving Father, becomes the One who guarantees this ethical idea and its fulfilment. Thus behind the preference of theological rationalists for the Synoptic Gospels, or the "Synoptic Jesus," which has been so often noted, there lies simply this misunderstanding : they imagined they could discern in Jesus a teacher of their own ethical and religious Rationalism, and they honour Him for the "sincerity of His character."

The falsity of this whole "Liberal" conception was not perceived by critics until the "eschatological school"[1] called attention to the eschatological, Messianic character not only of the teaching of Jesus, but also of His whole attitude and activity. The critics had not wished to notice this before

[1] Bultmann also, as a critic of the Gospels and as a historian, is still under the influence of the Liberalism which he has rejected. The assertion that the Messianic self-testimony of Jesus is non-historical, made by Wellhausen and Wrede, which Bultmann has also adopted, is based upcn presuppositions which Bultmann himself no longer accepts. Behind their ostensibly purely historical scientific attitude towards the Messianic problem lie the motives of Liberal Rationalism, those motives which made a man like Volkmar believe that this alternative was inevitable: "either mad, or not eschatological." It would be a very good thing if the whole "formgeschichtliche" analysis of the Synoptic tradition could be carried through once more without starting from the sceptical conception of the Christian tradition determined by that general view of life. I venture to think that in many respects the results would be very different! To-day along the whole line of New Testament research we need to re-examine not the middle terms but the major terms. Even in Bultmann's *Jesus* there are sufficient passages to show how, in a roundabout way, he is forced to attribute to Jesus Himself elements which at first he had ascribed to the theology of the Early Church.

because they looked upon the eschatological element as "madness" (Volkmar), and they did not wish to soil their honoured example of moral worth with the taint of madness. First of all, it was simply a broader world outlook and a spirit of greater detachment towards the person of Jesus which opened the eyes of critics to the recognition and admission of these features which they regarded as so alien. Gradually the conviction made its way that this message of general truths, which they had assigned to Jesus, had no place in His life at all. Rather, His whole speech and action was the expression of His eschatological expectation, in which His own Personality somehow occupied the centre. Hence He places us face to face with ultimate decisions—in a way which would be impossible to the mere teacher of a law; it therefore dominates His message of the coming Kingdom of God *entirely*, and is something wholly different from the modern idea of the ideal ethical community which gradually comes into being; therefore He claims that He is more than a prophet, and yet it seems that He does not say who He is, at any rate not clearly. Hence His message, as well as His forgiveness and His works of healing, are the expression of the consciousness of a divine power which is "very difficult to understand." Hence His speech about the forgiving fatherly love of God (alongside of the terrible proclamation of the wrath of God), is something entirely different from an ethical religious truth; it is the expression of His self-consciousness, with its apparently fantastic eschatological outlook, which is so remote from the mind of the man of to-day.

This is an approximate outline of the average scientific picture of Jesus at the present time, the historical "photograph," as the scientific apparatus of the present day is able to take it. It is neither the "Liberal" portrait of Jesus nor the Christ of orthodoxy. It is more concrete and more living than either of these, and yet at the same time it is also more remote and more difficult to grasp. Above all, it is not a biography—the condescending presentation of the Life of Jesus of the positivist and latitudinarian type should rather be called "romances" of the life of Jesus—but a concentrated collection of a series of fragmentary "snapshots." The meagre, fragmentary, and uncertain character of the tradition in all details has become clearer to us than perhaps to any previous generation. All this creates a new situation for faith: it is both easier and yet more difficult than it has ever been before to believe that this person was the Christ. It is more difficult, because the actual verifiable historical reality, and the "insight" of the testimony of faith, are more clearly distinguished from each other, and easier, because all that falsely supported the direct view of the God-Man, all that makes the historical "picture" of the Man indistinct, or even disfigures it, and gives it the stiffness and unreality of a Byzantine picture, has disappeared. Thus it would not be true to maintain that nothing has been altered for the believer by the labours of historical research. But still less can we answer in the affirmative the decisive question: does historical research make it impossible to believe that this Jesus was truly the Son of God?

The historical "photograph" is certainly primarily quite different from the "portrait" which is créated by the vision of faith. But what historian as such, as a scientific man, would dare to say this Jesus cannot be the Christ in whom the Church believes?

Our attention is usually called to two facts which are supposed to bring out clearly the "contradiction" between the historical view and the faith of the Church, or, to put it otherwise, between Paul and the Synoptic Jesus: Jesus said nothing openly about His eternal being with the Father, and He did not connect forgiveness with the fact of His death. Both these objections will be dealt with in greater detail later in this book. Here I will only mention the most important point. Why should Jesus—if He was what the Church believes Him to be—have spoken about this? Which of us has any right to try to define the standard for the human-divine consciousness of the God-Man, since no one of us can even faintly imagine what it means to be filled with the prophetic consciousness of a special divine mission? The fact that Jesus was quite conscious that He was incomparably more than a prophet[1] cannot be effaced from the historical picture of His

[1] See below, Chapter XIV: *The Historical Figure of the God-Man*, especially pp. 369 ff.

personality. Further, which of us can establish with any certainty how much of this thought about Himself Jesus shared with the masses or even only with His own disciples, if He were the Christ, when the tradition deriving from faith in Christ, the tradition of the earliest period, makes it quite plain that even to His own disciples He only gave hints and glimpses of the mystery? With regard to the God-Man, there can be no argument from silence, since this very silence itself may form part of the divine incognito. So far as Jesus speaks at all, He speaks as the One who fulfils the sayings of the prophets; it is His *munus propheticum.* Therefore His existence is more important than His doctrine, and it is of this that the apostolic testimony speaks.

So far as the second point is concerned, the argument is still less convincing. That Jesus did not proclaim forgiveness as a general truth, but—as in the whole of the Old Testament—that He proclaimed it as a special divine revelation, which was indissolubly connected with His message of the Kingdom which He ushered in, forms part of the actual situation, which can be ascertained through scientific historical study. Why, however, should He anticipate that event in His life in which the meaning of His existence would culminate, and be fulfilled, by a proclamation which no one could then have possibly understood? Would not such an announcement have endangered the truly historical, and thus the truly human character of His existence? Might it not be that the Church, which had never fully understood the meaning of the Johannine narrative, never took the humanity of the Son of God quite seriously, and so through a misunderstanding of the Johannine story of Christ unconsciously fell a prey to a certain kind of Docetism?

We dare not say more than this. For even the "scientific photograph" is anything but complete. We will only say this: even if we assume that a case might arise in which we would be forced to accept the picture of Jesus which to-day is valid for the historical critics as objectively right—and here the differences among the critics and the pictures they give us are well known—and even if the situation were such that Jesus had "only" done and "only" said what the radical critics of the

New Testament will admit as historical reality, who would then have the courage to say: This man cannot be the Christ in whom the Church, Paul, and John believe? Why should it not be possible that he who wrote "born of a woman and subject to the Law," "born of the seed of David according to the flesh" would not have admitted to-day that the scientific picture of Jesus is more or less true of the "Christ after the flesh"?[1]

We certainly do not mean that the point to which these most extreme critics would reduce the acts and words of Jesus in the tradition corresponds to the amount of historical reality which is available for us. Rather it seems to us that in this criticism the leaven of the outlook of Liberal theology is still at work, and that it still dims their historical vision. We are convinced that Jesus was not only (as Albert Schweitzer and many others also admit) filled with a Messianic consciousness which sounds strange to us, but also (for those who had ears to hear, and that not only now and again, and not only towards the close of His life) that He testified that He was the Messiah, even though evidently in a manner which was in keeping with the incognito of His whole existence. We believe certainly that He wrought deeds before which we who know a good deal about psychical healing would stand amazed and baffled and know no explanation, and we do not see how for historical reasons anything convincing can be brought against these facts. Only our own historical views do not come into the picture at all. But the systematic theologian may perhaps, without seeming immodest, request the historian to listen to him when he again and again points out to him the philosophical limitations attaching to all historical work, thus reminding us that if the historian were also a believer, and were fully conscious of his faith, in his scientific work also much would become plain which he had not seen before, and he would not longer "see" much which he thought he saw. The historical instinct is an imponderable which is also strongly influenced by one's general view of the world and by faith, and upon the historical instinct finally all historical scientific work depends.

[1] On the decisive point, the limit of historical reality and the reality of faith: the Resurrection, see below, pp. 345 and 583.

Once again: the changes which in our opinion are certainly to be expected in the picture drawn by historical science are not the point on which I would here lay the most emphasis, but the fact that even the present-day scientific picture— so far as we can speak of such a picture at all—is not opposed to the Christian statements of faith, even though the great stumbling-block still remains that faith asserts that this man is the Son of God. To-day, after a century of historical criticism, the stumbling-block is essentially no different from that which it was at the time when "the Jews" were "offended" by it.

 Finally, one question still remains with which we must deal briefly; although it is of little specific weight, it played a large part in the period of historical interpretation, and, in so far as this period is not yet wholly over, still plays a part: the question of comparative religion. In itself the formulation of the problem from the point of view of comparative religion is justified, and also necessary, even in the New Testament. The historian must first of all have explored every avenue in order to explain an historical phenomenon in the light of its environment before he can admit that it is peculiar, not capable of historical explanation, and can then sever its connection with the historical standpoint and set it over against it. No one to-day will deny that not everything is original in the New Testament, and that not all can be made comprehensible merely from the connection with the Old Testament. Above all, the language of the primitive Christian tradition is that medium which was used by almost the whole of the intellectual life of that world so far as educated people were concerned. Thus it is not surprising that the religious language of the New Testament also is that of Hellenism, and he would be a poor historian who would not guess that behind this use of the language there lay something more.

Our knowledge of religious Hellenism and of the thought of the New Testament need not be very profound to perceive the vast difference between the spiritual structures which in both cases are concealed behind the same terms. Who would think of connecting the myth of the dying and rising divine saviour—in which the chief point is the regular recurrence of the event—with the story of the crucified Jesus of Nazareth who was crucified under Pontius Pilate, where the characteristic element in the story is the fact that it took place once only? Who does not see directly that the Logos speculations of Philo and the Logos gnosis of the Mandaeans,[1] just because they have no historical subject, must have a quite different meaning from the Johannine Logos doctrine, in which all the accent is placed upon the words "was made flesh"? People are eager to follow up this line of explanation so long as (and in so doing they are ready to find even the wildest improbabilities probable) they do not see the unity between Jesus and the witness of the Primitive Church, or between the witness of the first Christian community and that of Paul. As soon as this has been perceived, then all these external causal relations are regarded as irrelevant; hence, at the most their significance becomes subsidiary, and may be relegated to the sphere of "occasions." The light way in which occasionally the most improbable explanations belonging to comparative religion were swallowed, while the smallest difficulties in the explanation from the point of view of the unity of the subject were "sifted" out, hardly does honour to the achievements of historical research. Pseudo-history has here found a very fertile soil, which it still, to some extent, possesses. Pseudo-history flourishes wherever men are unable to perceive the decisive categories and the special character of the structures which are determined by them. It is, however, unnecessary to go into this question in further detail, since we are here confronted with no established results of research, but only with a mass of bold and extreme hypotheses. It is true, of course, that the lexicographical results

[1] I agree entirely with the excellent observations of Bultmann (*Christliche Welt*, 1927, pp. 502–11) on the importance of the knowledge of the history of religion as an "indispensable preliminary task," but I do not come to the same optimistic conclusions as he does, namely, that in this way "one's views will be brought into the right direction" (p. 510). On the contrary, I would say that it gives rise to endless misunderstandings and very inadequate "explanations." For the distinction Bultmann makes between matter and form is unfortunately unfamiliar to most of those who take part in the explanation of the New Testament in the light of the general history of religion—unless it be in a manner which from the very outset regards all that is definitely Christian as part of the "form."

196

are of great value for detailed exegesis, but they do not exercise any marked influence on the whole.

The historical scholar who has to wrestle day after day, at close range, with these individual problems is inclined to regard every attempt of the systematic theologian to understand the position of research and its significance for faith as a violent handling of the multiplicity of history, and a hasty simplification of the complicated state of the problem. There are two things which he ought always to remember: the first is this, that he himself never goes to his work without, in the main, having already adopted a certain "position." For only from a collective and general view can he gain fruitful hypotheses for the details of his work. It is sufficient to point out an undertaking like that of the *Religionsgeschichtlichen Volksbücher*[1] in order to make clear to what an extent modern theology believed it could use its scientific results for its view of Christianity as a whole.

Secondly, he ought not to overlook the fact that on our side the complicated nature of the problem, and the complete inconclusiveness of research, the uncertainty of all individual solutions, and the fact that the historical task is never ended, are explicitly recognized. It was not *we* who put the question about an historical conclusion; on the contrary, we are critical about any such assertion, since we are of the opinion that it is just here that science can never find rest, because its object transcends itself. Rather from the other side the Christian faith is continually called in question by appealing to a scientific conclusion of this kind. Thus our task was only to examine the conclusion offered to us by the other side with regard to its extent. Faith, however, with the presentation of which we are here concerned, is based neither upon positive nor upon negative scientific results. It simply explains its own position towards the statement that scientific results make faith impossible, and, it is true, it does not do this in the sense of a general smoothing out of difficulties, but, on the contrary, in sight of and looking towards the fact that faith to-day and at all times must go through the possibility of "offence." The "material" for offence is always different, and yet essentially

[1] A series of popular presentations of the "results" of New Testament criticism from the Liberal Christian point of view.—TR.

197

it is always the same: that the man Jesus is God. To-day the problems of historical relativism are in the foreground; to-morrow it will be something else. From this point of view, in this sense we have spoken about "results." Research goes on, and the task of scrutinizing faith must therefore be undertaken afresh in each generation. But in its essential features—faith knows this, and *only* faith knows it—it will never have any other issue than this.

BOOK TWO

THE PERSON OF THE MEDIATOR

CHAPTER VII

THE DIVINE WORD

(i)

THROUGH God alone can God be known. The knowledge of God comes only through revelation. This assertion is not peculiar to the Christian Faith, it is found in all religions. The Christian faith, however, claims that only in it, that is, in the revelation of God in Jesus Christ, does this assertion attain truth and reality. No proof can be adduced in support of this belief; indeed, those who ask for proofs simply show that they do not understand the statement, for a revelation which could be proved would be no revelation. It would be based upon some general truth outside itself. But a static truth of this kind—a general truth—would be the very opposite of revelation, and any doctrine which might be based upon it could only be called "revelation" by a gross misuse of terms, and a gross misunderstanding of the real meaning of revelation.

On the other hand, however, there is one point which can be proved, and it is this: by "revelation"—and therefore also by the term "God"—Christianity means something totally different from all forms of religion or philosophy. Further, it is also true that this sense of the uniqueness of faith is not an accretion, evolved in support of its claims, or a later theological theory, but an integral part of faith itself. A real Christian faith is impossible apart from the conviction that here, and here alone, is salvation. For the Christian faith is related to an historical event which took place once for all. The very fact that it arose in this way constitutes the revelation. This event is not merely the starting-point of faith, it is also the foundation upon which it is built. It belongs to the essence of the Christian faith that it is based upon this solid foundation, that everything depends upon this fact, upon this event which took place once for all. It is indeed quite possible to confuse

201

other forms of religion with Christianity; but that it is a confusion is proved by the fact that this kind of "Christianity"— in spite of its real desire to be Christian—is related to all other forms of religion and philosophy exactly to the extent in which it differs from Christianity. The inquiry contained in the earlier part of this book has led to this conclusion.

In all this, however, we have been obliged to assume that people already know what is meant by this unique fact, this fact which constitutes both the foundation and the content of the Christian faith. No one ought to object to this; on the contrary, all the language of Christian theology presupposes the knowledge of this basic fact of revelation; if this were not the case its terminology would be that of the general philosophy of religion. Christian theology cannot be built up gradually, line upon line, any more than the Christian creed has been composed of isolated clauses. Christian knowledge is not a mechanical structure, composed of separate pieces; it is an organism in which the whole precedes the parts, that is to say, the whole is already contained in each part. Thus each article of faith, each theological idea can only issue from the whole and return to the whole, just as the circulation of the blood starts from the heart and returns to it again.

Hence the theological elucidation of the significance of this fact for the Christian faith must also spring from the same source; its task is simply that of following that circular course in thought and reflection, and then of describing what it sees— without any alteration whatsoever—in order that it may make the meaning of this fact clear to the human consciousness. When this process has been completed it also provides a convincing proof of the truth of the statement that revelation— in the Christian sense of the word—means something entirely different from all forms of religion and philosophy. This proof is, in so far, a proof to Christian faith of its own truth, as it elucidates the meaning of the fact upon which Christianity itself is based. It is, however, no proof in so far as, in order to make it complete, faith must always be present. In what sense, however, we can speak of faith as "being present" in this connection can only be established at the close of this study.

When we speak of revelation and the knowledge of God in connection with Christianity, it is always assumed—even if it is not explicitly stated—that we are dealing with a vital living fact. For to Christian faith it is impossible to think of the revelation of God merely in terms of the discovery of truth; essentially it means the uprush of life itself; when, therefore, this revelation breaks in upon the soul it does not affect one side of the nature alone—as, for instance, that of the intellect—but it seizes the inner core of personality. Here there is no "Light" which is not also "Life," no faith which does not bring obedience in its train, and trust and godly fear, no knowledge or discernment which does not involve personal decision as well. Where this does not take place there must be some radical misunderstanding of the message of Christ, and therefore no right faith.

This is so because the revelation is not a miracle to be contemplated with amazement, nor a mystical feeling, nor an irrational emotional experience, nor an intellectual conception, but a Word of God, or rather *the* Word of God, the absolute demand of the Lord Himself, entailing a grave responsibility upon those to whom it comes. If this were not the case, this "revelation" might easily be confused with "mere knowledge" as an intellectual process, or with happiness as an emotional experience. But it would not then be the Word of GOD; it would not be the final truth, but only a preliminary truth; not the real experience of salvation, but a passing phase of happy feeling. So far as the witness of the Scriptures is concerned there is no suggestion in them of any such misunderstanding. In the Scriptures it is always assumed, as a matter of course, that the knowledge of God consists in the communication of salvation, and that this alone constitutes the knowledge of God. To know God means always and first of all to know the Lord Himself, and to learn to discern His Will in all its salutary moral earnestness.

This is the fact: the Word of God. Or, to put it the other way round: the Word of God is the fact. For this alone corresponds to the real relationship between man—in the present form of his existence—and God: that if this Word is to be audible to man it must be *given*. Again: the witness of

Scripture knows of no other "Word of God" save that which has been given, and given in the form of an event. It is assumed that man does not himself possess this Word. If he did, all would be well. If he were actually in possession of the Divine Word, he would also have come to himself.[1] For he was created in the Divine Word. If he is in the Word, then he is in his rightful place in the divine order; he will then know the meaning of his life, and will not have to search for a clue to the riddle of existence. If he knows the Name of God, he will also know his own name. At the present time, however, the very opposite is the case. Man does not know himself because he does not know his God. He does not know the meaning of his existence, his life is in disorder, he is eccentric, thrown out of the true order of life; hence he is part of the order in which death rules, and all is in disorder. He is separated from God; that is, he is a sinner.

To admit this means that we do not possess the Word of God, and the lack of this Divine Word spells disorder, ruin, and corruption, the darkness of ignorance and non-being, the awful condition of those who are without God and without hope in the world. Hence salvation must obviously be something entirely beyond the power of man to achieve, whether by reason or feeling or action: the Word of God must be a free gift, through which God imparts Himself in saving power to the soul.

It is with this transaction that Christian faith is concerned, or rather, it is within it that faith lives and grows. Faith is

---

[1] This is the fundamental idea in Kierkegaard's book, the *Brocken*, the point at which sin is recognized as an entity for the theory of knowledge: If man is a sinner then he is not in the truth, then he cannot know the truth, he cannot even know that he is not in the truth. This is precisely the doctrine of the great theologians of the Early Church, like Athanasius, for instance. Christ the Logos is the Truth; man has fallen away from this Truth. Therefore "no Other could bind man to the Holy Spirit but Thou, who art the express image of the Father, in whose image we also were created in the beginning. . . . Hence God had to step forth into the midst, in order that He might set free those who were sighing under the curse. . . . This is the cause . . . of the appearance of the Word in the flesh" (*Contra Ar.*, I, 49). The Word—the personal Word—of God is the principle of Truth as it is of the Good. Cf. my work: *Philosophie und Offenbarung*, pp. 37 ff.

related—quite consciously and definitely—to this actual Word, this Word which is an event. *To be determined by this event, this fact of the Word, this Word Incarnate, is faith.*[1] It does not form simply one article in the Christian creed: "In the beginning was the Word, and the Word was with God, and the Word was God . . . and the Word was made flesh . . . and we beheld His glory." It would be truer to say that this description covers the whole content of faith, the Divine Revelation as a whole. Of course, it can be described in other terms, as we see from the accounts of the teaching of the Apostles. But if ultimately *this* is not what is intended, the message is not the authentic revelation of Christ. Formulations of truth exist which are rather "one-sided"—which stress the less important aspects of the truth—but this formulation of the Christian message goes to the very heart of the matter; it is absolutely central. Why this is so, and the significance of this point of view, we must now proceed to consider.

(ii)

Is it possible to maintain—as is done by a certain pragmatic and realistic conception of the Gospel—that it is merely due to an unfortunate accident that in the Gospel according to St. John the miracle of revelation is expressed by the idea of

[1] In this statement and the following observations I hope to do justice to the many criticisms which have been levelled at my book *Die Mystik und das Wort*, because in it these critics have detected in the idea of the "Word" a certain oscillation between Idealism and Biblicism. I cannot wholly escape from the force of this criticism, but must confess that in that work I did not distinguish sufficiently clearly between that which was decisive, or intended to be decisive, and the introductory matter. This made it possible for a view of my intentions to arise like that which is expressed in the able, speculative book by H. W. Schmidt: *Zeit und Ewigkeit* (1927) (pp. 76–98). My attention was only called to this book shortly before the present work was published, therefore I cannot discuss it here. I believe, however, that these observations of mine will render any further discussion superfluous. The same applies to the majority of the rest of my critics, who, almost without exception, have fastened their attention upon that weak passage (which, however, I do not regard as so specially important). The Introduction (to the subject) can only be of decisive importance to one who bases his faith and therefore his theology upon it, whereas to me this preliminary study is an important but not a fundamental concern.

the Logos, which was also the leading idea in the Greek philosophy of religion? Or does this denote the beginning to that "Hellenizing process" which, according to the more recent school of thought, is supposed to have determined the history of Christian dogma?[1] Or is the Christian revelation—as Hegel's school of thought conceived it—simply the culmination of the process which had been set in motion by Greek Idealism?

[1] In the most recent phase of research into the history of dogma, in which Bousset may be named as the first theological representative, the Ritschl-Harnack thesis of the Hellenistic-Platonic character of the Logos conception has been replaced by the differentiated theory of the historical development of myths, which claims that the historical origin of the Christian conception of the Logos is the mythological idea of a personal Logos, as it was present in Hellenistic popular Gnosticism, and in the "Redeemer" mysteries of the Hermetic type. Latterly, the sources established by Bousset (Persia, Egypt, Greek Hellenism) have been extended by the addition of the mysterious triad of Manichean, Mandaean, and Iranian influences. To the non-specialist, of course, it is impossible to form any estimate of this question; on the whole I regard this theory as an important supplement to the earlier theory. The "Christian myth" has at least as much in common—as will be shown further on (see below, pp. 377 ff.)—with that mythology as with this speculation, and both are inwardly related through the Logos conception (see Bousset: *Kyrios Christos*, p. 306) as a *Word* of revelation. What, then, is the relation of Christianity to this? "Christianity has not contributed any original element to this, it has only (!) added one point: it has applied it in all its fullness and variety to the Person of Jesus Christ" (Bousset, p. 316). Actually "only" this! And in so doing everything has been changed. For henceforth the Idea is no longer merely an Idea, and the mythology is no longer mythology; the rational Idea of timelessness has been replaced by a unique event, and the mythological quasi-events have been replaced by the unique real event. Just as, in any case, the $\sigma\omega\tau\acute{\eta}\rho$ $\tauο\tilde{\upsilon}$ $\kappa\acute{ο}\sigma\mu\upsilon\nu$, the world-Redeemer of John, "can be explained formally and from its content by Caesar-worship" (Bousset, p. 245), so also that which Irenaeus—or John!—calls the Logos, can be explained by reference to Hermes, Thoth, or the Iranian seers. There is nothing, really nothing, to be learnt from these historical genealogies for the real positive understanding of the Christian idea of the Logos; all that this can lead to is an immense amount of misunderstanding. In spite of this, in that which has been made known by these historians we see one fact of vast significance: no other than the one which Bousset himself formulates as the interpretation of the Early Church: "That which Greek philosophy, Hermetic beliefs, and the worship of Thoth dimly felt from afar has here become truth: this force which binds God and man together has appeared in Jesus of Nazareth!" (On this, cf. my *Religionsphilosophie* on the Problem of the History of Religion, pp. 64–76.)

If this be so, argue the supporters of this theory, it is absolutely fitting that the central conception of Greek philosophy should become the decisive conception for the Divine Truth in the thought of the New Testament, and also, later on, in Christian dogma.

So much, to begin with, is clear: the Greek conception of the Logos is not an accidental phenomenon in history; it is not the product of an intellectualism which could be omitted from the process of history without being missed; it is an absolute necessity for thought; it is the fundamental conception of all thought; indeed, we might even go so far as to say that it is the basic idea of humanity itself: the principle of all meaning of intelligible speech. By this I mean the principle which transforms the making of words into language, vegetable existence into conscious life, mechanical ideas into thought, instinctive and animal existence into human life. The idea of the Logos is the hidden presupposition behind all thought, all search after truth, all reflection, all questioning, all mental effort. Something of extraordinary significance takes place when man first becomes aware of this central point around which all his thought and reflection must revolve if it is to have a meaning; when he begins to understand that nothing conditional exists apart from the unconditional, nothing finite without the infinite, nothing relative without the Absolute. "In Him we live and move and have our being." Apart from participation in the Divine Logos, there is no reason, no humanity. The idea of the Logos is no "invention of the Greeks" (Scheler), but it is the principle through which alone we are able to distinguish invention from truth, the principle of all truth, the full perception of the fact that the spiritual plane is unconditionally superior to that of mere existence.

It is, of course, true that so long as we regard the Logos conception solely from the point of view of logic we shall not discern the depths of meaning which it contains. From the point of view of thought alone man contemplates and enjoys the world; he still forms part of it; he has not found his own independence, which only becomes a spiritual fact when the self attains self-determination, in the deliberate concentration of all its powers on action. Thought which is merely speculative lacks moral depth and true freedom. Man only attains consciousness of freedom and of true humanity through the moral law, through the moral Logos,[1] through the idea that the fundamental meaning of life lies in personal responsibility. It is only through the moral sense that the Logos becomes an inescapable challenge instead of a static object of contemplation —of θεωρία. From the point of view of theory ideas do not affect my personal existence; they do not affect me in any way, they reign majestically in Olympus, unmoved and aloof; and those who desire to understand them must search after them for themselves. But the Moral Law, the practical imperative, does touch my personal life; inevitably it forces me to accept my personal responsibility. The Moral Law is related to the actual moment and to my own personal existence.

In the very nature of the "Law" or of abstract thought, however, lies the impossibility of its ever becoming actual and personal. The speculative character of thought is opposed to the concrete character of personal volition. This shows its connection with objective thought. Even the moral idea of the Good is a mere idea; it is no real imperative. The Moral Law conceived as an *a priori*, as a principle of immanence, does not create a real sense of responsibility. I am still alone with myself. I am still engaged in a monologue. Conversation has not yet begun. For in true conversation—in real responsibility—it is essential that I should receive something from without: a real word, the Logos as a Logos which is altogether apart from my own thought, something over which I have no control. This means, however, that the Logos comes to me in an irrational way, along the path of actuality, as a word that is *given*. Otherwise even morality is only intercourse with oneself, *Icheinsamkeit* (solitude of the self), as

[1] The later history of dogma, following Ritschl, has always equated the Platonic-Stoic-Philonic Logos conception, a metaphysical World-Idea. In essentials this may well be correct; yet we ought not to overlook the fact that this Logos as the centre and origin of the Ideas is at the same time an ethical principle. That thereby the ethical is subordinated to the theoretical is not only a Greek characteristic but ultimately a characteristic of all Idealism which is consolidated into a system. The system as such— whatever it may be—means the superiority of the theoretical-aesthetical element over the ethical element

Ferdinand Ebner so aptly puts it; it is self-love, self-regard. Nothing save a real relation to a real *"Thou"* can dispel this solitude of the soul; only a real conversation, in which we are actually addressed by another person, can make us responsible; this alone would be absolutely timely, personal, and therefore wholly serious.

But the voice of this Other cannot be a human voice. For all human intercourse is an attempt to escape from the seriousness of reality. All human association is an attempt to flee from the Infinite. A really serious situation could only arise if the unconditioned moral Logos were to enter into conversation with me, were to address me, to demand obedience from me, and that not as an equal, but with a voice of absolute authority.[1] This Word would not inquire my opinion about the Good, but would impart it to me as a secret. So long as I stand over against the Moral Law I am merely humanity in the abstract, man as an academic conception, not myself in actual reality. This comes out most plainly in the fact that the immanent Moral Law arouses in us the sense that it is absolutely possible to achieve the Good. The abstract, *a priori* Moral Law addresses us as though our minds were still unsullied by experience of any kind. Hence, although it speaks of duty, it fills us at the same time with an inspiring sense of freedom and autonomy. Thus it deceives us, and we do not perceive that our minds are no longer like blank pages in a book; we do not realize that we are not free. The moral superficiality of the Moral Law from the point of view of Immanence is this: that it does not permit us to realize that we are real human beings, but that it regards us as hypothetical "subjects," or as individuals who are still free to deal with the claims of the Good as they please. This assumes that we possess a dignity

[1] This is the point at which I believe that I can detect in Gogarten's thought—which is otherwise in so many ways related to my own—a somewhat dangerous directness, a direct identification with the historical element. The whole thought of Gogarten is anthropological—certainly with a theological intention, but yet in such a way that the misunderstanding which is never fully overcome in any theology which starts from man, is not sufficiently clearly set aside. Yet a discussion with Gogarten at this point would lead us too far afield. Gogarten's great merit is that in his latest writings he has laid stress on the fact that there can be no rela-

which in reality we lost long ago; it idealizes us by implying that we still possess the power of beginning from the very beginning; it confuses our present selves with something which once was true, but which is so no longer; hence the affinity which exists between this conception of immanental moral ideas and intellectual abstract thought and the sphere of aestheticism. This kind of morality is itself a semi-aesthetic phenomenon: the idealization of humanity by means of thought, a fair but hollow make-believe. This conception of religion as a system of immanental moral ideas is widespread and popular because it does not destroy the veil of illusion, because it still permits us to deceive ourselves about the hideous reality of sin.[1]

Within the sphere of thought governed by the idea of the Immanent Reason, that is, of the moral law of reason, it is impossible to find a real moral challenge, or to come to actual grips with the problem of evil. As we have already seen, it is of the essence of moral immanental thought that man possesses the power of judging for himself on the question of evil; thus man is both judge and accused criminal at the same moment. Hence it is impossible for him to believe in the seriousness of the breach between man and God; in the depths of his being he is convinced that he tends towards good and not towards evil; this being so he finds it impossible to take the whole problem of evil very seriously, at least so far as he is concerned as an individual. It is impossible to combine the consciousness of sin with the sense of the immanence of goodness which characterizes moral Idealism and its immanental theories. The "Categorical Imperative" likewise is not a real imperative!

tionship of faith to God which does not go through man. The other idea, however, is just as necessary, namely, that there can be no real relation to man—no realization of the "thou"—which does not go through God. Only the "thou" illuminated by the Divine Light really becomes to me a "thou"; only through faith in God does a human being become to me a "thou," and only through the knowledge of the *God*-man Jesus Christ does the Man Jesus become Christ to me.

[1] Expressed in theological language the error of Idealism consists in the fact that the Primitive State is confused with the present reality, thus the non-recognition of sin, the confusion of the idea of man with his (present) deepest inwardness.

Once more the sense of autonomy which invests man with legislative authority over himself is the critical point at which decision must be made: either a real conversation, a real imperative, which sweeps away human autonomy altogether, and replaces it by the pure authority of the Divine Word, or autonomy, which means the removal of the barrier between us and the Divine, the loss of the sense of God as the "Wholly Other," hence also no real conversation, no real challenge. Autonomy, the principle of immanence, the principle of the self-sufficiency of the human reason, is the exact opposite of the real communication of the Logos, and of real self-knowledge.

(iii)

The Logos as the principle of Immanent Reason, although it is absolutely necessary as an idea for the understanding of all that is human, ignores the real human element in life. Equally it ignores the real God. The Idea of God, the Logos of the Idealistic philosophy of religion, at all periods of history, is not the personal God. It is that through which the deepest element in our nature is identical with the divine. Thus it is that which we can actually know of ourselves about God, through our most profound and interior reflection; for that very reason it is not the personal God, but that element which we possess in common with God. It is not God's "Proper Name," but it is that which communicates Him. Clearly, this means that the God we meet is not the Creator, the personal God. Since the common human element which we can postulate *a priori* of every fellow human being, "by ourselves," is not his personal being, his "proper name," how much less can we know of God, God Himself, of His Proper Name by means of interior reflection. For whereas we can know the essential nature of our fellow creatures through our own nature, just because they are our fellow creatures, and thus have the same nature as ourselves, we cannot know the essential nature of God, by ourselves, since He is not a fellow deity, and we live on an utterly different plane of existence. Once again, it is the principle of autonomy which obscures this truth because it implies that we ourselves are on a level with God. Thus knowledge of the real personal God is only possible through a personal self-communication of God, through revelation, in which He imparts to us what we ourselves could never know—not even by any attempt to probe to the foundations of life, by any self-directed effort of thought and interiorization—through the communication of His Proper Name, of His secret. All knowledge of ideas, knowledge of the Logos in the immanental timeless sense, in the sense of continuity between our knowledge and the Divine Being, can never be a knowledge of the personal God. Such knowledge is only possible through a personal revelation within time, breaking through the continuity of the Logos connection, by the incomprehensible marvel of revelation in the sense of something which is non-general, non-logical, in an event which is absolutely unique.

Real conversation then ought to be of this character: the absolute Truth, which is at the same time the Absolute Good, both of which are identical with the Being and Will of the personal God, should be communicated to us as the divine secret of His Will; and communicated to us, indeed, in such a manner that God should be to us so real that we ourselves would also and at the same moment become real, that is, that we would no longer see ourselves in the glorified light of an illusory moral freedom and autonomy but in reality, as sinful creatures. Only thus would this conversation become truly personal, really meant for us alone, and therefore truly serious. This, however, includes one final point. We cannot recognize evil as evil until we are no longer enmeshed in evil. We can only recognize the Fall as such when we ourselves have returned to the origin. For only then are we in the truth, and thus in a position whence we can really *see* the evil. Thus this divine self-communication would at the same time mean a re-absorption of man into his original connection with God, in order that in this both God Himself and our real condition might become evident.

The Christian religion is summed up in the revelation of God in Jesus Christ. The Logos became flesh: the Logos as a temporal event in human history, and for that very reason the personal Divine Presence, and His self-communication, the manifestation of that which is an impenetrable mystery to the mind of man, in spite of the fact that it is the foundation of his life and the element in which he exists, against which he rebels because it brings to his consciousness his sense of limitation and of sin, although it is his salvation. The Word which became flesh is the personal original Word of Grace, bringing with it life and light, through which those who received Him received power to become the Children of God.

Therefore we cannot say that this is the Greek Logos, nor can we say that this Logos has nothing to do with it at all. In reality it is that principle of ultimate truth which the Greeks—the Idealists of all time—mean by the "Logos."[1] But

[1] The relation of the dogma to the Greek doctrine of the Logos is extremely complicated. Certainly the modern history of dogma deserves praise for the way in which it has drawn our attention to these relations and has thrown some light upon them. To some extent, however, the Ritschlian historical Positivism which stigmatized every statement about conditions which did not lie within the historical and ethical sphere as "metaphysic" or speculation, has also caused a great deal of confusion in the estimate of the Logos doctrine. In the doctrine which dominates the thought of the Church the cosmological Logos conception plays no part. This conception is essentially Johannine and not Philonic. In spite of this, it is a fact of some significance that Irenaeus, Athanasius, and the Cappadocians also speak of the Logos, just as it is no accident that John calls Christ the Logos. The Eternal Son is the Eternal Word of God, the One in whom God has disclosed His Eternal Purpose, His Eternal Thought. Jesus Christ is therefore the Redeemer, because He is this Eternal Word of God. Through translation into Latin and even into German, all trace of the cosmological conception of the Logos has been effaced; all the more powerfully, however, has the meaning of the "Word" in the scriptural sense—of the Word which is salvation—which expresses the Purpose of God and His Voice speaking to man—been emphasized. But even Irenaeus and Athanasius speak of the Logos as Augustine and Luther were to do later on: the Logos is the Eternal personal Revealer. The misunderstanding of the more recent history of dogma is based firstly upon an erroneous equation: the relation of the Eternal Revealer to the Creation of the World is described as a "cosmological speculation," whereas here the Creation is not a cosmological idea at all, but purely one of faith. Secondly, the anti-intellectualistic bias of Ritschlian theology hinders the understanding of the meaning of knowledge in faith. Only from the point of view of knowledge can the scriptural and ecclesiastical conception of the Logos be evaluated. The Christian faith is above all the knowledge of God; hence the eternal Revealer as the Son of God is at the same time the Logos. Not through this relation to knowledge and to the Creation, but through the lack of any relation to historical revelation, and thus to historical decision, is the speculative Greek Logos conception

it is also in sharp contrast to it, in so far as here the illusion is destroyed which implies that along the path of speculation about the Logos, the way of immanental philosophical reflection, of the contemplation of ideas, or, as one says nowadays, "the contemplation of essence," man can reach this end along any path whatsoever which leads without a break from the human up to the divine. But only because this divine Logos Himself, in an incomprehensible way, in a way which is a stumbling-block to the intellect, *comes* to us: no, *came* to us in a contingent historical event, is it possible to know Him and to share in His life.[1]

Therefore *Logos* cannot be translated otherwise than as the Word. For this is the difference between the Word and the Idea, that the Word is a real, sensible, and mental concrete event, and therefore is a personal communication. That we can only have fellowship through the Word—and not through spirit directly or through an idea of the Logos—reminds us that we are creatures and not the Creator. The fellowship of the Creator with the creature through the Word of the Creator, the real, spoken Word, the Word which is an actual temporal event: this is the revelation of which the Bible speaks, and of which the religious philosophy of Idealism, whether Greek or modern, does not speak.

distinguished from the Logos conception of the Scriptures. Just as definitely also is it distinguished from the Logos personality of the mystery religions and the Redeemer mythology. This conception is certainly distinguished from the philosophical conception by the element of personality, through which, on the other hand, it enters into closer relation with the Christian conception. But it lacks the presupposition of strict Monotheism on the one hand and the relation to the historical-personal fact on the other. Cf. the note on p. 273.

[1] The same may be said of the mythological Logos conception. Christ is the fulfilment of these mythologies as well as of Idealistic speculation. It might be said: the Logos mythology is the postulate of a Christ, the Christ for whom man longs. But to the extent in which the piety of the mystery religions was content with this it is evident that its adherents were not aware of the actual seriousness of the human position. Ultimately it is profound trifling, but indeed of such a kind that objectively it does express the whole need of humanity.

(iv)

Whereas philosophy has usually perceived this contrast quite clearly, and has frankly rejected this connection with a personal Bearer of the Word as theological prejudice and obscurantism, a theology which, in essentials, is really in agreement with philosophy, has tried to effect a reconciliation between it and theology. This subject has been fully treated in the first part of this book, hence at this point a mere reminder will suffice. The simplest form of mediation is that which is suggested by ordinary Rationalism: the Idea, which is true in itself, is supported by the corresponding exemplary life of the One who proclaims it. The same idea appears in an improved form in the conception of the religious hero or the religious genius, common in Romanticism. In neither instance is there any idea of a contingent revelation, of the real communication of a secret. For the difference between the genius and other men is merely one of degree; it is therefore always "accidental" and temporary in character. Even the genius belongs wholly to the sphere of natural possibilities open to human beings.

A second attempt arose out of the concern with history: this is the conception of historical positivism, of Christ as the "firstborn among many brethren," the idea of Jesus as the Founder of Christianity. The "Founder of the Christian religion" has nothing to do with the Revealer of the New Testament, because He merely represents an historical beginning, not the fact itself. He is not Himself the Word, but He brings the Word, He is the One who "first of all shapes the idea," and now the idea itself is here, and is self-evident, quite apart from the One who brought it; it is timeless truth, and is therefore not revelation; it is truth which regards Jesus merely as a remarkably effective exponent and herald of the truth, to which He has also given an incomparable personal expression; in principle, however, objectively it is wholly independent of Jesus.

There is nothing accidental in the fact that down to the present day no serious attempt has been made to interpret the Person of Jesus—the meaning of the fact of Christ—from the *prophetical* point of view.[1] For it is as clear as daylight that Jesus did not wish to be a prophet, but that He asserted that He was more than all the prophets, not merely in the sense of intensification of degree but also in the sense of a new quality. If, however, we take the conception of prophet seriously, as the prophet Himself and the whole Bible takes Him seriously, as the One who proclaims the secret of God, the One who makes known the Will of God, which no man could know apart from this proclamation, then there is no such thing as being "more" than a prophet. The "more than a prophet" idea could only mean this: the unity of the Divine Word with the Person; thus the Person does not only, like the prophet, possess an authoritative Divine Word of revelation, but He *is* this Word in person. This, however, is what Christ is, as the Scriptures and the Christian Church testify to Him.

Modern theological thought can only believe that it is achieving something for the interpretation of Christ by dwelling on the idea that He is "more than a prophet," because it does not take the idea of a prophet at all in the real serious sense. The prophet is confused with the religious genius, that is, with a person who represents a maximum of religious humanity.[2] Genius is the universally human raised to the

---

[1] Bultmann also ought not to be understood in this sense. For to him the Prophet of Nazareth, if I understand him aright, only means the humanity of Jesus Christ the Son of God. This is essentially a scriptural and not a modern view.

[2] How entirely natural it is to the thought of the present day to regard "Prophet" and "Genius" as identical terms—thus how easily the transcendental element which the Bible suggests when it uses the term "Prophet" can be twisted into something Immanent, may be illustrated by some extracts from Weinel's *Jesus in 19 Jahrhundert*: "There are, however, men in whom religion is a burning flame and a leaping fire, full of a wild beauty and awakening power. They are the prophets." "That which the genius is in the sphere of art the prophet is in the sphere of religion and morality." In point of fact no genius—were he Bach or Michael Angelo—possesses authority; there is not one who imparts a divine secret which apart from him would remain a sealed book. Rather the genius is precisely one who stirs the depths of *universal* humanity; we understand him because we have all experienced the same thing. It is precisely the great genius who has many others who know what he means from their own experience. Of Jesus,

highest degree, and a religious genius means the highest point of human capacity for religion, that is, of the moral and religious possibilities of knowledge which are latent within every human being as such. Hence—and this corresponds to the second possibility which was indicated above—the prophet and a discoverer of religious truth are mistaken for each other. If this were true in the religious sphere, the prophet would be what Euclid is in the mathematical sphere.

Such men do exist, it is true; from the historical point of view, even general moral and religious truths are positive, that is, they did once enter the mind of man for the first time at a certain point. But this is not what the Bible means by a prophet, and this is not what the prophet says about his own vocation. For he asserts that he has an authoritative divine word to proclaim, a message from God ("Thus saith the Lord"), not a general religious or ethical truth, which, as it happened, had not been discovered before, but a truth which, by its very nature, could not have been discovered by man at all, because its content is a divine mystery, and lies outside the realm of human possibilities of knowledge. Thus the prophet asserts that he has received a real divine revelation, and that in virtue of his divine commission it is his duty to communicate it as a divine secret which is now to be disclosed.[1]

who is supposed to be a "Prophet" of this kind, he says further: "That which only burned brightly in other hearts for a few hours and was then once more stifled by the cares and pleasures of daily life, soared in His great Prophet-soul like a leaping flame, in which everything else—the pleasures and the sorrows of earth—were consumed." Only, Weinel thinks that in order to complete this description it is necessary to use another category: "a quite distinct type of person, who emerges in Jesus in great strength and purity: the Saint" (pp. 136–8).

[1] Usually people try to discredit the statements of the prophets in the Bible by pointing out that there were false prophets. For our part we would draw from this the exactly opposite conclusion: that there are false prophets presupposes the existence of true prophets. The impossibility of measuring the falsity or the truth of the prophetic message, and its claim to inspiration, by rational standards, does not in the least prove that it is impossible to distinguish between false and true prophets. It is the same as with faith: if a Catholic and a Protestant argue together about the true faith, an impartial third party cannot act as judge in this controversy, but in spite of this a criterion of right and true faith does exist; but it can only be grasped by faith itself.

No one can be prevented from rejecting this view of the prophet's vocation, which is in accordance with the general conception of the Bible and of Christianity; and, in particular, no one can hinder the critic from pronouncing this state of mind to be self-deception, 'caused by lack of psychological knowledge, which is further proved to be erroneous by the fact that the prophets contradict each other; nor can one prevent the critic from substituting the conception of the "religious genius" for that of the prophet. Only, in that case, for the sake of clearness, the conception of prophet should be entirely renounced, since this second conception means something entirely different. The prophet is not the highest summit among the heights attained by mankind, who receives the divine light before other men precisely because he is the highest peak; but a prophet is an ordinary man, who—in virtue of the divine will alone—is honoured by God to receive a word whose content no man could possibly discover to be truth by his own efforts, a truth which is guaranteed simply and solely by the fact that it is *God* who utters this word. Hence the essential element in any prophet is not what he is, but what he has received, and what he must receive again and again, if he is to remain a prophet at all. The distinctive element, therefore, in the prophetic "word" is not that it occupies a pre-eminent position within history, that is, that it is the first time this general truth has been disclosed, nor by the fact that it represents a maximum of human attainment: namely, the intensification to the highest degree of those religious and ethical powers which are to some extent the common heritage of mankind; but the prophetic "word" differs from all that is produced by the life of history by the fact that it is a *new quality*: a word from the other side, the communication of a divine secret, and therefore authoritative. The word of the genius has no authority in the strict sense of the word. Rather in a hundred years' time it is destined to become a commonplace. Both the discoverer of truth and the way in which the discovery was made may be forgotten; but, in spite of this, the truth discovered by the genius remains true. It has permeated the general intellectual life of humanity. The greatest poet is the one who is able to express what the best minds of his own day feel dimly and cannot express, or at least cannot express so fully and so felicitously. The religious hero will always be honoured, it is true, for through him alone will a thousand others first perceive what the religious life really means. But he himself will desire that all should become what he is, and his influence will be shown by the fact that others will become more and more independent of him; all that he has to do is to "wake them out of their first sleep" (Schleiermacher). He is a "mediator" only until others have reached sufficient independence and maturity. This we express by saying he has no authority. He is only *primus inter pares*.[1]

The word of revelation, however, is an authoritative word, something which, in principle, is wholly different from all general religious and moral truth. A prophetic "word"—even when it is naturally mediated along human psychological lines—is God's own word, ἴδιος λόγος, the letters which form His Proper Name, which no man can know unless it be disclosed to him by God Himself. As opposed to the idea of something timeless it is connected with time, in distinction from the idea which is unmoved, it is the word which has "come."

To us the fact that God's Word has come to us and its actual truth are indistinguishable. The word of revelation is true in so far as it comes from God, and it is acknowledged by us as true in so far as we acknowledge that it is a word which has come from God. It is the fact that it has come from God which makes it legitimate, not its content as such. For that which only claims the right to exist on account of its content is a general timeless idea. To recognize the word of revelation as true means to admit also that it has come; and this means that we listen to it with the knowledge that this word has actually come from God. This is what the prophet means by his *N'um Yahweh*, "Thus saith the Lord." To him it is true, in so far as he knows that it has come from God, thus in so far as he knows that he possesses a divine commission, a divine revelation. It is precisely this difference from all that is merely

---

[1] On this point, cf. the work of Kierkegaard (unfortunately far too little known) entitled: *Der Begriff des Auserwählten*. Translated by Th. Haecker, Hellerau, 1917.

general religious truth which gives it the quality of a revelation. Therefore it is an authoritative word. The fact that this word has come to us from above, and that it has been communicated to us, means exactly the same as saying that it is an authoritative word.

For since it is authoritative its relation to us is different from that of truth in general. It cannot be *known*—in the usual sense of the word: it can only be *believed*. That which can be known, that which is continuous with our own knowledge, and can be connected with it, is not revelation nor is it faith; it is knowledge and intellectual truth. All this is connected with the idea of immanence. The word of revelation, however, is transcendent; it comes to us from the other side; therefore it cannot be connected with our present knowledge as though there were no gap between us and it. It breaks through the limitations of the sphere of my own knowledge. Its truth, therefore, cannot be "judged" or estimated; it can only be *believed*, accepted on trust. But this faith, this attitude of authority, cannot be applied to any human guarantee or human assurance as such; for such an authority would be false and heteronomous; it can be given to none save God alone. Or, to put it differently, this "word" can only be accepted as an authoritative word of revelation where it is evident that it comes from God.

Faith only exists where a "word" is accepted by the soul, or rather, where this "word" captures the soul because it comes from God, and its truth is thus self-evident. At this point we abandon our "inquiry"; for any truth which can be humanly proved to be true by a process of examination and inquiry is, *eo ipso*, not revelation but an intellectual idea. Faith does not come into the reckoning at all.

Faith is thus the relation to the Word which has come; therefore in faith the relation to the content of the Word cannot be separated from the givenness, from the source of the Word. The prophet, or, to put it more exactly, the divine commission to the prophet, and the authority of the prophet which is based upon this commission, is the source of the Word of God. This is the givenness of the Word in contrast with the non-givenness of thought. The teacher of the idea, the genius who discovers the idea, stands in no necessary relation to the idea itself. It is possible to sever the idea from its original historical source just because its discovery simply means the point at which the original discovery was made within the sphere of history. We are here concerned only with the intra-historical phenomenon of priority and positivism. The prophetic word, however, cannot be severed from the prophetic event, from the givenness of this Word; otherwise it would cease to be a prophetic word at all, and would be transformed into a general truth; this means that, *eo ipso*, it would cease to be a Word of God. At the same moment it would also cease to possess authority.

Thus a "Word of God," as distinguished from a general ethical and religious truth, is a word which must be believed; this means that it is a word which has come from God, whose authoritative, revelatory, objective character cannot be severed from its content, and indeed helps to constitute its truth. The authority of the Word does not exist apart from its content, neither can the content of the Word exist apart from the authoritative objective character. Or, to put the same thing in another way: the Word of God may be described either as something which is contingent and communicated, or as a truth which is vitally connected with the event of revelation. Whereas where general truths are concerned the manner of their entrance into history does not matter one whit—even for truths of a general ethical and religious nature—for the word of revelation it is precisely this manner of its entrance, namely, the divine commission to the prophet, the divine communication, the prophetic event, the miracle, which constitutes the decisive element. For here we are not dealing with historical positivism, but with something which does not lie within the possibilities of history at all; with an event which has broken through the surface of history, or, as Barth is fond of expressing it, with a vertical message from above. We do not deny, of course, that even the prophetic "word," in which the Divine Word is plunged into the current of history, is itself determined by history, and is manifested in a human and imperfect form; on the contrary, we recognize and affirm it. On this account, however, it still remains a "word" from the region which lies beyond all historical possibilities, an authoritative word of revelation.

(v)

When, however, we concentrate our attention upon the relation between this prophetic word and Christ, and between Jesus Christ and this prophetic word, from both these aspects we can perceive that there is a further point to be noted.[1] The prophetic revelation points beyond itself to something which is "more than prophetic," and Jesus Christ points back to the prophets as to those who stand behind and below Himself. The prophetic word of revelation is thus conceived from both points of view as a provisional message, as a transitional phase, like the first flush of dawn before the sunrise, incomplete in itself. This has been the view held by the Christian Church from the very beginning, and this also represents the thought of the New Testament concerning the relation between Christian revelation and Old Testament prophecy. At this point, therefore, it will be necessary to bring out this relation more clearly on the basis of the previous course of this inquiry, and at the same time to test the validity of our previous statements by this fact.

The prophet of the Old Testament had what no one else had or could have unless he were a prophet by vocation; he had a divine word of revelation, whose truth depends wholly upon the fact that it is a word of revelation; this "word" can never be transferred to the sphere of general truth without a complete distortion of its original meaning. Hence because he alone—not in virtue of that which he is in himself, but in virtue of the fact that he is the chosen mouthpiece of God—has this word, the prophet stands between God and man as a new fact; indeed, he represents a new category, in contrast to

[1] I am quite conscious of the fact that in thus relating to each other the Logos, the Word of God, Prophet, Christ, and the story of salvation, as the Coming of God I am treading in the footsteps of Irenaeus. If anyone should feel inclined to call my work "theology of the type of Irenaeus" I would be quite inclined to accept the description. Only I would have to remind my critics that between Irenaeus and the present day there have been Augustine, the Reformation, and Kierkegaard.

the whole natural sphere of humanity and history: he is the mediator of the divine truth of revelation. He is the place at which God deposits His Word, the organ through which God makes it audible in the world as His Word. Once it has been severed from this "place" it is no longer the divine word of revelation; its meaning has changed, and it no longer signifies what it did when it was perceived at this "place" as the Word which comes from God Himself, an authoritative Word which is an actual event, which has actually been "issued" as a Divine Summons. The prophet is a mediator between God and man.

This position of the prophet as the mediator has been expressed in an incomparable and magnificent manner in the story of the giving of the Law on Mount Sinai. Moses alone is worthy, high upon the summit of the mountain amid the clouds, to receive the Word of God. The people themselves were unable to bear this direct contact. They were not permitted even to touch the mount upon the summit of which this revelation was taking place. What Moses heard on the mount was a secret, a secret which God alone could reveal. For who should know the will of this God save him to whom it is specially revealed? It is this will which is here revealed through the mediator, Moses. Even though this is expressed only in the simple code of the Ten Commandments, still, by the fact that at this particular time and place it was given and received as a revelation, it differs in principle from every kind of rational humanistic ethic as, for instance, from the *notiones communes* of the Ciceronian ethic. It is a personal gift of revelation from the personal God, therefore it is not merely a law, it is also the institution of a covenant, the revealing presence of the personal God, who wills to be near His people as their own God.

This designation of the prophet as the "place" at which the divine revelation is given is typical of the revelation of the Old Testament as a whole. It is because this is a real event, a personal communication of the mystery of God, that the prophet stands between God and man as the concrete point at which this event takes place; he stands there as the mediator of the revelation, who possesses the Word and communicates it to others. The fact that the mediator is himself the place at which the revelation is given shows plainly both the concreteness and reality of the event of revelation, and also its transitory character. For who is this mediator? Who is Moses? Who is Isaiah? Is he a saint? Or is he one of the *homines religiosi,* who are held up to us as examples? As prophecy only appears in this form in the Old Testament, so, on the other hand, there is no trace in the Bible of a phenomenon common to other kinds of religious literature: the revered peaks of religious attainment, the experts in "religion," the holy men.[1] The sobriety of the Old Testament conception is finely expressed in the fact that the divine word of the prophet belongs to God alone, while the personality of the prophet himself is detached from every suspicion of holiness or divinity. The prophet is a man like ourselves, a sinner like ourselves, a weak, erring, struggling human being, who writhes under the burden of his divine commission. He is the exact opposite of the mystic who. in his communion with God, experiences moments of ecstasy and spiritual consolation. He is simply an instrument through which the voice of God speaks, an instrument without any value of its own. The gaze of the people is not to be directed towards him at all, but simply and solely towards his message, which is the revealed Word of God, just because it *is* the Word of God. His private experiences, his personal sanctification, his personal communion with God, and the special holiness of the man of God which is the fruit of this experience and this communion, which plays such a large part in all other kinds of religious literature, are passed over in silence. One thing alone matters: the Word itself, as a revealed word, and also that the prophet himself should maintain the disciplined and self-denying attitude of one who knows his own nothingness, and therefore surrenders himself utterly to God to be His mouthpiece, to "spend and be spent" wholly in His service.

For this very reason the prophetic revelation cannot be final. Actually it is not the revelation itself, but simply points towards

---

[1] That in the Old Testament, properly speaking on the margin of the prophetic type, there are reminiscences of the *homines religiosi* cannot be denied. But these oscillations on the margin disappear wholly in the great prophets.

it. The prophet only possesses the Word, he is not the Word itself. He has it—in the simplest and most austere sense of the word. This is what constitutes his position of authority. At the same time this means that his authority is limited. He is not himself the authority. The person who is here, and the cause for which he is here, are still two separate things. Hence in him the Word is not yet really present. He must point forward in his prophetic utterance to a Word which will take place, and he must wait with expectancy for this fact of revelation. The prophet is not himself the place where the revelation takes place; properly speaking, this process takes place in a higher sphere. He himself is subordinate to the Word, like all other men. It is true, of course, that in contrast to other men his "word" is an authoritative utterance. But he himself is only a means, only an impersonal instrument. He is not himself the mediator in person.

Hence through all prophecy there runs a golden thread which points forward, more or less clearly, to a manifestation of the presence of God in which alone the meaning of the prophetic revelation will be finally fulfilled. Prophecy is Messianic. Whether the prophet as a psychological individual is himself conscious of this or not, his message points forward to the future where the Word and the Person will not be separated, where the mediator of the revelation will not possess the Word outside of and above Himself, but within Himself, because He Himself *is* the Word. What is meant is the event in which the Person of the Mediator is the actual source whence the authoritative Word is proclaimed without having to be "given," first of all, a Person who, when He is asked concerning His authority, will no longer need to point away from Himself, but may rightly point to Himself. It was the aim of the last of the prophets to prepare the way for Him "who was to come." With a passionately humble gesture he pointed away from himself towards Him whose shoe-latchet he felt himself unworthy to stoop down and unloose. This gesture manifests his insight and his fidelity. The prophet knows that he is not the ultimate, the real, definitive, final revealer, who need wait no longer, one who does not need to wait to receive anything else, who need no longer point forward, the One in whom all prophecy is fulfilled, the One to whom all the speech of the prophets has pointed, the One who is Himself the Word of God, a new category, not merely a maximum amount of that which had existed previously—not a final and still greater prophet, but the Word Itself, the Word which all the prophets have foretold, present in His own Person, uttering His own message. As a human being the prophet himself has no authority. The ultimate truth of his message is not bound up with his personality. No one has authority save the God who Himself speaks to us. God does not delegate His authority. There are no intermediate courts of appeal. The idea of such courts belongs to paganism, indeed it is paganism: the idea of continuity between God and the world. This is the denial of the real, living, personal Creator God. There are no inter-mediate courts of appeal between God and the creature. Even the most sublime human spirit is still a creature. Even the highest forms of artistic, philosophical, religious, and moral inspiration are still "creaturely."

If this kind of inspiration is to be called "revelation," then the word can only be used in this sense: that all that is produced by human reason, all the fruits of Humanism, constitutes a species of general revelation, something "universal," and is therefore not an actual revelation at all; it is simply the dis-closure of some divine elements placed within the world, but not the disclosure of the divine "Proper Name," of the Divine Secret. Hence in principle all that is human stands upon the same level, from the primitive impulses of humanity in an African bushman up to the highest genius of a Goethe, a Bach, and of the "heroes of religion." But from this plane of humanity no ladder of ascent leads us on and up to God. Even the prophet, as a man, is a "creature." It is only his "word," so far as it exists at all, in so far as it is a "given" word, in so far as it came down from above, from the world beyond, that is something which does not belong to creaturely existence, but is divine.

But in the prophet's case this descent from above is only incomplete and partial; it is not yet a real existence. It only becomes this at the point where it is personally real, where it has actually arrived, and is no longer merely on the way, at the point where person and cause are one, where the Logos and objective existence coincide, where the Word is not merely uttered in the form of thought—but becomes flesh. Only the Word which becomes flesh is really the Word. Here alone the abstract, timeless, and impersonal element is wholly removed, here, where God speaks personally, because He Himself speaks in a person: *in* a Person, not merely through a Person, *as* a Person, and no longer merely about a Person. Here the authority which can give the final decision is no longer outside the personality, in a "word" which is above the person, but He, the Person Himself, is the rock of offence, the stumbling-block, *the* authority, of whom it is said: "Blessed is he who is not offended in Me." The Word, as the word of revelation, is only completely a Word of God where it is completely personal.

Once again, however, we must remember that what has just been said about the personal Revealer must not be confused with the modern view of the ethico-religious idea manifested through personality. The fact that Jesus Himself lived what He taught has no connection with revelation in the Biblical sense of the word. All this lies within the sphere of human possibility,[1] and is only differentiated from the rest of humanity by differences of degree. Through this no divine secret is disclosed, it is simply that the meaning of the idea which, in principle, every human being knows, or could know, is made clear. In a certain sense this equation of idea with personality can be measured; it is simply a question of estimating the value and purpose of some visible phenomenon by an invisible idea or standard. Here, therefore, there is nothing essentially new; nothing genuinely decisive takes place, but simply something which might happen at any time and under any circumstances, although nowhere in so complete a manner. Even the most perfect ethical and religious personality can never be an authority for us. This "revelation" is on a different level from the prophetic plane. It is general revelation of a

---

[1] It is only possible to assert the sinlessness of Christ in the strict sense of the word if one is a believer in His Godhead. It is not a statement of something which is perceived, but of something which is believed. Faith cannot be based upon it; on the contrary, only upon the basis of faith can it be asserted at all.

peculiar clarity, visibility, and power, but it is not the "Word of God," in the sense in which the Bible uses the phrase. A human being may be as moral and religious as he likes, he is still merely a man, and as such he has nothing to tell me about God. For either he merely tells me something which I can examine for myself afterwards, and then he is a "teacher," and stands on the same level as I do; the only difference between us is that he is a few paces further on. Or he may really communicate to me something of a real mystery of God: then he can only do this in virtue of a divine commission, thus it is not he who speaks as himself; indeed, it does not really matter to me *who* he may be at all. His word is a prophetic word. But there is a further possibility: He Himself may be in His own Person this Divine Word, coming from the realm which lies beyond all human possibilities. Then He cannot be man, a man like the rest of us, including the man of genius and the prophet, but He must be the Son of God, He in whom the word of revelation, the secret word in which God speaks His own Name, a human being, has actually become flesh: He is the Christ. Then He speaks and acts as God Himself, with divine personal authority, no longer in virtue of a divine commission, but in virtue of His Divine Being, as the Son, to whom the Father "has given to have life in Himself." This is the perfected Word, the one which has actually come unto us, the Word in which the divine truth and righteousness, which was separated from us by the great gulf made by the Fall, comes to us Himself and imparts Himself to us as truth, righteousness, life: the Word in which God gives Himself personally to us, because in the Word He is personally present, as the bridge over the gulf between us and Him, as the Mediator.[1]

[1] This is the connection between the Logos conception (the ecclesiastical conception, not that of Philo) and the doctrine of the Incarnation which has been so completely misunderstood by the later history of dogma. "If our Teacher, the Word, had not become man, we would never have been able to learn in any other manner what is of God. Also we could not learn it in any other way than by actually seeing our Teacher and hearing His voice with our ears, in order that we . . . might have communion with Him, by receiving increase from the Perfect and from Him who was before all Creation" (Irenaeus, V, 1). "Owing to His love He is always known

(vi)

It is this Word alone which can be both the object of faith and a rock of offence. We cannot "believe" in ideas; we *know* ideas. We can incorporate ideas, general truths, into our own structure of truth. Ideas form part of our mental existence, and therefore of the world as a whole, whether they are theoretical, aesthetic, or ethical ideas. They do not force us to confront a real tribunal, for as autonomous personalities we are always seated on the bench ourselves. Therefore we can never run into any danger of condemnation. We are never entirely exposed, never stripped utterly bare. For the idea is always the presupposition of our own existence, thus the basis of our own being, our deepest spiritual foundation. We are never quite at the mercy of the truth, never subject to a wholly impartial verdict. We can always find some standing ground, we can hold the last line of defence against attack. We must not surrender. We still have "firm ground" under our feet. The sense of continuity has not been broken.

When, however, the Word comes to us with authority, with an authority which is purely divine, addressed *to* us alone, a "Word" which does not also proceed *from* us; thus when it really only *comes*, and is not at the same time already present within us—when all ideas of "immanence" have been renounced—when we are confronted by the word of revelation as it stands over against us as the Other, as the Judgment, in which we are in no wise the arbiters of our own fate, where we are absolutely subordinated and in no way at the same time co-ordinated, where we stand thus over against God: here—and here alone—we must surrender unconditionally,

through Him through whom He made all things; this however is His *Word*, our· Lord Jesus Christ, who in the last times became man" (IV, 20, 4). The Logos doctrine of Athanasius is the finest of all in its systematic, and at the same time non-speculative existential character. Athanasius above all has clearly worked out the idea that man, created in the Word of God, has in it his life-principle—granted by grace—and since he has fallen away from the Word can only be restored by the Word coming to him again. "God's Word had to come Himself." Only the Logos could make good, since He alone reveals God and in this revelation brings back the life which had been lost.

here we are absolutely helpless, there is no longer any ground under our feet. Here we depend absolutely on the hand of Him who can hold us or allow us to fall, just as He will. Then the decisive thing will be this: are we going to try to defend ourselves, or are we going to let God have His way with us absolutely, that is, are we going to believe? or are we going to be "offended"?

To cling to the immanental relation with God means that we do not believe, that we are "offended." For it means clinging to the belief in the unbroken continuity between man and God, the refusal to admit the existence of the gulf which lies between man and God, the refusal to confess our sin. He alone really confesses his sin who has surrendered the last line of defence, who does not withdraw into himself and take refuge in the depths of his own being, as a fortress secure against all storms, who breaks with the immanental relation with God, with every kind of affirmation of the "God in us." For he alone really surrenders, he alone declares himself "a liar, that God alone may have the truth." We cannot come to this decision in our own strength, by means of reflection and "inwardness" alone. We can only come to this decisive point where the Word, as a divine communication, really comes to us, with irrational actuality, breaking through the inner continuity, thus in the presence of the Divine Word.

On the one hand lie all the immanental possibilities: speculative, metaphysical, mystical, and ethical. All have this in common: they do not wish to hear of a Mediator, of the Word which is *given*, of the necessity for being bound to the fact of revelation. They are all forms of self-assertion, assertion of the self over against God, assertions of an ultimate innermost possibility of self-defence, forms of self-assurance; the assertion that at least in the inmost depths of human personality continuity between man and God does exist. Speculation completes this continuity by the fundamental process of thought, God is the Idea of ideas, to which we attain along the *via negationis*, through the conception of the Absolute. Mysticism achieves this through the practical *via negationis* by withdrawal from all "images" of the sensible world, by the introversion of the soul to its central depths, where God and the soul are one. Moralism—whether it be that of the Pharisee or of the Stoic—while it admits the faults of external behaviour, withdraws to the last line of defence, which consists in the disposition, and there it asserts its connection with the Divine Will, the deepest and most sincere intention, which gives God a reason to overlook for its sake all that is otherwise lacking in the soul.

Hence all three reject the Mediator, the given element, the truth and possibility of life which comes from the region beyond ourselves, from God alone. On the other hand, it is precisely the Mediator before whom and through whom the decision is made. He who needs no Mediator needs also no mercy. He is not really willing to receive righteousness as a free gift. Rather he wishes to find it in the depths of his own soul. The Mediator is the judgment on all immanental possibilities. He is the Word which humbles us, since He makes all self-defence impossible for us. Only he who recognizes the Mediator really accepts the impossibility of a healing of the rent from the inside, from within the depths of the human soul, and thus admits the reality of guilt and sin. He alone accepts the grace of God, the fact that God alone can achieve anything, and in so doing he recognizes the "Proper Name," the secret of the personality of God. Not till then does he bow before the authority of God, when he really gives glory to Him. He alone knows what faith means. Just as the Word of God is fulfilled in the Word made flesh, so faith is fulfilled through faith in the Mediator. Here alone (and not till this point has been attained) is there the possibility of deciding between being "offended" and the attitude of faith.

CHAPTER VIII

THE DIVINE NATURE

(i)

FAITH in Jesus Christ constitutes the Christian religion. The entre and the foundation of the whole Christian faith is "Christology," that is, faith in Jesus Christ, the Mediator. The Christian Church was aware of this from the very beginning; the pagan world perceived it too, as is shown by the fact that the pagan inhabitants of Antioch called the early followers of the new religion in their midst "Christians"; all down the ages the Christian Church has always proclaimed this to be the foundation, the fundamental fact upon which she is built. There has never been any other Christianity than this, in which faith in Jesus the Christ constitutes both its foundation and its central point. To regard this "Christology" as an intellectualistic aberration from the original "ethical religion of Jesus," as the fatal beginning of a speculative process, as a degeneration from simple piety, shows very plainly that the meaning of the Christian creed has been entirely misunderstood. In this connection the defenders of Christianity are not concerned with speculation at all; they are not thinking about satisfying the metaphysical sense of scientific need; their whole concern is with the Word of God. Jesus is the Logos. He is the Word God has to speak to us. Essentially, Jesus Christ is not a doctrine—the ethical and religious doctrine of the Rabbi, Jesus of Nazareth—but an act of God, the self-manifestation of God, the final culmination of all the acts of revelation of the old covenant, and their fulfilment, the highest, personal, peculiar Word of God, in which, as at no other point, man is confronted with the decision.

The form of religion which the thinkers of the Enlightenment set up as the true religion in opposition to the Christian Faith of the New Testament, as the "religion of Jesus," or the "Gospel of Jesus," is actually a mere doctrine, a mere idea, a general system of ethical and religious truth. The irony of the situation is this: that those who are most suspicious of the Johannine-Logos-Christ as the product of "Greek speculation," are precisely those who, basing their argument on the real Greek conception of the Logos, attack the New Testament idea of the Logos. For what else is the Enlightenment idea of the "religion of Jesus," of the idea of the Kingdom of God, which Jesus "formulated for the first time in history," than religious Idealism, a relation to God which is not based upon a real historical revelation, but upon a conception of general, timeless, ethical, and religious truth? Even the appeal to the special religious power which is said to issue forth from the Person of Jesus does not alter this statement in the very least. For all that is meant is that this power is a secondary phenomenon, a kind of spiritual by-product. If it were more than this, this Person Himself would become the final revelation, and we would no longer be standing on the plane of the "religion of Jesus," but on that of the Christian faith in Jesus Christ as the revelation of God. If it be a real fact that Christianity is sharply distinguished from a general religion, whose highest representative and teacher is Jesus, then in actual fact nothing remains but this, which is levelled as a reproach at Paul: "The actual appearance of Christ, the entrance of this Divine Being into this world, would have to be regarded as the central fact, as the actual fact of redemption" (Harnack).[1]

In point of fact, that is exactly what the Christian creed does mean by its confession of faith in Christ, and it is precisely this creed which is the very opposite of a doctrine. Precisely where belief in the Incarnation of the Word exists, all speculation about the Logos—both ethical and theoretical—has broken down. For the Incarnation of the Word, and the Word made flesh, the Person of the Mediator, places us in the presence of decisions of which the followers of a moral general religion, of the so-called "religion of Jesus," have not the faintest idea. Only through belief in the Word made flesh can the intellectualism, reflective speculation, and aestheticism of the Greek philosophical spirit be rooted out. No moral law, no religious ideals, no Idea of God, however sublime, is able to do this. This alone can be done by the effectual

[1] *Wesen des Christentums*, p. 116.

Word, the actual revelation of God, the decision for or against the Mediator.

Thus the question: "What think ye of Christ?" is in no sense a deflection of interest from the main body of Christian truth. From the beginning this has always been the central question within the Christian Church, and from the very outset the Christian answer to this question has always been the same: it is "the power of God unto salvation," as Paul defines the Christian faith. The question, "*Who* is He?" means the same as the other question: "What has God to say to us in Him?"; the one cannot be answered without the other. The first answer to the question: "Who is He?" was this: "He is the Divine Word." Rightly understood, this reply contained the whole truth. He is that which God has to say to us—what can there be beyond that? But the converse is also true: What God has to say to us is just this: He has to tell us what *He is*. Unless you know who He is, you cannot know what God has to say to you. When you know who He is, then indeed you possess no mere speculative theory, with no reference to your life; when you acknowledge Christ in faith, you are acknowledging your King, and God is telling you something about yourself and about your life which "eye hath not seen, nor ear heard, neither hath it entered into the heart of man to conceive." When you know who He is, you know who God is, you know who you are, and what God wills to do for you and with you, and you see your real condition. If you have received this grace, that, in response to this question: "Who is He?" you can reply: "I know and acknowledge in Him the Name which is above every name"—you have been set upon a new plane of being, and your whole life has been changed. For the question, "Who is He?" is the same as the one which says: "What part, then, does God take in this whole process, what happens?" That this question can degenerate into an intellectual speculation simply means that it is always possible to state and answer this question lightly instead of seriously, in a frivolous manner instead of in the spirit of one who is seeking God, which means that the questioner is not really listening to the message of the New Testament at all, but simply pretending to listen.

Christ, Who is He? The doctrine of the Church replies: "He is true God and true Man, and for this very reason He is the Mediator." Here we are primarily concerned with the first part of this question, with the assertion of the Deity of Christ; or, to put it more exactly, in the sense of the Christian message: with His Divine Nature. Particularly in the last century and at the present time this "doctrine of the Two Natures" has been hotly attacked. Looking back over the centuries at the history of Christian doctrine, certain scholars noted the conflicts which have raged round this doctrine, and they saw how profoundly they had divided and shattered the life of the Church. They perceived the apparently insuperable logical difficulties with which theology had been wrestling from time immemorial. Above all, these modern thinkers looked at these formulas from the outside and were absolutely unable to understand them; hence, they regarded them in a spirit of hostility. Then they threw all the blame for the ensuing intellectual degeneration, with its results, upon this "wretched" doctrine of the Two Natures. In any case, one of the leading points in their theological programme was this: Christian theology must be freed from this pernicious doctrine of the Two Natures.

Their chief charge against this doctrine is that it amounts to a kind of metaphysical materializing. They argue that whereas the Gospel is concerned with the Will of God, the whole interest of ecclesiastical Christology turns rather on questions and forms of being, that is to say, on metaphysical problems. These, it is true, satisfy a certain intellectual necessity, but have nothing to do with the Christian's believing interest. Above all, however, this doctrine is said to be based on a conception of salvation (the doctrine of the deification of human nature[1]) which is alien to that of the Bible, and cannot be combined with it.

Although there may be a great deal of truth in this criticism of certain ecclesiastical theological doctrinal formulas, and the diversion of interest which resulted from it—and it cannot be denied that in the Christological controversies of the fourth and fifth centuries there was a certain deflection of interest

[1] See the Appendix to this chapter, pp. 249 ff.

235

of an intellectual kind—at the same time we ought not to over-look the real object of their main attack, and the conception which lies behind it; on the other hand, too, we must examine what is the nature of the conception of Christ which is offered us as a substitute for that of the Church. This substitute is simply the "modern" conception; therefore their attack is not directed so much against the special formulas of the doctrine of the Two Natures as it is against the New Testament conception of revelation itself, whether "Pauline" or "Johannine." The question, "*Who* is He?" has been entirely set aside, and replaced by the other: "*How* does He come to be what He is?" Thus the question of the being of Christ is replaced by one which concerns His appearance in history. This means that we have quitted the plane of revelation for that of phenomena within history, both moral and religious; thus quietly and unconsciously the Biblical conception of revelation has been replaced by the modern idea of the symbol, that is, by something which gives concrete expression to an idea.

It is important to realize the significance of this change: it means that this hostility to the doctrine of the Two Natures, to the "metaphysic" of the ecclesiastical doctrine of Christ, conceals a far more fundamental opposition to the scriptural and Christian conception of revelation in general. The fundamental contrast of the Christian faith between the creature and the Creator, between sinful "creatureliness" and the divine world of redemption, αἰών οὗτος—αἰών μέλλων, with the bridging of which the witness of Biblical Christianity is concerned, is exchanged for a relative antithesis, that between Nature and ethical Spirit, between being and value. Hence the redeeming revelation itself can be regarded as historical as such, as an historical phenomenon, namely, as the personal perfect representation of the moral religious idea, and as the goal of this redeeming event of revelation, an historical final purpose, the kingdom of moral and religious perfection. Indeed, both forms of hostility, to the conception of the Logos on the one hand, and to the conception of the divine nature of Christ on the other, are really based on the historical positivism or the phenomenalism of the modern interpretation of Christ, and the criticism of the formula of the Christological dogma is only the occasion which is utilized in order to discredit the Christian view of revelation as a whole with some show of justification.

This proceeding has been assisted by a circumstance connected with the history of language: indeed, this may possibly have been the cause of the whole hostile movement against the doctrine of the Two Natures: the change of meaning in the word "Nature" (*natura, φύσις*). When the ancient doctors of the Church spoke of the "Divine Nature" of Christ they meant nothing "natural" in the physical sense at all, but simply and solely the quality of His Being. The Divine Nature means the divine quality of being, *being* in distinction from mere appearance, the subject as distinguished from its predicates, the *Who* in contrast to the *How*. We have almost entirely lost this meaning of the word, and we know why this is so. To the extent in which the contrast between the creature and the Creator disappeared from the view of the modern man, as a result of his fundamentally monistic outlook, the relative antithesis Nature versus Spirit, Nature versus cultural achievement, became important. As a consequence the word "nature" has taken on for us the sense of merely physical, natural, or material. Hence to us the early ecclesiastical formulae, both those which concern salvation and those which define the Person of Christ, sound far more material and naturalistic than they are intended to be. At the same time we cannot deny that much materializing metaphysic also entered into the ecclesiastical definitions. The central idea of the doctrine of the Two Natures, however, has nothing to do with naturalism, or with the materializing of revelation and of salvation, and we are here concerned with this central thought alone.

(ii)

Revelation is the disclosure of the divine secret. It is not the communication of intellectual knowledge, of a doctrine about God, but God's own personal Word, in which He makes known His own secret will and purpose, and in which He permits us to know what are His intentions towards us, and what "is the state of His own mind" (Luther); the Word in which He Himself names the Name which no man can name, and in so doing, in communicating His Name to us, He makes us His Own, makes us sharers in His secret. Revelation is the Word from the other side, from a region beyond that which is accessible to man; the divine Word in distinction from all other ideas, which, thanks to "general revelation," we have a certain right to think about God. Within the sphere of that which is historically possible, within the human sphere, the sphere of the moral and religious ideal and its more or less perfect realizations in "experts in religion," in "saints," and in other "*homines religiosi*," revelation is not a maximum, but it is something entirely new, a new category; it is that, namely, which as God's own Word enters into this realm of human values from God Himself. Although this Word of God must also be mediated to us through human history and psychology—the miracle of revelation is not a prodigy—yet none the less on that account it is fundamentally different from anything historical, human, or ethico-religious.

The Word of God comes to us from the further side, from beyond the border-line which separates God and man; it is God's own Word about Himself, His secret, based on the fact that He alone is God; it is something in which the world, man, and human reason have no part, that which is reserved to God Himself, that which separates Him, the Creator, from His creature. The Word of God, revelation, means the issuing forth of this hidden One from His concealment through God's incomprehensible self-communication. Thus it can only come absolutely from God Himself, and, indeed, in a sense which differs entirely from all that is created, natural and historical, which also comes from God. It means that the barrier between God and the creature is thrown down; it means the coming to us of that which was from all eternity, over that gulf which no human being can cross, which no religious, ethical, mystical, or speculative exaltation can carry us over, the entrance into history of that which, by its very nature, cannot enter into history, because it is eternal.

This Word which comes to us from the realm which lies beyond all human and historical possibilities, is here, as a person; Jesus Christ is this Word from the other side. Thus

He Himself is the One who has come "down to us from above," whereas all the rest of us, even those who stand out like mountain peaks among religious humanity, yes, even the prophets themselves, are all of them "from below." This is what is meant when we are told that He is the "Word made flesh." Here there is no longer merely a prophetic Word from beyond the creaturely frontier, from within, from the secret of God, but a person; this Word which has come to us from beyond the natural frontiers of our human life is a personal being. Hence in principle this event is absolutely different from all other events in history, from all forms of religious and moral human movement. It is the movement of God towards man, not the movement of man towards God. It is a divine event in a sense which is quite different from the sense in which the natural and the historical may be called divine, because its movement originates with God. For the natural and historical event moves within the limits of the life of the creature, but this event means the breaking through this frontier.[1] This is what makes

[1] This interest in the divine nature of Christ has never been more clearly expressed by anyone than by Luther—whose faith, since Ritschl's time, people have tried to place in opposition to the ecclesiastical doctrine of the Two Natures of the early Church. As one example amongst many let me quote here a passage from Luther's *Commentary on the Epistle to the Galatians*—and indeed from a classic passage in this work: "And here seest thou how necessary it is to believe and to confess the article of the deity of Christ. . . . For to conquer the sin of the world, death, the curse and the wrath of God in His own Person (*in semet ipso*) is not the work of a creature but of the Almighty. Out of this there results necessarily, that He who personally (*in se ipso*) conquered, is truly and by nature (*vere et natura*) God. . . . Because the Scripture ascribes all this to Christ, therefore is He Himself life, righteousness, and blessing, which is of the nature and the substance of God (*quae naturaliter et substantialiter Deus est*)." The passage closes with an explicit allusion to the central Christian truth: "Therefore when we teach the people that they are justified through Christ, that Christ is the conqueror of sin, death, and the eternal curse, we bear witness at the same time that in His nature He is God" (op. Lat. 30, pp. 22 ff.). This is also the view of the ancient doctrine of the Incarnation. Quite in the same sense as Luther Irenaeus observes: "The Redeemer is Jesus Christ, who Himself, apart from all other men, is called God and Lord . . . and the Word made flesh" (III, 19, 2) "by Nature" God (IV, 1, 1). "Through the Word, through which God made the world, precisely through and in this He also gives to men salvation" (III, 11, 1). "It is the same Hand through which God creates and completes" (V, 16, 1).

239

it a revelation, the Word becoming flesh. This event does not belong to the historical and natural sphere,[1] but to the revealing word of the prophets; it is the fulfilment of their predictions, it is there in the reality of which they could only speak.

Ideally, as well as in actual experience, there are several prophets, a small number of chosen individuals—a few selected, not elected, persons. But the Incarnation of the Word is in its very essence a unique event, and this Incarnate Word can only be One, or it is nothing at all. There is no higher category than the prophetic category, save that which (by its very nature) is exhausted in one solitary example, which is either the decisive element which takes place once for all or not at all: the Mediator, the Reconciler, the Son of God.[2] For He is the one ultimate meaning of all that the prophets have foretold.

Hence His uniqueness is something quite different from that which the modern man means when he uses the word "uniqueness." For uniqueness in the modern sense means something relative and gradual, the "uniqueness" of the *primus inter pares*. Here, however, there is no idea of a *primus inter pares*, but of One who is essentially the only One, the $\mu o \nu o \gamma \epsilon \nu \grave{\eta} s \ \upsilon \acute{\iota} o s$, who can have no equal, whose uniqueness lies in His very nature. He is the Only One, because, in principle, He is different from us, who are creatures; He is unique in the fact that He comes to us from beyond the frontier of creaturely existence, because He comes to us from the side of God, from the "bosom" of God, from "within," from the mystery of the divine self-existence. Just because this is what He is, He is

---

[1] It is of the essence of the Christian knowledge of revelation that the presence of the divine revelation should be set over against the world, in spite of the fact that God is present in this world—apart from His presence in revelation. We must distinguish between the providential government of the world, to which history and also the history of religion belongs, and the particular event of revelation and of salvation, although even the sphere of the divine government of the world, of the life of nature and of history is full of traces of God's presence. Modern theological Monism, however, regards this antithesis as a denial of general revelation.

[2] At the same time we must remember: We know this, we have this knowledge of that which is decisive, because it has happened, and to know this means that we perceive this "foolishness" to be the wisdom of God.

the revelation. Otherwise, at the utmost He would *have* a revelation, like a prophet. He who *is* the revelation is the only One, just as he who has the revelation is one among a few elect souls.

(iii)

Hence His authority resides not merely in His Word, which has been given by God, but also in His personal existence. His authority is not like that of a prophet, something which has been lent to Him, any more than He has received the Word of God. He does not need to wait for the divine command; He does not need to receive revelation over and over again. The distinction between Christ and the prophets consists, indeed, in the fact that He does not need to do this, because in Him Person and Word, and indeed the essential Divine Word, the mysterious Word, the Word from the other side, are all one. As Person He belongs to the same place as that to which the prophetic word belongs, although incompletely. As a Person He comes out from the secret of God, as the prophetic word also comes. Therefore He Himself possesses the authority which is ascribed to God alone. He Himself stands on the other side of the frontier, beyond which only God Himself can stand.

Here, too, the one thing that matters is to pay attention to this "place." For the place is decisive in the question of authority. In all that belongs merely to the realm of ideas, there is no question of a place, or of what happens, because here no secret is disclosed. Here we can speak of *semper et ubique*, and that which we perceive in this way is (logically or ethically) "evident," luminous. Therefore here there is no authority. All authority within the sphere of humanity is a usurped authority; at the most it has meaning and justification as a passing method of education. It is destined in the course of development to be set aside. Man and the human sphere, even the "Divine" within the human and the natural sphere, cannot be the seat of authority. Autonomy corresponds to this latter sphere. For over against all that is human, human-divine, or every kind of Idea, as participators in the same

241

"Immanent Divine" we take our stand as equally qualified partners. But when we are confronted by the Divine Word of revelation autonomy ceases. Here we have no standard by which we can measure truth. Here truth is communicated to us.[1] Hence it must be one or the other: faith or the "offence of the cross." A Word whose source guarantees the fact of its truth is the Word of revelation which possesses authority.

He alone who is Himself the Word possesses this authority, and, in the full sense of the word, *is* this authority. Hence, so far as He is concerned, the question, "Whence is He?" is not only justifiable, it is the ultimate question, which decides the whole problem of His person. It means the same as the question: "Who is He?" It concerns the authority of the Word of God if the answer to this question must be made not with any reference to His appearance within history, to the human, ethical-religious "How," but with reference to His secret. The mystery of the Person of Christ is the decisive element in His significance. For the mystery of His Person means the same thing as His coming to us from God, as the fact that His existence means transcending the frontier between the creature and the Creator from the side of God. When we speak of the mystery of His Person, however, we are not playing with words, we mean something absolute. The secret of Christ has nothing to do with the romantic idea that each individual, above all the world-historical great individual, the genius, the "daemonic man," is mysterious, unfathomable. It is the mystery of *God* that is meant when we speak like this, not the mystery of the individual creature; the other dimension, the dimension of authority, the dimension which we suggest by the expression: beyond the frontiers of creaturely existence, beyond the possibilities of human and historical existence.

[1] Certainly this statement contains a great danger, to which Wilhelm Herrmann was never weary of pointing, the danger of an intellectualist orthodoxy. As soon, however, as we perceive *what* is here "communicated" and what it means to receive this communication: that we are here concerned with the actual speech of God to us and with the decision of faith, intellectualism is ruled out, whereas on the contrary the polemic against this statement almost inevitably leads to a wordless immediacy and hence into a romantic subjectivism, which is still more unsatisfactory than any kind of orthodoxy.

It is the essential mystery; there is nothing accidental about it; it is the mystery in which the One stands over against all others.

Because revelation is God's own Word, which breaks forth from the Divine Being in its very essence, therefore He who is the Word made flesh is, essentially, the mystery of God. Only thus does He stand really over against all men, as the μονογένης, as the "only" Son, not as the *primus inter pares*. It is thus that the Scriptures bear witness to Him, it is thus that the Christian religion believes in Him. His secret, His authority, the fact that He stands on the further side of the frontier between man and God, or that He comes to us from beyond this frontier: all this means the same thing, that is, His Godhead. Only God Himself is essentially in absolute contrast to humanity as a whole; authority can be ascribed only to God Himself; in Him alone can we believe; to Him alone ought we to pray; from Him alone should we expect forgiveness and redemption. If any human being were to treat another human being as a god in this way, he would be a polytheist, that is, in the language of Christianity, an idolater. Even the most sublime character among men can never become an authority to us, nor be worshipped. In the fact that the Christian worships a man as the supreme authority, he expresses the absolute and unique mystery that this man is God.

(iv)

We are here concerned with the question of being, not with that of value, with the nature (using the word in the old sense), not with the spirit (using the word in the modern ethical sense). Therefore, we are not concerned with the question *how* Christ came to be what He is—this concerns His humanity and not His deity—but *Who* He is; now this means His deity, as a mystery, which faith alone can perceive. This, therefore, is why faith alone knows the authority of Christ. Absolutely, the question with which we are here concerned is that of the Divine Being of the Christ, not merely with His disposition which can be judged as one that is in harmony with God. A disposition, even the most perfect, the most full of ethical and religious love, is a definition which can be applied to the creature, contrasted with the Creator; it means obedience, not authority.

Disposition belongs to the plane of humanity, of history, human nature. When we speak of the disposition of Jesus Christ, we are speaking of His humanity, not of His deity.[1] To call this His deity simply means the denial of His deity. When the Christian religion, the witness of the New Testament, speaks of the Deity of Christ, it carries a very different meaning from that which it carries in the sphere of disposition (Ritschl, Herrmann), or of piety (Schleiermacher). The idea of disposition belongs to the sphere of natural theology, not to the Christian doctrine of revelation. The perception that the life of Jesus expressed perfect love, this perception of His ethical and religious temper, and of the trust which this inspires, is not connected with faith at all; it is simply an "opinion," in accordance with the general human ethical standard. Thus in saying this we are only acknowledging His humanity. His deity, however, means that in Him God Himself is acting, that His forgiveness is the forgiveness of God, His divine proxy, His authority, the secret of His Person. Not because He shows forth perfect love does God show Himself in Him. If we judge like this we are using the ordinary human standards. We "estimate" whether He acts rightly. He does not communicate any secret to us. But whether this man who loves is acting in the place of God, as the One who is empowered to act in His stead, as the One who is able to express the mystery of God, and who has the right to do so or not, whether His forgiveness is really the forgiveness of God, this question about His ἐξουσία or authority, this is a question which belongs to the realm of faith alone. The answer to the question: *Who is He?* alone makes the manner of His appearance amongst us—His historical humanity—a word of revelation. Only because, and in so far as, He is recognized as the One who comes to us from the inmost heart of the

---

[1] That in Phil. ii. 5 by "mind" (φρονεῖν) something quite different is meant, namely the purpose of love of the eternal Son of God, becomes self-evident in the further course of the passage.

mystery of God Himself, does His Love really tell us something about God which otherwise we would not know. If it were like the sufferings of a St. Francis, Golgotha would be a moving story of a human martyrdom, but no more; only as the Cross of the Son of God is the Cross the sign of reconciliation.

We can never discover the secret of the Divine Word from a consideration of His ethical and religious manifestation. The "moral judgment of Jesus from the point of view of His vocation" never "carries with it the religious judgment of Him as the revelation of God" (Ritschl). It is its presupposition, but never its basis. The basis is the mystery, the divine mystery of His Personality, which "flesh and blood cannot reveal unto thee."

The manner of His coming is the historical manifestation. The question of His personality, of His authority, lies "behind" the historical reality of the phenomenon, in the new dimension of that which "comes from God," which we—like the New Testament—can only express in terms of Being, and not in terms of disposition. This is what Luther means when he emphasizes, again and again, that Christ, as contrasted with those who through Him became the children of God, is Himself "naturally God."[1] The Christian testimony uses such terms of Being in order to make clear the difference between our relation to God and the relation of Christ to God. All these terms of Being, of "coming," and "having come," mean the same thing: that in Christ the Word comes from the other side, the mystery, the inmost being of God, the non-historical, the non-human, the self-existent Divine, the Proper Name of God: in a word, God Himself. Divine Nature means that which is of the nature of the Divine Being, of a kind which stands beyond the difference between the creature and the Creator on the side of the Creator Himself, and thus is "of His Own," that which has a relation to God which is not like that of a man, through the disposition and spirit, but that which is related to God—as God Himself.

---

[1] We might here use the word "substance," were it not for the fact that it is burdened with as naturalistic a sense as the word "Nature." To the early Fathers "substance" meant nothing material, but the subject of the predicates which is not absorbed into the predicates.

This is the secret of the "only begotten," or "only Son" who was "in the bosom of the Father"; this is He who "being in the form of God, counted it not a prize to be on an equality with God," in whom "there dwelleth all the fullness of the Godhead bodily," this is He "through whom and by whom were all things created." This is the One who has come. The prophet does not "come" in this sense. The prophet has a message which has come, and he therefore becomes a man with a commission, an ambassador. But he himself does not "come," it is only his word which "comes." The coming of Christ always means this breaking through out of another dimension into the sphere of history; the coming of the Person now corresponds to the coming of the Word.

The expressions which we use to describe this dimension upon which everything depends, are as a whole either metaphysical or mythological. But their origin and their meaning are neither metaphysical nor mythological, although the non-believer naturally can see nothing else in them. They are not metaphysical because they do not arise out of the realm of thought at all, they do not spring from the sense of the need for explanation, nor from any particular sense of need at all; their aim is simply to establish firmly the conviction that here we are concerned with God's own speech and action, and with that alone. They are not metaphysical because they do not claim to be incorporated into an intellectual system, but the exact opposite: their aim is to shatter every intellectual system. They are not metaphysical because they do not unite God and the world into the unity of a theory, an intellectual whole, but because they reveal the opposite, the contrast between God and the world.

They are, however, also not mythological, because mythology in particular has nothing to do with the Word of God, with a unique decision, with the actual address made to man at a particular moment, but with something general, with something which recurs again and again, something which is never real, because it never deals with a unique event. They are inadequate, they are a childish and stammering attempt to express truth, as is all that we try to say about God; but they are necessary, in order to express that which they have to express: that third dimension behind the surface of history, the point of insertion between the eternal and the historical, not as a point which *is*, but a unique event which happens, the divine self-existence coming into being for us, in distinction from all kinds of general revelation, which do not contain the thought of God as He is in Himself, but that of His relation to the world, which therefore can never give us news of what takes place "within the realm of His Majesty," nor of the nature of God's purpose towards us.

These are the expressions which describe the plane of the revelation, the realm whence it originates, the nature of its coming, the secret of its being. We do not indeed know, and the Apostle John would have been among the last to claim that he knew what those words mean: "Who was in the bosom of the Father." But this expression tells us just as much about the personality of the Divine Mediator as we need. The testimony of the New Testament has a great variety of such expressions—in Paul, in the Epistle to the Hebrews, and in the Johannine writings themselves. Perhaps it was not wise of the ecclesiastical doctrine to select one of these—the idea of the Logos—and then to construct a dogma from it. In so doing it has weakened the force of the fact that all these expressions mean something which cannot be measured by ordinary standards at all. On the other hand, however, it has rendered a great service to humanity by calling the attention of mankind to this point: it kept the Christian revelation pure, preserving it from becoming tainted with the pagan idea of continuity, avoiding strictly any weakening of the idea of revelation in the sense of a mere phenomenon within the sphere of history. This was the heart of the conflict in the great Trinitarian and Christological controversies of the past; and this is the crux of the problem to-day.

The expression, "Divine Nature," also serves this interest. In this term the common element in all the Christological conceptions of the New Testament is maintained: Christ confronts us all as the One who is Himself God, as One who does not seek God as we do, but who brings God to us, as One who does not tremble before the judgment of God, but who knows that He is Himself on the side of the Judge of the whole world, not as One who must endeavour to enter into the Kingdom of God, but as One who in His own Person brings in the Kingdom, even though in a hidden way. He is One who descends to earth, instead of ascending to heaven like the rest of us. He is not One who has to make up His mind, but is One who is the focal point of all decision, the "only begotten," the "only" Son of God.

Every attempt to destroy this quality of His Being, which is defined in the "Two Natures" doctrine, weakens and finally completely destroys the scriptural belief in revelation. Thus we are forced to this conclusion: If Christ really is the revelation of God, in the same way as the prophetic Word is the revelation of God, save that He is the Word in Person, making known the Will and Mind of God through Himself, instead of through a merely spoken word, then in His own nature He is God. For He who reveals the Proper Name of God is Himself God. He who brings to us the secret mystery of God, the mystery which apart from His coming would be for ever hidden from our sight, is indeed supra-mundane and supra-human; His place is "yonder," where God is; His "Nature" is as Divine as ours is human; in the mystery of His Person the secret of the personality of God is revealed; yet such a revelation is indeed wholly beyond our understanding. He is not a creature, but is Himself the Creator.

The Modern Interpretation of the Dogma of the Divine Nature of Christ

The present exposition of this theme is deliberately and uncompromisingly opposed to the modern conception of this dogma introduced by Ritschl and Harnack. It is my aim to prove that this modern view is a disastrous misunderstanding; and I shall try to prove this statement by a renewed study of the meaning of the ancient doctrine of the Early Church. The central point of the controversy is the interpretation of the doctrine of the deity of Christ, or to put it more exactly, of the divine nature of the Redeemer. The preceding chapters, which are of a positive character, are designed to prepare the way for a reinterpretation of the ecclesiastical doctrine on right lines; it would therefore need to be completed by a critical and controversial discussion of the views of recent historians of doctrine. But it would be impossible to do this within the limits of this work, so I will confine my attention to one example, trying to show how at one single point the modern history of dogma has changed the meaning of the doctrine of the Early Church, to such an extent that finally, with some hope of success, it can be set up in opposition to the message of the New Testament. I choose the doctrine of Irenaeus for several reasons. First of all, because Irenaeus may be described as the first great theologian of the Early Church; indeed, he has a greater right than any other to the title of the founder of the theology of the Church. All the others build on the foundation which he has laid. Further, in spite of the fact that his extant writings are few in number, he may be described as the most fertile and creative of the early theologians, for in his writings he gathers up the whole wealth of the New Testament witness to Christ, Johannine as well as Pauline, the specifically New Testament elements as well as those which are drawn from the Bible as a whole, combining them into a unity, in a way which was possibly never equalled until the time of Luther. Thirdly, the doctrine of the Word and the Person of Christ are so closely connected in his thought that his Christology is always soteriological, and his soteriology is always Christological, so that, here, if anywhere, the accusation that the ecclesiastical doctrine of Christ was deflected into the paths of metaphysical speculation can be refuted. And, finally, he is above all remarkable in this, that among the representatives of the theology of the Reformation it was the strictly "Reformed" (Calvinistic) thinkers in particular who revived the specific and fundamental ideas of Irenaeus, in order to make clear theologically the renewed scriptural understanding of the divine revelation of salvation. This circumstance would in itself necessarily make us surprised to hear the argument that Irenaeus is a typical representative of the ancient Greek interpretation of salvation;[1] it would make us suspect the suggestion that the doctrine of Irenaeus is derived from the Hellenistic "realistic Gnosis,"[2] and from an intellectual ethical form of Rationalism, such as is supposed to have been represented by the Apologists.[3] The line of argument represented by Ritschl and Harnack, which dominates the whole of the modern history of dogma, can be summed up in the following theses:

(1) (*Fundamental argument*): The dogma of the Early Church is dominated by a "physical" (also "magical," "mystical," "naturalistic," "mechanical") conception of salvation. Salva-

---

[1] It is true that in Harnack's treatment of the subject we notice that he only brings his charge of naturalism against Irenaeus's doctrine of redemption with certain reserves. In one place he says (*Lehrbuch der Dogmengeschichte*, I, p. 562) that here and there in his main doctrine Irenaeus "verges on" "soteriological naturalism." But what Harnack really means by this becomes clear not only from his treatment of the subject as a whole, but also by the way in which he argues from this very passage that Irenaeus does not really "fall into" Naturalism: firstly, because he supplements his doctrine of the Incarnation with that of the Atoning Work of Christ by the use of Pauline ideas, and secondly, because he also employs the rationalistic-moralistic ideas of the Apologists. But "for Irenaeus the centre of gravity always lies already (!) in the reflection that Christianity is real redemption, that is, that the highest good imparted by Christianity is the deification of human nature through the gift of immortality." Thus the specific doctrine of Irenaeus is the general Greek naturalistic doctrine (I, p. 560).

[2] Harnack, loc. cit., I, p. 593, and in several other passages.

[3] Ibid., loc. cit., especially pp. 588 ff.

tion is a "redemption which is achieved in a physico-magical manner by means of the Incarnation";[1] the doctrine of salvation is "the idea of the deification of the children of Adam as a mechanical result of the Incarnation."[2] "Redemption, as seen in its ultimate effect, was conceived to be the abrogation of the natural state by a miraculous transformation of our nature," "the supreme Good was definitely distinguished from the morally Good," "this does not contain the idea of atonement, for atonement can only be conceived where the division between God and man is regarded as an opposition of the will."[3]

(2) (*Proof from the effect of salvation*): The effect of salvation is characterized by the watchwords: ἀθανασία, φάρμακον ἀθανασίας (also ἀφθαρσία), θεοποίησις—thus immortality and the deification of nature as a "physical condition."[4] Therefore the desire for salvation centres round deliverance from death as the result of sin, rather than from sin itself.[5] The Ignatian description of the Eucharist as the φάρμακον ἀθανασίας is often quoted as an instance of this materialistic view of salvation, as a proof "that the Lord's Supper, in some way or another, communicates ἀφθαρσία in a physical manner," and passages from Justin and Irenaeus are also quoted in which the Eucharist is described as "heavenly Food."[6]

(3) (*Proof from the cause of salvation*): To this physical effect of salvation there corresponds the equally physical cause of salvation, namely the Incarnation of the Son of God or the Logos, which, as has already been said, includes within itself the "idea of the deification of the sons of Adam as a mechanical result of the Incarnation"; by the fact that the God-Man unites Himself physically with human nature, this human nature itself is "mechanically," automatically deified.

(4) (*Inference from the Work to the Person of Christ*): Hence it is important for us to realize that Christ Himself is of divine nature, which is thus combined with human nature in the Person of the Mediator. It is true that "the explicit formula of two substances or natures in Christ is not stated by

[1] Loc. cit., p. 545.   [2] Loc. cit., p. 562.   [3] *D.G.*, II, p. 47.
[4] *D.G.*, I, p. 561.   [5] Loc. cit., pp. 591 ff.
[6] Loofs: *Dogmengeschichte*, pp. 101, 145, 147.

251

Irenaeus,"[1] but even "Irenaeus could not persuade himself, against his own better judgment, to divide the *one* Jesus Christ after the manner of the Gnostics";[2] he thus prepared the way for the "Two Natures" doctrine, which was already fully developed in Tertullian.[3]

(5) (*Explanation of the Doctrinal Complex of Irenaeus*): In addition to this Gnostic-realistic, physical doctrine of salvation, which absolutely constitutes the heart of the theology of Irenaeus, as of later dogma—even when the dogma presents itself as a result of various compromises—there are also two other series of ideas in Irenaeus[4]: the moralistic rationalism of the Apologists and a mass of Biblical material loosely connected with it, as, for example, the doctrine of the reconciliation of God which "is proved wholly by passages of Scripture,"[5] especially Pauline passages, about which, however, it is suggested that there can be little idea that Irenaeus shows "any real understanding of Paulinism."[6] Above all, the rationalistic moralistic elements are most evident in the doctrine of the Primitive State; they are grouped round the view that freedom is designated as the goal of the act of Christ, and on the other hand that Christ is described as the Teacher.[7] These inconsistencies, however, do not belong only to the system of Irenaeus, but, although they are "absolutely evident," "they have never been removed and have not been permitted to be removed from the ecclesiastical doctrine of later centuries; hence the attitude of Irenaeus is here typical" (p. 588). It is curious that Harnack, who has a high opinion of the intellectual power of ecclesiastical theologians like Augustine, Athanasius, Gregory of Nyssa, and others, passes so easily over the circumstance, that even in the time of the Reformation it was precisely these "inconsistencies" which were maintained with fervour, and were even, by a retrospective movement, produced anew. This leads us to a critical revision of the theses of Harnack. We will begin with a general

---

[1] Harnack, loc. cit., I, p. 600.
[2] Harnack: *Dogmengeschichte im Grundriss*, p. 119.
[3] *D.G.*, I, p. 601.   [4] Loc. cit., pp. 562–4, 609–11.
[5] Loc. cit., p. 611.   [6] Loofs, loc. cit., p. 148.
[7] Harnack, loc. cit., pp. 588–92.

thesis: His first thesis is wrong; hence all the others are wrong.[1]

(1) The first thesis—which determines all the others—is based upon the presupposition that this disjunction exists: either ethical or physical. This disjunction does not exist, because the antithesis between Nature and Spirit is not, as modern Idealistic theological thought maintains, the really serious antithesis, but it is merely a relative distinction subordinate to the true antithesis between God and the creature. Spirit and Nature are the two forms of creaturely existence which are willed by God. It is true, of course, that through sin their mutual relation is one of hostility instead of vital tension; but the real reason for their hostility does not lie between them but above them, that is, both sin, and also the possibility of its removal, redemption. Therefore all that the Bible says about God and His revelation of salvation lies beyond this antithesis between the physical and the ethical, between Nature and Spirit. This antithesis between the physical and the ethical (mental), between knowledge and morality, is that of Idealism. The Christian faith presents us with the antithesis between God and the world, Faith and Reason (including the moral element), the Divine Nature and the nature of the creature, in which all that is now called "world" and "creature" is also defined as the realm of sin. The reason why Harnack confuses this Idealistic antithesis with the Christian one—and in so doing misinterprets the actual Christian conceptions—is this: he is influenced by the Ritschlian character of his theology, in which an ethical rationalism, a one-sided rational idea of God, a conception of revelation and salvation has replaced the Christian faith in revelation as an improved form of Christian thought (see above, Chapter II). It is this reinterpretation of the antithesis which also determines not only his interpretation of the Bible but also of dogma. The Christian statements all refer to situations which lie on the

[1] In saying this we have no desire to cast any doubt at all upon the great value of the services rendered by Harnack and his school in the sphere of research into the history of dogma; as an expert in dogma and as a scholar Harnack is far beyond all praise of ours. But as an *interpreter* of dogma he betrays very clearly the limitations of the theological school of Ritschl.

further side of the antithesis between the physical and the ethical, beyond Nature and Spirit in the moralistic Idealistic sense. The relation of the Creator to the world is not—as Harnack and Ritschl conceive it[1]—a question of cosmology, but of faith and salvation. Revelation and salvation are not moral terms; faith is not a moral form of behaviour. This does not mean, however, that they are in any sense "physical"; indeed, they are absolutely different from the creaturely element which is determined by this relative contrast: they mean that the barrier of the "creaturely" has been broken down by the advent of God; they mean the restoration of a new being by redemption, and the creation of a new subjectivity in faith. This is why the Christian articles of faith are stated in two ways; those who do not know that they are really one, that is, those who think in terms of the relative contrast between Nature and Spirit, regard them as inconsistencies. "Ethical" terms alternate with "natural" terms, those which describe Being alternate with those which describe a certain disposition, "mystical" terms alternate with "rationalistic" ones. And yet the real meaning is never anything natural, ethical, mystical, rational at all, but that third element in faith which includes both knowledge and disposition of the will, being and will, possession and movement. We find this distinction in the New Testament, within the Pauline doctrines; we find it, however, above all in the difference of emphasis between John and Paul, between the expressions which describe Christ as the bringer of life, light, eternity, being-in-God, and those which describe Him as the bringer of reconciliation, grace, and resurrection; at one time the writer will speak almost entirely of His Being and of the Incarnation of the Word, and at another all the emphasis will be laid upon His atoning work through His death. That there are no inconsistencies here but merely two ways of expressing the same thing, will become clear in the course of this work. All that can be done here is to show briefly some particular misunderstandings of the interpretations of Irenaeus, as they are determined by that fundamental misunderstanding.

[1] Cf. with Irenaeus's doctrine of Christ as the Word of Creation, Harnack, I, p. 583.

(2) The second thesis, about the "physical" effect of salvation, itself contradicts many of Harnack's other statements about Irenaeus. For instance, is salvation, which is created objectively through the Incarnation, subjectively mediated? If there really were a physical effect there could be no subjective mediation at all. Salvation would not be connected with faith, but it would become the portion of every human being quite naturally, "mechanically" as Harnack says. That there can be no question of such an idea in Irenaeus, Harnack himself gives evidence. Salvation is the portion of believers only.[1]

---

[1] Harnack hardly gives any idea that Irenaeus has not only a doctrine of the Incarnation but also a doctrine of faith, of the Spirit, and of the good works which are the results of faith and the Spirit, by which also the doctrine of the Church is determined. Irenaeus shows clearly that the effect of the Incarnation is not physical when he says distinctly in V, 10, 2: "*homo per fidem insertus et assumens spiritum dei, substantiam quidem carnis non amittit, qualitatem autem fructus operum immutat.*" "But as many as feared God, and were anxious about His law, these ran to Christ and were all saved." (IV, 2, 7.) Cf. also the detailed arguments about the faith of Abraham in IV, 5. We tend to forget that the Fathers of the Church had a very different task from that of the Reformers; it was their duty to secure the objective aspect of the Gospel against false doctrines, whereas the Reformers had to secure the subjective aspect. The Fathers discharged their duty so excellently that the Reformers were able simply to take over their work without having to lay the foundation afresh. Therefore when Seeberg, in an otherwise penetrating estimate of Irenaeus, says: "On the other hand his mind was unable to grasp the meaning of the idea of justification" (*Lehrbuch der Dogmengeschichte*, I, p. 434), he goes too far. If one looks at individual statements of Irenaeus and measures them by the standard of the Reformers, then doubtless Seeberg's opinion is correct. But if we take into account the fact that Irenaeus was fighting on a front which differed totally from that of the Reformers and of Paul, and that, on the other hand, even the Reformers when they were fighting against other errors than that of the "righteousness of works" used expressions absolutely similar to those used by Irenaeus, and finally, when we examine the intention of Irenaeus as a whole, which is directed wholly towards the objective establishment of salvation in Christ, then it seems as though Seeberg's view may be unjust to this Father of the Church. Perhaps it would be more correct to say that Irenaeus tends to formulate his ideas about the subjective aspect of faith somewhat carelessly, so that it is difficult to discern clearly what he really thought about the doctrine of justification, and that his expressions are open to misconstruction in detail, so that we might conclude that he means the *infusio gratiae.*

Secondly, and above all, it is a future gift. It consists in a hope.[1] In so far, however, as it is present, it consists in faith and in personal fellowship with God and Christ, which is given in faith, and through this with the believers in the Church. It is the Spirit of God, "working the will of the Father in them, and renewing them from their old habits into the newness of Christ,"[2] who "unites us with God,"[3] the Spirit whom "the Lord poured out, for the union and communion of God and man."[4] It is for us "through faith to receive the Spirit of God into our hearts."[5] To Harnack this faith seems to be something quite secondary—just *fides quae creditur*—it "simply (!) embraces the correct perception of the nature of the incarnate Logos, because this perception of faith includes the assured hope of a change of human nature analogous to the divinity of Jesus Christ, and therewith everything worth striving for."[6] But to one who is not already prejudiced by the Schleiermacher-Ritschlian objection to the *fides quae creditur*, namely the belief in the divinely revealed Word, the statements of Irenaeus about the faith will seem in essentials to be thoroughly evangelical, indeed Pauline, though they may perhaps lack some of the existential personal energy and point of similar statements by Luther or Calvin. We must not forget that it is

[1] It is almost incomprehensible, and can, indeed, only be understood when we remember the wholly non-eschatological character of the thought represented by the Ritschlian theology, that Harnack does not perceive the necessary connection between the doctrine of Irenaeus on the Incarnation and his "recapitulation" theory, and his eschatology; Harnack regards the latter as an "archaic relic, which is absolutely opposed to his speculative manner of reflection on redemption" (I, p. 615). Actually, on the contrary, the whole doctrine of "recapitulation" is eschatological, like the thought of Scripture as a whole: the gulf which Christ bridges in the Atonement is only finally closed by redemption. But this redemption is the fulfilment of all things in the Return of Christ. It is exactly the same in the teaching of the Reformers. To the extent in which they set the act of Atonement in Christ at the centre of Faith, they are eschatological, and they make no distinction between faith and hope. On this point, see my quotations in *Die Mystik und das Wort*, pp. 271 ff. What Harnack says about a "double conception of Christ which extends back to the Apostolic Age itself" is based upon a complete misunderstanding of Christian eschatology as well as of the "Pauline" faith in redemption. Both mean exactly the same thing.

[2] III, 17, 1.   [3] III, 17, 2.   [4] V, 1, 1.
[5] V, 9, 2.   [6] Loc. cit., II, p. 48.

the Word which was made flesh, and which is only effectively redeeming in so far as it is perceived. "For to this end the Word of God was made man, and He who is the Son of God, Son of Man, that man, blended with God's Word, and receiving the adoption might become the son of God."[1] It is the knowledge of Christ, faith in that which God in Christ has done, it is the Word preached by the Church and accepted by faith; it is the Holy Spirit, who effects love, a new life, a new will, who, according to Irenaeus, unites us with the Christ who became Man. In all this there is no idea of any physico-mechanical process at all.[2] Moreover, it is not true to say, as Harnack does, that Irenaeus does not possess a perception of sin sufficient for an adequate presupposition for a doctrine of

---

[1] Irenaeus: *Against Heretics*, III, 19, 1.

[2] From among the countless passages which prove how little Irenaeus was thinking in terms of a "mechanical" physical effect of the Incarnation I will give merely a few examples: V, 8, where he is saying that the possession of the Spirit is an effect of the act of reconciliation, "This, however, does not take place by a casting away of the flesh, but by the impartation of the Spirit." "If, therefore, at the present time, having the earnest, we do cry 'Abba Father,' what shall it be when . . .?" But this Spirit must be proved by works of righteousness. "As many as fear God and trust in His Son's advent (to Irenaeus this faith was the most existential thing there is) and who through faith do establish the Spirit of God in their hearts—such men as these shall be properly called both 'pure' and 'spiritual,' etc." (V, 9). Through faith and the Spirit man becomes living and "conformable to the Word of God." "Inasmuch therefore as without the Spirit of God we cannot be saved, the apostle exhorts us through faith and chaste conversation to preserve the Spirit of God." He goes on to prove in detail that the flesh cannot inherit the Kingdom of God, but that all must take place through the Spirit (see V, 9), "For this cause too, did Christ die, that the Gospel covenant being manifested and known to the whole world, might in the first place set free His slaves; and then afterwards . . . might constitute them heirs of His property, when the Spirit possesses them by inheritance." "Unless the Word of God dwell with, and the Spirit of the Father be in you, and if ye shall live frivolously and carelessly as if ye were this only, viz, mere flesh and blood, ye cannot inherit the Kingdom of God." "Now he says that the things which save are the name of our Lord Jesus Christ and the Spirit of our God." We bear the "Image of Him who is from heaven" in so far as it is true of us that "ye have been washed, but ye have been sanctified, but ye have been justified in the name of our Lord Jesus Christ and in the Spirit of our God" (V, 8–11). "To believe in Him is to do His will" (IV, 6, 5).

atonement. For Irenaeus also the Fall is the real sin (none of
the doctors of the Early Church, not even Augustine, has such
a deep sense of the fact that the sin of Adam is the real sin of
us all), and that this sin is disobedience against God.[1] Hence
the obedience of Christ is the act of atonement, because it
was our disobedience which created the gulf. It is only for this
reason that Irenaeus lays such stress on the original and
determinative freedom of man—to such an extent that Harnack
suspects him of being a moralistic Rationalist—namely, in
order that the Fall should appear to be really an act of will,
of disobedience, and not as Fate. And although Irenaeus,
like the Reformers, in his doctrine of sin lays the main emphasis
upon the present sinful nature (of man), the sinfulness of the
flesh, yet he does not omit to point out that this sinful nature
works out in the form of "sins."[2] The fact that (like Paul
and John) he describes this condition in particular as death—
death out of which the soul escapes through the spirit, which
is thus not merely death in the sense of physical corruption—
does not imply the naturalism[3] of his conception of sin; on
the contrary, it is a sign of its evangelical depth. "Communion
with God is life. . . . Separation from God is death."[4]

(3) The ultimate cause of all misunderstanding lies in the
misinterpretation of the doctrine of the Incarnation. Harnack
confuses the unique character of that which took place in
Christ with a magical objectivity. (This argument ought to
be applied equally to the death of Christ as well as to the
Incarnation.) The advent of God the Word in the flesh is
said to be a physical event, although in the significant passages
in question Irenaeus says distinctly not only that it proceeds
from the love of God, but that it also reveals the love of God,
that it brings out into the light the great plan of salvation
and the will of God, "in order that all may in Him see the
Father, for that which is invisible of the Son is the Father,

---

[1] Cf. for instance: "Those persons therefore who have apostatized from
the light given by the Father, and transgressed the law of liberty, have done
so through their own fault . . . so that they do themselves become the cause
to themselves that they are destitute of light, and do inhabit darkness"
(IV, 39, 3 and 4).   [2] E.g., IV, 27; V, 498.
[3] Harnack, loc. cit., p. 594.   [4] V, 27, 2.

and that which is visible of the Father is the Son."[1] "The Hand of God which formed us in the beginning—and now forms us in the womb, the same in the last times sought us out when we were lost, gaining His own lost sheep, and, taking it upon His Shoulders, with gratulation restoring it to the troop of life."[2] This "union between God and man" should be "received into our hearts through faith." To Irenaeus, as to the Bible, the Incarnation means the coming of God to man; to him the Being, the Person of the Son of God, according to its divine constitution, is as important as His Work, as it was to the Reformers.

It is also quite wrong to say that Irenaeus regarded the Incarnation by itself, severed from the life of the Saviour, severed from the Death and the Resurrection of Christ, as the divine act of salvation. It is due to a complete misunderstanding of the doctrine of the Incarnation that Harnack is able to say that "as the consequence of dogmatic thought," "only the manifestation in the flesh . . . but not a special work of Christ"[3] can have significance. This statement prescribes what Irenaeus is supposed to have regarded as important, but Harnack has failed to listen to what Irenaeus really says, and to find out what actually did seem important to him, and indeed this is due to a misunderstanding of his doctrine of the Incarnation.

Like Paul in his classical passage in the Epistle to the Philippians, Irenaeus also regards the Incarnation and the Death on the Cross as a divine-human movement of humiliation, and, like Paul, Irenaeus looks at this from the point of view of the obedience of the Son of God. But those who have no understanding of the Incarnation, who regard the Cross as a moral act of the human Jesus, must inevitably see these two ideas falling asunder never to be united—the one is ethical, the other physical. In the teaching of Irenaeus, however, this is not the case, any more than it is in the New Testament itself. The other charge brought against Irenaeus is that of Rationalism, because he calls Christ the Teacher (this is supposed to be due to the influence of the Apologists). But if we examine the passage quoted by Harnack a little more closely we find

[1] IV, 6, 6.   [2] V, 15, 2.   [3] *D.G.*, I, p. 610.

259

that not a trace of Rationalism remains. Here is one of these passages:[1] "No otherwise could we learn to know who God is if our Teacher, the Word (the Logos)[2] had not become Man. For no man could tell us anything about the Father, save His own Word." (Note how very clearly Irenaeus sees what it means to be the Logos: "what God has to say to us.") "Also we could not otherwise learn it, unless we were to see our Teacher, and hear His Voice with our ears, in order that we might become imitators of His actions and those who fulfil His words, who have fellowship with Him," etc.[3] Then follows a very powerful passage about atonement through the blood of Christ. Another passage which Harnack quotes as evidence of the "apologetic-moralistic" line of argument in Irenaeus is "He restored freedom . . . He re-created the human race". what on earth has this to do with moralism? But it must be

[1] Loc. cit., p. 592.

[2] On this point, see the particularly important passage in Book 2, Chapter XIII: "God Himself . . . is the Word"—*verbum ipse Deus*. The Word is not a mythological personality, but God Himself, in His revealed aspect: "And His Word knows what His Father is, as far as regards us, invisible and infinite; and since He cannot be declared (by anyone else), He does Himself declare Him to us; and on the other hand it is the Father alone who knows His own Word. . . . Wherefore the Son reveals the knowledge of the Father through His own manifestation. For the manifestation of the Son is the knowledge of the Father; for all things are manifested through the Word. . . . For this purpose did the Father reveal the Son, that through His instrumentality He might be manifested to all, and might receive those righteous ones who believe in Him into incorruption and everlasting enjoyment" (IV, 6, 3 and 5). Therefore "fellowship with God is to know God" (IV, 20, 5). "But as regards His love. He is always known through Him by whose means He ordained all things; now this is His Word, our Lord Jesus Christ, who in the last times was made a man among men . . ." in order that He "although beyond comprehension and boundless and invisible, rendered Himself visible and comprehensible, and within the capacity of those who believe, that He might vivify those who receive and behold Him through faith." The creature "learns everything from His Word, that there is a Father who embraces all things." "The redemption through the Son is the redemption through the Word of revelation" (cf. IV, 20, 7). The Incarnation can only be redeeming in so far as it is revealing, thus in so far as it creates faith; the Incarnation means the reality, the Word, the eternal Truth, and both in unity the real revelation of God (cf. the penetrating statements of Seeberg, loc. cit., pp. 405 ff.).

[3] V, 1, 1.

understood thus if the other series of expressions are regarded as magical and physical. If we want to know what ethical Rationalism means we can read a certain book on the *Essence of Christianity*, but not Irenaeus! We need not be surprised, after all this, to find that finally the whole doctrine of the second Adam,[1] in spite of 1 Cor. xv, is ascribed to the influence of the rationalistic Apologists, and declared to be impossible to combine with the doctrine of the Incarnation.

(4) At this point it is obvious that the fourth argument cannot be sustained: namely, that the doctrine of the "Two Natures" drags faith in Christ down to a naturalistic level. Anyone who knows with what ardour a man like Luther, in particular, clung to the doctrine of the Divine Nature of Christ,[2] needs no further proofs from Irenaeus. To Irenaeus "Nature" means that which belongs to the existence of God and to the existence of man. Thus it means "God Himself," and "man himself." That God Himself in Christ came to man and was not merely a man with a divinely good and kind disposition; and that He really came to man, and did not merely speak to him, this is what Irenaeus means, in the same sense as Paul, John, Luther, and Calvin. *Vere homo, vere deus.* Nothing different is intended, but this certainly without moralistic perversions, as divine—and hence precisely not physical but personal—"Being," not in the sense of "value," or disposition. Few doctors of the Church have also taken the humanity of Christ as seriously as Irenaeus—and in this, too, he stands

---

[1] Harnack has not the least understanding of the "mystical Adam-Christ-speculation." Therefore he makes it the antithesis of the Doctrine of the Primitive State in Irenaeus (pp. 593 ff.), whereas in reality both are most closely connected with each other. Although he knows that "Paul also was familiar with this idea" (p. 596) he thinks that "Irenaeus was preserved from the logical inference of an *apokatastasis* of all individual human beings by his ethical views" (p. 596). How everything here falls asunder which in faith—and hence also in the teaching of Irenaeus—is a necessary and connected unity! Irenaeus has as little of an "Adam-Christ-speculation" as Paul; for what is here meant is that in Christ the injury caused by the Fall has been made good; that is, the central statement of the Christian faith. Only to unbelief, which does not perceive the inner necessity for this connection, can this be regarded as "speculation." To faith, as once more we see most plainly in Luther, this is the very essence of the faith itself.   [2] See above, p. 239.

very close to the Reformers—yet few, on the other hand, have defended the *vere deus* as unconditionally against all modifications of any kind.

(5) After all this, there is nothing left to say about the fifth argument. In spite of the fact that in the formal sense Irenaeus was not a systematic theologian, yet—like Luther—he was a systematic theologian of the first rank, indeed, the greatest in the Early Church, if this is what it means to be a systematic theologian: to perceive connections between truths, and to know which belongs to which. No other thinker was able to weld ideas together which others allowed to slip as he was able to do, not even Augustine or Athanasius. But he did not take any trouble to articulate into a theological system the sets of ideas which were connected with their own groups; this cannot have been in the least accidental, any more than it was in the mind which is so nearly akin to his, that of Luther.[1]

The conclusions we have drawn from one example might be applied equally well to all the standard ecclesiastical teachers of theology, although with certain differences. The

[1] This would be the point at which to define one's position with regard to Bousset's original and often more pointed interpretation of the thought of Irenaeus (*Kyrios Christos*, pp. 333–62). In many sections of this book we could find material to controvert the statements of Harnack (for instance, this passage dealing with the main thesis of Harnack: "Still we ought not to speak of an undue emphasis on nature in Irenaeus's theory of redemption," p. 338); but on the whole we see in it, as in Bousset's history in general, a destructive criticism which goes still further, which is itself so remote from the subject that to it all that is an inner unity seems to be a mosaic of the most heterogeneous historical and traditional material. To follow out in detail the analyses which at first sight appear so searching and keen but which in reality only touch the external surface of the question, and to provide an apt interpretation showing how the supposed antithesis between the theology of Irenaeus and of Paul can be reconciled, by one which does not affect the outer fringe of the subject only, would take us too far afield. Yet I would like to emphasize very strongly that I do not regard the work of historians of this kind—namely of those who possess no inner relation to the subject, and therefore cannot really understand it—as useless on that account. Just because their attitude is so remote and objective they often serve a right understanding better than those who meet the question half-way. Thus few have done more to prepare the way for the understanding of the Christian confession of the earliest forms of Christianity than the author of the *Kyrios Christos*, who perhaps among all modern theologians was furthest away from it.

fundamental structure of thought, the meaning of the Logos, of the Incarnation, and its necessary union with the doctrine of the Cross, the meaning of the knowledge of the faith and of the Church is exactly the same in all essential points in an Athanasius as it is in an Irenaeus. Differences do exist, but they concern only individual formulas, and they can mostly be explained from the difference in the historical environment against which the Faith had to explain itself theologically. In Athanasius also there can be no question of a naturalistic doctrine of redemption. The Word came down to us from heaven "in order that as It is the Father's Word and Wisdom so also It might become to us holiness itself, life itself, the Door, the Shepherd, the Way, the King, the Leader, and finally the Saviour and Life-maker, the Light and the Providence of all." It would be quite easy to match every statement of Athanasius with an exact parallel from our own Reformers, which would prove indubitably that we are here concerned with the inmost sanctuary of our faith, with that which can only be redeeming truth in so far as it is appropriated in the most personal form of faith. Where, however, it is not understood what the "Word" means, and what is meant by the Incarnation of the Word, it is almost unavoidable that this unique event should be confused with a physical or magical event, and thus be contrasted with the inwardness of the moral temper. Yet this misunderstanding is not due to the theology of the Church Fathers, but to the Rationalism of their modern interpreters.

This is essentially the position, not only with regard to Irenaeus, but the ecclesiastical doctrine of Christ as a whole; and this is what lies behind the "interpretation" of this doctrine by Harnack. In spite of his incomparable knowledge of the material, and of the admirable way in which his knowledge is used to throw light upon many points, as a whole his interpretation is a complete and absolute misunderstanding, caused by a fundamentally erroneous conception of the Gospel. At the same time we would not deny that the Ritschlian-Harnack theory that dogma has been influenced by Greek thought is based upon much sound observation. It is not *sine fundamento in re*. But it does not concern—as Harnack thinks it does—the decisive fundamental conceptions of Christian dogma (the doctrine of the Logos, the doctrine of the Two Natures and the doctrine of the Trinity); rather these have been precisely the necessary methods of thought which have prevented the Christian message from coming too fully under Greek influence. The modern Rationalism of a Ritschl or a Harnack is far more Greek than the doctrines of Irenaeus, Athanasius, and Cyril. For what these modern teachers mean is the Idea (that is the moral idea) in concrete historical garb, whereas all the Fathers of the Church meant to express the uniqueness of the revelation of Christ, which is as contrary to the "ethical" as it is to the "physical" interpretation of this doctrine.

CHAPTER IX

THE DIVINE PERSON

(i)

THE doctrine of the divine nature of the Mediator necessarily implies the rejection of all attempts to make the Revealer merely human; indeed, as we look back at some of the modern teaching of recent years we might say it implies the rejection of all ideas of religious hero-worship. Let us on no account make an historical personality an object of reverence. Although it is true that all that is covered by the term "historical personality" belongs to the realm of Divine Creation, it still belongs to the realm of the creature which has fallen away from God. An "historical personality" means a vessel for the redeeming power of God, but it is not itself the redeeming content. If Christ is to be worshipped as divine, then certainly He is not to be worshipped as an "historical personality," for this would be to idolize a creature—in other words, idolatry—but His claim to be an object of worship lies in His Divine Nature. If we are merely concerned with His "personality," all we mean is summed up in His own words: "Why callest thou Me good? There is none good save one, even God."

What we call "personality" belongs to the sphere of historical perception. History is the arena in which personalities play their part. Anyone who wishes to be a good historian and a good biographer must have a fine sense for the personal element in general and a real and penetrating understanding of one personality. Personality is the flowering of humanity. In a very special sense this is true of the religious-ethical personality, of the inner life. Personal religious-ethical experience constitutes the inmost line of history; it is no less than this—but really it is also no more; it is never revelation, or redemption. For in the inmost depths of personality there dwells not God, but sin; sin, however, could not exist apart from consciousness of God; indeed, the stronger the consciousness of God the deeper is the consciousness of sin. But for this

very reason the power of redemption does not reside within
personality. An "historical personality," with its genuinely
personal, ethical-religious life, with all that can be described
as its "inner" life, can never constitute a revelation. For
revelation is quite remote from this whole plane of existence;
genuine revelation is something totally different. It is a
prophetic word from beyond this human and personal plane
of existence. And if the revelation belongs to a higher category
than this "word," then it belongs to the realm of Divine Being,
Divine Nature, Divine Authority. It lies behind the whole
realm of personality, even behind the "interior life" of Jesus,
regarded as the mystery of the Divine-Human Person, the
Divine Nature of this human personality.

We may therefore assume that personality, in our human,
historical sense of the word, belongs to the humanity of the
Son of God, not to His deity. Personality—as the element
which is accessible to everyone—is the human aspect of His
Person which can be known by every good historian; it is the
incognito of His deity, which, on the contrary, cannot be
known by the good historian, but can only be known by those
to whom it is "given." His personality, probably even His
ethical and religious personality, has been more or less
known by all; even our classical writers, who rightly recognized
that they did not hold the Christian faith, knew this. They
did not perceive the mystery of His Person, the "only begotten Son," His Divine Nature and authority, the revelation.
But they were honest enough to acknowledge this difference
themselves, hence they did not regard themselves as believing Christians. The discredit for the confusion of thought
which exists was due, not to them, but to the theologians.
The process by which this was achieved was the struggle to
throw over the doctrine of the Divine Nature of Christ, and
the attempt to identify the "historical personality" with
revelation.

Now, however, a very curious situation has arisen, to which
we must turn our attention. This modern conception of
personality—which believes it is obliged to fight against the
doctrine of the "Two Natures" as "non-personal," metaphysically material—distinctly defines the relation between

ourselves and Christ in comparatively impersonal terms: He is, namely, only the Bearer of the Idea, or of the principle. "In Him for the first time the Idea took shape." This is the fate of the purely historical human conception; no efforts to evade this destiny will ever succeed. In the struggle between the Idea and personality, personality, as the weaker party, has been defeated. For the Idea possesses the quality of absoluteness, and personality does not. The function of personality is simply to illustrate and "form" the Idea. Although we may intensify the expressions which reverence personality as much as we will, it will still remain true that the essential value of the historical personality consists in its conformity to the general principle. Only with the aid of the principle can personality attain its highest intellectual and spiritual significance; it lives by the power of the Idea. For from the historical point of view man is the Idea of humanity, that is, even the greatest personality is simply the expression of universal humanity, which for that very reason iš superior to personality. Thus from this point of view even Jesus is no more than the highest personal expression of the Idea of love, or "fidelity to vocation," or piety. He may be its discoverer, or its most perfect representative: but more than this He cannot be. Hence ultimately He has no independence apart from the Idea; He remains its historical "vehicle," to use the language of the Liberal theologians of the older school.

But can "person" have any other than this human meaning, with its reference to the Idea? It is evident that within the sphere of history and humanity no other meaning is possible. In the sphere of revelation, however, *through* revelation, it has another meaning. If Jesus Christ is the Revealer, in the Christian sense of the word, if He is the Word from "yonder," then He is the Revealer, the Word, *not* as the bearer of an Idea, but as a Person: not as a "personality" in the historical sense, but as the authority, as the most intensely personal Word of God. But the meaning of "Person" in this respect cannot be understood from a general conception of persons or of personality, but only through faith. For faith alone knows the meaning of the mystery of the Person or the authority of the Revealer. Here alone does the word "Person" attain its

267

full meaning. For here "Person" means simply the divine personality, the personal God. The personal God is He who is only recognized as God in the personal revelation, the God who is known, because He makes known His Proper Name, His mystery, nothing that forms part of any "conception of God"—the God to whom our only attitude can be one of faith and trust.

(ii)

Apart from this revelation God is always known only impersonally. For He is known on the basis of the Idea, from the point of view of the world, from the point of view of the human mind, from the point of view of that which God has imparted to the world of Himself in the Creation. But that which we can thus discover for ourselves, in a kind of ascending scale, is not the Proper Name of God. Since God is perceived in continuity with the world and man—and all perception of God apart from revelation is perception of this kind, of His continuity with the world and with the self—He is perceived only in that which is communicable, according to His immanent presence in the world : this means that He is not perceived as He is in Himself; "the state of His own mind"[1] remains an unknown mystery.

---

[1] Ritschl has often been praised for laying so much stress on Melanchthon's statement (so typical of the thought of the Reformation) : "*hoc est Christum cognoscere, beneficia eius cognoscere,*" by rejecting all "speculations" about the inner nature of God, and confining himself wholly to the knowledge of His work in Christ (see, for instance, the *Dogmatik* of *Nitzsch-Stephan*, II, pp. 515, 520, 541). This view contains a fatal error. Luther used certainly to warn people against "useless" and "high speculations"; but he meant something quite different from the view of the modern Historical Positivists; he was contrasting "speculation" with "revelation," for it is revelation alone which discloses to us the inward nature of God which we could not deduce from His works, God as He is in Himself, the secret of God. "*Sed docemus postea ex scriptura,* what God is in Himself . . . *quid est deus in seipso* . . . *quid* He is in Himself . . . *deus vult etiam ut agnoscamus eum etiam intra* . . . which He is inwardly." This is the point at issue which distinguishes the revelation of Scripture from Natural Theology (*W.A.*, 49, p. 238). What Ritschl calls the Christian revelation, Luther would put without hesitation under the heading of Natural Theology. Luther, indeed, does not disclaim interest

This knowledge of God, then, is an impersonal, universal conception, in which God is regarded as the "ground" of the world, the "ground" of the soul, the Logos in the philosophical sense, the universe, the "All" of the mystic. The neutral terms in which mysticism and Idealism are accustomed to express their conception of God are not accidental. The personal, the "living" God is not this kind of God; He is the God who names His own Name, the God who reveals Himself. He alone is the Creator God, because He alone is the One who stands over against the world and man. The God who is known in continuity with the self and the world may be the "ground" of the world, but He is not the world Creator. For in order to know the world Creator we must renounce all ideas of continuity between Him and the world idea—even with the Moral Law. Creation means that there is an absolute barrier between God and the world. In so far as God is the Creator and Lord of the world—the Creator of the world who made it out of nothing—it is impossible to know Him through the world itself. The God who can be known through the world is always merely the Demiurge,[1] the maker of the world, or the world's "ground," its "Necessary Being" as the Schoolmen rightly express it. But none of these expressions describe the living God of faith, the personal God, who created the world because He willed it, and as He willed.

in the Trinitarian Idea of God, nor in the doctrine of the Divine and the Human Natures in Christ—rather his whole interest of faith is directed towards these mysteries—but he does disclaim interest in the speculative interpretation and metaphysical questions of "how" this and that came to be, with which he was familiar, *ad nauseam*, through Scholasticism. On this point, see Theodosius Harnack, *Luthers Theologie*, I, pp. 58 ff., 266 ff.

[1] The Aristotelian metaphysic which underlies the dogmatic teaching of A. Schlatter, would suit a Catholic dogmatic system better than a Protestant one. Can we really disregard as insignificant the Kantian statement that from the world itself we can only deduce a Demiurge but never the God who is sublimely above the world? The fact that the Christian can grasp God in the world through faith is something quite different—as Calvin points out in the early chapters of the *Institutio*. That is the scriptural conception which also corresponds to the historical reality. If God could be known from the world, then there would be no longer any search for God. That God may be known in the world is known to faith through revelation.

The personal Creator-God, however, whose real Name is concealed from the whole world which was created by Him, in spite of all the glimpses which the world gives us concerning Him, this Creator makes Himself known when He names His own Name, when He reveals Himself in His personal Word. This personal Word, however, of which the prophets bear witness, but who is not Himself present in their testimony, is present, even if only visible to faith, in the "Word made flesh." In the Person, in the mystery of the Person of the Revealer, the personality of God is unveiled, and here alone, where it is at the same time concealed. The personality of God is "most hidden yet most manifest," that is, it is revealed to faith alone in the disguise of an historical personality, which as such, as a phenomenon which can be recognized within the sphere of history, is precisely not the true personality, namely, the personality divine.

Therefore here—and here alone—does all subordination of person to Idea cease. The Mediator is not merely the bearer of an Idea. The revelation of God in the Mediator cannot be severed from the Mediator. For this very reason He is called the Mediator, because He stands in this peculiar relation to the revelation, because the revelation can only be received *in* Him, and not merely *through* Him. He Himself is the revelation, as He Himself is the Word; He is what God has to say to us. For what God says to us in Him is not "something," but Himself, the personal God, His own Name. This Logos is not an Idea but a Person, not something general but particular. This is the stumbling-block, that a personality, an isolated historical fact, is asserted to be the absolute truth, the revelation. "Blessed is he who is not offended in Me." This personal fact produces an entirely new kind of relation, as fundamentally different from all other intellectual relations as the personal Logos differs from the Logos which is merely an Idea: faith, this new relation, is a relation which is genuinely personal and creates genuine personality.[1] Only now can we rightly understand why faith lays so much emphasis on its claim to

[1] A "person," in the full sense of the word, is not an entity which exists in its own right; one becomes a person through the call of God, "heard" in the decision of faith.

be the one really personal decision; it is the decision in the presence of the Divine Personality, in the presence of the personal Word and demand of God, of the Lord, who by the very fact that He speaks to us demands a personal decision —a decision which no Law, no Categorical Imperative, has the right to demand.

Here everything depends upon the Person. The Person is not the Bearer of something else. It is Himself, the Word, the Revelation, the personal Presence. The Person Himself is the Word, not any particular purpose for which He may have come; this personal Word comes from beyond the human sphere, and in His coming to us from "beyond" He is God's gift of revelation. God gives Himself in the revelation; it is His own Being which He imparts to us, His own Person, His very "heart." Therefore the relation between the word of revelation and the Person is not accidental and transitory as it is in the case of the Idea, but it is necessary. Indeed, it is not a relation at all, unless we can call identity a relation. It is the relation to itself. Here that which is revealed and the Revealer are one. Just because this is so, it is in the full sense of the word a revelation. But this Person is not the historical personality who can be perceived as such. The historical personality who can be perceived is the incognito under which the Person is concealed—from those who do not believe. It is the mystery of the Person, which, as such, can only be known by faith.

(iii)

If, however, the Person is that which is revealed, not an idea which can be detached from it, nor a general principle, then, too, the Person is that which "comes" to us from that dimension "yonder." The Person Himself—the authoritative, and thus the Divine Person—is the Word from the other side, the Word from above; the Son who was in the bosom of the Father. For if we could distinguish between the Person and His message, we would be led inevitably back to the principle of logos (reason), (and would thus deny revelation). That which is eternal is the Eternal, that which is revealed is the Revealer, and the Revealer is revealed in the real historical personality of the Mediator with which He is mysteriously, indirectly identical. He Himself, not only His message or His Gospel, is from above, from eternity, from beyond the whole sphere of creaturely existence. For He Himself, His coming, constitutes the content of the Gospel. That He came unto His own, that "we beheld His glory, the glory as of the only begotten of the Father, full of grace and truth," this is "Light and Life," this is "the truth which came by Jesus Christ."

The Christ who came *is* the Gospel. Thus His Person, as the "One who has come," is the Word of God which has "come," in the sense in which the prophetic Word "came." What is meant is not the manifestation of His personality which everyone can see, but the mystery of His Person. The mystery of His Person consists precisely in this, that He is of a different origin from ourselves, that He is "from above." Whoever listens to the answer to the question "Who art Thou?", to whom the mystery of the Person of Christ is revealed, has received the gift of faith. To him it is "given to understand the mysteries of the Kingdom of Heaven." He can believe, because he stands in the presence of the personal divine authority. All the statements of the New Testament about Jesus as the Christ point towards this dimension of authority, towards His origin, as the One who has come from God Himself. Properly speaking, they all denote the parabola from the supra-sensible world, whose angular point touches the world of sense in this event of Jesus Christ. In order to understand this contact, this historical personality of Jesus, aright, that is, in faith, it is necessary to perceive this "parabola," that is, the knowledge of the region whence He has come, and whither He returns. Only thus can we really perceive in this familiar personality the mystery of the Christ; only thus is the relation of authority possible; only thus do we perceive that this Jesus is the Christ, "whom flesh and blood hath not revealed unto thee."

The mystery of the Person, authority, the dimension behind history—this is what is meant in the Christian faith by the deity of the Person of Christ. For authority can be ascribed to God alone. Either we interpret the word "authority" merely in a non-literal, superficial sense, or we mean the divine authority, the authority which can be ascribed to God alone. If it is Jesus the "Kyrios" to whom we pray: *"Maran atha, Come, Lord Jesus!"* then He is God. For we pray to God alone. The One worshipped as *Maran* by the Jew—he who knows the second commandment, he who knows better than any other that it is allowed to give worship to none but God— Him does he worship as the only God.[1] We are here confronted with the mystery which is firmly held and preserved for us in the doctrine of the Trinity, whose aim it is to secure the Unity of God against polytheism, and the reality of the divine revelation in Christ against all mere symbolism. God Himself reveals Himself personally in Jesus Christ. This is revelation in the complete sense of the word: the identity of the One who reveals and of that which is revealed. Here God Himself speaks, but not in a mere message—for here there is more than a prophet—but in the existence of this Person. It is this which constitutes the mystery of revelation, and also its authority, the absolutely new element, in its very essence absolutely unique. If this were not the meaning of revelation, then Christ would be a mere symbol, merely the bearer of an Idea, of a Gospel which could be detached from His own Person. But this would not then be a revelation; for He would then be less than a prophet, not more. It is only this identity of the

---

[1] It is an extraordinarily superficial view to assert that the faith in Jesus as Lord (*Kyrios*) arose out of the general Hellenistic idea of gods who were transformed into human beings. We might, indeed, put the question the other way round: How was it that in the midst of this polytheistic mythological religious world an absolutely rigid monotheism, which is the presupposition for the Christian belief in Jesus as Lord (*Kyrios*), was able to thrive at all? Only in the Christian faith in Jesus as Lord (*Kyrios*), only in faith in the God-Man Christ, is the Monotheism of the Old Testament taken quite seriously. Paul is a more rigid Monotheist than Isaiah, because only through the revelation in Jesus Christ is God known truly and personally as the Creator who is above the world. Cf. Luther *"fatemur fester unum deum esse quam gentiles"* (*W.A.*, 49, 238). Only in the faith in the Incarnation of God does the contrast between it and the Hellenistic mythology become unconditionally clear and sharp. The uniqueness (once-for-allness) of the revelation, which is identical with the reality of the revelation, makes the separation between God and the world complete. The absolute transcendence of God is only completely fulfilled in the faith in the Mediator.

divinely authoritative Word and the Person which constitutes the fact that He is "more than a prophet." Thus His Person is not the transparent veil through which gleams the divine, but He is Himself the Divine; hence He is not that which is divine, but God.

The distinction between the divine and the personal-concrete is the underlying thought of Idealism. It is Idealism which claims the right to erect a barrier, however delicate and slender, between eternity and time, to which therefore even the highest form of the temporal is only an appearance, only a transparency or symbol of the eternal. From the Christian standpoint there is no need to reproach Idealism for this; the real error lies in the other direction, namely, that Idealism regards the difference as so slight, when in reality the gulf which yawns between the creature and the Creator is deep and vast. The distinction between "idea" and "appearance" is far too slight to express the contrast between God and the world. The real error of Idealism is this: that a method which it usually applies rightly but inadequately it applies wrongly to One who is really and only both man and God, One who does not merely represent the divine as a specially perfect symbol, as a transparency which is particularly transparent; for the One who breaks through the barrier which for ever separates the creature and the Creator is the One, the only One, in this unique event which is therefore the turning-point in the history of the world. That here too Idealism separates what it otherwise separates rightly, that it does not perceive the unique character of this event: this is the "Greek" revolt against the "foolishness" of the Gospel.

The recognition of this folly as the truth is the Christian faith. Hence to it everything depends upon the reality of this identity, on clearing away the last traces of symbolism. That which is otherwise regarded as "daemonic" (Tillich) is here and here alone precisely the obedience of faith and the insight of faith: the identification of a point in the Here and Now with the eternally divine, of a human reality, of a personality, with the Divine Godhead. Faith is concerned supremely with the non-separation between the Revealer and that which is revealed. Hence not only is that which is revealed eternal, but the personal Revealer also, for both are one.

(iv)

If, however, we intend to take the fact of revelation seriously, a further point needs to be stressed: it is the revelation of that which was previously concealed. Thus that which is revealed and the Revealer are identical, it is true, and yet there is a distinction. There is One who reveals and One who is revealed. They are identical, they are one and the same, the One God. But God, in so far as He reveals Himself, is yet different from that which is revealed, otherwise revelation would not be a real happening. The divine authority of the Revealer is the personal authority of God. There is no other authority. And yet the Revealer does not stand merely on the same side as God, the revealed, but at the same time He stands "alongside" Him as the Revealer of that which otherwise is not revealed. Thus this suggests the theme of the doctrine of the Trinity, an idea which arises just as necessarily from the idea of revelation (when it is taken quite seriously), as it suggests an impenetrable mystery. It is the exact opposite of intelligent understanding. It warns us that precisely when we take the knowledge of God in Christ as a revelation of God, then first are we seriously faced with the mystery of the revealed God. The dogma of the Trinity is not the result of a false intellectualist Greek Logos doctrine, but it exists the moment that we really believe that God was in Christ, the moment that we take this statement of Paul's quite seriously, and do not try to modify it in an Idealistic symbolical sense till it becomes the humanistic idea that in Jesus the "Idea . . . took shape." If what the Pauline and the Johannine doctrine of revelation states is true—and what, in a less clearly defined manner, was the common Christian creed of the primitive Christian communities, who believed in the "exalted Lord"—then the question concerning the relation between the revealing and the revealed God cannot be evaded. Of course, like the New Testament itself, we can stand still before it and confess that we do not understand it, that it is God's own secret. Ultimately the doctrine of the Trinity does not mean anything else. But the aim of this doctrine is also to preserve from error the power of this mystery, the real mystery of faith. The point is this:

we are summoned to stand in humble, reverent silence in the presence of a real mystery, not in the presence of an illusion.

This doctrine is not an explanation; it makes no attempt to explain anything; but it does intend that nothing pagan or Jewish should be proclaimed instead of the mystery of Christ. This was the reason for the fight against Arius and against Sabellius. The doctrine of the Trinity is a theological doctrine, not a scriptural proclamation ($\kappa\acute{\eta}\rho\nu\gamma\mu\alpha$). It is not a message to be preached. It is a defensive doctrine, which would not have been necessary at all if the two fundamental statements of the Christian creed had been allowed to stand: God alone can save, and Christ alone is this divine salvation. There the matter might have been allowed to rest were it not—as Calvin remarks in this connection—that those who "say" this, secretly "murmur" something entirely different.

At the present day Arianism is no longer a vital issue, but Sabellianism is still vigorous and needs to be confuted; on this point, at any rate, Schleiermacher spoke out frankly, and admitted that he was a Sabellian.[1] Sabellianism in the broadest sense—we are not here concerned with all the lesser distinctions of the history of dogma—means the denial of the reality of the revelation; it is "Judaism." Translated into our own terminology we might say that Sabellianism transforms revelation into a mere symbol, a *mimus theatralis* (Hilarius). It is not that the reality of Jesus is denied, but the deity of Jesus is understood in the merely symbolical sense and not in the realistic sense. Jesus is only revelation in a relative sense, not in the absolute sense; this means that He is only revelation in the general sense, in which revelation is not interpreted literally. The modern conception of Christ is essentially that of Paul of Samosata. In fact, we might describe this theologian as the first Ritschlian, or, in a more general way, as the first modern theologian. Christ may indeed be the Revealer of

---

[1] Instead of using here the correct general term of "Monarchianism," I use the narrower term "Sabellianism"; I do this really in view of Schleiermacher, who described himself as a Sabellian. In the exact sense in which the word is used in the history of dogma Schleiermacher's doctrine is in no way Sabellian. For in Schleiermacher's doctrine it is not the true Humanity which is imperilled but the true Deity.

God, but not in the sense which is demanded by the transition from the prophet to the One who is "more than a prophet," but in the sense of a modification of the prophetic element, namely, that Christ was merely the possessor of a specially great but impersonal divine power and divine spirit. Revelation is impersonal, the personality is not the revelation. The relation between the Christ and the revelation is that of a perishable veil. The unique character of the revelation is denied. In principle, what took place in Christ could happen again and again. Jesus is nothing more than a man who was specially highly endowed by God, a personality with "a quite remarkable religious and moral disposition of the highest power and purity" (cf. p. 99). But it is possible that another might one day come who would be endowed with yet higher powers and who would thus outstrip Jesus. The union of Christ with God is purely ethico-religious. Thus in so far as the problem of His Person is considered there is no idea of a revelation in the Biblical sense of the word at all, hence no idea of decision, of the essential and unique, of the crisis in history which either happens once or not at all. The man Jesus is in no sense really the Redeemer. For no human being can be a redeemer since he himself stands in need of redemption.

Here also we perceive how fluid is the distinction between Arianism and Sabellianism. In practice they constantly merge into one another. If we say, "Still, He is the Redeemer but he is not God," that is Arianism. Redemption is postulated quite seriously and absolutely, but there is a definite refusal to admit that the Redeemer in this sense can only be God Himself. Or perhaps it is said "God alone is the Redeemer," but, since Jesus is not God, the redemption through Jesus is not taken quite seriously. Either it is true that the redeeming revelation is present in Jesus Christ, in His existence as a Person, and then God Himself is present, the redeeming God, and not a man who himself needs redemption, or, on the other hand, people may say, "It is nonsense to say that Jesus Christ is not a man in need of redemption, and that He is God Himself": then redemption through Jesus Christ cannot be quite real, for this would mean something quite relative, something which is present all the time, even if perhaps not to the same extent.

To take the personal reality of revelation quite seriously is the exact opposite of Sabellianism. To take the divine nature of the Revealer seriously is the exact opposite of Arianism.

The divine personality, in whom the hidden God makes Himself known unto us, is not a mere *prosopon*, a *mimus theatralis*, a transitory phenomenon in the form of God, a transparency, a symbol, but it is itself the personal eternal God. It is this idea which finally completes the Christian conception of revelation.

The Sabellianism of the present day certainly desires to free us both from the difficulties of the "Two Natures" doctrine and from the doctrine of the Trinity. It is as crystal-clear and "simple" as is all the theology of the Enlightenment type. But it has bought this clarity and transparency very dearly, for it has been obliged to renounce the whole Gospel. For this theory weakens and modifies the fact of Christ till it becomes merely semi-divine, merely a human event of a very remarkable character. We must either have rational clarity and simplicity or paradox! The logical absurdities of the doctrine of the Two Natures and of the Trinity express the inconceivable miracle of revelation. It would not be a divine revelation at all if it could be grasped by the mind, if it could be "perceived," if it could take its place among our other activities of thought and experience, and thus be established on these lines. Revelation in the New Testament sense cannot be anything other than illogical, since it breaks through the continuity of our thought, as indeed it breaks through the continuity of the human and natural sphere in general. There was no need to wait for the Socinian schoolmasters and scoffers of the period of the Enlightenment to call the attention of Christendom to the logical inconsistencies of these fundamental doctrines. Indeed, thinkers of the calibre of Athanasius and Basil did not need to have these difficulties pointed out. But they knew that they were defending these illogical truths as the most precious treasures of the Church. Not out of a morbid love for the absurd and the paradoxical, but because they found that these contradictory statements expressed the fundamental paradox that God became man. This is the Holy of Holies of the Christian Faith.

(v)

But it is not only the Christian conception of revelation, but also the Christian Idea of God, the knowledge of the personality and the love of God, which is completed by the idea of the Trinity. We saw already how closely the knowledge of the personal Creator-God is connected with the personality of the word of revelation.[1] It is only possible to know the truly personal God in the God who manifests Himself in the personal Word of revelation. In the last resort, the God of Idealism—both of ethical and speculative Idealism—and of mysticism is always impersonal, because continuity exists between Him and the world, between Him and the Self. This continuity is destroyed by two expressions: "creation out of nothing" and "revelation." Revelation, however, is the presupposition for the knowledge of the Creator. The continuity of thought must also be broken through, in order that it may be seen that the continuity of Being has been broken through. So long as men believe that it is possible to know God apart from any special revelation, without any special event of revelation, they believe that He can be known in continuity with themselves (subjective Immanence); He is therefore regarded as a force which is continuous with the world (objective Immanence), as a mere Idea, not as a personality. Hence the distinctive note of scriptural thought, which runs right through the Bible, is this threefold character of God: the personal God, the Creator, the God who reveals Himself in His personal Word.

But the genuinely personal Word is only the Word which has become Person. There alone does God pronounce His own Name, where He gives Himself wholly to the finite. Is this

[1] The Old Testament certainly ought not to be quoted as an authority against this statement. All the nations surrounding Israel lived also in the world and knew somehow or another that there was a divine mystery in the world. But for them more or less the world and God flowed into one another. Polytheism, nature religion, is primitive Pantheism. The knowledge of God as the Creator and the Sovereign Lord was gained in Israel not from nature but from revelation. The Old Testament knowledge of the world-Creator arises not out of the world but out of the Word of the Prophets. The Word, sin, creation, and the hope of redemption form a connected chain. If one of these links were lacking the others would not be there.

really God? Is He like this? Or is this person only a divine instrument of revelation (*Prosopon*)? Once again the question of the reality of the personal revelation becomes the final question. Is it God in His inherent Reality? Is it really His own Proper Name which is here made manifest? or is it merely the form which contains something entirely different? Is the self-communication of God something different from God Himself, or is it precisely this God who communicates Himself, who is the real and true God, the Essential Deity, the Divine Name? Is the form in which God comes to us something which differs from His real Being? Or, on the other hand, is this will to descend, to seek for fellowship, to give Himself, the actual will of God, so that both His "coming" and His "being," His self-revelation and His independent inherent Deity, His self-communication and His Essence, are one and the same?

It is this question which is answered by the decision about the personal character of the revelation, by our attitude towards the mystery of the Person of Christ. In the Bible "revelation" is never conceived as mere form, but always, at the same time, as content. The fact that God reveals Himself *is* His Love; in the very fact that He comes down to our level, that He comes to us, that He seeks us, He reveals His heart, His will. It is only when we see that the Revealer really is God Himself that we perceive that God is One whose inmost essence is Love, whose inherent Reality is personal, and that It exists for us. God manifests Himself to us in revelation as the One who communicates Himself, as Love. Because the communication, the Word, is Himself, therefore in Himself He is One who gives Himself. But that He is the One who communicates Himself we cannot conceive otherwise than through the thought that in Himself—and not only in relation to the world—He is loving, self-giving. It is this truth which is expressed in the Christian doctrine of the Trinity—the real doctrine, the doctrine of the Church, not the pseudo-doctrine of modern theologians. The Word, the process of self-communication, exists eternally in God Himself. When God reveals His being to the world as One who gives Himself, as Love, this is what He is in Himself, in His very Nature.

Therefore also this relation between the Revealer and that which is revealed exists within Himself from all eternity, as the inherent and essential Reality of the Divine Nature. The eternal Logos is that in which God expresses Himself. This is the element which is common both to the philosophical and to the Christian doctrine of the Logos. But the decisive difference is this, that the philosophical form of this expression is incorrect, that it is not meant as a real personal communication, as the Incarnation of the Logos, and that therefore even the expressed Logos is not the personal Logos but an Idea. To the form of immanent, reflective knowledge, without a personal fact of revelation (Logos philosophy) there corresponds its content: the impersonal character, the nature which does not communicate itself, the non-love of God. The speculative Logos is a world idea. Likewise in the Christian religion to the form of the personal communication there corresponds its content: the personal loving will of God as the very essence of the Divine Nature. The Triune God alone gives Himself within Himself, and therefore is in Himself Love and Personality. Hence the very same abyss lies between the philosophical and the Christian interpretation of the Logos as that which lies between the immanental thought of God and belief in revelation.

There is, however, one final observation to be made. The Trinitarian conception, which is already implied in the thought of revelation, when it is seriously entertained, expresses something further, and again only places one element in the idea of revelation in the right light. Although God in Himself, and not only in His historical revelation, is One who gives Himself, the One who loves, at the same time He does not cease to be the Other, the hidden God, the One who wills to reveal Himself, thus the One who even in the act of revealing Himself still remains mysterious, the God of majesty, the Source of all, even of revelation, whom we cannot comprehend as such, whom we cannot understand, but whom we can only worship as an unfathomable mystery. Revelation does not mean that for the believer the hidden God has been resolved into the revealed God.

God is not simply Love. The Nature of God cannot be

281

exhaustively stated in one single word.[1] The Father is not swallowed up in the Son as the passing phase is resolved into the final one. The dim background behind the figure of the Son must not be allowed to disappear, otherwise faith would lead us astray into a false security. *Certitudo* develops into *securitas*. We ought never to regard the truth that God is Love as something we can take for granted, but as a truth due to the great unfathomable will of God. God loves whom He wills. To know His love means to belong to the elect. Even in His love God does not cease to be sovereign Lord. It is this great and vital truth which is expressed by the doctrine of the Trinity: that we do not substitute a simple inevitable static condition for a state of motion and freedom. God is the Father and the Son. We are to believe in God as Love; this means we are to have unity in duality, in a duality which has to be constantly overcome by faith. God is not simply Love. He *defines* Himself as Love. Love is His Will, not His Nature, although it is His eternal Will. As His Nature,[2] however, even in Christ, we must worship His sovereign Majesty and His Holiness. This twofold tension must ever be preserved: God is LOVE; but also, GOD is Love. Only in this way can we think the personality of God. Only the God in Three Persons is truly personal. The non-Trinitarian God is simply the rigid Idea of God.

The question still remains: why do we speak of a God in

[1] Thus when Ritschl deliberately suppresses the idea of the holiness of God alongside of the love of God, this is not merely a special element in his doctrine of the "attributes of God," but a fundamental contradiction to the scriptural knowledge of God. It not only renders his idea of God incomplete and in need of correction, but it makes it something fundamentally different from the Christian idea of God altogether; it is rational and one-sided in contrast to the paradox of the Christian faith. It is the rational idea of purpose which is independent of revelation, in contrast to the freedom of God which only unveils His secret in revelation to whom He wills.

[2] That is the distinction which Luther makes between the *natura* and the *voluntas Dei*. For instance, on Gal. (I, 47): "*non jubet scrutari naturam Dei, sed agnoscere voluntatem ejus propositam in Christo.*" Certainly the distinction between the hidden and the revealed under the concepts of nature and will is not without its dangers, as when even Luther can teach that "The Divine Nature is nothing else than a furnace and the passion of such love" (*W.A.*, 36, 424).

Three Persons and not of a God in Two Persons? It is, however, neither our task nor our intention to develop a doctrine of the Trinity at this point. All that we have tried to do is this: to make clear the connection between the personal nature of the revelation and the personality of God. Therefore the question of the Holy Spirit can only be mentioned in passing. Revelation is a happening, and indeed a personal happening, thus it is transitory. Revelation means, indeed, that the very Nature of God, in His inherent Reality, was made known "to us," and thus was recognized. It is impossible to speak of revelation without speaking of faith. Even the distinction between an objective and a subjective element is only possible from the point of view of faith. What, however, is this subjective element?

Revelation means that God speaks and man is silent. God Himself acts, God alone acts, we merely receive, we merely endure. God Himself steps on to the stage, and we retire. Everything depends upon the fact that it is God alone who speaks. We cannot reply. Where should we find the basis for an affirmative reply? How would it be possible for us to judge the Divine Word or to pronounce upon it? God Himself must answer the question which we cannot even put rightly to ourselves, but which in its full force is addressed to us. This is the revelation, this is faith: that God answers for us. This is what it means to believe: that we have nothing more to examine and weigh up, that even our "yes" cannot be regarded as our own choice, but simply and solely as God's own speech and God's gift. Faith, the power to believe and not merely the content of faith, is the gift of God; this is the testimony of the Bible. This does not exclude the fact that faith is decision, decision of a fully personal and active kind. How could it be anything else than this? But at the same time this decision is a gift, the highest activity of the self is the gift of God. This echo of the word of Christ in our heart, as the speech of God in us, is the Holy Spirit.[1]

[1] It is possible to assert absolutely that the spirituality of the Christian faith is evident (in the sense of a *vestigium* or *adminiculum*), in the fact that in it the polar tension between objective and subjective is complete; faith is at the same time the most objective thing there is: *verbum externum*, historical fact, and also the most subjective thing there can be: God's Spirit in us; the *verbum alienum* and the Word as God's own Voice speaking in the heart.

That this also must be understood as something real and actual, and not only as something semi-divine and semi-real, is expressed in the doctrine of the deity of the Spirit. Even the foundation of this process in its peculiar character, as contrasted with the objective Revealer and with that which is revealed, is, as the subjective foundation of revelation, no mere phenomenon of merely historical extent, no *mimus theatralis*, but it is eternal. Faith is as far from being a psychological phenomenon as ·the Christ is far from being an historical phenomenon. It is the same God who speaks to us in the Christ without and in the heart within, the "Christ for us" is the "Christ within us," and neither exists without the other. It is the Spirit of God who testifies to the Word as truth, and it is the Word of God which mediates the Spirit.

Now we have reached the point at which we can see how foolish it is to describe the Christian doctrine of the Logos, of the Divine Nature, and of the Trinity as metaphysics. Metaphysics deals with theoretical objectivity, hence it is something aesthetic and intellectual, $\theta\epsilon\omega\rho\iota\alpha$. Faith, however, faith in the deity of the Word, and in the Divine Nature of Christ, is the very opposite of theory—there is naturally a theory of this faith!—but it means an extremely personal decision and a very literal divine personal presence. At this precise point the attitude of a mere spectator is excluded; it is precisely the mere spectator who is incapable of seeing what is here meant. Only the person who is taking part in all this can know Christ as the Christ. "No one can call Christ Lord save by the Holy Spirit." For only one who is no mere onlooker needs Him, only one who shares in this matter knows how much he needs Him, the Revealer and the Mediator of the reconciliation, the One who brings to the soul what he has sought in vain, that without which life is meaningless and unhappy. But it is the fate of matters of faith that they are constantly held to be something quite different from that which they really are by people who are not personally interested in them. So it seems likely that to the very end of time the reproach will be hurled at us again and again that we are here simply spinning metaphysical or speculative theories.

CHAPTER X

THE SELF-MOVEMENT OF GOD

(i)

THE revelation contained in the Bible is the proclamation of the self-movement of the absolute unchangeable God, the proclamation of the personal, living God, the One who reveals Himself. The God of abstract thought, of mysticism and of ethics is the θεὸς ἀκίνητος πάντα κινῶν, the deity who is absolutely unmoved, and in repose—although not on that account inactive. The truth about this God is "static" truth. The deepest foundation of the world, of the Self, of the soul, the law of all laws does not move. The Idea *is*. The Deity of the mystic "is"; the God of the Moral Law is Himself, as identical with the Law, as rigid as the Law. To predicate motion on the part of the Absolute is, as the Neo-Platonists of all time have known very well, an intolerable contradiction. For movement means striving, and striving means to seek for something one does not possess, and this implies imperfection. The God of the Christian faith, the Three in One, the Living God, is in Himself motion, because in His very Nature He is Love. It is not the world which first causes the motion; for if this were the case then the movement would not be really that of God, but of the world. But it is God Himself who is moved; the Father loves the Son and the Son loves the Father. This love constitutes the very essence of God; it does not come into being first of all in relation to the world, but it reveals Itself to the world as the Divine essence. The world is, therefore, not the necessary correlate of God, but it is the contingent creation of His Will. In the Son the Father loves the world, as He has created it in Him, the Logos. The Son, the Logos, is God in respect of His attitude towards the world, His power of communicating Himself, the principle of Creation, Revela-

285

tion, and Redemption. In the Son, as the Son, God is the self-moved, the God who Himself descends into the world.

The Bible is the book in which the ever-recurring theme is this strange assertion: that the God who has created the world and who fills all things, who holds all things within His hands, the Omnipresent and the Almighty—*comes*. The Coming of God is the real theme of this book, and of this book alone. People have always drawn attention to the "historical character" of Biblical religion. This observation is not wrong, but it does not touch the heart of the matter. What we to-day call historical interest is alien to the spirit of the Bible. Israel has not produced any important "profane history" like Greece and Rome. The real concern here is something which is quite different from the concern for history. This book deals with world history in the most comprehensive sense of the word, or to put it still more clearly, with divine history; it is concerned with the coming of God into the world. Therefore it would be better to say: the Bible is concerned with revelation and with final history (*Endgeschichte*). The Bible is eschatological through and through, even where the eschatology is given first of all in the form of historical pictures. In the last resort, what is always meant is this: the coming of God, the coming of the Final, the Ultimate, which is at the same time the actual restoration of all things.

Revelation is the coming of God in the Word; the Kingdom of God, redemption, the end of the age, the Messianic era, all mean the coming of God "in power." The common element in both is this "coming"; the point of intersection in both, the final purpose of the prophetic revelation, and the beginning of the coming of the Kingdom of God, is the coming of God in the Word, which is a personal advent, the Incarnation of the Word. "The prophets prophesied until John"; but "he that is least in the kingdom of God is greater than he," although "among those who are born of woman there has arisen none greater than John the Baptist." The whole of the Old Testament and its revelation is Advent. The New Testament is the Christmas message. The Old Testament is written in the light of the expectation of the coming Word, the New Testament in the light of the Word which has come. Indeed, in so far as the Word has now actually come, contact with reality has already begun; the Kingdom of God, and thus the coming of God in power, has begun. But in so far as it is only here in Him, in hiddenness, it is still to some extent in the future, something which is yet to come.

The coming of God, as a descent, as a condescension, as the founding of the divine fellowship, the founding of the covenant, the divine search for that which He does not need, is incomprehensible love. The coming God is the loving God, and only the coming God is the One who truly loves. For He only is the One who Himself goes forth to seek; the One who Himself moves in search of the beloved; the One who cares about the beloved with tender solicitude. This "coming down" of God, this condescension, this coming of God to men, is the proof of His unfathomable Love, which is something quite different from the goodness of the Creator, which even the natural man can to some extent understand. It is the Love which gives its very self, the Love which pours itself out for the sake of the beloved. It is the Love which is all the greater the less claim the beloved has upon It, the less it is worthy of such love. Hence the coming of God as Love can only be fully known where it is the coming of God to sinful man, the seeking of those who have fallen away, of those who have been unfaithful. Here alone does the divine Love unveil its whole incomprehensible wealth and richness: where God gives Himself to the sinful creature, in order that He may once more and indeed fully restore the fellowship which had been broken between man and God—in the Atonement.

(ii)

Hence it is precisely this central theme of the revelation of the Bible which rouses the opposition of all systems of religion and of all philosophies. The philosophy of religion has always rejected the doctrine of the coming of God as mythology— whether His coming has been depicted as that of revelation or as that of completion. "We must most decidedly renounce belief in the Son of God . . . the God who came down from Heaven, in order to become a man, an infant, a crucified man, and then for a second time to become God; this is pure Greek mythology. . . . Our way of thought has become too sober to indulge in ideas of this kind."[1]

It is the fixed basis of all philosophy, that the Absolute is and must be unmoved, because otherwise He would not be the Absolute. Mysticism also and ethical Rationalism express the same opposition. The deepest depth of being does not move. We may be able to sink down into Him but He Himself does not rise up to us. The Law of all Laws does not alter. It is difficult to give any reply to the argument about mythology, or against the idea that motion contradicts the idea of the Absolute. In actual fact, the self-movement of God does stand in opposition to the idea of the Absolute, whether this idea be conceived logically or ethically.

We can only reply that the admission of this contradiction as true is the condition apart from which neither the Living God nor the God of love can be known. That the absolute God is at the same time the One who comes, the hidden God is also the One who is revealed, the God of the stern and rigid Law also the One who forgives; this fundamental antithesis in the Idea of God, which is expressed in the central dogmas of the Trinity, the Incarnation and the Atonement, is certainly the characteristic sign of the scriptural Idea of God. As an idea, this thought has no meaning. But it does not even claim to be an idea; it is based upon the revelation of this God Himself. If people still choose to talk about mythology in this connection, well, they must do so; but it is God's own mythology, His own "travesty," as the New Testament itself conceives it: "He emptied Himself and took on Him the form of a servant."

There is, however, another reason why the term "mythology" is not acceptable. The very element which is characteristic of the whole of the Biblical revelation, the element of uniqueness, is absent from the myth. It is true, of course, that in the Bible there are many prophets, and therefore there are many "revelations"; but they are all witnesses to the one Word, and indeed to the Word which is to come, of that Word which has actually come, as a unique event. One God, One Mediator

[1] Keim: *Geschichte Jesu*, p. 365.

between God and man, one act of reconciliation. "If Christ died, then He died once for all." This sacrifice, as the Epistle to the Hebrews points out again and again, was offered once for all. This "once for all," this absolute seriousness of an actual event, of something which has actually happened, is a feature which is alien to all kinds of mythology. On the contrary, the main feature of mythology is its cyclic character. Therefore the mythical element is absolutely different from the historical element; there is no mythological religion which has an absolute interest in a fact of history, whereas the Christian religion of revelation stakes everything on a fact of this kind. And by a "fact" it means something which happens in the most external, matter-of-fact, sense of the word, something which has actually happened. "The Word became"—not merely Man, but "*Flesh.*"

Instead of referring to this cyclic movement we might also point out the connection between mythology and polytheism on the one hand, and between revelation and the strictest monotheism on the other. Many gods are the necessary background (and usually the necessary *dramatis personae*) of the myth. The process is played out essentially in the imaginary world of the gods. The presupposition for the revelation of Christ, and for its interpretation is the most uncompromising and unconditional monotheism, the Yahwism of the Old Testament, faith in the God who is jealous to preserve His sole glory, and the impassable gulf which lies between the creature and the Creator, who therefore will not even permit an image or a picture of God to be made, because if this were allowed the separating barrier would have become too thin. This God, the absolute Sovereign, who makes any continuity between Himself and the world impossible, this God is the One who comes. His coming is therefore no kind of visible process in some mythological world of shadows, or in heaven, which might form the scene of a myth; but in so far as we are thinking of it as a happening, and not of the everlasting mystery of the purpose of God, this event is something quite simple, earthly, and human, a fact which any chronicler could report, without having the least idea that in this event something divine had taken place. The "coming," however, the movement between eternity and time, itself leaves no room for the growth of fantasy. The simple statement: "The Logos became flesh," covers it entirely. As a myth this is indeed somewhat meagre.[1] On the one hand, Eternity—beyond the time-process—and on the other, time with its sober record of an historical event; and between them both a flash of lightning, the invisible connecting link, which at the same time proclaims the direction of that Advent which culminates in the profound words: "The Word *became* flesh."

The fact that this took place once for all means that it is really the Absolute with which we are here concerned, and not some mythical semi-Absolute; it means, too, that the event *really* happened, and did not merely seem to happen, as in a myth. Nothing else in the whole world is unique in this sense. For this event alone has no connection with other events. In itself it is absolute. For it is the Incarnation of the Word, the coming of the Son of God, the Atonement. The world cannot and must not be reconciled a second time. The more spiritual the character of the event—as we have already seen—the nearer it approaches to uniqueness. But the very nature of history excludes any idea of a unique event. The human element, as such, is also the universal element; it means that which connects all, and is common to all. It is precisely in this union between the unique event and the common element that history consists, in the interplay of the Idea and personality. Hence the absolutely unique event cannot be historical in this sense; it cannot consist in a blending of thought and personality of this kind. In so far as the fact of Christ is conceived in these terms it is not really unique, it is not a turning-point; at the most, it is merely the culmination of a process. It is only unique in so far as it is the event of the Incarnation of the Son of God, the coming of God Himself, the point of intersection of history and eternity, thus it is both history and the abrogation of history by eternity: history —"the Son of David according to the flesh," in its visible

[1] For the extension of this myth into concrete expression, which at isolated points has also penetrated into the Gospel tradition, see below, pp. 322 ff., and 577 ff.

fulfilment before our eyes; eternity—"the Son of God according to the Spirit"—in the reality of faith.

(iii)

We can only really understand what the Bible means by the coming of God, and this unique event, when we interpret it from the point of view of the presupposition of the Bible itself. The presupposition of this movement is the gulf between God and man, the abyss which lies between the holy God and the sinful creature. The Incarnation of the Son of God is determined by sin. God comes. He must "come." He will come, because the creature has turned away from Him. This does not mean the perfecting of the Creation—this indeed would be movement within continuity—but the restoration of a fallen Creation. Throughout the Bible the coming of God always means the summons to "return"; it means that a link which has been broken must be mended; it means the restoration of something diseased (which was originally sound) to health and wholeness; it means redemption and reconciliation. This summons to "return" reveals the fact of discontinuity, and the strongest expression to describe this discontinuity is just *sin*. Sin is the gulf which separates God and man. It is sin which determines the nature of the divine movement, giving it the character both of an invitation to "return" and of a gracious "descent."[1]

This is the presupposition for the eschatological character of the scriptural faith in revelation: the fact that sin is taken seriously, that this gulf is seen to exist. Neither Speculation, Idealism, Mysticism, nor rational Moralism see this gulf. They do not take sin seriously. Above all, they do not take it seriously in its personal centre: guilt. They may, of course,

---

[1] May I be allowed once again to refer to Irenaeus? His doctrine of "recapitulation" is indeed unique in theology in the way in which it reveals the connection between the Creation, the Fall, revelation, and redemption as a divine movement which is regressive. The fact that modern historians of dogma cannot understand his point of view at all is a clear proof of their Monistic (non-eschatological) evolutionary point of view.

be conscious of imperfection, and they may therefore admit the necessity for some kind of development. Or they may admit that sin exists as bondage to the senses, and to the world, and therefore they may seek for deliverance from this by introversion, by sinking down into the ground of the soul. Or they may acknowledge sin in the shape of departure from the norm, in isolated actions, and may therefore desire improvement. But they do not recognize the defect which constitutes a positive obstacle to communion between God and man, between man and his goal, and, indeed, an obstacle of such a character that man cannot lift a finger to help himself, because, since it belongs to the past, it has passed out of his control altogether; this obstacle, this defect, is guilt. To the extent in which the sense of guilt exists, the possibility of understanding the Christian idea of the need for the Mediator also exists.

If, therefore, we are to understand revelation as the self-movement of God, we must first of all see clearly that, in his own strength, man cannot possibly move towards God. The motionless character of the non-Christian God is illustrated most fully by the fact that outside the Christian religion all movement is a self-movement of man towards the unmoved Deity. The descending movement is Christian; the ascending movement is non-Christian. Luther often calls the movement which is effected by speculative knowledge of God as a "climbing up to the Majesty on High." That is the right way to describe it. All thought is a continuous movement towards the Absolute. Its aim may be God—namely the Idea of God as the foundation of all Being and of all Thought—but it is never the living, loving, merciful God. Mysticism also is an ascent —or rather, since here the slow progress of thought is exchanged for a swifter motion—it means that the soul soars aloft towards God. The soul must leave everything behind; she must cast away every hindrance, she must be detached from all, then, infallibly, her search will be rewarded, as surely as the wind blows into the room when the window is opened, as surely as we are warmed and illuminated when we place ourselves in the sun. If "grace" is mentioned at all in this connection— and in this experience the inflow of the Divine is indeed

God's doing—in any case it is "grace" which has been attained by man, grace which can infallibly be attained[1] by following "the way" of mystical practice; it is grace in which forgiveness plays no part, the *gratia infusa*, not the gracious word of mercy and pardon.

Finally moralism also is a "way," a self-movement towards God; it consists in the gradual approach to the ideal through moral self-improvement; this effort does seem to succeed, although the rate of progress is very gradual. Although the individual may remain to the very end some distance from the goal, yet the section which has been achieved is the guarantee of fulfilment; it has practically been attained in one's own strength. Even if, perhaps, it is not exactly "good works" upon which the soul depends, there is at least the confidence that the good disposition will be finally rewarded, and this guarantees the attainment of the goal. And it is felt that this is a *real* guarantee. For otherwise one could not be sure of the goal. We may and must expect with complete confidence that assistance will supplement that which is lacking in our present endeavours; otherwise we would either eat our hearts out in a terrible uncertainty, or we would be obliged to receive this certainty as a gift.[2]

Thus the idea of self-movement towards God is everywhere supported by the certitude of self-sufficiency, of the continuous "way" to God, and of the possession of adequate strength, of continuity between man and God. Man trusts in his own self-

---

[1] Should the objection be raised that a mystical doctrine of grace does exist which does not teach that the soul can mount to heaven by its own efforts, nor lay stress on "inwardness" or ecstasy, but which preaches absolute quietism, as, for instance, the *prapatti*-mysticism of Hinduism, we might reply that in it everywhere the fundamental idea is that of identity. The instances of a supposedly Theistic mysticism which are adduced by Otto themselves testify to this. It is quite plain that Otto himself only recognizes this mystical idea of grace, and not the conception of grace which is taught in the Bible and held by the Reformers, especially since the publication of his latest work, *West-östliche Mystik*.

[2] This moral self-sufficiency is the element which is common to Stoicism, later ethical Idealism, the religion of Zoroaster, and the Pharisaism of later Judaism, as it is described by Jesus in the Parable of the Pharisee and the Publican, and as it is stated in all its naked truth in the Parable of the Labourers in the Vineyard.

movement because the gulf is not perceived, or, to put it the other way: men feel that this self-movement *must* exist which leads to the goal; therefore an impassable gulf cannot be *permitted* to exist. This is the spirit of self-righteousness, or righteousness of "works," the self-confident optimism of all non-Christian religion, to which even a so-called pessimism like that of Buddhism, or a "doctrine of grace" like that of certain Hindu sects, does not in the least constitute an exception. For in the first instance there is ascribed to man the moralist self-movement which leads to the goal, the self-redemption from *Samsāra*; in the second case all is indeed made dependent upon the grace which gives, but this is simply the "infused" grace of the mystics; it does not mean the reconciliation of the holy God with the guilty sinner. All "faith" which lies outside Christianity is self-movement, ascent, and is therefore in no sense an act of venturing faith; this element is lacking, just as much as the element of revelation, that is, of the self-movement of God.

In the Bible, however, revelation is described as the self-movement of God, as a descent, as an act of condescension. God does not simply wait to be sought, He Himself seeks man. The characteristic element in the Bible is this: in the intercourse between God and man the initiative belongs to God. He moves towards man. This is His "coming," a divine event—not in the sense of the Gnostic-theosophical process of "becoming" within the Godhead, but a divine story of God's dealings with the human race. Thus the character of this movement is the coming of God to man, or, to put it more exactly, the descent of God to the sinful creature. This is the whole point of the Christian revelation, for in every other form of religion the subject is treated from the opposite point of view: how can man come to God? This change of direction also provides the basis for the other characteristic feature of the message of the Bible: that *God* is central, and not man. For salvation lies in the movement of God, in what God says and does, not in any human activity at all. Hence we are here as little concerned with religion as we are with morality, or with mere speculation. In the Bible religion is rendered valueless by God. The final meaning of the doctrine of justification is that the concept of religion is stripped of all meaning by the divine act of revelation and reconciliation. Because everything depends upon the coming of God, therefore, and this is the third point, from the very outset it is a movement towards the whole world. Not the flight of the individual soul out of the world but a coming of God into the world, to His people. Thus here not only is religion swept away, but also all the individualism which is connected with religiosity, the instinct to seek God by flight from the world, in order to establish one's own soul in security. The restoration of the Kingdom of God is the point at issue; this, indeed, includes the deliverance of individual souls, but from the very outset it is something universal, something which embraces the world and humanity as a whole. Hence here the decisive point of view is no longer that of the happiness, rapture, or even the improvement of man; all this is subordinate to something greater still: the sovereignty of God, the fulfilment of the will of God, the breaking forth of the divine Light and Life in the whole of creation, the Glory of God. All this is implied in the direction of this movement; the self-movement of God to man, to the world.

It is this truth which is proclaimed in the simpler and more well-known phrases: *sola gratia, sola fide, soli deo gloria.* The mystic also can have these words on his lips, subjectively he may mean them quite seriously. But in spite of this we cannot really take him quite seriously when he does so; it lies in the very nature of mysticism—just as in that of moralism and speculation—that it cannot take this quite seriously, because to it God is not the One who moves, but man, because God does not "come" but is in "repose," and simply "is," whereas man alone moves along the "way" which annihilates distance. *Sola gratia* means: God alone walks along the way, not man; God annihilates the distance which separates Him from us, God comes to man, not man to God, and this is so because God alone can walk along this path, because He has a dimension which is far beyond the range of all human "walking"; He is infinite.

(iv)

We can only describe this coming of God by two expressions, which suggest both the fundamental tendencies of our existence, as "knowledge," and as "life." The coming of God is the self-manifestation, *revelation* and self-communication of God for life, the restoration of personal fellowship with God, atonement and redemption. And both mean that He comes. This is the subject of the Bible. The knowledge given to mankind is not "something," but God. It is not some particular kind of "salvation" or "Good" that is given to him, but the "Eternal Good," the salvation of the divine life. The love of God is His self-communication and His self-communication is at the same time His self-vindication, His holiness. Apart from this coming of God in revelation man cannot know God, and apart from this coming of God in atonement and redemption man can have no communion with God. But both mean the same thing. Apart from the revelation to man, God is the *deus absconditus*, the hidden God, the God whose Heart man cannot know, whose Nature he only knows so far as he knows it from himself and the world—yet these are sinful and corrupt—hence the God he knows is the angry God. Without the Atonement, however, apart from the explicit declaration of the will of God, which posits a new relation between fallen man and the Creator, a man has no right to think of God otherwise than as the angry God.

Both God's ways of giving Himself, in revelation and in the act of reconciliation, are an act of self-communication from spirit to spirit, from person to person. The gulf between God and man is not physical, it is wholly and absolutely personal. For sin means personal alienation. Man is alienated from the origin of his being, from that with which he could be united: the Word of God. In the Word of God man has been created. In the Word of God he has his personal principle of existence, from the Word he fell, namely from that in which God Himself gives Himself to men. This is why the coming of God must mean His coming in the Word, the coming of the Word of God; but this "Word" is not an impersonal "principle," nor an Idea of God, but it is the personal Being of God, the Divine Logos.

Thus the coming of God means that His Word is always coming nearer until at last it is really here in Its own actuality, no longer as a certain knowledge about the Word—as among the prophets—but the self-existence of the Word, in personal existence and authority. It is really and actually God Himself who wills to come to us; and it is really to us that He intends to come. To the extent in which it is the real coming of *God*, it is the coming of the "glory of the only-begotten of the Father, full of grace and truth"; in so far, however, as it is really a coming to *us*, it is the coming of the Son in lowliness, in the form of a servant, in the "likeness of sinful flesh." For God wills to come to us where we actually are. He does not condescend to some high region of human existence, to some "ideal" humanity; for such altitude would not really be our sphere, it would be at the most one aspect of our existence, isolated ideologically from our existence as a whole; it would not be the personal reality in which we live. There He would not be really known to us as He is Himself, nor would we truly know ourselves. Between God and ourselves there would still remain the cloud and smoke of illusion. God wills to come to us in reality, that we may know Him as He really is, and that we may know ourselves as we are. He wills to meet us at the place where we can be found. This is why He comes in the lowly guise of human existence. There He really meets with us, and this is why, after we have been finally unmasked, we arrive at the knowledge of Him and accept Him. Thus the manner and the aim of the divine coming is *nostra assumsit ut conferret nobis sua.*

It is the self-communication of God to us. Hence on His part there is an act of giving, and on our side an act of acceptance. This is the meaning of the divine "descent," this is the direction of His search. Because He seeks us truly, He follows after us until He finds us where we really are.

In this self-emptying alone His self-giving, His coming unto us, is perfected. That which is the most absolute contrast to the Absoluteness of the Divine Being must itself receive this Absoluteness. Here alone does God reveal the unfathomable depths of His love, the infinite desire with which He wills to give Himself to us—here alone, where He gives Himself so utterly that we might almost say that He "gives Himself away," as He lays aside all His glory—here, where the Creator of the world is merely "as one that serveth," as one who gives His life "as a ransom for many," as the Good Shepherd who goes on and on, after His lost sheep, "until He find it." That the King should don the beggar's cloak in order to persuade the beggar that He wishes to be his Friend—this condescension is His love. Indeed, His coming, as a whole, is nothing but love. Hence this complete act of self-giving, an act which transcends all that our human minds could ever grasp, manifests the infinite and unfathomable perfection of His love. This love of His is, at the same time, simply His unconditional will to reveal Himself, His Deity, His Divine Nature, and to make it evident to man. And in the act of revealing His love, His Name is hallowed.[1]

(v)

Here alone, therefore, do we perceive the complete contrast between this living personal God of Love and the unmoved rigid Being of the God of the philosopher, the mystic, and the moralist. The mystic may speak as much as he will about the love of God, yet the love to which he alludes is never the love of God who stoops down to man, who runs to meet him, who seeks us sinners until He finds us. It is not the God who forgives the sinner by taking the guilt on His own shoulders. It is not the God who "humbles" Himself in order that He may be with His sinful creature in its lowliness. It is never the Merciful God. The God who dwells aloft in sublime repose,

[1] This is the main theme in the doctrine of the Incarnation of the Early Church. Not that a magical transformation of human nature has taken place, but that the love of God became visible upon earth in His coming to us: this is what Irenaeus, Athanasius, Cyril, etc., really mean, and also Luther and our classical hymn writers. On that account we are here concerned, not as in Historical Positivism with the love of the human Jesus as such, but with the love of God which speaks to us in the coming of His Son, in His coming in lowliness, in this movement "from above," the love of the eternal Son of God who humbled Himself and took upon Himself the form of a servant.

is, measured by this standard, a God without love, the Olympian, who in supreme indifference reigns, sovereign and alone, upon His celestial heights, until some soul soars up to Him by the energy of his own thought, or meditation, or ecstasy, or through his own moral strivings. This God, who is sufficient to Himself, who has no longing desire for mankind, this Lord of the Heavenly House may perhaps be pleased to receive guests, but He does not search for the unfaithful who do not wish to have anything to do with Him. He alone knows what the Divine Love really is who knows the God who "comes," the God who Himself comes to men as they are, the God who reveals Himself in the Incarnation.

Therefore here alone can we speak of faith. Faith is the attitude of those who simply receive. It is the very opposite of all self-knowledge, self-assurance, or self-possession. A man only really believes where everything depends upon his receptivity, where he is utterly dependent and helpless. By this I mean something quite different from the "feeling of absolute dependence" advocated by Schleiermacher. This phrase sounds far more Christian than it really is. It means nothing more than the consciousness of causal determination; it is not the admission of a personal relationship. Faith, however, is a wholly personal attitude towards the divine Personality. Therefore, properly speaking, this presupposition, the act of standing before that gulf knowing quite well that it is absolutely impossible for me to cross over; to be brought to the point where I despair of ever healing the wound of my own existence in my own strength, or to bridge this gulf in my own power—this experience constitutes, as it were, the ante-chamber of faith. The knowledge of sin and guilt, in the Christian sense of the word, is the implied presupposition of faith contained within faith itself.

For he alone who knows this impossibility in its whole existential horror, and in its terrible sense of judgment, is in the right state of mind to perceive the coming of God, to accept the fact that God must do everything. But this admission is already the beginning of faith itself. Faith—so we said in an earlier passage—is the relation to the coming Word; in its fullness it is the relation to the Word of God who has come.

By this time it will have become clear that this view does not imply any particular "Christological theory." For this coming of God, this self-movement of God, this act which God alone performs, can only be perceived by him who is conscious of the need of his own existence, by one who feels the water rising to his chin, and who cries unto God "out of the depths." God can only be known *de profundis*. But *in profundis* there is no other God than the One who gave Himself to the utmost humiliation for our sakes. When a soul really knows no way to God then he is ready, and he alone, to believe in that God who Himself has come to him in the depths. The soul which is really and honestly despairing will find no help but in this faith. Hence he alone knows what it means to depend wholly upon God alone. For a soul who depends on someone else, and not only upon the God who comes to him Himself, depends secretly upon his own efforts, or he does not even see how great is the distance to be overcome.

The same truth might be stated the other way round: a man can only be brought to a full sense of his own complete helplessness when he admits that "God Himself must come to me, hence I must indeed be so far away from Him that I cannot possibly find the way back by myself." Only when he hears the message of revelation does man become conscious of the questionable character of his natural knowledge of God; only in the message of reconciliation does he see his guilt. It is only this proof of the divine love which has the power to break down his human pride and his pride of reason. The revelation creates faith, not faith the revelation. Despair does not necessarily imply deliverance. Despair does not in any way prove that God is merciful. All that I learn from despair is that I am despairing. Indeed, it is the essence of despair that we can see no way out at all.

So long as I still trust in my own knowledge, in my natural knowledge of God, I do not wish to hear about revelation. Hence I am far from faith. I regard it, as Fichte said of prayer, as a childish phase which precedes the mature knowledge of manhood. Even in the knowledge of God faith means absolute dependence upon God's giving, namely, on that self-giving of God which we know in His revelation, interpreting the word in the sense which is opposed to its immanent meaning. Faith is therefore the very opposite of proof. Proof means security of thought, the secure casting of the anchor of new knowledge in that which is already known. Or we may express the same thing in terms we have used already: the continuity of thought, or the co-ordination of the new element into the context of thought. Intuitive thought may well be the daring leap of the mind which precedes the slower process of thought; in so far as it is intuitive thought and not mere fantasy, the corroborative proof, the rational argument will come along later as a support, behind the intuitive pioneer, to restore the connection. But faith means the renunciation of this connection altogether. Faith cannot be established upon a settled basis. It does not stand, it depends. It depends on the Word of God alone, which can be trusted because it is the Word of God. He who does not trust this Word, does not see it as God's Word and does not believe. It is impossible to believe and at the same time to ask for proofs. Faith is pure dependence upon revelation.

This does not apply only to the justifying process in thought alone but also in action, in practical existence. The moralist is the man who knows how to justify his behaviour, and who considers that it is justified in the sight of God. But he who knows himself to be a sinner, to be a guilty being, finds that this kind of justification breaks down. He has "nothing with which he may pay his debt." Therefore all his hopes of being enabled to turn towards good depend on the divine action alone; that is, on forgiveness; on forgiveness, that is, which is a real transaction, which is not merely inferred on the basis of that which is present at the moment. Thus he depends on forgiveness as the revelatory Word of God, on the pronouncement of forgiveness as an actual fact.

Therefore faith, in the full meaning of the word, as pure dependence on the gift of God, exists only towards the coming God, who does all things Himself, who does all things alone, who imparts Himself to the soul. The philosopher therefore does not talk about faith, but about knowledge, the mystic speaks of visions and experiences, the moralist about the right disposition. Faith belongs to the sphere of Biblical revelation.

Faith belongs to the personal God, the Creator God, revelation, the Word of God, the coming of God. It is an improper use of the word, which weakens its force, if we use the word faith in the religious sense—apart from this connection. Faith means standing still on the edge of the abyss because it is impossible to walk any further; and it means standing still before the self-movement of God, as the only possibility of reaching the goal. Therefore faith only exists where a man can say: *sola fide*, *sola gratia*, and this means: faith in the God who has come to us, the Mediator.

CHAPTER XI

THE ETERNAL BASIS AND THE TEMPORAL EVENT OF THE INCARNATION

(i)

REVELATION is absolutely unique, therefore it is absolutely decisive. This is so true that we could reverse the statement and say: the one absolutely unique and decisive fact is revelation. It is only since Christ came, and through Him, that both uniqueness and absolute decision have been in existence. It has often been observed—and rightly so—that only through Christianity has the world become conscious of the problem of history; but usually when this remark is made the ideas with which it is connected are far too vague. The key to the understanding of this very significant fact lies in the conception of uniqueness, which is identical with that of absolute decision. This conception does not belong to the sphere of Natural Science. All our study of nature is directed toward overcoming the idea of uniqueness; our whole aim is to be able to discover and apprehend the laws of nature. In nature anything that is unique can safely be ignored; it is non-essential.

In history this relation is reversed. Here the unique is the really constitutive element. The historical scholar seeks to discover the special distinctive quality in every human phenomenon; he searches for the features which will never recur, which are not general; his interest is centred on the elucidation of peculiar, individual elements or characteristics. This is why he re-tells the story of the past. As soon as the unique element in his story ceases the charm of history has vanished. If everything seems to be *tout comme chez nous,* historical interest dies a natural death. And yet it is also true that the elements which are only strange, peculiar, individual, have just as little power to grip our attention. The interest of history depends quite as much on what is common to humanity as it does on what is unique. Indeed, really great history is precisely that which combines the highest quality of common humanity

with the highest element of uniqueness, as these are illustrated
by the great personalities and events of world history. They
are the most interesting of all. Are they, however, more than
that? So long as we are mere spectators of world history the
only categories in which we think are those of interest and
admiration. But it might also be possible to look at history
not merely from the point of view of a spectator who enjoys
a fine spectacle, but really seriously. Then we would listen to
find out "what it has to say to us."

Only then does the problem of history become significant
for us: nothing has so much to say to us as history, but its
message is not decisive. When we have discovered what history
really is, we realize that we cannot seek for the decisive within
history. History represents the common human element in the
form of uniqueness. But the relation between these two elements
consists in a certain tension. The element of uniqueness limits
the common human element, and the common human element
limits uniqueness. Genius, for instance, because it is still
common to humanity—even although it may be rare—is not
really unique. By the very fact of its individuality, however
significant this individuality may be, the greatness of genius is
still a limited greatness, and possesses a limited significance.
Hence, although genius has much to say to us, its message is
not decisive. An epoch in world history or a great event has
immense, but not final, significance for us. As we confront it
we are still conscious of our freedom, of our independence in
principle.

But revelation is absolutely unique, and at the same time
eternal; hence it is decisive. If it were eternal only, it would not
be decisive. For in that case it would be the common element
which lies behind all that is common to humanity as a whole.
It would not be an event at all, but only an idea, which would
shine through the events of history as their "background."
That which is merely significant is never decisive. On the other
hand, if revelation were wholly and *only* unique, then it would
be so absolutely remote and unintelligible that we could have
no relation to it at all. It is decisive because it is both unique
and eternal.

It is only because it is eternal that it can be absolutely

unique. Between eternity and nothingness there lies merely the natural and the historical, both of which are relative; neither the one nor the other is absolutely unique. The natural element is clad in the uniform of Natural Law; the historical element is, it is true, strikingly individual, but just in so far as it is significant it is only relatively unique. The eternal element alone can be absolutely unique. But since this is so, since it thus fulfils the essence of history, at the same time it also abrogates history. It fulfils the meaning of history; that is, in it is actual that which in history only "strives" to be actual: it achieves the union of the unique and the significant. Therefore it is decisive. It is the "fullness of time." It belongs, however, to the nature of the "fulfilled" time that it should only take place once. History, as such, knows no fulfilment, but only the striving after fulfilment.

It is therefore inevitable that this fulfilment of history should lead to the abrogation of history. It is impossible to introduce the eternal into the chain of historical events as though it were a specially precious and magnificent pearl. The weight of the pearl would break the chain. The eternal as an event, the revelation, as such, possesses no historical extension. The eternal in history, the revelation as the absolutely unique, cannot be perceived in terms of historical extension. Revelation is not the actual fact which is made known through history: the life of Jesus and the historical personality of Jesus—but the invisible secret of the Person of Jesus, hidden behind the veils of history and of human life, not the Christ after the flesh but the Christ after the Spirit, the "Word made flesh."

But this Word means—and it is with this meaning that we are here concerned—the End of history. The Word is the Word of the beginning, "before" all history, and that of the End which lies "behind" all history. All history seeks for that which takes place in Jesus Christ, and is "here." Hence, it means the fulfilment of history. But all history too flees from that which is "present" in Jesus, and therefore it means the abrogation of history. In all history what should happen never happens. This is what keeps history in existence. If what ought to take place should actually take place, then history would cease, the end of the ages, the time of fulfilment would have come. History, like the Odyssey, endures so long as home has not been reached. And by its very nature history can never attain its goal. For it moves always on this side of the gulf which separates man from his origin and his goal. Where this deep gulf is transcended, there is the end of history, the source of history, and its goal has been reached; there history comes to a standstill, for the fullness of time has come. But around this event, as round a rock, swirl the tides of history, and then the current flows on.

But by the very fact that this unique event has actually taken place the whole of history henceforth has been modified. The problem of history has arisen, history has become problematical. What is still more serious is this: historical man, as such, has become problematical. The uniqueness of revelation has set its seal upon history, which it did not previously possess, the seal of the possibility and the necessity of decision. Before Christ there was no final decision, because the ultimate had not yet been presented to man; all that faced him was the historical element. Now, however, there stands within history, but as the alien element in history, which cannot be perceived from the merely historical point of view, the fact of revelation, the "revelation of Christ" as the "sign which shall be spoken against," "for the fall and the rising again of many." The stone which the builders have rejected has become the chief corner-stone, but at the same time also described the stone thus: "on whomsoever it shall fall it shall grind him to powder" (Matt. xxi. 42, 44).

The sense of the seriousness of existence was in the world before Christ came, but final seriousness has only existed since then, because only through Him is there an ultimate decision. This means that henceforth every historical element has gained a new quality. We have a new consciousness of time and history; but only in faith do we really possess this. The *moment* gains the quality of an absolutely decisive moment through Christ in so far as we are related to Christ, in so far as we "see" what His coming means, in so far as we receive the Word which in Him has become "flesh." To say that history has become problematic means: whereas previously men lived simply within history, absolutely immersed in it, we have now, so to speak, raised our heads above history, and we can see the mist in which history is enveloped. We see the *riddle* of history, of historical existence, and we see the *sin* of history and of historical existence. We know Adam, the "first Adam," because, and in so far as, we know the "second Adam."[1]

This is something quite different from the hostility to history which appears in Idealism of the kind which has no use for history, or in mysticism of the type which is still more opposed to history in all forms. For whereas the revelation of Christ lays a heavy burden of responsibility, with absolute seriousness, upon the actual moment of history, mysticism relieves this tension. To say that mysticism is non-historical means that it is non-decisive. For the mystic "time is like eternity"; when he descends into the divine abyss all consciousness of time disappears. There is no decision there, but only "being" since God "*is.*" Indeed, everything is already decided, or rather, there never was anything to be decided. Time and all demand for decision are regarded as transparent illusions. All motion

[1] It has often been pointed out that the idea of world history and of thought in terms of world history, arose out of eschatology in general or out of Old Testament prophecy in particular. Primarily there are two factors which constitute the presupposition of the idea of world history: firstly, the unity of the meaning of the world as it is determined by the idea of Creation in "Monotheism," and belief in the reality of historical events. The Idealistic philosophy of history may be aware of the unity of meaning, but it does not recognize real events. For according to its view everything is development, hence there is no decision. But even the Old Testament (not to mention the religion of the Parsees) does not know fully the complete Christian conception of history. For on the one hand there is not yet complete openness of vision for the people as a whole, and on the other hand the decision is not yet fully there: the "decisive element" is still lacking, the event that took place once for all, and hence also the idea of the Final Judgment. Where, however, this idea has begun to dawn—in later Judaism —there it is permeated at the same time with strong nationalistic elements and is lacking in the seriousness of the prophets. It is, however, fulfilled in the "Now" of the Gospel.

To how great an extent the idea of history, the understanding of what it means to have history at all, is dependent on faith and unbelief, is shown by the naturalization of the conception of history during the last fifty years, and the deification of history in the period of historico-philosophical Idealism. Against this even the idea of individuality taught by Troeltsch does not help us, for it finally becomes merged in relativism, and in the place of decision it places intuition (the cosmos of individualities).

is regarded as unreal. All appears to be steeped in the one divine light, which does not differ from darkness because no darkness exists. History has nothing to say to the mystic at all. He sees in it no dawn of an approaching decision; he has no eschatology. He sinks down into an eternal repose. We only need to think of India to know that we are describing a real state.

The revelation of Christ is therefore absolutely decisive, for in it the non-historical, the eternal, breaks[1] through into time at one point, and in so doing makes it a place of decision. By this I do not mean the event in world history which we call the "rise of Christianity." This is a very important event, it is true, a "very decisive" event—taking the word in a relative sense; but it is no more than this. It is quite possible to hesitate to say whether it is as important as, for instance, the fusion of East and West due to the compaigns of Alexander, or as the fall of the Roman Empire. It is one turning-point among many in the course of world history. This is not what I mean. For this is only the echo of the real event of Christ, which, however, as such, cannot be perceived as an historical event at all. Christianity has only become so important because so many have seen in Christ more than an event of history, namely the unique revelation of God. If we were to set the modern conception of Christ in the place of the primitive faith in Christ, Christianity would soon disappear from the chronicle of the historian. The power of Christianity within world history is the radiance of faith in Christ, of faith in the absolute, decisive, unique revelation.

[1] The "breaking through" would be in reality—as is often charged against us—"Supranaturalism" if we were here concerned with the insertion of a new supernatural "section." But in so far as the "breaking through" does not in any way result in any visible historical phenomenon, but only in the mystery of the Person of Christ on the one hand and in faith in this mystery on the other, it does not lead to the isolation of a "section" of eternity in the midst of time, which indeed would be supranaturalism in the bad sense. Hence it is so important to distinguish between the Christ *in* the flesh and the Christ *after* the flesh.

(ii)

This faith, however, includes within itself the knowledge that this Word which "came," which "became flesh," is the eternal Word. The Word itself, as the personal Word, as the Son of God has His origin and His duration in eternity, so also this happening, this coming, also has its origin in eternity. This thing that happens breaks forth from the being of God as He is in Himself, from the mysterious depths of the Trinity; how could it be otherwise seeing that it is really the coming of God? How could it otherwise possess absolute decision, or be the final guarantee? This is why the Scriptures speak of the "eternal purpose" of the Incarnation, of the reconciliation and redemption of Christ. Truly no speculative interest, no mythological side-issue here emerges, but faith itself, revelation itself in its entirety. For only that which is based on the eternal is revelation, and only that which wills to be anchored in the eternal sphere itself, and knows that it is thus anchored, is faith.

History in the human sense is a matter of indifference for faith. It is "flesh." Christ as an historical personality is the Christ after the flesh. The life of Jesus, the story of Jesus of Nazareth, as such, is a significant event within the human sphere, but it is no more. But the "coming" of the Son of God in the flesh, the fact that the Son was sent forth into the world, this event which moves between time and eternity is, as the origin of the Christ, as the mystery of His Person, the proper concern of faith. For this coming constitutes the Person of the Mediator: for here and nowhere else can Jesus be known as the Christ. All other knowledge is on the historical plane and is represented as an extension of humanity, as a human phenomenon—however sublime this may be. The fact of His coming, the shining thread which extends from eternity into time, and is perceived by the eye of faith—it is this which distinguishes faith in Christ from admiration for an historical character.

Not only the Logos Himself, the Son, has His origin in the eternal, in the mystery of God, but also the event of His coming. The "impulse" of this movement, that which gives it power, direction, decisiveness arose in eternity. Only thus can we finally dispose of historical positivism; only thus can we avoid the misunderstanding which arises when we regard the historical element as important in itself. Just as faith can never become the full certainty of the *sola gratia* without becoming aware of eternal election, so also the knowledge of revelation can never be directed purely towards the "Christ after the spirit" without becoming aware of the eternal origin of this historical element. This is no unauthorized extension of the interest of faith into an inaccessible region; on the contrary: here alone is the sphere of faith. A happening of this kind, this dimension alone is the object of faith.

The statement that this movement itself arose in the eternal sphere needs further elucidation. For this idea of an "eternal purpose" is still exposed to the danger of a "Judaistic" interpretation, which would utterly destroy the reality of the revelation. It is absolutely true that the source of this movement is within eternity, that is, both the will to send the Son and the willingness to be sent belong to that mysterious realm. For not only the One who sends is God, but also the One who is sent, the Son. It is the Son "who although He was on an equality with God, thought it not a prize to be equal with God, but emptied Himself and took upon Himself the form of a servant. . . ." To regard this as a "speculative" idea means that one is still held in the grip of historical positivism; that one has not yet discovered the dimension of faith. If *this* is empty speculation—as quite naturally it must seem to unbelief —then the whole of the Christian religion is speculation, everything, that is, that goes beyond the ascertained facts of history. But faith only begins where the historical perception ceases; faith and perception are mutually exclusive. That which can be perceived is never the object of faith, and that which is the object of faith can never be perceived.

If then the Sent One is really God—and this is faith's witness to Christ—then also the fact that He was sent and the willingness to be sent constitute an eternal process, however little we can imagine what this means, although we can only express this in a very stammering way, like children who cannot speak plainly. I am not saying this for the sake of saying it, but in order that, where it needs it, faith, to be real faith, may be strengthened. God does not send a man, but His Son. It is not a man who obeys Him, but His Son. This is why this "sending" and this "willingness to be sent" cannot be regarded as an event within the sphere of history. The fact that Christ was thus "sent" is not a movement within history, but it means that the eternal enters into history, it is the entrance of the non-historical element into the world of history. "When the fullness of the time had come, God sent forth His Son." Here another dimension is indicated from that which is suggested when it is said that God "sent" Elijah with a message to King Ahab. Here what is "sent," in the New Testament sense, is not Elijah, but the Word which came to Elijah. But in Christ the Word has become a Person. The dimension from which the Word comes in the Old Testament is the same as that from which the Son comes in the New Testament; it is not a dimension in the world of history at all, but the dimension of the eternity of God directed towards history.

Therefore both the "sending" and the "being sent" are eternal. As Luther would say, "The proceeding began in heaven." The obedience of the Son is not the obedience of an historical personality, but the presupposition on the basis of which this personality could become historical. Not only the commission, but also the reception of the commission, arises within eternity. If it were not so, this would not be the movement of God towards man, but the movement of an historical figure, which would only be caused by God in the same way as any other historical movement is caused. It would not be revelation, but providence, God's rule over the world. Thus only from the idea of the Trinity can the whole fact of revelation be understood. This does not mean that a detailed doctrine of the Trinity, or even the mere conception of the Trinity, forms part of the Christian message, for such a conception cannot be found within the New Testament. It is, however, true that the whole of the testimony of the Apostles is full of the Trinitarian idea, and every Christian statement is rooted in it, namely, in the idea that between Christ and God there is a relation which differs from that between Christ and us, a relation in which from the very beginning Christ was on the side of God over against us, as the divine authority, as the Lord (*Kyrios*) whom we worship.

(iii)

That we are here concerned with the very opposite of the speculation of the mere spectator can be known by anyone who recalls Luther's glorious hymn, "*Nun freut euch lieben Christen gemein*," in which for anyone who "has ears to hear" the necessary connection between the eternal purpose of the Incarnation and the existential need of man is suggested drastically and clearly enough. That the Christian, with his belief in salvation, needs to mount so high is only the reverse side of the fact that he feels his need more deeply, and is more fully conscious of it than others. Because he alone knows what the gulf is, he alone knows what is needed to bridge this gulf. Luther's hymn proves that the doctrine of the eternal purpose of the Incarnation is through and through non-speculative, practical, and existential.

Because the Christian sees history as a whole separated from God—not from the providence, sustaining power, and sovereignty of God, nor from His immanence in the world, but indeed from His saving presence—because he sees, brooding over all that is historical, the "wrath of God," like a dark cloud out of which at any moment there might break forth the final disaster, judgment, and damnation, therefore he knows at what point the saving movement must begin. But the fact that the whole of eternity must be set in motion for his sake shows him the depth of his need. This thought of the divine self-movement—of the movement of the eternal purpose of God and of the eternal obedience of the Son which begins in eternity—as the means to the rescue of the sinful creature is as a human idea audacious beyond all measure. Indeed, if man could regard himself as so important that he could demand that on his account the whole of heaven should be set in motion, this would certainly be the height of human arrogance. But there is no question here of a human idea at all, but of something which takes place within the self-movement of God, which indeed is identical with the manifestation of this Will of God. Since, however, it is God's own revelation, and not a human idea, from a human interest it is transformed into a divine interest: it develops into the divine interest of the self-manifestation of God, of the dominion of God. But the boldness of the soul which believes that we are intended to take this incomprehensible interest quite seriously, this absolutely disproportionate estimate of worth by God Almighty for us "worms," for these "lost coins," which from His point of view can have no value, the boldness to believe that "God had pity in eternity for my misery beyond compare"—this boldness is faith.

On the other hand, the positivistic conception, which looks at the whole subject from within history, is a clear proof of the fact that the real need of man is ignored without a glimmering of understanding of its existence or of its reality, that the gulf has not even been perceived, and—this judgment cannot be evaded—how little men take the words sin and guilt seriously. The only reason why men expect "redemption" from a process which has taken place within history is because they have not felt the need which lies behind history, because, on the contrary, they regard history as the really normal, as that which ought to be. This means also that it is not historical man as such, not our present manner of existence as such which is wrong, eccentric, chaotic, sinful, but only certain features within it, which could very well be removed by careful thought. There is no belief in the corruption of our actual human historical condition: men not only oppose the doctrine of Original Sin because they dislike the idea it conjures up, but because they do not believe in its central thought, in the state of corruption, in the Fall, in the break, in the destruction of the coherence of life. Hence they do not conceive "redemption" as a "return" at all, but as something future, as a speeding up of development, which is posited as identical with the "fulfilment of creation." So utterly different are these two points of view.

(iv)

In the previous chapter we pointed out the connection between the "coming" of God and the summons to "return." This has become still clearer with the perception of the clearer relation of this event to the eternal aspect of the question. Because the coming of God is a real coming, because therefore actually "heaven is moved," then this "coming" must mean "coming back." The break did not form part of the original creation, it means rather the falling away from it. The coming of God, whose intention it is to overcome this separation, is thus a process of restoration. Otherwise His "coming" would be unnecessary. The Incarnation of God, and the eternal purpose of the Incarnation, is not based upon an imperfection which has been inherent in the world from the Creation, which as such might need redemption; such a conception of the Creation would be Gnostic and Manichean, and entirely alien to the message of the Bible and of the Church. The purpose of the Incarnation refers rather to sinful fallen humanity and the creature than to the creature as such. The coming of the Son into the world is not a coming into God's Creation, but into sinful creation. It is not the perfecting, but the restoration of creation. It is connected with closing the gulf which yawns not between the creature and the Creator, but between man who is sinful and a wrathful God. It is not creation as such which needs redemption, but the fallen creation. Hence the work of the Mediator is that of reconciliation. Revelation and reconciliation are one throughout the whole of the Bible. But the Creation as such, *qua* good creation, had no need of a Mediator.

Thus it is the mercy of God, the faithfulness of God towards His unfaithful creature which the Incarnation brings to us as redeeming truth. Apart from this "coming," from this self-movement of God, apart from it as a divine movement which arises in eternity, we know nothing either of this mercy or of our need for it. It is only through this whole fact that we learn what our need is. And that God is like this, that His love is so deep, so unconditioned, we can only come to know

314

from this His condescension. It is only when we see how low
God has to stoop that we see how far we have fallen. Without
this real happening both the gap, the gulf, and also the Divine
Love, seem to us far too small. The incomprehensible element
in this estimate of worth, which contradicts all laws of proportion, is the *tertium comparationis* in those parables of the
shepherd who seeks for his lost sheep, of the widow who turns
the whole house upside down for a tiny coin. This disproportion
shows the difference between the living merciful God of the
Biblical revelation and the "Absolute," the "Basis of the world
or of the soul" of thought and of mysticism, and the moral
principle of ethical Idealism.

This disproportion between the "worm Jacob" and the
sovereign Lord, this incomprehensible movement of heaven for
our sake—this is the revelation of the living God, the marvellous
Word of the Scriptures, Jesus, the Christ.

CHAPTER XII

THE FACT OF THE INCARNATION

(i)

THE central truth of the Christian faith is this: that the eternal Son of God took upon Himself our humanity, not that the man Jesus acquired divinity. Those who have been able to follow what has been said so far in this book will understand why faith lays so much stress upon this distinction. For this distinction concerns the fundamental character of the movement: is it a movement from God towards man, or is it a movement from man towards God? Or, to put it in another way, is it the self-redemption of man, the ascent of man, or is it redemption through God, a descending movement, is it a righteousness of "works," or is it the gift of "grace"? The direction of the movement is the decisive question for faith as a whole. The fact that this movement implies descent is the element which, in principle and unconditionally, distinguishes the Biblical revelation from all other forms of religion or philosophy. It is all-important, in fact, everything depends upon this: that the termini of this movement should be rightly defined, and not the other way about. The origin of the movement is in eternity. Thence it issues forth, its goal is historical humanity; towards this also the movement is directed. Hence the event of revelation can only mean that the eternal Son assumed our humanity. *Nostra assumsit ut conferret nobis sua.*

This, however, implies quite clearly that the process cannot be either historical or natural. It lies beyond the sphere of all human-intellectual or natural-causal happenings. Thus in principle it is an event which cannot be perceived, that is, it is one which can neither be understood nor explained. It is a divine secret; it is absolutely unique, and therefore cannot be compared with any other happenings; hence it lies outside the sphere of the imagination. To put it more precisely: it is impossible for us to define the relation between this event and the natural happenings which it conditioned, i.e. the facts of the history of the life of Jesus. All that we can say is this: this mystery is the presupposition of this Life, and indeed of the whole Life. Possibly its closest analogy would be the Creation, but this analogy itself, if we do not confuse it with the causal process of becoming, but regard it in the Christian sense, is completely invisible, an absolute mystery of God.

The total significance of this event is expressed in the statement that the Logos assumed human *nature*. This statement has been misunderstood by modern theology, with its lack of perspicacity, and taken to mean simply "naturalism." But the early Fathers meant by "nature" simply the totality of human existence as the possibility of personal life. "Human nature is all that makes up a human life." Jesus Christ is true Man; His life lacked nothing which formed part of human historical life. It does not mean that a "section" of human and natural life has been removed and in its place a "section" of the divine life has been inserted. At least this is the central tendency of the doctrine. That the Church did not remain entirely true to it will be shown immediately by an illustrative incident of considerable importance. The life of Jesus is not a blend of natural and supernatural elements. So far as the historical and visible side of His life is concerned it is quite natural and historical.

The Christian doctrine has, however, laid equal stress on the fact that although Jesus Christ assumed human nature, He did not assume human personality. Here too, as far as possible, the Church protested against a false view of the supernatural, as though it were possible to insert a divine section into an otherwise natural condition. No, even from the human psychological point of view Jesus is wholly and truly Man. The opposing doctrine of Apollinaris, which indeed allowed that Jesus had a human body and a human *psyche* (in the Aristotelian sense), but not a human spirit, was rejected as heresy, as a corruption of the Christian conception. The "complete humanity" was defended with passion against all such minimizing attempts by the very same people who had also tried to defend His deity against the minimizing attempts

317

of the Arians. Translated into the language of to-day this means that as an historical personality, as a subject of history, Jesus is completely human. For by *Nous* the ancients meant exactly what we mean by historical personality, the sphere of humanity.

(ii)

One thing only was rejected: it was affirmed that Jesus Christ has no human Personality. We cannot sufficiently admire the sureness and delicacy of this definition. It corresponds exactly to the scriptural idea of revelation. The *Nous* is the rational nature, the means of communication which arises out of the historical connection and unites with history, that whereby the Person makes Himself visible and clear from the human and historical point of view. The *Nous* is the historical manifestation of the mystery of the Person. Everyone possesses a mystery of personality, which is in no wise identical with his historical personality, with the individual human character which is visible to the historian or to the biographer, and can be grasped by him. This mystery of personality lies behind all historical and psychological perception. It lies even behind all self-perception. As human beings we all wear masks, and we see each other and ourselves through masks. We are mysteries to others and to ourselves. And indeed this mystery does not consist merely in the sense of individuality; that is our natural mystery, not the mystery of personality. There is the mystery of our created being which separates us and always should separate us from each other. But it is not this with which we are now dealing, but with the personal mystery of responsible being. For to be a person is to be a responsible being. Our mystery is the inmost point of our actual existence, of our self-determination, of the self which is not "given" but self-determined. For our mental endowments constitute nature, personal possibility. We, however, are not personal only through this "given" element, but this endowment only develops from a possibility into a reality by means of our own personal act, our own decision. Thus it is action as a whole, not individual acts in the historical sense (for these are only the expression of personal being), the fundamental, original act, which constitutes the mystery of our personality.

Here alone is the seat of sin; again, this means sin in the total sense, that sin which is the source of all sins, which we cannot perceive psychologically, that which lies "behind" all that is sinful from the historical point of view—the Fall. The fact that we all wear masks which we cannot lay aside is the result of this original Fall, this original personal act. This is our secret, of which we are afraid, because although it is true that we do not see through it, yet we have some suspicion of the nature of that which lies behind it. We cannot unmask ourselves because we are no longer sufficiently true. But there is a place or point at which we are unmasked: before Christ, in faith. There we see the secret of our personality, there alone where we know the mystery of His Person, where we see Him as the Son of God. Our personality, however, remains an object of faith, not an historical form. For as persons we cannot be known, only believed. Our being, as persons, is determined by our attitude towards God.

The secret of our personality is that having been created by God in His image, in His Word, we have fallen away from God, away from His Word. This is our "eccentricity"; it is this that constitutes our present historical reality, and at the same time our mask.

It is the mystery of the Person of Jesus Christ that at the point at which we have this sinful "Person" He has, or rather is, the divine person of the Logos. For "person" means precisely that which we cannot *have*, but must *be*. Christ has indeed assumed human nature, but not a human person. Thus He may have assumed the possibility of being tempted—the possibility of sin which is connected with the historical personality—but He did not assume the corrupted personality spoilt by Original Sin, that is, the necessity of falling in temptation. To fall in temptation—in spite of Original Sin— is never a natural fact, but always and only a personal act. Hence it is said of Christ: He was tempted in all points like as we are—yet without sin. He stepped into the abyss. He entered wholly into human life, even descending to the deepest depths of the "sinful flesh." He allowed the powers of the abyss to work their will upon Him—but He did not make the abyss wider, for that would have destroyed the meaning of His coming. He came in order to enter into the abyss and thus to build the bridge, but not in order to make the gulf wider by His action, to break down the dykes by committing sin Himself. Hence, although He assumed human nature with its possibilities of being tempted, even an historical personality after the manner of men, He did not assume human personality in the sense of the ultimate mystery. Instead of the human mystery of personality, sin, He possesses the divine mystery of personality: divine authority.

(iii)

But, even though we are forced to state that Jesus Christ only assumed human nature, but not human personality, still we must insist as strongly as ever that this means the *whole* of human nature. In laying such stress on the completeness of His human nature we are not proclaiming a "physical conception of salvation," a naturalistic corruption of the thought of salvation—and thus of the thought of sin; on the contrary, we are stating a profound truth which the modern man has completely lost. Through the conception of "human nature" there is an effort to work against the individualistic isolation of mankind. As sinners men are not only isolated individuals, but—even when they no longer know it—they are members of a solidarity. This is true not merely in the sense of the modern theory of environment, or of the doctrine of heredity. Both these theories weaken the idea of the responsibility of the individual. But the Christian conception of solidarity is one which is not natural and not historical, one which is not visible and cannot be proved, but can only be believed. This is what is meant by the doctrine of Original Sin: a solidarity in sin, of which we have no historical knowledge, which, however, lies at the basis of all historical experience. We are not only sinful men, we form a sinful humanity. We are sinners because we are human beings; the idea of a sinless historical human life is from the Christian point of view an impossible idea, which shakes all specifically Christian statements of faith to their very foundations.

We must recognize this solidarity, this human character of sin before we can estimate its weight. It is at this point that the question is decided for or against Pelagianism, which at bottom means simply either self-redemption or redemption through faith alone. On the other hand, the knowledge of this solidarity is the only possible means of overcoming religious egoism. You were not created simply as an individual —as an isolated individual—nor can you be redeemed as an individual. God always deals with humanity as a whole. The wonder of redemption is only known for what it really is when we see that the God who sees us before Him as sinful humanity has had mercy upon us all. This is what is meant, and not something physical, by the doctrine that the Son of God assumed human nature. By doing this He made it evident that humanity as a whole is the object of His activity; it already implies the universality of the divine will of redemption, the significance of the fact of Christ.[1] Whether this central thought of the doctrine of Christianity may have been connected with certain sacramentarian or magical elements is of no interest to us here. In any case, in the dogma of the Early Church such elements were never of final significance, because people always saw that although this union of the Son of God with human nature[2] was indeed intended for humanity as a whole, it only profited those who believed. It is thus a personal transaction between the Divine Person and the person of the human being who believes. The chief point is always that of decision.

In Christ God deals with humanity as a whole, He assumes the whole of human nature, because only thus can He lay hold of sinful humanity. And He deals with the whole of humanity because from the very outset His will of love is universal; it is directed towards the whole. The Fathers of the Church did

---

[1] It is obvious that this does not imply any "Universalism," any unconditional salvation of all, which would diminish the seriousness of the Judgment. We know the universalism of the divine will to reconcile and redeem only in a sense which calls for decision, thus as a will which it is possible to disobey.

[2] Cf. the Appendix on the Dogma of the Divine Nature of Christ, p. 249.

well to say clearly that the Incarnation of the Son of God was not an event which affected humanity at one point alone, but that the whole situation of humanity has been altered by it. It is not only the decision of the individual for Christ which is important, but that which alone makes this decision possible: the coming of God to humanity. The Incarnation is the great miracle: it is absolutely objective; it is utterly impossible to divert it into any subjectivistic direction at all. The great fact of salvation, the miracle of Christmas,[1] consists precisely in what modern subjectivism rejects as "sacramental magic," that which precedes all human relation to Christ, namely, the relation of God to us, the assumption of our human nature, the bridging over of the gulf between the human-historical existence as such and God.

(iv)

But in the past this amazingly glorious message has been burdened with an idea which is apt to obscure the meaning of its central thought: I mean the theory of the Virgin Birth. It is, of course, true that this idea plays no part in the Christological conflicts of the Early Church. Even great heretics

[1] Luther's warning against useless disputations about the doctrine of the Two Natures is not merely a prescription, as if a doctor were to warn his patient against eating too much. We ought not to discuss this at all. The whole problem is seen from a wrong angle when this is done. A miracle of salvation is turned into a metaphysical problem; the existential question: What took place? is turned into the inquisitive inquiry: How did it take place? From the very outset to ask how it is possible that God should become man is a wrong question. We find no trace of this question in the New Testament at all (apart from the theory of the Virgin Birth). The New Testament simply announces that this has happened. So also the whole modern Kenosis doctrine has wrongly stressed this question of possibility and the laws which govern the functions of a divine-human Person, instead of stressing the fact itself, as it is present to faith: namely as the presence of the divine salvation in the Personal Word: Christ. Just as in the case of the doctrine of Inspiration, people have wanted to look into the divine mechanism (to see how it works) instead of listening to the divine Word itself. Hence I have not entered into the question of the "substance" of the divine-humanity, but have only tried to trace out simply the meaning of the word "revelation": if revelation is taken seriously, then the divine-humanity must be what it is said to be.

like Paul of Samosata accepted the Virgin Birth—in itself this is a sign how little this doctrine is apt to protect the precious treasure of the faith from being squandered. Of late this question has become increasingly prominent in theological discussions in which the great ideas which lie behind the dogma are no longer rightly understood on either side. It is easy to understand that in lay circles this theory constituted a simple conception of the Incarnation, which could easily be grasped, and was therefore highly prized, and that it was upheld and obstinately opposed to all rational and ethical attempts to water down the conception of the "deity of Christ." Here, however, this is not the point at issue; we are concerned with the actual fitness of the term to express what it sets out to express.

In earlier days this discussion used to be cut short by saying briefly "It is written"; that is, with the aid of the doctrine of Verbal Inspiration. To-day we can no longer do this, even if we would. Particularly in connection with this question of Parthenogenesis it is well known that the New Testament tradition is rather precarious. This so-called fundamental dogma is not mentioned either by Paul or by John.[1] Paul only mentions the two points which lie, so to speak, to the right and the left of the mystery of the Incarnation: Jesus Christ was sent from God in the fullness of time; He humbled Himself and took upon Himself the form of a servant. And, He was born of a woman and was subject to the law. At another time he says still more plainly: He was born of the "seed of David" according to the flesh, but a Son of God according to the spirit. John, who certainly would have felt quite free to complete the tradition in the dogmatic sense from his own knowledge of the facts, is completely silent on this point. To him it is sufficient to say "the Word was made flesh," and "I am come from above." The whole of the rest of the apostolic literature, including Mark, is also silent on this question. Apart from the two passages Matt. i. 18–25 and Luke i. 35, in the whole of the New Testament there is no trace of this idea or of any

[1] With regard to the doctrine of the Virgin Birth even Luther recognizes that the Scriptures "do not lay so great stress on it," since Paul does not mention it (*W.A.*, 46, 19).

interest in it. Both these passages, however, belong to that part of the New Testament which even the most conservative scientific theologian who bases all his arguments on the authority of Scripture would to-day hardly dare to use as a scriptural proof, apart from the fact that there are many indications that, even in this respect, even these early passages of Matthew and of Luke once read very differently.

These arguments, however, are not adduced here in order to attack the doctrine itself, for this would be wholly out of keeping with the spirit of the rest of this book. All that is intended here is to show once more that the process of producing arguments and proofs based on Scripture, which is also untenable on general grounds, is here especially unfortunate. This statement also implies a second point, which is only of slight importance: as an historical account which the Church is supposed to have received from the parents of Jesus, the idea of the Virgin Birth scarcely comes into consideration at all. There is practically *no* historical evidence at all for the argument that this doctrine is based upon a statement of the parents of Jesus. They, however, were the only people who would have been competent to give the necessary information, if this doctrine is supposed to be based upon a "report" of this kind. On the contrary, everything goes to prove that this doctrine arose rather late, thus that it arose for dogmatic reasons and not out of historical knowledge. Here then we have reached the point where the question really belongs. The doctrine of the Virgin Birth would have been given up long ago were it not for the fact that it seemed as though dogmatic interests were concerned in its retention.

The first reason was this: it was argued that natural procreation is contrary to the divine significance of the Incarnation. Let us be quite clear on this point. The question is not: Is the birth of the Person of Christ a divine saving miracle, the miracle of the Incarnation or not? But it is this: Are we obliged to represent to ourselves the divine miracle of the Incarnation of the Son of God as a Virgin Birth or not? We are, namely, absolutely certain of the miracle of the divine fact. But that this miracle can be further explained by the addition of a biological factor, namely, development of life in the womb of the mother without male seed: the controversy rages round this biological interpretation of the miracle. Our double thesis is this: firstly, the divine miracle does not permit us to offer detailed explanations; the fact itself should be enough for us; the way in which it happened is God's secret. Secondly, the Son of God assumed the whole of humanity; thus He took on Himself all that is human, all that lies within the sphere of space and time. Procreation through the two sexes forms part of human life. It is a process in time and space; we can know whether it has taken place or not apart from faith. If we do not know about it, this has nothing to do with faith at all; it simply constitutes a gap in our knowledge.

Therefore we answer the first objection thus: The majestic wonder of the Incarnation of the Son of God is not made greater but smaller by the biological theory of the procreation through one sex alone. The idea of a Parthenogenesis is an attempt to explain the miracle of the Incarnation.[1] If, however, it were to be used to support the opposite thesis, namely, that it is obviously unworthy of the Divine Son to come thus, in such a human way, into the world, we would not hesitate to describe this argument as Docetic. Thus the Son of God *did* enter the world in an unworthy way! This is the fundamental element in the idea of revelation in Scripture. Even His origin had neither form nor beauty, it also took place in the form of a servant.

With more apparent justification men have pointed to the connection between this theory and the doctrine of Original Sin. But it is really difficult to see to what extent the birth through a sinful mother alone[2] could be an indication or a condition for the sinlessness of the Lord, nor why the procreation through two sexes should have proved a hindrance for God

[1] The equation of the miracle of Christmas with Parthenogenesis on the part of the "positive" theology has led to the result that the opponents of the Christian faith can easily take refuge behind their hostility (not unjustified) to the idea of a Parthenogenesis. This is the way in which polemical discussions are usually carried on.

[2] This idea is connected with the biological error of the ancient world, that in procreation the male alone is active, and the female receptive and nourishing, whereas to-day, on the contrary, biology gives instances of natural Parthenogenesis.

to create a sinless God-Man. All the arguments in this direction are obviously made to fit a dogmatic idea to a traditional fact, although actually it was strongly opposed to the fundamental idea of the doctrine of the "Two Natures." The doctrine of Parthenogenesis is one of those attempts to insert a divine "section" into something which is otherwise natural, a supernatural fact, and indeed a fact which can be perceived, of which two people could know something without faith.

In stating this it is not my desire to enter into controversy about the doctrine; rather I would here express my indifference to this as to all other attempts to explain the miracle of the Incarnation. We have no desire to attempt to explain the way in which God works His marvels; we simply stand amazed before the Fact itself, without thinking it necessary to combine with this certain inquisitive biological ideas. Not because we think that a parthenogenetic birth is impossible, but because we do not consider this biological curiosity to be of the essence of the matter at all; and because we know that the testimony of the Apostles supports this view, we, for our part, pass by this doctrine without attacking it.

We have no desire to attack it because this doctrine, owing to its simplicity, has often been the means of distinguishing between the language used about the God-Man in the actual New Testament sense and the improper use of language on this subject in the modern sense. It is better to retain the matter in a somewhat unsatisfactory form than for the sake of the erroneous form to give the whole matter up. All depends upon the miracle of the Incarnation of the Son of God—in the strictly Pauline and Johannine sense; but nothing depends upon the manner in which it took place. The history of this doctrine will probably resemble the course followed by the doctrine of the authority of Scripture. So long as the doctrine of Verbal Inspiration is the only intelligible form in which the Bible can be described as the Word of God—in distinction from all other literature—then it is better to hold firmly to it than that on account of this erroneous form the whole precious content of the doctrine, the scriptural principle of the Christian Church, should be thrown away. The time may, however, now have arrived when these two vessels are no longer necessary, and not only so, but the time may have now come when instead of being a protection for the content they have actually become a danger. Both forms are attempts to make the miracle at least to some extent rational. Therefore they are forms of little faith, not of great faith, and there is no reason at all to consider oneself a "believer" in a special sense because one holds these views.

CHAPTER XIII

THE SIGNIFICANCE OF THE HUMANITY OF CHRIST

(i)

How far modern thought has drifted away from the understanding of the paradox of Christ comes out particularly
clearly in the fact that the newer conception regards the discovery of the complete humanity of the historical personality
of Jesus of Nazareth as a great embarrassment for faith,
indeed, as if it were something due to the more recent "scientific" views, which must inevitably lead to the destruction of
the faith in Christ of the Early Church, and thus of the faith
of the New Testament. This view is based on the assumption
that the faith of the Early Church was connected with a Byzantine super-human picture of Christ, and of the life of Christ,
which preferred to erase all concrete human features from the
portrait. The exact opposite is the truth. As if it were not the
disciples in particular—who knew the Man Jesus better than
we with all our historical research—who worshipped Him as
the Exalted Lord! Faith is as much concerned to preserve the
belief in His true unlimited humanity as it is to preserve the
belief in His Deity. The Church, and the theology of the Church,
may not always have understood this, but in any case at the
highest points of Christian perception, and particularly in
the theology of the Reformation, this truth was perceived.
This was expressed not only in a general way in the dogma of
the true humanity of the God-Man, but it was preserved in
practice by the exposition of Scripture, and through preaching,[1]

[1] At this as at so many other points Irenaeus and the Reformers meet.
Before Luther no one ever took the *vere homo* so seriously as Irenaeus. In
this he is approached possibly only by Tertullian, whereas later thinkers
may have indeed held firmly to the dogma since the doctrine of redemption

even though from time to time this fundamental insight may have been somewhat obscured.

The common element of all religion is that we have to do with God. The God who in inaccessible transcendence reigns beyond the stars, the Infinite, the Absolute, the One who is beyond all thought or imagination, the Unnamable: this is the God of the highest forms of intellectual religion, and of the philosophy of religion. The God who appears among men in marvellous theophanies and, although at first concealed, suddenly makes known to them His Deity and thus arouses in the worshipper the awe and terror of the Numinous: this possibility of recognizing God in this direct manner constitutes the essence of pagan mythology. But the God who, although He cannot be grasped by the human mind, though He is infinite and self-sufficient, comes down to the level of humanity in the form of a real historical man, in the lowliness of an earthly human existence, and meets those to whom it is given to dis-

reaches here its highest point, but for the rest fought less for the true humanity than for the true deity of Christ. It is well known how Luther used to speak about the humanity of Christ. He speaks quite openly about His childhood, about His gradual growth and development, even in the spiritual sphere, pointing out that so far as His humanity was concerned, "Like any other holy man He did not always think, speak, will everything, like an almighty being, which some would fain make Him out to be, thus mingling unwisely the Two Natures and their work, for indeed He did not always see all clearly, but was led and aided by God" (*W.A.*, 10, 149). "He ate, drank, slept, waked; was weary, sorrowful, rejoicing; He wept and He laughed; He knew hunger and thirst and sweat; He talked, He toiled, He prayed. To sum up: He used everything for the need and preservation of this life, He wrought and suffered like any other man, save that He was without sin; otherwise He endured good and evil things like anyone else, so that there was no difference between *Him* and other men, save only this, that He was *God* and had no sin" (*W.A.*, 46, 498). In spite of this there is some truth in the language used by moderns when they say that in the ecclesiastical doctrine and teaching the humanity of Jesus has not been done full justice, that in point of fact the failure to distinguish between the picture of Christ as proclaimed by the Church and the Jesus of history, above all, the confusion of the Gospel of John with an historical description of the life of Jesus, has done a great deal to obscure the true humanity of Jesus Christ by His true Deity. The doctrine of the Virgin Birth has also helped to "mingle unwisely with one another" the historical and the pneumatic elements. The reaction is seen in "modern" Christology in which the humanity of Jesus is confused with His Deity.

329

cover who He is in this form: this is the God of the revelation of Scripture. The condescension of God, the theme of the whole Bible, would be a mere theophany, a divine miracle to stir our amazement, and thus exactly the very opposite of an existential, absolutely decisive contact, if the self-manifestation of God were not at the same time also a veiling, if it were not a complete entrance into the reality of human life upon earth.

This is the decisive element in the revelation of Christ: that the Eternal Word, the Eternal Son really became flesh. A strong word is here chosen in order to suggest the lowliness of His true humanity. "Flesh" is the strongest expression in the language of the Bible, which is used to express the state of human lowliness, a condition which is most remote from the divine glory. To this Paul has added a still more daring expression: in the "likeness of sinful flesh." Belief in the veiled presence of the divine within the non-divine, in that which is not only unlike, but absolutely opposed to it, could not be expressed more strongly. And the author of the Epistle to the Hebrews, a writer who witnessed particularly powerfully to the deity of Christ, is not afraid to translate the abstract expression into concrete terms: He was tempted *in all points* as we are, in our weakness, yet without sin, He who "in all things" was "made like unto His brethren."

The self-revelation of God in this complete concealment of His glory, this absolute indirectness, this paradox, this element which is an absolute contradiction to all logical thought: of this the Christian faith has been conscious, and has preserved it as its sanctuary, its possession of salvation, the very truth of God given to it alone and in it alone. "Thus Christ also held man together in Himself since He the invisible became visible, the one who could not be conceived became apprehensible, the one who could not suffer became passible, the Word became man."[1] "So He lived through the stages of man's life, for the sake of infants He became an infant, for the sake of children He became a child . . . for love of young men He became a young man . . . and finally He went forward to death, in order that He, the firstborn

[1] Irenaeus, III, 16.

from the dead, might Himself in all things have the preeminence."[1] "In this consists the knowledge of the divine mystery, that thou shouldst know as God Him of whom thou knowest that He is man, and Him as Man of whom thou knowest that He is God."[2]

We are all familiar with the fact that Luther grasped the idea of the lowliness of Christ with all the fervour of his faith. On it indeed redemption as a whole depends. For our sake did He stoop so low, "like Him has no man gone so low."[3] For "He will and must be in all places."[4] "It is indeed true that He was also forsaken by God, not that the deity was separated from the humanity (for deity and humanity in this Person who is Christ, the Son of God and the Son of Mary, are so united that even in eternity they cannot be separated or severed), but that the deity withdrew itself and concealed itself, so that it seemed, and he who reads might say: 'Here is no God but simply a man, and even a sorrowful and despairing man.' Thus the humanity was left alone and the devil had a free access to Christ, and the deity withdrew her power and left the humanity to fight alone."[5] "According to His divine being He is always equally great; but according to His appearance and revelation He is not always equally great. . . . In the day of His flesh He was small."[6]

"He is God, but He chooses to become this particular man. As has been said, this is the most profound incognito and the most impenetrable impossibility of recognition that can be; for the contrast between God and an isolated individual human being is the greatest possible contrast; it is infinitely qualitative. This, however, is His will, His free will, and therefore it is an incognito maintained by omnipotence. Indeed, in a certain sense, by the very fact that He permitted Himself to be born into the human race, He has bound Himself once for all: the impossibility of piercing through this disguise was maintained in such an almighty way that He Himself, to a certain extent, was under the power of His own disguise, wherein lies the literal reality of His purely human suffering; this was not merely in appearance, but, in a certain sense,

[1] II, 22.   [2] Hilarius de Trin., X, 60.   [3] *E.A.*, 18, 172.
[4] *W.A.*, 23, 703.   [5] *E.A.*, 39, 47.   [6] *W.A.*, 34, 2, 127.

it showed the supremacy over Him of the absolute incognito which He had Himself adopted. Only thus can we mean it seriously when we say that He was true Man, for which reason also He goes through the extremity of suffering, that is, He feels Himself forsaken by God. Thus at every moment He is not beyond the possibility of suffering, but He really suffers and He experiences the purely human element, so that the reality proved itself still more terrible than the possibility, so that He who had freely assumed this disguise, suffered as much as though He had been arrested and imprisoned by others, or as though He had imprisoned Himself in this incognito. . . . The unrecognizability of the God-Man is an incognito which is firmly maintained by omnipotence, and the divine seriousness appears precisely in the degree in which He Himself, from the point of view of purely human experience, actually suffered under this concealment" (Kierkegaard).[1] "The object of faith is the God-Man, just because the God-Man is the possibility of 'offence.' "[2] "If we get rid of faith, or of the possibility of 'offence,' at the same time we also get rid of something else: the God-Man. And if we get rid of the God-Man we get rid of Christianity."[3]

It cannot be helped that those who know nothing of faith should see in all this nothing but intellectual laziness, a morbid love of paradox, a complete aberration of the intellectual life, a degeneration of the sense of truth. Again, we cannot prevent this paradox from being confused with all kinds of irrationalism. All we can do, for our part, is to show the connection in which this indirectness, this paradox, stands within the idea of faith itself.

(ii)

Revelation means the assumption of the temporal by the Eternal, of finitude by the Infinite, of personality by the Absolute. Then does this mean an actual change? No. Through the revelation God does not become anything other than He is. Otherwise how could this be a revelation of God,

[1] *Einübung im Christentum*, pp. 118 ff.
[2] Ibid., p. 130.　　　　[3] Ibid.

how could we know God in the revelation? Nowhere do the Scriptures assert that "God became a man." There has never been any suggestion that a miracle of transformation took place. But what is said is this: "the Word became flesh." The divine personal authority, that in which God expresses Himself and Himself addresses us: all this, in a way beyond all understanding, is present in a human personal life. Thus it is a man who addresses us with a divine claim, with divine authority, as though He were God Himself. He does not come to us as One who is endowed with a divine message, with a divine commission; no, what we mean is that event in which a man, in His own Name and in the Name of God, speaks to us, a man in whose Person we meet with the personality of God. It is this unique event which, to be unique, *can* only happen once, and therefore is an incomparable fact: this is the revelation.

This revelation, however, at the same time, by its very nature, must be a veiling. Precisely that which constitutes the fact that God really addresses us, in order to reveal Himself to us, also means that He does not speak to us directly. It is this very nearness of God—this absolute nearness of God— which at the same time constitutes His distance from us. May we not say, indeed, that anything would be easier to believe than this: that God Himself should speak to us in Person through the personality of a carpenter's son! God cannot really meet us personally save through a person. But can He Himself really meet us thus? The question whether this *can* take place becomes meaningless if it really does take place. So we need inquire into this no further. For we are speaking from the standpoint of those who have faith, not from the standpoint of those who only desire to believe. We do not preach faith, we only seek to elucidate it further. What we here desire to make plain is simply this: that this revealing encounter, this divine address and approach, is something very indirect, something which takes place mysteriously behind a veil. Precisely in that element in which revelation as revelation is perfected is also its complete concealment: the human personality. As a revelation it is complete because a real personal approach can only take place through a real person whom we meet personally. As a veiling, however, it is complete, because to us there is nothing more ordinary, less striking, more familiar, than a human person like ourselves, thus the very opposite of something which must first of all be given unto us. Certainly, in a sense, every person is a mystery; but in all the round of existence is there anything more familiar and homely, more like ourselves, anything more like our double than our fellow man? No creature, either in heaven or on earth, no reality is so near us. We do not think there is anything easier to know, of ourselves, than our fellow man. Therefore, nothing would seem more opposed to a real revelation than our fellow man.

What is the meaning of this fact that veiling and revelation coincide? That God remains a mystery to us even in revelation, that even in imparting His very Self to us He withholds Himself, that even where He comes closest to us He must be sought, that even where He is most fully present we have not the power simply to take hold of Him without further ado. This is the "guile" of God, which is simply another word for His Grace, His Love, which wills nothing other than this, that we should possess Him in reality and in truth. For a God who even in revealing Himself were not at the same time the hidden God, the mysterious, the Lord, the One who cannot be possessed, would not be the God who as perfect Love is also the Holy and Unapproachable.

(iii)

We shall understand this better, perhaps, if we start from the human end. The indirectness of the divine self-communication means that God does not force Himself upon man, that He does not overwhelm him with His creative power, but that He summons him to make his own decision. This is why God comes in the Word, and, it is true, in the completion of the Word, in the Personal Word. The Word is always an indirect communication, a communication which demands our own activity as well. Direct communication would mean the passive transference from the one to the other, like the relation between two pipes which communicate with each other. All sensible communication is of this kind. It makes us passive. There is nothing to "appropriate," nothing to decide. The more indirect the communication the more spiritual, the more decisive it is. In order to make intellectual truth my own, I must apprehend it by my own act. If I wish to understand a moral idea—if, indeed, I want to understand it as such at all—I must affirm it by my own act of decision. In both instances there can be *no* direct communication. The one who imparts—the "teacher"—can do no more than set the self-activity of the scholar in motion. And yet all thought, even of the most immaterial kind, is not yet truly spiritual because it does not summon me to a real decision. In this sphere of thought I conduct a monologue, I am not really addressed by anyone else. I remain within something general which I already possess. All that is present is only the movement of memory (ἀνάμνησις), of inwardness or personal reflection, but for that very reason there is no real movement, no decision. Reflection leads always to a state in which one really was already, in which one has always already decided. This is the essence of the immanental philosophy. The Idea simply means ἀνάμνησις, "*Er-innerung*," "re-miniscence," that is, an act in which one remains within the orbit of self.

Decision, on the other hand, ought to mean an act in which the self is left behind, a flying leap, rather than a gliding motion. The act of decision ought to mean a definite move forward, stepping over a boundary line, the act of leaving all our previous experience behind. It should be a venture, an act in which the soul really steps out into the unknown. Something of this seems to be indicated in any real contact between one person and another. It would almost seem as though in this act we really could "get out of ourselves." It ought to be so, but we do not really reach that point. We do not really decide in the presence of other persons because to us they only represent the universal, and thus they are akin to us—they tell us general truth; and on the other hand, in so far as their claim on us is accidental and unjustified, all that passes between us is nothing but chatter. Real decision could only take place where a person and absolute justification

335

or necessity (that is, the necessity which is otherwise possessed by ideas), were to confront us as *necessity* in the form of what is from without or accidental, a word from without but absolute. Then only could we really go forth out of ourselves, make the leap toward the Other, leaving self behind. There alone would we feel obliged to "venture," because we would be no longer supported by any universal truth, by any necessity of thought. There alone would we be utterly without reserve, unable to find our way, unable to find a firm foothold anywhere; if, indeed, we could ever be reduced to this—when we would be driven to depend wholly on something other than ourselves, at that moment we would believe. Faith alone is genuine decision.

Faith, however, corresponds to the most indirect form of self-communication, to that of revelation. The revelation is the Word which is the personally present Absolute. This communication is in the highest degree indirect; for it is the self-manifestation of God in a human being. The communication of an intellectual teacher is also indirect, in so far as he cannot force me to think. It is, however, not wholly indirect. For he really does express his message. It is the direct speech of thought. To the extent in which it is truth which I myself must think, it is indirect. To the extent, however, that it is an expressed idea, it is offered to me directly. It is teaching. This direct teaching, however, corresponds objectively to the fact that I possess this truth, of myself. Even the prophetic revelation was not complete because it was not a completely indirect communication. In the fact that it is the Word of God which the prophet proclaims, it is an indirect communication, which addresses our faith—it is, however, indirect in a quite different degree from the communication of ideas. But to the extent in which it is an expressed "word," it is the direct communication of ideas. Indeed, the prophet says *N'um Yahweh*: Thus saith the Lord. It is due to the incompleteness of the revelation that he must say this. Exactly to the extent in which it is not wholly indirect, it is also not a complete revelation. It is therefore only the communication of the Word through thought, not the Word itself; it represents an intermediate stage between thought and revelation, between teaching and personal contact. Where, however, the Word itself is present, as the Person of the Logos, in a human personality, there only is it wholly concealed, yet wholly present. The same element which discloses it wholly at the same time conceals it wholly, that is, the personality, whose inmost centre is the Divine Person.

(iv)

Thus here the form of the communication is mystery. Jesus Christ has not imparted Himself directly, in order that the decision to which He calls us may be really the decision of faith. The category of this life—in contrast with every other life—is mystery, in the essential fundamental meaning of the word, the "incognito." Only because the deity of Christ appears in the incognito of His humanity is it possible to have a relation of faith towards Him, a real decision. A complete disclosure would leave no room for faith; it would be sight. But such a manifestation would no longer be revelation through the Word—in the "Word made flesh"—but either God in a form "possible to be known directly," a pagan miracle; or God Himself without the "concealing" of His Majesty, God's coming in power for Judgment. The mystery of Christ is therefore the point of contact between the One who appears within history and the personal mystery of the God-Man. He who rightly understands the mystery of the Messiah knows what is the mystery of the God-Man.

It is possible to mistake Christ for some other human being. This alone makes it possible for us to *believe* in Him. It is this possibility, indeed this extreme probability, of not being recognized which creates room for faith. For instance, to use a parabolic illustration: Just as the electric light shines more brightly the narrower the wire through which the current must pass, so also the fact that it is impossible to know Christ makes faith possible. Knowledge is found wherever there is security, whether it be the security of sensible perception, the security created by proof, by the logical processes of thought or the *notiones communes* of the Idea. All these forms of security are different brands of self-assurance. In knowledge I can always depend upon something. I know that I am supported. That which seems mysterious has become clear; we now see "through" (evidence). Here there is no longer any mystery. Even in the presence of the Moral Law we are not overwhelmed, but we are exalted by the consciousness of dignity, of repose in the Idea. But in the sphere of faith it is not so; here there is no security; here there are no sensible or mental points of support; here is no calming of the mind; nor any self-assurance; faith is a venture; it means hanging on a thread, not standing on solid ground; it is an attitude of complete dependence, and, indeed, of dependence upon Another, and it is therefore the abiding mystery within the revelation. This does not mean that faith is uncertainty, but that it always has uncertainty on its left hand. Faith only exists where there is nothing to be seen, for it is seeing in the dark. *In istis tenebris Christus fide apprehensus sedet sicut Deus in Sinai et in templo sedebat in medio tenebrarum* (Luther).[1]

Faith, that is, true decision, exists at this point alone: where the Word cannot be recognized as divine in virtue of its luminous character, but where it illuminates simply and solely in virtue of its inherent divine being; where this man, Jesus, is not "judged" as the Son of God on account of His perfect moral character, but only where the incomprehensible perception of His coming from God makes known the divinity of His manifestation; where no mediating medium of a uniting directive tendency exists any longer between the personal authority of God and the personal obedience of faith, but where the spark leaps forth directly, without any conducting wire, the lightning which springs from the divine eye to the human, from the authority of God to the obedience of man. That is, faith exists only in the presence of the Mediator. Direct contact between God and man exists only and wholly in a mediated relation; that is, in dependence on the Mediator.

God can only reveal Himself as God under a veil. For only in this disguise, in which faith is the only possibility (and yet from the human point of view is not a possibilty) is man driven to cast himself wholly upon the gift of God. There alone is God Himself the Only Doer. There alone man receives

[1] Gal., I, 191.

nothing from God in virtue of his humanity. There alone man is in the condition which disposes the soul for the Presence of God, that is, he is empty. At the point where the mystic prepares himself for the reception of the divine grace man is not really empty, for there he glides—apparently—gradually through introversion into the divine. There he finds the divine—so it is claimed—in the ground of his own soul. He is not really the recipient of God's gift, but he steals his way in —so the mystic claims—by his own efforts into the divine mystery. He gains divine grace—so he claims—surreptitiously. It is just because this experience is claimed to be immediate, without any need of a mediator, that it is impossible that it should be a real experience of the divine presence. The real desire of the mystic is fulfilled not along his own line of experience at all, but at the very opposite pole: through faith in the Mediator.

In faith alone is man really stripped of himself, because here alone does he really leave himself wholly behind; because here he has no spirit of self-confidence or of self-justification left, but he is wholly dependent on what he receives. But this abandonment of self, this "leap of faith" cannot be achieved in his own strength; it is not a human possibility at all. As a human possibility this leap is simply a defiant desperate *salto mortale*, a leap into the real darkness and void, a spasm, a bare statement. Real faith is more than this, and it arises only through the objective possibility of this venture, the divine promise, the new possibility, which is a divine gift. Therefore, from the point of view of faith, this act is not really a "leap" at all, for the soul which makes this venture finds itself supported and upheld. No human being can pierce the mystery, the incognito of the Mediator, but "verily flesh and blood hath not revealed it unto thee." It is here that the new event has taken place, viz., that through Jesus, the Man, the eternal divine Son has spoken to man with divine authority. Here is the supreme venture, the intensest moment of decision; but it is a venture given by God, a decision created by God.

Therefore in this event God remains the Unfathomable. As the One who comprehends Himself He remains the One who cannot be comprehended, as the One who gives He remains the Inexhaustible, as the Merciful One He remains the Sovereign Lord who can do as He will. As the Loving One, He is also the Holy, who even in giving still asserts His sovereignty, who is not Himself One on whom claims are made, but One who makes His own claims, who does not allow Himself to be possessed, but Himself possesses, who alone grants His grace as the manifestation of His sovereign will, of His glory. God comes to man in the Mediator; this is the self-movement of God in which revelation consists. But this Divine Advent in the Mediator is no commonplace existence, no visibility, no release of the tension, no given fact, but, as the mystery of His existence, credible only to faith, it is at the same time the highest tension because it is the most complete veiling.

(v)

Hard on the heels of faith, therefore, follows the possibility of "offence." The Idea of God never "offends" anyone. The sentiment which accompanies it is rather that of enthusiasm, the ecstatic feeling of rising on wings to the divine heights. We may regard this Idea as folly or illusion, or we may regard it with cool scepticism, if we will, but it does not arouse real resistance. It does not strip man of his pretensions; on the contrary, here he sees himself in the glory of his likeness to God. He sees himself as a participator in the divine nature; he is free and self-directed. His attitude towards the Law, and towards truth, is that of one who is on an equal footing with God. In faith, however, through the revelation in the Mediator, man is stripped, emptied, annihilated, humiliated to the utmost, in order that God may really be able to impart to him His own nature, that He alone may give Himself to him, through Himself.

It is this which causes men to stumble at the Mediator, the God-Man and His claim. It is indeed possible to pass Him by, without recognizing Him, but not without receiving a prick at the heart. The nearer His mystery approaches the more urgent grows the danger of being "offended." Pilate was too remote from Jesus to be really "offended" in Him. But the religious Jews were offended by His claim of which they were aware and because they were aware of it. They could not endure the Son who, as the "heir," reminded them of their stewardship and of their unfaithfulness, and who wished to deprive them of their trust. That is why they crucified Him. No prophet ever said: "Blessed is he that is not offended in Me." This is the Word of the Mediator. The One who can "cause us to stumble" is the Mediator; only when we are confronted by Him is there the possibility of being "offended." For there is no Other who can force men to come to a decision about Him when they are confronted by Him. The Person about whom it is imperative that we should make a decision, for or against faith, is the Mediator, the One before whom, in whom, we decide before God and in the presence of God.

The possibility of faith means also the possibility of "being offended." The full humanity of the Son of God includes both these possibilities. If the Son of God could be "known directly" there could be neither faith nor the possibility of "being offended." The Son of God in whom we are to be able to believe, must be such a One that it is possible to mistake Him for an ordinary man. To break through the ordinary limitations of humanity would be to break through the possibility of faith. This is why faith is as deeply concerned to preserve belief in the complete humanity of the Mediator as in His complete Deity, and in each case for exactly the same reason. This has been maintained by the ecclesiastical doctrine, from the point of view of dogma: true Man and true God. But it has not always carried through its principle rightly. It may well have been that the first occasion for this was provided by the New Testament traditional picture of Christ itself.

The Gospels were written by faith for faith. Their aim is in no way "historical"; they have no intention of giving a mere "report" about the way these things took place. They bear witness to the Word of Life "which we have heard, which we have seen with our eyes, which our hands have handled"— this is the point of view not only of the Johannine narrative, but also of the Synoptic narratives. The picture is "distorted" as soon as it is read from the point of view of a profane historian, as soon as it is confused with an ordinary biography. From the point of view of those who know what did take place, the Gospel narratives are correct. The more this point of view emerges and becomes dominant, the greater will be the discrepancy between that which the historian expects and that which the narrative inspired by faith actually gives.

On the other hand, to the extent in which the understanding of this point of view disappears, the confusion becomes the more dangerous. If the Johannine picture of Christ is conceived as a plain narrative, as an obvious description of fact, which can be perceived as true by everyone whose senses are sound—and this includes "a feeling for that which is truly great"—then it is an extremely misleading picture. It is this incognito of the God-Man in particular which is threatened when Christ's human form is confused with His Divine Humanity, perceived by faith. In that case the Johannine Gospel would become an absolutely Docetic book, and its leading theme, "we saw His glory"—if it were taken to mean that they perceived it directly—would be Docetic also. Indeed, this would mean no less than renunciation of the belief in the humanity of Jesus altogether. The great theologians of the Christian Church have always been aware of this danger; but they have never been able to avoid it entirely. So again and again they have regarded a truth which could only be perceived by faith as a tangible picture of reality. This was the cause of the conflict between the defenders of the historical-critical view and the Biblical-Kerygmatic view of the life of Jesus. This question does not further concern us here; it has already been fully treated in the preceding pages. The important point for us, in this connection, is this, that whenever this mistake has occurred, immediately the idea of the humanity of Jesus has been obscured. The idea that Christ was "true Man" still formed part of the Creed, it is true, but the interpretation supported by the gospel history did not correspond with it, hence this theology was confronted with the necessity of thinking of a divine-humanity in which the divine was mingled in some way with the human—and this in spite of the ἀσυνχύτως of the Creed. The dogmatic connecting link evolved the fatal doctrine of the *communicatio idiomatum*, by means of which the statement of faith concerning the unity of the divine with the human was transformed into a metaphysical theory.

(vi)

The doctrine of the Two Natures itself is right, but it is this metaphysical misunderstanding which causes difficulty. It is dangerous, not merely because a conflict with historical science thus actually became inevitable, but, above all, because it seemed as though the divine-humanity would have to be posited as an independent entity. Thus the God-Man as the *God*-Man could be perceived by all. The indirect character of the manifestation had been destroyed. The incognito had disappeared. The deity was materialized, the decision of faith was ruled out, just as the doctrine of Verbal Inspiration materialized the authority of the Scriptures and ruled out the decision of faith. Revelation became a theophany, the Incarnation an actual transformation of the Divine Logos—in so far as the humanity was taken seriously at all, as, for instance, in the Kenotic theory.[1]

This metaphysical misunderstanding is due to the fact that here the same tendency was at work which we have already noted in the development of the doctrine of the Virgin Birth, namely, the desire to explain the Divine Humanity of Christ, to make it metaphysically clear. Here—and in this Ritschl is absolutely right—metaphysics have really entered into the

[1] It is well known that a certain difference exists between the Reformed (Calvinistic) doctrine and the Lutheran doctrine on the relation between the human and the divine natures in Christ. The element which they hold in common is the decisive one, the acceptance of the Creed of Chalcedon: the two natures are not mingled, but they are united in one person. The Lutherans, however, taught the *communicatio idiomatum*, that is, the blending of the two natures in an historical individual, Jesus Christ, while the Reformed theologians held the opposite view. In this exposition I believe that I am presenting the meaning of the Reformed doctrine: in so far as Jesus Christ can be known historically, in so far as He belongs to the human sphere, He is Man. His Deity is the secret of His Person, which as such does not enter into the sphere of history at all. Biblical criticism, so it seems to me, has made the Reformed view the only possible one; for it cannot be doubted that it is this view which above all concentrates on the thought that Jesus, as an "historical personality," is man. At any rate, whether the Kenosis doctrine of the Lutheran type can achieve the same without falling into absurdities has not been proved by the supporters of the Kenotic theories of the last century.

343

sphere of faith and have corrupted it. A necessity for decision is turned into a need for explanation. A relation produced by the authoritative personal Presence of the Word of God is turned into a magico-material substantial Presence. The doctrine of the Two Natures becomes the object of purely external, theoretical, semi-scientific discussion and explanation. Faith becomes intellectualized, and it is henceforth possible to discuss the Deity of Christ in the same way that a physical phenomenon could be discussed.

This does not mean that this point of view predominated among the great theologians of the Church, nor among the simple believers who accepted the dogmas of the Church as they were given to them. It only meant that real knowledge of the Deity of the Mediator, through faith, was somewhat dimmed, but this modification of belief had great historical influence. The reaction of the nineteenth century against the metaphysical element in the conception of Christ, the emphasis on the true humanity of the Son of God, which was the main result of the rise of historical criticism, was on that account absolutely justified. But whereas in the earlier ecclesiastical doctrine at least the essence of the matter was preserved, although its outer covering was suspect, in the reaction of the nineteenth century, the essence of the matter itself was discarded simply because its outer covering was unacceptable. For now the genuine revelation, in which all depends upon the source of its authority, was transformed into a quasi-revelation, a mere historical phenomenon, which could be judged purely from a historical point of view, in which all that remained of "revelation" was the concrete representation of the Idea, the ethico-religious personality, the religious hero, the symbol. If the earlier view led to magical and material conceptions of the spiritual mystery, the later views dispelled the mystery in a positivistic sense. Whereas in the earlier phase of Church history revelation tended to develop into metaphysics, in the later phase, revelation was reduced to ordinary human history. The Byzantine figure of Christ on the one hand corresponds to the humanitarian interpretation of Jesus on the other. Yet we owe a debt of frank gratitude to this anti-metaphysical theology and to historical criticism for breaking

344

through the rigidity of dogma, and it is to them we owe the fact that once more the question of the true Deity of the real Man, Jesus Christ, has become a living issue.

The metaphysical question is this: how can a man also be God? The New Testament gives no reply to this question; it does not attempt to give one; in fact, it takes no notice of this question at all. Even the account of the Baptism of Jesus is not an attempt to give an explanation. The account of the baptism does not explain how it has come to pass that the Man Jesus is the Son of God, but it bears witness to the fact that it was thus attested by God. The Apostles did not trouble their heads about the problem of the possibility of combining divine personality with human nature, or if they did think about this at all they did not regard it as sufficiently important, or good enough to mention it to their Churches. It was enough for them to know that He is both true God and also true Man, not only from the physical but from the mental and spiritual point of view, in no way absolute, unlimited, all-knowing, all-mighty, but a weak man, who suffers, is hungry, one who has tasted the depths of human anguish and despair; in brief, a human being, whom it is only natural to regard as a mere human being.

(vii)

It is this Man, in whose personal existence the Divine Person meets us—through faith. The Person of this human personality does not resemble a human being; here the humanity of Christ ceases; indeed, this Person is not historically visible at all. He can be seen by faith alone. Since the means by which this Person communicates with the world is the human spirit—as the ecclesiastical doctrine rightly defines it—there is always the possibility that this Person, who speaks to us, personally, through this spirit, through this personality which is composed historically of body and spirit, may be mistaken for a human person. But why does this possibility exist? It is not in any way due to this Divine Person. The possibility of making such a mistake, the inability to perceive the divine within the human personality is due to man, to unbelief. The act of man, his responsible act, is that of unbelief, not of belief. Unbelief is that state of mind which refuses to learn; it means the closed mind. To him "who has ears to hear," Christ says, "I am the Christ." To refuse to listen means that we are obstinate; it is sinful disobedience. But it is only to the believing soul that Christ says who He is. He Himself discards His incognito to faith, in faith. This is why, as the Christ, He remains concealed within history. Where He discloses Himself history disappears, and the Kingdom of God has begun. And when He unveils Himself He is no longer an historical personality, but the Son of God, who is from everlasting to everlasting.

This is the meaning of the distinction between "*in* the flesh" and "*after* the flesh." He alone can know the Christ who came "in the flesh" who does not know Him "after the flesh." For the historical student, for the historian and biographer, He remains the Rabbi Jesus of Nazareth, or the religious genius. This is the "Christ after the flesh," and to know Christ in this way is to know Him "after the flesh," even when such knowledge consists in the most profound and penetrating understanding of the personality of Jesus. But to know the "Christ come in the flesh" is to "know Him according to the Spirit"; this is the knowledge of faith, the knowledge of the Eternal Son of God as the "Word made flesh."

Real decision does not exist on the plane of history. For that is the sphere in which men wear masks. For the sake of our "masquerade," that is, for the sake of our sinful mendacity, Christ also, if I may put it like this, has to wear a mask; this is His incognito. It corresponds to our sin. So long as we do not take off our mask He retains His disguise. Both disguises are laid aside at the same moment. Where Christ discloses Himself, in the revelation, in faith, there also He removes our mask in faith. Or, to put it the other way round: when we know ourselves as we really are, as sinners, then we also know Him as the Mediator. Through faith we come to see what lies behind our historical mask, the secret of our personality, that is, sin. At that point, however, through the revelation of Christ, we perceive also that we belong to God. At the very point where we know that we have fallen away from the Word, in which and for which we were created, where we recognize the fact of the Fall, and of the sin which caused it, there also we know ourselves again in the Word, and now as new creatures we are once more taken up into the Divine Word, as those who have been reconciled. This knowledge of sin, however, is only possible through this knowledge of the Word. Repentance and faith, *mortificatio* and *vivificatio*, are one, an indivisible act of revelation. Both imply the one decisive act, and this act is the meeting with the Divine Person in Christ through the self-revelation of God, in which we also—in a two-fold sense—are revealed as we truly are.

We do not perceive the mystery of our person so long as we do not perceive the mystery of the Person of Christ. We look at ourselves also from within history, and thus from the human or natural point of view. We do not know the depth of our problem, even although as human beings we are always conscious of it to some extent.[1] We do not penetrate into the depths because we are afraid of them. For in these depths is

[1] Here the connection between the so-called "Adam-Christ speculation" (Harnack) and the doctrine of the Incarnation is clearly visible, as above all it has been emphasized by Irenaeus—following the precedent laid down by Paul. On the one hand the Word is the Revealer of God, but on the other hand the Word is also the archetype of human destiny. Man has been created "in the Word." The Word is his personal principle of being. Only in the Word are we personal. Here ethical Idealism and Christian Faith coalesce, as indeed the doctrine of the Primitive State is common ground to both. The doctrine of the *imago Dei*, from Plato to Hegel, has been the root principle of Idealism. But the profound difference is that which Idealism does not admit, that which lies between us and our origin, the "something in between" which determines the whole of history and our historical reality in contrast to the Idea. We have fallen away from the Word in which we were created; this is why we no longer know ourselves, and the natural knowledge of humanity is either falsely naturalistic or falsely Idealistic, falsely Determinist or indeterminist. The true knowledge of the real nature of humanity is given to us in Christ, who as the Mediator is also the restorer of human truth; that is, He is man determined by the Word, and united with the Word. Hence He is the true Man, the Firstborn among many brethren—*as such* He is the *primus inter pares*, but only in so far as He is recognized as the God-Man, who can never be *primus inter pares*, and only in so far as the likeness refers to that which lies on the further side of history. What Christ is "by nature" man is—or becomes—through grace.

sin. This is the key to the understanding of our existence. Sin itself, however, cannot be perceived from the point of view of history. The mere knowledge of sin from within history—the "Pelagian" point of view—is always something relative and individualistic; when it goes further than individualism it falls into Naturalism (social guilt, influence of environment, etc.). The real knowledge of sin is the knowledge of Original Sin, which lies as such behind the surface of history. The knowledge of Original Sin as an *a priori* of our own and of all history, agrees with the knowledge of the fundamental ground of all history which comes to us in Jesus Christ. The merely historical knowledge of sin hides from us our own reality just as much as the merely historical view of Jesus conceals from us His divine reality. Both are due to our lack of seriousness, to our clinging to the relative, to the phenomenal, to the historical appearance. Both mean that our attitude is merely that of a spectator, as opposed to that of decision, which alone takes place in faith—and therefore in that other third dimension.

The decision takes place where the historical plane has been transcended by the event of the revelation of the non-historical, of the eternal Word of God, which is personal in character, just as we too, through this event alone, become really personal. As merely historical human beings, as members of the human society we are not really personal, because we only compare ourselves with a universal truth, and not with the concrete Word of God. We live under the illusion that we are self-determined and free, and this illusion conceals our sinful reality beneath its fair falsity. We do not shoulder the real responsibility for our actual existence. For to do this we would need to take the whole weight of sin upon our shoulders. Hence as human beings who are determined by thought alone we are as unreal as we are non-personal. We can only become personal through faith, through decision in the presence of God Himself —and not in the presence of the mere Idea of God—through the decision made in the presence of His personal reality, and moreover through His personal reality in the revelation through the Mediator. We become truly personal, indeed, at that point where we overcome all that is merely historical, or, rather, where we ourselves are vanquished by the power that is super-historical, which is revealed to us through the historical element, that is, in "the flesh."

(viii)

The revelation is the Person, or, to put it more exactly, the mystery of the Person of Jesus Christ. Historical positivism is making a last attempt to save itself from the fatal consequences which ensue when history, as such, is made the absolute criterion, when for this mystery of the Person of Jesus Christ it substitutes the inner life of Jesus. It is at once too little and too much. It is too little: for the Person is not the mere subjective reflection of the life within, the interior life. On the other hand, it also says too much; for the inner life itself belongs to the historical setting, which encircles the mystery of personality. A person may therefore possess a very penetrating understanding of the inner life of Jesus without being touched in the very least by the mystery of His Person. The "interior" psychological point of view belongs just as much to the Christ "after the flesh" as the view of the "external" pragmatist historian. Or, to put it the other way round: nothing is more remote from the Christian as such than to regard Jesus as a problem in psychology; and it is significant that the Gospels betray remarkably little psychological interest in the Person of Jesus Christ. Of the inner life of Jesus, in particular, they say almost nothing.[1] Even the psychological element is not a mystery, but it is an object which can be

---

[1] What we call "psychological" and "historical" to-day is described in dogma as "human nature." The great theologians have evinced no interest in the psychology of Jesus—save in so far as they were concerned to prove that it was truly human—because to them the psychological element did not constitute the mystery of the deity of Christ, but the plain fact of His humanity. A secret, and indeed an unfathomable, essential secret—the mystery of revelation itself—means the co-existence of this psychological-historical and this eternal-divine personality. To try to fathom this means from the very outset to draw the Divine Person into the human sphere. A "psychological interpretation" of the divine-human consciousness is a *contradictio in adjecto*. For whatever can be understood psychologically is thereby labelled "human." It was the error of the Kenosis doctrine of last century that it tried to give a psychology of the God-Man.

349

directly known. The "mystery" of which the psychologist speaks is only something relative and passing; it is only a mystery so long as it has not been discovered, but this can be done through the work of psychological interpretation. The question must be decided in one way or the other: either the mystery of the Person of Jesus is the Absolute which we think it is, and then there can be no question of a psychological inquiry at all; for it is not only the inner life of Jesus which is mysterious, but His whole life, both in its unity and in its direction. Or it is possible to study His character from the psychological point of view until the essential element has been discovered; in this case there would never have been any mystery at all.

The mystery of the Person of Jesus must be identified with the mystery of His cause. The decisive point is not what He *felt* about His significance, but what His significance actually was. This does not mean that we would deny the importance of the question of the self-consciousness of Jesus; but this question is included within one which is still more comprehensive. The significant element in Jesus Christ, in His life, as it can only be known from the point of view of faith, is the fulfilment of the Word, the perfect existence of the Word of God. From the point of view of faith this Life can be known as the communication of the divine mystery of the eternal purpose of God. But this disclosure does not consist in the Idea, the abstract doctrine, but in this Life, as it was actually lived. Further, this disclosure is not the historical phenomenon, as it can be conceived and interpreted by man as such, but the meaning of this Life as it can only be conceived by him who sees in it the coming of God to man, the act in which the limits of "creaturely" existence have been transcended.

But this unity of the Word and the Fact must necessarily be personal in character. For this is precisely what this Person means: significance, the "Word," as an active reality. This life only has significance as something actually achieved, saturated with the sense of a personal will, and tending in this direction. In the apostolic message this meaning was summed up in the simple expression: obedience. But this was not meant in the ethical sense, in the sense of obedience to a vocation, which

we can "estimate" by the usual ethical standard (Ritschl).
For this obedience does not refer to a task within history, but
to the "coming" of Christ, to that movement which extended
from the world beyond into this world. It is "Messianic"
obedience, and this is something which lies wholly outside all
human, ethico-religious categories and analogies.

This "obedience" of Christ means at the same time unconditional sovereignty over the whole human sphere. Through
this obedience the significance of this Life, the cause itself,
becomes a personal significance, a personal will, the identification of the Self and the Cause. This will is the uniting factor
in this Life which gives it significance.

But this will is at the same time knowledge. Otherwise it
would be arbitrary and arrogant. Not only does the Christ
will to make this cause His own, but He knows and admits it
as His own, this cause which no human being could call his
own without committing the crime of blasphemy. For to know
this cause as His own meant that He knew Himself to be the
"only Son" of God. It is not that through the knowledge of
the cause to which His life is to be given, and His obedient
acceptance, does He, a human being, become the Son. This
is a misunderstanding. For if this latter interpretation were
the true one, it would not refer to the question with which
we are here concerned at all, with the movement from eternity,
but it would refer to a moral idea which, at bottom, was always
the concern of everyone. It is impossible to *become* the Son.
He only can be the Son if He *is* the Son, and in the very nature
of the case, in this sense, there *can* only be one Son. If a human
being were to arrogate to himself, in appalling self-deception,
the title of the Son, the absolute and only Son, who through
the self-movement of God completes Himself in humanity:
then he would be either a madman, or a blasphemer, or a
harmless visionary, who uses a name whose significance he
does not know, which he confuses with something relative.
Political Messiahs belong to this latter category.

The Jews of the time of Jesus were near enough to the matter
to understand something of it, to understand something of
what was taking place. They saw the alternative rightly:
either the Son of God or the very height of blasphemy.

Tertium non datur. It was easier to deal with the political Messiahs. Their whole existence bore witness to the fact that their claims did not extend to this final stage of wanton blasphemy. But Jesus was different. They had to take Him seriously. The alternative was perceived quite clearly. This historical parenthesis ought to make clear what is really at stake when we speak about the "Messianic consciousness." It means the claim to belong to a plane which extends far beyond the range of ordinary human possibilities. And indeed it means more than this; for as soon as a man makes this claim at all, the verdict has in fact already been pronounced: it is blasphemy, a wanton insult to the majesty of God. Every decision of the will in this sense is a blasphemy, because it means going beyond the borders of creaturely existence. That is why we say that this will of Christ to obey constitutes at the same time the knowledge of His Being. He alone can be obedient, as SON, if He already is the Son. To know this and to will to obey God mean the same thing.

Thus the self-consciousness of Jesus is really decisive. But we can only understand this expression rightly if we understand it not psychologically but purely positively, as the unity of Person and Cause. This unity is present in the Christ—if He is the Christ. It is not His self-consciousness which makes Him the Christ, but His self-consciousness is only one element in His Messiahship. Hence the transference of the question to the purely psychological sphere, the modern discussion of the Messianic consciousness, is always a sign either that we do not quite understand what it is all about, or that from the very outset we regard this Messianic consciousness as the visible expression within the temporal and historical sphere, of some quality of historical greatness (such as *primus inter pares,* Founder, Discoverer, Genius, etc.). We also evade the decisive question if, instead of looking at the Messianic category itself, we pay attention to the various forms in which it was expressed historically. In point of fact, to say that Jesus was "more than a prophet" says everything. For if we take the idea of "prophet" seriously, and if we take the words "more than" seriously also, that is, as sharply categorical definitions, with no sense of gradual development behind them at all, as terms which describe the wholly Other in contrast to all human, ethical, or religious definitions—this Other which is the Word from beyond time and space, and the Word in a Person from the realms beyond time and space—then to be "more than a prophet" must mean that He is the Son, the eternal Son, the One in whom the Person and cause are one, the One in whom God does not merely express His own Name in Word but in Person, the One in whom God Himself is personally present, the One whose authority—in the strict sense of uniqueness—is identical with the personal authority of God.

Modern thought, which is so remote from understanding this point of view, has always believed that it was possible to play off the statements of Jesus in the Gospels, in which He plainly subordinates Himself to the Father, against this unity. Only it is curious that those who think like this were never disturbed by the thought that the early leaders of the Church knew all these passages too, and that they were not in the least disturbed by them. But modern theologians misunderstand the early Fathers to such an extent that they regard their very statements as an evasion, which only betrays their embarrassment: they point out, namely, that the Fathers made those passages which imply subordination (to the Father) refer to the human and not to the divine nature. This statement is the only fitting one, in this connection, and it is the very opposite of an evasion. It belongs to the very nature of the incarnate Logos, to the very nature of the Son who goes through the world in the form of a servant, that He should subordinate Himself to the Father. (Cf. pp. 544 ff.) This subject will be treated in another connection. The whole historical appearance of the Son of God is, as such, that of "one who serves," in a subordinate position; it is the means to an end, not a self-end. But this service also implies authority. The Mediator *is* the Mediator just because—as One who belongs to both sides—He can stand at the same time both with God above men and with men beneath God. He would not be the Mediator apart from this two-fold character—it is precisely this dual character which is the characteristic of Mediatorship. Hence there is no reason at all to argue that this admission of "subordination" implies an "embarrassment."

Thus the course of our thought returns once more to the beginning: the mystery of the Person of Christ is the mystery which faith alone, as such, can perceive, and to faith it remains a mystery, even in this act of perception. We have not attempted to explain the Messianic consciousness. To do this would simply mean explaining the Messiahship away. We have merely tried to describe the meaning of the word, and, indeed, in categories which are only intelligible to faith. By means of this description the mystery is not solved, but it is intensified. It is precisely this fact which baffles the human mind: how a human being could be, could possibly regard himself as, the Messiah in this full sense. It is at this point that the question arises which the Jews answered in the negative on the morning of Good Friday. That they acted thus and did not seek the evasions which modern theology has at its disposal—the modification of the Messianic claim to mean some relative historical greatness—redounds to their credit. They recognized that here was an absolute challenge; that they must decide in one direction or the other, that there could be no middle path. They knew the immense significance of the Messianic claim; but in this claim they did not recognize the divine authority, because this recognition would have been too humiliating. This question necessarily arises, where this claim is really made. Hence our next task will be to examine the historical question.

CHAPTER XIV

THE HISTORICAL FIGURE OF THE GOD-MAN

(i)

WHEN the fullness of time had come God sent forth His Son "born of a woman, born under the Law." He "emptied Himself, taking the form of a servant, being made in the likeness of men; and being found in fashion as a man, He humbled Himself, becoming obedient even unto death, yea, the death of the Cross." The divine self-manifestation is enclosed within a real historical human life. This human life is the place in which God wills to meet man. Revelation and faith are vitally connected with this history. Hence because this meeting-place exists, there is a real revelation, and apart from it—in the strict Christian sense of the word—there is no revelation. This is the unique element in the revelation of God, and this uniqueness constitutes its reality. This does not mean that this life, in its historical extension and its visible character, as such, constitutes the revelation. If this were so, the extent of our knowledge of this history would constitute the extent of our faith. Then faith and revelation would be simply a *quantum*, and every item in this life, every detail in the life of Jesus in its passage through time and space would be a part of the revelation. But in that case revelation would not be absolutely unique, but something extended, multiple, like other kinds of history in general. This direct identity between the life of Jesus, the history of Jesus, and the revelation does not exist. The "flesh" is not the "Word," although it is practically impossible to separate this "Word" from the "flesh." The identity which exists between the two is not direct but indirect. But it is quite certain that this indirect identity does exist, so that we who believe, in spite of the fact that this history is not itself the revelation, are absolutely bound to it and interested in it.

Let me make this clear by an illustration: the circles which are caused when a stone is thrown into the water are not themselves the action, but if there are no such circles then it is quite certain that no stone has been thrown into the water. The historical extension and visible character of the life of Christ do not in themselves constitute the event, but without this visible history there would also have been no event at all. This history is composed of countless "accidental" elements, of which we know only a very few—we need only remind ourselves that our knowledge about the life of Christ before His public Ministry is an almost total blank; again, we do not need much reflection to show us that what the Gospels actually tell us in so many words about His life would only fill a few days of His life. It is only these "accidental" elements, which we know in such a fragmentary manner, when they are all gathered together, which constitute the life of Jesus as a real human happening. If they, in themselves, were the essential thing, then we would be in despair over the miserable paucity of the narratives which have been handed down to us; for every bit of the tradition which had not been preserved would mean that we had lost so much revelation. But it is certainly essential that there should be such actual elements, however "accidental," and, indeed, these elements in particular and no others; for if it were otherwise we would be dealing with an idea, where it is essential that it should be free from all accidental historical elements.

The central element in this Life, which makes it absolutely decisive for us, is the "Word" which this event contains. But this "Word" is not an idea, a truth, a thought, but a personal reality. The Word is the Son, and the Son is the Word. The Person cannot be severed from the historical appearance, however little it may be directly identical with it. The Person determines the character of the historical appearance of the life, as it determines the picture of this character which can be grasped historically. It is not merely the Person who gives the special character to this Life; the history also, into which it enters, helps to determine it: the country, the people, the period, the historical inheritance. But just as no biographer or historian conceives his hero simply as the product of historical factors, but regards the essential element in him as something independent of all these factors, and places

the "personality" of his hero over against all these co-deter-
mining factors, giving to this "factor" all the more weight the
stronger and more independent the personality, so it is obvious
regarding the Person of the God-Man, that although historically
It cannot be visible in itself, yet its historical visibility, its form
and appearance, the life in its characteristic course helps to
determine it, and thus in it, even if not visible, it is yet suggested. To those who know what all this means, who know
the indirect nature of the revelation, the fact that this characteristic element, which the historian can handle, is capable
of such widely differing interpretation, constitutes a sign, a
vestigium divinitatis. This visible historical aspect—to which the
whole of humanity belongs—is of such a kind not merely in
the fact of human existence as such, but above all also in the
characteristic definiteness of this human life in particular, that
it conceals the Divine Person quite as much as it reveals It.
But in any case these widening circles, which show that a
pebble has been thrown into the pond, are not absent, even
though the connection between cause and effect cannot be
perceived by the profane eye, but may now be guessed at,
and now denied.

(ii)

It is therefore not surprising, indeed, it is only what we
should have expected, that there should be no uniform historical picture of Jesus.[1] Unless, from the very outset, the perception quickened by faith seizes on the essential and right
aspects of the Life of Christ, which thus produces a view—
even of the human aspect of the life of Christ—which is, on
the whole, uniform, the variety of interpretation is absolutely

[1] I believe that Windisch (*Zeitschr. f. system. Theol.*, 1927, p. 47) must
have misunderstood the point of my similar observations in the lecture
on *Die Absolutheit Jesu* if he takes them to mean that by this reference
to the scientific situation I wish in some way or another to *prove* the
absoluteness of Jesus. I hope that this illusion may have been dispelled
by the detailed observations in this book. If there is here any question
of proof at all, then it is rather only in the opposite sense: this scientific
situation corresponds certainly to that which may be expected from the
point of view of the Christian faith.

endless, that is, where the picture of Jesus is contemplated from the "purely human" point of view. This point has already been discussed in an earlier part of this book. In spite of this, however, we do not regard the attempt to construct a scientifically objective picture, as is done by the newer school of historical criticism, as valueless. In point of fact, here also— though in a very relative manner—there is a certain historical scientific objectivity in the way of conceiving the facts. At the same time it is evident that this endeavour not only (as is the case in all historical research) does not completely attain its end; that is, it never arrives at an absolutely recognized objective "picture," but also that, apart from this general relative factor, it is confronted by special difficulties in relation to this "object." In saying this I am not alluding to the paucity or unreliability of source material. Compared with other historical personalities, the sources for the life of Jesus may be said to be neither particularly meagre nor particularly unreliable. There is another circumstance which is far more characteristic: the nearer objective research comes to the heart of its object, the personality of Jesus, the more it tries to approach His "inmost intention," the more embarrassed it becomes.

For here it is confronted by certain stubborn facts which it cannot fit into its humanistic and psychological scheme at all, facts which will not bend themselves to the desired uniform method of interpretation. It is then at this point that the various scientific schools of thought or tendencies separate and follow different lines of interpretation. For instance, to name only the outstanding types: there is one school which regards Jesus essentially as the Teacher or Herald, and at the same time the exemplary representative of a moral and religious "inwardness," the Fulfiller of the "ethical religion of the prophets," who was concerned only with the attitude of heart and will of every individual human being towards the God whom he proclaimed. The specific ideas of the Gospel which do not fit into this circle of ideas, and eschatology in particular, as well as the hints and suggestions which Jesus threw out about His own Person, are then either rejected as later interpolations or they are pronounced to be the non-essential form of this message, determined by conditions of time and space; the self-consciousness of Jesus is then interpreted in the light of these ideas. This leads certainly to a fairly uniform picture,[1] but at the cost of a violent mishandling of the historical facts which alters the story beyond recognition.

Hence another tendency, which was less concerned with giving an interpretation which would be intelligible to the modern mind than with historical correctness of presentation, laid particular emphasis upon those features which had been pushed aside by the previous type of thought, and set them forth as the essential features of the Life of Christ; thus out of this material they constructed the picture of a fanatical "Prophet" of the imminent final Messianic Kingdom, claiming that Jesus believed that He had been sent by God to usher in this Kingdom. It is impossible to adapt this theory in any way to the modern way of viewing ethical and religious questions. On the other hand, other equally essential features do not fit into this picture of an excited enthusiast, in particular those which the first school of thought emphasized as decisive, namely, all those elements in the Gospel story which again and again attracted thinkers of the rational, ethical type of the Enlightenment, elements which led them to see in Him their authority, and their Example in all that pertains to religion and morality.

In all this I do not mean to say that a purely human picture of Jesus is impossible; if this could be proved it would indeed be disastrous, and would flatly contradict all that we have said about the faith. The historian will still regard his picture as right, and will in the last resort always find a way out of his difficulties by the favourite device of appealing to the "inconsistencies of man,"[2] without it being possible to disprove his arguments. To the believer, however, this remarkable

[1] The severe strictures passed by Albert Schweitzer on this Liberal-Christian picture of Jesus, which almost amount to a charge of perversion of history, are well known. If Schweitzer's criticism has not been as effective as it should have been the reason must be that his own presentation of the theme is so one-sided, which gave those whom he attacked cover behind which they could take refuge from his otherwise devastating attack.

[2] An allusion to the poem *Homo sum* in *Huttens lezte Tage*, by C. F. Meyer, a well-known modern German poet.—Tr.

situation in historical science is a sign (*vestigium*) that it is impossible to do real justice to the historical phenomenon of Jesus from the objective neutral scientific standpoint; it can only be achieved from the point of view of faith. Thus from the purely systematic point of view we would be obliged to sum up the result of these reflections in the following statement, based solely on systematic considerations: a uniform interpretation of the life and character of Jesus is an impossible task, from the point of view of scientific study, because the hidden unity of this life, which, as such, is also the key to the full understanding of this history, the Person of the God-Man, is not human and historical at all. Thus, from the purely historical point of view, the historian cannot recognize Jesus the Son of God; but he also finds it impossible to fit this historical picture into his "analogical continuum" in a satisfactory manner, that is, to explain it, because the unity which would be determined by this interpretation does not lie at all within his sphere of knowledge—and we might add: does not lie within the sphere of that which we usually call interpretation at all. For the historical appearance of the Mediator is also determined by the mystery of the Person of the Mediator; thus, ultimately, to every historian His Person remains an insoluble problem. The mystery of the Person of the Mediator always disturbs the views of the secular historian, and the historian cannot do otherwise than notice this disturbing fact again and again, yet without understanding it, and as a man of pure science without being able to accept it. It is therefore a most audacious undertaking for a theologian, that is, for a believer who is also a scientific scholar, to try to sketch even in briefest outline a picture of the historical personality of Jesus. It is impossible for him to do this as though he were a secular historian; he cannot sever the other reality which he knows as an invisible reality through faith from the historical picture which he sees before him. Moreover, he can only see the historical visible reality, the "picture" of Jesus from the point of view of a believer. Therefore he brings to his task presuppositions which the others do not bring with them, and which he cannot base upon "scientific" grounds. He is, however, confident that the opposite view is not a scientifically tenable one; that is, that it is *possible* for others to see things in a different manner—his own view is not capable of "scientific" proof—but that their scientific view does not *force* them to different conclusions. Thus the attempt must be made, in spite of this difficulty, in order to show that the Christian faith is not opposed to the reality which can be historically known, as is so often asserted. In so doing we are naturally obliged to confine our attention to a few leading points.

(iii)

"Born of a woman." "Born of the seed of David according to the flesh." From the very beginning, that is, with the beginning of its reality in space and time,[1] the Incarnation of the Son of God implied that this life would follow a human and natural course. We have already considered the logical implications of this point of view in reference to the birth of Jesus. If the idea of a Virgin Birth had really meant anything to the Apostle Paul he would hardly have laid so much stress on the fact that Christ was "born of a woman," as an element which He shared with all other human beings, and on His origin from the "seed of David." Yet this expression means more than this; it implies the perfectly natural character of His human development. Legend and pseudo-scientific research into the Life of Christ have always busied themselves particularly with this question of the *development* of the personality of Jesus. The New Testament ignores this aspect entirely, as a matter of supreme indifference—save for the stories in Luke's

---

[1] How completely modern scholars of the first rank take it for granted that they can employ rational standards to decide what is possible and what is impossible, is shown, for instance, by Johannes Weiss in the statement on the pre-existence of Jesus in connection with the idea of His human birth. "Strictly speaking, both are ruled out. . . . For in a birth there comes into being a new entity which had not hitherto existed" (*Urchristentum*, p. 378). As if the Fathers of the Church and the Reformers who taught the doctrine of the deity of Christ did not know this already. It was this very fact which seemed so impossible that they regarded as the miraculous fact of redemption, the truth which is truer than all that which is *not* logically excluded.

Gospel about the infancy and childhood which, for their part, however, emphasize the purely natural character of Christ's development. Evidently the New Testament regards all this as part of the "flesh," and thus we have no need to know the particular details. It simply presupposes the fact of an ordinary human development as something quite natural, as part of the Incarnate state.

The same observation, however—and this astonishes the modern man—applies to all psychological-genetic questions. Everything which has been put forward, even by outstanding scholars, about the inner development of Jesus in the period of His maturity, belongs rather to the sphere of Gospel romances and imaginative *Lives* than to the picture which is based on scientific grounds. Especially is this true of all hypotheses about the way in which the Messianic consciousness arose. Naturally no one is forbidden to think about this question. But he should make it quite clear that in putting forward such daring hypotheses the limit of scientific knowledge has been reached. Of the manner in which this consciousness arose we *know* absolutely nothing. Only one who does not believe in the Messiah will attempt to make a psychological construction, which always means a natural explanation. A natural explanation will, of course, be interesting to those who share this general point of view, and more or less necessary, but it is very far from being a *scientific* achievement. These hypotheses have about the same value as the materialistic hypotheses concerning the way in which the spiritual arises out of the material. Hence they remain mere hypotheses, because here there is nothing to explain, because these matters lie in a region which is outside the possibility of all scientific explanation.

From the scientific point of view it is a particularly dubious proceeding to use the story of the Baptism of Jesus as the basis for a construction of this kind.[1] In the form in which this

[1] Bousset, above all, has vigorously attacked the still popular interpretation of the Baptism of Jesus as a psychological biographical fact (*Kyrios Christos*, p. 265). The statement of Weinel that: "We must admit that He, like all the Prophets, had His hour of vocation" (*Ntl. Theol.*, p. 207), shows how easily "critical" scholars *postulate* what they do not *know*. Is it not possible that after all the distinction between Jesus and the Prophets may be precisely this fact, that for Him there was no such solemn hour of vocation?

incident has been handed down to us it does not lay itself open, in the very least, to such treatment. The alterations in its structure which are needed in order to turn it into a basis of this kind are, from the scientific point of view, of the most questionable nature. Still more hazardous, however, is it to use the story of the Transfiguration for this purpose. If such procedure can be dubbed "scientific," then all we can say is, the borderline between historical science and romance must have been effaced.[1] As a purely human consciousness the self-consciousness of Jesus must certainly have arisen at some particular point in time. But just as it is impossible to determine the moment when a child first becomes conscious of its own existence as a self—and anyone who has understood the idea of the Self will no longer inquire into its causal explanation—so it would be equally irrelevant to know at what exact point in time the Messianic self-consciousness of Jesus arose. It is not without good reason that the Biblical witnesses of the Life of Jesus had no interest in these psychological questions. They had something more important to do.

(iv)

"Born under the Law." The statement, "born of a woman," shows how Jesus was bound to the conditions of natural existence. In this phrase, "born under the Law," Paul is defining His limitations as a human being. The birth of Christ is the sign of His creaturely character, given to man; the Law is the sign of His special quality among the creatures, of His moral and religious humanity. What does the picture of the humanity of Jesus show us? Even as a human being, Jesus, as a man like ourselves, is subject to the Law; since, according to the view which Luther so often and so emphatically stated, He was a "weak" human being like ourselves, who had to eat and drink, who got tired, so also He was a man who had to submit to the will of God, and who had to struggle, who was

---

[1] Pfleiderer's remark (*Urchristentum*, I, p. 664) in connection with the confession of Peter: "this idea of the Messiahship was still so new to Him, that He shrank back from it in fear, and sought to defend Himself from it," belongs to the imaginative type of the *Life of Jesus*.

"in all points tempted like as we are," a man whom we see asking God, listening to God, praying to God, thanking God, one who was neither omniscient nor omnipotent. His soul could be "sorrowful unto death"; He could tremble and faint, and plead with God to remove from Him the bitter cup of suffering. He was a man who lived as a Jew in the late period of the ancient world; who shared the views of His time, and expressed Himself in the language of His people; in brief, in the full sense of the word, He was an historical personality.

But already the reader of the Gospel narratives, whose eyes are open to perceive the "truly great," is forced to stand still in amazement before this remarkable Figure, perceiving in this historical picture some of those ever-expanding "circles" which point back to something which cannot be explained. In his own way he feels he must confirm the apostolic word of testimony, that He "was obedient even unto death, even unto the death of the Cross." Let us try to analyse this impression in greater detail.

There is in Him no trace of that discrepancy which usually appears particularly clearly in people of a high ethical type, that hiatus between their desire and their actions, between their ideal and their life, between their knowledge and their obedience. He makes the highest demands, with such sternness and in such a completely natural way, assuming, as a matter of course, that He belongs to a different order, that we can only conclude that a man who can speak like this has either forgotten his own obligations towards the Law altogether or else he knows that he has fulfilled the Law. It is impossible to discover any hiatus between His teaching and His Person. Here we approach the subject of His sinlessness, yet we know that this is the subject not of an empirical historical opinion but of faith. But the picture of the reality does not contradict the view held by faith.

Students of the Gospels have constantly been impressed by Christ's freedom from all Jewish national peculiarities both in His character and in His behaviour. In His complete detachment from all historical institutions, such as the family, the State, the religious community, as well as from race, custom, etc., the trammels implied by social position, riches, etc., there is something almost timeless and supra-national about Him, in spite of the fact that He is, and intends to be, a Jew; so that it is as easy to represent Him as the classical Sage (Strauss, Wellhausen) as it is to represent Him as a Hebrew Prophet. And yet this is not due to any lack of clearness and concreteness in the Synoptic Gospels; they certainly do not represent Him in a "Byzantine" light. It is true, of course, that nothing at all is said in them about His virtues—and the omission is, very significant. In this instance it is really true to say that "moral greatness is always self-evident." He is shown to us in many different and many extraordinary situations; in every instance He always manifests not only complete self-possession, but in each situation He reveals His complete adequacy, the same inimitable originality revealed in the mastery of a particular situation. This gives to His figure an aspect of regal repose and dignity, of absolute self-possession and mastery of all that is non-spiritual and accidental, which might almost appear inhuman, if behind it we did not feel at the same time an immense passion, an intense energy of will and feeling. There have indeed been some who have reproached Jesus with being one-sided. And, indeed, this is true enough if to be "one-sided" means to subordinate everything to the "one thing needful," to the one supreme Cause, and inevitably such an attitude must seem one-sided to the humanitarian moralist. It is the "one-sidedness" of One who regards God's interests as paramount, to whom His Cause is supreme.

The beautiful phrase of Goethe: "Far behind him, remote and insignificant, lay that which holds us all in thrall—all that common is and low"—is an exaggeration when it is applied to Schiller; yet if it were applied to Jesus it would seem banal. All self-assertion, all fluctuation between self-affirmation and service has ceased in Him. For it was not this that lay behind the conflict in Gethsemane, but the struggle with the conviction that the way of complete failure is the one which is ordered by God, and absolutely necessary. The natural way in which all the temptations of Satan glance off Him harmlessly like blunted arrows, although it may not be an isolated instance, is still the striking representation of that which we perceive in His story. The Buddha may also have been a "completely selfless" man. But let us not forget this: in the Buddha selflessness is a self-end; the aim is the extinction of desire. In Jesus this selflessness is coupled with a passionate positive energy of purpose and will. The rhythm of His life contains quite as much of the spirit of a breathless race towards the goal as it contains that of complete repose; it is characterized quite as fully by the prophetic saying: let us hasten! the time is far spent (*ultimum tempus*), as by the completest self-possession and repose. Thus His selflessness is combined with a royal sovereign will, which the Roman centurion recognized as something akin to his own military authority.

The highest instance of this *coincidentia oppositorum*, however—of which even the keen secular historian will say: it is "unique in kind"—is that of the intensest sternness of moral judgment and of infinite forgiving love. The nineteenth century saw the latter only, and it relegated the preacher of judgment and of repentance, the one who arouses the true fear of God, to the background, and placed in the foreground the One who proclaimed the Fatherhood of God. Since the rediscovery of the eschatological element, however, this other aspect has received renewed attention. In point of fact, both these elements are found in Jesus: the terrible warrior and destroyer of resistance against God—no one ever attacked the religious leaders of His day with more severity—and a Friend of sinners and of outcasts, who showed forth a love which was unintelligible to those who saw Him, and indeed roused great hostility against Him. From Him also the fire of the wrathful God streamed forth, still more powerfully than from any of the great prophets, or from John the Baptist; but the element in Him which was new in Israel was His love of sinners, free from all taint of proselytism; to the rigid observer of the Jewish Law it was this which constituted the great stumbling-block. This unconditional, unlimited fellowship with bad people, this forgiveness (which they regarded as "careless" because it laid down no conditions at all), which He expressed towards sinners, could only be practised by One who was not afraid of being misunderstood, by One who knew that in Himself evil could not find a single cranny by which to enter into His soul, that it had not the least affinity with His spirit in any direction or at any point. In His own Life He expressed the truth that in the Gospel the Law is fulfilled as well as abrogated.

Another "coincidence" of a very significant character has often also been pointed out: His nearness to men and yet His remoteness from them. Who could more easily make the claim to have been truly human than He, the discoverer of the child? The child is indeed human absolutely, human without any additional quality, without any achievement which distinguishes one human being from another. Hence for Jesus the child is the closest illustration—an illustration which is almost the living embodiment of that which it signifies—of the true attitude of man towards God. The disciples, in their well-meant efforts to save their Master's time and strength, thought they could distinguish between what was important and what was unimportant and tried to keep the children away from Him, yet He always had time and strength to give to these, to the "least of these," His little ones. What a loving understanding His parables betray for all the small things of life, and all the natural creation, for all that is close to the ordinary life of men as men! How free His language is from all rabbinical sterility and learned abstraction! To how great an extent all romantic preservers and guardians of the life of the people in its simpler forms might rightly appeal to Jesus for support at so many points! Here we see no radical desire for progress, no strained efforts to pass beyond present conditions, no attempt to bury natural life and feeling under a weight of abstract ideas and theories.

And yet, in another sense, His whole life is one of extreme detachment. He does not shun the reproach of extreme lack of family feeling, in reference to the family in general, as well as in connection with His own relatives. He does not make the slightest effort "to preserve the sacred possessions of His people." His words about the tribute-money constitute a double refusal: He rejected both nationalistic patriotism and the attitude of enthusiastic wholehearted recognition of the authority of the ruling State. He is a stranger in this world; He has no profession, and He tears His disciples away from their callings and their natural conditions; He possesses no home, no income, and no property. He does nothing which could bring Him even the slightest praise from those who care supremely for civilization, although unlike those who have "left the world" in India, for example, He is no ascetic, but was reproached by His enemies with being a "winebibber and a glutton." He is unmarried, and He praises the celibacy of elect souls, but He consorts without the slightest embarrassment or self-consciousness with women, under the very eyes of those who in all periods will try to read evil into a man's dealings with women, in their desire to ferret out supposed impurities; He went to be the guest of women, and allowed them to wait on Him. He speaks the harshest words against being bound to those "sacred possessions," and yet He makes no attack upon anything. He honours pious customs and traditions, but He breaks through them if by so doing He can help any human being. He shares human experience to the full, and yet He is completely detached. He stands in complete reality in the midst of the real world, without breaking a single thread which binds it to the creation, and yet He is free from all; He is rooted in nothing, and yet He has not been torn up by the roots.

He stands in the midst of the ethical and religious tradition of His people. He honours it. The Scriptures are to Him the revelation of God. The Law is to be fulfilled, to the last jot and tittle. The Temple also, the place of the sacrificial worship—in criticism of which the prophets went almost to the limits of rejecting it altogether—is to Him worthy of reverence, indeed it is holy. In the synagogue He teaches in the manner of the Rabbis. And yet—He passes all this by, and sets over against it the One thing which He proclaims and represents in His Person, as completely incomparable. We can only faintly imagine to-day what it must have meant to a pious Jew to hear these words: "Ye have heard that it was said to them of old time . . . but *I* say unto you." If He had been a man of the type of Socrates, the contemporary of the Sophists, this would not have been extraordinary. But He was Himself a teacher of the Torah; He was a member of the synagogue, and was Himself "under the Law." We do not know exactly what were the words He used when He said the Temple would be destroyed. But evidently this was a point at which He was attacked when He came to His trial. His mere existence, every one of His words, threatened all present existence, by their concentration on what is ultimate. It is not in the least surprising that He, who was in no sense either an iconoclast or a revolutionary, should have been condemned on such a charge. It was quite appropriate that it was not the legal representatives of the State and the civil order, but the representatives of religion, of the Jewish religion of the Law, who recognized His revolutionary character. For they alone understood the menace which went forth from Him.

(v)

Only now can we deal with the problem of the Messiahship of Jesus. Once more it is of the very nature of the case that here in particular it is impossible to reconstruct an historical "picture" which will be universally accepted. For here we reach the point at which the historical and the suprahistorical elements come into contact with each other, where the "circle" which the historian is still able to perceive—the inmost central circle—becomes the point which he no longer sees. Here, therefore, the judgment of the historian becomes completely uncertain. The history of research into the life of Jesus is a story of toilsome endeavour to see Jesus truly, and at the same time to see Him purely from the human point of view. These two things cannot be achieved at the same time. If we admit His Messianic claim as historical and real, then it seems as though His ethical and religious humanity, to which sobriety of outlook seems to belong—is obscured; this simply does not agree with that aspect of His life, with the impression of rigid sobriety and unbending discipline. If, however, for this very reason we ascribe this claim to the later theology of the Church, then we are in conflict with the whole of the Christian tradition, and are confronted by insoluble historical problems.

Hence no particular view, however much it might try to express nothing but the exact historical truth, could ever count on general acceptance. In spite of this fact, however, and in spite of the uncertainty of the tradition, such an attempt must be made. The fact that general agreement is impossible does not prevent accuracy. Where we are dealing with reality which can be ascertained historically, we ought not to allow ourselves to be robbed of the right to our own opinion on questions of actual historical fact through the influence of an extreme radicalism in the criticism of tradition. Once again we would emphasize this point: our faith is not based upon this historical picture; it is not founded upon our historical perception of the inmost circle. But even the historian ought not to reject, *a priori*, the possibility that here the believer might for once be less prejudiced from the historical point of view, because he is not dominated by the view that everything must fit into the "analogous continuum." We place no limits to criticism, but we do certainly call attention to the fact that a limit is set by historical reality.

Thus we too are confronted by the question to what extent the—historically ascertainable—mystery of the Person of Jesus is expressed in the historically ascertainable incognito of His historical reality and, although always veiled, may yet gleam through all the coverings of His "form as a servant." In the previous pages we have already dealt with this question of the divine shining through the human. To him who sees, that is, to him who believes, every word, every act of Jesus, every peculiarity of His character is a sign of the mystery of His Person. But not all these circles are equally clear because not all are equally near to the central point. Let us try to approach the inmost of the concentric circles, always with the consciousness that we are not here concerned with the "point" but with the circles; that is, with the historical radiation of the invisible divine mystery, and thus also with something which is the object of legitimate historical criticism.

Thus we begin with the general observation that the "Messianic consciousness" only forms part, but not the whole of this inmost circle. The question whether Jesus regarded Himself as the Messiah does not of itself decide the further question of His Messianic consciousness in the broader sense. The "Messiah" is a name; the "Son of Man," the "Son of God," are other names. But even with the Name the "circle" is not yet fully outlined. To describe this fully we would need to draw into the range of our reflections His bearing, the manner of His speech and behaviour, His silence and His passing by, the way in which He discussed problems with the leading men of His day, and, above all, His deeds of power, since, indeed, in all this His special self-consciousness is to a certain extent visibly expressed historically.

The first point we note is this: that Jesus intended to be more than a prophet. According to the statement of Jesus, John the Baptist is the greatest of the Prophets, but he is also the last of the series. On this side there begins something absolutely new, something incomparably new and great, so new that there can be nothing which will exceed it. With Jesus the new age which closes history has opened; the Kingdom of God has begun to appear upon the earth. To the question of the Baptist: "Art thou He that should come?" the reply is guarded, but to one who knows, it is an unmistakable "Yes." Jesus speaks about His own authority in a way which was different from all the Prophets, in a way, indeed, which would not have been fitting for a prophet. For the prophet has no ἐξουσία, no personal authority. Jesus describes Himself as One who has broken into the house of the strong man, and has bound him. He speaks of His mission,[1] not like a prophet with a definite commission, but with reference to His existence as a whole. Therefore He says also—what no prophet had ever said, or had any right to say—that His "coming" is not spatial at all; His existence *is* His "coming." Hence in Him the Kingdom of God "has arrived," and—turning to the Pharisees—He added: "it is in the midst of you." Jesus Himself explains that these unexampled powers which are exercised by Him are a sign of His authority. By this ἐξουσία He forgives sins. Not in the Name of God—that would have aroused no resistance— but in His own Name, appealing to the authority which is

---

[1] When Dibelius (*Formgeschichte*, p. 91), commenting on the "Johannine" passage in Matt. xi. 26, says: "He comes, Himself of a different origin and kind, to the children of men, in order to lead them out of the corruption which forms part of their very nature," and then describes that as a typically Gnostic idea, then likewise every word and saying of Jesus which expresses His specific consciousness of His mission would be described as "Gnostic." In point of fact, this "Gnostic" element constitutes the very heart of the Gospel itself. (See below, the section on "Christian mythology.")

vested in His own Person, which is likewise proved by a mighty work of healing. Hence He says plainly—what no one before Him had dared to say: "Blessed is he who is not offended in Me."[1] So far as His Person was concerned, the people seem to have felt baffled. There was no category in which they could place Him. So they gave Him fantastic names, drawn from their own popular eschatology.

Did Jesus call Himself in a special sense "Son of God"? The critics of the present day tend to answer this question in the affirmative. The arguments against it are weaker than the tradition and the difficulties which arise out of denial. "Ultimately it seems probable that Jesus did feel Himself to be Son of God in a special sense" (Weinel).[2] Jesus Himself alluded to the mystery of His relation to God. As the "Son" He contrasted Himself with the "Servants," the Prophets who were sent before Him. He "held Himself to be the decisive and final revelation of God" (Weinel).[3] Only when we see this do the special eschatological names which He also assumed become significant. Doubtless we are intended to conceive His Entry into Jerusalem and the Cleansing of the Temple as "Messianic" acts. His Messianic claim was the subject of His trial, as "King of the Jews" He was crucified, and the usual inscription, with the announcement of the crime (for which the criminal had been condemned) ran as follows: "Jesus of Nazareth, King of the

---

[1] Even Bultmann, whose critical knife would excise more from the tradition (particularly at the point of the Messianic consciousness) than most other critics of the present day, appears to admit that this saying is historical (*Jesus*, p. 198). But this is not the saying of a prophet. This identification of personal authority with the Word is the new thing, the new category, which is above the prophet, and we know now what it means when the word prophet is taken seriously (see above, pp. 216 ff.). On the other hand, the conclusion of Bultmann's book: "whether he has been sent by God—that is the decision," weakens its force. Even in the sense of the arguments of Bultmann himself it ought to have been put like this: "Whether he is the One whom God has sent"; for (even for Bultmann) everything depends upon this—that we are here concerned with ultimate things, whereas with a prophet we are still only concerned with the penultimate. I have already said that I believe that the radicalism of Bultmann is the result of premises which he now explicitly rejects; hence I cannot accept his arguments (see above, p. 190).

[2] *Bibl. Theol. d. Neuen Testamentes*, p. 207.   [3] Loc. cit., p. 202.

Jews."[1] The controversial discussions in Jerusalem are difficult to understand except on the assumption that He was regarded as an aspirant to the Messiahship. The confession of Peter: "Verily Thou art the Son of God," and the reply of Jesus: "Blessed art thou, Simon Barjona, for flesh and blood have not revealed this unto thee, but My Father which is in heaven," is to-day seldom ascribed to the later theology of the Church; it bears too plainly the stamp of something which could not have been invented.

Indeed, even the title of "Son of Man," which has an eschatological ring about it, seems to hold its own with criticism, however one may feel about this assertion of Jesus, which certainly exceeds all merely human claims.[2] According to the tradition (which is here not at all improbable), this stupendous admission was the actual underlying cause of His condemnation. To sum up: the historical picture of His self-consciousness is one which almost verges on delusion, and yet on the other hand is connected with an absolutely sober, reflective, and humble way of thinking.

(vi)

These facts—whose historical details are still uncertain and are therefore a most unsuitable foundation for faith—are the points which suggest the existence of that innermost circle. It may sound fine to say: "Faith has no interest at all in these facts"; but this lofty indifference is forbidden to us by faith. It is of importance to us that this "circle," which is so indistinct that many historians cannot "see" it at all, should really

[1] Cf. Bertram: *Die Leidensgeschichte Jesu*, p. 77.

[2] Weinel, loc. cit., p. 216: "To the mind of the ancient world it was quite usual to attribute that which is mysterious and forceful in man, that which is of genius, to the forces of another world, to the indwelling of beings from another realm." P. 224: "It is quite natural that it (namely Jesus' consciousness of His mission) should assume the forms which were provided by the religious thought-world of His people and of His period." In any case the Jews did not think this, for they were horrified and exclaimed: "He has blasphemed against God!" and even the Gospel of John does not seem to have regarded this claim of Jesus as something quite "usual."

exist. We do not build our faith upon it, but as believers who also desire to look at the historical aspect of the question, we do *see* this circle: the Messianic claim.

Historical critics who are not believers, who do not admit the claim of Jesus to be the Christ in the sense of the witness of the Church, have tried to deal with this fact in various ways. Some deny it altogether, that is, they say that the Messianic claim was invented by the Church later on—but this leads them into the various difficulties which have already been mentioned, although this theory does enable them to extricate themselves from the difficulty of giving an explanation of this strange phenomenon. Others seek to explain the Messianic claim in a "spiritual" sense, that is, in the sense of religious theories of Immanence. But this path which was followed by the older Liberal Christian school is trodden by few to-day. The third type of critic admits the actual fact of an unusual eschatological Messianic claim of Jesus, but he tries to explain it as the form adopted under certain circumstances, suited to the period, for the self-estimate of a religious genius of the highest type; he then urges us to be tolerant of this curious phenomenon, reminding us of the circumstances in which Jesus lived, in those days; this theory likewise—though with more respect for history—seeks to transform this phenomenon into immanental religion. Such critics admit, it is true, that Jesus regarded Himself, in a sense which to them seems quite fantastic, as the Son of God, as a Being of a higher order, but they try to make this fact intelligible by explaining it from the psychological, historical point of view—from the point of view of the mentality of the period—as the form in which an extraordinary religious genius could regard himself.

The fourth type—[in our opinion the historians whose historical intuition is most to be trusted, who do not let themselves be led astray by their own particular point of view]—state frankly and plainly, *either* that Jesus was as Matthew describes him *or* that He never existed; then in truly modern fashion they adapt this picture to their own view by regarding Jesus as the victim of a "Messianic dogma"—we may observe, in passing, that it is not clear why this particular man, Jesus, should have applied this Messianic dogma to Himself. At the same time the Messianic statements of Jesus are represented as realistically and mythologically as possible, and therefore as fantastically, in order to avoid the error of the Liberal Christian immanental interpretation.

It may be quite impossible to decide, from the scientific point of view, which of these views is more correct than the others. We must leave it to the historians to come to a mutual agreement about the debit and credit account. All we have to say is this: in actual fact this situation corresponds to that which we might expect. The most plausible historical theory, the one which is suggested by the phrase, "Messianic dogma," is that which, among all the views of secular historians, may be regarded as the one which comes closest to the view of faith. It regards the mystery of the Messiahship—judged from the human point of view—as a wholly fantastic phenomenon, and leaves it at that, without being able to reach any closer understanding. It does not seriously try to explain it psychologically but leaves it as it is, in all the strangeness of its historical objectivity.

This is more or less the point of view of the believer also as he looks at the history of Jesus and at this inmost "circle." He understands that here the opinions of the historians, both in those which concern actual facts, as well as in questions of their significance, must go different ways. He does not count at all on the possibility that a unity could here be created along purely scientific lines. He does not even claim that he himself has a still surer method at his disposal. He only knows: *this man is the Christ*. Not because he says so himself—for what he himself says is history, it refers to the "circle," and not to the "point," and therefore it belongs to the sphere of relativity. But to the man who knows already that this is the Christ, that Jesus said this, that most probably He made such statements about Himself, statements of such a "fantastic" nature, this is a proof, and to a certain extent a confirmation (*adminiculum*) of his conviction that this is what He really is. It would be still more curious if the situation regarding this inmost circle were different from what it really is—according to our most reliable historical knowledge. Thus, as we try to sum up, we see that it is quite in order that the historians should argue whether Jesus ever existed at all—for to come "in the flesh" means to come into such an existence that later on people will be bound to argue about it; likewise over the question: did He regard Himself as the Messiah?—for it belongs to the real Messiah that later on people will be able to argue whether He did really regard Himself as the Messiah—for how should the Unique be expressed otherwise than in some form which is not unique, thus in some form or another offered by history. However, among all the forms at our disposal there could indeed have been none more suitable to express this unique fact than that in which the Old Testament eschatology expressed the unique, the decisive fact in its personal form. It too was cumbered with historical elements and was not clear, but it was the one which existed. The controversy about its meaning forms part of the nature of the fact which is expressed by "the form of a servant" of the Son of God, by the "Word made flesh," of Jesus Christ, so that the historian too might not be excepted when it is said: "Blessed is he who is not offended in Me."

APPENDIX

THE "MYTHOLOGY" OF CHRISTIANITY

It is obvious that all the Christian credal affirmations concerning the divine activity in revelation and in salvation are "mythological"; that is, quite definitely they are inadequate. Christian theologians have always been fully aware of this, and even the simple Christian believer knows as much about this as is necessary. At this point, however, we need to keep our eyes wide open in order that this admission (1 Cor. xiii. 12) may not allow us to glide imperceptibly into a trend of thought which would destroy the Christian faith. We need only remind ourselves of Hegel, and of the way in which he transformed the "symbolic ideas" (or "presentative conceptions") contained in Christianity into "notional scientific truth," to receive a warning which cannot be disregarded. The Christian knows that all his statements about the Faith are mythological, but he also knows that this is the only form in which they can be expressed and preserved; on the other hand, he is aware that every kind of "notional" scientific formulation actually becomes more inadequate and more dangerous, precisely to the extent in which it seems more scientific. "Therefore it is my simple counsel," says Luther in an Easter sermon,[1] "that thou let it be with simple words and childlike pictures and that thou trouble not thy head about what the high and learned minds say of these things, who will have all things without pictures and will probe everything with their own clever reason. . . . Therefore I leave all reasoning and all high and searching questions and allegories and speak simply and as a child about this article of belief. . . . Must we not indeed grasp all that we do not know by means of pictures, whether they give a true picture or not of that which they try to represent? Wherefore, then, should we not learn to understand this article by means of pictures, since otherwise we cannot under-

[1] *E.A.*, 3, 281. In spite of the fact that the tradition concerning this sermon is very uncertain, I venture to quote this passage because it bears unmistakably Luther's stamp upon it.

377

stand or know it, because indeed the picture helps to preserve the right and pure understanding?"

To faith this is sufficient. But from the point of view of scientific thought we need to enter into a more detailed discussion of this question.

(i)

In the problem of Christian "mythology" the one point at issue is the specifically Christian idea of revelation. The form of the Christian statement of faith corresponds exactly to the relation of Christianity as a "revealed" religion to the Idealistic or mystical idea of revelation on the one hand, and to the belief in revelation of the non-Christian religions on the other hand; this point came out clearly in the first chapter of this book. The Christian "myth" is neither the abstract ("notional") conceptual statement of the philosophy of religion, nor is it "mythological" in the sense of pagan mythology. Indeed, the difference with which we are here concerned is not merely one of degree; it is quite evident that it belongs to an entirely different category.

The idea of revelation in the philosophy of religion has no relation to time. It deals with the static Idea, with the ground of the world, with the ground of meaning, the ground of the soul, of which we are always conscious because it is always present, with the God who "is," who is always there, to whom all that we need to do is to open our souls. Here revelation is no real happening. Pagan mythology, on the other hand, is certainly concerned with actual happenings, or rather, it knows of an unlimited number of events which are both divine and temporal. The Divine and Eternal Being expressed in the temporal form of an occurrence is indeed the essential characteristic of the myth.[1] But because heathenism believes in such an infinitely varied divine series of events, it has no conception

[1] Measured by the Christian conception of history both the myth and the Idea belong to the same category; both are fundamentally wholly timeless. The irrational element which is expressed in the mythical consciousness, as distinguished from the rational Idea, is not that of act, of history, but of Nature. Like the Idea it is itself "static" truth. The myth is a symbol clothed in the form of an event, a substantive in verbal form;

of one serious decisive event; all its conceptions are based on the idea of recurrence. Its underlying thought is governed by the course of nature, not by the decisiveness of history. The "notional" abstract philosophy of religion and the spirit of mysticism both represent a relation to the Divine in which nothing happens; mythology one in which much "takes place" but nothing decisive *happens*. The Christian "myth," however, expresses the idea of a unique and decisive event.[1]

Whereas pagan mythology is infinite in variety and extent, and places no check on the vivid fantasies of a fertile imagination, to which fresh inventions can continually be added with-

in so far as it expresses an event it is in the sense of something which continually recurs and which takes place always and everywhere. The myth-conceptions of Bachofen and of Schelling here lead to the same result.

[1] It is unnecessary to emphasize the fact that the conception of the Unique (*Einmalige*), represented by the Romantic philosophy of history (to-day by Rickert) on the one hand, and by the Idealism of Leibniz on the other hand, both woven into a unity by Troeltsch, has nothing at all to do with our conception of uniqueness (*Einmaligkeit* = once-for-all-ness). The Romantic conception of the Unique is simply that of individuality, and therefore it is a natural conception. For individuality is the manner of being of all life. We can also say: it is an aesthetic conception; for individuality is that living element which is the object of contemplation. It is, of course, true that history also as such presents us with the picture of individual visible life; but this is not that which distinguishes it from the being of nature; it only distinguishes life (in Nature and in History) from scientific abstraction; but this does not mean that history has been understood in its character as *res gestae*.

This is also true of the more serious conception in individuality in Leibniz. It differs from the Romantic conception in this, that the individuality here is of metaphysical and not merely of phenomenal dignity. Whereas the Romantic conceives individuality like Spinoza only as something which has been refracted, which experiences the universal through the material (*principium individuationis est materia*), for Leibniz it is the original form of that which most really *is*. But it is obvious that in the teaching of Leibniz it does not possess a specifically historical but a general metaphysical significance. It is common to the being of Nature and to History. Quite rightly he does not use it for the definition of the historical as such. It is a metaphysical, theoretical object of contemplation. It designates an act, an activity, only in so far as all being is active, not a distinction of the historical from the natural. It has not the quality of decision, an actual deed, in the personal sense. But this, however, is truly historical. Because revelation alone is genuinely personal—namely divinely personal—it is the decisive element, the absolute event.

out in any way injuring the preceding ideas, the Christian "myth" is *one*. It describes one movement, and indeed a movement of a quite definite unique kind, which by its very nature can only be interpreted in one way. It is therefore as rigid as a mathematical formula—although it is not abstract—and it offers no scope to an imagination hungry for variety. Thus—if we compare it with the mythologies of the pagan world—it is an "abstract myth," as abstract, namely, as it can be and yet be combined with the personal and dynamic character of the revelation as a whole. This is one of its characteristics. But its other characteristic is equally important: it describes a movement which rises in eternity and returns to eternity, but which, at a certain point, touches historical reality, passing through a definite place in the time-series, which in this way gains infinite significance, to such an extent indeed that henceforth it is qualified as *the* decisive element. It is precisely this element which constitutes the unique revelation. This "point" in time is not mythical; it cannot be described as something fantastic which can be distinguished from ordinary actuality; on the contrary, it is the lowest point that can be imagined; it is a blank, a death. In the central point of the Christian "myth" stands the statement: "crucified under Pontius Pilate."[1] This form also, this union of time and eternity, is, like its content, unique, not only quantitatively, gradually becoming unique, but, in the strictest sense of the word, it stands alone. For this very reason it behoves us to be very cautious in our use of the notion of the "myth" in this connection.

(ii)

The Christian "myth" of the coming of God in revelation, of the Creation and the Fall as its presupposition, and of the

[1] This additional phrase, "under Pontius Pilate," shows the abyss which lies between mythology in general and the Christian "mythus" in particular. If we think of "redeemer-gods," Hellenistic-Iranian-Mandaean mythology, we are able to measure the significance of this apparently unimportant chronological statement. In mythology even the mystery of redemption remains an Idea, a possibility, a longing; in the Christian religion it is attested as *factum est*, as something which has taken place at the nadir of human history.

Resurrection and the coming Kingdom of God as its completion, denotes a movement. This means that God is here
revealed as the living God, and that history is the sphere
of decision. Further, this means that God is known as the
Absolute, and that the historical decision is the absolutely
serious decision. If history in general is installed in place of
this unique element, then history loses its decisive character
and faith merges into the pantheistic view of history associated
with Idealism—the Idealistic philosophy of history, the idea
of development. But if the unique element is not regarded as
a point, but as historical extension—taking the historical
personality of Jesus as historical, and no more—it also loses
its final character and, along this path, faith glides just as
easily into the Idealistic philosophy of history. Uniqueness,
invisible, non-extended uniqueness, is only another way of
describing the absolutely decisive character of this "movement."

In mysticism, in Idealism—even in the Idealism of the
philosophy of history—there is no decision. The Idea, even
when it is regarded from the point of view of its concrete[1]
presentation in history, has no relation to time. The Idea is
timeless;[2] thus it also transforms history into something timeless, by the idea of unfolding or development. The direction of
history is thus defined from the outset; whoever knows the law
of its movement (Hegel) knows its goal, and need not wait
therefore to see how the further course of history will shape
itself. Here there is neither judgment nor decision. Hence no

[1] The concrete expression of an Idea in history is wholly different from
revelation; for the correlate of that which has been thus expressed in concrete
form is a universal. History is not yet conceived as existential, as the sphere
of decision, so long as it is only conceived as the sphere in which the Idea
takes concrete form. The antithesis of the concrete versus the abstract is
essentially a theoretical antithesis; it is not practical and existential.
History is concrete, just as life itself is always concrete, but revelation alone
constitutes it the sphere of decision. In the midst, between both, there stands
here also the practical Idea, the ethical as a general law. In so far as it is a
practical law it guarantees decision, in so far as it is a general law, an
ethical Idea, it is precisely the character of decision which is lacking. The
utmost one can say would be this: That the moral law is the reflex in theory
of that which revelation means in practice.

[2] The Idea of Time in Idealistic philosophy, from Plato to Hegel, is
that which "in itself is negative" (Hegel).

philosophy of religion is able to comprehend those points at which the Christian faith recognizes time to be essential: *Creation*—the greatest stumbling-block to the philosopher, that is, unless it is confused with the *creatio continua*, and if the Pantheistic idea of God within the world does not take the place of the scriptural idea of creation out of nothing; *the Fall*— which is quite different from the transition from Paradisial immediacy to reflection; the *revelation* of the *"Word made flesh"*— which is quite different from the concrete form of the Absolute or ethical Idea; and the completion and dissolution of history in the Kingdom of God—which is something quite different from the Immanent "End" of all history, towards which the world is continually approximating. Therefore, whenever the philosophy of religion appropriates the content of the Christian faith and transposes it into its "scientific form," this content itself becomes entirely different, for the element of time and motion has been extruded, and the Christian content of faith is transformed into the timeless conceptions of Idealism; this takes place almost imperceptibly through the use of the Idealistic conception of history. Thus the actual Christian event becomes a state of *being*, final decision becomes development, the ideas of the Fall and of Redemption are changed into an evolution of human life from lower to higher forms of existence of the latent capacity for high achievement which humanity contains.

(iii)

But this situation needs further elucidation. Behind the static character of abstract thought there lies a fundamental connection with space and sensuous perception. There is just as clear a connection between sensuous perception and space, even where the purest and most "immaterial" kind of perception is concerned, as there is between decision and time. Space is the category of that which is always present, time is the category of that which is unique. Space leaves us unlimited time—it allows us to stand and gaze at our leisure. Time confronts us at every moment with a challenge: we must decide to do *either* this *or* that. The Idea is related to space, not to time; therefore all its symbols are spatial, like the word "Idea" itself, which has at its root the "thing seen," the spatial perception. It is true that over and over again philosophy— that of Hegel in particular—has tried to relate abstract conceptions to time; actually, the result was the exact opposite: it transformed time into a concept ("Notion").[1] It is no wonder that this attempt of Hegel's led people to apply to his speculations the term of the "mythology of the Notion." This "mythology" did not do much harm, however, since it was noted very soon that this system made an improper use of all time symbols. To speak of the "development" of notions, of their "unfolding," transformation, "return," etc., is only a *façon de parler*. Time never really entered into this process at all. The Idea is timeless; so it is spatial, for without one of these two forms thought cannot exist. All thought is either spatial or temporal. Spatial thought, or that kind of thinking which ultimately centres round "sight," round ἰδέα or εἶδος, we call conceptual (notional), scientific, etc.; while thought which is connected with time, we call "mythical."[2] Once more,

[1] Lit.: it "benotioned" (*verbegrifflichte*) time.—TR.

[2] On the borderline between the myth and the notion lies the most important conception of the Idealistic philosophy: that of the *a priori*. It is well known that for Plato himself it forms the connecting-link between a series of mystical-religious ideas and a series of rational philosophical ideas. Precisely that Platonic doctrine which comes nearest to Christian thought, that of the Fall, is only possible because Plato interprets the *a priori* and the idea of "Reminiscence" not merely as rationally timeless, but also as mythically in time. The conception of a falling away from the world of the Ideas to which the antithesis between the sense world and the Idea leads him, means more to Plato than a poetic form; here he introduces his Orphic religious ideas, which to him are realities. We find a similar phenomenon in Kant, wherever the *a priori* has practical significance: in the conception of the intelligible self, of the intelligible character, and of radical evil as "inherited guilt." Because this distinction between the intelligible and the empirical is of real practical significance to Kant, at this point he touches the time myth. But he remains undecided. The stringency of transcendental rationalism forbids, the seriousness of practical ethical thought commands, the recognition of the myth as truth. In the one case the *a priori*, precisely to the extent in which it is "static" truth, remains dominated by the ethical idea of law. In the second instance, in which practical earnestness is dominant, in some way or another it is an "event" which is intended, however one may resist the attempt to introduce it into the time series.

however, the genuinely temporal myth is not found within paganism but only within Christianity. For the pagan myth does not take time seriously; it thinks in terms of cycles and crude phantasies. It also desires to have images, but not decisions. Its tendency is aesthetic. It loves to gaze at the marvellous, to look at the amazing exploits of the gods, in which the only "happening" is an exhibition of the marvellous. Or, in so far as it is taken seriously—and the genuine myth *is* to be taken seriously!—the myth is "symbol,"[1] it is the transparent vehicle of "static" truth.

In both instances the "visibility" of the myth is the sign of its hidden timelessness. The Christian "myth," however, is that way of thinking in which the Divine, the Eternal, the Absolute is not placed before us as a mere object of contemplation, but one in which the Absolute comes to us with a demand for decision; hence it cannot be neutral; it is no mere abstract object of contemplation but a Person.[2]

[1] For the connection between Idea, Symbol, and natural event, cf. the most informing study of Bachofen: *Das Natursymbol als Keimzelle des Mythus* (Ausgabe Bernouilli, I, pp. 272 ff.). The myth receives an impulse towards the unique (*Einmalige*) (and thus away from the sphere of the symbolic and the ideal), towards history, on the one hand in the sphere influenced by the prophetic Mazda religion (Zarathustra!), and on the other hand in that type of Hellenism which has already been influenced by the Hebrew idea of history. It is about time that we should cease our continual inquiry into the question of the way in which prophetic religion is determined by mythology and reverse the question by asking how mythology is determined by prophetic religion. India, the classic country of the myth, which at least until the Middle Ages remained untouched by the prophetic idea of history (Zarathustra, Hebrew prophecy, Christianity, and Islam) does not admit any such approximation of the myth to the unique (*Einmalige*). The idea of identity leaves no room for historical decision. Here, therefore, we can see most plainly the meaning of the pagan myth.

[2] In his important article on the relation of the Gospel of John to the Iranian Redeemer-mythology of the Mandaeans (*Christliche Welt*, 1927, pp. 502–11) Bultmann makes some very noteworthy observations on the principles which govern our understanding of the nature of mythology. "In reality the myth expresses how man understands himself in his existence in the world; it expresses this because it throws on the screen of the imagination the images created by his longings and his dreams." It seems to me that here Bultmann ascribes too much to the myth in contrast to the Idea, and too little importance to the Idea as compared with the myth. They are more closely related than Bultmann admits, both positively and

For there is a further point which is also connected with time and space. That which is beheld from the spatial point of view is objective, neutral, a thing which can be seen; even a human being so far as we merely look at him is a "thing seen" (*Sehding*). But whatever forces us to make a decision is personal. Philosophical speculation, even when it is speaking about God, loves to use impersonal expressions: the Absolute, the Divine, the ground of the world, the *Universum*, the Deity. Hence wherever the Idealistic interpretation of Spirit is dominant it is regarded as "progress" towards the spiritual ideal when the expressions which imply personality disappear from religious language and are replaced by impersonal expressions. To transform religious conceptions into impersonal terms coincides with their removal from the sphere of time into that of space. They no longer present a challenge to personal moral decision; they have become subjects of contemplation, of theory.

What has just been said receives a remarkable confirmation when we reflect upon the ethic of Idealism. If what has already been said is true, ethics ought to occupy a remarkable position midway between timeless spatiality and decision within time. For as an ethic it demands decision, but as Idealism it is a theory. This is also actually the case. The more seriously the Moral Law is regarded—and this means the less ethics merge into aesthetics—the more definitely the characteristic expres-

negatively. For the Idea also (we need only think of Plato in this connection) intends to give an explanation of the way in ·which man interprets his existence and not merely an explanation of the world, and on the other hand the myth is indeed, as Bultmann himself suggests, a projection of the longings of man, a "dream and phantasy image," which expresses this longing. On this account we should note especially the continuation of Bultmann's idea: "Unless God *really* reveals Himself this knowledge of God remains negative, indeed, it is only self-knowledge." We would like to add, however: This self-knowledge is as transient and as superficial as that of Idealism. For even self-knowledge can only be complete where God really speaks to man. To the extent, therefore, that in the myth also time, the moment—under the form of a merely mythical, not real happening—is dissolved, it does not challenge man really and truly to decision. It is therefore only symbolic instead of conceptual, an intuition of the Eternal instead of a decision, a counterpart of the theory and the Idea, an aesthetic phenomenon.

sions assume temporal character, the more they become "mythological." Perhaps the most familiar instance is the "Categorical Imperative." Further, the conceptions of responsibility, of moral challenge, of demand should be described as incipient myths. It should also be noted that phrases denoting the act of seeing (*space*) are gradually being replaced by those of hearing (*time*). We are approaching the Word and leaving the Idea behind. The act of *seeing* represents our relation to things, the act of *hearing* represents our relation to persons. Thus the idea of the Good leads to the idea of the Imperative, to the demand, the claim. The act of seeing, even the contemplation of the Idea, is theoretical and impersonal; the act of hearing, listening, and obeying is existential and personal. Wherever man begins to "listen" seriously, in the moral realm, there Idealism has ceased, and faith in revelation has begun. Or, to put it the other way round: the moral Imperative, the act of hearing, can only begin to be taken seriously where there is something to hear, where there is revelation. Serious, critical ethical Idealism[1] is the point at which spatial abstract impersonal thought abandons its own claims, gives heed to time and to the moral challenge, and the barrier between it and all that is truly personal disappears.[2]

(iv)

The Christian "myth" is that form of thought in which time is taken absolutely seriously; hence it is the only type of thought in which God is regarded as truly personal, that in

[1] Bultmann's phrase about the "purely negative knowledge of God" which he applies to the myth might be used with still more force of this critical ethical Idealism, which indeed is not realized anywhere in its pure form, not even in Kant. Its incomparable importance for purposes of introduction consists precisely in its *idea of crisis*. On this point, compare the book by Heinrich Barth, *Philosophie der praktischen Vernunft*, which appeared while this book was passing through the press.

[2] The Bergson philosophy of Time is a purely aesthetic affair, therefore in spite of its hostility to spatial thinking it cannot get beyond spatial conceptions; the dynamic is only Time within the spatial; hence the philosophy of Bergson is really concerned only with the intuition of Time. It is not concerned with questions of decision and of personal reality at all.

which the Word, as the Word of God, and as the real Personal Word, is the decisive factor. Thus it is the Myth of the Word. For this very reason all that is "mythological" (in the usual pagan sense of the word) has been removed. Sensuous perception has vanished; the "Word became flesh"—this is a poor kind of myth, measured by the standard of the requirements of the imagination. Here also there is no room for the mere spectator or for theory; for here the one thing that matters is the decision of faith, obedience to the Word. Hence the Christian "myth" differs from other forms of theory or mythology because the Word does not proceed *from* man, but comes *to* him. This unique historical event, Jesus Christ, in whom it takes place, of whom the Christian "myth" speaks, and on whose account this "myth" exists at all, is not a process of thought or a figment of the imagination, but historical reality. Thus its origin lies neither in thought nor in the speculative imagination, but in history, and indeed in the unique element in history, in an historical event which merely touches the fringe of history, in the "Christ according to the spirit," who is the Christ "in the flesh." The Christian "myth" can therefore desire to express nothing save the absolute seriousness of this encounter, of the revelation of God in Jesus Christ. On the other hand, every attempt to come through without the Christian "myth" must end in this, that the absolute seriousness of that which here took place has been destroyed by the space-symbolism of conceptions and the non-seriousness of theoretical perception.[1]

The "movement" which the Christian "myth" describes is characterized by four points: the *Creation*, as a beginning which

[1] Hence the instinctive distrust of all scientific theology displayed by practical faith. It scents from afar the danger which lies behind all scientific treatment of faith, the danger that the mythological form—which for the truly serious expression of faith is the only form—might be sacrificed in the interest of a supposedly purely formal requirement, to its purely intellectual aspect, as indeed has actually happened over and over again. Scientific theology is only Christian where it uses scientific reflection in order to be able to dismiss the claim of the scientific conception as incompatible with the matter of faith, and to reflect upon the ultimate validity of the mythological expression from the point of view of the nature of faith itself.

qualifies temporal reality as divine; the *Fall*, which constitutes
the negation of temporal reality—that is, as the knowledge
of the original relation of the Creator to His creatures which
has been personally disturbed, indeed destroyed, as a universal
fact which affects all history *qua* history; the event of revelation,
the coming of God as *Reconciliation*, through which man's return
to the original relationship again becomes possible through
decision, that is, through Word and Faith; and finally,
Redemption, as the conclusion of the possibility of decision by
means of the actual removal of the contradiction. These four
points are indissolubly connected with one another. Each one
can only be known together with the other three. These four
points form a unity. This unity contains nothing that is
irrelevant. And secondly, they are all completely concealed
from ordinary perception; indeed, they are only present at all
in the decision of faith. If any one of these points is regarded
as a "theory," or as a "speculation," or as etiology which gives
an answer to a curious inquiry, then that point has been misunderstood. These four points are all statements of faith, of
such a nature that only "in Christ" are they possible at all.

Further, in this connection we ought to observe that all
these four points belong to the same "dimension": they all
refer to the dividing line between time and eternity; not,
however, as a static relation, but as an actual event. The
static relation betwen the eternal and the temporal is not
myth, but symbol. Hence the symbol for the sensuous perception, the Christian "myth," is that in which time is significant,
in which decision is required. Symbols belong to the general
"world view" (*Weltanschauung*), the Christian myth belongs to
the decision of faith. Hence, because it is not concerned with
the static relation between time and eternity, but with events—
closely related to each other—which take place between time
and eternity, even the use of time phraseology is inadequate. If
we use the image of the "process," this terminology describes
something which, in distinction from all other happenings
of any kind, does not merely "take place"—that is, is not
"historical"[1] but something which actually happens, which,

---

[1] From this point of view it should be clear why it is that I avoid the
closely related conception of "saving history." It does not take into

indeed, *has* happened, in a very remarkable way. Perhaps we might express this most clearly by saying, in a somewhat broader sense, that it is an "eschatological" event, super-history.

For the same reason this "myth" is also completely remote from all sensuous perception, in spite of the fact that, in order to suggest that the event as a whole is decisive, it uses certain visible elements. The briefest and the most abstract definition and yet the one which most fully corresponds to the truth is contained in the Johannine phrase: "The Word became flesh." The need for some kind of sensuous perception is not ignored. On the other hand, however, the character of this event is distinguished quite plainly from all idea of static Being, of the absolute Idea; the absolute decisiveness of the event is distinguished quite clearly from all the timeless space-symbolism of the Notion. Finally, these four points not only form a unique indissoluble unity as a whole, but each one, by the very nature of its meaning, must be unique: there is only *one* Creation, *one* Fall, *one* Atonement, and *one* Resurrection. At the same time, since we are here dealing with existential statements of the Faith and not with theories, all these four points are also universal; this means, they all concern everyone, and they are absolutely individual; that is, they are matters of faith, in which, so far as he is a believer, everyone shares, and no one is merely an onlooker. Indeed, all four points are concerned with the same decision in which faith exists. Hence they are all summed up in the one Word, the one Logos.

(v)

The revelation in Jesus Christ is central: this is the final, decisive, unique event which affects me, a human being living within the world of time. But I can only understand the nature of this event from the point of view of its presupposition. For the event of Christ, as the coming of God, corresponds to the

account that this "history" is not historically tangible, is not extended historically in time, but that it constitutes the invisible element in this definite historical element, as I have tried to make clear in the distinction between personality and the secret of the Person of the Mediator.

Creation which has been ruined by the Fall; for it is the Atonement, the healing of the wound caused by the Fall, the bridging of the gulf between God and Man. This gulf means the absence of continuity between the divinely created existence and its Creator, the broken connection, both in its external and obvious effect (evil and death), as well as in its secret personal cause (guilt as the centre of sin). In order to make this "break" quite clear, we have to reject every "solution" which depends upon the maintenance of the idea of continuity; thus it means that all these "solutions" are branded as illusion, sham, or superficiality. All assertions of continuity conceived in personal terms mean a righteousness of "works." Therefore to reject it means primarily a life-and-death struggle with all attempts to establish a "righteousness of works," with all its religious and ethical ideas of an "ascending development." All speculative attempts to find a solution, even although more on the fringe of the subject, belong to this category; indeed, we might say that every immanental synthesis (and this means every possible synthesis which could be made by man) belongs to this category. This is the negative side of the knowledge of Christ.

The positive side, however, through which alone this negative knowledge is possible, means that the gulf which separates man from God has been bridged, that is, that the original fellowship between man and God has been restored. Here also, lest the idea of continuity should secretly be reintroduced in the guise of the terms revelation and reconciliation, the transcendent character of this proceeding must be stated unmistakably: this restored fellowship is a "vertical relation." This emphasis on the other-worldly character of this act does not do away with the Divine Immanence in the world—even the sinful world is the scene of the divine activity—on the contrary, it presupposes it (see above, p. 31), but it does certainly presuppose the existence of this "gulf," the fact that the divine order has been disturbed, the absence of a present salvation and the saving knowledge of God. But this movement of God towards the world is not a physical process, and the restoration of unity is not a magical process; it consists in the presence of the Word of God, that of His presence in Person, which leads the soul of man to personal decision. It is only through this act of personal decision that this event is recognized as decisive. This is the Christian idea of revelation—hence the Christian "myth"—the actual coming of the Word, the Incarnation of the Word, the divine personal Presence in the sinful temporal human reality.

Hence, for this very reason, this is no "historical event,"[1] no "historical personality" as such—for how could this gulf be bridged which separates all history from its origin?—but it is the crossing of that frontier which separates all history from God, thus it is that event which takes place between time and eternity; it is that event which belongs to the same "dimension" to which the Creation, the Fall, and the Resurrection belong: that of primal history, super-history.

If we wish to avoid this "mythical" element, we must avoid Christianity itself; we then find ourselves once more within the sphere of the Idealistic philosophy of history. Here Jesus Christ is only an historical factor within the universal movement of history, an "impulse" within world history, and no more, therefore at the most an extraordinary, singular phenomenon, representing humanity at its highest—but not unique. In the New Testament witness the question is always being asked: Whence comes the Christ? This question is constantly asked because we are here dealing with a process outside of history which breaks through history. This dimension is that of the

---

[1] The definite fashion in which Karl Barth in particular has developed this distinction between an "historical event" and the Fact of Christ has given rise to a great deal of misunderstanding and controversy which was not really required by the facts of the case. Our critics have not realized that if we accept the point of view of an "historical event," the event of revelation has become subordinated to a universal order, that of history, whereas it is in reality a category by itself. It is neither Idea nor History—just because it is the decisive event—but the unique (*Einmalige*) which, as such, cannot be part of history, but which means the judgment on and fulfilment of history. Those who have seen how Historical Positivism has obscured the meaning of the Christian witness just as disastrously as non-historical Idealism, will only be thankful for Barth's obstinacy upon this point. An "historical event" can also be perceived like other historical events. It is thus never a matter of faith. History is just as little the category which is superior to revelation as experience is the category which is superior to faith. Thus everything depends on the right understanding of this point.

Word of revelation, of authority, of faith, of decision, of the unique. This decision does not belong to the historical Christ. Hence we no longer "know the Christ after the flesh." That He is the Christ means that in Him this self-movement of God towards man, towards history, has been recognized.

Thus everything depends upon this event, for which all the categories which belong to this time-reality are inadequate. This is why we can only speak about it in a figurative manner, why we can only use "mythical" terms. As space-symbolism inadequately describes the static condition of Divine Being, the Idea, so the time-myth, the historical event as an act of God, inadequately describes the action of the personal God and His movement towards man. This time-myth—and this is very important—is God's own act. For He Himself comes in the shape of the historical event, in the guise of historical personality, to man. Thus this "inadequate" method of expression is God's own act and language; He Himself originated this "myth." For this historical human being is God. This language is certainly inadequate, for this is the divine incognito; but the fact remains that He *is* God. This pictorial language is the Word of God Himself: His coming in the form of an actual man. This is the difference between the Christian "myth" and all other forms of myth or symbolism: God Himself, the unknowable, has made Himself known; He Himself has placed the sign of identity between our finitude and His Infinity, between this historical existence and His eternity. This "myth" is His word; it is no human invention.

But for this very reason, because this Word is an act of condescension, the appearance of God in another form, "most hidden, yet most manifest," a Presence in incognito, therefore this event of the Word points towards another event, one in which this indirect revelation becomes direct; this truth that can merely be believed becomes a visible reality: thus even in the Word of revelation, in the Word of the Person of Christ, the Coming of God has not been completely fulfilled. Decision is possible. The unique element in the revelation is the fact that genuine decision is possible. The fact of this possibility, however, the fact that this temporal event can be interpreted in two ways, means that the present time is a provisional period. History is still history, indeed it is only truly history in so far as by history we mean that time is to be taken seriously. No other possibility of taking time seriously exists. Neither the philosophy of Ideas, nor the philosophy of religion, does that. In the full sense of the word we can only be "serious" when we believe in the truth of the Christian "myth."

(vi)

Modern theology has allowed itself to be deluded by Idealism, and has come to conceive this "myth" in "scientific terms," and in so doing to rob it of its content. The truth of the Gospel has been sacrificed to the static conceptions of space-symbolism, or to the illusory dynamic of the philosophy of history; this has taken place under the supposed stress of scientific necessity. The fact that this has been done in all good faith does not alter the fatal results to which this per- version of truth has led; the harm that has been done is not repaired by the knowledge that in so doing men thought that they were rendering the Gospel more suitable to the age, more attractive to the ways of modern thought. What it really comes to is this: that men wished to put away from them the folly and the stumbling-block of the Christ "myth." They did not wish to incur the reproaches of those who think that the only form in which truth can be presented to men, and to educated people, is through thought presented in scientific terms—in the abstract, impersonal conceptualism of space symbolism. This temptation has assailed Christian theology on a previous occasion: in the Early Church, when the truths of the Faith were debated in the light of Greek speculation. Upon the whole, the Church of that day conquered this temptation—thanks to men like Irenaeus, Tertullian, and Athanasius—in spite of all the concessions which were made. The Church rejected the Gnosticism of the Alexandrine school, which regarded the scientific conception as a higher truth than the mythical form of the scriptural message of the Church. The Early Church insisted on the necessity for a "childlike faith"—though pos- sibly not with the vigour with which this was done by Luther later on—conscious that such a faith contains a higher wisdom than all philosophy.

It was not until the time of the Enlightenment that the dyke broke down which had kept the faith of the Church distinct from the thought of the world: Christian dogma was submerged in the flood, and for the past two hundred years the process of the "liberation" of Christianity from "myths," and the transformation of the Gospel into the abstract terms of the (logical or ethical) Idea, or into the language of mysticism, to which this is akin, has been going on. The destiny of Christian theology will depend upon whether it is able to arrest this process of disintegration and return to the view of the Bible, the Early Church, and the Reformation, namely, that the Christian "myth" is the truth—the truth which, here and now, in the historical world, in the realm of decision, for us is final.

The Church herself is not altogether free from responsibility for the fact that the dyke broke down, for she herself did not present the truth of the Gospel sufficiently clearly. This comes out very plainly when we put the question about the relation between time and eternity in the Christian faith. At all points at which it was necessary to keep quite distinct that which takes place on the level of history and that which takes place on the border-line, the Church sometimes failed to preserve the distinction; this means that she did not always resist the temptation to indulge in speculation on her own account. The Church did not always keep herself wholly free from speculative views and from a mythological point of view (in the bad sense of the word)—this took place both with regard to the Creation and the Fall, as well as in connection with the relation between the historical and super-historical elements in Jesus Christ, and in eschatology. Hence it was inevitable that the conflict with science should arise. At the first point, in the doctrine of Creation, perhaps the main result was the rejection of the elements connected with the *Weltanschauung*; in the three others, however, the fight still continues—in so far as it was not "solved" by the leap into historical positivism, which meant that the whole truth was renounced—; it rages most hotly round the central point: the relation between historical research and the faith in Christ. It is here that the final decision must be made. This too is the point at which we must reach clear convictions about the Fall, eschatology, and also about Creation.

It is here that the discussion is most difficult, because this is the point at which faith and science meet on common ground. Science has nothing to state with respect to the Creation, the Fall, and eschatology; wherever Christian doctrine comes into conflict with science on these questions it must be a false kind of doctrine, a speculation, a theory instead of an article of faith. In the problem of Christ, on the contrary, an impartial, tolerant attitude is impossible, otherwise the σάρξ ἐγένετο would lose all its significance. But, on the other hand, wherever faith really recollects itself, and does not allow itself to be drawn into historical positivism, the conflict is solved. Faith in Jesus Christ is not dependent on the courtesy of history; but it does acknowledge the necessity for historical research. In what sense this statement is intended has been fully explained in the previous pages of this book.

Hand in hand with this reflection on the connection of the Christian faith with the mythical form of the statement—we would say rather with that which takes time seriously—goes another, which is most closely connected with it: the rediscovery of the language of the Bible. Our theological language has been corrupted by "Greek" thought because we have been more afraid of the anthropomorphism of the Bible than of the abstractness of scientific conceptions. The next generation of theologians therefore will have to learn not only from Luther but also from Oetinger and Bengel; their scientific work will consist in this, that they will have to show why the Biblical knowledge, if it is stated differently—I mean, if it is transposed into another mode of expression—thereby becomes different in fact. Christian theology will have to lose its fear of anthropomorphism and its respect for abstract intellectualism. But this simply means that it must continually rise above its own scientific habit of mind. For in science we use abstract terms; therefore we also, for the sake of scientific intelligibility have transformed the concrete personal myth of the Gospel into an abstract myth, not with the idea that thus we would come nearer to the truth, but in order to restore the connection between our abstract way of thinking and the thought of the Bible. The meaning of this procedure is—and we hope we have to some extent made this clear—to show that the childlike myth of the Bible is the truth which has been given to us by God Himself.

BOOK THREE

THE WORK OF THE MEDIATOR

CHAPTER XV

THE PERSON AND THE WORK OF CHRIST

(i)

"God so loved the world that He gave His only begotten Son that whosoever believeth in Him should not perish, but have everlasting life." The coming of the Son of God is His work. His existence is the redeeming revelation. The work and the person of the Redeemer are an indissoluble unity. When we speak of the one we speak of the other; when we understand who He is we understand His work; it is impossible to understand who He is without comprehending His being as God's act for us. The Gospel actually consists in this very unity: in this unity of word and fact, of truth and reality, of person and cause, all of which are elements which outside this revelation are everywhere separate from each other. He *is* the Truth: but this "is" means life; vital, vigorous, effective. This truth is not "static," it is an event, a deed. Both these statements are equally important: that He is the Truth, and the fact that He is the Truth is itself an act.

Hence the contrast which modern theology has drawn between the "magico-natural" conception of salvation of the Eastern Church, and the "ethico-practical" conception of the Western Church constitutes a serious misunderstanding. We are not dealing with an absolute distinction at all; the difference is simply one of emphasis. The intention of both is the same; the apparent differences are due to the fact that different aspects of this truth are emphasized at different times. A real antithesis could only arise if the paradoxical unity which transcends the antithesis between nature and spirit were lost. If that were to take place, then all that would be left would be two forms of interpretation: the magical, material objective interpretation, and the rational, ethical subjective interpretation. What was said above about the doctrine of the Two Natures is also true in this connection : in principle the dogmatic definitions of the Early Church are right; but the doctrine has not been able to steer clear of certain malformations. These malformations, however, do not occur only in the direction of magico-natural sacramentalism; they appear just as frequently in the direction of rational subjective moralism.

In principle, however, the Early Church is absolutely right: the great miracle over which Christendom rejoices is the Christmas miracle of the Incarnation, the coming of the Son of God, the Incarnation of the Word; and this means the *Person* of the Mediator. That *He* is here, that the God-Man exists, this is salvation, this is revelation. If it is this "Being" that we mean, then we can confidently make our own the boldest statements of Indian or Greek philosophers, all that the speculative Idealists and mystics of all ages have said in their most exalted moments about the eternal Divine Being, about the "abiding ground" of Eternal Being contrasted with the ceaseless flux of earthly becoming. The false element in their views does not consist in their claim to find salvation and truth in the Divine Being. If there be any salvation at all, on what could it be based if not on the Being of God? If an ultimate redeeming truth does exist, could it be other than the eternal truth of God? Even the Bible itself knows no other : God is our refuge, God the Eternal and the Unchangeable. Revelation simply means the knowledge of this Eternal God. This is not where they go wrong; their error lies in the fact that they think that they already know and possess this God, the Eternal Truth.

The fact that Christ is the centre of the Christian message does not mean that the central element in this message is no longer the Eternal Truth and the Eternal Being of God. Nothing is more foolish than to try to play off "Theocentric" and "Christocentric" standpoints against one another. As if it were not this very "Christocentric" message of the Gospel in which God is absolutely central! If Christ means anything at all, it is simply and solely because through Him God is revealed, the eternal Unchangeable God, in His very Being. This is all that matters; nothing else counts at all. If we make a hole in a dark wall through which the heavens become visible and the sunlight streams in, we do not say that this window is opposed to the heavens and the sunshine. Jesus Christ is the window through which we can see God. When the Christian message says with emphasis, "Look to Christ," it does not mean "look away from God," but "look away to God where God really is," for if God is contemplated apart from Christ, if Christ is ignored, then God is not seen as He really is. Zeal for Christ is zeal for the true God; the exclusive element in the Christian creed: "in no other is there salvation . . ." is simply the exclusiveness of Divine Truth. Because the truth of God is one, and one only, and because in order to see this truth we must stand at a certain point, is the reason why we must make such exclusive claims for Christ.

But that which we are to see in Christ is absolutely nothing other than God, and indeed God's Eternal Being. ὃ ἦν ἀπ' ἀρχῆς, "that which was from the beginning . . ."; it is of this we speak, this is the whole meaning of the Gospel. Therefore the Gospel which is most evidently "Christocentric" begins with the words: "In the beginning was the Word." This is the point of view from which the writer intends all that follows to be read. His point is this, that the whole interest and significance centres in the Word which was from the beginning, the eternal truth, the truth of God. Fichte's saying, rightly understood— but certainly *not* in the sense in which the writer intended it— that it is only the metaphysical and not the historical element which saves us, is absolutely right, that is, if by the "metaphysical" we mean the real truth of God (which can only be known through Christ). Christ is really simply the window through which "the eternal Light streams in"; this is His significance, and His alone. Because in Him the Word which was from the beginning became flesh—for this reason, and for this alone, He is the Christ.

The Christian message therefore does not divert interest from the eternal to the historical sphere; on the contrary: through the "historical element"—and we now know what that may mean—our attention is directed towards the eternal; and indeed precisely towards this "static" truth of the eternal, unchangeable Being of God. This truth is not a theory of creative evolution, or of divine development, or of a theogonic process, it is the message of the Word "which was from the beginning." If this were not the Word from the very beginning, then it could never be the divine, the redeeming Word. It is this which connects the Christian faith with religion and speculative philosophy of every kind: the fact that man seeks to take refuge in the Eternal, in the Unchangeable, the longing to escape from the stream of endless flux, which as such is fleeting, and therefore unblest. Wherever we hear this cry for the eternal, if it be a real cry, there we hear accents which are akin to the Gospel. The contrast between the temporal and the eternal is not weakened by the Christian Gospel; on the contrary, it is still more sharply accentuated than elsewhere. That redemption can be found only in the eternal cannot be expressed more clearly than in the central Christian doctrines of the Triune God, of His eternal purpose, and of eternal election.

(ii)

Thus the difference between the message of Christ and the teaching of mysticism and of speculation does not lie here, but in the fact that in the Christian message this Eternal Word is not regarded as a truth which man, "at bottom," already possesses, but as a revelation, as something "given," as a Word which has "come." This Word *is* Christ. The ancient Fathers of the Church were not mistaken when they used to underline this word "*is*." He *is* the Word. "I *am* the Way, the Truth, and the Life." "I *am* the Door." "I *am* the Light of the world." His Being is itself redemption. To His Being we may and must point when we are speaking in a Christian way about salvation and the truth. This is not naturalism, a magical conception of salvation. If the Divine Being of God is the redeeming truth, then the Divine Being of Christ is also this truth. No human action is necessary. The activism of the West—I allude to the contrast between the Occident and the Orient—is not more spiritual than the quietism of the East. Both tendencies need rebirth; thus the Western theological definitions of the mystery of Christ are in no way more Christian or more spiritual than those of ancient Greek theology. In both there lies the danger of misunderstanding, but both also can be understood aright. Later theology, however, has certainly not understood the theology of the Eastern Church. That in itself would be enough to suggest that it has also deprived Western theology of some of its content.

The Incarnation is the fundamental Christian truth; not only the Greek Fathers of the Church were conscious of this fact, but also our Protestant forefathers.[1] The best Protestant hymnology also bears witness to this fact. We need only remind ourselves of the Christmas hymns of our Church:—

> "Gott wird Mensch, dir Mensch, zugute,
> Gottes Kind, das verbindt
> Sich mit unsrem Blute."[2]

---

[1] It is one of the most astonishing things about the modern view of the history of the Reformation that the absolutely fundamental significance which this early Patristic central idea of the Incarnation possessed for the Reformers in general and for Luther in particular is overlooked; if the question is not overlooked altogether it is then assumed that the Reformers were in this respect "rather naïve," and limited by the outlook of their day; hence it seems quite a simple matter to eliminate this idea from the theology of the Reformers without altering the nature of their theology in any way. It is a good thing therefore that the edition of Luther which has at last been published by Theodosius Harnack leaves no further doubt on this question. It is unnecessary to prove this point in detail; here it will be sufficient to point to Luther's well-known exposition of the ladder to heaven in his Commentary on Genesis (indeed, this illustration is often used by Luther when he is speaking of the mystery of revelation as a whole) whose central idea is this: that "the secret of this descent down the ladder is that in Christ "God and Man are truly in one and the same Person." . . . "The ladder is therefore the marvellous union of the Godhead with our flesh. . . ." On this is based "the immense and indescribable dignity of the human race . . . because God has united Himself with human nature through this marvellous union," etc. That also for Calvin this idea had not lost the significance which it had in the Early Church, the twelfth chapter of the second book of the *Institutio* is sufficient evidence. At the same time we must admit that in general the theologians of the Reformation preferred to regard the Incarnation from the point of view of the doctrine of Satisfaction. But the indissoluble connection between these two "main articles" of the Christian Faith is also expressed by them with complete clearness and decision. It would be very valuable if the corresponding proof could be produced from the practical religious literature of the period of the Reformation. This ought not to be a very difficult matter.

[2] Lit.:   "God becomes man, for thy sake, O man,
        Child of God, who unites Himself
        With our flesh and blood."   —Tr.

The existence of the God-Man, as such, constitutes revelation and salvation. This is why He is called the Mediator, not primarily on account of His work, but because of what He is in Himself. He is the Mediator because in Him the eternal Word is present, in Him the eternal Light enters into our world, because in Him the eternal purpose of God, the mystery of God becomes known, because in Him we can see God. "He that hath seen Me hath seen the Father." Of course, this means he who sees Him as the eternal Son of God, who sees Him in the mystery of His Person, who recognizes Him in His unconditional divine authority, and this means, who knows Him as the One who is from above, not like ourselves, from below, One who has "come," the One "from the Other Side," the One whom we have not seen, if we only know the life of Jesus in the moral-religious historical sense, thus One whom we do not really "see" if by this we mean—however successful the attempt may be—merely an understanding of the inner life of Jesus. The "Self" in whom we see the Father is the "only One," the "only begotten," the Eternal Son, not the historical visible personality.

That He has actually come to us, that He is given to us, that He is here, it is in this that Christendom should rejoice evermore. For this is what we lack: Himself. Not some status which God may graciously aid us to acquire, some kind of position in the world, or the possession of some kind of spiritual title to salvation, but *Himself*: God, in so far as He wills to impart Himself to us. The "Son" means God Himself as the Word. In Him we have been created. We have lost the Primal Word, and in Him the meaning of our existence, the Image of God, the fact that we belong to God, fellowship with God; the divine inheritance has been squandered. We have lost our home, we have left the Father's house, we are now homeless outcasts. That He Himself, He in whom we belong to God, He in whom we know God and ourselves according to the truth, He in whom is the meaning of our life, He in whom God names His own Name and thus our name also, is here once more among us, and that we can know Him, that He is in fellowship with us: what else could be desired as salvation? He is, of course, only present to faith and not to sight, He is here in hiddenness, not yet in glory and power. And yet "We beheld His glory." That this is possible, even though only with the eye of faith, that it can be seen in Him, is the grace which ought to suffice for the believer.

(iii)

We may thus speak of the Being, of the "mere existence," of the divine-human "Nature" of the Mediator without falling back into a metaphysic of being, into speculation or mysticism, because this Being includes within itself the fact that He has come. Only as the One who has come is He the Son. The duality of His being, the "Two Natures," means simply that the Eternal Word has come. Therefore it is precisely this Being which stands in contrast to mysticism and to speculation: it is the Being of the Mediator. By the very fact that as the Mediator, as the God-Man, He stands before us, we are confronted by the fact that of ourselves we could not know God. If the Christian religion speaks of the Eternal Word, and the Eternal Son, it does not speak of Him like the Platonist Philo, nor like Hegel, nor like Meister Eckhart, for it is speaking of Jesus Christ. We differ from Platonism in this, that we know the Eternal Son and the Eternal Word only in Jesus, in this real historical fact: the life of Jesus. We differ from historical realism in this: that in this Jesus we know and confess in Him alone the Eternal Son, the Primal Word, the Christ after the Spirit.

The humanity of the Son of God means that He has really come, it means the contingency, the uniqueness of the revelation. The divinity of the Son of Man means the eternity of the Word, the personal Presence of the Eternal God in Him. Therefore whoever speaks in a Christian manner about the Being, about the existence of the God-Man, is speaking at the same time of that which is revealed, of the divine self-movement, of the act of revelation. The incomprehensible co-existence of the predicates, God and Man, is simply the incomprehensible fact that the Eternal God comes, that the eternal truth is one which has become such for us, and that we only rightly

understand it as that which has come and has become, thus
that we cannot sever it from the fact that it has come without
destroying it. There is no surer method of thoroughly damping
the ardour of all speculative arrogance and metaphysical
pretension than to look steadily at the message of the Being of
the God-Man and at His dual Nature. In this monstrosity of a
God-Man we know our own deformity, in this contradiction we
see our contradiction, in this problem we see our own problem,
the problem of humanity, evil, sin. For we need the Eternal
Son as One who has come, as One who has come in time, and
in human historical form, that is, in the form of a servant, just
because we are sinners. The Incarnation is the divine and
merciful answer to our falling away from God. The Mediator
in His Person, by His very "constitution," is the mediation
between the Creator and the fallen creature, in a double
connection: as the Mediator of revelation and the Mediator
of reconciliation.

Here therefore there can be no question of a metaphysic,
because here we are dealing with the Word and with faith,
with sin and reconciliation. We may also say, because we
are here concerned with the whole personal relationship of
faith between the personal God and our own decision. For
faith alone can know the Mediator as the Mediator, the decisive
act in which man is stripped bare of all pretensions by God,
and in the presence of God; and this as one who of himself
can neither know the truth nor live in it, nor can attain to a
life in the truth, as one who is in a condition in which one
expects deliverance alone through the act and speech of God.
Recognition of the Mediator means the actual breaking down
of our nature. This is why the natural man says "anything
but this!" This too is what intellectual reason says. Everything
within it revolts against this attack on its pride. The truth as
something which has come into being, as something which is
"given" through history! The Eternal Truth bound up with an
accidental fact of history! And just as hotly does the moral will
rebel against this also—and still more passionately because it
is more personal: righteousness as something which is given
to us as a free gift, what *I* ought to do done by another and
reckoned to me as though I had done it, the right attitude to

God won through that which another has done! Faith consists in conquering the "offence" and the "folly" constituted by the Mediator; for faith means allowing oneself to be humbled, and the boldness with which we accept the unspeakable mercy of God. This the Mediator is in His Person, because in His Person we meet the personal God. There is no other possibility of coming into contact with God. "No one cometh unto the Father save through Me." For the meeting must be real and personal; otherwise we remain by ourselves, carrying on a monologue with ourselves, with our own ideas. But God can be met only there where God personally and really comes towards us Himself. This is the Mediator. Only through the most grievous misunderstanding is it "possible" that the very faith in the Mediator can be perverted into a metaphysic, because by its very nature it desires to secure the existential, personal character of the meeting of the human soul with God.

(iv)

While we lay so much stress on the fact that the Person of the Mediator is in itself the revelation, at the same time we do not wish to suggest—as will be seen directly—that we either ignore the "Work" of the Mediator or even relegate it to a subordinate position. We do certainly mean, however, that we reject subordination of the opposite kind. Melanchthon, in his first edition of the *loci*, enunciated the following statement, which is not only well known, but we might almost say, from the theological point of view, epoch-making: *hoc est Christum cognoscere, beneficia ejus cognoscere.* Certainly the statement is right, and it is important in so far as it is directed against scholastic casuistries, against the metaphysical perversion of the doctrine of Christ. In this sense we might render it thus: it does not matter how the divine and the human Natures in Christ are united with each other, or how they can co-exist, but what does matter is what we have in this Christ; how Christ speaks to us, not what we think about Him, is the problem for faith. This is evidently the real meaning of the statement of Melanchthon. His formula, however, has a shade of meaning which not only could easily lead one astray, but has actually done so. It contains the germ of the whole anthropocentric point of view of later Lutheranism, and this simply means of religious egoism. Man occupies the centre of the picture, with his need for salvation, not God and His glory, His revelation; thus God becomes the One who satisfies the needs of man. Not in vain has Ritschlian pragmatism so often appealed to these words. Christ is needful in order that men may be helped, God is the guarantee of the value of human life.

This is not the view of the Bible. God reveals Himself for His own sake, in order to create His Kingdom, in order to manifest His glory,[1] in order to restore His own order, His dominion. The Bible is the book in which the glory of God is the first concern, and the salvation of man comes second. In the self-manifestation of God, in the dominion of God, the salvation of man is also included, but it is not the other way round. This is salvation, that man should once more learn to set God at the centre, that he may once more be able to say with real conviction: whatever God does He does well. That God and His cause may be his first concern, and man and his salvation a secondary consideration, because he knows that God Himself, just in His unconditionedness, *is* the salvation of man. Not because Christ brings us *beneficia* is He the Son of God, but because He reveals God to us do we know ourselves also as sheltered and healed in Him. Opposition to metaphysical speculation is indeed "practical" knowledge, and the Christian faith is—as Kaftan used to teach—"a practical concern." But the "practical" nature of faith ought not to be confused with a coarse or refined Eudaemonism. That God Himself really and personally meets with us, this is the practical, essential knowledge. This is the true antithesis, not religious

[1] What can we say when a historian of dogma like Otto Ritschl thus explains to himself the fact that in the theology of Calvin the dominant idea is that of the Glory of God? "In this fact there is a transference of the vital idea of glory whch means so much in the national life of the French to the concrete colouring of his Idea of God" (*Dogmengeschichte des Protestantismus*, III, p. 172). Then was Anselm of Canterbury a Frenchman, for the same idea is prominent in his teaching? And what about the Prophets of the Old Testament?

pragmatism, which places man's self-end in the first rank and God, in the last resort, simply as the One who guarantees this end; which means that God becomes simply a means to an end.

Hence it is important that the doctrine of the Person of the Mediator should not be subordinated to that of His Work. The Mediator, in His Person, is not a means to an end, but a self-end. For He is the revelation of God. He is not merely—as, for instance, in the doctrine of Anselm—the instrument of the reconciliation. The doctrine of the Incarnation, the Christmas message, is as important as the doctrine of "satisfaction," the message of Good Friday. Neither can be separated from the other, for both mean this, that God comes. He comes to us Himself; and He really and actually comes to us, to us in our low estate.

(v)

The Being of the Mediator is the gift and the act of God. The New Testament bears witness to the Mediator as the great gift of God. God sent Him; He gave Him, He gave Him up. This refers not merely to the death of Christ, but to His whole existence, as indeed His whole existence is regarded from the point of view of "humiliation." The fundamental feature of the whole message of the Bible is this: that God is known through His action. But by this action is not meant His activity in the world in general, His preservation and rule over the world, the sphere of general revelation. In this sphere God appears to us in a sort of twilight, here God does His "strange work." Here He is not known as Himself, in His inner Being, as He is in Himself (*Ansichsein*). But by His action is meant His special action, His act of revelation. For this is the aim of this act of God: that He makes Himself known. His action means that He issues forth, He comes. The most important element in His action is always His own presence in this action, and the secret aim of this action is always this: that He may "dwell" among His people. This "dwelling," however, is not a physical but a spiritual state: "they shall all know Him." "The knowledge of the Lord shall cover the earth as the waters cover the sea." "His light shall break forth as the morning." The purpose of this action is the vision of God, the final revelation.

His Action is therefore the same as His Speech. The real gift of God is always His Word; but the message of prophecy does not fully express this intention. For it is still only a word about the Word. The real Word is the personal Word, which is identical with His personal Presence. This Word, as a personal Presence, is Christ, the Eternal Son, the Word which was from the beginning. Therefore He is the fulfilment of all the action and all the speech of God. As "Himself" He is the meaning, or rather the One who is meant, though here and now in faith and thus in the disjointed character of this earthly existence, but then in completion. If the prophetic revelation is already the work of God, the act in which He comes near to His people, then, far more, the revelation of Christ is the revelation which consists in the Person of Christ. To have Him means to have God. To have Him is the same as having Him given to us. His life is the divine effectual Word.

For in Him, in His existence, God has really found a firm footing within humanity. It is not as though humanity were not already in His Hands; even the heathen are His instruments whom He uses as He wills. But here we are speaking of a different kind of presence, of the Presence of God in revelation and in salvation. This Presence begins for us in Christ, through His "assumption" of human "nature." In Christ God takes the part of man in spite of the fact that man has fallen away from Him. This is not merely because Jesus *says* this, but by His very existence as the God-Man. For in Him God has entered into a new relation with man, He has united Himself with man.

It would not be difficult to slip into the magico-sacramental misinterpretation which turns redemption into a physical or hyper-physical event, and thus into an event which has no connection with the "Word," and thus presents no challenge to the human will. But this is not what is meant. Human nature—as we have seen—is not the physical nature of humanity; it is rather the world of history. By the fact that the eternal Logos became historical, became an event, an existing fact, within the reality of time and space, one historical personality among us historical personalities, by the fact that He became flesh, He has bridged the gulf which separates historical life from the eternal world. The fact that He has thus bridged the gulf is the whole point. How this happens, how it comes to pass that an historical man is the Eternal Son, who has "come," this is the secret of God. Those who know that this mystery, this marvel, is the Divine Intention will not feel inclined to try to probe into the mystery any further. But faith holds fast to the fact that it has happened, that in the Jesus of history we can behold the Eternal Son, that in Him God Himself can meet with us. Faith is not concerned with the Incarnation as a metaphysical problem. But the knowledge that in Jesus Christ the barrier which separates us from the Creator has been transcended, so that now God really meets us personally, constitutes the real knowledge of Christ.

God's act is the Incarnation of the Son of God. God sent Him, God gave Him. But this would not be the sending forth of the Eternal Son if this act were not also His own act. It is the act of the whole Trinity. The Son is not only the One who is sent, but also the One who willingly permits Himself to be sent. He is the One who has "emptied Himself." It is His act, both here and on the other side of the border-line between the two worlds of history and of eternity. He is here not simply as One who suffers and endures, but also as One who is active in the midst of His passive acceptance. He would not be a real person but merely a material instrument if His life were not also His own act. Therefore His whole life is His act, His Passion is revelation. As the personal act of Jesus Christ it is an act of revelation. But it is not only the act of God in so far as it is the life work of Jesus, as in the historical sense it is the personal act of Jesus. Neither the Birth nor the Crucifixion are in the historical sense acts of Jesus Christ, but they are indeed the act of God, and thus also the act of the Son, namely, precisely because they constitute His humiliation, His giving Himself to the flesh and to death. His historical life, and His action in the widest sense—thus, for example, also His teaching—is certainly a moment in the revelation, but it is not the revelation itself. The revelation, the *work* of the revelation, is the whole, which cannot be conceived in historical terms at all. Hence it is not the story of Jesus which is the object of the Christian faith, but the revelation of God in the Person and Work of the Mediator, as it is attested by the Church as a whole. Only he who sees this as a whole beholds the "Christ after the spirit." He who sees the historical only— just because he does not see it as a whole—does not see the Christ at all, but merely the life of Jesus, the "Christ after the flesh." He may indeed see the action and the Being of Jesus, but in this action and in this Being he does not see the revelation of God, even when he uses Christian terms to express what he sees.

This distinction is vital for the understanding of the historical activity of Jesus.

(vi)

Finally, there is still one more question to be discussed, which, if it is brought into the discussion at the wrong point, causes untold confusion: the question of the relation between special and general revelation. There is only one Logos. This Logos can only be known in Christ. But this Logos is the principle of all knowledge, and, above all, it is the central truth in all religion. Here everything depends on the order of the series: whether we say Christ is the truth of all philosophy and of all religion, or all that is true in philosophy and in religion is "Christ." In the latter instance the principle is superior to the illustration, and the revelation of Christ is merely an individual form of a general truth, a concrete instance of an idea. Thus from this point of view the idea triumph over the revelation, the impersonal conquers personality.⁵The truth of Christ becomes the special expression of the general revelation, alongside of other more or less equally justified forms; the historical illustration, the Person of Jesus as the bearer and discoverer of this idea, which is in principle detachable from His Person—this is the fundamental thesis of the modern view.

The Christian view, on the contrary, is that the revelation

in Jesus Christ, this unique event, is the truth just because it is unique, by the very fact that it is connected with this time, this place, and this Person. But in asserting this we do not mean—as is so often laid to the charge of Christianity—that on this account we would claim that all philosophical, mystical, and general religious knowledge of God is not true. It is not absolutely untrue, but it is partial truth, half truth. Christ is here "divided." But that is an awkward comparison from the spatial and mechanical sphere. That which is divided can be brought together and formed into a whole. But this is not what is here meant. For when a living creature is divided it can never be put together again and formed into a whole. By the fact that it has been divided it has been killed. It is not merely in pieces, it is at the same time altered and spoiled; it has lost its original significance.

Thus the whole of the history of philosophy and of religion, is a field which contains scattered elements of truth. It is the task of the Christian "philosophy of religion" to produce the proof for this general assertion. Philosophy recognizes Christ as the Eternal Logos, even though as an impersonal principle, yet still according to His absoluteness. Hence the Johannine conception of the Logos cannot be absolutely contrasted with the Platonic conception. Only the relation between them is the opposite of that which is usually claimed to be the case: Plato can only be understood in the light of John, not John from the point of view of Plato. For Platonism is a Christian truth which has been detached from the main body of truth. The historical relation between the two conceptions of "the Word" has nothing whatever to do with the matter. The subject with which the Gospel of John is dealing does not come from Plato—just as little as it has originated in the Mandaean Gnosis. John uses the Logos idea, which he reshapes from the very foundation, stamping it with the character of that which is personal and historical, in order that he may thus express the way in which he understands Christ. The old theory that Plato was a preparatory stage for Christianity, or that Plato drew his wisdom from Moses, is just as false historically as it is actually true to say that it is Christ, whom he, so to speak, perceived dimly from afar.

413

Likewise all living religion—which has not been watered down by rationalism and legalism—takes from the truth of Christ the moment of revelation in the sense of the contingent, "real," realistic means of the communication of knowledge and of life. But the more strongly this reality is present, the less it is watered down by speculative or mystical ideas, the more accidental does this revelation become, so far as its content is concerned: never quite without some elements of divine truth, but never without nonsense alongside of truth, the whole chaotic mass of polytheism, with its fantastic and frequently non-moral mythology, and its equally weird and wild rites of worship—as well as so much that is great, which commands our genuine reverence.

Thus even outside the Christian revelation of the Bible man is not without God nor without truth. But in his search for truth the closer he approaches to the centre, the more his energies seem to fail, the more it becomes clear to him that even his search for God is always at the same time a flight from God, and that his service of God is always at the same time trivial and self-centred. The Logos is also not outside His creation: for in the Logos it is created, and therefore it bears traces of its origin. But our collective knowledge of the world and our collective relations to the world are all interwoven, in the most complicated manner, with sinful illusion. Hence the knowledge of God in the world "outside," and in the relations of man to the world, only give us a confused picture of their divine origin; indeed, it does not yield a *theologia naturalis* which would be suitable as a basis for a Christian theology. The *analogia entis* might indeed have been the normal relation between God the Creator and His creature. But this normal relation no longer exists; it has been obscured and corrupted by the falling away of man from God. Confidence in a natural theology of this kind could only endure so long as the Christian consciousness was strong enough to oppose the destructive tendencies of a knowledge of the world based purely upon its own efforts. Since this support has been lost we can see how much there is in these "necessary truths of reason" so far as religion or theology is concerned.

Christ is the Truth and the Life. Hence He is the source of

all knowledge. All truth is ultimately the truth of Christ. That which is true is true through the Logos who was in the beginning; the Logos, however, is not the One whom philosophy likes to read into the Johannine statements, the eternal principle, but the Eternal Son who reveals Himself to us in Jesus Christ.

CHAPTER XVI

THE PERSON AND TEACHING OF CHRIST

(i)

PRIMARILY and pre-eminently the work of the Mediator is revelation. "I made known unto them Thy Name" (John xvii. 26, R.V.). This is the meaning of the Incarnation of the Eternal Son of God. The Word became flesh. "God, having of old time spoken unto the fathers in the prophets, by divers portions and in divers manners, hath at the end of these days spoken unto us in His Son, whom He appointed heir of all things" (Heb. i. 1–2, R.V.). The sending of Christ is the fulfilment of the mission of the Prophets. Knowledge of God, of the eternal will of God, of His eternal purpose for humanity, of His will to complete His perfect work, is the aim which Christ serves. But this purpose and this means of realization are co-extensive. The revelation of God is the self-manifestation, the self-authentication of the Eternal Son.

This is why He came. He Himself—that we might know Him and in Him the will of God—is the purpose of His coming. The self-end is not the Mediator but the revelation of God, the Word, the manifestation of God in the Son. The fact that the Mediator took upon Himself the form of a servant is something transitory, and subordinate to this purpose. It means service, and therefore the life and work of Jesus Christ expresses both this subordination to the Divine Purpose and the fulfilment of this Purpose. This does not mean that first the one and then the other was manifested in turn. The whole of the life of Christ, at every moment, runs along this parallel line of serving God and reigning with God, which can indeed be distinguished according to the point of view, but in reality can never be separated. Every word and every act means both "I am serving God, and in Myself I make God known." A recent historian has pictured this Life of Jesus as "acts of the Messianic consciousness." And in a classic phrase full of deep significance the Gospel of John makes the Lord Himself express it thus: "My meat is to do the will of Him that sent me, and to accomplish His work" (John iv. 34, R.V.).

An explanation of the connection between the Christian faith and the picture of the Life of Jesus has often been made more difficult because two quite different things have not been kept distinct: the point of view, and the psychological historical method. The point of view is the self-revelation of the Son, the self-glorification and self-authentication of God, the "I AM"—the Eternal Being of God—which is served by the historical manifestation. The psychological historical method, however, is precisely this historical manifestation. The historical activity and self-giving of Jesus, just as much as the assumption of the "form of a servant," is the incognito of the Son of God. Thus here also there is no direct identity; it is indirect. The "form of a servant" and the self-affirmation cannot be directly perceived, and the form of both should not be confused with the matter itself, just as little as—if we may here anticipate —the point of view of suffering and active obedience should be confused with the psychological picture of passive suffering or of active assault on evil. The psychological historical features are in all these cases not the matter itself but only signs, hints which faith alone can rightly interpret. To establish statistically, for instance, how often Jesus speaks of Himself and how often of the cause He serves, as of something higher than Himself, would not provide us with the least illumination on this point. To what extent *both* are intended in every word, in every deed, cannot be understood from the details but only from the whole, and here again not from the historical and psychological point of view, but only from the point of view of faith, although the psychological historical glimpses are scarcely to be mistaken, since they are capable of one interpretation only. Here also the incognito is preserved. We are not intended to *see*.

(ii)

The historical appearance of Jesus was primarily that of a Jewish Rabbi, a Teacher of the *Torah*. At least, this is one external aspect of His historical figure. He taught in the

synagogues like the Rabbis, or like the "teachers" who
wandered about the countryside and taught in the open air.
He also taught the Law, the Will of God. Thus He placed
Himself wholly within the continuity of the divine revelation.
"That which God spake in times past by the prophets. . . ."
This also He taught in the external, biographical sense. But *is*
He really a Rabbi? Can the conscientious historian bring
himself to retain this title? The people, in any case, thought
otherwise. He "speaks with authority," they said, and "not as
do the Scribes." One sign of this difference and of this authority
can be stated immediately: His whole teaching is characterized
by the phrase: "But I say unto you."

It is possible to misunderstand His teaching and to regard it
as rabbinical in character. It is possible to find parallels to
most of His sayings which sound either exactly the same or
are very similar. Hence we have no right to assert that His
teaching is absolutely different from that of the Rabbis. But it
is not difficult to perceive the difference. For just as it is
characteristic of the sayings of the Rabbis which resemble the
sayings of Jesus that they are hidden within a chaotic mass
of trivial sayings, so it is equally characteristic of the sayings
of Jesus that they are not hidden in any such tangle. The
people, in any case, noticed the difference, and even the
historian who drags in these parallels perceives something of
this. The Christian tradition has made us all readier to detect
the fact that here the manner of speech is quite different. But
this concentration upon the essential, this "inwardness," this
immense simplification which has often been observed—these
quite correct observations do not say the decisive thing: here
everything is said with the utmost incisiveness; this is no longer
the teaching of morality, but the proclamation of the unconditioned Law of God, which does not fit into this world at all,
because already, in its finality, it unveils the Last Things.
The "eschatological" historical school is not wrong in its
assertion that this ethic is wholly eschatological in its tendency.
In fact, to the finality of this claim there correspond only the
Last Things. Friedrich Naumann, too, was quite right when
he said that he despaired of the usefulness of this ethic for the
cultural life of our day. In reality there is here no cultural

ethic, nor any standards, in the presence of which any human achievements could exist. This ethic itself belongs to the chapter about the Last Things, concerning which we usually find only a few embarrassed statements at the close of some book on dogmatics. In any case, the man who calls this ethic impracticable has understood it far better than the man who speaks easily about its beautiful inwardness and simplicity. Here everything, even the most ordinary matter, is placed in the weird glaring light of the Last Day. The ethic of the Sermon on the Mount only resembles the rabbinical teaching in its outer form; inwardly it is concerned with the Last Things, with the Kingdom of God.

We are accustomed to require an ethic to be practicable. If this is what we want, then we should turn to Aristotle! The ethic of the Gospel is not practicable because it is serious.[1] To take morality seriously, or, more correctly, to take the Will of God seriously, leads to the despairing admission that it is impossible to do it. But the impossibility is no excuse. The phrase "You ought and therefore you can" is a saying of the ancient Serpent. It is the language of Pelagianism which adapts the Law until it becomes practicable. It is impossible to do the Divine Will, because we are sinners, because this historical existence is a sinful existence. Therefore the commandments of the Sermon on the Mount do not fit into it, however much they may be the standard which is the only one for us. Only the impossible is worthy to be obeyed. For only the impossible is the Will of God. That it *is* impossible is due to sin.

Jesus does not trouble about the worldly categories of "possible" or "impossible." He is no schoolmaster, nor is He a pedagogue. He is the One who fulfils the Law, who fulfils all things. The Will of God is the unconditioned will,

---

[1] It is not sufficiently recognized that "serious" is a categorical and not merely a psychological definition. It is possible to be "serious" about aestheticism, but aestheticism categorically excludes seriousness. The Christian faith is the only thing which is absolutely serious—although naturally many a non-Christian is more serious than the average Christian —because it alone takes God absolutely seriously, because it alone knows decision. For it alone knows the Unique (*Einmalige*), the decisive event, which can never be repeated.

and what can be called good in the sight of God must be
the unconditioned Good. Jesus does not take any interest in
intermediate conditions. He is concerned about reality as it is:
sinful, wrong; and with the final Kingdom as it ought to be:
completely good. We may seek in vain within the Gospel for
fine shades of meaning. Light and darkness, the righteousness
of God and sin, heaven and hell: the rest is for those who
have time to think about other things than the one thing
needful, for the "leaders of civilization." From the point of
view of the life of modern civilization, it is true, the Sermon
on the Mount leaves much to be desired. In actual fact,
however, it has no gaps because it gives no instructions at all.
It gives isolated examples of the one Good, the absolute Good,
the Impossible.

(iii)

It is therefore not true that Jesus was a Rabbi. For He does
not speak about the Law of which the Rabbis speak. He does
not speak about truths at all. He witnesses to a reality, namely,
the coming Kingdom of God. A part of His proclamation of
the Kingdom of God is His so-called ethic. His whole historical
activity, however, is determined by the watchword "Repent!
for the Kingdom of Heaven is at hand." This was the summons
of John the Baptist, the last of the prophets. So Jesus places
Himself in the succession of the prophets, not as the preserver
and exponent of that which they proclaimed, but as One who,
like them, proclaimed a new message. This is how the majority
of His contemporaries seem to have understood Him. Hence
He who speaks thus about the coming Kingdom, can He be
anything other than a prophet like John? In the message of
the Bible, eschatology and the Law of God belong together.
Together they form this unity: the covenant of God with men,
the royal sovereignty of God over men. But we ought to pay
special attention to the order of both magnitudes. Just as the
Mosaic Law was introduced by the divine promise "I will be
your God and ye shall be My people," so that the Law is thus
a part of the Covenant, and not the other way round; so it
is also with the message of Jesus. The point of view which

420

is superimposed is not the Law of God but the Kingdom of God. First in importance is not the human task, but the gift of God; not the attitude of men towards God, but the attitude of God towards men. This is the message of the Kingdom of God: "God is coming." And this is the call to repentance: "Receive the invitation to the great Feast!" "Go, work in His vineyard!" There is a decision, a final decision. How could one speak of the Kingdom of God otherwise than in terms of the most urgent decision? The category to which this decision belongs is that of *the actual moment*. Man has no right to think, "I have still time." The Last Things stand at the door, for you and for me, for this generation as a whole. Of the day and the hour knoweth no man—but indeed this is not said in order to modify the urgency of the summons.[1]

The Will of God in the Law and the Kingdom of God belong together. Here, however, we perceive the fulfilment of a characteristic element in the whole prophetic message: the reversal of all valid standards. The publicans and the harlots will go into the Kingdom before the righteous Pharisees; the Samaritan before the Priest and the Levite; the sorrowful publican before the righteous Pharisee. "Blessèd are the poor in spirit, blessèd are they that mourn, blessèd are those who

---

[1] Once we have recognized that in eschatological thought Time is an intensive quality—and thus how far removed from the idea of mathematical Time which has to do with watches and calendars—it will be no longer possible to say that Jesus and His Apostles were "deceived" in their expectation of the Parousia. The "soon" of the eschatological Hope cannot be expressed in the terms used to describe mathematical astronomical conceptions. If we confuse this neutral material idea of Time with that existential decisive idea of Time, then certainly there is nothing left but to admit that the prediction was not fulfilled, and therefore that it was erroneous. But at the Judgment the "error" of the Apostles will hold its own against the "truth" of their critics. Seriousness and "soon" are indissolubly connected. The "soon" is an intensive quality, that is, it increases with the increasing seriousness of God. The chronological "soon" and the truly historical "soon" cannot be compared. Where God is truly known, there at the same time the speedy coming of His Kingdom is recognized. In the literal sense the critics are indeed right: Jesus and the Apostles did identify this "soon" with a point in the time-series; and this definition of a special time has proved to be incorrect.

421

hunger and thirst after righteousness." We are to turn round
and become as little children, in order that we may inherit
the Kingdom of God. Thus the movement leads completely
backwards, not forwards. The ethically intelligible scale of
wages no longer has any meaning, and the man who does his
"duty" is no more than "an unprofitable servant." In the
presence of God man can have no claims at all.

Even the holiness of the ascetic has no value in the Kingdom
of God. Man cannot determine his worthiness for the Kingdom
by his own moral achievements; this comes to him simply
through the mercy of God. The movement is not one of ascent
but of descent, that of the shepherd who in incomparable
self-devotion searches after the lost sheep "until he find it."
There is more joy over a sinner who repents than over
ninety-and-nine just persons who need no repentance. The
Kingdom of God is like unto a woman who gets excited over
the loss of a small coin, and turns the house upside down in
her search, and when she has found it raises a loud cry of joy.
The Kingdom is like that father who has more joy over the
return of the prodigal than over the virtues of the decent son.
Here the new element is not the message about the loving,
kindly father, but it is this reversal of standards, this complete
devaluation of all that "ethical religion" is accustomed to
regard as decisive. Therefore it is just at this point, in the
attitude of Jesus towards sinners, that the stumbling-block
appeared.

The Rabbis also used to teach about forgiveness, rather in
the way in which "ethical religion" in all ages has done. But
they did not understand the revolutionary meaning of this
doctrine. They did not understand that by it their whole
position was threatened at its very root. This is why they
regarded the preaching of Jesus and His practice of forgiveness
not only as something new, but as an ethical and religious
offence. That it was an offence to them shows that they had
perceived the revolutionary contrast between this teaching on
forgiveness and their own ideas—this contrast to their whole
idea of God—whereas to-day most people do not notice this
at all. Here again it is the unconditioned ultimate way in
which the thought of forgiveness is thought out to the very

end[1] which characterizes the message of Jesus, only that the inversion which lies in this finality is clearer than elsewhere. It is always possible to speak of the Law as of a general truth, but where forgiveness is concerned this is impossible. Where the word of forgiveness is unconditionally pronounced, there—if it is to make sense at all—it can only be uttered with authority. Here is the really new element in the teaching of Jesus: He does not teach forgiveness as a general truth, but He grants forgiveness as a fact. His parables of the Prodigal Son, of the Lost Sheep, and the Lost Coin are the commentáry on His own behaviour, the answer to the question of the Pharisees who were scandalized at His careless way of consorting with sinners, so much so that He was called the "Friend of publicans and sinners."

(iv)

Once again, however, a step forward has been taken which leads out beyond the second sphere, that of the prophets. No prophet has ever himself forgiven sinners, and when Jesus was asked by what authority He did these things He replied by deliberately working a miracle of healing as a proof of His authority. Does it not seem that the Synoptic narrative, which here, in face of this double proof of authority, asserts that the hostility of the Pharisees and the Scribes began at this point, must correspond with historical reality? But however that may be, this assumption of divine authority is not an isolated instance. Rather it is the determining element for all that is peculiar to the teaching and behaviour of Jesus. Jesus is not, like the prophets, one who simply proclaims the coming Kingdom of God. He is One who dares (even though

---

[1] Bultmann (*Jesus*, p. 185 ff.) states the decisive point of view for the New Testament idea of forgiveness. "If something new is to happen there is only one thing which can help; real forgiveness can only take place "where it is understood as God's free act . . . as an event in time." But he obviously does not see the connection between a real event and personal reality, with reference to personal authority. Involuntarily, therefore, his idea of forgiveness slips back into the sphere of thought. If forgiveness must really be *given*, then everything depends on the fact that it is given with *authority*, and by a definite person to whom I am bound by this gift.

423

deliberately in a hidden way) to speak of the fact that the Kingdom has come. It is, of course, true that He is not thinking in terms of the rational-ethical conception of the Kingdom of God as an "immanent force," or as a realm of inwardness, but as the transcendent Kingdom of God, the one which comes from the other side, the marvellous Kingdom,[1] which breaks through the world of history, the αἰών οὗτος, the final Kingdom—which cannot be confused with any religious force within the world or with any morality—which has come in His Person. This is why the "prophets have prophesied until now"; this is why the judgment on the towns which have seen "this" and have heard it shall be more severe than that pronounced on Sodom and Gomorrah; that is why here the command of God is proclaimed in its ultimate eschatological intensity; this is why John as the greatest of the prophets still stands on the hither side of that which has now come.

Where is this other-worldly wonderful Kingdom? Who can doubt how this question should be answered? It is here in Him, in the midst of you, O Pharisees! It is here, where your blasphemy is directed. Here where the signs which are recounted in the answer of Jesus to John are actually taking place. Here where One dares to set forth not merely a general

[1] The mythological catastrophic images of the New Testament are attempts to express something that cannot possibly be imagined, something so amazing that it transcends all the startling events within the limits of history, the wholly Other of the Final Event of all. To-day we would express this in a rather less naïve manner, but we would not essentially express it any better. Jesus regards His own Mission in connection with this miraculous event, in spite of the fact that He knows that historically it will end in death, that is, that it will not take place in the realization of that miraculous event. From this point of view we should gain a new appreciation of the miracles of the New Testament. To the immanentism of modern religion miracle is an embarrassment; it does not know what to do with it. To the religion of the Bible miracle is central, because in revelation it is concerned not merely with something inward, but also with the actual event of the restoration of the Creation. Everything depends, in the most crude sense of the word, upon this miracle; but this miracle was first of all proclaimed in the coming of Christ (we are here concerned with Reconciliation and not with redemption, with faith and not with sight) and on that account His miracles are only "signs," but still they *are* signs. As such they should be studied and pondered with as much earnestness as His words. In so doing we do not anticipate the historico-critical problem.

Law but the ultimate truth in a personal address. Here where He is, who lays the foundation-stone of the New Community in the community of His disciples.[1] The controversy about the "Messianic consciousness," that is, about the word "Messiah," has obscured the more important question: Can the historian come to any other conclusion than this, that Jesus attributed to Himself just as much finality as His whole message is a final message? Whether we mean this by the term "Messiah" or not, Jesus knew Himself as the One in whom the kingdom which had been predicted ends and the Kingdom of fulfilment begins: not in the sense of an epoch in world history, thus not in the sense of the "Founder of the Christian religion," but in the sense in which it is determined by the wholly eschatological conception of the Kingdom of God. The wholly Other, the other world, is present in His Person. That is why He forgives sins, that is why, in answer to the question "Art Thou He who should come or look we for another?" He says, "Blessèd is he who is not offended in Me." This is why, in contrast to the prophets who are the "Servants" of the Lord, He calls Himself the "Son" and the "Heir." Jesus is not a Rabbi—which He appears to be; He is not the prophet—for which most people hold Him: He is the Son, according to His own claim.

To argue therefore, as some do, that the Father alone, and not the Son, belongs to the Gospel as Jesus Himself proclaimed it means that historical reality has been completely ignored. The very opposite is true: His whole message is simply His action determined by His consciousness of Sonship, understanding the word in the definite eschatological, transcendent sense. Only from this point of view can we understand His whole

[1] On this point cf. the very important study by K. L. Schmidt, *Die Kirche des Urchristentums* (*Festgabe* for Deissmann), which comes to the conclusion that "the question whether Jesus made His disciples into an ἐκκλησία must be answered in the affirmative" (p. 293). That from this point of view an anti-critical light falls upon the extreme historical criticism of Bultmann, and on the other hand—not out of conservatism, but from scientific necessity—that "conservative" work. like that, for instance, of Kattenbusch (we might also instance Kahler) again comes into honour, has been suggested by K. L. Schmidt himself (pp. 291, 295, and loc. cit.).

behaviour. His message cannot be separated from His Person at any point; by "Person" we mean here not the historical personality but the mystery, the divinely authoritative Person. Since He thus proclaims the Will of God, the Kingdom of God, forgiveness, repentance, in so doing He is at the same time proclaiming Himself. His whole message is an act of authority, in the eschatological sense, a Messianic act, a self-authentication of His authority. The view that His language about forgiveness is meaningless, or indeed false, if it be severed from connection with His Person, applies equally to the whole of His work as a teacher. He is not merely the herald of something which is to come, like all the prophets, but, since He proclaims nothing different from that which the prophets foretold, save with this difference that in Him what is proclaimed is already present, He is the herald of Himself as the One in whom the dominion of God, the "other-worldly" element, the wholly Other, is actually present. Hence He does not point forward to a greater one who is to come; this is why He does not divert attention from Himself but towards Himself, this is why He does not turn men away from His Person, but binds them precisely to Himself and regards the decision which is made in His presence as one which is made in the presence of God Himself. In this perception we have at last got beyond the question whether the Kingdom of God be transcendent or immanent, seeing that in Him the transcendent and the coming Kingdom is present, because it is present only in Him— in Him as the One who has come—thus it is both present and future, the Word that has come, and the Word that *will* come.

When we have reached this point, however, we are able to look steadily and boldly at those facts which characterize the close of His life. Here the "eschatological" school has swept away many of the prejudices of Rationalism, but it has not yet made an absolutely clean sweep. For historical reasons there is in essentials nothing to be said against the Synoptic narrative. The Confession of Peter and Jesus' attitude towards this, the fact that this Confession coincides with the first prediction of His sufferings, the journey to Jerusalem as a march to death, the Messianic consciousness partly revealed and partly concealed, the open announcement of the Messiahship to His disciples, and, above all, the Last Supper as the institution of the New Covenant[1]: all these are features of the life of Jesus and of the tradition which, like all original historical sources, are always at the mercy of scepticism, but against which no really convincing arguments can be brought on scientific grounds. They agree exactly with the rest of the picture which has been handed down to us by the most ancient records. They have not really been attacked on historical grounds, but from the point of view of preconceived opinions, by a theology which did not know what to make of the whole Messianic eschatological message, and yet wished to retain Jesus as the Teacher and Example of their rational and ethical form of religion, in order that they might still have some connection with the New Testament, after the whole of the testimony to Jesus as the Christ had been thrown overboard. These general presuppositions of the earlier school of research into the life of Jesus, once they had become interwoven with the whole web of historical research, became a scientific tradition, and, following a law of inertia in the history of intellectual culture, they are still effective, even among those who do not share the point of view represented by these presuppositions; they prevent real historical insight, and they confuse our feeling for what is historically genuine.

(v)

But even if the Synoptic picture of Jesus is in essentials accepted, does there not still exist a great difference between

[1] The study on the Lord's Supper by K. L. Schmidt (*R.G.G.*[2], *Abendmahl*) also gives the impression of a losing battle fought by historical criticism as it retires from the field. If we exchange the false critical question ("is it not possible that things might have happened differently from the way in which the tradition records them?") for the healthy critical question ("do strong reasons exist to give us cause to suspect the tradition at this point?") then scarcely anyone would venture to support the hypothesis of the "original Lucan text" (which only regards as genuine tradition Luke xxii. 15, 16, 18) against the tradition of the Church which was attested very early, still less since that "original Lucan text" is in no way in opposition to the rest of the tradition on the Lord's Supper, and thus makes it quite unnecessary to eliminate it.

this picture of the teaching activity and doctrine of Jesus and the apostolic proclamation of Jesus, the Christ? It is quite certain that this difference does exist, but it exists precisely to the extent in which it should exist, if Jesus is really the Christ to whom the Apostles testify. Jesus would not be the Christ of whom the Apostles speak if this difference did not exist. The testimony to Jesus Christ *cannot* be the same as the historical self-testimony and the historical picture of Jesus, precisely if and because this Jesus is the Christ to whom men bear witness. For the believers' duty to bear witness to Christ is quite different from the task of the Son of God when He was in the form of a servant; it was His mission to carry out, in the hiddenness of an historical life, the divine work of revelation, and in so doing to reveal Himself.

Is it not conceivable that the real position was something of this kind? that just because Jesus really was the Christ, He did not speak about Himself as the Christ in public? that just because His death has saving significance, He did not speak about it openly to the crowds, but only to His disciples, in order that His existence might be really historical? Would not this historical character of His life have been completely removed if during His earthly life He had spoken about Himself as though His death were already an accomplished fact?

The teaching of Jesus is not itself the Divine Word made flesh, the "revelation," in the strict sense of the word. As the One who teaches He is not the Mediator. To be the Mediator is His existence, and indeed the mystery of His existence, which, as such, is present as little in His teaching as it is in His historical "personality." It is the Church which speaks of the Mediator, of the revelation of God in Christ, not Jesus Himself. This is precisely the point of view of the Gospel of John. It intends to say to us: That which Christ has to "say to us," the actual Word of God, which speaks to us in Him, the Logos—this He is Himself, His existence, the Incarnate Son, and by the very fact of this Incarnation the hidden Son of God. Even His deeds are only important because they "say" this, and indeed as they represent *His* speech, the miracle of His presence. He Himself is the miracle of the bread (John vi.),

He Himself is the miracle of the restoration of sight (John ix.), He Himself is the miracle of the Resurrection (John xi.). How this is related to his historical speech—recorded by the chronicler—is in any case a secondary question. What Jesus said, if it be taken by itself, is just as far from being the revelation, the Gospel, as His historical personality, the picture of His life and of His inner life taken by itself is the revelation, the Mediator.

His actual "speech" belongs to the mystery of His Person. Even His teaching—which is recorded by the chronicler—is, like that of the prophets, simply an indication of the existence of this mystery, whether it explicitly deals with it or not. Certainly, as we have said, His whole teaching is saturated, illuminated by the fact of His Sonship, and the consciousness of His Sonship—for him, that is, who "has ears to hear." But this does not provide us with any standard for the estimate of His historical self-testimony—in the sense in which the chronicler records it. For even this explicit testimony to Himself could never be anything other than something indirect, simply an indication, a suggestion, a hint. No "historically verified word of Jesus" can be, as such, *the* revelation, the Gospel; no historically verified witness to Himself, no Messianic saying, as such, is the revelation of the mystery of His Person. As Jesus then (objectively) bears witness to Himself, even when He does not speak about Himself (historically, in the sense of an actual record), so also His (historical) self-testimony is not the Gospel about Jesus Christ, but the prophetic indirect indication pointing towards His own Word, which He does not pronounce, but which He *is*, which therefore He only "says" to him who knows who He is.

Hence the preaching of Jesus, and the preaching of the Church about Jesus Christ, fall into two different categories; they are necessarily different, just because this Jesus is the Christ. Therefore they cannot be compared; a statistical inquiry into the frequency of the witness of Jesus to Himself simply shows that those who make such an inquiry have not seen the point at all. It may very well be possible that the historical evidence for the self-witness of Jesus is more meagre than it seems to be from the Synoptic Gospels—even if we

leave John out altogether. For the question whether He is and
intends to be the Christ, this perception is of no importance
at all. So far as the historical evidence allows us to reconstruct
the picture of His teaching, Jesus seems (to some extent
deliberately) to have concealed His Messiahship, and perhaps
it was only towards the close of His activity that He alluded to
it somewhat more plainly. This would then be an indication
that even His prophetic word followed the course of events,
that is, that it was genuinely historical—in contrast to any
abstract scheme of teaching—and thus just like the rest of His
existence as a whole. But whether He concealed His Messiahship or made it known, His speech was always an indirect
communication,[1] and would be an indirect communication
even if it had taken the form of the self-evidence recorded in
the Fourth Gospel. The explicit (historical) concealment and
the explicit (historical) unveiling only form the two-fold
indication of the two-fold nature of His mediatorial existence,
which, as such, is both hidden and manifest, which, however,
certainly reveals a tendency, a purpose, to proceed from
concealment towards manifestation.

Thus the argument which claims that if Jesus had been the
Christ He would have borne witness to Himself in the same
way as the Apostles and the Church bore witness to Him, is
based upon a complete confusion of categories, of points of
view. Such a life of Christ, which would anticipate the witness

[1] On this question Kierkegaard's dissertation on "Blessed is he who is
not offended in Me," in his *Einübung zum Christentum*, is of decisive significance. The points of view are all exposed and worked out in a masterly
manner. But the application is often far less useful than the view of
principle—this is due to the paucity of information then available on
historico-critical questions. The fact that Kierkegaard makes full use
of the Gospel of John as an historical "source," forces him (in reference
to the indirectness and the directness of the communication) now and again
to use some very arbitrary arguments. But his *principles* provide the key we
need for our present situation: How can we combine the historical picture
which emerges from the Synoptic Gospels, the "photograph," with the
Christian witness of the Church which shows the truly historical Jesus Christ
—of whom the historical picture is only an abstract image? All we need to
do is to apply the idea of the indirectness of the communication, and thus
of the "incognito," in a more logical and decided way than does Kierkegaard himself.

of the Church, and thus the Cross and the Resurrection, would not have been a genuinely human life at all; or, to put it the other way round, an historical existence in which He would have said explicitly nothing at all about His Messiahship would have been no divine-human life. The former annuls the "being in the form of a servant," while the latter exaggerates the "incognito" or the "Kenosis." Between these two extremes, so far as we can tell, lies the historical reality. He, whose whole reality speaks to the one who beholds Him, saying "I am HE," has indeed explicitly expressed this "I am HE," but within the limits which separate the prophetic word from the apostolic word. Thus we may finally conclude that even in the most explicit speech of Jesus (that is, of that which could actually be recorded) He concealed Himself quite as much as He manifested Himself, and that in so doing, through the suggestions contained in His teaching, He expressed the essential meaning of the whole matter which is contained in the Word of God.

(vi)

The work of the Christian revelation, however, neither begins nor ends with the life of Jesus and the teaching of Jesus. But that which lies before and behind it is not of the same kind, in spite of the fact that it deals with the same subject—the Mediator, Jesus Christ. Thus the work of the prophets—or the work of the Christ in the prophets—is to point forward, the work of the Apostles is to point backwards to the witness to Jesus Christ. Just as Jesus Christ would not be historically possible for us apart from the retrospective explanation of the Apostles, just as the prophets stand between Christ and other men as those who bear authoritative witness to Him as the Coming One (naturally this does not mean merely the Messianic predictions), so the Apostles and their witness to Christ stand between Him and the rest of us, as those who bear witness to Him as the One who has actually come. The whole faith of all those of us who are neither prophets nor Apostles is based upon this twofold testimony. Without this testimony we would have no Redeemer.

Above all, however, there is still one more point to consider. The Apostles are the witnesses to the Resurrection. That they saw Him as the Risen One constitutes the qualitative difference between us and them, just as the prophetic vocation constitutes the qualitative difference between the prophets and ourselves. In virtue of this special grace it has been given to them to show to us, to whom it has not been given, the Christ. Without their testimony to that which we could not prove for ourselves, there would be for us no "historical picture of His Life"—for we owe its existence to the Church, which is based upon the apostolic testimony—nor would we be able, even if there were an "historical picture of Jesus"—think of that of a Tacitus or a Josephus—to discover in it the Christ. The Resurrection as an actual event is that unknown quantity which the secular historian strives again and again in vain to determine, in order to explain the transition from the teaching of Jesus to the teaching of the Church.[1] Without the reality of the Resurrection —for which indeed it is impossible to find a place in any secular historical picture, since the recognition of its reality depends upon faith, that is, the very opposite of secular history—the historian must try to place the decisive factors of the Resurrection faith before the Death of Jesus, and in the interior life of the disciples, in order to be able to explain the "Visions of the Resurrection" as the reaction from the extreme tension caused by the Death of Jesus, and thus to give a naturalistic explanation. This is the crux for historical research.

Faith does not feel this to be the crux at all. The disciples

[1] To how large an extent historical science is connected with the general world-view, and how impossible it is to write "objective" history becomes plain at this very point. As one example among many which might be given, let us quote Reitzenstein (*Das iranische Erlösungsmysterium*, p. 119): "Like Wellhausen, I can only understand the faith of the disciples in the Risen Lord, if for them the living (Jesus) were already not merely man but more than man. Here the belief in the Bar-nashā can provide the psychological explanation." There is a vast mass of "scientific" literature which at one blow would lose all significance if the Resurrection of Jesus could not be "explained in a psychological manner" but were a reality, that is, a literature which owes its very existence to the conviction that Jesus *cannot* possibly have risen. The modern world-view (which for its part has nothing to do with science) here forces a "correction" in the historical tradition.

believed in the reality of the Resurrection because it had actually happened. And because they have this Resurrection faith which can only be rightly understood from the actual event of the Resurrection, their preaching differs from the manner of Jesus' teaching. That problem which to the secular historian is the basic problem in the history of Christianity—how out of the preaching of Jesus did that of the Church arise?—does not exist for faith, but for unbelief it constitutes a problem which cannot be evaded and yet is insoluble.

We can therefore formulate the difference between an historical picture of Jesus—to be reconstructed, say, from the Synoptic Gospels—and the witness to Christ of the Apostles and the Church in the following terms: It is the difference between that which can be known of Jesus Christ outside and inside the knowledge of the Resurrection. That the Apostles were not concerned to make any distinction between these two things, which are yet one, is quite natural, and is as true of the Synoptists as it is of John. To none of them does an "historical picture" mean anything at all. With more or less historical accuracy they bear witness to Jesus Christ, whom they only really knew after the First Easter. When they bear witness to Jesus Christ they do this with respect to the whole revelation, not merely to His revelation within history, but also to His resurrection, which completes the historical revelation, and which alone makes it possible to know it. They tell the story of the Christ come in the flesh, from which the historian of the life of Jesus extracts the story of the Christ according to the flesh.

From this point of view, then, we can see how mistaken it is to desire that the faith of the Church should be based upon the historical picture of Jesus. Rather it should be based upon the collective revelation as a whole, which includes not merely the testimony of the Apostles but also the whole of that of the prophets. This is the meaning of the Reformers' principle of Scripture, in which was first expressed the full Christian belief in revelation—and thus also the knowledge of Christ as of the Revealer: the whole Scripture is the revelation of Jesus Christ. We need to use the whole of Scripture in order that we may understand the significance of that which has happened in Jesus Christ. Indeed, even the life of Jesus, with all His historical teaching, is not the revelation itself but the "flesh" in which the "Word" is revealed. To this Incarnation, however, the Christian Church does not reckon only the life of Jesus, this span of thirty years, or rather of three years or even of one year, but all that God has done to reveal Himself to us in the special way of which the Scriptures alone can tell us. Not in the life of Jesus, least of all in a picture of the life of Jesus which has been historically and scientifically corrected, but in the whole Scripture do we know the revelation of God in Jesus Christ.

SECTION II: RECONCILIATION

CHAPTER XVII

THE NECESSITY FOR RECONCILIATION

(i)

LUTHER certainly hit the nail on the head when he described Christian theology, as distinguished from every other kind of theology, and particularly that which is definitely Christian from that which only *seems* to be Christian, as a *theologia crucis*. The Cross is the sign of the Christian faith, of the Christian Church, of the revelation of God in Jesus Christ. The feeling of the Church has been quite sound on this point; but where she went wrong was in her frequent forgetfulness of the meaning of the phrase: *in hoc signo vinces*; in that over and over again she herself lost the key to the meaning of this sign. Luther contrasts the *theologia gloriae*[1] as a false theology with the genuine theology, the *theologia crucis*. The whole history of Christianity, and the history of the world as a whole, would have followed a different course if it had not been that again and again the *theologia crucis* became a *theologia gloriae*, and that the *ecclesia crucis* became an *ecclesia gloriae*.

The whole struggle of the Reformation for the *sola fide*, the *soli deo gloria*, was simply the struggle for the right interpretation of the Cross. He who understands the Cross aright—this is the opinion of the Reformers—understands the Bible, he understands Jesus Christ. "Therefore this text—'He bore our sins'—must be understood particularly thoroughly, as the foundation upon which stands the whole of the New Testament or the Gospel, as that which alone distinguishes us

---

[1] O. Ritschl's statement is misleading when, in connection with his remarkable explanation of the divine glory in the teaching of Calvin, he contrasts the Calvinistic theology as a *theologia gloriae* with the Lutheran as a *theologia crucis* (loc. cit., p. 169). For it is for the sake of the *gloria Dei* that Luther confesses his faith in the *theologia crucis!* And the *Cross* of Christ is for Calvin the basis of the knowledge of the *gloria Dei*.

and our religion from all other religions. For Christians alone believe this text. Therefore whosoever believes this article of faith is secure against all errors, and God the Holy Ghost is necessarily with him."[1]

The message of the Cross is the central mystery of the scriptural Gospel. It is not the task of theology to explain these mysteries: for if explanation were possible these mysteries would only be fortuitous mysteries, and thus not real and divine. But it is certainly the most important task of theology to bring out the meaning of these mysteries as clearly as possible. For it is only the meaning of these mysteries which gives us the right to regard them as the Word of God, and a divine Act of revelation, and only in their clear meaning can they be distinguished from all merely accidental, psychological false mysteries, from all that is merely emotional and irrational. Hence we have no right to be content to say that we can only behold the spectacle of the Cross with awe, as an unfathomable, unspeakable mystery. The word *Mysterium* must not serve us as an *asylum ignorantiae*, as a hidden recess in which all kinds of irrational and arbitrary ideas and mystical extravagances may be concealed. For the Gospel gives us a clear and open message of the Cross. It is not regarded as "something mysterious," but as a quite definite mystery. At this precise point, where God utters His most mysterious, unspeakable Word, let us listen and hear it plainly, and not let it fade away in an inarticulate devotional manner like the low murmur of the priest before the distant altar in some large church. What good does it do to speak in a semi-whisper about the mystery of the Cross, merely hinting at something numinous and mysterious, if behind this mysterious behaviour we are cherishing ideas which are absolutely opposed to the message of the Cross? The clear and open message of the Cross has nothing at all to do with ritual mysticism[2] or with things of that kind.

[1] Luther, *W.A.*, 25, 330.

[2] I regard the idea of cultus-mysticism which takes such a foremost position in the latest New Testament research as very apt to lead to misunderstanding. Whereas in Bousset it arose out of the endeavour to explain the Primitive Christian belief in Jesus as "Lord" (*Kyrios*) from the Hellenistic cults in which an exotic deity was worshipped as *Kyrios* ("Lord"), and thus as an indispensable connecting link between real cultus-mysticism

In the New Testament the Cross is mentioned quite definitely by men who knew exactly what they meant to say to those for whom this message was intended. For only in the Word, in its clarity and its distinctness, do we come to perceive how mysterious, how marvellous and incomprehensible God is in His revelation.

It was not merely in the days of the Reformers that it mattered supremely to understand the Cross, the divine act of Reconciliation, aright. This question is of supreme significance to-day. It is only when we test a theology by this standard that we can see whether it is Christian or not. Goethe must have known why it was that he hated the Cross. The darkness of Golgotha cast its shadow over the beauty of the world and of man, and spoilt it for him. It is only at the Cross that we see clearly both the "offence" and the "folly" of the Christian revelation. Here alone, at last, the intellectual and moral pride of reason is finally broken. From time immemorial this is why speculative Idealists have cherished a special dislike or even hatred of the Apostle Paul; this is why Liberal Theology, both of the older and of the more recent type, has tried to thrust a wedge between the Pauline doctrine of the Atonement and Primitive Christianity. For our attitude towards the Cross and the Atonement finally reveals quite clearly whether we believe in a "general" or a "special" revelation. It is the message of the Mediator of the Atonement which first makes the self-assured man so conscious of the humbling element in the thought of the Mediator, and thus of the idea of revelation in the Christian sense. It is the Cross, more than anything else, which differentiates scriptural revelation from all other forms of religion, and from Idealism of every kind.

and the religion of the New Testament (based on the consciously non-Christian presuppositions of Bousset), it is used by Deissmann and others on the presupposition that the Christian faith is in its very nature (not in its historical origin) Christ-mysticism, and, like all the theological work of Deissmann, it serves to strengthen the tendency to conceive Paul's plain statements of faith as secondary reflex statements, conceptions of faith in general, as fossilized deposits of something which was once living: religious *feeling*. How much labour the great theologians, and above all the Reformers, might have spared themselves if only they had possessed the simple mystical key of Deissmann!

(ii)

Throughout the nineteenth century it is possible to trace a line of theological thought which seems to be equally remote from the Rationalistic Idealistic conception of religion on the one hand, and from the Early Christian doctrine of Reconciliation on the other; this line can be traced backwards through the Socinians to Abelard; in recent times it happens to have joined forces, deliberately, with the great opponent of Anselm. This theology is that with which we are already familiar as the theology of reconciliation, which begins with Schleiermacher, reaches its high-water mark with Ritschl,[1] and, through the Ritschlian school, still continues to influence thought at the present day. Since it claims to be Christocentric it also asserts that it has formulated the scriptural idea of Reconciliation better, and in closer accordance with the principles of Scripture, than the orthodox doctrine of the Church has done. It is evident that theologians of this type are anxious to understand the meaning of the Cross of Christ. But it is just as evident that they have completely failed to understand the Cross. For the Passion of Christ is merely regarded from the humanistic religious point of view as the highest proof of the perfect religious or moral union of Jesus with the Divine Will. The Cross is thus the supreme proof of Christ's fidelity to God—a fidelity maintained through the severest trials. Though the whole of the life of Jesus is a singular proof of love and fidelity, the Cross is the crowning act of this life, its high-water mark, its fulfilment.

[1] The strong common element in the doctrine of Schleiermacher and of Ritschl is their conception of Reconciliation as a merely subjective process. Thus here, too, as at all points, Ritschl is somewhat nearer to the message of the Scriptures than Schleiermacher. Whereas for Schleiermacher the problem of guilt does not exist at all—justification is merely the subjective reflex of the beginning of redemption—in the thought of Ritschl the problem of justification is always central. But he even makes the *prius* into *posterius*: reconciliation *follows* justification, whereas in the scriptural thought of the Reformation it is the objective basis of justification. This, however, is not only the view of Ritschl. In this, as at so many other points, he is only voicing the views of modern thought and feeling in general; this is why discussion with him is entirely relevant to-day.

In themselves these ideas are scriptural, and they are certainly valuable, only they do not represent what the Bible means by Reconciliation. They go no further than the conception of the Idea made visible in history—of ethico-religious fidelity to vocation. Between this death and that of a Socrates, for example, the only difference is one of degree, not of principle. The death of Jesus is a sublime and noble martyrdom, one of the noblest which can be imagined. It is no less than this, but also it is no more. Thus it really represents a general principle, of which Jesus gives a supreme illustration. It is a demonstration of human love at its highest point—and, in so far as in all human love the divine love is manifested, of divine love as well. But thinkers of this type have no idea that this fact represents an actual *objective* transaction, in which God actually *does* something, and something which is absolutely necessary. Nor have they any idea that a new situation has been created by this event—not merely that a clearer vision of a truth has been given, a truth which could have been known before, although it was then less distinct—that through this fact alone the impassable gulf which yawns between God and man has been spanned by the energy of God's own action, and that here alone God reveals His secret, which had been hidden from the sight of mankind until that time. In this type of thought the significance of the Passion and Death of Christ is wholly subjective. It is suggested that as man beholds this picture of the Man who gives Himself up so completely, with so much love and faithfulness to God, the divine love and faithfulness will be manifested to him. The meaning of Reconciliation is here misinterpreted. This is the subjective view: Man, quite wrongly, regards God as an enemy, as a Judge who wishes to punish him. At the Cross man becomes aware of his error; here the idea that God is love conquers the idea of His anger. Thus here the only gulf which separates man from God is illusory, namely, it is that which human error has placed between itself and God. Reconciliation simply means the removal of a religious error.

Ritschl was conscious, and rightly so, that in developing this purely subjective doctrine of Reconciliation he was in opposition to Anselm and in agreement with Abelard. Like the

Socinians before him he draws the main force of his argument from the defects of the doctrine of "satisfaction" in the theology of Anselm, as well as from an observation about the use of forensic ideas, and the conception of the divine honour—a point to be treated later on in this work. His main error is this (as is the case with numbers of less important opponents of the Biblical and orthodox doctrine of the Cross) : that he set up the alternative—either Anselm or the subjective interpretation. Rightly understood, this alternative does not exist.[1] The doctrine of Anselm is a magnificent attempt, but it is neither the only possible one nor is it the only attempt which has ever been made to conceive and establish theologically the scriptural idea of the vicarious sufferings of Christ as a sacrifice and as a penalty. Anselm's leading ideas had already been clearly formulated by some of the most outstanding of the ancient Fathers of the Church,[2] but without the specific medieval emphasis. From the controversial point of view, therefore, it is far too easy merely to attack the doctrine of Anselm, which, although in essentials it coincides with the thought of the Scriptures, is yet at certain points open to criticism. Above all, it will be necessary to dispel the deeply rooted prejudice against the "forensic" elements, and the idea of the Divine Honour in Anselm's doctrine of the Atonement (and in all objective forms of this doctrine). We can only do this if we try to understand the idea of Reconciliation, both in the Bible and in the doctrine of the Church, by tracing it from its root.

[1] Even in the doctrine of Satisfaction we note—as in all the leading doctrines of the Christian Church—the modern form of argument with which by this time we are familiar: the critic fastens on some objectionable *expression* of the matter and thus justifies his criticism (here in itself justifiable) to his own conscience, and makes this a reason for rejecting the matter itself. In particular, criticism of the ecclesiastical doctrine of Reconciliation has been facilitated by the introduction of the idea that it affirms a change in the mind of God. The great Fathers of the Church and the great theologians show no trace of any such idea. See below, p. 470.

[2] The meaning of this fact has been obscured by the mistaken view that the Patristic doctrine of Redemption through the Incarnation has been supposed to be a (Hellenistic) substitute for the doctrine of Justification and Reconciliation, or even that it is irreconcilably opposed to it (see above on the modern view of the dogma), whereas it forms an indissoluble unity with it.

(iii)

Once more our starting-point will be the fundamental Christian belief that God has revealed Himself in Christ. Revelation means that God has come to us, hence it means condescension, self-emptying, since, in order to come close to us, He had to divest Himself wholly of His deity. It is a manifestation of Himself of such a kind that it is possible to pass it by without seeing it; it is a form of the presence of God which it is possible to mistake for the exact opposite, as the most complete absence of God's presence; indeed, this is how we must regard it if our spiritual eyes are not illuminated. In *Isaiah liii* this truth was fully perceived for the first time: "He was despised and rejected of men . . . We did esteem Him stricken of God, and afflicted." "When we see Him, there is no beauty that we should desire Him. . . ." This is the very opposite of a theophany, in the pagan sense of "the possibility of being known directly."

In itself the Incarnation already means being "in the form of a servant." But the mere advent "in the flesh" does not constitute the complete self-emptying, nor does it mean that Christ's coming to us is complete. In it the *nostra assumsit* has not yet been fulfilled. For to be born into this life—however little it may be worthy of God—is still, in itself, something beautiful; indeed, the physical nature of man—in spite of everything—is the most beautiful spectacle upon which the eye that seeks and thirsts for beauty can rest. It is only when the body is suffering from weakness and when it comes to die that it reminds us of finitude and infirmity.

And all forms of death are not equally horrible. The death of the youthful hero on the battlefield in the hour of victory, the death of the venerable prince of poets, which is like the falling of ripe fruit, whom the whole nation mourns with true homage, might be called a beautiful rather than a hideous death. But the Cross is in every respect hideous: the shameful death of a criminal, the obloquy of the death on the gallows, sheer torture. Is there any place where we would less expect to see the revelation of the merciful God than on the cross

441

of Golgotha? Is there an event further removed from any kind of apotheosis that we could imagine? Above all, this is so when we consider what this death meant also inwardly. No creature can suffer so much as man because no creature is so near to God. Man alone knows what hell means because he alone knows God. Only suffering bound up with God is genuine human suffering. Here alone is remoteness from God. This is the deepest point in existence known to us or which we can imagine: suffering and shattering contact with God being regarded as the bearing of the divine wrath. That alone, in the complete sense, is the *nostra* which Jesus Christ has accepted, since He, as Luther says, *sensu praesentissimo Inferni tactus est*,[1] that He tasted to the full the sense of remoteness from God, the presence of the angry God, since He felt Himself to be forsaken not only by men but by God. If the cry, "My God! My God! Why hast Thou forsaken Me?" were not so well attested, we might regard it as an invention of those who had traced the thoughts of the scriptural revelation really to its utmost limit. How could God manifest Himself to us in a more hidden manner than when He confronts us in a death of this kind?

But however great this "offence of the Cross" may be, yet, if the distinction is permissible, we can still say that it is a theoretical one. To the Greeks it is foolishness. The Greek spirit is too superficial, too aesthetic, to feel the full force of the "offence." It sees the "folly," but not the "offence"; the Greek feels that this cannot be imagined, but he does not feel the offence which this causes to the man whose whole ethical and religious passion is confronted by this challenge, the offence that it is to the will which is directed towards the Law of God. The full force of the "offence" *can* only be felt by the Jew, who has come so near to God through the whole divine process of education by which he has been trained. This is what constitutes the "offence": that here it is not only the Son of God who dies, but that He dies for the pious, righteous Jew, because only thus can he be saved. The actual depths to which human nature can fall are not revealed by the knowledge of death—not even by human death—but only

[1] *W.A.*, 5, 602.

by the knowledge of sin and guilt. That is the real *nostra*: death as the wages of sin, as the expression of the divine wrath, as the divine reaction against our sin.

It is not enough to say that we are far away from God, that our life is not like the divine life, that God has to come a long way to reach us; it is not merely the fact that we belong to a different order of being, that we are finite, which separates us from God. This would be a merely negative separation, a mere sense of incompleteness. The truth is rather that between us and God there is an actual obstacle, which blocks the way like a great boulder, an obstacle so great that we cannot push it out of the way by our own efforts. This obstacle is sin, or, rather, guilt. For guilt is that element in sin by which it belongs unalterably to the past, and as this unalterable element determines the present destiny of each soul. Guilt means that our past—that which can never be made good—always constitutes one element in our present situation. Therefore we only conceive our life as a whole when we see it in this dark shadow of guilt. Thus the sense of guilt means that our eyes have been opened to the intense seriousness of life. The more profoundly serious is our view of life, the less life is broken up into isolated elements, and the more it is conceived as a whole, the more it is seen in the light of man's responsibility, that is, of guilt. Guilt, however, is not in any sense something concrete (this may, perhaps, be regarded as the chief error in the doctrine of Anselm); it is something absolutely personal, it is the perverted attitude towards God, therefore it is something absolutely infinite, like the soul, like the relation to God itself. Sin is the perversion of human nature through the perversion of the human attitude towards God. In guilt we see this perversion as something which has actually taken place, which can never be undone; we are made to feel that this is an irrevocable, inescapable fact. The central point in every human being is his attitude towards God. So far as his attitude towards God is concerned his nature is perverted, spoiled, and lost. It is God's holiness and righteousness which makes us aware of this subjective fact as an objective fact; since our attitude towards God has been perverted, God's attitude towards us has also been changed. It is not merely subjectively, from

443

our point of view, that our guilt lies between us and God, but objectively, from the point of view of God. This is what constitutes its gravity.

For this reason, too, this obstacle which lies between man and God is infinite. Human guilt gains its infinity from God, just as our soul is infinite because it reflects the infinity of God. It is because God is so near to us that guilt is so terrible. The more we see that sin is sin against God, the more serious it becomes; and the more we see it as sin against God, the more we recognize that our sin is irrevocable, that is, it is guilt. Both "sin" and "guilt" express the truly personal relation between God and man. Hence the converse is also true: the more personal is our relation to God, the more plainly do sin and guilt stand out. The obstacle which blocks the way, the great boulder on the path, owes its weight to the divine nearness, through which guilt is maintained, so that it cannot be dispelled by any specious arguments: thus our sense of guilt is due to the presence of the Divine Holiness.

(iv)

Sin against God is an attack on God's honour. Sin is rebellion against the Lord. But God cannot permit His honour to be attacked; for His honour is His Godhead, His sovereign majesty. God would cease to be God if He could permit His honour to be attacked. The law of His Divine Being, on which all the law and order in the world is based, the fundamental order of the world, the logical and reliable character of all that happens, the validity of all standards, of all intellectual, legal, and moral order, the Law itself, in its most profound meaning, demands the divine reaction, the divine concern about sin, the divine resistance to this rebellion and this breach of order. The holiness of God requires the annihilation of the will which resists God. God is not mocked. If this were not true, then there would be no seriousness in the world at all; there would be no meaning in anything, no order, no stability, the world order would fall into ruins; chaos and desolation would be supreme. All order in the world depends upon the

inviolability of His honour, upon the certitude that those who
rebel against Him will be punished.

But this divine reaction is not automatic; it is not expressed
in terms of natural law—although it is according to law; it
is absolutely personal. Therefore God takes a personal share
in this reaction. It is not a coldly objective, impersonal, logical
process. But—like the love of God itself—it is a personal movement: God's zeal has "burst into flame"; He wills to destroy
all that opposes Him, indeed, as Luther, one of the greatest
heralds of the love of God, says, He even takes pleasure in the
destruction of this resistance.[1] This is His holy divine wrath,
the negative aspect of the Divine Holiness. The divine wrath
corresponds to our guilt and sin. Whether man's relation to
God is really conceived in personal terms or not is proved by
the fact of the recognition of the divine wrath as the objective
correlate to human guilt. This, then, is the obstacle which
alienates us from God. It is no merely apparent obstacle, no
mere misunderstanding; this separation is an objective reality,
the two-fold reality of human guilt and divine wrath. In this
reality both God and man are involved; in contradistinction
from the good Creation of God, this reality has been produced both by sinful man and the holy God. Therefore it is
certainly not an original true reality, but, all the same, it is
reality: the reality of wrath, in which God does His "strange
works," where, therefore, He cannot show Himself as He is
in Himself, but where He must show Himself as He is in relation to this sinful world. Only where man recognizes this
reality of wrath does he take his guilt seriously; only then does
he realize the personal character of God, and his own human,
personal relation to God. The rejection of the doctrine of the
wrath of God—as "anthropopathic"—is the beginning of the
Pantheistic disintegration of the Christian Idea of God.[2]
In the whole of the Scriptures, in each of its parts, and in all
the classical forms of Christian theology and of the Christian

---

[1] "He draweth one in and hath such a desire that in His jealousy and
wrath He is driven to devour the evil ones" (*W.A.*, 28, 559).

[2] On the significance of the idea of the wrath of God within the Christian
knowledge of God and in theology, see my article: *Der Zorn Gottes und die
Versöhnung durch Christus; Zwischen den Zeiten*, 1927, pp. 93 ff.

message, the full conception of the personality of God carries with it, indubitably, the recognition of the divine wrath.

The meaning of the divine judgment of wrath is this: corruption, absolute, irretrievable loss. That is our position as we are in ourselves. We do not feel it to be so. No human being feels it so, according to its truth, for to feel the wrath of God which corresponds to the truth would already be Hell. But objectively it is so, and the fact that we do not feel it is another form of our lack of seriousness. Hence the more serious we are, the more the sense of the divine wrath increases; and the less we see the divine wrath, the greater is our superficiality. This is the character of the gulf which lies between us and God. Once we have recognized this, once we have seen this gulf in its whole breadth and depth, we know that from the side of man there is no bridge, no possibility of crossing over to the other side. We cannot construct the bridge, for in this unfathomable abyss it would be impossible to find any solid ground on which to build. We can neither get rid of nor stride through the wall of fire which lies between us and God. Guilt is no longer in our power. Only one thing could help us: if God Himself were to intervene, if He Himself were to remove the obstacle—and this means forgiveness.

(v)

But what does forgiveness mean? I do not mean, what does this man or the other *teach* about forgiveness, but what *can* forgiveness mean, in actual truth, in positive fact? The divine law—the world-order—requires that sin should receive its corresponding penalty from God. God cannot approach man as though there were no obstacle, as though no block of stone had made the way impassable between us and Him. Indeed, it is the divine righteousness and holiness which gives this obstacle its weight, its objective reality, which is the reason why we cannot push it out of the way. Man cannot push this obstacle out of the way just because God alone has power over it. Forgiveness, however, would mean the removal of this obstacle, thus it would mean the contravention of the logical result of the world law; therefore it would mean a process more vast and profound than we could even imagine, a change far more vast than the suspension of the laws of nature. For the laws of nature are laws of the Divine Creation, external laws. But the law of penalty is the expression of the personal Will of God, of the Divine Holiness itself. Forgiveness, therefore, would be the declaration of the non-validity of the unconditioned order of righteousness which requires penalty.

Modern superficiality, which is due to Pantheism and Naturalism, evades this difficulty by an appeal to the analogy of human life. Good people forgive one another, how much more then must the good God be ready to forgive! The fallacy is not perceived. Good people forgive because they remember their own sin, because they know they have no right to judge others. They know that they ought to forgive. It forms part of the moral man's idea of duty that he ought to forgive. He ought—just because he is under the sway of the divine world order, which cannot be annulled. Precisely because God must be taken seriously, men ought to forgive each other, thus we ought to forgive just because God is not mocked. The intense moral reality of God, however, is seen most plainly in the fact that disobedience to Him must inevitably be self-destructive; it dashes itself to pieces against an immovable rock. It is quite ethical to say: "man ought to forgive," but it is in the highest degree non-ethical to say: "God also ought to forgive." "Dieu pardonnera, c'est son métier!" There is no more impious saying. But it only expresses the thought of all who have been influenced by the Enlightenment: "Of course God will do it. . . . How could He do otherwise, since He is so kindly!" As soon as anyone regards the forgiveness of God as a matter of course he is as audacious as Voltaire. This impiety is not modified if we say: "God forgives if we repent," for this simply amounts to a denial of guilt. What has my present repentance to do with my previous guilt? And it also amounts to a denial of sin; for the sinner can never repent in proportion to his sin. There are no human conditions in which we have the right to expect that God will forgive us as a matter of course.

If, however, we are unable to judge of the forgiveness of

God from our idea of Him, then we can know nothing at all about it from the human point of view. Whenever anyone thinks he has the right to lay down the law about divine forgiveness he does not take the question of human guilt seriously. For whoever takes it seriously knows that he can only expect from God the penalty which he deserves. If the conscience which has been weakened by Naturalistic ideas cannot perceive this truth clearly—the worse for *it*! But if we can expect from God nothing but punishment—and hope, at the very most, for forgiveness as a free gift—it is evident that we can know nothing of forgiveness unless it is explicitly revealed to us. To the free grace of forgiveness there corresponds the contingent freedom of the divine communication of forgiveness, which could not possibly be inferred by reason. It is only thus, as an unimaginable revelation, as a gift which could never be taken for granted, as a free, gracious gift, that forgiveness is proclaimed in the Bible. If all real personal knowledge of God is freely revealed, and thus a contingent communication, and therefore connected with the self-manifestation of God within time, this applies in a very special way to the revelation of God's Will to forgive. It is not a logical necessity to God to forgive. He can forgive or not forgive. Indeed, it is of the very nature of God to possess this freedom, this mysterious Will which men cannot understand. To know forgiveness is only possible on the basis of an explicit divine declaration, which breaks through all intellectual necessity, all legal idea of an *a priori* necessity. Thus forgiveness can only be revealed to us as something which actually *happens*, as a *fact*, as an amazing assurance of forgiveness from God Himself.

The same truth might be expressed by saying: forgiveness is the very opposite of anything which can be taken for granted. Nothing is less obvious than forgiveness. For anything that can be taken for granted belongs to the sphere of obvious truths, which can be deduced as necessary by the mind, *a priori* certainties, truths which can be inferred from given premisses. But any truth which can be logically deduced as a "necessary" truth belongs to the sphere of law. Such truths are based, in the last resort, upon the theological character of the divine procedure, upon the majesty of law as an expression of the Divine Will. But if any truth is obvious, certainly it is *not* forgiveness, but punishment. For punishment is the expression of the divine law and order, of the inviolability of the divine order of the world. It is obvious that every man receives his deserts.[1] This is the logic of the legal view of the world. This is all that can be posited from our point of view, that is, from immanent necessity, from the point of view of the human mind. The idea of forgiveness may remain in the background of our consciousness merely as a faint hope, but can only become a certainty through the explicit declaration of God in His Will.

But this means that forgiveness can only take place as a real divine act. The sense of acceptance, the certainty of forgiveness, can only legitimately refer to a divine act of revelation, to an explicit communication of this divine secret. Such an act would be the most inconceivable revelation possible, something so new that it could never be imagined. Further, this forgiveness would have to be imparted in such a way that the holiness of God, the inviolability of the law, and the logical demands of the penal order would still be maintained. Thus the perfect revelation of forgiveness can only be such as brings out with intense emphasis that it cannot and must not be taken for granted. This means that it must be of such a kind that it will express the reality of guilt, the reality of the divine wrath, and yet, at the same time the overwhelming reality of forgiving love.

(vi)

Thus in real forgiveness the gulf between God and man would indeed be spanned, but in such a way that in the very act of throwing this bridge over the abyss the depth and

---

[1] This is, if we may use the expression, the fundamental idea in the religious philosophy of the Reformers and in that of Luther in particular, that the God who can be known outside of Christ is the angry God, because He can be perceived from the *lex naturae*. The idea of the consistency of God leads not to forgiveness but to punishment. On this point cf. Th. Harnack: *Luthers Theologie*, pp. 283 ff.

breadth of the gulf would become still more evident. Real forgiveness would be an event of such a nature that in the very act of removing the great boulder which blocks the path its weight would become still more evident. It would be a transaction of such a kind that *only* in it, in its actual achievement, could we become *certain* of the divine forgiveness. But this is what the New Testament means by reconciliation through the Cross of Jesus Christ. This is the event in which God makes known His holinêss and His love simultaneously, in one event, in an absolute manner. We can, however, only perceive its full significance as a real act of forgiveness if we see that it is far more than a symbol, however impressive—one symbol among others—that it is *the* act of revelation, which, as an actual event, constitutes the basis of our faith in forgiveness. This is what is meant by reconciliation, if the word is taken in the Biblical objective sense.

In other forms of religion forgiveness is gained far more easily. It is simply asserted as a fact; that is, men allow themselves to expect it from God.[1] Thus it is taken for granted. If it were not taken for granted, then we would be forced to depend upon an event of revelation, then it would be impossible to assert it thus; we would be obliged to receive it as a real gift. Is it not possible, however, that there might be a "private" experience of forgiveness? an event of revelation which could be repeated every time afresh for each individual? That is, "revelation" in the sense in which the word is used by fanatics. But the revelation of the Bible in contrast to this individualistic fanatical type is open to all; it is an event which is intended for the world, and which takes place in sight of the whole

[1] If we study the history of religion with the question, "What does forgiveness mean here and how is it obtained?" we find that the law which governs this question is the following: that the more a religion rises from a sacrificial system into "more spiritual" regions, the easier forgiveness becomes, or as a rule the very idea of it disappears altogether behind mystical ideas or those of a philosophy of identity. If this does not happen then a rigid moralism, impressive enough in its way, is developed (Zarathustra, the Stoics) in which the thought of righteousness leaves no room for forgiveness at all. Thus either we find forgiveness connected with a (more or less primitive) sacrificial cult, or we find religion without sacrifice and without forgiveness.

450

world. It is an historical event, an Incarnation, and therefore, in principle, it is a unique event. For even sin is not a private matter for isolated individuals. Sin, as my personal sin, is always, at the same time, also the sin of the world. Hence the revelation of forgiveness, the event of forgiveness is that of which it is said: "Behold the Lamb of God, which taketh away the sin of the world."

Just as forgiveness is more easily obtained in other religions —or rather, seems to be—so also the conception of guilt is shallower. Anselm is absolutely right when he sums up all the teaching about forgiveness outside Christianity in one vigorous phrase: *nondum considerasti quanti ponderis sit peccatum*. We can see whether guilt is regarded seriously or lightly by the kind of energy or "work" which is considered necessary in order to remove the separating obstacle from the path. The more this is supposed to be done "for nothing," without anything happening, the more forgiveness becomes an "obvious," "necessary" conception, the more it expresses the view that lies behind the mocking phrase: *C'est son métier!* The more seriously guilt is regarded, the more it is realized that "something must happen," just because forgiveness is not something which can in any way be taken absolutely for granted. The more real guilt is to us, the more real also is the gulf between us and God, the more real is the wrath of God, and the inviolable character of the law of penalty; the more real also the obstacle between God and man becomes, the more necessary becomes the particular transaction, by means of which the obstacle, in all its reality, is removed. The more serious our view of guilt, the more clearly we perceive the necessity for an objective—and not merely subjective—Atonement. To deny this necessity means the *nondum consideravisse pondus peccati*.

The converse, however, is also true: only in Christ and not till then, has humanity been able to perceive this burden of guilt, this necessity for an objective act of Atonement. The gulf of separation, all that blocks the way between man and God, did not become fully evident in its immensity until the actual Atonement had taken place, through the Cross. In the revelation of Christ, in this one event, question and answer, need and the knowledge of need are present simultaneously.

Only at the Cross of Christ does man see fully what it is that separates him from God; yet it is here alone that he perceives that he is no longer separated from God. Nowhere else does the inviolable holiness of God, the impossibility of overlooking the guilt of man stand out more plainly; but nowhere else also does the limitless mercy of God, which utterly transcends all human standards, stand out more clearly and plainly. That God can be both at once, the One who "is not mocked," and the One who "doth not deal with us after our transgressions"; that neither aspect is sacrificed to the other, or can be subordinated to the other as a mere attribute; that God is equally the Holy One who asserts His unconditional claims, the One whose glory may not be given to another, and the Merciful One who gives Himself to the very utmost limits of self-emptying—this fundamental theme of the whole Bible is the message of the Cross, the truth which is not to be separated from the fact, but in it alone, in this actual happening, *is* the truth.

(vii)

That God comes, that He comes to *us*, means, that He Himself really and actually meets us as we are. This is why He comes down to our level, that He may really meet with us. *Nostra assumsit.* . . . That it is *God* who really meets us, and that He really meets with *us* means the same thing. He meets us at the point where we become "real," that is, where we stand before Him naked, stripped of all illusions and coverings or masks, with nothing to shield us from His gaze. This only happens where our inmost soul is exposed, where, in the presence of God, we have no excuses to offer, nothing to say. Our humiliation is complete when we perceive that in ourselves we cannot possibly reach God. This illusion, the illusion of religious people, is only finally destroyed by the Mediator of the Atonement. Everything else which religious thought has invented, in order to mediate between God and man, is more noble, is less humiliating for us, than the conviction that this Atonement is necessary.

The humiliation coincides with the perception that fellowship with God is not something which we can take for granted, but something which is incomprehensible and amazing. The more we take it for granted, the more, properly speaking, we take our place by the side of God. The summit of this arrogance is reached in the doctrine of identity: *Atma is Brahma.*

At the opposite pole to all this stands the Cross. The doctrine of identity—and the kindred systems of speculative Idealism and mysticism—maintain that it is not necessary that any objective transaction should actually take place, for God's attitude is eternally the same. There is no obstacle between us and God save our erroneous idea that it exists. Here guilt is denied. Its doctrine of redemption is not one of forgiveness— and still less of atonement—but this: it is the perception of the unity which was always there, the knowledge that this idea that there is some obstacle between us and God is an illusion; thus it is the assertion that fellowship with God is perfectly natural. This view fosters man's pride; it humbles him less than any other view; it does more than anything to increase and intensify his arrogant illusions. This is a permanent illusion; it is therefore the very opposite of realism.

The truly realistic view, which therefore is just as much opposed to Idealism as it is to Naturalism, is the judgment man passes upon himself when he admits that he is guilty. The more realistic we are, the more knowledge of guilt we possess. The more real man becomes, the more he acknowledges himself to be guilty. The more clearly we see that fellowship with God is *not* something which can be taken completely for granted, the more we see that it is "costly." And the "cost" is not paid by man. For how can sinful man himself undertake to bear the "cost" of restoring the conditions of fellowship! Thus this restoration of communion "costs" God[1] something; even on the part of God it is not taken for granted; even by Him it can only be achieved with

---

[1] Luther recognizes quite clearly that this is the very thing which constitutes the distinction between the Christian Faith and the religions of the world. "For I have said often that faith alone is not enough for God, but that the cost must also be there. The Turks and the Jews also believe in God but without means and cost" (*E.A.*, 12, 339).

"labour"—as a particular event. The heavier the burden of guilt the heavier the "cost," as Luther puts it; that is, forgiveness is the very opposite of something which is so natural that it costs no effort. The knowledge of the necessity for an objective atonement keeps pace with the progress of man in laying bare his soul to reality.

It is the same, therefore, with the knowledge of the real God. The real God is the personal God, the One who reveals Himself. Knowledge of guilt, the personality of God, and the reality of revelation necessarily belong together. The real God is the One who is absolutely holy, and absolutely merciful; the One, therefore, whom we can never reach by thought, who in this paradox, the highest paradox of all, is to us the mysterious, the impenetrable, the One whose attitude towards us is not governed by natural necessity, but is absolutely free, whom we can only know where He chooses to reveal Himself to us freely. His free revelation and His revelation in the unity of holiness and mercy is one and the same thing. Hence the perfect revelation of God in the Cross of Christ means both the perfect revelation of the incomprehensibility and impenetrability of His Being, of His Majesty, and of His freedom and generosity. He is the God who is to be feared and yet loved as no other Being could be loved and feared. Because forgiveness is His free gift we are forced to depend upon it as a contingent, absolutely "given" objective fact. Further, it is the vicarious endurance of the penalty of sin, because it is not merely the expression of the divine freedom, but also of the divine necessity and obedience to law. The Cross is the union of the divine freedom and necessity, and likewise the union of His holiness and mercy, of the infinite validity of the Law and the unlimited sovereignty of God, as the Lord of the Law.

CHAPTER XVIII

THE PENAL THEORY OF THE ATONEMENT

(i)

Two series of statements of a parabolic nature[1] determine the scriptural message concerning the fact of the Atonement: firstly, the parables which deal with payment of debts, which are taken from the practice of the law, with their ideas of satisfaction and penalty; and secondly, analogies drawn from the practice of the cultus, with their emphasis upon sacrifice and the shedding of blood. Both merge into one in the idea of expiation, and indeed of substitutionary and complete expiation, which constitutes the divine objective basis of the Atonement. The active subject in this process is the Person of the Mediator, whose Mediatorship does not receive its full meaning until this point. All these ideas have become wholly alien to the thought of the present day. We can explain this fact in two ways: either it means that in the progress of knowledge we have passed on to a higher stage of development, that these views represented a more naïve and primitive

[1] That in point of fact it is only possible to deal with these questions at all by means of parables, and not with adequate expressions, may be regarded as the main difference between the doctrine of the Bible and the orthodox ecclesiastical doctrine. The great theologians have almost all ranged themselves on the side of the Bible, perhaps Luther most of all, at least most plainly. For it is this and nothing else which explains the way he changes about from one "theory" to another of the most varied kind. He knows exactly that each one of them is necessary and throws fresh light upon the matter in hand, but that no single one is sufficient by itself or in any way adequate. We find the same thing, in still greater freedom, in the witness of the New Testament, and indeed in that of a man like Paul. All these expressions are radii of a circle which converge on the same central point without actually touching it. How can it be otherwise since it is the nature of all theological statements to be radii which converge on a central point, while the actual centre is hollow? God can never be fully defined. Orthodox theologians and their "liberal" critics have not understood this. It is due to this misunderstanding that here and there they can use such an unscriptural expression as "arithmetical treatment" of the question of Atonement. The defective system of Luther, in the formal sense, is also at this point the truer system in the real sense.

455

way of stating religious and moral truths, which a scientifically educated age is bound to express differently, and is indeed able to do so; or, on the other hand, our sense of alienation from these ideas may be due to the fact that some part of truth may be lacking; that some aspect of it may have become obscured or may have actually disappeared, some element of truth which can never be transformed into a general religious or moral truth, not because it is not quite true, but because the general truth, as such, is never the truth.

To put it briefly: these expressions sound strange to us to-day simply because we are accustomed to thinking in terms of general rather than special revelation; the only difference is that here, in the thought of reconciliation, which is the personal heart of revelation, this sense of alienation reaches its highest point. Hence it is only at this point that the idea of the Mediator emerges in its full significance, although from the very outset it has seemed to us to be the characteristic and final token of the contrast between general religion and the Christian faith. This idea—that is, if it is not entirely denuded of content—sums up within itself all that is non-modern, alien, and offensive in the Gospel proclaimed in the Bible. Through it, Jesus Christ the Crucified becomes absolutely central to the Christian faith; or, to put it the other way round, wherever Jesus Christ, in His Person, really and actually is this central point, there of necessity are we forced to use this word "Mediator."

It is not difficult to understand what took place when modern Christian thinkers began to be conscious of this sense of alienation from the older views; their first reaction was an attempt to weaken the significance of those conceptions within the New Testament which had become unintelligible, and, wherever possible, to interpret them as perversions, due to the later doctrine of the Church, and thus, whenever it was possible, to remove them from the testimony of the New Testament altogether. From the outset this attempt was doomed to destruction; and to-day its complete failure is admitted on all hands. This alien element *is* the witness of the Primitive Christian Church.[1] We can only get rid of it at the price

[1] May I here be allowed to anticipate the subject-matter of Chapter XXII?

of cutting ourselves off at the same time from the clear witness of the New Testament. Thus this has been the meaning of the theological movement of recent years; in this respect there seems very little to choose between the various well-known theological "tendencies" within the Church. Christianity has preserved a good conscience by the supposition that the "real content" of the scriptural testimony to Christ has not been destroyed by the rejection of these alien elements in the doctrine of the Atonement, but that, on the contrary, it has only "been made still more evident."

From the very outset, however, this argument is very precarious, for it cannot be denied that the witness of the New Testament, as well as of all the classic forms of Christianity—and especially of the testimony of the Reformation—regards these ideas as decisive. Students of Luther, for instance, are not to be envied who still venture to maintain that "actually" this objective doctrine of the Atonement, in the thought of the Reformer, is merely a relic of an outlived world of ideas, which is connected very loosely, and in any case not of necessity, with his central thought of the Faith, and may, therefore, be severed from the true faith of the Reformation as simply an element "due to the limitations of the period." That the onus of proof lies on the defenders of this statement, and not upon those who oppose it, is obvious in face of the actual and indeed unanimous witness of the Christian Church and of the Scriptures.

Although this seems quite evident to those of us who see nothing but self-deception in this minimizing process, it seems to be our duty to prove theologically, on the one hand, the indissoluble connection between this "alien" doctrine of the Atonement and the fundamental thought of the message of the Bible, and, on the other hand, to show the indissoluble connection between these modern endeavours to minimize the significance of this doctrine and the general system of modern thought, or "religion in general." Both these subsidiary aims will, however be attained naturally in the course of our progress towards one main purpose, that is, from our systematic reflection on the meaning of the message of the Bible.

(ii)

The doctrine of the Church—for reasons into which we cannot enter here—since Anselm's[1] profound and masterly example of the ideas which the New Testament provided for the explanation of the meaning of the Atonement, has emphasized almost exclusively the ideas of satisfaction and penalty. This one-sidedness is to be deplored. For the other ideas also represent glimpses into the meaning of the fact of the Atonement which are of great value. But the elaboration of the idea of penal expiation itself by Anselm was an act of outstanding importance, and it is no accident that the Reformers—and Calvin in particular—also followed the great Canterbury theologian along this line. Indeed, in a certain sense, that one-sidedness was not altogether blameworthy, for it led to this result: it emphasized in an unmistakable way that idea which certainly *ought* to stand in the very centre of the message of the Bible—the question of guilt, and of deliverance from it.

The idea of "penalty" corresponds to that of "guilt." If we want to understand the idea of penalty we must begin with the nature of guilt, to which penalty is a correlative idea. Both conceptions, however, are rooted in the knowledge of the Divine Law. The Law as an objective basis for thought is the point at which both the rational and the Christian knowledge of God meet. The Law is the backbone, the skeleton, the granite foundation of the world of thought. The perception of reliable order and of the rule of law, above all the perception of a moral law, constitutes the heart of all our natural knowledge of God. In the Moral Law the rule of world-law in general reaches its apex. For in it there is disclosed not

[1] The expression "punishment" is here used in the wider meaning which also includes "satisfaction" in the Germanic-mediaeval sense. For naturally punishment and repentance ought not to be contrasted with each other—as sometimes happens in discussions on the Anselmic doctrine—since indeed repentance is a legal sanction, a kind of punishment. That even Anselm should not be understood too rigidly (as if, indeed, he were concerned with this precise form of the sanction) is shown by the fact that outside his *Cur Deus homo* he utilizes the idea of punishment quite naturally. Cf. on this point the article on *Versöhnung* in *P.R.E*[3], 20, 562.

merely the law-abiding character of the form of the world, but the personal will which shapes the world. In the Law, in its inviolability, its absolute reliability, its unconditional logic, its absolute identity which endures throughout all changes in events, we are impressed primarily and chiefly by the eternity and the absoluteness of God. The Law means that the world is ruled by the purposive Will which co-ordinates all things, and is equable and self-consistent. The Moral Law in particular shows us that this Will is personally directed towards us, and, through its challenging "thou shalt!" awakens us to personal existence.

However, this is only true of the Moral Law when it has already been contemplated in the light of another law, the revealed law, without any limitation. For it is the limitation of the rational knowledge of law that it can never become fully personal. It is precisely the idea of accordance with law which sets limits to the knowledge of the personal God. The Categorical Imperative is not quite personal, because it is not a real Imperative, because it oscillates between a timeless idea—according to the analogy and with the characters of the logical Idea—and the will, which can no longer be conceived in the mind, but can only be heard in a real, personal summons: in the commandment of the God who reveals Himself. The Law is only understood in its superiority to the world where it is not itself the final court of appeal, but where it is regarded as the expression of the will of the Lawgiver, of the personal God. As such, however, it can be known neither in the world outside, nor in the spirit within—since there it never confronts us as an independent personal entity— but simply as a command.

Therefore the Moral Law of the Bible is different from the ordinary human moral law,[1] and in it alone the true meaning of the Law is fulfilled. The Law of the Bible is nothing in

[1] One must have very little judgment—even in the purely historic-aesthetic sense—if one can reduce the call to repentance of the prophets of the Old Testament and the moralism of an Epictetus or a Cicero to a common denominator like "moral religion" or "ethical Theism." For in the case of the former we can always hear the cry: "Glory to God in the Highest!" whereas in the latter instance ultimately we are concerned with man, his culture, personality, and reason. The Law never becomes a command.

itself; it is what it is as an expression of the Divine Will of the Lord, of the will of Him who is the Creator of the world. Therefore from the very outset it is concrete—not abstract, like the Kantian Moral Law—and personal. It cannot be confused with a timeless Idea. Therefore it does not need to be put later in relation to existence—the existence of the world and my own existence. For He who speaks to me in the Law is the Creator of the world, and He is my Creator; He who speaks thus to me speaks to me personally, as I am here and now. Hence from the very outset my relation to Him cannot be merely ideal, something which could be confused with a mere idea, but it is an existential relation. "The Law" cannot be my Lord, I cannot be its property; but God is indeed my Lord, and I am His property. It is only in this thought that we take the Law quite seriously; previously, apart from this personal aspect, the Law still suggests something unreal, the feeling that we are playing with an idea, the spirit of a spectator. The urgency of the demand of the actual moment is still absent from this conception of Law.

(iii)

God, the sovereign Lord, the One whose will is identical with Himself, and who can therefore be known as identical with His Will, who is the enemy of all caprice, whose Will can be relied on absolutely; this Lord, Yaweh, the "I AM THAT I AM" —this is the holy God of the Bible. Holy because the world and I are unconditionally His property, and upon whose claim to authority over me, upon whose "earnest will" (Luther) we can and must absolutely rely. This divine self-authentication of His unconditional right to own us, and of His Will, which of itself absolutely excludes every sort of sharing with anyone else, all halving of rights, all bargaining, all modification of demand, this divine self-affirmation is that which the Bible calls the Holiness of God. To this, therefore, belong the "zeal" of God as the exclusiveness of the sole divinity of God, and the "honour" of God, which means that this exclusiveness forms part of the being of God as the Holy, the Lord.

It is on account of His Holiness that God says: "My glory will I not give to another." For to "give His glory to another" would mean cleaving His Will in two. It is of the very nature of the holy God that He should be supreme, that His sovereignty should be absolute and unquestioned.

The Law is the manifested Will of the Lord God: eternally the same, self-consistent, unchangeable. The truth that this Will of God is a free, personal will is not more important than the other truth, that it is God's unchangeable, inviolable Will. Both together constitute the conception of the Divine Holiness, of the authority of the Will of God, absolutely law-abiding, and yet absolutely self-sufficient, to whom the world belongs unconditionally as His own property. This holy will of Law is the aspect of the Divine Majesty which is turned towards us. Therefore the Law belongs to the revelation and to the revealed God; but it belongs to the revelation of His Majesty, of that aspect of His Being which separates Him from us, in which He alone is God; the self-existence of God, the manifestation of His glory, of His own Name, that is, of that which is to be ascribed to Him alone, but really should be ascribed to Him before all else, is expressed in it. "Hallowed be Thy Name." All order, all significance, all beauty, all trustworthiness, all constancy, all fidelity and all faith, all truth and all good, are based both upon the Law, which constitutes the intrinsic content of His Will, and upon this unconditional self-manifestation in which the Law is rooted. "God cannot repeal His Law," says Luther. God cannot cease for one second to will to maintain His purpose unconditionally; if He were to cease to will for one instant the universe would collapse, unimaginable chaos would reign. The world is based upon the fact that this Will, this holy, personal Will cannot be altered. The glory of God is the unconditioned, supreme end, the highest purpose there can possibly be, because it underlies all purpose of every kind. It is the most objective purpose there is, because upon it are based all objectivity, all norms, and all validity. It is utterly foolish to try to connect it with any kind of subjectivity at all, or with any anthropopathic primitive thought, which is unworthy of God. The glory of God is the basis of the rule of law as a whole.

(iv)

Sin, however, is an infringement of this glory. The Law of God is the appropriation of human life by God. Through the Law, man is definitely described as the "serf" of God, as God's property. Through the Law the relation of man to the world and to his fellow men is indirect, refracted, "triangular" in kind. The line of connection always passes from man, through God, to man and to the world. The visible aspect of the Law, it is true, of the behaviour demanded by the Law, is right behaviour in the world and in relation to our fellow men. But the most important point is this: obedience to whatever the Will of God may command. It is always true that one thing is needful, the unconditional validity, the unassailable, inviolate Will of God, the Will which decides that God alone shall be supreme, that is, the glory of God.

Sin is the reaction against this normal tendency of life, the order for which we were created. Sin means making man supreme; it is self-will, thus it is rebellion against the divine order, the negation of the God-principle (namely, the sole authority and existence of God), thus it is the infringement of the Divine Holiness and Glory. Tested by this conception of sin it soon becomes clear whether the Idea of God is really personal or not. It is never personal where God is merely an object of thought, where knowledge of God is based upon knowledge of the world and philosophical reflection. Hence the conception of "sin" is not a philosophical, but a religious idea. The philosophical idea is called "evil." But evil is never so bad as sin. For it is not rebellion, it does not mean the severance of our relation with our origin, but it simply means opposition to the norm or to the Idea. Evil as severance presupposes the life-unity with the Creator, given by creative grace. Evil as sin means breaking away, the Fall, rebellion, lying, and ingratitude; it means the denial of the original truth, that is, disorder; it is like the son who strikes his father's face in anger, or—since this is daemonic evil and not human sin—it is the bold self-assertion of the son's will above that of the father.

Sin alters the attitude of man to God, and in so doing it alters the nature of man. Into this we cannot enter further here. But human nature is not altered only in the sense of natural law—as an ability to do good; this attitude is altered in the specifically ethical sense—in the sense that we cannot find our way back. It is only in this definition of sin that the full seriousness of the moral demand is expressed.

The change introduced by sin, however, does not only affect man, it also affects God. The fact that sin has happened is not forgotten and ignored, as though man could always keep going back to the beginning. Rather it is retained. It is taken into the reckoning; it is guilt. Only thus is the life of man conceived as a unity: your past still belongs to you, you can never shake it off, it comes between you and the new moment; you are no longer a blank page, you have your own history, and this history is identified with you as your present, your past sin is still put down to your account.

The idea of guilt expresses not only the solidarity of humanity, the totality of life, but also, and above all, the inviolable Holiness of God. God is not mocked; "whatsoever a man soweth that shall he reap." God does not forget. The constancy, the self-consistency of God, which is primarily one of the comforting and glorious things about Him, is a terrible thing in this connection. God does not forget; the injury to the divine order does not heal; this wound remains open eternally, though not in your memory—there it heals only too easily— but in the remembrance of God. All the expressions which are used in the Bible about "writing down," "entering in a book," etc., are meant to express this. It is just because the connection between God and man is so personal that guilt exists, working not merely causally (as Original Sin, *fomes*), but as the past which affects the present, and is reckoned as guilt (*reatus*). Just as previously it was comforting to know that we could reckon on God, so now it strikes terror to the heart of man to know that we *must* reckon with Him.

(v)

What, however, can we expect from God? What else indeed than the consequence which issues, absolutely logically, in accordance with the unconditional character and seriousness of His claim? If the Law lays down the conditions on which fellowship with God, and thus salvation, can be attained, then disobedience must express the opposite, and instead of salvation we can only expect ruin. Just because it is not an abstract law with which we have to do, but the concrete and personal Will of God, who from the very outset takes possession of the whole of existence, and determines the condition of existence as a whole, life and its state of happiness as the law of existence, so also disobedience to the Law must have life-significance, or, to put it more accurately, its significance points to death and ruin.

Divine punishment also issues, necessarily, from the Holiness of God; not, indeed, as a penalty which is deliberately intended for us, but simply and solely as the fulfilment of the Will of God. It is not an educative, paternal punishment, but the punishment meted out by a master, the punishment of a sovereign inflicted on a rebellious subject. God becomes the royal Judge, who utters the condemnation of the prisoner at the bar. Apart from ideas of this kind the Holiness of God means little or nothing to us. This idea belongs, therefore, to the fundamental elements in the Biblical message of the Old and the New Testaments.

This idea is intolerable to the modern mind, which has been spoilt by the sentimentality of the Enlightenment and the Romantic movement. In every part of the Bible, in the classic Christian message as a whole, the possibility is taken into account that God could annihilate His creature if He chose, that the holy God will punish disobedient humanity with final and absolute ruin. It is this idea which clearly differentiates the view of Law in the Bible from the humanistic view of law; the latter is so abstract that it disregards this life-and-death significance of the Law, and is only concerned with "the Good in itself." It lacks the relation to the Creator and Lord of the world and of life, and therefore the full existential character of the Law. Because the Law in the Bible is wholly existential—just as the Will of God is wholly directed towards reality—heaven and hell, blessedness and misery, cannot be severed from the idea of obedience and disobedience. But this does not mean—as the school of the Enlightenment and even Kant used to insinuate—that in so doing morality has been corrupted by Eudaemonism. This error is avoided by the fact that the ethical as a whole is related to the glory of God. This alone secures us against Eudaemonism.

(vi)

All the conceptions which have been hitherto employed: law, lord, sovereign, serfdom, property, guilt, penalty, judgment, are taken from the sphere of law. Hence they have always roused the ire of those who regard the Law as something to be depreciated,[1] and especially in the nineteenth century. All the terms in which we refer to God and the eternal are taken from some definite sphere of our own life. It is merely thoughtless to compare these "forensic" terms with "ethical" terms, to the disadvantage of the former: Rather, an analysis of the "ethical" vocabulary would lead us to the conclusion that the "forensic" terms form the original stock of every serious ethic. Alongside of them there are merely those which are drawn from the natural life—biological terms—and between them both, and also not insignificant in their ethical application, are the terms drawn from the spheres of economic

---

[1] It is strange how the rejection of "juridical" expressions to describe the religious relationship—as has been usual in theology since the time of Ritschl—overlooks the fact that the Bible is full of such juridical expressions, and indeed of such a kind that we could not imagine a Bible without them at all: guilt, remission of guilt, judgment, judge, punishment, accusation, condemnation, pardon, release, above all the two fundamental ones: the Law and the royal sovereignty of God. Evidently it has been forgotten that even Father, Kingdom, love, fellowship, have first of all a natural sense, and thus are used parabolically. Thus the question is not whether we wish to use ethical or juridical expressions, but which of the natural parables it is best to use to describe the relation of man to God.

and social life (for instance, to render an account—father—guilt).

The forensic expressions predominate because in them the Law denotes not merely an idea, a purely logical, ideal principle of order, but an ideal vital force. The *tertium comparationis* between the forensic and the religious sphere is the Law as the authority which controls reality. Hence in the language of the Bible in particular the forensic expressions play an especially large part, in the New Testament as well as in the Old Testament, in the Synoptic teaching of Jesus as well as in the writings of Paul and John. Indeed, is it not a fact that the central conception of the message of the New Testament, that of the Kingdom of God, is a parable drawn from the law of the State, since it really means the royal dominion of God?

Just as it is impossible from the purely empirical point of view to eliminate these terms from the thought of the Bible, so also our inquiry has shown us that the leading ideas of Christianity, those of law, holiness, and guilt, cannot be expressed without them, simply because wherever we are concerned with the subject of the Holiness of God we are dealing with this *tertium*: the authority of the Divine Will and the divine order, or of the Law over reality; the fact that God is the *Lord*. Hence it is no sign of great fidelity to the Scriptures nor of a deep understanding of Christian truth to think that we can attack any dogmatic formulae simply by using the word "forensic" as a term of reproach.[1]

---

[1] Ritschl—whom we quote once again as the most outstanding theological representative of this type of thought—begins by saying that the conception of the divine righteousness, in so far as it is supposed to mean something other than the "consistency" of God in the carrying out of His purpose of Love, is not a religious conception, but that it is a blend of the ethico-religious and the legal habit of thought. In a special way this is true, he says, of the idea of punishment and of a righteousness which punishes. Therefore it should have no place in Christian thought. How this is to be brought into harmony with the thought of the Bible is another question. But it is clear that this elimination only succeeds if a further assumption is taken into account: that God feels nothing but love even towards those who resist Him. It is an error to say that He punishes (*R. u. V.*[4], pp. 233–50). This idea leads to the conclusion that Ritschl himself draws (although not perhaps as clearly as we might wish): the sense of guilt is also an error, in so far as it is more than the subjective consciousness of discomfort of the man who

In reality, this opposition to the use of "forensic" terms is due to an entirely different reason; it is due to the fact that the idea of the Divine Holiness has been swallowed up in that of the Divine Love; this means that the Biblical Idea of God, in which the decisive element is this two-fold nature of holiness and love, is being replaced by the modern, unilateral, monistic Idea of God. That this is the real cause of this opposition, and not fear of forensic terminology, comes out most plainly in the fact that the juridical idea of penalty is not the only one which is attacked, but that there is just as much opposition to the non-juridical idea of the wrath of God,

feels his remoteness from God. Indeed, even this discomfort as such is not ethical, since it is connected with distrust of God, which makes man worse (*R. u. V.*, p. 62). These astonishing—but logical—statements are based on the argument that reward and punishment are ethically doubtful ideas (whereas really all that is doubtful is behaviour which is motivated by the ideas of reward and punishment) and that righteousness, in this sense, ought not to be predicated of God, because otherwise God would be bound by this as by a natural necessity (p. 236). As if the same could not be said, too, about the "Purposive Will" which Ritschl calls the Love of God! As if it were not the case that this consistency—which Ritschl stresses as its characteristic—expresses this constancy upon which man can depend! All this revulsion against law, righteousness, and punishment is based simply on the non-recognition of the Divine Holiness: that God asserts Himself and His Will, unconditionally, against all resistance. The relation of human and divine penal law is therefore the very opposite of that which these modern theologians recognize: the juridical idea of penalty is rooted in the idea of the divine penal justice and is only a pale reflection of it. If faith in the divine penal justice falls away (that is, the belief that God's Will is powerful, and that He intends to carry through what He wills even against resistance) then there remains certainly only the idea of purpose on the one hand, and the instinct of revenge on the other. The moral idea of righteousness has been destroyed. Rightly, therefore, Dorner, in his excellent criticism of the Ritschlian doctrine of Atonement (*Christliche Glaubenslehre*, II, p. 595), calls these arguments a "form of ethical Docetism," since, most improperly, they make a forcible separation between the natural and the moral aspects of the question. This is the Rationalism of modern theology, which is based upon the contrast between nature and spirit, whereas the faith of the Bible denies this contrast and places it at another point, which accentuates it far more sharply. That God possesses and exercises penal justice is a central idea in the faith of the Bible, in which there is expressed the fact that God is not only Idea but an active power, and indeed that His Will is a force which makes itself felt against resistance.

which is also removed from the Christian vocabulary. Opposition to this idea, therefore, is not directed against the formulae in which it is expressed, but against the very substance of the idea itself, namely, against all that the Bible means by the Holiness of God. To the modern mind the idea that God can be angry is as intolerable as the idea that He exercises punishment and judgment. Both these expressions, however, are intolerable because the modern man, through the influence of the thought of the Enlightenment, is so accustomed to think that God's function is to stand surety for human purposes. It is the genuinely theocentric Idea of God that men find intolerable. Actually, their resistance is directed against the Will and the Majesty of God.

A further reason is the naturalistic modification of ethical thought, which comes out very clearly in our modern theories of penal administration. Punishment is regarded as a relic of the primitive instinct of revenge. Thus such an idea may not be ascribed to God; at the utmost the only idea we can connect with God is that of educative punishment, in the service of love or of life. The harsh thought of the Bible—and of the New Testament!—that God, because He is God, can punish man, and, indeed, must destroy all that infringes His sovereignty, is an impossible idea for the modern mind. Because the thought of the Holiness of God, and the gravity of the idea of law, is no longer understood, men seek for such biological-psychological explanations. Superficiality makes its own God—a God who is of the kind it likes. So long as we continue to reject the scriptural ideas of Divine Holiness, of divine wrath, and of divine righteousness in punishment, the process of decay within the Christian Church will continue.

(vii)

Before the Enlightenment—this means before the Socinians—there was no serious discussion on these fundamental questions within the Christian Church. That God is the holy and just Judge, whose punishment is to be feared, was a general view of faith because it was unmistakably a main feature in the message proclaimed in the Bible. It is only possible to understand both the ecclesiastical and the Biblical doctrine of the Atonement on the basis of this presupposition. The problem is not whether there is a divine tribunal or not, but whether the necessity for punishment, the fact of being subject to this tribunal, to the divine necessity of destruction, is the general human situation.

When the idea of guilt is taken seriously this step has been taken. We are all guilty; and to be guilty means to fall under the divine condemnation, and to fall under it to such an extent that every attempt at human flight is impossible. If evil is once conceived as sin against God, and hence as determining man as a whole, then there can be no question of any idea of self-redemption, in any form whatever. Moreover, if sin is regarded as guilt, then the unfavourable verdict lies beyond human reach; it comes with the necessity of Fate; for "guilt" means that the fact cannot be altered. Guilt is an inescapable necessity of punishment. This is the situation, this is the real obscure *Nostra, sub specie aeternitatis.*

Hence the *Nostra assumsit* means that the Son comes under this condemnation. Does He wish to meet us? then *here* are we, and here alone. The divine revelation is determined by objective conditions, and, indeed, by conditions in which God and man are equally involved (see above, p. 445). The sphere of revelation is the reality, but this reality is one which is alien to the Divine Will. It is the intervening reality of human sin and divine wrath, and of the divine necessity of punishment. A revelation which did not take place at this point would be no real revelation at all. A divine truth whose light did not really break through the darkness of this atmosphere would not be a real light which could penetrate the darkness to reach us. When this light breaks in upon us we know both the reality of the atmosphere of sin and the reality of the coming of the light, and we know both at the same time. But the refraction of this light means the punishment of sin, the assertion of the Divine Holiness over against human guilt. At the same moment that we perceive the Divine Will to forgive we perceive also the Holiness of God, and thus the Divine Will to punish. And only where this fact, the Cross of Christ, is understood to mean the working out of this condemnation, do we see in it the revelation of the living, holy, and merciful God.

Nothing is easier than to caricature the statements of the Bible and of Christianity about the penal sufferings of Christ in such a way that behind these "theories" we seem to perceive the figure of some bloodthirsty Oriental monarch, or of some primitive Eastern divinity, with his whims and caprices. But in reality the absolute sovereignty of God is the presupposition of this revelation, and, wherever the idea of a "democratic God" is entertained, there will be no intelligent understanding of the meaning of the Cross. But the Sovereignty of God means the Holiness of God, the fact that God *is* God. The Cross is the only place where the loving, forgiving, merciful God is revealed in such a way that we perceive that His Holiness and His Love are equally infinite.

Here the Cross is not conceived as an idea; for everything here depends upon the actual coming of God. Man can indeed imagine an idea, by his own efforts, in spite of his sin and guilt; if ideas can help him he is not in such bad case. Forgiveness would then be a matter of course. For an idea always seems natural to him who has once found it. When an idea is discovered we know it was always there, that it was possible *semper et ubique*. An idea, therefore, only shows us something that "is," never something that is "becoming."

Here, however, the point at issue is this: that something which actually "is" actually *becomes* another kind of reality. Man is guilty in the sight of God, and God *is* holy. Here, therefore, there is no other solution on the basis of the "*is*" than Judgment. A real solution, real redemption out of this situation, cannot take place by saying that the situation is not as dark as it is painted, but only by a real alteration in the situation itself,[1] by means of a divine transaction. Hence

[1] The usual polemic against the ecclesiastical doctrine of the Atonement is an attack on a self-created opponent. Incapable of understanding this central thought of objective Atonement, there is substituted for it the idea of a change effected in the mind of God, an idea which seems easier, and arises out of primitive religious conceptions, thus of an Atonement whose object is God. Neither Paul, nor the Epistle to the Hebrews, nor any of the great Christian theologians nor any of the classic Christian creeds has ever represented this absurd idea of a change in God

this is the test by which we can find out whether a man's view of guilt is serious or not: it comes out in the way in which he regards revelation. Is it actually something which has really happened? is it the creation of a new situation or not? If the Cross merely denotes the removal of a religious error (namely, that God is not an angry Judge) then guilt is not taken seriously. If guilt is taken seriously, then there is no help save in a real happening, which really "cleanses" us from actual guilt.

(viii)

The New Testament is not afraid of pressing this general conception of guilt—this economic-legal image—still further. A debt must be paid. Man cannot pay. Guilt costs. Man cannot pay the price. The cost shows the real necessity for the transaction, shows that it cannot be taken for granted. And the character of this necessary event is determined by the character of our situation, by the actual penalty to which we have been condemned. A debt must be "paid," which lies utterly outside all human possibilities. The conception of the "cost" and the "price" denotes the objective condition for the revelation of grace, an objectivity which is alien to God, and yet is none the less retained by Him: the reality of wrath, the necessity for punishment. This must take place, the movement which leads to man must pass through this point. But this "necessity" forms part of the Divine Holiness.

through the Atonement; for the witness of the New Testament is quite clear that it is God who, through His Love, creates the Atonement. It is obvious that even in the thought of Anselm there can be no question of such a view. In spite of this, however, again and again we read —as for instance in the article in *P.R.E.*, which has already been quoted— that the "progress" of more recent theology since Schleiermacher consists in the fact that this idea of a change in God Himself through the Atonement has been overcome (p. 573). Thus only these two alternatives are recognized: either the pagan doctrine of the changing of the mind of God by the Atonement, or a subjectivistic conception of Atonement—whereas the whole classical Christian doctrine denies this very alternative, since it recognizes both the wrath of God and the Divine Love which blots this out. It is the same paradox and mystery as the doctrine of the Trinity.

Thus this "necessity" does not proceed from the side of man.[1] We cannot say "the Cross 'had to' happen!" But the Cross is the only possible way in which the absolute holiness and the absolute mercy of God are revealed together. God cannot make this process any "cheaper." It really "costs" so much because of human guilt and Divine Holiness. The mystical path would be "cheaper," for in it guilt is merely error, and God is nothing but love; there is no need for forgiveness; everything is all right, all you need is to know it. But this would only be true on the assumption that the idea of guilt is an error. The way of the Enlightenment also would be cheaper: God forgives everyone who repents. This view is based on the assumption that such people exist, and also, that neither guilt nor the Will of God to punish are real. Even the prophetic revelation of the Divine Will to forgive, regarded as it is in itself, that is, apart from its eschatological meaning, would be "cheaper," to the extent that here the Word is not personal, but is only expressed in language. There it is only the spoken word which confronts the resistance of man. But here, in Christ, the Person is Himself the Word, therefore He Himself must enter into rebellious humanity and become its victim, in order that He may thus complete His "coming," and pay the "cost." That even to God it "costs something" to reveal Himself, means that even for Him guilt is real, something which cannot

---

[1] The Fathers discussed the character of this "necessity" at great length. It is well known that in Anselm this necessity is deduced as something absolute, which springs out of the nature of God, with reference to His Glory. This is the non-scriptural element in his doctrine, that the Atonement can be thus deduced. (Still, it is based solely upon the divinely revealed idea of God!) But on the other hand the idea that God simply chose to act thus is likewise less than the thought of the Bible, since this makes the whole institution of redemption an incomprehensible arbitrary act of God, whose meaning cannot be perceived at all. Hence, we may conclude that the idea of the relative necessity which Calvin formulates (following earlier thinkers) (*Institutio*, II, 12, 1) is the right one; that is, from the point of view of the Christian knowledge of sin we cannot imagine any other possibility of Atonement than that which has actually taken place in Christ. We acknowledge this as the only possible one; but we cannot allow ourselves to express any opinion on the point whether God might not have had another. For such a speculation would be as useless as it is arrogant.

be ignored, not something which can be dismissed with a wave of the hand, that even He knows that He is bound by His own Law, although as "Lord" He stands above it free and supreme. God will not reveal Himself otherwise than in this way, that although He is free from the Law He is, at the same time, bound to His own Law,[1] as the One who, in the act of most sovereign transcending of the Law—in forgiveness—at the same time intensifies the validity of His Law as absolute.

Hence the Cross, conceived as the expiatory penal sacrifice of the Son of God, is the fulfilment of the scriptural revelation of God, in its most paradoxical incomprehensible guise. It is precisely in His revelation that the God of the Bible is incomprehensible, because in His nearness He reveals His distance, in His mercy His holiness, in His grace His judgment, in His personality His absoluteness; because in His revelation His glory and the salvation of man, His own will and His love for men, His majesty and His "homeliness" cannot be separated from one another. It is thus that He is God, the One who comes, the One who comes to us in reality: who comes in the likeness of sinful flesh, the One who Himself pays the price, Himself bears the penalty, Himself overcomes all that separates us from Him—*really* overcomes it, does not merely declare that it does not exist. This real event is His real coming, and therefore it is both the revelation of that which *we* are and of that which *He* is.

His "coming" means the unveiling of that which He is in Himself, "in His inmost heart." In the world neither the guilt

---

[1] The most difficult point in the doctrine of Paul and of Luther, and the one which is least understood, is this: that on the one hand God recognizes the Law as His, and thus never suspends it at all, and yet stands there as the One who freely grants forgiveness, as the One who is above the Law. The Law expresses the immutability and consistency of God, for the will of God is *immutabilis* (*W.A.*, 18, 615). In forgiveness, however, the same God shows Himself as the Lord who controls His own Law. "For if His Will had rule or measure, ground, or cause, then already it would no longer be the Will of God. For what He wills is not right because He should so will it or ought to will it, but on the contrary because He wills, therefore what happens must be right" (*W.A.*, 18, 712). Beyond the Law He has *noch eyn ander wort* ("yet another Word") which He has given as His real Will (*W.A.*, 36, 17). In spite of this, it is true that "He cannot repeal His Law." Both these are united in the Cross of Christ, and there *alone*.

473

nor the love of God can be rightly known. For the world, as it now is, is an interim reality, *mundus alienatus*, κόσμος δυσκόσμητος. Because we are *alienati* this is precisely why we do not know our guilt and do not know God. There may, indeed, be a knowledge of guilt outside Christianity, outside the revelation of Christ, but nowhere else does it attain this ultimate poignancy and gravity. For all other forms of religion—not to mention philosophy—deal with the problem of guilt apart from the intervention of God, and therefore they come to a "cheap" conclusion. In them man is spared the final humiliation of knowing that the Mediator must bear the punishment instead of him. To this yoke he need not submit. He is not stripped absolutely naked.

But neither does he know the Divine Love. Of course, everywhere there is a certain knowledge of the love of God. But how can it really be serious if God has not to overcome any real obstacle which stands in the way between Him and man?—if God does not really descend and run after man? That the Good Shepherd lays down His life for the sheep—this is the Divine Love. The self-movement of God is not only His revelation but His grace. The one fulfils itself when the other is fulfilled: in complete lowliness, in complete inadequacy, in the form of a servant, of the suffering Servant of the Lord, with His penal suffering. That this truth was perceived in the Old Testament and nowhere else shows that here alone is the new promise that points to Christ. But since there it is only foreshadowed, while only in the New Testament does it really take place: therefore the Old Testament is merely the *promise* which points to Christ. This is why the New Testament stands under the sign given it in regard to this event by Jesus Himself: that of the *New* Covenant.

CHAPTER XIX

THE EXPIATORY SACRIFICE

(i)

God, the Holy One, as the Lawgiver is the exact opposite of all disorder and caprice, and in existence as a whole His Law is the element which ensures reliability and objective validity, it is the element of positive rigour. Where this aspect is stressed exclusively in the interpretation of the Atonement, then the doctrine itself—as in the case of Anselm—tends to become one-sided and crudely objective. In the New Testament this one-sidedness is not visible. Alongside of the "forensic" comparisons or parables there is another line of thought which runs through the testimony of the Primitive Church, and this is the ritual idea. To the mind of our own day this comparison seems, if possible, still more alien than the previous one[1]; but it is just as important to understand this idea as it is to see the significance of the idea of penalty. For the idea of an expiatory sacrifice expresses the purely personal element—as contrasted with the objective and forensic aspect—far more clearly.

The Law of God sends man out into the world as the place where he has to prove his obedience to God. The Law therefore is the "rational" side of the divine revelation. Hence it is quite possible that man may pay so much attention to law that

[1] The contrast between "ethical" and "ritual" religion, which plays so large a part in modern theology, is a false antithesis. It corresponds to the ethical Rationalism of a religion of the type of the Enlightenment, but it is out of harmony with the thought of the Bible; it does not even harmonize with the thought of the prophets. The modern view of the prophets suffers from a false identification of rational "ethical Theism" with the prophetic message, to which goes back also the view that the prophets were hostile to the cultus as such. It was in harmony with the historical situation in which the prophets appeared that with great energy and one-sidedness they should emphasize the relative contrast between the ethical and ritual aspects of religion. But it is not true to historical reality to ascribe to them the idea that the cultus as such is not commanded by God.

475

God is forgotten. Non-religious humanism, or aesthetic ethics, is a case in point; all religion of the type of the Enlightenment which tends to identify the divine with the ethical—even if it does not go so far as to say the civic—illustrates the same tendency. The ethical element in particular, the consciousness of the Moral Law, tends to sever its connection with God, its foundation and its origin. This is why it is perpetually in conflict, historically, with the religious element, or, to put it more exactly, with the ritual element. The ritual side of religion is the reminder that our life is destined for the worship of God; the real meaning of all moral conduct should thus be simply to honour God, "to walk before God." Although moralism, or the ethical emphasis, may have a right to make its protest as a reaction against "ceremonial religion," yet, on the other hand, ritual religion has an equal right to protest against moralism, where in the end God simply disappears from sight behind social ethics and philanthropy, and is thus swallowed up in good citizenship. When we speak of the "East" and the "West," we mean this absolute antithesis, even within Christianity: as, for instance, the contrast between the Christian "Americanism" of the West, and the Orthodox Church of the East, with its elaborate liturgy.

The great commandment is two-fold; without being distorted it cannot be reduced to a single formula: it demands love to God and love to man, the service of God and the service of man. Even the actual form of worship has its own justification. For we are told both to pray and to work. The cultus is the service which is directed to God, as service to Him, the fulfilment of the "First Table" of the Commandments. Hence for the sake of the truth it contains the cultus is also capable of serving as a parable of the Highest Truth of all. The idea of morality is that I belong, through God, to my fellow man. The idea of the cultus is that I belong solely to God Himself. Hence, since the thought of the divine right over man has a quite personal meaning, because it designates a relation between God and man, which is not broken by a third element, the world, the centre of the cultus is sacrifice. Sacrifice means direct surrender to God without any thought of social usefulness. The sacrificial animal is killed and burnt for the god;

476

the wine of the sacrifice is poured out for him. All life belongs to God and is to be consecrated to Him, directly, to Him personally, to Himself.

The most important sacrifice is that which is intended to remove some obstacle which has come in between God and man: the atoning or expiatory sacrifice. In all forms of religion in which sacrifice is practised there is some sense of the vitality and personality of the god, or of the gods. Man is conscious that he is here dealing not with impersonal world laws but with active powers. He is conscious that "God" not only has rights over him, but above all that He has the power to destroy him. The existential danger of a broken relation between God and man is the presupposition of the expiatory sacrifice. It is felt that something must "happen" if harm is not to come upon man, a disaster which comes from God Himself. For the fact that the relation has been broken means that God is angry.

All these ideas—however primitive they may be—are not further from the truth on the one side than moral rationalism, for instance, on the other. Just as even the secularized moral law still points towards ultimate divine truth, so also the most debased cultus points to a truth, and indeed to a truth which has been completely lost by the representatives of the opposite point of view. It is the truth which consists in the remembrance of the free personality and freedom of God, which cannot be conceived in any terms of rational-cosmic law, of man as the personal property of God, of the necessity for the fullest personal, direct surrender, of the wrath of God as the reaction of the living God to the sin of man, of the necessity for a special sacrificial act, of a means of expiation, of a priestly mediation, that is, one specially directed towards God.

(ii)

Man is the personal property of God. God desires from him not merely a legally correct life, but personal surrender, even as He Himself, the Creator, grants to His creature not merely a happy life, salvation, but personal communion with Him, the Creator. Just because of this, because this original relationship is so personal, its destruction on both sides is also personal.

477

On the side of man, from which this "break" proceeds, it means *sin*. We have already seen that sin is quite different from evil, just because it has this personal character, because it is the self-willed destruction of the personal original divine relationship. "Against Thee, Thee only have I sinned." To one who speaks thus, there can never be any idea that this injury can be repaired by "doing better next time." It is an injury which no ethical means can ever heal.

For this injury is no mere "damage to property," it is an injury done to the Divine Person Himself. Therefore, in accordance with this personal sin is the personal reaction of God: that is, the wrath of God. Wherever these two points are regarded as equally serious, the living, personal character of God and sin, there men speak of the "Wrath of God." The God who is really angry, really loves. To reject the idea of the wrath of God also means to reject His Love. Then all that is left, both negatively and positively, is the abstract idea of law. The idea that God is angry is no more anthropopathic than the thought that God loves. The reason why the idea of the divine anger is always exposed to misunderstanding is because among men anger is ethically wrong. And yet, even among men do we not speak of a "righteous anger"? And does not the flame of righteous anger show that love also is truly personal? To banish all emotions from the sphere of the Divine Good is not the work of Christian thought but of "Greek-modern," that is, rational thought.

God is angry because He is personal, because He really loves. The Bible speaks so naturally about the divine wrath, even in the New Testament, because it is so full of the thought of the personal love of God, which is something quite different from the "rational moral purposive will." Once again, this is not a relic of primitive thought; this is evident from the fact that both Luther and Calvin felt the wrath of God intensely, as a present fact, and made others feel it too. They had this experience because they had received so richly the knowledge of the personal merciful God. But the idea of the wrath of God has become so alien to the thought of our own time, because in general the idea of the personality of God has become alien through Rationalism, because so often the conception of the law of the universe has been set in the place of the living God.

God is angry. What does that mean to the man who knows this? That a disaster is hanging over him which he cannot avert. He knows the cause: his unfaithfulness. But along with this sense of impending disaster goes also the sense of his impotence to avert this disaster by any merely interior or ethical means. The nearest approach to such an attempt would be an inward transformation at the very centre of the disturbance, which is indeed the personal relation, that is, to return to the original personal relationship. Ah! if only this were possible! But the way to this possibility is blocked by a double barrier: inability to achieve this, and also the feeling that it would not be permitted; in other words, sin which cannot be rooted out, and guilt which can never be made good. If ever the way to God is to be reopened and the normal relationship restored, something else will have to take place. This process would be expiation.

In the ancient rites and ideas of expiation something of this vital truth still lives; otherwise it scarcely exists anywhere else—in mysticism least of all. Of course, we are aware of the primitive nature and the inadequacy of all these religious means of expiation. But it is more than doubtful whether the rejection of these ideas in favour of a non-ritual religious ethic brings us any nearer to the truth than the practice of these rites. It is difficult to say which of these two is nearer to the truth: rational moralism, or primitive religion with its propitiatory rites; for both have preserved one element of truth and have lost another. Rational moralism recognizes the insufficiency of all human means of expiation; sacrificial religion recognizes the need for the expiatory sacrifice. Hence the truth resides in that expiatory sacrifice which is not offered by man but by God, and therefore, because it is a divine transaction, has been offered once for all.

(iii)

The conviction of the indissoluble connection between evil and wrong, between death and sin, permeates the whole of the Bible. It is summed up in Paul's phrase: "The wages of sin is death." Whether or no another category may exist, in which death is a natural phenomenon, in any case, human death, as we know it, is something which ought not to be. "For we are consumed by Thine anger, and by Thy wrath are we troubled. Thou hast set our iniquities before Thee, our secret sins in the light of Thy countenance." Precisely because human death is not simply the cessation of the biological functions, or physical dissolution, but is far more terrible than the death of the lower animals, it is the outward and visible sign of some profound inward disharmony. It is so absolutely opposed to all that is God's real will for man that it can only be understood at all if we realize that it represents the perversion of the relationship between man and God. The simple, "normal" fact of death itself does not do justice to the moral claim of the knowledge of God. Which of us has not wasted his life in some way or another? Who among those have been awakened to the knowledge of God would demand the right to live on longer? Would not such an one acknowledge that to be permitted to live on was an amazing fact? It is, of course, true that to people of the present day, who are accustomed to regard God from the point of view of life, instead of life from the point of view of God—that is, who regard God merely as One who subserves the demands of humanity—it is difficult to revitalize this truth. We behave like those tenants in the parable who had forgotten that they had only leased the vineyard, and that it was not their own property. But if it is true that we are only tenants, that is, that we have no rights of our own over the vineyard, but that we only possess a borrowed, limited right over life, how can we evade the conclusion that our lease ran out long ago, that long ago our death fell due?

Only death? Yes, but not merely biological death, which also falls to the lot of the animal, but human death, which is only experienced by those who have been created by God as immortal souls, death whose torment consists in the fact that it never ceases. It is this death which corresponds to the wrath of God, the death which we have never yet seen any man die. This is the death which God wills in His anger. This death, this terrible disaster, hangs over us so long as we are in a state of guilt, and thus are under the wrath of God. It is not the expression of a mood of God, or an emotion, which fades away as the years pass; but it is a divine necessity, a necessity, however, which is not based on any idea of fate, but solely upon the Divine Will. It is because He is the Holy One that He thus *wills* death.

Does He only *appear* to will this death? Is He concealing His real feeling? To think thus would be to play fast and loose with God. God is not mocked; whoever sows to the flesh shall of the flesh reap corruption. Only thus can we learn the lesson. This *is* the situation; it cannot be otherwise unless something takes place which would satisfy the divine anger, that is, something which would do away with the necessity for our death, which would provide an equivalent for our death. It is at this point that religion inserts the idea of sacrifice, with the right feeling that something must happen, something extraordinary, something which resembles human death, as a kind of forfeit for all that makes life precious, for the very substance of life itself. This idea of an *equivalent*,[1] which lies behind the idea of sacrifice, would not have exercised such an immense influence, it would not have been so widespread, dominant, and tenacious all through the course of history were it not for the fact that behind it there lies a deep truth.

Of course there is no human equivalent. Naturally every sacrificial cult, as an attempt to buy oneself off, only offers a "cheap" solution. But the search for an equivalent is not false. For it expresses the idea that only on this presupposition is it possible to live on at all, the feeling that we simply cannot go on any longer "without something." We cannot live without God. But also we cannot live with God so long as our guilt is

---

[1] It is quite possible that the reason why, among all the illustrations at his disposal, Anselm chose that of Satisfaction, was because it holds the balance evenly between the ideas of penalty and of sacrifice, and because it brings out particularly clearly the idea of an equivalent, On the other hand, if, in so doing, he allowed himself to be led astray into the attempt to reckon out this equivalent, we must not overlook the fact that he was concerned with one thing only: with an *infinite* guilt and an *infinite* expiation. The stress he lays on the word "infinite" shows the seriousness of the problem Anselm is handling.

not expiated. We cannot simply become "good friends once more." The wrath of God is not a mood, it is an actual force,[1] and it is a divine legitimate power, an objective necessity. Religion has never been able to find a way out of this dilemma: that every sacrifice is only an apparent equivalent, only an apparent solution of the conflict, and yet that there ought to be some "sacrifice."

God alone can make this sacrifice. He alone can expiate, can "cover" guilt as though it had never been; He alone can stop up the hole, fill up the trench; for there is something infinite about sin. Over and over again it seems to be forgotten that it is God Himself who expiates, who provides the sacrifice; this is the case whenever people condemn the doctrine of the Atonement because it represents the Deity as a "bloodthirsty, revengeful, Jewish God," to whom also Paul is supposed to have rendered homage. "Greater love hath no man than this, that he lay down his life for his friends." It is indeed God Himself who takes everything upon Himself. "He who spared not His own Son, how shall He not freely with Him give us all things?" Thus in the New Testament the Cross of Christ is conceived as the self-offering of God. It is God who does it,

---

[1] That the wrath of God, even for the loving God, is a reality, has sometimes been expressed in a drastic manner by the idea that sinful humanity had been sold to the devil, to which corresponds the mythology of being bought back from the devil, of a fraud practised on the devil, of an outwitting of the devil, etc. It is well known that even Luther was fond of these mythical expressions, because to him the one thing that mattered was the reality of the fact of the Atonement. Those who know how Luther even hypostatizes the Law as the personal enemy of God with whom Christ carries on conversations, will be cautious about ascribing all this simply to "primitive" ideas, or about holding a view which attributes all this merely to the poetic instinct or to the desire to popularize dogma. Rather in the thought of Luther, as in the Bible, the idea of Satan is carried to the utmost limit of Dualism which is possible within the Christian recognition of the Almighty God. In the idea of Satan the objective character of the disturbance of the world-order is expressed in the plainest possible way; but even to the Reformers Satan is never an independent power, but always merely the being which executes the wrath of God. Hence fundamentally this type of doctrine of the Atonement says exactly the same as the classic ecclesiastical doctrine, even though in it, thanks to its personal character, the mythological element can grow rankly and assume pagan forms more easily than in the latter.

it is God Himself who suffers, it is God who takes the burden upon Himself.

(iv)

But this act of expiation is real: God *does* something; He suffers; He takes the burden *really* upon Himself, there is a *real* transaction. Sin must be really "covered." If the broken thread is to be re-knit, the equivalent must be produced. In this sense of necessity the idea of sacrifice and the idea of penalty converge. But this "necessity" does not mean an objective law, but the freely personal Will of God; it is based not on an abstract law of righteousness, but upon the holy Will of God Himself. Because God is holy, something must actually take place in order that the past may be completely obliterated. Because God cannot simply overlook the insult to His honour, cannot behave as though it were nothing, because both for His own sake and for the sake of the right relation between God and man this "cause" must have its "effect," because only that which has an effect can be really known: for the sake of this reality something must really happen which would be an equivalent for the judgment of wrath, for the sacrificial death of man, in order that men may know that this cannot be achieved for nothing. Sin is not "nothing," it is objective, that is, even before God it is an actual burden, indeed even an infinite burden. The wrath of God is not imaginary, it is not a misunderstanding, it is truth. At the same time it is certainly neither the ultimate nor the primary truth. It is that which God is, so to speak, forced to do by man for the sake of His Holiness, it is His "marred, disfigured Face." But true as it is that sin is no illusion—in spite of the fact that its very essence is deceit—so also it is true that this divine reaction against it, wrath, is no illusion, however much it may contradict God's essential nature.[1]

To the reality of the fact of sin—as an actual disturbance of the divine order of life—there corresponds the divine fact of expiation, as the presupposition for the restoration of order.

---

[1] On this point, cf. the note on pp. 518 ff.

The idea of sacrifice, the idea of equivalence, as the central point of the idea of sacrifice, expresses this two-fold character of the reality of the disturbance. The extent of the injury to the world order is known by the greatness of the remedy. But the *reparatio* is intended not merely to express the magnitude, but also the quality of the disturbance. The disharmony is, in its necessary effect, fatal for man because it separates him personally from the source of his life. God, as the One who is separated personally from man, is the angry One; the necessary effect of this separation is the opposite of the effect of personal communion with God, absolute disaster, death in the pronounced human sense. That these disharmonies cannot simply be removed by the love of God, because the love of God is no other than *holy* love; that God is not merely the Merciful One but also the Holy One—all this is expressed in the sacrifice of the Son of God, in the actual sacrifice, that is, not simply in the *idea* of sacrifice. For this idea only has meaning if something has actually happened, as a real concrete historical event. Indeed, it is precisely this fact, that something *must* happen, which constitutes the meaning of the idea. Its whole meaning is summed up in the actual sacrifice.

Hence the fact of Christ helps us to understand both these facts, namely, that the religion characterized by a sacrificial cultus was always exposed to moral criticism on account of its evident inadequacy, and especially that it was never enough for those who were morally in earnest; and yet that, in spite of this, this form of worship was maintained even among the Jews until Christ came, in spite of, and alongside of, the religion of the Law and of the Scribes, the Temple alongside of the Synagogue. We also understand why Jesus Himself did not wish—any more than the prophets—to ban the worship of the Temple in His lifetime, that, on the contrary, He connected His own death as closely as possible with the sacrificial cult, with the sacrifice of the Passover, thus that He desired to fulfil this truth in Himself, like the Law, and indeed that this was inevitable.

Whereas to the man of the ancient world the idea of an expiatory sacrifice—even if in perverted form—was still direct and living, in these modern days we have to re-learn it again by way of Christ. It is due to the influence of Rationalism that the idea has disappeared so completely. For it is of the essence of Rationalism to admit no break in the world order, to believe in an unbroken continuity between God and the world. All the arguments of the Rationalistic theologians, from the time of Reimarus onwards, which have been used against revelation, apply especially to the idea of expiation: there can be no need for a divine intervention in the world order, because otherwise this world order would be imperfect. So completely has the remembrance of the break in the world order vanished that people even believe that it is possible to argue directly from the fact of unbroken continuity. The exaggeration of the Christian idea of Providence at the expense of the eschatological idea, as can be observed in the ecclesiastical Christianity of post-Reformation days, is certainly not free from blame in this matter. But, in any case, it is clear that the very presupposition upon which Rationalism rests is denied by the Christian faith, namely, that the world represents the divine order of things. No, it is in disorder, and this disorder is profoundly deep-seated, to such an extent, indeed, that the divine order has been almost entirely destroyed. The grave nature of this disorder, the necessity for a *reparatio* or *restitutio* is the fundamental idea of the Christian faith. This is expressed in two ways: in the necessity for a special revelation, and in the necessity for the Atonement.

Because the system of knowledge has been thus injured, God cannot be known "without further ado." An "extraordinary" divine institution, a special divine self-revelation is needed. Because the divine order of life has been disturbed, because fellowship with God has been broken, and the Divine Love has been squandered, an extraordinary transaction is needed in order to knit up once more the broken thread; thus a special Divine Atonement is required. Both Revelation and Atonement witness to the same truth; the intention of both is the same. But because the disturbance of life is still deeper than the disturbance of the system of knowledge, therefore the Atonement is the final and the most profound expression of the whole fact of Christ. That it had to happen, that such a "work" was necessary, that it has "cost" *this*, constitutes the final expression

485

of the discontinuity, of the breach between God and the world.

(v)

But this negative aspect is only one side of the truth. If the necessity for the expiatory sacrifice reveals to us the greatness of the gulf which lies between God and sinful humanity, the reality of the sacrifice also reveals, and not fully till then, what it means to say that "God is Love." All energy can be recognized by the strength of the resistance which it overcomes, by the "work" which it achieves. The Divine Love is known by the greatness of the resistance which it overcomes. Just as in the sphere of human life sacrifice and self-surrender are the only wholly satisfactory proofs of love, so is it also in the knowledge of God. If the sacrifice had been a mere analogy— as in all subjective or merely human interpretations of the sufferings of the Cross—then the love of God also would be a mere analogy, based upon wholly inadequate premises. If all that happens in the Atonement is that men are set free from the false idea that God is a judge, and they thus gain confidence in a God who is kind, then all God has to do is to overcome human error. A human fact is needed simply in order to give men an illustration of the Divine Love. The Death of Jesus has a purely demonstrative meaning. Nothing actually *happens*, but we are shown that nothing need happen, that God always might have been known as Love.

This is not the meaning of the Biblical message of the Cross. There something really happens on the part of God; God really overcomes something which concerns Him. Just as in the revelation His coming is a real coming, so also in the Atonement His overcoming is real, as real as the gulf which lies between Him and us. The same applies to the human response to this fact. Just as it is only in the real coming of God—in the reality of the revelation—that God is known as the One who really desires to have dealings with us, so still more in the overcoming of the reality of the wrath which lies between Him and us is He known as the incomprehensible, as the One who truly loves us in spite of everything. Only the God who loves us in spite of everything is the God of Love. Because Mysticism and Rationalism do not know this, they do not know the God of Love, although they may use this expression. That the Son of God comes to us through the fiery barrier of the divine wrath: this is the compassion of God, which the Gospel and it alone can make known to us.[1]

Just as guilt is lightly regarded where it is taken for granted that it can be overcome, so also there is no profound sense of the meaning of love where it has not to overcome any real obstacle. The Bible teaches us that God really has something to overcome, thus that His forgiveness is a real happening, a process of "breaking through wrath," as Luther used to put it. The very aspects of the Gospel which the modern mind regards as alien, primitive, or at least as unnecessary, are actually the essential aspects. The essence of the Gospel consists in this, that here is a real event, a sign of the real gulf between God and man and a sign of the real movement of God, an event which shows up both the seriousness of our position and the unspeakable wonder of the Divine Love.

Apart from this event, the "Love" of God would resemble the Platonic Ideas, or the conception of Aristotle: ἀκίνητος παντὰ κινῶν. God's Love would then mean simply the moral idea of purpose. But then it would not be truly personal. Such an idea would mean that fundamentally God is not touched by human happenings at all. He lives enthroned above history, above human sin and human suffering. He is not the God who has "heard the cry of His people and has come down to save

[1] As in the Christian belief in Creation the idea of the independence of the creature, and above all of man (made in the Image of God, freedom, individual responsibility) within the Almighty Power of God, is emphasized to the utmost extent, to the very verge of the idea of Omnipotence, so also in the idea of Atonement, the idea of the sinful independence of the creature is maintained and emphasized to the very verge of Manichaeism. But in the fact that things are brought to a head in this paradoxical way lies the centre of the Biblical message: the unfathomable love of God is here displayed. The greater the obstacle the love of God overcomes, the greater does the Divine Love appear. This is the "breaking through wrath." In the Old Testament we find for this the imperfect expressions: to lay aside His wrath; to forget or "repent Him of the evil"; "He will not be angry for ever"; that is, comparative expressions, which all suggest a relation to time.

them." He is far more like the world law, as described by
Fichte, than the God of the Bible—even though he may be
described in personal terms. That the Absolute God in person,
that the One upon whom is based the unchangeable law of
the universe, is at the same time the One who comes down to
us, that the Eternal enters wholly and really into history and
breaks through it: this paradox, which is altogether beyond
human reason and can only be believed as a whole, is the
revelation of the living and the truly loving God.

The self-movement of God towards man is the theme of the
Bible. This self-movement, however, is completed at the point
where it meets with the greatest resistance, that is, where it
is confronted by guilt, the objective element which separates,
the objective nature of which is itself only fully perceived in
the process of breaking down its resistance. At the very
opposite pole to this perception is the mystical idea or the
philosophical theory of identity, where nothing moves at all,
because all movement is only an illusion. Hence what the
mystic calls the Love of God and what the Bible calls the Love
of God are two different things. On the one hand there is no
conception of a love which loves "in spite of everything,"
while on the other hand this invincible love is the central
truth. On the one hand opposition between God and the world
is regarded as an illusion; on the other, in the Gospel it is
recognized as a reality, but it is conquered. But this process
of overcoming resistance—if it is not to be a purely dialectical
process and thus merely the solution of an error—must actually
take place and can only be known in this actual event. Hence
the real revelation and the real Atonement are closely connected with each other; indeed, rightly understood, they are
one. The God of Love, the One who loves us in spite of
everything, can only be known as He really is in this aspect
of His Love. For apart from this fact of Atonement He is not
the loving God at all. Apart from this perception of His Nature
He is the God of Wrath. Only in Christ is He the God of
Mercy. For "he who believeth not in the Son is judged already
and the wrath of God remaineth on him," not as an imaginary
idea but as a terrible reality. Whoever is not affected by the
Atonement remains severed from the God of Love, thus in the

reality of death, whose end is the second death. This shows, beyond a doubt, how serious this matter is, that we are here concerned not with a mere misunderstanding, but with life-and-death reality. If the wrath of God is a misunderstanding, the Atonement is merely a subjective process; it simply means the clearing up of a misunderstanding; this certainly leaves us in the dark as to how far it would really matter if this mis-understanding were not cleared up. At any rate, it seems fairly obvious that we need not expect it to lead to any very serious consequences.[1] If, however, the Atonement is an actual fact, then both the Divine Love and the state of sin must be taken seriously. The fact of the atoning revelation also shows the two-fold end, as something which really takes place: judg-ment for life or death, salvation or ruin. The Last Things have already begun to cast their shadow over history, and to this extent they have already begun. The actual fact of the Atonement—and it alone—makes the final fact of Redemption a certainty.

[1] We can perceive the transformation of the Gospel message by the modern spirit in the fact that the latter has retained only the ideas of love, forgiveness, and redemption, and has rejected the necessary correlative ideas of the gravity of judgment, holiness, and condemnation. The modern pseudo-Christian creed amounts to this: somehow or another in the end everything must work out well for everybody. Christ is, of course, the Redeemer, but it is possible to have redemption apart from Him. Of course, we must take the divine command seriously, but God will never condemn anybody. It is, of course, true that the Bible is the divine revelation, but in spite of this its fundamental idea, the combination of holiness and love, judgment and mercy, is false. The idea of an ἀποκατάστασις πάντων, in the sense of a good end which can be expected to take place naturally and thus not in the sense of Acts iii. 21 at all, which has *no* scriptural ground, and which in the whole course of Christian history has always been regarded as a superficial heresy, is to-day regarded as that which is really and characteristically Christian.

CHAPTER XX

THE MEDIATOR

(i)

THERE is nothing particularly remarkable about the fact that
a personality stands at the heart of the message of the Bible;
we can easily adapt our minds to this fact; indeed, itis in
harmony with modern thought. But the fact that this Person
stands absolutely alone at this central point, that in this picture
all other persons are, properly speaking, only like the setting
and the frame, that He alone is the content of the m essage
and that all that is decisive has been uttered in Him alone: it
is this exclusiveness which constitutes the stumbling-block. This
shows clearly that these two points of view stand for two very
different conceptions of personality. To the modern view of
the Person of Jesus this exclusiveness simply seems an impossible
exaggeration; it is like a person who raises his voice beyond
the ordinary pitch till it becomes a shriek. For the Christian
witness to the Person of Jesus this exclusiveness is part of
Himself. This is precisely what is intended. It is why this
Person is called the Mediator. If He really is the Mediator,
if we understand what this strange word really means, then
we no longer ask whether He alone ought to dominate the
picture. To be the Mediator means that He stands alone.

Thus when we speak of the "Person" and "the Work" of
the Mediator we mean exactly the same thing. He Himself,
because He is what He is, *is* the Revelation and the Atonement.
We do not need to posit Christ as the subject of a transaction
in order to speak of His work. If we speak rightly of His Person,
in accordance with His Nature, we also bear witness to His work
of revelation and atonement. He *is* what He does and He *does*
what He is, and both these statements mean that He reunites
man, who is separated, indeed practically severed from his
divine origin, with God. He does this by the very fact that
He is a Person, because and in so far as His being a Person
is, as such, already God's reconciling act. For He is indeed
the Incarnate Word, in Him and in His being God is the

One who has come to us. Thus in His very Nature the gulf between God and man has been bridged. He Himself is the bridge which God throws across to us, over which God comes to us.

This is the great, absolutely evangelical idea which dominates the older patristic literature on the doctrine of the Atonement. This doctrine has met the same fate as the doctrine of the Two Natures and the Anselmic doctrine of Satisfaction—it has had to endure being branded as thoroughly non-evangelical, pagan, naturalistically magical. Here, too, the fact that the word "nature" is misunderstood has a good deal to do with it, but this misunderstanding only arose because inwardly the doctrine itself had come to seem alien, remote, and unintelligible. We have no wish to deny that occasionally the Greek Fathers did mingle Greek intellectualism or ideas of ancient magic with the Christian doctrine, sometimes even to a large extent. But this does not in the least affect the fundamental tendency of their doctrine of the *recapitulatio*, of the "deification" of human nature through union with the divine nature. To them φύσις means the state of existence, or of "being," both in the broadest and the deepest sense of the word. To them Redemption means that in His Son God entered into human existence, that He plunged into the world of history in all its sin and corruption. This is what they mean by "physical union."[1]

[1] As an outstanding example of this Patristic doctrine of the Atonement we might mention the work, *On the Incarnation of the Logos*, by Athanasius. An analysis of its leading ideas would confirm what has been said in the previous pages of this book: how little, namely, the modern view of the dogma of the Incarnation does justice to the views and the deeply scriptural outlook of the great theologians of the Early Church, which Athanasius formulates thus in the early pages of his book: We need to recognize "that our guilt is the cause of His (the Saviour's) descent, and that our sin drew out the love of the Logos to man, so that the Lord came to us and appeared amongst men" (*de Inc. Verb.* 4). The Incarnation of the Logos does not mean merely the removal of a physical taint, but the restoration of the original image of God, and with this the original relation to God, and this not in a magical way, but by means of the renewed knowledge of God and the faith which is determined by this. The Incarnation is the exhibition of the loving condescension of God in the only way sinful humanity could understand (*de Inc.* 14–17)—a favourite idea of Luther's! The only point in modern criticism which is right is this, that in this patristic doctrine the idea of guilt is stressed less than the corruption caused by sin; but it is plain enough that the doctrine deals with the harm wrought by

This idea, however, is directly in line with the message of the Bible, as indeed it is expressed in the New Testament, although in other language. Here, in essentials, we are only concerned with proving the principle. In the main, however, this proof consists in a retrospective glance at what was said in the second part of this book. The Person of the God-Man, as such, is the revelation of God, the coming of God to man. As such, it says that God is on the side of man. If Jesus Christ is really the One to whom the Scriptures testify, the "Word made flesh," what then could this Incarnation, this descent into this world mean, save that the gulf which lies between man and God has been bridged? This gulf is indeed the great obstacle, the element of separation introduced by sin. Is the existence of this gulf actually denied by God in His coming? If this is so, what else is necessary to assure man of the Divine Will of reconciliation? Could the Atonement consist in anything else than in this?

Then is the Cross superfluous? This is a foolish question. For as the meaning of the fact of the Cross only becomes clear through our knowledge of the Person of the Mediator, so also, on the other hand, the Person of the Mediator can only be perceived as such through His personal activity on the Cross. We are not here dealing with two different objects, but with two different points of view, in the interpretation of the one reality. The Incarnation and the Cross form an indissoluble unity. The first is fulfilled in the second, just as the second begins in the first. The meaning of the Incarnation, the *nostra assumsit*, only becomes quite clear where this *nostra* means the utmost depths of human existence. And the self-surrender of the Cross simply means self-surrender to the lowest depths of human existence. The movement in which all consists is one and the same; all is directed towards spanning the gulf of separation.

This is what is so extraordinary about this Person, that in Himself He represents the divine self-movement; in His own Person alone, and this not in humanity (which we could

sin and that this harm has its centre in the spirit (God's image) of man; the reference to guilt, too, is not absent; it is merely in the background.

understand) but in His mystery, in the absolutely unthinkable
paradox of the divine-humanity. This union of opposites—
this real union of real opposites—is what we mean by the
paradoxical expression of the divine self-movement. Indeed,
this perception of faith that we are here concerned with a
dual Person, this contradictory personal unity, constitutes the
original element in the doctrine. In His Person a divine
happening is made known to us, something which we can only
express by the use of these mythological expressions. The
Apostolic Age, indeed, was under no misapprehension when it
placed increasingly all the emphasis on the Person of Christ
as the great Divine Miracle in its message. This did not mean
that it had in any way departed from the truths of the Gospel
in its original purity. This was the conviction of the Primitive
Church, and this is the testimony which has always stood out
clearly at all the classical periods in the history of the Christian
Church, as the very heart of her Gospel: Jesus Christ Himself.
That HE IS WHO HE IS, indeed that He *is* at all, it is this which
constitutes the Atonement.

(ii)

Jesus Christ is the heart of the Gospel because in His Person
He unites the human and divine natures. This means the
really human and the really divine; not in the way in which
to some extent every human being does this—for so long as
there is a trace of humanity left in a man there also some ray
of light from the Divine Image is still visible in him—but as
He alone can do it. His "being" as the Mediator, however,
cannot be severed from His "work" as Mediator; for this
Person is not static but dynamic. The element which distinguishes a person from a thing is its reality, its actuality.
His "being" as Mediator coincides with His vicarious action
and His vicarious suffering. As the Substitute He is the
Mediator.

The whole existence of the Mediator consists in making
Himself one with humanity in its sin and sorrow. The
Incarnation is no mere gesture; it is reality, stark and painful.
Jesus drinks the cup of human existence in all its alienation

from God, to the very dregs. Nothing is spared Him; He is
not the royal Son of God, who visits man wearing a disguise
which He throws off when things become too hot for Him,
that at the critical moment He may reveal Himself to the
amazed multitude as the Son of God. He rejects the idea that
when His position is most desperate He might be saved by
legions of His Father's angels. Everything must be fulfilled.
He will have no privileges; He bears no resemblance to those
"voluntary" workers[1] who are not willing to accept absolutely
everything which forms part of the lower position which they
have temporarily assumed.

Christ's identification with humanity does not only involve
suffering in the usual sense. Primarily it is a simple direct
proof of His solidarity with us. He does not separate Himself
from humanity. It is this which is His sign-manual, that He
does not separate Himself from us. He is the Friend of publicans
and sinners. The rest of us all want, at least in part, to cut
ourselves off from our compromising co-partners in humanity.
Where is the man who would not be a Pharisee? Which of us
does not desire a little throne where he can sit in judgment
on others?. But the Mediator joins Himself to the lowest dregs
of the population, to those doubtful characters from whom
others turn away in disgust and loathing. He bears the title of
"Friend of publicans and sinners." He is their "Friend," not
the one who "converts" them. It is possible they may be
"converted," but this is not why He seeks them. He seeks
them simply because He wants to belong to them. "To-day I
must abide at thy house."

In principle this attitude implies everything else. Since He
chose especially those who were not noted for anything in
particular, and who did not achieve anything in particular,
in whose existence was represented nothing but the absolute
human element, in its alienation from God, without any assets
to balance their deficiencies, He thus expressed His identification, in principle, with everything human. And He did this at
the point which matters most of all: at the central point, at

---

[1] This illustration refers to the fact that in Switzerland the sons of
industrial magnates will sometimes enter "the works" as "employees"
for a time.—TR.

494

the point where man is alienated from God by his sin. "The whole misery of humanity has seized hold of me"—in *Faust* this is, in the last resort, a mere phrase. In an absolutely unlimited sense it has been truth only in Him who has manifested it in deeds. "He had compassion on the multitude." He is the only One who has swept away all distinction between men, to whom, ultimately, such differences simply do not count. He only sees human beings—sinful, suffering, and poor. This is His philosophy of history, of civilization, of humanity; this is His existential attitude.

The final proof of His identification with humanity was given in His sufferings on the Cross. The Cross is no mere act of endurance, as one might bear a disease or a stroke of destiny. This feeling that the Son of Man "*must* suffer" means something both exterior and interior. He bears it willingly, He takes it upon Himself deliberately, He gives Himself up. The Church is right in laying so much stress on this willingness to suffer (or, to put it still more plainly, this deliberate acceptance of suffering)—using *Isaiah liii* to illustrate the point, as the decisive element in His sufferings. His Passion is not a transaction—as it certainly might seem to be in the doctrine of Anselm, a method of expiation ordained by God which gains its value from the costly nature of the sacrifice—it is a personal act; it is real, vicarious action, identifying Himself wholly with the human race. It is indeed a mode of action whose character is suffering (see pp. 509 ff.), but it is none the less a mode of action in which He gives Himself up wholly. This form of action, in which the one who acts is entirely one who suffers, we call sacrifice. Thus, even in its secular sense, this word is drawn from the language of the cultus. The suffering of Christ means both surrender for man and unreserved solidarity with the whole human race; but, above all, it means solidarity with that which separates humanity from God, with that therefore which from the point of view of God is a necessity, with the divine wrath, which works death.

The Mediator gives Himself up completely to this suffering of the wrath which comes to man from God. In this self-sacrifice His identification with humanity rises to its greatest height, in this giving of Himself to the real endurance of the divine judgment, the divine wrath. The mere achievement of death is not the main thing, as though we were here concerned with a human "sacrificial animal." "He was obedient unto death, even the death of the Cross." This obedience is just as important as the actual event. Here it is the idea of sacrifice in contrast to the forensic idea of penalty which is expressed; it is a personal act. The trembling and horror of Gethsemane form part of this sacrifice, and, above all, that last cry on the Cross: "My God! My God! why hast Thou forsaken Me?" It is real suffering; there is nothing make-believe about it; it is a real surrender, not a drama which had already been prepared in the heavenly world. Otherwise how could the truth of the ritual idea of sacrifice be fulfilled if it were not really true that a Man gave His life, that He endured painful renunciation, that in agony He gave Himself up? At the same time this sacrifice means something quite different from the ordinary human suffering of loss and death. It is not the torture and the Cross as such, but this complete collapse in shame and complete failure—it is this which makes the suffering of Christ of a kind that no man before or after Him has ever suffered the like. For when we said that death was far more terrible, and far harder, for man than it is for animals, this also applies to Him who really bore the sin of the world, and who, although He was nearer to God than we can ever imagine, yet bore a death such as none have ever suffered before or afterwards.

(iii)

Only he who is true man can suffer from his connection with God. To suffer in this way is the very thing that makes man as he now is. He who suffers most from his connection with God is most human. But the way in which Christ suffers from His connection with God is only possible to Him, because He does not act as a human being, in His own interest, but for God, as God's representative. The depth of Christ's suffering is due to the cause for which He suffers; because Christ knows that He is wholly identified with the cause of God, therefore He is in a position to identify Himself so completely with man, to give Himself so unceasingly to man, really to feel "the whole misery of man"—a phrase which on the lips of anyone else would be a mere phrase—to suffer and to die *for* humanity and not merely *with* humanity. It is precisely this sense of solidarity which the sinner lacks. Even those who care about it cannot achieve this unity with the rest. Pride and selfishness separate us from others. Inwardly, from arrogance, we are afraid of giving ourselves away, and outwardly the instinct of self-preservation prevents us from doing this. Christ is the only One who confesses His unity with humanity in the sight of God, and who acts in the sense of this solidarity. And in so doing Christ proves that He is standing on the other side of the gulf which separates us from God, and affects our present position as human beings.

Christ therefore is the man who is well-pleasing to God, the ideal man who was not affected by the Fall, the whole man, the "second Adam," in whom the nature of man is restored to harmony with the Divine Creation. This certainly only takes place inwardly, in the centre of His Being, in the intention of His Will, not outwardly, in His "form," which is indeed the "form of a servant." For He has taken upon Himself the likeness of "sinful flesh." But in Him, in His inner attitude, the Divine Image has been restored.

Yet we must take care that this truth does not become a point at which—as has so often happened in modern theology—unconsciously we glide off the lines and slip into the errors of Rationalism. The fact that Paul speaks of Christ both as the "second Adam," the "firstborn among many brethren," and as the "heavenly Lord" is sometimes explained on merely psychological lines by using the well-known phrase about the "inconsistencies of humanity,"[1] or the critics try to explain it historically as due to contradictory traditional influences (in reality, this explains nothing at all!). It was thought to be a clear issue, either one or the other, therefore they decided for the former in order that—owing to the support given by the Pauline testimony[2]—they might the more easily evade the

[1] See p. 359, Translator's Note.
[2] While in the earlier Liberal conception of Paul the Pauline statement about the Deity of Christ was weakened by pointing to the "archetypal man, Christ," historians of religion now say that "the relation between

second. In reality, in the thought of Paul on this point there is no contradiction at all, but it is strictly objective, logical, and consistent. Christ can only be the man in whom God is well pleased, the sinless One, the One who is truly and humbly one with humanity because He is also at the same time more than man, the Son of God. The very fact that He identifies Himself with humanity in such a vital way is the proof that by nature He does not belong to us. If He were man—that is, only man, as we are—then He could not identify Himself with humanity as He has done. It is only because He comes to us from the further side of the gulf that He is able to act thus. And no one can come to us from beyond the breach, from beyond the gulf, save God Himself. Of course, in order to perceive this clearly we need to assume that sin is taken seriously, that it is not regarded as a merely accidental element in human existence, but that it is seen in its real character, as Original Sin. To be a human being means to be a sinner. To predicate sinlessness of any human being, when one knows what sin really is, means that this man must be more than human. Only the God-Man can be the Sinless One.

This is the abstract formula, but we are not forced to argue from this point of view at all; indeed, we can very well start once more from the point of view of solidarity as a personal act. It is characteristic of the Mediator that not only does He identify Himself wholly with man, but also that He is absolutely united with God. He comes to men as the One who has no human aims; His whole purpose and desire is directed towards

the first and the second Adam is one of violent contrast. The first man and the second have nothing in common with one another save the name. And this community of name is something quite external. Paul, when he called Christ the ἄνθρωπος, had no intention of suggesting that both beings were connected with each other through the common possession of humanity." For behind this conception one may discern simply the Mandaean myth of the "Heavenly Man, the Divine Being, *Anthropos*" (Bousset, *Kyrios*, pp. 125, 140). Certainly in this as in other cases the knowledge of the myth is able to free us from the false-rationalistic-liberal conception; but we should pass from Scylla into Charybdis if we were to allow these "parallels" to lead us so far astray as to assert that Paul himself can be expounded in the mythological sense. For Paul holds the truth of the Deity of Christ just as firmly as the other truth that Christ as the Logos is also the archetype of humanity.

the things of God: the Kingdom of God, the dominion and the glory of God, that is His "cause"; and all this not in the human ethical sense of an ideal towards which one aspires, but in the divine sense, of the sphere from which one comes. Christ does not act merely as One who is absolutely united with men, but also as One who is absolutely one with God, as the authorized representative of God, who makes an unconditional personal claim on man's obedience. The fact that He appears in the "form of a servant" is only the incognito of His royal state. The Kingdom, the dominion of God, is not merely the cause of God which He serves, but it is likewise the sphere in which He Himself reigns. The whole rhythm and movement of His life is indeed that of One who comes, not of One who goes, it is a descent, not an ascent, it is the act of One who *brings* something to man, not of One who strives to *attain* some human end, it is a divine, not a human movement.

The fact that He is thus one with God, in such a way that the cause of God is absolutely His own cause (not in the ethical sense in which it gradually *becomes* His), this Messiahship of His (even though it be hidden), His divine claim on humanity as a whole, makes it possible for Him to make Himself the servant of humanity, who gives His life for the race. The fact that He is one with God constitutes the basis of His solidarity with man. Such an identification with humanity is beyond the power of any mere human being; this can only be done by the man who is God. Only the King can thus deal with humanity as a unity, only the Divine King can thus grasp the "whole misery of humanity" and make it His own. To give oneself to death like this for others can only be done by Him of whom "it is written" that He is the One to whom alone this part can be assigned, because He is the only One, the Unique Saviour.

(iv)

Hence His Death is a sacrifice offered by Himself. It is Messianic suffering, the suffering of Him who knows that His Passion and His Death are the Ultimate Act; it is the act of One who is aware that this is not merely an outstanding event in the whole history of the sufferings of humanity, but something quite specific; indeed, that it *can* only take place once in history, that it could not possibly happen again; therefore, too, it is necessarily connected with a quite definite Person, and this not in the universal human sense but in the theocratic sense, in the sense of the divine economy of revelation. It is the suffering of the Messiah, it is the suffering of the Person who can be none other than Himself.

This is true even of His life, seen from the point of view of His death on the Cross. The way in which He approaches sinners could not be taken by anyone else, and indeed no one else would have the right to take it. This also is not merely human solidarity, but it is the blending of the divine and human elements in His divine vocation. He is the Lord who calls Zacchaeus down from the tree and says to Him simply: "To-day I must abide at thy house." The whole "ministry" of Christ is equally an act of sovereign rule. It refers to man, it is true, but only for the sake of God. And this service of humanity is not exercised in the general ethical sense—"let man be noble, helpful, and good"—but in the Messianic sense: it is divine help, the help of God, in the strict sense of the word, thus it is help of a kind which we could never bring.

Christ's death may therefore certainly be described as an honourable instance of "fidelity to vocation"; but even this expression is not used in the general ethical sense. The characteristic element in His Passion is not that Jesus was true to His vocation in the way in which every one of us ought to be true to our vocation, but that He had this particular vocation, which no other has ever had before or since. Hence His death was not an accidental occurrence in which fidelity to His vocation was put to its hardest test, but His death is an integral part, we might even say the main part, of His vocation. He "came to suffer." His death is the fulfilment of that which had been foretold in *Isaiah liii* of the Suffering Servant of the Lord. Thus His Passion and Death is not significant as a moral test which He endured successfully—as an ethical event—but as a divine deed and a divine revelation, as a "Messianic event." It does not merely give Him the right to be called the Redeemer, it constitutes Him as the Redeemer.

Only thus can we understand the meaning of His sacrifice. It is the personal entrance into a necessity which existed in the presence of God and for His sake; it means making His own the Divine Will of revelation and of atonement, with the inclusion of this negative element of the suffering of death as expiation. It is "obedience"—not in the general ethical sense, but in the specifically Christian sense, in the sense peculiar to the Messiah, that obedience suggested by Paul's often quoted phrase, according to which the *whole* life of Christ is conceived from the point of view of obedience in suffering.

It is only this which makes this death vicarious. It is thus the exact opposite of that which—not wholly wrongly—the doctrine of Anselm is usually taken to mean: an objective-impersonal substitutionary transaction. What we said above about sacrifice as an "equivalent" is only protected from "false objectivity" of this kind by means of the idea of vicarious offering. For vicarious offering (substitution) is something entirely personal; it is personal in that dual sense which characterizes the personality of the Mediator. In this process the Mediator is acting vicariously both for man and for God. For the people He acts as their High Priest, who brings the expiatory sacrifice in the name of them all. But the ordinary priest does not act personally but impersonally. His surrender refers to an object, a means of expiation, which, it is true, is intended as the equivalent for the most personal sacrifice of all, but which can only be mistaken for this by those who regard the whole matter carelessly and without thought.

Personal surrender can only be that wherein the personality is sacrificed. But this is not to be understood only in an unreal secondary sense as the surrender of the human will to the Divine Will. For this surrender is the natural moral duty for everyone, hence it is not special, it is not the expiatory sacrifice through which the right to continue to live can be gained. Rather what is here meant is sacrifice in the sense of the real surrender of life, of existence, of our life blood, human self-sacrifice for the guilt of others. History and legend tell us, it is true, of similar analogies, of incidents in which men and women willingly went to death in order to set others free, or in order to expiate their guilt. They are significant suggestions of the reality which took place in Christ; but they are no more than this. For they lack the ultimate presuppositions of the universal and wholly serious knowledge of sin and guilt, and also, above all, they lack the rightful consciousness of One who expiates, of One who acts as the representative of God and humanity. They are not "Messianic" sacrifices. No human being is capable of offering a pure sacrifice, and no mere human being is empowered to act in the place of God. Only a divine act can help in this situation. But this divine act, if it is to have meaning, must be at the same time genuinely human, a real sacrifice, painful, carried through in anguish, desolation, and despair. Only the God-Man can here really be the "priest," since He is at the same time the "sacrificial Lamb."

This Passion is, however, vicarious through the personal solidarity, the close union which subsists between the One who suffers and those for whom He suffers. Only man can suffer from his connection with God, and only on this account can this sacrifice have meaning. The human element, in the deepest sense of the word, constitutes the "material" for this sacrifice; therefore it must be suffered in a truly human way. But this can only be achieved by God Himself; therefore the Person who thus acts, the Person in whom human nature truly suffers, must be the Divine Person. It is therefore wholly impossible to separate the human and the divine vicarious elements from each other. The existence of the one implies the existence of the other. This indissoluble unity of the divine and the human in the double vicarious offering is the mystery of the revelation of Christ, as it is the mystery of the Person of the Mediator.

(v)

Here God is dealing with humanity. This perception is fundamental. Nothing more is needed if this is taken seriously. To take it seriously means that we accept the fact that here something has actually taken place, that God is dealing really and truly with us, that God is not merely teaching us something, or clearing up a misunderstanding. It is meant seriously too, since in it it is really *God* who is acting, not merely a man from whose behaviour we can draw conclusions about the divine attitude towards us. Finally, this event is significant because here God really deals with humanity as a whole, and thus, that the event which here takes place is not merely an historic event, which concerns merely that particular generation and the world of that day, but "all who believe."

The idea of substitution gathers up all these elements into one. If the Cross really means the dealing of God with humanity, then we cannot interpret it in any other way than in the sense of the doctrine of substitutionary atonement. The Passion of this Man possesses divine significance if it is not merely human suffering but a divine act. It has divine meaning if it is necessary suffering, necessary from the point of view of God, a necessary suffering of man. It has divine meaning if through this necessary suffering of humanity the divine gift of salvation is given—communion with the divine life.

The assumption on which we base the statement that this human event is really a divine act is the divine humanity, the Person of the Mediator. It is, of course, possible to assign divine meaning to human life and suffering; but we do this in the sense of general revelation; thus these experiences form part of human life as a whole, and are thus unable to change it in any effective way. In instances of that kind we are not dealing with the question of God's salvation at all, but simply with some historical event possessing ethical significance. But if divine action in the sense of the revelation of salvation is what is meant, as a special act of God, then the statement of a divine act in the Passion of Christ only has meaning on the presupposition that this Christ is the God-Man, and that His death is the expiatory and substitutionary sacrificial oblation.

If this is the meaning of the Cross, then the Cross, and thus the Atonement and Revelation, are absolutely unique. If here the act really proceeds from God, and if it is true that here something was actually done, on the Cross, then this event is such that by its very nature it is capable neither of repetition nor of extension in time and in space. It is a "moment" and only *one* "moment." It is the decisive event, alongside of which there is no other. It is a point which only faith can see, but it is the point at which all else is decided.

The Cross of Christ is not the absolute turning-point simply as an historical event. The world has indeed become different since then in the empirical sense, but the difference is not decisive. The influence of the Cross has been felt in history, but only in a relative manner. It is a force in the great magnetic field of history, but not in any sense the strongest force. The world is not redeemed, still less "Christian." The course of history after Christ has been altered, it is true, and it is different from what it would have been if this had not taken place. But who would assert that the decisive factor in this course of history has been Christ? It is quite possible to defend the thesis that, historically speaking, Christianity has been a fiasco. True Christians would be the last to controvert this. Conceived as a schema of cause and effect, Christ is only a relative magnitude. This is due to the schema as such. There are no absolute causes and effects. The sphere of causality, of empirical happenings, is identical with the sphere of relativity. This holds good of the "internal" causes and effects as well as of the outward. Even in the matter of the conversion of Christians Christ has not succeeded. It would be impossible to argue back from the state of any Christian to an absolute cause. The theology of causality is necessarily relativistic. No Christian possesses absolute faith, no one is really wholly converted, if we regard these expressions empirically. It also forms part of the incognito of Christ that the final significance, the absolute turning-point, which His Cross means, can never appear historically in its effects.

The Atonement is not history. The Atonement, the expiation of human guilt, the covering of sin through His sacrifice, is not anything which can be conceived from the point of view of history. This event does not belong to the historical plane. It is super-history; it lies in the dimension which no historian knows in so far as he is merely an historian. It is an "event" which is only an "event" for faith. That it actually happened faith alone knows. It is not a fact which has its place in world history. It would be absurd to say: in the year 30 the Atonement of the world took place. But we can say: this event, which those who know history tell us probably took place about the year 30, is the same as that which we know through faith as the Divine Act of Atonement.

What matters is that it *did* actually take place. But if it has taken place, then it has happened once for all. We said that also about revelation and felt obliged to say it. But it is only because revelation is thus connected with the Atonement that it has this realistic significance, this clear character of some thing which has actually happened. If it was really necessary that there should be an expiatory sacrifice in order that God should once more direct His grace towards men, if the assertion that God *has* forgiven *me* is only verified when it appeals to this fact, then certainly the result is this, that the Christian revelation is distinguished from every kind of mysticism, Rationalism, or general religion, with a clearness which can exist nowhere else.

(vi)

This assertion, the connection of the Atonement with the actual achievement of expiation, which to the "natural man" seems purely arbitrary, is recognized in its necessity when we understand what is meant by expiation, when the phrases the "guilt of sin" and "the forgiving love of God" have their full weight. Neither guilt nor forgiveness is taken quite seriously where there is no emphasis upon the Mediator. There may indeed be no lack of "good will" or of "personal earnestness," but it is impossible to be sufficiently repentant where the necessity for expiation is not seen, and one cannot be confident enough where one does not know the reality of expiation through Christ. Expiation is that which separates the forgiveness of God and human guilt most widely and then brings them together again. That this should be necessary shows the depth of guilt; that this is real shows the unfathomable nature of the love of God. That this should be necessary we know only because it is real. And that it is real we only understand when we know that it was needed. Therefore the consciousness of guilt is the point of insertion for revelation. To repent is the presupposition of faith, but it is only completed in faith.

It is in this that our deepest humiliation consists. That which happened there leads us to refer the guilt of humanity as a whole to ourselves. If Christ dies vicariously, then He dies for all. Thus guilt is the guilt of all. It is, of course, possible for us to have some inkling of the solidarity of guilt apart from Christ; but—as history shows—we cannot grasp it aright. For in order to understand it we must allow our selfishness to be broken, which continually isolates us from others. In ourselves, psychologically, even as Christians, we never actually achieve the consciousness of unconditional solidarity. Even the true knowledge of guilt we possess only by faith, and moreover by faith in that which has happened once for all. For it is only possible to believe this at this point. The sacrifice of Christ is the only adequate ground of knowledge for the unconditional solidarity of guilt.[1]

Likewise it is the only ground of knowledge of the unconditional forgiveness of God. For unconditional forgiveness means that God takes the initiative, that He does not wait till we have fulfilled the conditions, till we "come." He Himself "comes." The Cross means that He, as the Forgiving One, really comes to us sinful men. Further, it means that He comes to all. His coming is His taking our side, and the side of us all. Only His coming breaks down the barriers which are opposed to His forgiveness. Because He Himself comes to us, we know, whoever "we" may be, that He really wishes to have fellowship with us. His coming to sinful men, however, is His breaking through that which is between us: it is expiation. Only when we know Him as the God who thus breaks through can we fully know Him as the God of Love.

This act of breaking through, however, either does not take place at all or it takes place once for all. The one thing that matters is that it has really taken place. But if it has really happened, then it has happened once for all. Historical humanity as a whole is the object of the divine dealing. All that is called history is included in it; only thus is it really

---

[1] The almost general recognition of human solidarity in sin which prevailed in the ancient world is a pregnant hint at the truth. But it is no more than this; for, like the modern idea of social guilt, at the same time it weakens the sense of individual responsibility.

the Cross of Christ. Therefore the believing recognition of this uniqueness, faith in the Mediator, is the sign of the Christian faith. Whoever considers this statement to be a sign of exaggeration, intolerance, harshness, non-historical thought, and the like, has not yet heard the message of Christianity. Such a one is still thinking in terms of the general revelation, and is still trying to fit the Christian witness into that system. Just as it is of the very essence of the Christian faith to believe that "in none other is there salvation," so also it is essential to believe that "it happened once for all."

To one who understands the Cross, as it is proclaimed in the New Testament, this uniqueness is included in his understanding of it as a matter of course. For this very reason it becomes the criterion of understanding. For this fact expresses most clearly and aggressively the opposition to the conception of general religion. No two points of view could be more violently opposed to one another than those represented respectively by the Idea and the Unique Event. If, as in modern historical science, the Idea is refracted, it then becomes manifold. History is the manifold expression—in principle the number of times is unlimited—the manifold incorporation of the Idea. Against this view of history the Christian claim stands out with the same harsh opposition: it is not something which can happen many times over, it is not the highest point in a series, but it is absolutely isolated because it is not an historical point: it stands for the super-historical fact of the divine of salvation. Therefore it is not without misgiving that we may use the term "saving history."[1]

[1] A tendency to regard the Bible from the point of view of the "saving history" seems to be present in Calvin's theology in the conception of an *oeconomia* and *dispensatio revelationis* (cf. the informing work of Schrenk, *Gottesreich und Bund im älteren Protestantismus*). But these very ideas, and above all the way in which they are used, show that Calvin was not concerned with the ideas which became later on so important in later theology of this type, especially in v. Hofmann, namely, the idea of development and the law of continuity. Calvin's interest is the very opposite: in spite of the difference between the Old and the New Testaments the unity of the two is the chief thing, "the differences . . . do not refer to the *substantia* of the covenant, but to the *modus administrationis* (Schrenk, p. 47). History in its flux, in its continuity and its relative gradations, ought not to be confused with revelation.

Revelation is thus placed within the current of historical relativities; there is always danger that in so doing the special element in revelation may be so sucked into the general current of the history of religion that it will disappear altogether. What *is* the special element in the Biblical revelation before Christ? Simply the prophecy which points to Christ. Only from the point of view of the fact of Christ can we understand the special element in the revelation of the Old Testament, particularly in its differentiation from all other forms of religious history. It is Christ as a fact, as the unique, it is the Mediator of the Atonement, the fact of revelation and atonement as a personal act of God, which in the Old Testament, not merely in the teaching of the prophets but also in the Mosaic cult, gleams on the horizon like the rays of dawn before the rising of the sun.

The prophets do not proclaim ideas but an event, namely, that God Himself will "come" and will Himself wash away sin. *Isaiah liii* should not be interpreted as an idea which is complete in itself, which, as such, it is sufficient to know, but as a report beforehand of a real happening, in which the One who acts is actually God Himself, although the visible actor in the scene is the "Servant of the Lord." "Surely He hath borne our griefs and carried our sorrows; the Lord hath laid on Him the iniquity of us all, and by His stripes we are healed." This chapter of Isaiah is not isolated in the Old Testament; it is the quintessence of the Old Covenant. The Old Testament in its many-voiced choir of prophecy, of the prophetic history and message, is the special element which points towards the unique event which took place in Christ, just as, on the other hand, the New Testament simply means looking back to this same event.

The Scriptures of the Old and New Testament do not themselves constitute the unique event. They are varied, extended, a literature and a history. But the meaning of this literature and this history, in distinction from all other literature and history, is the testimony to this unique fact of Christ, of an Atonement accomplished in Him once for all, which is itself an incomprehensible historical "moment" between two intelligible historical periods, and at the same time the eternal purpose of God which transcends history. The unique element in history is none other than the eternal which is beyond and above time. But it is in accordance with the character of this imperfect world that this eternal element must be given to us as something special, as really special, that is, as something unique, that the reconciling revelation of God is the Mediator.

(vii)

Finally, in connection with the thought of vicarious sacrifice there is still one misunderstanding to clear up, which refers to the relation between "suffering" and "action," between the death of Jesus and His life as a whole. Great harm has been caused by the fact that in the course of Christian history the vicarious sufferings of Christ, upon which, in point of fact, the witness of the New Testament makes everything depend, has been conceived falsely, in a directly psychological manner. People often ask: "Did Jesus really come only in order to die?" "Is His whole life only the preparation for this closing act of suffering and death?"

This question is intelligible once the whole process has been transferred from the supra-historical sphere to the historical and psychological sphere. It becomes still more natural when the Atonement through the death of Jesus (as at least seems to take place in the doctrine as propounded by Anselm) is conceived almost as a celestial legal "transaction," and the existence of the Mediator almost only as the existence of the "means" which was necessary for this "transaction" and thus entirely objectively and impersonally. It should, however, never be forgotten that this objective impersonality was never what was intended—the Passion hymns of the same Church which produced this doctrine constitute the clearest proof of this statement. Even the doctrine of Anselm only desires to state the abstract formula, the point of view for the real, personally vital event which is recorded in the New Testament, and especially in the story of the Passion.

Further, even the most abstract form of the doctrine of the Atonement never isolated the death of Christ in the way that modern critics claim that it did. For it was always plain that

509

the presupposition for the effectiveness of the expiatory sacrifice of Christ was its moral testing in His life. The so-called "active obedience" was always regarded—even by Anselm—as the indispensable condition for the significance of the so-called "passive obedience." This is an approach to the right doctrine, even if it is still an unwarranted abbreviation of the "life" of Jesus in favour of His "death." The contrast is a wholly erroneous one. Rather, the whole life of Jesus, or better still, the whole existence of the Mediator, should be regarded from this double standpoint of suffering and action. The well-known passage in Philippians which speaks of His obedient suffering unto death, even the death of the Cross, might and should have been used to illuminate this whole question.

The Passion of Christ does not begin with His entry into Jerusalem. It does not begin in history at all, but on that mysterious border line between time and eternity. It begins with the "self-emptying," with the "coming" of Christ. The Incarnation should be regarded from the point of view of "suffering." The "form of a servant" is itself the Passion, the descent into the lowliness of human existence, which culminates in the Cross. If the life of Christ is looked at thus—that is, not historically—then it does not matter if we say that the Cross is simply the crowning fulfilment of the whole. The way of the Cross belongs to the Cross just as the Cross belongs to the way of the Cross. What Bengel says of the Resurrection— everything in the Scriptures *spirat resurrectionem*—may be applied also to the Cross, all *spirat crucem*. All Christ says and does should ultimately be understood *sub specie crucis*—if it is to be understood at all—or it will not be understood, or it will be misunderstood, merely conceived from the historical point of view. The "Cross" is the total expression of the life of Jesus. Hence because for faith everything depends on this downward movement of God, this self-humiliation and self-contraction, this *Kenosis*, to faith the *oboedientia passiva*, as the Ethos of this movement, is certainly the higher aspect. Only this expression ought not to be understood in a psychological-biographical sense at all. It states nothing concerning the historical realization of this movement of God. Therefore the psychological question "passive or active?" leads us nowhere.

On the contrary, from the historical and historico-psychological point of view precisely that which dogmatically belongs wholly to the sphere of faith as passive obedience is visible, above all, as the highest activity, as an output of great energy. Here we see and feel the elements of conflict and victory, of haste and expansion, of pleading and seeking, of an urgent and aggressive movement, in which the Leader strides forward in hot haste. It is a heavenly offensive against the historical sphere dominated by the "Prince of this world," the αἰὼν οὗτος. Did not Jesus once compare Himself to a man who breaks into the house of the strong man armed, binds him and robs him? At another time He compares Himself to a man who throws his firebrand on to the earth in order that he may set everything on fire, and longs for nothing so much as to see everything alight with this flame! He is one who came not to bring peace but a sword, one in whose service no one is allowed to look back because everything goes forward at such a pace. It is not an excited or fanatical rushing forward, but still it denotes extreme effort, the use of all one's powers, an almost breathless striding towards the goal which characterizes this short historical episode which we call—in our exaggerated way—the "life of Jesus." We are glad that to-day we no longer see in Jesus merely the gentle Shepherd with the lamb upon His shoulders, but first and foremost the royal Hero who wages a dangerous battle and who is filled absolutely with the will to conquer. Here there is nothing of the Indian renunciation of the world, nothing of mystical ascetical indifference to the affairs of this world.

The confusion of the dogmatic interpretation proper with the psychological and historical view of the matter has led to a dangerous emphasis upon the elements of suffering in the life of the Saviour; this may perhaps have done a great deal of good in the wild days of the Middle Ages in Germany, when there were savage passions to tame, but in the long run may have ended in weakening Christianity, just as Buddhism tends to do. The psychological historical picture of the "Life of Jesus" shows us intense energy, an unconquerable will in the conflict for the Kingdom of God. It is a very good thing that historical criticism has released this genuine picture of Jesus and His earthly life from the pious frescoes which had bene painted over it. There is no question that to-day we see once more this historical picture of Jesus more plainly than most of the generations which have preceded us.

But if that is all we have gained, we have really lost more than we have gained. For all this is indeed only the form under which He appears to us, it is only the incognito which awaits recognition by faith before it can be laid aside. The meaning of this activity is this: the divine condescension, and thus the Passion. Not the suffering of the Man Jesus—that is only one element—but the suffering, the sacrifice, in which the existence of Christ, as such, consists, the self-emptying of the Son of God. The relation of the heroic life of Jesus (as seen from the outside) to this is that of an incognito, but, indeed, as such that in it the other can be visible for faith. For that conflict is still, above all, a renunciation, a giving up of that which holds man in chains, a refusal to be detained, a refusal to enjoy—detachment. This life is not "positive," in its essence it is negative. The positive, energetic element consists in the intensity with which men are thrown out of their usual conditions, rooted up out of their soil, made uneasy, thrown into confusion. But here nothing is "built up." There is no sharing in their activities. The characteristic element is indeed that which drives humanitarian thinkers to despair: the complete lack of all emphasis on the "values" of civilization, or even of any interest at all in actual culture. Civilization—the total content of the positive—is not denied as in India, as little as Creation is denied. But here something else matters, so civilization is ignored. Everything is ignored which, in the human sense, is positive. All goes out into the void, into that which can come from God alone. The whole endeavour of man is to be directed towards making himself ready for that which is wholly Other.

Hence this activity means rather letting things happen from the resistance of man than an actual struggle. No methods of carrying out His aims are used, and none are sought. Violence, which is indispensable to every "positive" will, is explicitly rejected. For to use means would be to use this world. But the wood of the world is unfit for the building of what is new.

Here, indeed, we see no anxious monastic renunciation of the world, no asceticism, no fear of woman, of riches, of eating and drinking, and the innocent joys of life. On the contrary, there is a striking contrast between Jesus and John the Baptist, in His freedom towards all these things. But still less than anxious renunciation do we see any sign of joyful and decidedly optimistic acceptance and unrestricted use of this world. Albert Schweitzer rightly calls our attention to the fact that in the life of Jesus there is a total absence of all plan of action, of any kind of organization. Anyone who wishes to influence this world in the positive sense, in the sense of building up, who wishes to bring something to completion within the world, must plan, organize, arrange. Of all this we see no trace at all. Jesus undertook nothing; He left nothing behind Him; He achieved nothing, and indeed He did not try to achieve anything. In the end, in spite of all the profound differences, this life still resembled the life of a Buddhist monk more than that of a man of the West with all his practical energy. The Christ stands in the world as the One who endures and tolerates it.

Why? Because Jesus came, it is true, in order Himself to represent the new man, the new age, but, since it was still within this old world, in a negative form. The Cross remains the sign of this revelation, even on its positive creative side. In a world which is set against God, in a period in the world in which Satan is regent, the divine cannot be otherwise represented without the risk of being misunderstood. The modern man, however, has no understanding at all of this negative aspect because he does not know that contradiction, that gulf which is in this world. He believes in building up, in direct progress; he knows nothing of the fact that the world, and man, must first of all be broken before God can create the new world and the new man; even when he reads *stirb und werde* in a beautiful poem, he does not take it to mean anything more serious than that we must be prepared for constant change. Hence to him the Cross, in which this summons to "die" is taken literally, is the stumbling-block which he cannot overcome. And in this sense are we not all "modern"?

That a death—this most hideous dreadful death—must redeem, and has redeemed us, this is the non-modern, anti-modern Gospel of the Bible. Therefore the obedience unto death of the Christ is more important to faith than "active obedience." Or rather, the two cannot be compared. In the obedience of suffering, of which faith speaks, it is not the historical and visible event which is meant but a process which faith alone can see. But faith sees this event in the picture of a life which is both active and passive, active in suffering and passive in action, in the life of the obedient "Servant of the Lord," who is the Lord Himself.

CHAPTER XXI

THE ATONEMENT

(i)

RELIGION of every kind is concerned with redemption. For in all forms of religion man seeks to rise above himself; he seeks deliverance from the condition in which, apart from redemption, his life is passed upon the ordinary commonplace level. Even the soul which finally finds repose in a monistic acosmistic system of identity, in a Pantheistic *amor dei intellectualis*, finds something which he did not possess from the outset, even if the repose which he finds consists in the discovery that he had been "in God" all the time. Thus all ethical religion also strives towards a state which is better, worthier, and truer than the present state, towards a release from one's present condition. Every kind of effort to achieve salvation, whether through knowledge or strenuous exercise of the will, or through ritual acts, starts from an initial condition out of which the soul desires to rise, because he regards it as unsatisfactory, and also because he feels unhappy in it. All forms of religion seek for deliverance from this condition, that is, for redemption.

But it is not always perceived that the real root of the evil which man seeks to overcome is a wholly personal wrong relationship between God and man: the guilt of sin. It is generally admitted that everywhere man seeks to be delivered from distress and suffering, from death and infirmity, from want and ignorance; further, it is also usually admitted that we need to be freed from impurity and folly, from bondage to the senses and from selfishness, possibly even from irreligion and from godlessness. But all this is seldom traced back to the one root: sin against God, personal guilt, from which we can only be released by forgiveness. Thus in the "spiritual" forms of religion in particular the prayer for forgiveness is rarely heard. And yet it does occur. Even though it may be one petition among others, yet over and over again a soul will persevere so ardently in its search for truth that he will finally

515

discover that this is the real need, the one that lies behind and above all other needs. Very impressive testimonies exist which show how in all ages there have been men who have sought for forgiveness from God.

But the message of Christianity does not consist in pointing out our paramount need for forgiveness, nor in declaring that God is really ready to forgive us. Just as our sense of the need for redemption is deepened by our sense of the need for forgiveness, so also in the Christian faith this is deepened still further by our sense of the need for atonement. Guilt is too great to be removed by forgiveness pure and simple. Before this can take place something else must happen, upon the basis of which forgiveness can become possible. But this condition—this is the new element in distinction from all ritual atonement— is a state which only God Himself can produce. This paradox, a condition prior to God's action but which God alone can fulfil and which He really does fulfil, this is the Christian view of our spiritual need and the way it is met. Hence it is a perception which, if it is not to contradict itself, can only be based upon fact, upon the fact in which this takes place. The Christian doctrine of forgiveness is based upon the fact of atonement.

Reconciliation presupposes enmity between two parties. To put it still more exactly: reconciliation, real reconciliation, an objective act of reconciliation, presupposes enmity on both sides; that is, that man is the enemy of God and that God is the enemy of man. Sin is thus described as enmity towards God, which, for its part, provokes the wrath of God. The enmity of man towards God is not only, and is not first of all to be regarded from the subjective side, or from the side of consciousness. It is possible to be an enemy without knowing it. Man is the enemy of God not only through his consciousness; it is rather his actual attitude which constitutes his enmity. He is God's enemy because he disturbs the divine order and throws it into disorder, because he spoils the creative work of God, and the cause of God, because he conspires with the "Adversary," with the evil Power, and allows himself to be used by it for purposes which are hostile to God. Man works against God before he knows what he is doing. But this is not "sin of ignorance"; for even this ignorance is sinful.

But this enmity also exists subjectively, though in very different degrees and forms. The human consciousness reflects the objective situation. Gradually there rises to the surface of consciousness the conviction that the root of sin is not fate, nor a natural condition, but an act: an act of defiance, disobedience, or distrust. The reflex of this in consciousness is a bad conscience, and fear in the presence of God. It is quite true to say that the universal fear of God does not spring from the rational ethical sense, or from a "bad conscience," but from the "sense of creatureliness." But that our sense of "creatureliness" over against God possesses this negative character shows plainly that sin is deeply rooted in our nature, behind all the particular ethical instances of its presence. The story of the Garden of Eden hints at a truth which stands out clearly in the knowledge of Christian truth: that *this* creaturely feeling was not the original feeling. No man is without it; but this only shows that no man is free from sin.

Thus even for human consciousness our relation to God is something which has been spoiled; man lives in "dispeace" with his Creator. The psychological images to describe this unrest are very varied. This unrest is the one constant element, the fundamental undertone in all the interior life of human beings. "Our heart is restless until it finds its rest in Thee." This unrest runs through the whole gamut of psychological phases, from frivolity, that is, from the flight to distraction, to that of suicidal despair; from easy-going comradeship with God, which yet cannot stand any test, and in this proves its unreality, to the point of the open renunciation of God and the hatred of religion in every form. The dogmatic theologian cannot deal further with these psychological symptoms of deep unrest; their importance is rather for the practical spiritual adviser. The dogmatic theologian sums them all up under one heading: Enmity towards God, and thus in their ultimate meaning—though this may often be unconscious—not according to the psychological form which this enmity may assume externally. This is how the Bible also regards them. "The lusts of the flesh are enmity towards God"; this is its judgment on human nature.

(ii)

But there is also enmity on the side of God. In the disordered situation created by man God does not merely suffer and look on from a distance. He "reacts" against this disturbance of the order of Creation, and in the Bible this divine reaction is called the wrath of God. The Divine Holiness, the unconditioned will of God to affirm itself, transforms this disturbance of the divine order into something objective: the necessity for punishment. For His Holy Will is unconditionally active: if it is not effective for blessing or salvation, then, in consequence of the human break in the divine order, it works in the opposite direction, and produces disaster. But this will is personal. God is present in this anger, it is actually *His* anger. For God is not mocked. That something has been interposed between God and man objectively, not merely subjectively in the consciousness of man, is thus not a pagan idea, but it is the view of the Christian Bible itself. It alone brings the seriousness of the sense of guilt to a head, by showing that, even if it were possible, it is not enough simply to turn round and go in the opposite direction. Guilt means that something has taken place with which man is impotent to deal. The simple act of turning "right about face" is not only impossible—since sin has poisoned the very nature of the will—but also it is not permitted. A veto has been imposed from the other side. This is what guilt means, the objective obstacle which alienates man from God; thus guilt means hostility on God's part.

This objectivity of guilt, this divine reaction against sin, is the reason why reconciliation must take place, why it must consist in something more than a mere change of mind on the part of man.

In what sense, however, can we speak of reconciliation objectively? Is God reconciled through the blood-sacrifice of the Son?[1] Criticism usually identifies both these ideas,

---

[1] Modern criticism of the ecclesiastical (and Biblical!) doctrine of the Atonement starts from the statement: "sinners cannot be conceived at the same time and in the same connection both as objects of love and of wrath" (H. Stephan, in connection with Ritschl's doctrine of Atonement, *Ev. Dogmatik*, p. 566). On the other hand, Th. Harnack regards it as the "main-

without further inquiry, with the doctrine of Atonement. But it is a remarkable fact that the New Testament never once says that God is reconciled. God *reconciles*, but He is not reconciled. He *reconciles Himself*, but in this process He is only the One who acts, the One who gives; He is not also the One who receives. In spite of this, the Atonement is indubitably an objective happening, an act of expiation, it is not merely a subjective process, or the clearing up of human misunderstanding. God reconciles Himself in Christ to man. Here we stand in the presence of the central mystery of the Christian revelation: the dual nature of God.

God, so far as His relation to the world is concerned, as the One whom we can know, in so far as He is immanent in the creature, is the angry God. Just as truly as sin is real, and cannot be explained away, so also God's anger is real, and it cannot be denied or explained away. But the wrath of God is not the ultimate reality; it is the divine reality which corresponds to sin. But it is not the essential reality of God. In Himself God is love. But no one knows this love. No one can or ought to know this love. It is that which can and should be known only by him to whom God wills to reveal it. This is the secret of the Trinity, the love of the Father in Himself and in itself. It is God's own heart, the love which does not first need a world to love in order to exist.

spring" of the Reformation view that Luther "ventures confidently to step right out into the centre of the deadly tension of this antithesis" (*Luthers Theologie*, p. 336). Actually it is this which constitutes the fundamental contrast between the one-sided Idea of God of modern theologians and the paradoxical revelation of the Bible. "Spiritual men (*spirituales*) learn to distinguish . . . between God and God, and learn to reconcile the wrath of God, or the angry God, with sinful man" (Luther, *W.A.*, 40, 11, 342). Only where this dualism exists, only where God is known as One who "outside Christ" is really angry, but "in Christ" is "pure love," is faith real decision and the Atonement a real turning-point. Therefore the dualism of holiness and love, of revelation and concealment, of mercy and wrath cannot be dissolved, changed into *one* synthetic conception, without at the same time destroying the seriousness of the Biblical knowledge of God, the reality and the mystery of revelation and atonement. All the Christian mysteries rise at this point, in reality they are only one: the mystery of the living God. Here arises the "dialectic" of all genuine Christian theology, which simply aims at expressing in terms of thought the indissoluble nature of this dualism.

This love can therefore only be made known to us through a special revelation. But this revelation simply means that the Divine Love "breaks through" wrath. Here, in the world, God is the *deus absconditus* who effects His *opera aliena*. Here He is the angry God, because by sin He is separated from us. But His nature is not wrath, but overflowing, unfathomable love. He is thus revealed in the Son. This is the place where the love of God breaks through the wrath of God. This revelation of the divine mystery of love in the midst of the reality of wrath is the "propitiation" (ἱλασμός).

God cannot and will not contradict Himself. Even as the God of love He cannot deny His wrath. His activity in the world, His law, and the *opera aliena* are all really, and not apparently, His work. This He will not renounce. But at the same time He wills to save the Creation, which, judged by the Law of righteousness, would have fallen a prey to death. The objective aspect of the Atonement, therefore, may be summed up thus: it consists in the combination of inflexible righteousness, with its penalties, and transcendent love; thus it means that the world-dualism caused by sin, which issues finally in death, is declared valid, and at the same time the overwhelming reality of the Divine Love is also justified. Hence as the classic passage in *Romans iii* puts it, the ἱλαστήριον, the propitiation, is also the "proof of His righteousness." Hence this is the meaning of the Cross: the reality of wrath, which is yet in some way a subordinate reality, and the far more overwhelming reality of the love of God.

In Christ alone is this true, only in Christ is it possible to praise God as unconditional love without endangering His Holiness. Only in Christ is the Divine Love truly known; only here is it the revealed love, which has broken through all obstacles to reach us. It is only true where it is the exact opposite of a general truth. For as a general truth it either removes the aspect of holiness, or it is limited by the idea of holiness. As a general truth it is not the mystery of God which we call love. It is characteristic of the mystery of God that it can only be made known through a special revelation. Hence it is quite possible to speak of the love of God apart from Christ, but where this is done something quite different is intended. For we can only speak truly of the love of God where the truth comes to us along this path: where love breaks through wrath, and where in thus overcoming the reality of the world it also determines the character of our perception of love. Thus, as Luther says, the real knowledge of Christian truth can only exist where God can be distinguished from God, that is, where God in His reality in the world and God in His revelation, "the Law" and the "Gospel," are distinguished from each other. In Christ we know that God is love, and nowhere else. Outside of Christ the God who is operative in the world remains the angry God in His *opus alienum*. "He who does not believe is condemned already and the wrath of God abideth on him."

The objective reconciliation is the presupposition of the subjective; expiation is the presupposition of justifying faith. The Christian faith has always been firmly persuaded that "in Christ" there is forgiveness of sins. It is not afraid of describing this objective state with drastic expressions drawn from trade, such as the right of purchase, gain, provision of necessaries. The main point is not that these expressions are used, but the significance of the ideas which they are supposed to contain. They all describe a process of "breaking-through" as the objective basis, the possibility, and at the same time the reality of forgiveness. They are abstract formulas for the same truth which the picture of the Crucified, or the story of the Passion, places visibly before us. They suggest the point of view from which this reality, this Word, can be understood, just as the historical picture insists on the actuality, the factual character of this Word. The forgiving love of God cannot become real to us without the picture of this event, nor can the story of this event convey to us the forgiveness of God apart from this Word. The doctrine is the story and the story is the doctrine, hence it is esoteric history, which will not disclose its meaning to any mere historian, and esoteric doctrine which no philosopher can understand.

In this event forgiveness takes place. Whoever has seen this will have seen through the misunderstanding which has dominated Liberal Christianity down to the present day: namely, that in the end the "Pauline" doctrine of Atonement came back—even though by "an immense *détour*" by way of forensic and ritual traditions—to the "simple" thoughts of Jesus about the divine forgiveness. This *détour* is indeed the heart of the matter: the knowledge that God comes, that forgiveness happens, that it *must really* happen, because our guilt is real. Here therefore forgiveness has a quite different meaning from that which it possesses where it is spoken of in connection with a general idea of truth. The supposed *détour* corresponds to the difference between the Idea of God in general religion and the Living God of Revelation.

(iii)

But this emphasis on the objective character of the Atonement does not rule out the necessity for a subjective process; indeed, this subjective process is really the aim of the Atonement. On the side of man something really needs to be removed and re-created. This may be called reconciliation (atonement) in the narrower sense. It is not primarily the sense of guilt which has to be removed, but the actual stain of guilt itself. Many men have scarcely any sense of guilt at all; it is not aroused in them until they come into contact with Christ. And it is in Christ alone that we all come to know what our guilt really is. The first element, therefore, in the act of reconciliation is not the removal of this subjective sense of guilt, but the knowledge that our guilt has been purged, or, in the characteristic language of the Old Testament, that our "sin is covered." In the language of the New Testament it is expressed by saying that the creditor's account is torn up before the eyes of the debtor. It is an act of God, the majestic act of an absolute monarch which is here made known; it is not a subjective feeling, a peaceful state of mind, from which possibly some objective inference may be drawn.

The positive reverse side of this process of "covering" sin is called justification, the divine declaration that so far as God is concerned there is no longer any obstacle between us and Him. God once more speaks to man in tones of mercy and not of anger. He speaks to man as to one who belongs to Him, and not as to one who is cast out from His presence. He speaks to him as one who is His own, and who is to be the sharer of His life. It is only God's own Word which can do this. For to us this is incomprehensible. God addresses man as just, and thus He makes him "justified." He lifts him up into the state of "justification." Just as the touch of the royal sword transforms a burgher into a noble, so the divine declaration of forgiveness raises the sinner into the state of righteousness. His Will ignores entirely all that is so real to us that we know we could not overcome it. He declares it to be nothing, and promises that it shall actually become nothing. It is not because He foresees the final destruction of sin that He declares sin is nothing; on the contrary, it is because, by His Word, He cancels the existence of sin, that sin must finally disappear. For in reality what God speaks comes into existence, and when He declares anything to be non-existent, it is non-existent. His Word both creates and renews the life of the world.[1]

This Word is Christ. In Him the divine creative and redeeming Word speaks to us. That this Word, the Alpha and the Omega, speaks to us once more as to those who belong to Him: this is the reconciliation, the central point between the Fall and the Redemption, the central point at which redemption begins. It begins through the atonement because it is based on the Word, because we are here concerned with a personal relation, and not with a process of nature. Redemption without atonement is in the last resort the conception of sin as something natural, like disease. Forgiveness without atonement means that sin is conceived simply as error. The Word is the reality which restores what was lost, wounded,

---

[1] Holl (*Luther*, p. 124) illustrates his idea that the verdict of God in justification is "analytical" in character, by the parable of the sculptor, who sees in the block of marble what he can make out of it. This idea is exactly contrary to the idea of the Bible and of the Reformers. God's gaze at us does not mean that He sees in us possibilities which stand out among others—otherwise His creative work would be simply to draw out that which is already there—but it is itself the creative act which calls into being that which does not exist. But Holl is right in saying that even in Luther's faith justification and (future) redemption are not to be thought of apart from each other.

broken: it is this which constitutes the Atonement. The mere word of forgiveness apart from its actual reality is mere Idealism; to assert the reality of redemption without the Word is merely natural religion, which includes all forms of Pantheism, even of the most "spiritual" kind. Thus the central point, where the subjective and the objective aspects of Atonement meet, is this: the Word of divine justification. As a Word it means nothing unless it is heard, and, indeed, heard in such a way that it is believed. Faith in justification is the central point in the Biblical message, because the relation between God and man is a truly personal one.

Justification is the most incomprehensible thing that exists, All other marvels are miracles on the circumference of being, but this is the miracle in the centre of being, in the personal centre. Justification means this miracle: that Christ takes our place and we take His. Here the objective vicarious offering has become a process of exchange. Apart from this transaction, forgiveness is not credible; for it contradicts the holiness of God. Justification cannot be separated from the "objective atonement," from the expiatory sacrifice of the Mediator. Indeed, justification simply means that this objective transaction becomes a "Word" to us, the Word of God. When I know that it is God who is speaking to me in this event —that God is really speaking to *me*—I believe. Faith means knowing that this fact is God speaking to me in His Word.

(iv)

It is only in this subjective experience, in faith, that the Atonement becomes real. But this subjective experience is completely objective in character. For this is what it means: that my "self" is crossed out, displaced, and replaced by Christ, the Divine Word. This is that *"fröhliche Wirtschaft"* ("happy exchange" or arrangement) (Luther) by which Christ becomes mine and I become His. *Nostra assumsit, ut nobis sua conferret*, Luther was not the first to say this. The phrase from Irenaeus which has been chosen as the motto for this book: "for the sake of His infinite love He has become what we are in order that He may make us entirely what He is" is not merely the basic thought of his doctrine of "recapitulation," but in a variety of forms it is the main theme of the Christian message of the Early Church. "In His forgiving goodness," we read in the *Epistle to Diognetus*[1] "God gave His Own Son for us as a ransom, the Holy for the unholy, . . . the Imperishable for the perishing. For what else could cover our sin save His righteousness? Wherein could we, the unscrupulous (lawless), the godless, find justification save in the Son of God? O marvellous exchange, O incomprehensible work! The lawlessness of so many was to disappear in the one just One, the righteousness of One should justify many sinners." "That the Logos became flesh," says Gregory of Nazianzen, "is in my opinion as much as to say that He became sin and a curse, not indeed transforming Himself into this, but in this manner taking upon Himself our transgressions and bearing our sicknesses."[2] Or, in the pregnant language of Augustine: "*de te sibi mortem, de se tibi salutem, de te sibi contumelias, de se tibi honores.*"[3] These are simply different ways of expressing the Pauline phrases: "Christ Jesus who of God is made unto us wisdom and righteousness," and "I live, yet not I, but Christ liveth in me." This does not mean that Christ is a merely mystical force—if this were so, this dynamic force would remain relative like all that is dynamic; but "He is my *righteousness*." What Christ means to me cannot be measured by the standard of my own poverty-stricken experience—what would that mean to one who knows like Paul (*Rom. vii*), that "in his flesh there dwelleth no good thing"—no, the standard is the Word of Christ, the Promise of God, which is worth far, far more than a mere mystical force because it is absolute. But this Word, which in faith becomes mine, is not opposed to the idea of dynamic force; for it is indeed "a power of God"; but the *absolute* character of this force, which is effective as an energy and can also be felt, is not felt and experienced, but is accepted on trust, as the promise of God, and it is upon the absolute character of this force that everything depends.

This objective attitude is the distinguishing mark of faith.

[1] Chapter ix.   [2] Ep. ad. El. i, 14.   [3] On Psalm lix.

This is peace. Psychologically speaking, the one who believes is not simply satisfied; his heart still remains a "restless thing," the ebb and flow of feeling and emotion, the sense of exaltation and impotence, the sense of confidence followed by reaction, the oscillations between hope and fear, happiness and depression, do not cease. The state of the Christian is one of "confident despair." But this despair is *confident*. All these inner moods and feelings as they rise and fall toss like the waves of the sea over an immovable sheet of rock, upon which these words are clearly inscribed: "I belong to Christ, in spite of everything. In spite of myself, in spite of my moods and feelings, in spite of all my experience of my own impotence, even in the sphere of faith. I belong to Christ not because *I* believe in Him, but because of what Christ has said, through the Word which God has spoken to me in Him, the Mediator."

Thus it is the objective character of the fact of Christ and of the Word of Christ which gives its character to this subjective experience. In this respect we might compare faith with ecstasy: ἔκστασις. Faith also is to be outside oneself, but in a quite different manner; for the ecstasy of mysticism is a psychical experience which lasts for a few moments and then passes away again. But faith, so far as it is ecstasy, is independent of all subjective experiences. It means that one is placed at a point outside the stream of experience, on the further bank, which therefore cannot be touched by the stream of experience any more, because where I stand is not the position *I* have chosen; it is not my doing, but it has been chosen by God, because it is God's act, in an objective fact, because it is the Cross of Christ, or what is the same thing, the Word of the Scriptures.

Once again, it is evident that here the idea of the Mediator is decisive. It is the idea of the Mediator which gives to justification its objective character, and thus certainty to faith, that stability which cannot be moved by any subjective changes. He belongs to both spheres; to the objective world of history, in which my subjectivity can alter nothing, and to the sphere of the deepest interior life. He is a fact of history, and as part of the past an unchangeable fact. "It is written." But He *is* this Fact, the Reconciler, only as the Word of God, that which only "is" in so far as it is heard, and is then the most actual, the most intimately present, and the most inward fact there is. That God speaks through Christ to me, and that He thus speaks in me, is an absolutely present, and thus an absolutely subjective experience. It is the speech of the Holy Spirit. But the fact that it is *Christ*, in whom and through whom God thus speaks to me, is the most objective fact possible. The former experience is the goal of mysticism: immediacy, the breaking-down of the wall of separation, the overcoming of the distance between God and myself: *Christ in me*. How very easy it would be to confuse this with mysticism! And yet, how can we make this mistake? Are we not here concerned with Christ the Crucified, the sacrifice which has been offered once for all, apart from anything I have done? With something which is really, actually, and outwardly a brute fact, with no "inwardness" at all about it, a death. That it is this with which I am united is the absolute opposite of mysticism, for it means union with something objective, with a means, which stands between myself and God, and through which alone I can have communion with Him—this is mediacy pure and unrestricted.

Complete immediacy in the midst of complete mediacy: this is the paradox of reconciliation, of justification, of faith. It is not that we can say that the Christian faith possesses a mystical aspect as well as an objective and historical aspect; this would be a very crude way of describing the situation. Here we are not concerned with connecting two essentially alien elements, nor even with an organic synthesis. However paradoxical it may sound to say so, the one *is* the other. The Christ, who as an historical figure is the One who offered His life on the Cross as an expiatory oblation and sacrificed it once for all, is also the One who speaks to us in the intimacy of faith. It is thus that He "dwells" within us; it is thus that He is now really our righteousness and our life—in so far as we believe.

It is only due to misunderstanding that there can ever be any opposition between the ideas of "Christ for us" and "Christ in us," since in each instance something quite different is meant by "Christ." It is also impossible to supplement the one by the other, as Pietism tries to supplement orthodoxy. No truth will ever be born out of two misunderstandings, out of a combination of mysticism and orthodoxy; the true knowledge of the Christ of the Gospel will not issue from a mistaken idea of "Christ for us" and an erroneous idea of "Christ in us." Orthodoxy with a dash of mysticism as a corrective would scarcely come nearer to the truth of the Gospel than orthodoxy and mysticism separately.

As the Mediator, Christ, in His Person and His Work, is the unfathomable mystery of God, into which we cannot and ought not to penetrate, so also the Atonement in its paradoxical combination of the subjective and the objective, of the historical and the present, of the Word and the Spirit, is the unfathomable mystery of God. It is the mystery of the Triune God. That God speaks for us is the mystery of the Son; that He speaks in us is the mystery of the Spirit. That which is expressed outwardly and that which is spoken within the heart, the Christ for us and the Christ in us, are one and the same God. This is the reason why faith, which is most subjective, personal, and interior, is at the same time also most objective; and that the Atonement, which is so wholly objective, unique, confronting us as something alien and exclusive, is at the same time the most subjective and the most personal fact there is. Indeed, we are already on false lines—although in the doctrinal presentation of the subject it can scarcely be avoided—when we separate the thought of the fact of salvation from the appropriation of salvation. The rubric: "appropriation of salvation" is used frequently in dogmatics only when the conception of salvation has already been falsely materialized, and has become a rigid orthodox doctrine. Salvation is neither doctrine nor conviction concerning a doctrine, but the Word of God in Christ as it speaks to us in the heart; indeed, it is God Himself as He speaks in us. But both doctrine and conviction are merely human things.

(v)

In us God speaks His Word. This "us" is not a space. It is our Ego. If then it is the Word of *God* which is manifested in faith, then it must also be manifested in *our* faith. We must be able to say: *I* believe. God gives faith, God's Word is the content, God's speaking in me is the form of faith; but it still remains true: *I* must believe. In this union of faith, however, God remains God and man remains man. There is no fusion; the unity is that of the truth. God gives the reply to the question asked by man; here "question" is to be regarded in the existential sense. Only where man really asks for God will he receive the answer. The presupposition of faith is repentance. It is of course true, that in the last resort even repentance is the work of God and is only fulfilled in faith. But it also precedes faith—faith in the specific Christian sense. At the outset it belongs to the "human" sphere, to the Law. At the same time, however, it is judgment on the whole human sphere; it means turning one's back on it; it is a negative movement. Repentance is not like all other human movements, a movement of ascent, but a descent. Therefore, on account of this direction, repentance, the sense of guilt, the sense of being in the wrong, the sense of needing God, the feeling of poverty—constitutes the point of contact for faith, for the Word. It means openness to God.

Hence repentance is the presupposition of atonement. The sacrifice of the Old Covenant is of value in so far as it is an expression of this readiness for repentance. The sacrifice itself is simply the "filling-up" of the hole which is made known to us in repentance. To be willing to repent means that one is willing to make atonement. In this is included the willingness to avoid evil, but not the other way round. Whoever wills really and truly to make atonement will in future avoid occasions of evil. But the mere resolve: "I will not do it again" does not remove the sense of guilt; the will to expiate, the admission of the necessity for atonement is something new.

It is the sign of real readiness to repent. It is only in this faith in the Atonement that repentance is completed. The gift of a "broken and a contrite heart" is not bestowed until a man sees that nothing can help him save this one incomprehensible sacrifice. Only by this sacrifice does he measure the greatness of his guilt, and this sense of guilt is repentance. At the present day we know by experience that

529

the loss of the idea of expiation has completely disintegrated the moral consciousness. It has often been remarked that at the basis of the moral degeneration of the present day lies the loss of the sense of guilt. But men rarely admit that the sense of guilt itself is perverted when it has lost the sense of the necessity for punishment and expiation. This digression may serve to help us to a right estimate of the New Testament thought of sacrifice as it is held by most people to-day, according to which it is a relic of a sub-ethical cultus and the legal spirit, if not a wholly primitive instinct of revenge, and of an equally primitive belief in blood-magic.

To repent means to recognize the necessity for punishment and expiation and to be willing to accept it. Therefore forgiveness without expiation injures the moral sense. The ultimate point in the inward process of reconciliation is therefore the fulfilment of the necessity for atonement. Without this even the sense of forgiveness can never be established quite honestly and quite surely. The Bible and the literature of Primitive Christianity do not say a great deal about this, because at that time the moral sense of guilt was still so strong that the idea of punishment and expiation was unquestioned.

It is due to Rationalism, and still more to Naturalism, that these profound truths have been obscured for the modern man. It is no accident that it was the Rationalist Abelard[1] who first of all evolved a doctrine of the Atonement of a purely subjective kind, without any idea either of expiation or of penalty; it was no accident that his doctrine and his protest against the ecclesiastical doctrine of "satisfaction" were eagerly adopted and carried further by those typical Rationalists, the Socinians, that during the period of the Enlightenment the doctrine of the Atonement almost entirely disappeared, and could not be regained even by German Idealism. All these systems lack the one necessary presupposition for the understanding of this doctrine: the profound sense of guilt, the earnestness of repentance.

[1] By the Abelard doctrine of the Atonement we mean the one which is specifically associated with his name and peculiar to himself, without entering into the controversy which rages round the question to what extent we can find in his doctrine traces of another conception. Cf. Seeberg, *Dogg.*, III, pp. 229 ff., and Baur, *Lehre von der Versöhnung*, pp. 191–99.

(vi)

Through its connection with repentance the Atonement points backwards, to the present state of man. But as the beginning of redemption it points forwards. We have already pointed out that the fact that the Atonement is so absolutely central is a sign that in the Christian religion the relation between God and man is really personal. For guilt and forgiveness are the most personal matters that can ever be imagined, since they refer solely to the personal relation between God and man. But the realism of the Idea of God does not permit us to remain at the thought of justification. The Word of God, the promise of God, means something which is not contained in itself as a mere Word; it points forward to realization.

First of all, things must be set right at the centre, in the personal relation between God and man. This is the Atonement. But once this has been righted, really and truly, inevitably this implies the transformation of the whole of life. Or, to put it the other way round, this central position has not been fully restored unless reality as a whole is placed upon a new foundation. For man is a physico-spiritual being, that is, he is a being irrevocably connected with the sensible world. The central point of the misery of the world should be sought in the realm of man's personal relation to God. But this central point of the personal life with God cannot be isolated from life as a whole. From the centre, misery and wretchedness streams out into the world, and from the world it streams back again.

We do not live in sin through the will alone, but also through the body, and indeed through the world. As the cosmos is poisoned from the centre outwards, so also it again poisons the centre. In the main, therefore, bondage to the body also means a permanent state of bondage to sin, in spite of forgiveness, in spite of the Atonement, which in forgiveness and faith is really effective. Hence Atonement can only be a first stage. It points beyond itself as the Word of perfect restoration and fulfilment. Forgiveness also includes the promise of redemption. The Mediator does not intend to stand between God and ourselves. He desires to unite, not to separate. But He wills to unite us wholly. He is the Door; therefore through this Door we are to go into a new world: to the Kingdom of God, to perfection.

The Word of reconciliation would not be effective, it would not be the Word of God, if it were not the beginning of redemption. Faith is power, energy, the principle of life, the moral power of renewal. But faith is only faith, it is not sight, and the Word is only the Word, it is not the content of the Word. Between both there lies once more a turning-point. For effective though faith may be, it can never grow into sight. However powerful the Word may be, it can never be the reality which it proclaims.

We possess God's presence in Christ in a refracted, concealed way; owing to the sinful reality of this world, the rays of His Light reach us refracted by the murkiness of the atmosphere of this world. We perceive the God of Mercy at the place of horror, at the Cross. Therefore, even faith is a kind of possession in the midst of non-possession, certainty in uncertainty, comfort in despair, joyful confidence in repentance, the love of God in the fear of God, the immediacy of God in a wholly mediated manner, the Divine Word, the Word that is near, in the Word of the Scriptures, in a book, in fellowship with other people in the Church. Here also the Mediator and faith in Him are central; between that which is and that which shall be, forming both in His own image. For this very reason He is the Mediator, because He shares in both, because He has to point in both directions. He has a share in the sinful corrupted world and He has a share in the divine eternal world of perfection. He is the Bridge between both. The Bridge, however, is there to be crossed.

The contradictory nature, so characteristic of all evangelical credal statements, the dialectic, the affirmative in the negative and the negative in the affirmative, which is so hard to understand in thought—alas! still more so in life—this effect of refraction from the sinful world on the light of the divine truth, is also the token of the eschatological element. Hence the Christian faith points beyond itself to the End, to the resurrection of the body, because in itself it is inconsistent. Christ the Crucified cannot be the End of the ways of God; faith as seeing "through a glass darkly" cannot be the end of the revelation of truth. The dialectical and contradictory element requires a solution, but it demands a solution such as no one could master even in thought. The dialectic of faith remains unsolved, in contradistinction to the dialectical philosophy. The fact that it remains unsolved means that we are waiting for the solution which God alone knows and God alone can give. It is not that this hope has to be added to faith. Indeed, faith is itself simply the certainty of that which is to come; as such it is power and joy, as such it is a present possession; but only as such.[1] Hence Faith and Hope are the same; they are merely two different aspects, which look in different directions. Both refer to the one Word of God: Faith, since it stresses what we now possess, and Hope, since it points towards that which is promised to us. The promise, and nothing else than the promise, *is* the present possession. The Atonement is simply the beginning of Redemption. But just because this Atonement is the beginning of redemption, redemption itself is also definitely distinguished from everything else which is called by this name, even if this distinction does not permit us to picture this future to ourselves. If we could do this we would have already attained our end, then it would not be a future hope. This does not mean that our hope is indefinite. There is nothing indefinite about the hope of resurrection, eternal life, complete fellowship with God. It is sufficiently definite for our hopes; but it is not sufficiently definite for our imagination. It possesses the definite character of the Word, but not the definite character of sight.

Repentance and hope are the obverse and the reverse of the one faith in the Atonement. Real repentance is the perception that all we can do is to hope. It means being poor

[1] The distinction between axiological and teleological eschatology in Althaus (*Die letzten Dinge*[3]) seems to be derived from a relic of the tendency to expound the Gospels in a Platonic manner. Certainly—as Althaus (p. 25) reminds me—we can speak of *having* faith and of a *presence* of fellowship with God. But this "having" is in the form of hope, and that which is possessed is in the form of that which is believed, thus not of that which is seen. "As dying—and behold we live," "confident despair."

in spirit, it means knowing what we lack and the sense of our imperfection; it means the knowledge of the gulf which lies between us and God, it is the sense of distance, of the fact that we are still so far away. Whoever truly repents is thrown wholly upon hope. Repentance and waiting correspond to each other, therefore repentance is that which belongs to faith in the coming Kingdom of God. The sacrifice of the Mediator— to put it in another way—therefore is necessary because only "in Christ," and indeed in the Cross of Christ, can we really repent. To repent is to die; but we cannot die of ourselves. The mystical process of "dying to self" is a righteousness of "works," it is self-affirmation. We only really repent when we know that we can never be penitent enough, that we do not feel the seriousness of the situation sufficiently to be penetrated with the intense earnestness which such repentance demands, when we realize that Christ must repent for us. If we could repent as we should no atonement would be needed, for then repentance would be atonement. Then the righteousness of God would have been satisfied. But this is precisely what we cannot do. We can only do this where we can "be righteous," for to be "righteous" and to repent mean the same thing. The point or "place" at which this happens is Christ. We are baptized into His death. We are "buried" with Him into His death. This is not sacramentarian mysticism but simple faith in the Word.[1] We must let God tell us in the death of Christ what our position is. The fact that we take this Word from Him is itself faith, repentance, the state of being "buried" and "dying" with Him. It is precisely the objectivity of the Atonement, that expiation is necessary, in order that we may be led to real subjective

---

[1] When Heitmüller (*Taufe und Abendmahl im Urchristentum*, p. 19) admits "that the same effects which are ascribed to baptism also seem to be simply connected with faith," but explains this "inconcinnity" by the familiar statement that "Paul was not a systematic theologian," we ought to remind ourselves that real Sacramentalists always regard the Sacrament as the chief thing, as the highest point of their religion, and that they could never say like Paul: "I thank God that I baptized none of you, save . . . besides, I know not whether I baptized any other." For the real Sacramentalist it is impossible to ascribe "the same effects . . . also simply to faith" apart from Baptism, even if he is in no sense a systematic theologian!

repentance. For only thus do we come to see what our real position is. Only as those who have been reconciled, for whose sins expiation has been made, are we ready to repent, just as we are only justified as those whose sins have been expiated. So long as we think we can ignore expiation and attain forgiveness without it, our repentance is not really serious.

We say exactly the same thing if we emphasize the other side of the question; if we say that repentance is only possible to those who hope. So long as we are depending on something other than Hope we are not yet as empty as we ought to be if we are to correspond with the truth; we are still trying to fill up the hole which God alone can fill. But we can only say, "all we can do is to hope," if there is really something to hope for. For no man is so stupid as to risk everything for an uncertain hope, or even for a blind hope. We can only risk all for hope where we have a certain hope, and where our hope includes everything. Only the promise of God in Christ, only the hope of real redemption, and the certainty of this hope in revelation can loosen the convulsive clutch with which we cling to the valueless present. The Atonement means our redemption and our life, as well as our humiliation and our death. Death and Resurrection, judgment and liberation constitute the content of the word of reconciliation.

CONCERNING THE SUPPOSED CONTRADICTION BETWEEN PAULINISM AND THE MESSAGE OF JESUS

WE believe that by demonstrating the inner connection between the various forms of the Christian doctrine of the Atonement a detailed argument to prove that this doctrine itself is based upon the New Testament testimony of the Apostolic Churches has been made superfluous. Whenever this view has been rejected it has been due to purely dogmatic reasons. Because the orthodox doctrine itself had been rejected the effort was then made to explain it away by proving that it was not based upon the teaching of the New Testament. Wherever critical scholars—for instance, in the old Tübingen School—had thrown off their allegiance to the Christian faith and to the Church to such an extent that they no longer felt it necessary to base their faith upon the New Testament at all, there, in principle, they admitted in a quite unprejudiced manner that in spite of differences in detail the "Pauline" doctrine of the Atonement and the orthodox doctrine were agreed in all essentials. Thus we may "take it as read" that in essentials Paul held and taught this doctrine. A more detailed study of this question belongs to the domain of Biblical Theology.

On the other hand, there is another problem which, both on account of its actuality and of its difficulty, needs rather more detailed treatment. Certainly, so we hear it said, Paul did teach this doctrine, both as regards the Person and the Work of the Mediator. Taken as a whole all this is "Paulinism." But if we admit this, so runs the argument further, and do not try to alter the thought of Paul (like a certain school of Mediating Theology), and if we also admit the critical work which has been done on the Life of Jesus, we cannot avoid the conclusion that the difference between this doctrine of Paul and the whole teaching of Jesus Himself is absolute. Thus at this point which you "Paulinists" have again thrust into the foreground, in any case one or the other must be true:

536

either Jesus or Paul. How can this be combined with your conception, since you cannot admit that there is a contradiction between Jesus and the Christian testimony about Him?

This absolute contrast between Jesus and Paul is supported by two arguments: the first is positive, and is based on the teaching of Jesus on forgiveness, the second is negative, and deals with the lack of any definite reference on the part of Jesus to His sacrificial death, in those sayings of His which belong to a reliable tradition. The first argument gains its cogency from the supposed perception that Jesus taught forgiveness as a general truth, as a self-evident truth about the Nature of God. This, however, is an absolute misrepresentation of the case. From the very outset this is impossible, since Jesus stands upon the ground of the Old Testament. When a religious Jew speaks of forgiveness he does this on the basis of the divine revelation. It is always a special condescension of God, it is His merciful and gracious dealing with His chosen people, the proofs of His grace in Moses, the prophets, and other men of God, and the divine leading of this people seen in the light of this revelation, upon which the pious Jew bases his faith in the forgiveness of God. Thus he sees clearly that forgiveness must be a definite *act*, that it cannot simply be taken for granted as the natural result of some idea of the kindness of God. The Jew knows that a general statement: "God forgives because He is a kindly Father," would be a blasphemy, a mockery of the Holiness of God. That God does forgive is a marvel, a miracle, it is not something which can be taken for granted, and the religious Jew discovers this "miracle of grace" in the prophetic revelation and in the history of his divine deliverance. "He made known His ways unto Moses, His acts unto the children of Israel"—so runs the classical passage in the Old Testament doctrine of forgiveness in the 103rd Psalm.[1]

[1] To how great an extent even in later Judaism the consciousness of divine grace was connected with ideas of a "saving history" is discussed by Köberle: *Sünde und Gnade im religiösen Leben des Volkes Israel bis auf Christum*, pp. 613 ff. It was a vital fact that forgiveness was connected with expiation through the sacrifice of the High Priest (p. 614). Wherever mercy was concerned—and "forgiveness was included in the thought"—there is

But Jesus does not speak of forgiveness as a religious Jew, but as the Messiah who has been sent by God. If His whole message is an "act of the Messianic consciousness," so much more His language about divine forgiveness. He *is* what He says about it; His speech cannot be separated from His existence, from the mystery of His Person, from His authority. If what even the pious Jew knows about forgiveness is based upon the divine revelation in "the Law and the Prophets," then the words of Jesus about forgiveness form a veritable revelation of God in act; for He is more than a prophet. What He says is valid only because He says it. That He speaks about the forgiveness of God is—like everything else, only here it is clearer than anything else—God's own merciful action. Here forgiveness actually takes place, and the certainty of forgiveness is connected with this happening.

Forgiveness actually takes place through Him. It is this which constitutes the stumbling-block, the fact that He forgives, that He has dared to "interfere" with this prerogative of God—as the Pharisees see it; that He administers this royal privilege as though it were His own—as faith admits. He does not forgive in the Name of God, He does not appeal to a higher Court. He Himself *is* this higher court of appeal: this consciousness of authority shines through all His acts and through all His speech. He has "come" to the lost sheep of the House of Israel. He is empowered to do for them what only God can do. His forgiveness is His supreme proof of authority, and hence it is the stumbling-block. It is, in the highest sense, an "eschatological" event; it is the presence of the Kingdom of God. Hence His parables, which are supposed to express the general idea of forgiveness, are also only to be understood in this connection. They illustrate and comment on His action.

always the thought of "mercy on Israel," even when the question is that of the forgiveness of the heathen (p. 616), that is, of grace granted specially in connection with the whole revelation of salvation. "Apparently the motives of this faith are . . . very varied; at bottom, however, they all go back to the election of Israel. Whether this is actually mentioned, whether the reference is to the covenant with the fathers of the nation or to that of Sinai, to the merit of the patriarchs and prophets . . . fundamentally it is all the one same familiar idea: the historical motivation of the national hope of salvation" (p. 617).

They contain anything but a general doctrine; rather they are meant to show that what Jesus does is really the act of God. He is the Good Shepherd who goes after His sheep. God, indeed, is the Shepherd; but this "going after" by the Shepherd is fulfilled nowhere else save in the historical acts of Jesus. Thus the question whether *God* does things like this arose out of the acts of Jesus. The point of His parables therefore is this: they are meant to show that His acts are the acts of God, that His attitude towards sinners is the attitude of God Himself.

If, however, in His existence as a Person, He is the Revealer of the Will of God, then this applies to His existence as a whole. It is a unity. The fact that He existed, and that He existed thus, is His "coming" and His Passion. Or, to put it the other way round: in His Passion His coming is fulfilled. When Jesus speaks of "having come" and of "being sent," He is speaking of His Mediatorship. That God has "sent Him to the lost sheep of the house of Israel" means that His existence saves them from the guilt of sin. We cannot positively assert that in the later Jewish picture of the Messiah, with its vivid features of Messianic redemption, the close of this evil era, and the activity which will usher in a glorious future, the removal of the curse of sin was a central thought[1]; but on this point, as on many others, the assertion that Jesus took over the contemporary Messianic dogma just as it was, without changing it in any way, and applied it to Himself, has been proved to be a wholly untenable and imaginative statement. Rather, it was of the very essence of His own conception of His Messianic vocation that His position was authoritative also with reference to the problem of sin and guilt.

[1] True, even in the early Christian period Jews applied the idea of the Suffering Servant of the Lord to the Messiah. "It cannot be controverted that in the second century after Christ, at least in certain circles of Judaism, there was a certain familiarity with the idea of a suffering Messiah who suffered for the expiation of human sin" (Schürer: *Gesch. d. jüd. Volkes*, II, p. 650). Cf. *Testament of Levi*, ch. 18, the idea of the Messianic Priest-King, of whom it is said: "At the time of his priesthood all sin will vanish and the godless will cease to do evil. And he himself will open the doors of Paradise and he will remove the sword menacing Adam, and will give to the holy ones to eat from the tree of life . . ." (Kautzsch, *Apokryphen*, II, p. 471).

People usually overlook the fact that the Messianic claim as such, and still more the Messianic claim of Jesus Himself, includes everything which the prophecy of the Old Testament had predicted about the eschatological nearness of salvation, of the nearness of God, of reconciliation and redemption. To be the Messiah did not mean merely to be a figure which either accompanied or interpreted the great process of redemption, but the Messiah was the decisive active Person, in whom the reality of this process is incorporated, in which, indeed, it is realized. The unique character of the Person of Jesus, as compared with all the prophets—who yet, on their part, were already mediators of the divine revelation and the divine grace —does not only increase the mediatorial claim in exactly the same proportion, but—just because of its uniqueness—only then allows it to have its full meaning. He in whom the Kingdom of God has "come upon you" (ἔφθασεν), He in whom the Kingdom of God "is among you (in the midst of you)," stands, therefore, as the Mediator of that which is coming from God, between God and man, as the One in whom the transition is effected, and the One to follow whom is the condition of a share in the new era. It is He in whom the old aeon with its curse is ended, it is He in whom the new aeon with its salvation has dawned, and is actually present. All this must be remembered if we wish to understand the fact that Jesus Christ did not *teach* forgiveness as a general truth, but actually *forgave* sinful men with authority, and proclaimed forgiveness as God's will and God's act.

Yet another misunderstanding needs to be removed. People are fond of pointing to the Parable of the Prodigal Son to support the view that Jesus taught the forgiveness of God as a general truth. Quite apart from the fact that this kind of thing would be wholly impossible within the message of the Bible (and this means primarily the Old Testament), we ought to note in particular that the *tertium comparationis* in the parable is not *how* God forgives, but that His forgiveness is granted to those whom the average Jew, and the Pharisee in particular, regarded as outcasts; thus the point of the Parable is the unconditional character of the forgiveness of God, which was also the stumbling-block in the Pauline proclamation of forgiveness. Although this parable may throw no light upon the special problem under consideration—save the fact of the silence of Jesus about His Mediatorship, with which we shall be dealing directly—on the other hand, the two other parables in this chapter prove quite clearly that it is God who seeks the lost, that the initiative begins with Him, that this denotes a real movement on the part of God, a movement of the kind which has always been meant in the Old Testament by the "sending" of the messengers of God. The forgiveness of God is not something nebulous and intangible, it is something which "comes," which is "offered," and this offer is God's incomprehensible gracious act, His search for the lost. Jesus often expressly describes Himself as this chosen authoritative organ of the God who seeks men, as in other parables He makes it quite clear that He is the One in whom God offers His mercy, in whom He Himself invites men, through the life of the One who represents Him. Even to the prophets this execution of the divine commission of forgiveness meant something fundamentally different from a general doctrine of forgiveness; in the case of Jesus this means still more. It is connected with His "sending" as the Messiah, a "sending" which, even in comparison with the mediatorial work of the prophets, is something quite different: it is absolutely new, and unique, in the strictest sense of the word.

When this has been understood it is possible to understand the setting of the parable of forgiveness as well, and, we may remark in passing, this makes it historically credible. These parables are, therefore, the very opposite of a general doctrine, because they are the commentary on His own acts, and because the content of these parables is only intended to justify the action of Jesus. Hence their point is this: "You are wrong to reproach Me for My intercourse with sinners as though it were godless behaviour, for I am behaving towards sinners as God behaves; indeed, there is still more in it than this, for, actually, *God* is acting through and in My action." Thus these parables do not seek to disprove the divine forgiveness as the act of God; on the contrary, they are intended to show that the concrete, historical, and Messianic action of Jesus has the divine sanction. These parables can only be understood aright when we realize that they are intended to show this truth: not merely that such behaviour is *not* inconsistent with the character of God, but that, on the contrary, only in such behaviour can the character of God be really known.

This proves that the first of those two arguments falls to the ground. What is the position, however, in reference to the second, the argument from silence? Why did Jesus not speak plainly about the connection between forgiveness and His death —as Paul did, and, indeed, as the Christian Church did even before Paul came on the scene? We may reply with a counter-question: Why should He? He is not Himself an apostle! His task is not retrospective, like that of an apostle; it is His duty, as Messiah, to *be* the central point, tested and tried, between prophetic prediction and apostolic witness. His teaching is not the Gospel, save in so far as it is a moment in His Being, an element in His revealing existence. This existence, however, was intended to be truly historical, and therefore truly human, such that in it the "before" and the "after" have real significance, and cannot be altered or transposed. To live historically means to live with a forward look, thus not to anticipate the future as though it were already the past. The death of Jesus is proclaimed after it has taken place, when people can look back to it. Precisely as we realize that His message kept step with His life and did not hurry on ahead, that it was no proleptical expression but an existential commentary, we shall not be astonished that Jesus did not proclaim beforehand the mystery of His death. Indeed, we accept the view of the Reformers that He Himself was still wrestling with this mystery in Gethsemane;[1] for we do not allow the *vere deus* to make us forget the *vere homo*. If He *had* spoken about it, who would have understood Him? We do not sufficiently realize that such a proleptical way of speaking would be fantastic, arbitrary, and unreal.

We do, however, regard it as a well attested historical

[1] According to Luther, the Deity of Christ during His Passion and Death was "wholly hidden within Himself and lay quite still, and it did not put itself forward nor did it shine forth" (*E.A.*, 3, 302), but "the Deity withdrew His power and allowed the Humanity to struggle on alone" (*W.A.*, 45, 239).

tradition that Jesus only spoke to His disciples about His death towards the close of His active ministry, and that in a few rare hints He suggested that His sufferings according to the Scriptures were part of the Messianic plan of God. It ought to be regarded as a sign of the genuineness of the tradition that the sayings of Jesus about His sufferings and death are placed right at the end of the story, and that they are placed in connection with the knowledge of His Messiahship. Jesus speaks about death from the very moment when it begins to cast its shadow before Him, at the moment when the actual reality has to be faced. This is in harmony with the existential reality of His discourses—whether in public speech or in private conversation with His disciples. And He speaks of it as of a mystery which (in a very special way, it is true) is only for those "to whom it is given to understand the mysteries of the Kingdom of Heaven." He made these statements under the same limitations which surrounded His communication of the mystery of the Messiahship.

Therefore we cannot admit that, so far, any convincing evidence has been brought against the genuineness of the accounts of the Last Supper in the Synoptic Gospels and in the First Epistle to the Corinthians, although I am well aware of the difficulties raised by the four-fold account which has been handed down to us by the tradition. When we look at the history of criticism it is scarcely possible to doubt that the cause and impelling motive behind the critical disintegration of the tradition was not the manifold character of the actual tradition itself, but the dogmatic discomfort which criticism itself felt on this point. For it was at this point that the theory of the inconsistency between the doctrine of Paul and the teaching of Jesus Himself broke down, the theory to which Liberal Christianity clung with all its might, because it alone seemed to leave it a little justification to appeal to "Christ," and hence to have some right to the name of "Christian," while in every other way it taught the very opposite of all that had been called Christian right down the history of the Church from the time of the Apostles. The narratives of the Last Supper could not be genuine. At least they had to be worked over until they were no longer a menace to that particular theory.

I have no desire to suggest that such ideas were in the minds of any of the scholars who were engaged on the labour of research into the Life of Jesus from the Liberal Christian point of view. In their minds there is no doubt that the scientific question was always foremost, and we do not deny that for one who already shared the Liberal views it was possible to draw these conclusions in all honesty and fairness, so long as men saw in them merely a scientific principle, which on account of its apparent success seemed to justify their scientific work.

Once these theological prejudices have disappeared, however, and the fact that this is so is certainly due more to radical criticism than to orthodox apologetic—when all this has been cleared away, from top to bottom, then we can see clearly how little weight can be attached to the purely historical scientific arguments on this point compared with the tradition. Paul's phrase παρέλαβον, "I received of the Lord," written scarcely twenty years after the death of Jesus, and referring to an event in the life of Paul which can only be separated from the death of Jesus by a very few years—this phrase παρέλαβον, in its solemn asseveration, which suggests that the one who utters this expression is putting forth all his force to make himself believed, will indeed weigh more heavily in the scale with anyone whose mind has not been distorted by prejudice, than all the hypothetical constructions of the critics. This does not mean that the literal words of the Pauline tradition are beyond the reach of criticism, for this tradition must be compared with the other traditions. But it seems to me that the common element in the tradition, which is at the same time its actual kernel, has certainly been authenticated, as far as this is possible in questions of this kind.[1]

[1] At the same time, it must be confessed that the careful consideration of the probable manner in which the four (or five) types of tradition arose (if we regard the text of Luke, which also was handed down without the word about the cup, as the fifth) makes it very difficult to say what the "Lord's words of institution" really were, even quite apart from dogmatic prejudice. Indeed, naturally there still remains as the ultimate possibility (which cannot entirely be set aside) the sceptical solution, as it is offered by K. L. Schmidt in the article in *R.G.G.*[2], from which we have already quoted. Only to us it seems that the explanation of the actual fact is far more difficult in the sceptical than in the (relatively) more conservative

We need to re-examine the meaning of the scene of the Last Supper in the light of the confidence which has been regained by criticism in the question of the founding of the Church, in some such way as has already been done by Kattenbusch. For this point is evidently connected with the position which the Eucharist occupied in the most primitive form of the Church, as is also attested by the Pauline "παρέλαβον," and not by it alone. "The Eucharist is the act of foundation of His ἐκκλησία, of His Church, as such." If this statement of Kattenbusch is right it throws a great deal of light upon the meaning which the Lord Himself gave to this meal: it is the meal at which the New Covenant was founded, and it is so *sub specie mortis Christi*.

Thus the Mediator expressly stated His Mediatorship (as His apostle was expressly conscious of having received it from Him Himself) at the point at which His active ministry was almost over, where death was imminent, and was therefore, naturally, the subject of conversation; there, and not earlier, but actually there, where it corresponded to the actual situation. Thus the astonishing thing is not the unreliability of the tradition but, on the contrary, its reliability, so that even in its later strata (our present *Matthew* and *Luke*) it has preserved this existential order of the communication of the mystery so securely that at this central point it resisted for so long the temptation to allow myth or imagination to creep into the tradition. The uniting factor between the witness of the Apostle Paul and the Message of Jesus Himself can, in the nature of the case, only be like a very slight thread, a minute point. As such it has actually been handed down to us. The fact of the silence of Jesus can be used as far as it is based upon the actual facts, and no further. Thus the negative argument from silence falls to the ground like the positive argument.

Once again I must reiterate a point which has been fully treated at an earlier stage of this book: faith in Christ is not based upon this constantly fluctuating historical foundation. All that we have just been doing is to meet the excuse that

interpretation, so that we have to take into account the continued influence of dogmatic prejudice in order to explain why the former view should be preferred.

the discoveries of historical research, and especially the argument from silence, confront us with an opposition between the Pauline message and the message of Jesus which cannot be overcome. There could be no question of this, even if the position with regard to the story of the Last Supper and the collective teaching of Jesus about His death were of the character which many critics assert it to be. Belief in Jesus Christ, the Mediator, does not mean that it is necessary to believe that He Himself spoke explicitly about His death and its meaning. He is the Lamb of God, even if He did not *say* so Himself. All that is necessary is this: that what we know of the historical teaching of His life should not directly contradict this statement. But people will assert that this contradiction exists as long as they believe that Jesus was One who proclaimed general truths of religion, and among these the truth of forgiveness by God. The picture of His life presented to us by history, however, does not speak for, but against, this conception, and thus the contradiction automatically disappears. The difficulty of explaining how it was that the community of the disciples which knew the Jesus of history far more intimately than we ever could were yet able to believe in this meaning of His sufferings and death, if it had really contradicted His own teaching, is, in any case, incomparably greater than any difficulties which can result from the retention of the historicity of the Synoptic narrative.

To those who believe, the only difficulty which arises out of the actual historical situation is simply that which belongs, essentially, to faith itself, namely, the stumbling-block that the death of a human being can have absolute significance for all other human beings. It is not historical science but faith alone which can decide whether Jesus is really the Mediator through His death on the Cross. Or rather, it is not faith which decides this question, but it consists in the final admission that God says this in the Word of Christ and that thus it is so. Experience, however, so far confirms this faith that again and again all that can be brought against it from the side of historical science in the course of research by history itself is either dismissed altogether as irrelevant, or is at least rendered highly conjectural.

SECTION III: THE DOMINION OF GOD

PRELIMINARY NOTE

IT is not our intention to make a complete presentation of the Christian faith of the Church from all points of view. Rather from the outset our concern has been directed towards the central point, where time and eternity merge into each other and become one, and where the Christian faith took its rise: the Incarnation of the Word. But we cannot see this "historical" central point at all without perceiving the movement from eternity, nor the movement back towards eternity once more. The significance of Christmas and of Good Friday is only perceived in the light of Easter. The Resurrection constitutes the boundary line of the historical reality and activity of Jesus Christ. We must therefore still deal with this boundary line, and with this movement. But even when this has been done the scriptural testimony to Christ is far from being exhausted. To deal with this fully, however, would mean developing the doctrine of faith, of the Church, and of the consummation to their fullest extent. This would take us far beyond the limits of this book. In the following pages, therefore, all we can do is to establish the initial point whence these further ideas of the Faith could be developed.

CHAPTER XXII

THE HIDDEN KING

(i)

The revelation of God is the manifestation of His Sovereign Will. For God is the Lord. He is indeed "Spirit," but not the "Essential Reason" nor the Idea of Ideas, but the Creator-Spirit, the Lord God. He is Spirit not in the meaning of that which can be thought, but as power, as energy, as will. The world is not related to Him as a correlate—as His real aspect, as Pantheism conceives Him; for if this were the case He would be as much conditioned by the world as the world is by Him; He would be as much passive as He is active. God is the Lord; this means that He owns the world; it is not alongside of Him but beneath Him, He is the Creator who has called the world into existence out of nothing, because He willed it, and as He willed it. The Lord God and the Creator God are interchangeable terms. Only as the Creator can He be the Lord, and only as the Lord can He be the Creator. He is Sovereign; above and alongside of His Will there is absolutely no other court of appeal. The world is not His counterpart; man is not His partner; Reason is not the Law which binds Him.

This is what the Bible means when it speaks of the living God. The living God is the personal God. Personality does not mean a limitation of God; on the contrary, it means His unlimited absolute freedom, the freedom and self-mastery of the Divine Will which can be restricted by nothing at all. "I am the Lord, and there is none beside Me." If we think of "It," we at once make it passive; it is our object. We must, however, say more than this; whatever we can conceive in our minds becomes an object to us, and therefore an "It." We cannot think of personality since what we think becomes impersonal. Personality must meet us. Hence philosophical Theism does not exist. That which bears this name is a blend of faith in God and philosophy, drawn from Pantheism and the knowledge of the God of the Bible. To thought there corresponds only something which is thought, never a personality. Personality and conceivability exclude each other. We can only know of the personality of God through His personal contact with us through revelation. Hence, too, there is no mystical Theism, no individualistic God-mysticism.[1] The mystic may indeed find in the depths of the soul or of the world the "Ground," the "essence" of being, and in his experience of the irrational he may indeed find the "Holy," but never the living God.

The Lord—the personal God, the Sovereign—can only be known where He makes Himself known. Here also God is active, the One who gives Himself; He is not passive, like One who is found. Revelation takes place where God takes the initiative in the relation between God and man. This is the God of the Bible, the God who comes, not the One to whom one comes; He is the One who gives, who gives Himself, not the One from whom one takes; the One who gives without reason—simply because He chooses to do so—the One who freely chooses, the One who elects. Real knowledge of God, knowledge of the real God, only exists where God reveals Himself. Therefore knowledge of the God of revelation is not theoretical; it cannot be gained through a process of meditation. To the personal reality of revelation there corresponds its personal activity. God's Word is not an Idea but a personal address. We cannot regard him from the detached point of view of a mere spectator; we cannot say "I'll think about it" when He makes His demands upon us; the only possible response for us is that of obedient submission.[2]

[1] There is, however, an empirical, philosophical Theism, but only in so far as some elements are borrowed from faith. The philosopher desires to anchor his Idea of God in a principle; by this very procedure it becomes impersonal. The so-called (Theistic) God-mysticism, however, is an offshoot on the one hand of Theopanism,* and on the other hand of Polytheism, and it oscillates between the two. See my *Religionsphilosophie*, pp. 70 ff.

* This term is used to distinguish the view that *God is all* from the view that *everything is God* (Pantheism).—Tr.

[2] Hence Christian theology which understands itself can only consist ultimately in a continual self-annulment as a theory of the Faith. Doubtless it does consist in "talking about" these questions, but it does this in such a

For in Revelation God expresses Himself; thus He expresses Himself as the Lord, or rather He speaks to us as the Lord. His Word is the expression of His Will, it is absolute, it is the word of the Lord which has absolute authority. What else should God reveal but Himself, but His own Will? And to what end should He reveal it save to make it valid? God reveals Himself because He wills to reign. The first aim of His speech is that He should rule. To believe, therefore, simply means to obey—that is, to receive the word of the Lord as really addressed to *my* soul, to "take it to heart," to submit to it, to yield to the attraction of His Will, and to renounce utterly all attempt at resistance.

(ii)

We must, however, hasten to observe that this sovereignty is most remarkable in character, not in the least like that which we would expect from a Lord and Sovereign. He had no need of us, why then does He seek for us? He could indeed force us; why does He speak to us as those from whom He wishes to receive our willing consent? He not only respects our personality, but He wishes to be as near to us as possible, so near that He is in our very heart. He communicates Himself to us, as though He had need of us; He runs after us as though He could not do without us. His behaviour resembles that of a king who wrapped himself in the garment of a beggar, and then implored the beggar to be friends with him; it is thus that He reveals Himself to us as Lord. This obedience—the acceptance of His gifts of grace—He requires, and it is thus that He requires it. What amazing sovereignty, what a transcending of the law of dominion—revealed in His own manner of dominion! Not only does He Himself wish to be truly personal, but He also wishes to make us truly personal like Himself. As Lord He has the power to annihilate us—and we would have no right to say: God should not do that! But

way that it continually points away from this theoretical sphere to the practical sphere; it is theoretical speech to show that the Faith is not a theory and is existential, and, further, to show why this is so.

550

as the loving God He wishes to draw to Himself us who are alienated from Him. This is why He "comes." This is why He reveals Himself, this is the meaning of His desire to be sovereign Lord.

And yet the fact remains: He wishes to make Himself known as love, as far as this is possible; but He must also make Himself known as the holy righteous Judge when this is inevitable. He desires to make Himself known personally, whether in the obedience of faith or in the traces of His impersonal absolute majesty. In any case, He must reign! It is of His mercy that He sends His Word before Him, and allows it to work for a long, long time before He makes an end. But some time or another He will make an end, and no one has the right to say "there is still plenty of time!" His dominion, however, in this interim period, in His Word, is not "according to His Majesty," but as the hidden King. As He conceals Himself within His revelation, making Himself near to us and like us, in order to be near to us, so also in this revelation His royal power is hidden. Indeed, the nearer He comes to us in the revelation, the more veiled is His royal majesty, hidden from the eyes of those who do not believe, all the more majestic to the eyes of those to whom in faith He reveals Himself.

Royal sovereignty, but veiled—this, then, is the category to which the revelation of the Mediator belongs. Even the prophetic revelation of the Old Testament is both. That it is the Lord who there makes His royal will known does not need to be expounded any further. Here there is no possibility of philosophical speculation or of mystical contemplation. Here is a royal claim, and the obedience of faith, the word of the Master, and listening with fear and trembling. Here is the living personal God the Creator, who makes known His Name and will maintain His honour. But here also, just because He really makes known His Name, because He comes near unto His people, because He takes the initiative and not man, here also is condescending grace, fatherly nearness, heartfelt pleading, a gracious restraint, a merciful veiling of His glory, *attemperatio*, adaptation to man, which could not endure the Divine Majesty. Not in the fire and in the whirlwind does He will to reveal Himself, but in the "sound of a gentle stillness"—even in the Old Testament. And yet in the Old Testament it is only a spoken message about this near and merciful God who will not destroy the "worm Jacob," the time is only promised when He will Himself give to His people a new heart, when He Himself will write His Law in their inward parts, since He desires to be quite near to them, like a father among His children. Therefore the standard form of revelation still remains the prophetic call to repentance, the imperative. For the Word has not yet become flesh. There is still more resignation than conviction, for the real indicative is lacking—the personal reality, existence *in persona*, in the Person of the Mediator.

In Christ, however, the King Himself is present, and therefore His royal majesty is still more veiled than in the word of the prophets. For if it seems almost incredible that a human being can have received the Word of God personally—and this is the claim of the prophets—it is still more incredible that a human being should actually be the Word of God himself. The human form is the complete concealment of the royal majesty. Certainly the disguise in which God Himself can become real to man is real if he believingly admits it. It is the disguise which is wholly suitable for the divine purpose of revelation. But that this is the divine purpose of revelation, this nearness, this unconditional love, can only be perceived from the revelation itself.

(iii)

Even in Christ the Mediator, God wills to assert Himself as King. His Will is to be done, His Kingdom is to come, His Name is to be hallowed. Christ is the hand with which the Lord of the Creation again lays hands on the creation which has been separated from Him by sin and thus rendered desolate; with this hand He will re-establish the order which had been lost. The meaning of the revelation in Christ is the restoration of the order of creation and its completion, it means *restitutio, reparatio, recapitulatio*. This "*re-*," this return to wholeness, is the decisive element in the New Testament message still more than in the message of the Old Testament. It is here made known far more fully in its fundamental principles. It means the return to the first beginning—at the same time, however, it also means going further than this. This return means repentance, being accepted once more into the family of God, atonement; it means, however, at the same time, to come out of the state of banishment from God, redemption.

Through sin the world is under the spell of powers which are hostile to God. Sin is indeed not only actual in the will, it is also potential, materialized, it has become nature, it is interwoven with the life of nature. Its most realistic expression is death. Death is the wages of sin, therefore it is the enemy of God. All that belongs to it, all that is of the realm of sin and death is the disorder which is opposed to the dominion of God, which God in His revelation wills to overcome.

The centre, however, of this disorder is the human heart, the false attitude of the human ego to his Creator. The assault of God is therefore directed at this central point of the hostile attitude. It is the key position. It is concerned with repentance and forgiveness. But at the same time it is to be made manifest that the divine assault is directed against the whole reality of the world which is hostile to Him, that the Divine Will to rule is directed in all respects towards the renewal of the world. The main attack is directed against the disobedient heart, but only in order that in it the seat of all disorder may be touched. This assault of God upon the world is Jesus Christ. This is the meaning of revelation and atonement. He is the Divine King who thus establishes His sovereignty, and in so doing sets humanity free from the powers which are hostile to God and therefore also hostile to life.

At the same time we know now that we must not look for this sovereign will merely where it confronts us directly, in the royal summons and command, but also supremely, and in its full sense there only, where the King rules as the One who gives, who gives freely, who gives Himself away. For in this concealment of His royal majesty, precisely there where it is most opaque, is He "nearest" to us, there He is perfectly near and perfectly real. There, where the world sees the exact opposite of dominion and victory, namely, only defeat and impotence, there He triumphs, there the power which is hostile

to God is decisively beaten, once for all, to such an extent
that to him who has seen this, to one who believes, all that
happens afterwards seems merely like the engagements fought
by the defeated enemy as he retires from the campaign, whose
complete defeat has thus become a certainty.

The real historical figure of the Revealer is therefore that
of the hidden King, of the Divine King whose incognito is the
suffering figure of the Servant of the Lord. In the following
pages, therefore, it is our task to indicate how in the history
of Jesus royal majesty meets us in the disguise of historical
lowliness.

(iv)

It is the Divine Sovereign Will of God which is revealed in
Jesus Christ. Hence Jesus is the fulfiller of the divine legislation.
He did not come to destroy but to fulfil. The Law is not the
Moral Law, as thinkers of the type of the Enlightenment tend
to think, at all periods of the world history, but the personal
Will of God. This law is divine; it is revealed. Since it becomes
known as revealed it is different from the *lex naturae*, from all
idea of the moral law of reason. It is the personal claim of the
Creator on His creature, it means the making of a covenant.
The Law is the gift of God. The Bible knows nothing about
a general moral law of reason, and the message of Jesus also
knows nothing of it.[1] It is the *Lord* who speaks, and it is the
Lord who *speaks*. The Law is given, it does not float in the air
like a general idea above reality, it enters into history as
personal reality. It is thus that the message was delivered by

[1] Under the influence of the modern-rationalistic point of view the
legislation of the Old Testament has been regarded as though it were the
same as the moral law of reason, the ethic immanent in consciousness; the
prophetic communication of this Law was regarded solely as the psychological form belonging to that period of history, to which one need pay no
further heed. Actually, however, the Law of the Old Testament is something
quite different from the moral law of reason just because it has been
communicated, because it is a prophetic revelation. It is God's assurance
of fellowship. Even the general revelation, the *lex naturae*, is expressly
referred back to the revealing act of God (see, for example, Rom. i
and ii).

the prophets. Thus in final utmost pointedness it was delivered
by Jesus. This is why it was so remarkably simplified, condensed, gathered up into a unity, because in all law the one
thing that matters is this: to obey and to love God. This
means likewise that it affects the real human being as he really
is: it means that he is to love his neighbour! For the fellow
man, or to put it still more accurately, his neighbour, is the
ethical reality which is given to man.

"This is the Law and the Prophets." An abstract statement,
a general formula? No, the exact opposite: liberation from all
that is impersonal, the entrance into the sphere of that which
is alone real, the personal manner of existence. This means the
setting aside of all and every kind of "law" in the general sense
of the word. This summons places man wholly at a given point
in time, in the present because it places him wholly in the
presence of God. Here nothing more can be arranged—*a priori*—
or decided. The decision is taken at the moment because it
can consist in nothing else than in listening to the call of God.
All casuistry—and what can the Moral Law mean other than
a system of casuistry of a more or less complicated kind?—
is here excluded. For in each "case" all that matters is that
we should listen to the call of God.

Jesus only gives examples—incidental examples, although
they are chosen with some care—to explain what it might
mean to obey God in reality. In these examples we can see
how unconditional, how unreserved, how little suited to the
cultural needs of man the Divine Sovereign Will of God is,
how completely all human self-glorification, all sensible selfish
self-will of the Ego must vanish in the presence of the Divine
Will and the rights of our neighbours which have been
appointed by Him. Here there is no longer any question at all
of the claims of man, of the right to control his own destiny.
Claims and Law belong to God alone. Precisely in this that
He so wholly binds him to Himself does God honour and love
His human child. That this child should belong wholly and
utterly to God, this is the covenant of God with him and the
eternal meaning of his life.

The prophet proclaims this Will of God as the Divine Personal Word which he has been charged to deliver. Jesus, how-

ever, proclaims this message in His own Name: "But *I* say unto you." He makes no distinction between Himself and His message, He does not present His credentials as did the prophets when they began with the words "Thus saith the Lord." He does not point to some higher court to which He can appeal for authority. He dares—without the shadow of a suggestion, however, that in so doing there is any daring at all—to express those ultimate claims without suggesting that He Himself was in any way summoned to obey, be subordinated, or judged. In this giving of the Law he "who has ears to hear" can detect the voice of the present Divine Lawgiver Himself. Jesus takes up the call to repentance uttered by John the Baptist, as though He were only continuing the prophetic work of the latter. But as here we hear nothing of any greater One to come after Him, we see, on the contrary, that Jesus regards disobedience to His call to repent as incomparable obstinacy, and sets it above all the evil committed in previous days. Why? Because only in Him is the world confronted with the Lawgiver in person, and in spite of this—as it were to the very face of God Himself—it has defied Him. It is not only the ultimate challenge because it is He who utters the summons to repentance, but it is also ultimate in the absolutely personal urgency and stringency with which He challenges man to make this decision; and, lastly, because Christ is not merely the last in the series of God's messengers, but because He is wholly Other, because the majesty of the Divine Lawgiver speaks through Him.

(v)

Therefore, as we have already seen, His message about the Law of God is inevitably connected with His proclamation of the Kingdom of God. The royal dominion of God—this is the central point of His message, everything else turns on this, both His action and His speech. This is the point at issue: this conflict, this "breaking in" of God (Matt. xii. 29), this act of "casting fire on the earth" (Luke xii. 49–50) in order that God may claim His own property, that the Lord of all the world "comes" as Lord and King. Here, too, the predictions

of the ancient prophets are fulfilled which foretold this advent
of the Divine King, His dominion, the fact that He would
dwell amongst His people, and the marvellous character of His
Presence, so different from anything humanity had hitherto
known that it could not be imagined.

Here also, however, the "Word of the Lord" has become
different. For it is no longer merely a word of promise for the
future; it also points toward the present, towards the presence
of God in Himself, even though still hidden from mortal sight.
The great truth which the prophets foretold in their Messianic
and eschatological language, a truth which is utterly different
from a moral sphere of reason of any kind, in Him had begun
to be miraculously present. This is why so much stress is laid
upon the miracles. They are proofs of the presence of the
Creator in power. Jesus does not refuse to work miracles, He
simply refuses to use them merely for purposes of display or
ostentation, because the Divine Presence is manifested not in
order that men may stare at It, but that It may be obeyed,
so that men may repent and return to God. To Jesus Christ
the possession of power and of divine sovereignty was no less
important than to conquer the powers that are hostile to God,
and to restore the divine order. He *commands* the fever, He
commands the demons. He is the victorious Divine Warrior;
the demons are aware of this power when He confronts them;
it is this which causes them to fear and tremble.

It is at this point that we perceive most clearly the absolute
difference between what is here described as the "rule of God"
and the modern ideas which have gathered round the phrase
the "Kingdom of God." To the modern mind "inwardness"
is everything, the "purely ethical"; the healing miracles are
either regarded as non-essential or even as rather intrusive
secondary phenomena. The modern man is not thinking in
terms of sovereignty at all, of the rule of the Creator in power,
of the restoration of creation as a whole; he is thinking merely
about the transformation of man within the limits of history,
a change which leaves the natural and historical foundations
of human life unaltered. To him the Biblical realism of actual
faith in a living Creator seems quite remote. What does he
care about the "external"? Indeed, he does not know that the

557

inward and the outward cannot be separated, that even the forces which are hostile to God are not merely inward, but that they are also outward; he knows nothing of the corruption of the natural bases of life, nothing of the prophetic hope of the "new heaven and the new earth." He has isolated what ought to be from what is because his idea of God is not that of faith in the Creator, but that of Idealism, to which the world has always been something external, something to be depreciated. The primitive Christian tradition, however, was absolutely right in laying so much stress on the actual miracles of Jesus—although she may not have always kept herself quite free from that thirst for the marvellous against which Jesus always warned His hearers. It is, however, most impressive to note that Jesus did not only speak and teach; He proved His divine authority, and exercised it as the hidden King, who is not merely Lawgiver but also Creator.

As the One in whom God is present, not merely in word, but also in person, even though this presence may be a veiled presence, Jesus taught and healed. Therefore He also called a new community into being. The confidence with which He thus called men out of their ethical relationships in life and drew them to Himself has something irresistibly regal about it. For we must never forget that we are not in the atmosphere of India, the land of ascetic mysticism, where the flight from the natural created life of fellowship is in harmony with the religious idea of the people, and is therefore regarded as quite ordinary; but we are in the sphere of the Old Testament, among the Chosen People, to whom the Fifth Commandment is especially sacred.

Thus to override the moral ordinances of life is permissible only to one who feels that he has been summoned to this by the call of God, or to one who because He is more than a prophet may dare thus to call others, as God Himself used to call the prophets. Only those who when they heard the call "Follow Me!" perceived in it the royal tones of a king, even though they may not have been fully conscious of this at the moment, could, or should, have obeyed it.

He called them out in order that through them and in them He might lay the foundation stone of a new edifice. The glimpses of this process which we can glean from tradition are few and meagre; evidently the Church also felt this created a problem, so she gave as her explanation the idea that the Church could not be extended until the coming of "another Comforter." Still, this does not prevent us from coming to the conclusion that He gathered His own, the people who were "His," and that in them He planted the consciousness that they were a separate community. The question whether Jesus Himself founded the Church may be answered in the affirmative, not only in the dogmatic sense, but also in the historical sense.[1] He founded the New Covenant, not as an *ecclesia invisibilis*, as those who regard the Church purely as an invisible spiritual body would have us believe, but as a real community, a "people," however unassuming it may have seemed at first, whose constitution is "the blood of the New Covenant."

This brings us to our last point. The royal Will of God is the will of Him who makes His covenant with men. It is the will of grace. Therefore the noblest prerogative of sovereignty which Jesus exercised was that of forgiveness, and of intercourse with those who from the point of view of moral principles were outcasts. Explicitly He asserts His authority to forgive sins as His own sovereign right and connects it with His authority to heal. But this authority is certainly the one which is most deeply veiled.

To be the friend of publicans and sinners—He who was absolutely holy—to come down to their level, and to dwell with them, this is the royal bearing of One who rules while He gives Himself away, who asserts Himself by sacrificing Himself, who manifests His holiness and His righteousness by offering Himself as the expiatory sacrifice. "The Son of Man came not to be ministered unto, but to minister, and to give His life a ransom for many."

Hence His sufferings and His death are not only the fulfilment of the revelation of the hidden God, not only the reconciliation of the angry God, but they are also the most perfect mark of the power of One who triumphs in the act of defeat. It was

[1] Cf. the works of Kattenbusch and K. L. Schmidt which have been cited in the above pages.

thus that the Christian Church understood it; by death He overcame death. His death means "breaking through," not merely through wrath, but also through the effect of wrath, the corruption of death. His Cross is not only atonement but redemption—even if concealed. It is the foundation-stone of the Kingdom of God, not that of the Church Triumphant, however, but that of the Church Militant. It does not only "justify" the sinner, but it also makes him righteous; it overcomes not only guilt, but sin, it means the creation of the new man. But this new man "remains hidden until the Last Day" (Luther). That, however, this death is the victory over death can only be asserted if it really *is* so, and only by one to whom this fact is an actual event. The Crucified is known as victor in the Resurrection from the Dead.

CHAPTER XXIII

THE KING MANIFESTED

(i)

THE Gospel of Jesus Christ, as Paul shows us in the briefest compass in the second chapter of the Epistle to the Philippians, is a movement from God to man. In this passage Paul seems to be describing with his finger the course of a parabola, which begins from above, descends, and then once more ascends to its original plane, and then says: "*This* is what I mean!" But this illustration is intensely personal; everything depends upon this movement. Whoever beholds it—and this movement cannot be seen with the intellect, nor with the imagination, but only with the whole heart—believes, and knows what the Gospel means.[1] As we have already said, the region whence it came is the dimension of revelation, the mystery of the word of the prophets, and the mystery of the Word made flesh. "Whence hast thou thy message?" This was the question by which a prophet's authority to speak in the name of Yaweh used to be tested. "Whence art thou?" is the question by which the authority of Christ is tested.

A glaring contrast seems to exist between this claim to have come from eternity into time and the earthly scene in which His "coming" ends: "If He be the King of Israel let Him come down from the cross that we may believe on Him!" Between the claim that He is the Son of God and the act of hanging on the cross there is no greater or harsher contrast. This scene seems to brand the claim to be the Son of God as a lie. Yes, if we are of those who do not see clearly the dimension whence He came, who do not perceive that this descending

[1] "The centre in the thought of Paul is an historical-superhistorical divine act, or a complex of divine acts, which communicates to the whole human race a finished salvation. He who believes in these divine acts— the Incarnation, Death, and Resurrection of a celestial Being—receives salvation" (Wrede: *Paulus*, p. 93). When anyone misunderstands faith in Christ like this certainly one cannot expect that such a man will be able to see that it is precisely this faith which means the utmost ethical participation.

movement is necessary, in order that what was above may be realized below. It is a foolish contradiction, an absurdity, if we do not notice that this contradiction is our own, that this movement is determined by the fact that it is we who have torn asunder the two spheres, who have separated the world "above" from the world "below." Because the Jews would not allow themselves to be told this, because they did not perceive that *they* were the lowest point towards which this divine self-movement was directed, that it is they who determine the steepness of the gradient which lies between the divine world "above" and the divine-human world "below"; it is because they are not ready to repent that they do not perceive the region whence it comes, this is why they do not believe that He is the Christ. The very fact in which the full knowledge of the divine origin of this movement becomes evident to faith is to them a proof that this assertion of the divine origin of this movement is false. The source and the aim of the movement are inseparable; it is because He comes from thence that He is now here, at this lowest depth of human reality.

But this parabola extends in two directions. As it comes out from eternity towards us so also when it has reached the lowest point of the curve it strains upwards again to return to the region whence it came. The meaning of the eternal origin of this movement and of its realization in the human sphere can only be known by one who realizes that this eternal origin is also the final goal, the one which is really intended. The movement is from God to God, but it is a real movement, therefore the curve must pass through this deepest point. For it must be a real movement for us; for *we* are there, at the lowest point. If this movement from God to God is to have significance for us, then it must pass through this lowest point, as through our own place. If, however, it is to have this significance for us—from God to God—then this deepest point must also be the turning-point where the descent turns into an ascent. The Crucified is the One from above—this alone gives meaning to His Cross. Otherwise it would simply be a remarkable incident. The Crucified returns to the region whence He came: through this alone does it become credible that He really did come to us from above. The meeting with the Risen and Exalted Lord, the Easter message alone makes the statement, the "Word," whole and significant, the Word in which the whole Christ-revelation exists. In it alone that movement is fulfilled, and thence it receives its meaning: from God to God.

Apart from Easter, all would remain shrouded in darkness. Without Easter the Jews were right when they mocked Him for His claim to be the Son of God: a criminal who had been hanged!—Son of God! Easter alone brings out the fact that in this "form of a servant" the King was really concealed.

Therefore the message of Easter is the Christian message, and the Christian Church is the Church of the Resurrection. This is true from the historical point of view: it was not until Easter had taken place that the Church was formed. On Good Friday there was no Church; all the disciples of the Lord were scattered as sheep that have no shepherd. It was the fact of Easter which drew them together. It was this fact alone which made Peter truly understand the truth that had previously simply shot through his mind like a flash of lightning: "Verily Thou art the Son of the Living God." Easter alone made a full belief in Christ possible. If the "movement" were to be real, its meaning could only be fulfilled at the point where it was perfected. A speculative belief in Easter? What nonsense! As a woman can only sew properly with a knotted thread—for otherwise her work would be in vain—so if Christ be not risen, really risen from the dead, and has actually been "seen" as the Risen Lord, all Christian faith is vain. Everything else is pure fallacy. Positively as well as historically—this coincidence is necessary—Easter is the foundation stone of the Christian faith and of the Christian Church.

(ii)

Easter discloses the meaning of the life and the sufferings of Christ; this meaning is Resurrection. It is not that we say: *also* resurrection, *also* the eschatological element, as necessary to round off the whole, the "Last Things" as the closing chapter in Christian doctrine. Nothing is at issue but the

Last Things. The meaning of the "movement" is indeed the
coming of God, the dwelling of God among His people, the
royal rule of God. Thus it is not something historical, something
which can take its place among the existing historical natural
presuppositions. In this event the rent is indeed to be healed,
the gulf bridged. This division, however, runs right through
the whole of historical existence; it does not only concern that
which the individual human being does wrong within the
historical presuppositions, but it concerns these presuppositions
themselves. The point is the overcoming of Original Sin, not
only of individual sins.

The theme of the Old Testament is not the history of a
people as such, neither is it world history as such, but it is
divine history in the people of Israel, and divine history for
the world through the people of Israel. But divine history
means the end of history. The fact that in the Old Testament
this eschatological element is not clearly perceived beneath its
historical veil is because it was essential that first of all the
whole realism of faith in Creation should be firmly established against all temptations to allow it to dissolve into a
"purely spiritual" religion concerned solely with the other
world. To the historical man the message is directed, it is to
him that God wills to come, it is him whom God wills to
redeem. At all costs this "coming" must be defended against
all temptations to be thought of as a "going." The movement
is one from the world above to the world below; it shows the
loyalty of God towards His Creation, which He does not leave
in the lurch, and the seriousness with which the historical
human being and history are firmly maintained as the sphere
or the goal of the divine revelation.

The possibility which characterizes all forms of "higher"
religion outside the Bible does not exist here, the possibility,
namely, of getting rid of the coarser, lower part of man's nature,
or at least of leaving it to take care of itself in order to take
refuge in eternity with his precious soul. This "possibility" is
simply the fruit of a fertile imagination! It is simply untrue.
As though the lower part of our nature were not also part of
the Creation, and as though we could make this lower part
responsible for evil! Once sin has been recognized in its true

colours, this evasion is no longer possible. Man is a unity, body and soul. The Creation of God is a unity, the spiritual and the natural belong to each other. Together they broke away from God, together they must be redeemed, if there is to be true redemption at all. The coming of God means a coming into full reality, whereas the religious movement of man is always an attempt to flee from reality. This historical realism of Old Testament eschatology is due to the same cause as the personalism of its Idea of God and of Revelation. "God comes" means: He comes to the whole Creation, He comes really, and He must come if there is to be a real redemption at all.

But however strong may be the emphasis which is laid upon this historical realism, on the other hand the reality of redemption is emphasized just as strongly. The whole creature is to become a sharer in the divine "coming." In it the whole of history is to be fulfilled. The individualism[1] which is supposed to have begun with Jeremiah—as a preparatory stage for the individualism of the New Testament—is a purely fantastic idea. The Bible never knows any form of redemption save that which is universal. Private forms of redemption are not contemplated. The Day of Yahweh is the same for everyone, and the Covenant of Yahweh which is then to be fulfilled is a covenant with His people. But the content of this covenant lies beyond all the possibilities of historical imagination, beyond all natural analogies. Man receives a new heart, the Law has become to him no longer something which is opposed to him, but it is written within upon the fleshly tables of the heart; it has become his own; and all, small and great, shall know the

---

[1] The contrast between the Old Testament and the New is usually wrongly understood on both sides. The "Socialism" of the New Testament which lies in the idea of the Church, namely, that there is salvation only within the community of Christ, is misunderstood; and the individualism of the Old Testament summons to repentance is also misunderstood. For it cannot be denied that the conversion of the nation, in the sense intended by men like Amos, Hosea, or Isaiah, is regarded as an inward experience in the heart of the individual. The distinction arises at a different point; that is, out of the "people," as an equally theocratic and national fact, the "people of the covenant," the purely theocratic ἐκκλησία is severed from the national element.

Lord. He will be present in a wonderful way, in such a way that even the dumb creatures will feel it as an unusual enhancement of their own nature and as a removal of all that disturbs and annoys. The knowledge of the Lord will cover the earth as the waters cover the sea. The Mountain of the Lord will be higher than all mountains, and to it shall all nations make their pilgrimage. Peace and justice will exist, life will have found its fulfilment, its meaning.[1]

If we wish to understand the eschatology of the New Testament, we must carry with us into it all this realism of the Old Testament. It is, of course, true that it can be understood from itself alone, but repeatedly we modern men who have been infected by Rationalism and by Mysticism fall into the temptation offered by "purely spiritual religion." As we can only rightly understand Christ from the word of the prophets, so we can only understand Easter, and the meaning of Easter, from the point of view of the Old Testament hope. It is, of course, true that the Ultimate, the wholly Other, the Unimaginable, the non-finite, the non-material, the non-temporal is proclaimed: absolute eternal life. But all this is meant in a realistic way, not ideally, not in a "Greek" manner. Therefore at the central point of the hope of redemption stands the proclamation that death has ceased to exist.

(iii)

It is a remarkable fact that modern religion—whether it be coloured with moralistic, speculative, or mystical ideas—ignores the problem of death. Our classical writers, and in particular their chief, Goethe, avoided the question of death as much as they avoided the problem of radical evil. Plato welcomed death

---

[1] It is not correct to say that it is only the later Judaism which knows a transcendental eschatology. For the mythological superlatives and "exaggerations" of the prophetic eschatology ought to be understood wholly as attempts to burst through the merely historical framework. The phrase concerning the "new heavens and the new earth" in "Trito-Isaiah" is by no means the only example of the kind; this can be perceived as soon as we have learnt to interpret the intention of the "mythological" statements of the prophetic eschatology aright.

as the Deliverer. The mood of Socrates towards death is one of a superior humour. In the New Testament, on the contrary, it is regarded as the Enemy. Death and the Devil belong to each other. Death is only regarded as the Deliverer where man does not believe in the good creation of God, where humanity is separated into two halves, soul and body, where the body is despised as the prison-house of the soul.

Disloyalty to the body is profoundly unscriptural. It belongs wholly to the opposite tendency: to the idea of the ascent of man with its asceticism, not to the idea of the divine descent with the message of redemption. Redemption of the body, not *from* the body, is the message of the Bible. For the body is the creation of God. The body is the delimitation between God and man, and it also constitutes the reality of man as a human being. To leave the body to look after itself in order to return to the Deity is a Pantheistic idea, it is not part of the scriptural faith in Creation.

Death is the Enemy just because it tears body and soul asunder, those two parts which together make up the being of man. It is true, of course, that this death is only the last and harshest appearance of that which, in a more hidden way, makes up the character of this existence as such. For this process which rends body and soul asunder is always at work. We have a non-spiritual sense-life and an abstract spirituality. This anomaly, however, is due to sin, for through sin the Will of God, the spiritual content of life, becomes the abstract law of Reason, and the sense-life becomes a lawless, "savage" independent force. So much we are able to admit. But in faith we know that all death is the result of sin, although *how* this is so we cannot understand. The origin of death, like the origin of our existence and the origin of sin, lies beyond the sphere of our own experience. We cannot fit this element into our picture of history, it always lies behind it. For "history" also means, above all, the regular succession of the generations which come and go through the cycle of birth and death. Without death we cannot conceive of history. Death as well as law is one of its fundamental constituents.

For this very reason redemption cannot exist within history. Death in the narrower as in the wider sense forms an inherent part of history as much as its cause, which is sin. Death is the visible aspect of sin.[1] A redemption which does not remove death is by that very fact stamped as an illusion. Redemption within the sphere of history is a self-contradiction. For from the point of view of history it is true that "in the midst of life we are in death"; indeed, still more, in the midst of life, at the heart of life, death gnaws secretly at our vitals. Historical life is life which contains and nourishes the seeds of death.

The mystic who ignores death and asserts that true redemption consists in being "in eternity at every moment" is just as superficial as when he ignores the forgiveness of sins, and asserts that he has already received the grace of God. In each instance he ignores reality.

Redemption, if it is to be regarded seriously, cannot therefore mean anything less than the cessation of death, not only the cessation of cessation. Death, from the point of view of the Bible, is not this abstract idea of the cessation of existence. Death is always regarded as the wages of sin. Death and sin merge into one another. The "eccentricity" of life, that man is no longer in his right place, that his life energies are in a state of revolt, that the organic connections both between the individual and the community, as well as those between corporeality and reason, have been severed: all this means death as well as sin. In the reality of experience, death and sin come under one heading. Since we hunger for life, we hunger just as much for liberation from sin as from death. Our life is a mixture of death and life. But this disintegration is just as much sinful as it is "natural." Just as the question about the

---

[1] Of course, in this connection the argument which tries to prove that death was in the world before sin—whereby our attention is directed to geological-palaeontological chronology—has not the slightest weight. For that in this empirical historical world death is always present is a self-evident fact. But the *prius* and *posterius* of the statement of faith has nothing whatever to do with this scientific chronology, with this *post* and *ante*. We have no hope of being able to register the date of the Creation of the world and of the Fall in the calendar of the palaeontologist! Every kind of scientific cosmos, including its chronology, is as much affected by sin as by the Creation. Evolution is true within the reality which is determined by the Creation and the Fall. It is not Time itself nor the created world which is sinful but *this* earthly life and *this* world of time.

origin shows the connection between death and sin, so also is it with the question about the goal. History first begins outside the gates of Paradise, as life which is under the curse of death and the Law.

Death is the real aspect, and guilt is the ideal aspect of sin. In the act of dying, what it means to be severed from God, from Him who is life, becomes visible outwardly. In the definition of "guilt" we know from within what it means to be separated from God. Death is the materialized form of separation from God; the complete dissolution of the body is the sensible end of that which began in sin. The *terrores conscientiae*, the pangs of hell suffered by the guilty conscience, are the inner result of severance from the Creator. The heart of this whole disturbance and destruction is the false attitude of man towards God. For the attitude towards God is the being of man. His being is not independent. He is whatever he is able to be at all through his attitude towards God: the image of God, the reflection of the Divine Word. Therefore the process of healing must also begin here, at the centre: it consists in this, that God starts afresh from the original attitude of man, which he has abandoned, and restores him again to that fellowship with the Word in which he has been created. This is the process of the reconciliation and justification of the sinner. By it the fires of sin are, properly speaking, extinguished: "we therefore have peace with God." This is the decisive element. Reconciliation, however, is more than this; it is at the same time the beginning of redemption.

(iv)

But it is not the full reality of redemption. For forgiveness does not cancel the actual effects of sin. The ruin which began with sin still takes its course, even where the guilt of sin has been forgiven. Even he to whom forgiveness has been granted remains a member of the sphere of history, and drags himself along under its curse. The realistic side of sin, that which we call death, in the wider and narrower sense of the word, still remains active in his life. His sin has been "covered" by God, but the roots of sin have not been eradicated. Living fellowship with God has been promised to him, and in this promise it is present in the *Word*; but it is not yet present in *power*. We still live by faith and not by sight. But the Word which has been given unto us means power, faith means sight. Reconciliation means redemption, redemption from death—Resurrection.

Atonement as a process stands within the historical sphere, and is subject to the limitations of the historical sphere. It does not extend effectually to the physical nature of man, nor effectually to man as a whole. It is essentially an inward and individual process. It breaks through this inwardness, it is true, through the new moral power it confers, and it also breaks through the individualistic isolation of human life by the formation of the new community, the Church. But both these changes only occur within historical limits. We remain sinners and we remain individuals, in spite of the New Birth, and in spite of the Church. The real working out of the new life which has taken place in Christ is more a foretaste and a suggestion than an actual effect. Therefore the Christian remains above all one who hopes. What he hopes for, however, is the disappearance of historical barriers, of those disintegrating effects which we sum up under the heading of death, and of which death in the narrower sense forms a part.

The real hope of the Christian is not of a life after death, but of the removal of death from life, of the resurrection of the dead, death being swallowed up in life, the victory of divine life over death. Apart from this eternal life would only mean passing death by, stealing away from the sphere of death. This cannot be the "End." For if this were all the creation of God would remain rent, and the sovereignty of God limited. Death is not something which exists alongside of the creation; it is the disturbance of the creation itself. The restoration, the divine fulfilment, cannot be other than the removal of this disturbance which has intruded into the created world and has set its seal wholly upon it. Just as little as there can be any redemption which ignores the question of guilt, but must pass through guilt, so also redemption cannot ignore death but must pass through the fact of death. Just as a conqueror does not conquer the country by ignoring the strongest fortress in the enemy's land—knowing that he is not a real conqueror if the enemy's fortress lies in his rear—so the Greek-Rationalistic and the Indian mystical idea of a redemption which ignores the fact of death is a half-truth which cannot be combined with the royal Will and the unlimited sovereignty of God. A redemption in which the soul alone is saved from death might just as well be described as a defeat as a victory. This idea of the mere immortality of the soul belongs to the idea of the "ascent" of man, not to the divine self-movement towards man and the world.

Death, however, is the bolt which shuts the door without mercy upon the historical life. We do not know what lies on the other side of death, what lies beyond death; we cannot imagine what life would look like which was not marked with the stamp of death. We can only express what we think in futile negations, which say nothing, save that we have become aware to some extent of the negations which death brings into our life. A negation of negations, that is the formula for our ideas of eternal life. "And God shall wipe away all tears from their eyes, and there shall be no more death, neither sorrow, nor crying, neither shall there be any more pain, for the former things are passed away."

Life without cessation, joy without sorrow, power without limitations, fellowship with God without disturbance, time without passing away, physical life without the flesh, sight without the pale cast of thought, without the paradoxes of faith, knowledge no longer "as in a glass darkly" or in a riddle, but "face to face, even as we are known"—all this might be expressed in one sentence: God will be there, and we shall be with Him. He will be our God, and we shall be His people. This is the meaning of the whole history of revelation, something unimaginable, unthinkable, something one could only imagine if one already had the experience, because to be able to think this would mean to possess it, to know that the goal of history is the end of history. We cannot avoid conceiving this goal as the ultimate point in history, as the end of history.[1]

[1] He who on account of the "mythological" character of this *Futurum* and this *Praeteritum* substitutes a *Praesens*—ostensibly in the sense of the Gospel of John—falls a prey once more to the old Hegelian transformation

For the end of history cannot itself be an historical event. Just as little as we can fit the Creation and the Fall within our historical picture—and can only speak of it in the *perfectum praeteritum*—can we force the Redemption, the Final Act, into the framework of historical events, and must therefore speak of it in the future tense. If we *could* fit it into history it would not be the Final Act, the event which bursts through this framework of history.

We may think of the final catastrophe which will mark the close of history in as heightened a dimension as we like: it will still remain within the dimension of history; therefore it is not what we mean at this point. We cannot bring this event, as such, into the time schema at all; for as an event in our time-series the dawn of eternity would not be the dawn of eternity. Eternity is just as little the continuation of time as it is that which precedes time. Eternity and time cannot be compared. Our temporal life is a crooked fragment of eternity. We ought not to make the attempt to force eternity into it. Eternity, or rather the resurrection from the dead, remains close to us at whatever point in historical time we may be. It is only separated from us by a thin wall along which we pass as we pass through time. "Some time or another" it will break through; at any time this might happen—how could we assert the contrary?—but we do not know how we are to imagine what this "some time or another" will mean. "We shall be as them that dream." Or rather, our life will seem to us like a dream out of which we awake. Can we bring the dream world and reality together into a temporary relation? Yet this is only a poor analogy. For reality is no dream.[1]

of the Gospel. It forms part of the existential seriousness of faith that it confesses the Fall as *Praeteritum* and the Redemption as *Futurum*, in spite of the fact that these "times" cannot be read simply from the clock of this world and be registered in the calendar of experience. On this point, see the section on *Christian Mythology*, pp. 377 ff.

[1] Cf. the remarkable words in the Apocalypse of Baruch (lxxiv. 2-3): "That time is the end of that which is corruptible and the beginning of that which is incorruptible. . . . Hence it is far from the evil and near to them who die not" (Kautzsch, op. cit., p. 440).

(v)

Therefore we cannot imagine what the Resurrection of Jesus Christ means. It is as invisible, as unthinkable, as the Incarnation. The Apostles did not make any attempt to explain it to us. They testify to the fact, but they do not describe how it happened. They attest this fact as the completion of that movement which proceeds from eternity and leads back to eternity, passing through the deepest point at which the wrath of God gathers itself up as the complete despair of the soul and the complete tearing asunder of the unity of body and soul. The death of Christ is not like any other death, but it is the death which, as the wages of sin, could only be experienced by One who knew God. This point remains doubly mysterious, impenetrable to our human minds. No human being can possibly imagine the death which Christ died. The Bible and the doctrine of the Church suggest it by the use of the word "Hell." The *terrores conscientiae* of which everyone knows something, but which only a man who has wrestled with God like a Luther has tasted, are—as Luther himself often emphasized— still a foretaste, a distant analogy of that which Christ passed through. This death which every human being experiences, or rather the death which every human being experiences who knows something of the wrath of God, is indeed a foretaste of what death as the "wages of sin" really means.

This is the deepest point in which alone the reality of man is reached, as it is from the point of view of God, and as we can merely guess at it. Through this "place" Christ has passed. Since He reached it—the point which no human being has ever reached, since whoever reached it would thereby be destroyed—He also penetrated beyond it in virtue of the power through which He reached it. The profoundest depths and the greatest heights lie very near to one another. It is not an accident that the Doctors of the Church could not agree on the question whether Christ's "Descent into Hell" meant the deepest depths of humiliation, or the beginning of His royal sovereignty. We should not desire to know more than this: that it was through this "place" that Christ returned to eternity, into the glory of heaven. He revealed Himself to His Apostles

573

as the glorified One, as the heavenly Lord, in His majesty. In this manifestation alone did they become certain that He was the King who previously had been hidden. This self-attestation became known to them as the completion of the movement whose witnesses they had been, as the border line between time and eternity. This is the Easter message: that to them has been made known the "Name which is above every name," as the true Name of Him whom they knew in the form of a servant, that Him whom they saw as the Lowly One they have been allowed to see exalted to the right hand of the Father, that from this sight they have learned to see in its true meaning that which they had seen previously, the lowliness of the King in the form of a servant. It is only because this is true that there is Advent, Christmas, Good Friday. Easter is the ground of knowledge for the apostolic knowledge of Christ. Hence the apostolic witness to Christ is the basis of our faith in Christ, and the basis of the Church.

We are not witnesses of the Resurrection, hence our faith is based on their testimony. Let us not be surprised at this! If it were not so, it would not be the unique revelation of God. This "heteronomy" is the same as the fact of the real revelation. It is an error, which it would not be difficult to expose, to believe that through the historical picture of the life of Jesus any one of us can become an eye-witness of the Christ and His Resurrection. For we have no other picture of the life of Jesus than that which the Church composed, based on the testimony of those who had actually experienced the Easter fact. The Easter message is inextricably interwoven with the picture of Jesus. The Gospels depict Jesus as only they could depict Him who had really experienced Him as the Risen Lord. And they have only depicted Him *because* they knew Him thus. Whoever bases his faith "merely on the Synoptic Gospels themselves, and not upon the testimony of the Apostles," deceives himself, since in this picture of the life of Jesus without knowing it he has already received the Easter message.

And yet there is a sound element in the revolt against the mere heteronomy of a faith which is based simply upon the testimony of the Apostles, that "He is risen." It has evidently been in accordance with the Divine Will that through the picture of Jesus which the Church has preserved for us we also should have our share in the "autopsy" of the Apostles. We also, in virtue of this tradition, can ourselves bear witness to the Risen Lord, but not only through this "picture of the life of Jesus." For the witness of the Apostles to Jesus Christ, like the prophecy of the prophets about Christ, is not only a report to us that others have seen Him as the Risen Lord. Rather this testimony, this Word about Christ, in the perception of faith becomes to us the very Word of God, and the presence of the Exalted Lord. Not because the Apostles witness to Him as the Risen Lord do we believe in Him as the Risen Lord, but He who made Himself known to them as the Risen Lord, and in this knowledge gave them the witness to Himself, gives Himself to us in this their testimony that we may know Him as the Risen Lord. It is not the historical credibility of the Resurrection narratives which bears witness to Christ, but the self-testimony of Christ conveys to the believer the historical credibility of these narratives. Hence to all those who read these narratives only with the interest of students of secular history they will always remain incredible, whereas faith will be undisturbed by all historical criticism.

Easter, the Resurrection of the Lord, is not an "historical event" which can be reported. If it were, could it be Easter? Easter is not an occult process, for whose reliable description by eye-witnesses we would need as ideal a group of eye-witnesses as possible, under strict supervision. What use are "eye-witnesses" for the event of Easter? What sort of an occult process do people imagine it to have been that it could be described in semi-scientific terms? Easter, the Resurrection communication of the Christ, is itself revelation, the divine self-testimony, which, as such, allows of no objectivity because it is addressed wholly to faith. To know and to believe in Christ as the Exalted Lord is one and the same thing. Those to whom this first perception was given were the Apostles, the original witnesses. But their testimony is not that of eye-witnesses but of witnesses of faith. Their witness is based upon the fact that they have received this revelation, which can then become the basis for our faith. They do not report the Resurrection; they bear witness to it.

575

(vi)

But what about the Easter stories and the empty tomb? This point must be made quite clear first of all: that the empty tomb, which certainly any secular eye-witness could observe (in contrast to the theological controversies which usually circle round this point), plays no part whatsoever in the New Testament as the foundation for faith in the Resurrection. Paul does not mention it, none of the Epistles mentions it, and in the Gospels, even where it is admitted as an actual fact, the certainty of the Resurrection is never based upon it. The Apostles certainly had other reasons for their faith in the Risen Lord than that of an empty grave! If the Resurrection were conceived merely as an occult happening, then certainly the empty grave would be the main point in the argument. That this is nowhere claimed in the New Testament is the best possible proof that all ideas of this kind do great injustice to the testimony of the New Testament.

Secondly, it is no accident that the only people who are named as witnesses of the Resurrection are disciples or believers. How easy it would have been to introduce some "impartial observer," as would have been the case if we had been dealing with an occult event. If, in the meeting with the Risen Lord, we had been dealing with a mere "perception," then certainly the neutral observer would be the most valuable eye-witness. In spite of the fact that at a very early date imagination began to weave pious fancies into the narratives of the Resurrection, and also that there are, without doubt, certain apologetic tendencies in the Gospel narratives, yet of this, which might so easily have happened, there is no trace at all. It was clear to the Church, even in a period when legend and apologetic were already busy, that there is no question of such neutral ocular testimony for the Resurrection.[1] Faith and faith alone knows what the Resurrection means.

[1] What would have been easier than to expand the story of the watchers at the tomb in this fashion? For they would have been the very eye-witnesses who were most needed, since they were wholly disinterested and impartial. But of this we find no trace. It is said, it is true, that they felt the earthquake, were afraid, and saw the angel, but that is all.

On the other hand, we cannot deny that the historical tradition presents us with some difficult insoluble problems. This is not the case with the point of view of the general world outlook. He who believes in the Deity of Christ cannot be affected henceforth by any scruples of this kind with reference to the Resurrection, as it is reported in the Gospels. But there does remain a question which no honest person can ignore: does Paul mean, do the earliest Apostles, whose testimony has only come down to us in a very fragmentary way, mean the same thing as that which our present Gospel narratives report to us? Must not the conscientious critic—even if he is a believer—admit that there are important signs that the first experience of the Resurrection did not take place in Jerusalem but in Galilee? Can we so easily pass over the fact that Paul places his meeting with the Risen Lord, which is so different from that which is described in the Gospels, on the same footing with theirs, and that this account is thus accepted by them? May we, with our faith in the Resurrection—which we will not here discuss any further—dismiss the historical question whether the Resurrection testimony of the primitive Apostles and of those "five hundred brethren" may not have been more like that of Paul than that which is now recorded in the Gospels? Have we this right, in view of the undeniable inconsistencies in the tradition?

We do not possess this right. For we never have the right to overpower the sense of truth by faith. Whoever asserts that the New Testament gives us a definite consistent account of the Resurrection is either ignorant or unconscientious. It is impossible to co-ordinate the different narratives into a unity, and these inconsistencies do not lie merely on the surface. Just as little, however, do they affect the heart of the matter, the real, physical resurrection. For just as it is true that Paul teaches the resurrection of the body, but not the resurrection of the material substance of which the body is composed, so it is true that the Christian testimony to the Resurrection is nullified apart from the assertion of the physical resurrection, without, on that account, saying that it necessarily combines with it a statement about the material body of Christ. As truly as our body will decay and become corrupt in the grave

577

—and yet we shall rise again in the body—so truly faith gives us no reason to state that the testimony to the physical resurrection of the Lord is bound up with credible testimony to the fact of the empty grave.

But neither can we be responsible for the assertion that the first Apostles, when they bore witness to the Resurrection, certainly did not mean what the Gospel narratives have handed down to us in the tradition. On the contrary, on this point there is some important testimony, above all, from Paul himself. For even he emphasizes the words "risen from the dead" in connection with the phrase "buried," and "risen on the third day according to the Scriptures," i.e. the connection with the general Jewish idea of resurrection. So we must be willing to admit that there is no uniform answer to the question "What, then, did really take place?" and that probably it is not intended that there should be such an answer. For whatever may be "reported" or "attested" in human language, in whatever images this "process" may be described—all these are only faint suggestions of what the Resurrection, the Resurrection of Jesus Christ, really means as the basis of our resurrection. Easter, as an event, stands in a category by itself; it is something which we can sum up under no current heading, which cannot be fitted into any of our ideas and images of thought and experience.

The belief in the Resurrection, the witness to the Resurrection of the first Christian community, belongs to the best attested facts in the Gospel tradition. This belief itself, however, is defenceless and exposed to a purely natural "explanation." To speak of the Resurrection itself as "one of the most sure historical facts in the history of the world" is just as senseless as the opinion that scientific knowledge can overthrow belief in the Resurrection. Rather the situation is similar to that which pertains to faith in the Deity of Christ: the historian is confronted by a problem which he may indeed arrange in an orderly way, but which he cannot fully explain in a satisfactory manner. For the attempts to explain the Resurrection appearances (visions) from the point of view of psychology are not only without the very least historical basis, but they also remain, when they are tested for psychological probability, in the highest degree unsatisfactory. No psychologist or historian has yet been able to represent as in any way, or to any extent, probable how a group of disciples, which had been broken up by a terrible catastrophe, the shameful defeat of their Master, could have come from purely inner reasons to such a faith which was finally condensed into visions. We can, it is true, never maintain that such a natural psychological happening as is constructed by the usual explanation of the Easter fact, which is the hypothesis of the Liberal Christian type of thought, is impossible; but there is no unprejudiced historian who does not feel how embarrassing it is to try to give a natural explanation of this fact. For in order to do this one has to make everything which the witness of the New Testament puts down as the *effect* of the Resurrection into its *cause*: faith in the fact of the Divine Sonship of Jesus. The historian who can be moved to replace the connection of facts as it is described by the Primitive Church by the opposite point of view can only be moved by general philosophical reasons, and not by historical reasons. The embarrassment is the same as that which is felt in the endeavour to interpret the Person of Jesus. This perplexity must be admitted, although, on the other hand, this must not be made a proof for faith. It is certainly a "proof" to the faith which already exists, but it is no proof to one who is not yet convinced, and faith is not based upon it. For faith is based on nothing but the witness to Christ, which is always the witness to the Risen Christ, whom faith knows to be the Word of God.

(vii)

The Resurrection is the *telos*, the goal and the meaning of the life of Christ. As in a game, the thrower's aim is that the missile should hit the mark, apart from which it would be altogether valueless, or as the meaning of an address finally consists in this, that what ought to be said *is* said, so the Resurrection is the meaning of the coming of Jesus Christ. The whole revelation is eschatological. This is the mystery of the divine purpose, the "end of the ways of God"; eternal glory, the life everlasting. "For this purpose the Son of God was manifested that He might destroy the works of the devil." The "works of the devil," however, in their result, in their *telos*, mean death—death as the expression of power, of the power-side of the reality of sin, just as guilt is its inner side and its hidden ground. Hence the Resurrection of Jesus is the proof of the superior reality of the Divine Will of redemption over that of the reality of wrath.

To the people of our own day the realism of the Biblical and the Reformers' "mythology" sounds remote, although it is the most sober form in which that which is intended can be stated. It cannot be better expressed than thus: Christ has broken through the gates of death and has robbed death of its power. We usually expound this in a subjective way by saying that He has redeemed us from the fear of death, and has given us the certainty of life eternal. But the myth says more than this. Just as truly as the wrath of God is a reality, and the Atonement therefore a fundamental happening, the creation of an actual new situation between God and man, so also through the Easter fact something actually *happened*; it was not that something was merely *said* which ultimately might have been said otherwise.

For the "movement" of the Christ-event is indeed not an idea, but a real movement, and by the fact that it has actually taken place through Him—the Mediator—it is achieved for us and on our behalf. The way which has been opened up by Him is now open and free for us. It is not merely that apart from Easter we would not know anything about eternal life—as we now know it through Christ—but that for us there would be no eternal life at all. For if this movement had not been carried through to the bitter end (to its *telos*), then it would mean absolutely nothing. As truly as this movement must be actual in order to be the revelation and atonement of God, so truly also must its end, its completion, be actual. "If Christ be not raised, then is your faith vain, ye are yet in your sins." This means that nothing has happened. That our life has this *telos* is only based upon the fact that the life of Christ came to this *telos*.

But we ought not to isolate the Resurrection from the whole

revelation of Christ any more than the Cross. What Bengel says of all the words of Jesus—*spirant resurrectionem*—is true of the whole life of Christ. This is the ultimate meaning of it all. What else does the Cross, the Atonement, mean than this, that we have been accepted by God for eternal life? *Futurae vitae consignatio* is justification. But this *consignatio* does not receive its final valid divine signature until the Resurrection. The phrase "the Cross" means absolutely and inclusively victory over death. But the Cross would not *be* the Cross of Christ without the Resurrection. Easter is the point of perspective, in reference to which alone all that the Gospel says is right. Take this one element away and there is nothing left; this one element is something which has really happened, and as something which has really happened it has been "seen."

It would therefore be a mistake to inquire into the particular meaning of the Resurrection. Its meaning is the meaning of the whole Gospel, and it is absolutely in accordance with its nature that in the New Testament sometimes it is our own resurrection and sometimes the state of justification, as the "being made righteous," which is related to the Easter fact. Both are equally applicable. On the other hand, it would not be wrong to say that Easter also means for us the victory over death as doom. For Christ is not merely the Logos, He is not merely that which God has to say to us, but He is at the same time also the Mediator, and thus the "Firstborn," the Firstborn among many brethren. Thus His way becomes our way. His Easter means our Easter. His way is thus not only the basis but also at the same time the type of our way.

We cannot and ought not to try to understand the Resurrection of Jesus Christ without at the same time thinking about our own resurrection. "If there be no resurrection from the dead, then Christ is not risen"—thus runs the remarkable argument of Paul. This does not mean that the general faith in resurrection is the presupposition, or even the ground, for faith in the Resurrection of Jesus. What Paul means is the very opposite. But the Resurrection of Jesus would be to us merely a story if we were not to know it in its "power," its meaning, the *beneficium* of Christ. It does not mean that first of all we can know that Jesus is risen, and then afterwards:

"then this means that we also shall rise again." It is precisely against this kind of separation in thought that Paul is aiming his remarks in the First Epistle to the Corinthians. Christ's Resurrection is only credible, and only then really known, when we see it breaking through death as such which is also our own death. The "power" of the Resurrection is not something secondary alongside of the event or its nature. At Easter this is what took place: our breaking through into eternal life.

For Jesus Christ is no private individual, and His destiny is not a private affair. He is indeed the Mediator. Since He Himself goes through death, He carries off humanity as His spoil with Himself, that is, those who through faith become His own, who through election are His. Through His Resurrection alone are we translated "out of the Kingdom of darkness into the Kingdom of His dear Son." That only through belief in the Resurrection did the Church, historically, come into being is only the historical reflection of the fact that it is based only on the resurrection in Christ. As truly as Christ *is* the turning-point and does not merely talk about it, so truly is the Resurrection the turning-point within this turning-point; the turning-point of our world. If in the message of Good Friday we have to lay special emphasis on the *factum est*, we have to do the same in the message of Easter. But we can only do this, we can only lay this emphasis, if it has taken place *for us*. A mere fact has not this right, but only the fact which at the same time fulfils the meaning of the word.

The theological "realists" are right: at Easter something, something decisive, did take place. Luther's Easter hymn is not too realistic, too strong, or too concrete. It is precisely with this that we are concerned, that "one death devoured the other." If the reality of the wrath of God—which is at the same time the Kingdom of darkness—is a reality, so also the breaking through the reality of wrath is a reality, not merely in the act of Atonement, but in the Resurrection. For both of these mean a breaking through. But a breach is nothing in itself. It is a hole, through which something else now becomes visible. We cannot see the "hole in itself." We can see the kind of hole which has been made by the fact that the other side becomes visible. Therefore the theological "Idealists" are also right: Easter is what it means, it *is* what it manifests to us. But just because it really *is* the other side which is revealed to us at this point, which comes to us, it is evident that just here, where we know what Easter means, we feel most powerless to say it. For how can we express the "Other"? Indeed, how can we even grasp it? If we could grasp it, then how could it be the Other? Just because the Resurrection of Christ is ours, it is not an "historical" event. The historical element is only the margin of the hole, which in itself says nothing. We cannot do anything else. Even the Apostles could do no more than lead us to the edge and say: Look there! Look through the hole and see that He has gone through, and indeed properly speaking from outwards within and not from within outwards. For the breach comes from the side of God, from the further side. God raised Him up; as the One who is restored to the divine world is He attested to the vision of faith. But since this factual character thus characterizes the "edge of the hole" in the historical world, so it points already to the Other, to the Light, in whose radiance alone we can know the reality of the "breaking through." This, however, is something which even the Apostles cannot state in so many words.

It is a *Factum*, certainly, but not one which can be fitted into a series; it is one which can be fitted into the succession of historical events as little as the facts of the Creation and the Fall, the Incarnation and the Atonement. In all this whatever becomes historically visible is only the echo of this happening. It is super-history, eschatological history, hence it is no longer historical at all. Again, it is a *perfectum futurum*. This statement may make the logician's hair stand on end. That is all in order. For everywhere in the narratives of the Resurrection we read that they were terrified. We cannot understand this "Perfectum" without the "Futurum" nor the "Futurum" without the "Perfectum." This is the abstract way of saying what the mythological expression says: "Christ has broken down the fortress of death, He has destroyed the gates of hell." This is what *is*, and yet—we live by faith and not by sight—it is only for the future. By faith we live now in the city which is to come, which Christ *then* founded.

But this means that we await the Resurrection. As we, as

sinners, are those who have been made righteous through Christ, whose righteousness will be hid in Christ until the Last Day, so also as dying human beings, and as those who will die, we are sharers in the Resurrection of the Lord. "It doth not yet appear what we shall be." The decision has been taken, but only as that which must be taken repeatedly, as one between faith and unbelief, between obedience and disobedience, between "offence" at the "folly" of the Cross and knowledge of the divine wisdom. The turning-point, although it has happened, is only *ours* if we ourselves turn round. This "turning" is the state of faith, the state of being a Christian. This act of "turning" makes one a believer. It is not that one *has* turned oneself, *has* known, has believed, has wrestled through. Certainly this "has" is the meaning of faith, but faith is always only in *actu*, it is the existence of the decision. Therefore it is precisely the "is" of the Resurrection of Jesus which has qualified our life as struggle, turning, decision, as an ever new beginning, an ever fresh receiving, an ever renewed search. Here we have no continuing city, but we seek one to come.

(viii)

The Christian Church makes a distinction between the Resurrection and the Ascension; and her instinct is right, however unsatisfactory the narratives of the Ascension may be from the historical point of view. The Resurrection is not the Ascension. For the Resurrection is the presence, the return of the Risen Lord, to show Himself alive by many infallible proofs, but the Exaltation is the movement in the opposite direction: the final conclusion of the story of revelation. In the Resurrection Christ turns His Face towards us from the Other Side, in the Ascension He has His Face turned in the other direction, away from us. The story of Christ has now reached its end. The movement has returned to its origin, the circle is complete.

The Exaltation of Christ is that which is to be believed on the basis of the manifestation of the Resurrection. It is not itself that basis. It is true, of course, that the Risen Lord is

the King, who has now thrown off His disguise, who speaks
to man no longer from His lowly position but from His glory.
But in so far as He makes Himself known to His disciples as
the Risen One, He still belongs to the sphere of earthly reality,
as the One who closes His own work of revelation. The Risen
Lord is becoming exalted, One who will return whence He
came. The Ascension has nothing to do with the conception of
heaven, of the kind current in olden time, of a three-storied
universe. For us who no longer hold this view this article of
faith is just as necessary as it was for primitive Christianity.
Through it the revelation which closes in the self-manifestation
of the Risen Lord is known to be ended. It is just this idea
which is necessary, if we are to know the Christian revelation
to be unique. The Church does not expect further appearances
of the Risen Lord.[1]

The Easter message is the foundation upon which the
Church is built. The laying of this foundation is not a
continuous act. Faith tends towards mysticism if this fact of
the closure of the revelation is not recognized, if the line of
separation which is drawn by the fact of the Ascension is
partially effaced, and if men maintain that it is possible to
hold direct immediate communion with the Exalted Lord
not mediated through the Word. This is the fanaticism which
would turn the believer into a prophet.

The Exaltation is the goal of the movement of revelation:
from God unto God. Hence Christ is only the Exalted One as
the One who was upon earth incognito, in the guise of a
personality which could be interpreted in two ways, in hiddenness: the King. This is the "Name above every name." Only
in the fact that we here know Him as this do we know the
meaning of revelation, the dominion of God. The first Christian
confession of faith ran thus: Christ the Lord. To believe means
to have a Lord, a King, who really, that is unconditionally,

---

[1] This applies also to Paul, in distinction from all "Christian" fanatics.
Paul does not base his personal faith as a Christian on his vision of the
Lord, but his apostleship. But he does not regard the apostleship as the
highest grade of Christian experience—that is, as something after which
everyone should strive, because it is really intended for all—but as an office,
which is given to few, and is limited to a definite period.

585

without restriction, is King, an absolute Lord with no democracy. The meaning of the revelation is the dethronement of the self, of the rebel, by the rightful monarch. The whole of revelation is simply the divine reconquest of the rebellious province. *Regem habemus!* The days of anarchy are past.

Why do we say *Christ* is King, and not simply God is King? Because the One who has come to us, the One who has come near to us, the revealed God, not God in His hidden majesty, is the One who wills to be our King. It is of the mercy of God that He does not visit us in His majesty, but as the One who stoops down to us on our own level. The royal sovereignty of the God of Majesty would mean that we should be annihilated. The sight of God in His majesty would consume us as by fire. It is the mercy and compassion of God which gives to us the Mediator as King. It is the God who is reconciled to us in Christ whom we are to know as our Lord and King.

But this is not all. Only in Christ, too, we know the seriousness of the Divine Royal Will. The God whom the natural man knows outside the revelation of Christ is the distant God whose Will does not concern us nearly as individuals. His Will is like flashes of lightning on the distant horizon. It does not yet apply to us, there is still time, we do not take it quite seriously. He is like that lord in the parable who is indeed the master of the vineyard, whose stewards are men, but about whom they are not obliged to think seriously. It only becomes serious when the master sends his servants and warns the men through them; and it becomes final and total seriousness when he sends to them his own son. The revelation of God in Jesus Christ is the Will of God expressed in a way which man cannot escape and which penetrates to him through all obstacles. It is not until Christ confronts him that man is forced to come to a decision; therefore it is not until the problem of Christ is in the forefront that we can know whether a man is serious in his relation with God or not. All wish to be religious in some way or another, all wish to have some kind of religion. But whether in this piety the chief point is God or man, the Will of God or self-will, is only decided when the soul is confronted by Christ. Therefore God also is our King: God who in Jesus Christ the exalted Lord is our King. The royal sovereignty of God is unknown outside the revelation in the Scriptures, outside Christ.

(ix)

Christ is the King of His people, whom He calls His own, the people beloved and chosen by Him: the Church. Hence when we speak of the Kingdom of Christ we must and should also speak of the Church. This, however, lies outside the range of the intention of the present work. We can only suggest in a few words what ought to be said in this connection about the matter.

From the very outset the revelation of the Bible is not concerned with the individual as such. The individualism of philosophy, of mysticism, and of moralism is alien to the spirit of the faith of the Bible. It is always regarded as a matter of course that the "people" of God are meant. The imperfection of the Old Testament is not that the people and not the individual soul receives the revelation, and is the object of the divine reconciling and redeeming process, but that this people is primarily a nationally limited magnitude.

Therefore the New Testament fulfilment of the revelation was not in the direction of deepening the personal religion of the individual, but was an extension of the "people of God" to the world of the Gentiles. We understand the struggle of Paul so little not because we take his universalism for granted, but because we no longer take seriously the idea of a people of God, chosen by Him. Paul takes this idea absolutely seriously, and he was able to carry out his ideal. But he takes it seriously in the idea of the universal Church.

The *ecclesia* is the people of God, chosen and elect, set free from national limitations. It is the Kingdom of this King, of Christ. It is not merely an idea, a magnitude present to thought, as though in reality Christ had only to do with the individual. It is, rather, exactly like the people of Israel in the Old Testament, the object of the Divine Will of revelation. The proclamation of the Gospel did not take place under the motto "let each man see for himself how he can be saved," but it was a continuation of the message of the prophets:

"the Kingdom of God, the royal rule of God will come, God wills to have an obedient people!" Hence the Church is not an aggregate of individual believers; it is the unity of believers based on the Divine Will, as it is founded on its *principium*—or rather, in its *princeps*—Christ, the Head of the Church.

The Church is not a means to an end, it is itself the end. The institutions of the Church, the constitution of the Church, the apparatus of the Church—all this is means to the end. But the Church itself is not a means, just as little as the body is the means for the limbs. If we want to use the terms "means" and "end" in this connection, we ought rather, in the spirit of the New Testament, to say the individuals are organs, members, the "means" of the body, the Church. But we must not press this figure too closely. Ultimately the body itself exists only in, not outside of, its organs, apart from the "organizing principle." In the Church, however, this means Christ. Everything serves Him, it is true, for He is the King, and not the first citizen in the republic. Just as we say Christ and faith belong to each other, so we ought to say Christ and the Church belong to each other. Rightly understood, the statement of Ritschl, that the Kingdom of God is the correlate of the divine love, is good scriptural language. But the Kingdom of God now means the Church, just as the Redemption now means Atonement, and communion with God means faith. The Church is the community of those who have been reconciled, justified, of those who believe. But its original name was the community of those who are "called."

In this Church, in this faith, Christ is the fundamental principle through the Word and as the Word. For the Church is "founded upon the foundation of the Apostles and prophets, of which Jesus Christ is the chief Corner-Stone." Christ wills to rule through His Word alone; for only as the revealed God will He now be our King. There cannot be and there ought not to be any "communion of the Christian with God" which ignores the Word, but only upon the foundation of the Word; therefore also no obedience, no work for Christ which ignores the Word, but only upon the basis of the Word. That which holds together the people of God, that which founds the community, that which summons to obedience, that which creates the power to obey, is the Word, the Gospel of Jesus Christ, as it is attested as God's Word by the Holy Spirit, speaks to us, comforts, judges, warns us, and, as something real and effective, shows us the way. This is the manner in which the King rules over us, until His coming "in power."

For the Word is not the end; not even the Word made flesh. Just as certainly as the Incarnation of Christ has as its goal the Exaltation, so also shall faith merge into sight. History, even Church history, is an interim process. It is neither a beginning nor an end. It is an intermezzo, a *provisorium*. There is nothing more stupid than the assertion that faith is the end. Faith points to the end, seeks for the city which is above; Justification and Atonement aim at Redemption, hope awaits its fulfilment, the Church fights as the Church Militant in the midst of a world which does not wish to submit to Christ, towards the end, aiming at victory—but all this is not the end itself. To be content with this, and to leave the end uncertain is the very opposite of faith. Faith means being eagerly intent on the end, even for the end of faith itself.

The sovereignty which Christ exercises during this interim period is very limited. Indeed, it is more like fighting with the rebellious than like ruling over an obedient people. This interim period is due to the sin and disobedience of man and the longsuffering of God, which leaves time for decision. But there will come a day when this period will be over; there will then be no longer any time for decision, or the decision itself would not be real. The Day will come when God will stand forth in His majesty for all those who are not hidden from His eyes by the presence of the Mediator in whom they have taken refuge. This will be the Day when the tares will be separated from the wheat, and that which is hidden will be revealed. Until that Day the Kingdom of Christ is hidden— in the world, not to faith. Then, however, it will be revealed to the world, in the world in which it will restore the original divine order, which in this restoration will be at the same time perfected. That Christ is known in faith as the King must mean that He will be known as the Victor, whose victory

will no longer be hidden but revealed, who will redeem His
Word in reality and in power.

But in order to speak (even to some degree) adequately of
these things we should need to deal with the questions of faith
and the life of faith, with repentance and the New Birth, with
Sanctification and Hope, with the Church and the Final End.
We should also speak of Christ and His Work. For what else
does faith, repentance, New Birth—what else does the Church
and the Final End mean, save the royal work of Christ, the
work which He does as the Exalted Lord in His own Church?
Our suggestions have been simply intended to show that in
order to know Christ it is necessary to think about matters
which are not usually regarded as the "doctrine of Christ."
But what has the doctrine of Christ, to which our endeavours
have been dedicated, to do with the practical and simple faith
in Christ, and what has all this to do, above all, with the
obedient following of Christ? This book must close with a brief
reply to this burning question.

CONCLUSION

CONFESSING CHRIST; BELIEVING IN CHRIST; FOLLOWING CHRIST

THE whole Gospel of Jesus Christ is the exposition of the First Commandment: "I am the Lord thy God, thou shalt have none other gods but Me." Whenever anyone really listens to the First Commandment and admits its reality, he already possesses the whole truth that the Scriptures and the Gospel of Jesus Christ contain. This is the whole meaning; it has no other. Whoever understands what this means: "I am the Lord thy God; thou shalt honour, fear and love none save Me" understands everything which it is of final importance to understand in this life. The whole message of the Church, if it be a true message, simply aims at intensifying the force of this First Commandment. The Church has no other task. This includes all her teaching, both in dogma and in ethics. When this commandment is obeyed, then all is well with her both in her faith and in her active life. But all is not well with the Church when she thinks this is not sufficient; when she says that this commandment is only law, and what matters most is that the Gospel shall be preached. There is no other Gospel than this "Law" itself.

Then is the Gospel of Jesus Christ superfluous? Did Christ come into this world for nothing? Yes, unless through His coming this First Commandment be understood and accepted. But this is the very reason why He came, and it is for this very reason that the Gospel consists in our knowledge of Him; this is why He became man, was crucified, and finally rose from the dead. His whole revelation is designed to serve the First Commandment. It is thus and for this reason that He is the fulfilment of the Law: as Mediator, Revealer, Reconciler. For indeed even He wills to be known as the κύριος χριστός, as the *Lord* Jesus. He does not wish to have any mere hearers, but *disciples* who do His Will. It is a terrible misunderstanding, the worst, the most subtle fraud ever perpetrated in the Name of God, if we think that everything does not depend upon this obedience, if we hold that through faith in the Mediator, in justification, this obedience has become either superfluous or a secondary matter. Faith *is* obedience—nothing else—literally nothing else at all.

Now what does the First Commandment mean? Does anyone understand it? Does anyone take it seriously? Does anyone ever take its tremendous claim literally? It was not accepted by the Jews, or they would not have rejected Christ. They rejected Him because they could not tolerate this claim. The "natural man" cannot understand the First Commandment. It is just because he is so ignorant of its meaning that that which constitutes the Gospel had to take place. The Mediator is the One who—as the Mediator—first makes us able to hear the First Commandment. We do not hear this voice of God—or we do not hear it without hearing it wrongly—save through the Mediator. Apart from Christ the First Commandment seems empty and trivial; we do not fear it as we should, indeed as would be only natural if we could understand its real meaning, if we had really heard it for ourselves. We regard the Name and the Will of God in a superficial way until Christ takes this Name, pronounces It Himself, shows us Its meaning through the Word made flesh, the Crucified and the Risen Lord. Thus, just as we are obliged to say the Gospel is simply and solely the exposition of the First Commandment, so we must also say, apart from this actual exposition of it by God Himself, in the story of Christ, the First Commandment would be unintelligible to us; it would be unreal.

This then is our position: without the Gospel of Jesus Christ we do not know what this means: "I am the Lord thy God, thou shalt have none other gods but Me." We need Christ the Mediator in order to be able to know and recognize the Lord God as Lord. This "coming" of God is necessary—for us who are what we are—in order that the commandment may be taken seriously. This is why the Jews rejected Him: because they perceived that now God's Will would have to be taken seriously, far more seriously than they wished to take it. This is why the modern man is prepared to think of God in a general way, but not of the Gospel of Jesus Christ, the Mediator, because here the Divine Will comes too close to him, nearer than is comfortable for his self-will; hence his opposition to the Mediator.

It will therefore be suitable to conclude our treatment of this subject with some observations upon the two-fold thesis:—

Firstly: The message of Jesus Christ, the Mediator—the content of dogma—is only understood and taken seriously when it is understood as the exposition of the First Commandment, when the "Dogma of Christ" constitutes the basis of the "Christian ethic."

Secondly: Obedience to the Will of God—that is, moral obedience—is not taken seriously until we believe in the Gospel of Jesus Christ the Mediator.

I must, however, hasten to add that in all this I am only summing up the ideas which have guided my argument concerning faith in the Mediator. I have no intention of adding an "application" of this theory to the "ethical problem"; I am simply giving a retrospective summary in order that I may show that as a whole I have never been dealing with anything else, or at least, that I had no intention of dealing with anything save with the moral problem itself.

Thus the first point is this: that every article of the Christian faith, rightly interpreted, always has an ethical bearing; that is, a true and vital ethic must be based upon a true and vital creed. The mistake of modern theology did not lie in the fact that it sought to establish a close connection between ethics and faith; where it went wrong was that in the endeavour to establish this connection it allowed the Christian revelation to be dominated by a rational ethical idea; in so doing, it endangered the truly ethical character of the Gospel by permeating it with the abstract and superficial spirit of ethical rationalism, and, at the same time, it misrepresented the ethical significance of the Christian message. On the other hand, we can have nothing but praise for the intention which actuated this endeavour. This intention, which is wholly admirable, arose out of the desire to free the Christian faith from a kind of sterile intellectualist orthodoxy, which was indifferent to ethical problems and shirked the travail of personal decision in ethical questions. The aim of modern theology has been to show the indissoluble connection between ethics and faith; indeed, understood rightly, the absolute identity between the two.

This intellectualism, however—as the whole of Church history bears witness—has always accompanied the testimony to Jesus Christ, the Mediator. This danger lurks wherever the confession of faith in Jesus Christ is formulated into a creed and elaborated by a scientific theology. It is not that in themselves either dogma or theology imply or involve an intellectualism of this kind, On the contrary! If we examine the impelling motives in the history of dogma we shall see that the opposite is true: Christian dogma has acted as a kind of breakwater, erected by the Christian Church as a defence against the seething ocean of intellectualism by which it was surrounded. Christian dogma is not a product of the Greek rational spirit; on the contrary, it is the fortification erected to keep it out. The same applies to the recent tendency to attribute excessive emphasis on dogma to the Reformation. Here again, originally the whole aim of the Reformers was centred on one single point: by every means in their power to force man to quit the attitude of a mere spectator, to leave theory behind, and face the real challenge of life. The doctrine of justification does not compete with the concern for ethics; rather, it means the definite rejection of all lack of serious concern with ethical questions. Just as the controversies in the Early Church about the doctrine of the Trinity meant the rejection of the speculative arrogance of reason, so the controversies of the period of the Reformation meant the rejection of the moral arrogance of reason (righteousness of "works"); both, however, are actuated by the one central concern for ethics.

The significance of dogma is always negative. It is only on account of her weakness that the Christian Church always needs dogma. The aim of dogma is simply to protect the message of the Gospel, to defend the faith from destructive misunderstanding. Rightly understood, it is the sum total of negative statements: God is not this or that. Hence at every fresh period in the history of the Church it needs to be reformulated, not because the content of the message has altered but because the misunderstandings and perversions against which the same message always has to contend are different. Thus a dogma of to-day would need, above all, to make its position quite clear with reference to the religion of immanence and evolution. In discussions of this kind lies the justification for the existence of dogma. It is a wall of defence; a wall of this sort is important, but it is not the most important element in the Faith. It is not that which it is there to conserve. Dogma is not itself the Word of God and faith.[1] It is merely the discussion of faith with unbelieving error by means of thought. This process of discussion is carried on by theology. Hence theology is worth far less than faith. Its significance also is negative; its task is to create room for the Divine Word. The positive element consists solely in the proclamation of the Divine Word itself, in the actual fact that God is speaking in His Word. Dogma and theology exist for the sake of the Christian message, not *vice versa*.

Where this relationship has been reversed, thus where dogma is confused with the actual message, the danger which threatened the Faith has turned into the devastating evil of intellectualism. Here the wall of defence has killed the life which it was there to protect, or at least has almost stifled it; here the wood which was intended to support the tree has used up all the vital sap. This is the corruption of faith by orthodoxy. Faith has become doctrine, a matter for the intellect, the play of thought, scholasticism. This disaster is not due to the dogma, the formulated creed of the Christian Church; for without dogma the world invades the Church and lays it waste; the disaster is due to the fact that the dogma, the merely intellectual expression of the divine truth in Christ, has itself been deified. The fact that God's Word is not a static theory, that it is not a Word which man can manipulate as he chooses, but that it is a living personal challenge has

---

[1] Just as the use of a telescope is that by limiting our vision it directs it (for anyone who looks at the inside of the telescope sees nothing at all), so the function of doctrinal formulas is to direct our spiritual faculty of hearing in the right direction, namely, to the point where man is silent, and God Himself speaks. He who desires to evade this directive limitation, he who desires to hear "outside" the doctrine, simply hears nothing at all.

been forgotten. When dogma has ceased to be witness, that is, to point to something behind and above itself, then it is fossilized into a concrete "Word," a fetish. Or, if we say that the ethical meaning of the Word of God has been forgotten, we mean the same thing. The Word is no longer a challenge; it has become an object for consideration, a theory.

The Church cannot be sufficiently grateful to those who are aware of this silent process of ossification which is going on under their eyes, and who raise their voices in warning against it, for the sake of the faith which is expressed in the dogma. This confusion of faith with theory means that something terrible has taken place; it means that under the pretext of being very ardent for the divine honour, the divine truth has been obscured by a subtle web of human falsity and error, while man has made things as easy as possible for himself. For even the most paradoxical forms of belief in the doctrine of the Trinity and of the Atonement, once they have been turned into theories, are only too easily used as an escape from reality, from conflict with a real resistance, into the airy spaces of the sham reality of mere thought.[1] Thus the doctrine of Justification, which represents the highest kind of moral earnestness, becomes a pillow upon which the lazy and cowardly conscience lays down its head and falls asleep.

This is not due to the fact that the doctrines of Justification, of the Trinity, or of the Atonement are not true; rather it is due to the fact that men do not want to hear the truth of God—the voice of the Lord—in these doctrines because they do not wish to obey it; all they want is to possess this message as a static truth which they can use as they will, and con-

[1] This is shown above all by the fact that the dogma is not "really" believed, that instead of walking with the aid of the map one is content to *read* the map only, and to ascend the steep and winding ascent in "thought" alone, but not in reality. Instead of existentially allowing one's heart and life to be determined by the words of the Faith, one merely glances at them. This is like receiving guests into one's house but not allowing them to go further than the ante-room. We must learn to interpret intellectualism from the negative point of view, that is, as a way of preventing the Word from penetrating into the personal centre, where it desires to be. "Faith" of this kind is an act of acceptance which is yet the very opposite of surrender.

template as a mere object of thought. The content of the creed is the same as the message of Christianity, when the conceptions of the message and the creed are in right condition. But the aim of dogma is simply to "define"; it does not proclaim anything. It merely expresses something; it does not address a message to actual persons. In this process of definition it exercises a useful function in the Church—for without it the Church would become merged in the world; but its function is one of service—it exists for a higher end than itself, that is, it exists for the sake of the message. It is not more than the message, but less, since it states merely the truth which can be expressed intellectually—it does not possess the existential reality of speech, of personal address. For this cannot be defined or asserted; like life, it is only real when it is in motion. Just as living beings can be preserved by chemical means—but only as those who once lived, who resemble those who are alive in everything with the one exception that they are no longer alive—so in dogma the intellectual substance of the Christian message can indeed be preserved, and this indeed is a right and necessary process, only we must always remember that although it may resemble it verbally, it is not the real message itself.

Dogma expresses what ought to be proclaimed in the Church. This statement seems to contradict the statement which I have just made that essentially dogma only possesses a negative function. But this contradiction is only apparent. It is not the content of the dogma which is negative, but its function. The content, however, cannot be grasped from the dogma itself, but only from the proclamation of the message, in faith. The creed is not there in order to produce faith, but in order to express it. But this "expression" in the creed is not itself the Christian message; it only suggests it. It is the fence which protects the path to the left and to the right, but it is not the path itself. It is intended to show the right path, to fence it off, but it cannot itself be the path. Compared with the Word of God which is preached and believed it is like a good map; it is only "legible" to one who knows the real Word. Only the believer can be taught by dogma, only for him is it a "doctrinal law" because he alone knows its origin. To him the statements

597

of dogma are simply signals to halt; they say, "Do not pass beyond this sign!" But it is not the dogma which binds him, but the truth to which the dogma points. The dogma is not itself the authority; it does not speak for faith, but about the faith of the Church, and thus to the individual it becomes a sign-post, which has been erected by those who as believers have preceded him, and are alongside of him now—the Church—as a warning to believe in the right way; and this means to listen to that which has helped others to believe.

The great danger of dogma is that too often it transforms the sign of the thing it represents into the thing itself. When this happens, a process of listening to a personal message becomes a neutral process of theoretical learning and the acceptance of certain intellectual truths. The formulation of the truth has been mistaken for the truth itself.

Once this has taken place it certainly is difficult to perceive any connection between faith and ethics. For what connection can there possibly be between a truth which is interpreted and accepted in a theoretical sense and the sphere of ethics? For this always means that the fundamental significance claimed by Christianity for faith and life is transferred to dogma; this leads to a very dangerous over-estimate of the value of the intellectual element in religion, and to an inordinate esteem for mere knowledge as opposed to actual behaviour. Where this confusion takes place it spells death to the moral element in religion, because the real basis has been changed.

There is no worse foe to morality than dogmatic orthodoxy.

But the fault for all this does not lie with dogma itself—it is not due to the fact that a Church expresses its faith in a creed, as every true Church is bound to do; the reason for this fatal confusion lies rather in the fact that the meaning of this creed is no longer understood, and that the creed is confused with the message, that it becomes more important than the message, instead of being regarded as a subsequent consideration. For the word of the message itself, whose truth is defined in the dogma, is not exposed to this misunderstanding. Where it is really the Word of God which is proclaimed—the same Word which is defined in the dogma—there is nothing which can be appropriated in an intellectual neutral manner, nothing which provides a subject for mere knowledge and speculation, but it is the claim of a person on a person, which the one who hears makes his own, body and soul. For it is simply the exposition of the First Commandment, and indeed an exposition which only takes place in order to make it possible for the commandment really to have its full weight. It is thus that the "teaching" of the Bible is given. The "Knowledge of the Lord," "the Word of the Lord" is always meant in a practical sense—and particularly in that which is really taught here.[1] The Will of God is made known—to the human will. It is the Will which takes possession of a human will by means of the Word. It is a doctrine which can only be appropriated by an act of decision. The message about the Creator is not a theory of the way in which the world came into being, which we can discuss like any other theory, but it is the personal Word of the Creator, who, because He is the Creator, is my Lord. The Incarnation is not a mythological theologumenon which is meant to explain how Christ can be regarded as God; but "to see" what this "coming" of Christ means is the same as to know our "place," to be aware of our real situation, and thus to perceive the divine mercy, through which He thus condescends to us. The doctrine of the Atonement is not a "theory of sacrifice," but it is the unveiling of our guilt in its truly

[1] It was fear of orthodox intellectualism which hindered a man like Wilhelm Herrmann from perceiving the meaning of the decisive Biblical category of the "Word." In the Bible revelation is never an "impression" which is merely perceived afterwards in the Word, as though the Word were something secondary to the revelation itself, but the revelation is in the Word, in spite of the fact that the human word, by the very fact that it is human, is merely the veil which conceals the Divine Word. The definite Word, the definite content of thought, is not a reflection on the revelation, as though it were itself simply an "impression"; but it is precisely this definite Word which is the revelation. That the Word is the place where the revelation is found, that revelation can be found only in perceiving this Word, and must really be found in it: it is this perception which distinguishes living faith both from the false immediacy of mysticism and from the false mediacy of orthodoxy. It must first of all be found; it is not a matter simply of logical understanding and acceptance; *God* speaks it in a human word. But it must be found in the definite Word, in the fact that it can actually be heard and understood: God *speaks* it in the human word.

fatal character, and of the incomprehensible Act of Grace by which God has taken our part. How hopelessly men must have misunderstood the meaning of the Reformation if they have not seen that the doctrine of justification through faith alone does not mean merely comfort and reassurance for the burdened conscience, but above all the creation of a new moral individual, of the "workman" who not only ought to do good works but wills to do them.

It is quite clear, however, that as soon as we begin to think *about* these doctrines, instead of submitting ourselves to them, our attitude becomes wrong. They have become objects to us, when the shoe ought to be on the other foot: we ought to be objects to them. We appraise them, instead of allowing them to judge us. Our attitude towards them has become that of a spectator, and this means that our relation to them has become purely intellectual. They are no longer "the Word," but a theory, an object to be looked at coolly from the outside. And the result is that now we master them instead of letting them master us. To assert about these theories that they alone create the moral will is certainly a disastrous misapprehension.

Once things have reached this pass even the most colourless ethic of the Enlightenment is better than this kind of dogmatism. But here we are not dealing with this kind of thing. Here we are not inquiring into the ethical significance of dogma—there is such a significance, although it is of a subordinate kind—but into the significance of the Christian witness of the Scriptures and of the Church, and concerning this we certainly maintain—with the Scriptures and the Church—that it alone really creates moral obedience. I will expound this second thesis under six headings.

Firstly: Only in the Mediator Jesus Christ do we know ourselves as we really are.[1]

Self-knowledge is a decisive ethical factor. So long as we cherish illusions about ourselves we cannot act ethically. Apart

[1] This does not mean that outside of Christ there is no self-knowledge, but it does mean that outside of Christ there is no self-knowledge which goes to the root of the matter.

from Christ man tends to judge himself and the world of human beings around him either from a cynical determinist point of view or in an enthusiastic ideological manner.[1] In the first instance he sees the brutal realities, the instinctive biological factors and complications of human historical existence. "The machine is kept going by hunger and by love." He sees the way in which Nature is a law to herself, in detail, and in the great historical forces, the terrible way in which the human will is bound hand and foot by instinct, fate, and society. He is a "realist." He sees a great deal, but there is one thing which he does not see—the one truly human reality—the solidarity of human guilt, godlessness as the root of evil, death as the wages of sin. In the second instance the "idealist" sees indeed the difference between humanity and *Bios*, between spirit and instinct, between what must be and what ought to be. He sees the responsibility of the individual. But he does not see the complications of evil, the bondage of the enslaved will, the way in which man is bound into a whole by guilt and sin. He is so dazzled by the idea of primitive humanity, by the idea of man, that he does not see the real human being, who is as different from the ideal human being as is the spoilt work of art from the perfect work. He does not see what has happened. Through this all his expectation and behaviour is Utopian, just as the conduct of the other is paralysed by fatalism.

If the statement, common to all ethical doctrine, be true, that self-knowledge is the foundation of all moral behaviour, of all ethical improvement, then it is at this point that every ethical system proves itself inadequate which does not recognize that man has been created by God, and has fallen away from God. Every system? Yes, every form of religion which is not "revealed," or, to put it more exactly, every system of thought that does not mean faith in the Divine Revelation and in Atonement through an historical Mediator. For man can only

[1] Pascal is right, there are two systems of ethics only, Epicureanism and Stoicism, with an endless number of variations and blends, which are of no importance for our subject. The one desires to understand duty from existence, the other to master existence by duty. From the Christian point of view both are distorted sections of the one truth.

601

learn to know himself through the knowledge of the divine movement in which God stoops down to man, in which God Himself bridges the gulf between Himself and man. We only know what our real position is by that which God does in us and for us. We do not fully realize that we are slaves until we see that we have been "bought" by God, "bought with a price."

Only in the Christian view of sin does righteousness affect equally that which the Realist sees and the Idealist beholds. The Realist sees—distorted by this one-sidedness—Original Sin and the original curse, but not as sin, or as the curse. The Idealist may perceive the original state of man and his freedom, the idea of humanity, but he does not see that this freedom and this origin have been lost. The one sees the present reality apart from its origin, the other sees the origin apart from the reality. The one may perhaps see the complications, but he does not see the responsibility of the individual; the other sees the responsibility of the individual apart from human solidarity. Hence both these human ethical theories are not finally serious, for the one eliminates the elements of responsibility and freedom, and the other the elements of guilt and the complicated character of sin. The one leaves man to perish in the midst of existing conditions, the other promises him an illusory redemption by setting the spirit free from bondage to the senses.

The Christian view of human reality, however, is connected with, and created by, the knowledge of the Divine Revelation and Atonement through the Mediator. We only fully perceive our need of redemption and atonement at the actual moment when it takes place, only at the Cross do we know our guilt as human beings, without any excuse; our impotence to redeem ourselves without fatalism, and our original glory and destiny without sentimentality. For it is in the Mediator that the original Word once more addresses us as those whom He had lost and has now received back again. From this standpoint we perceive that as Realists we had forgotten the Creation and as Idealists we had forgotten the Fall, and how impossible it was for us, by our own efforts, to make a fresh synthesis.

Secondly: Only in the Mediator is the will of God, that is, the Good, known as Love.

All human ethical systems suffer from the disharmony due to the impossibility of effecting a combination between reality of life and rationality, of Eudaemonism and legality, of abstract spirituality and spiritual concreteness. All attempts to get beyond this dualism have been shattered and will also in the future come to nothing—in spite of all the material ethical values which flourish so prolifically. The impotence of Eudaemonism as a moral principle need not be discussed any further. But the Idealistic ethic also is unable to disclose to us the meaning of the Good.

It is greatly to the credit of the Kantian ethic that with the austerity proper to a philosopher it has resisted the temptation to force a synthesis of which rational thought is incapable: the synthesis of inclination and duty, love.[1] For this possibility lies outside the range of human law. Law is the only, the highest, the best that can be said from the human side about the Good. Man may talk about "love," but he will still remain under the influence of that which the philosopher calls respect. Love is a divine, not a human possibility. For God is love. Love can only exist where it is given.

Therefore love is the Word of the Divine Revelation and Grace. It is, of course, true that mysticism also speaks of love, but in so doing it means something quite different. It does not mean the love which really goes out of itself, which stoops down to help others, the love which seeks and saves—how could mysticism know about this? It does not mean the Divine Love as the coming of God to us. It knows indeed only the God to whom one comes oneself through recollection and introversion. It does not know the God who Himself moves, but only the God who "is." The God of Love, however, is the God who comes, who seeks, who saves, who communicates Himself, who reveals Himself, *qui nostra assumsit ut nobis sua conferret.* Love

---

[1] Through the entire history of ethics there runs an attempt to achieve this synthesis (which corresponds to the synthesis of Idealism and Realism in theoretical philosophy, in Pantheism): the solution of the contradiction in the aesthetic sphere. The latest great example of this is provided by Schiller's letters on aesthetic education.

can only be known in the God who forgives. But the forgiveness which really takes place—and it alone reveals the loving God, since it alone is serious—is the Atonement through the Mediator. For the Mediator is the One in whom forgiveness is not merely *spoken*, but actually takes place. The love of God is known only in the Mediator.

In this love, however, the meaning of the Good is revealed. Love is the fulfilling of the Law. But only the Divine Love is the Good, and this means only the love which reveals itself in its coming, and in revealing itself communicates itself. This downward "movement" is itself identical with love. In it the world as it is, man as he is, are both judged, and yet restored. For in this "coming" man sees how far away he is—there is no sharper judgment than forgiveness—and in this "coming" his distance from God is overcome: the Atonement is the restoration of fellowship. This Divine Love itself is the Good, in which all discord is removed. It is "good" and the "Good," it is life and the meaning of life, it is the affirmation of the world and victory over the world; it is the "Yea" which preserves and the "Nay" which criticizes and destroys; it is the most conservative force in existence, for it confirms and upholds the created order; and it is the most radical, for it is the re-establishment and re-creation of all that exists; it is the "Yea" to man as he is, to the sinner in whom this his being is absolutely denied, and the "Nay" to the sinner in which he is once more called back into the Divine Being.

It is into this movement that one is taken up in faith. Indeed, faith consists in being absorbed into this movement. Hence faith is not the demand of love—which, as Kant rightly says, it is futile to demand, although, as the sole Good, it would be the sole thing which might be demanded with real justification —but the fact that one is placed in the Divine Love, that one receives this movement as a gift. Hence faith cannot be separated from love. To supplement faith by love is about as sensible as it would be to supplement the door by the room into which it leads. Faith simply means entering into the Divine Love. When this takes place, however, the moral movement also receives a wholly new character.

Thirdly: Only in Christ the Mediator is it possible to see and love one's neighbour.

We have already pointed out that apart from Christ ethics are either spiritual in an abstract manner or unspiritually concrete. This concreteness is simply that of natural individualism, the realism of the natural man. It is not something ethically concrete, but simply the concrete instinctive life, thus something which is impersonally concrete. On the other hand, the spirituality which is humanly possible is the abstract spirituality of the principle, of the Idea, of Law, the character of the legal man whose life is governed by principle, who judges life pharisaically and forces it into his own forms. This ethic is never concerned with man as one's "neighbour," but only with man in general; between him and me there is always an "It," a something abstract, a "case." I never see the individual as he is in himself, but always as the representative of something else, as a "case," and I never deal directly with him, but try to "apply" the law to this particular case. Therefore as a human being my "neighbour" is never this particular individual here and now. I do not love him, I merely respect him.

For to love him would mean seeing him as he is here and now, accepting him as he is at this moment. Love cannot be anything other than that which God does to us; that is, it means the coming of God to us, preservation on the negative side, and apprehension on the positive side. To love means to accept this man *as he is*, "in Christ," as one who has been judged in Him and granted the grace of God, above whom there stands the word "sinner," "fallen being," but also the word "justified," or "one who has been restored." Love also means going out into the world, in order to lay hold of it for God. Hence love (we know now that there is no other that deserves to be called love save love in Christ) is both so deeply concerned with this world, in contrast to Stoicism, Platonism, and Mysticism, and yet so much more radical in its denial of the world than all philosophical ethics, which in the last resort still pay court to the world, and allow themselves to be caught by it, and mysticism which does not really come to grips with the world at all.

Love is concrete, for love is actually concerned with my

neighbour in his need, not with a "case." It does not need to ask how the law can here be translated into concrete terms, for it does not know how to think in abstract terms; it does not know of the contrast between nature and spirit. It is indeed the Will of the Creator which has made both, spirit and body, things and human beings as *one* creation. And it knows nothing of an abstract law which already exists, but only of the present Will of this Creator and Redeemer—God. Therefore—as Luther always says rightly—it always does just what comes to hand. It does that which has to be done, here and now, which for that very reason cannot be known beforehand. It takes our neighbour seriously by the very fact that it does not look at him from the point of view of some legal plan, but places him in this absolutely peculiar situation in order to do for him just what can only be done to him thus, and which none but I ought to do here and now.

To come into touch with my neighbour in this whole-hearted way, however, is only possible through that movement from Christ towards us; indeed, it is simply the continuation of this movement into the human sphere. Hence the remarkable negations in the great hymn to love in *1 Corinthians xiii.* Love is no human possibility, it is the denial of all that might be regarded as love from the purely human point of view. It is possible only ἐν Χριστῷ, in the position in which I, and my neighbour through Christ, are placed by faith. Only thus is this complete nearness remote from sentimentality and weakness, and this complete other-worldliness not an abstraction remote from the world. In Christ alone can we venture so completely to say "Yes" and "No." But when all this has been said the decisive word has not yet been uttered.

Fourthly: Only in faith in Christ the Mediator is our arrogant self-will broken and God honoured.

All natural ethics are, in the last resort, self-assertion. This is not only true of the eudaemonistic ethic, as is quite natural, and as is also admitted, but also of the Idealist ethic of law. There is a more subtle form of Eudaemonism, the romantic principle of individuality, of self-expression, the self-affirmation of the "deeper" or of the "more spiritual" self, of the "true nature," in the sense in which Rousseau used the word, and in which it is used to-day by educational reformers who have been influenced by him. It is only its lack of clarity that enables this philosophy of life to exist at all. For a "spiritual self" of this kind is not an entity; it only becomes such through self-determination. Above all, however, this philosophy of life lives upon its superficiality; for its underlying article of faith is this: man is good. Nothing else shows so plainly the superficiality of this point of view than this statement.

The Idealistic legalistic ethic saw through this obscurity and this superficiality. It makes distinctions; it is critical. Hence it distinguished between the empirical and the "intelligible" self. But it is this very distinction which constitutes the same evasion of reality. For which self is here the sinful guilty self? It cannot be the "intelligible" self, for this is identical with the Good; it cannot be the empirical self, for this is not free, and is therefore not responsible. Behind this distinction lies the ancient theory of Platonism, which in its distinction between soul and body evades the problem of evil. The real human being, however, is precisely the one who, although he is not free, knows he is responsible, and although he is "spiritual," knows he is sinful and guilty. Even Idealism does not recognize this reality. Therefore in it the final basis of morality is self-respect. Even the Idealistic ethic is self-affirmation.[1] Therefore its last word is autonomy. Indeed, in it sin in its original form comes out most clearly and plainly, grown to its full size: the desire to be as God, the desire to will life from within, to be emancipated from the Divine Grace, from the attitude of dependence, from the Giver.

The sense of complete dependence on God, the recognition of the primal relationship, that God alone has all and that we of ourselves have nothing, that all that is good can only be received: this is the *sola gratia* of faith. Only in faith is the lie destroyed which says that man stands alongside of God as His partner, as His co-legislator, as one whose deepest self is

[1] We must not draw our comparison from the later Idealists who have been influenced by Christianity, but from the Idealists of the ancient world; the impression of a naïve self-righteousness and self-reference is overwhelming.

at bottom identical with the divine. Only in faith does man recognize God as Creator and himself as creature. Only in faith therefore is God honoured, and His Name hallowed, and He is recognized as Lord. Only in this absolute dependence is both the illusion of the immanental theories and the arrogance they breed exposed and denied.

All this, however, is only true if we take the word faith in its fullest sense, and this means faith in justification through faith alone, and thus faith in the Mediator. For this is justification: that we have no good thing in ourselves, but that whatever we have must first of all have been received, that righteousness is not our own, but the righteousness of Christ, which is made our own through the Word of grace. The mystical doctrine of grace, therefore—however strikingly Pauline or Augustinian its phrases may sound—is no real doctrine of grace, because it is not concerned with forgiveness but with "infused grace." But this means that the guilt of sin is treated lightly, that the obstacle which separates us from God is not admitted, the gulf is not perceived. The sight of the gulf, and the perception of the necessity for a bridge over it which shall proceed from the side of God, simply means that we need the Mediator. If, however, sin is not admitted, then the sense of need is not perceived; this means also that at the decisive point to be thrown upon the grace of God is not admitted. The relation is an impersonal one. If it were personal, then the guilt of sin would be admitted as that which above all constitutes the personal separation. How can God be honoured in such a relation, which ignores the serious element in the personal relationship?

Man is only truly dependent as a sinner, that is, as one who is under condemnation, when as such he knows that he is absolutely dependent upon the word of release. Only through the character of the release—of forgiveness—does grace become really personal. The justification of the sinner by being set free and declared just by God Himself: this is grace. But this word of justification is only taken seriously as an award, as something which is not taken for granted, if it is taken seriously as an actual event, as the act of Atonement. Only the knowledge that this must take place, that this is necessary, that we must be "bought with a price" which is so costly, breaks down the pride which believes that in reality our position is not so bad, that at bottom we are all right. Only through the Mediator do we become absolutely dependent on what God does and on what He gives. For apart from faith in the Mediator, in some way or another we have to forgive ourselves.

Faith in the Atonement which has taken place through the Mediator makes us humble. Here alone is the continuity between us and God abrogated, in order that it may be restored by God alone.

We remain proud so long as we do not believe in the Mediator, and it is only pride which does not allow us to believe in this message of the Mediator. In faith in this happening man is stripped naked, and, in this process of stripping, God is honoured as the sole Giver of life.

Here the innermost line of defence which man throws up in his fight against God is surrendered, here man has to capitulate unconditionally. This capitulation means the breaking down of self-will before the Divine Will. Man ceases to be a competitor with God when he says: Christ is my righteousness. This, however, is the whole point of the moral struggle: there is no other good, no second good. The Will of God alone is good, and the only good is to make it possible for the Will of God to have its full weight. This is evil: "*my* will be done, my name be honoured, my dominion come!" This is good: "Thy Will be done; Hallowed be Thy Name, Thy Kingdom come." *Tertium non datur.* "Thy Will be done" does not become true for us until we believe in the divine communication of Himself, the Good, in the Mediator.

For here at last man renounces the claim to be able to carry on his business at his own charges. The unreserved admission of one's own bankruptcy is the presupposition of the real entrance into the sphere ruled by God, as, on the other hand, to take the fact seriously that God alone matters is the presupposition of this declaration of bankruptcy. Repentance and faith are the same thing. Both mean the cessation of the false independence of man and his return to the original attitude of dependence. This return is the only thing which has an independent moral value. All other values are merely derived from something else.

That life depends wholly on grace is not "one aspect" which needs to be completed by the ethical element, but it is itself the ethical element. For this is the recognition of the Divine Will, which is itself the Good, alongside of which there is no other independent Good, such as a Moral Law to which the Divine Will also is obliged to bow.

Fifthly: Only through faith in justification does the Good, from being a postulate, become a reality.

The naturalistic ethic tries to construct ethics from the point of view of being. It is therefore not really an ethic, but only a maxim of prudence. The Idealistic ethic interprets the moral law as an obligation. Hence in it the Good always remains merely a postulate, a demand, a law without power to enforce itself, and therefore, finally, ideology. In the faith in justification, however, the ethic is founded on the being which God declares as our being: the sinner is the righteous. In this respect the Christian faith is like Naturalism: it starts from a given fact, not from an abstraction. But this given fact is not something which has been given by nature—not even divinely given, as mysticism and sacramentalism suppose—but one which is given in the Word of God. By the fact that it is given in the Word, faith is like Idealism. But this Word is not an idea, it is not something to which man must first move himself; it is the Word of grace, from which therefore he is always to start.

This is the new element in the Christian Ethos: we always start from the Good, namely, from the righteousness which we have—in Christ. Living in grace means that we must begin with this "is," that the "is" is not only the goal at the end of a long road, but the starting-point to which we must constantly return.

Already we possess righteousness, namely, that of Christ, thus that which we do not possess of ourselves, but which is ours through the pronouncement of God. This dignity is not one which is still to be attained: "What Christ has given to me is worthy of love." This is our "wreath," our "crown."

This is the language of the Christian man, this is the new pride, which is at the same time a new humility; for man has not attained that which honours him by his own efforts but as something from outside, as *gratia gratis data*; a pride which reaches higher than the most audacious pride of the Idealist, and a humility which thinks more humbly of our own possibilities than any kind of realistic resignation.

This, however, makes another point clear. In all other ethical formulations of a problem the question always concerns the object of the action. This is a superficial view. For the object of the action is not the chief point, but the whole point lies in the doer, not in the deed. For it is not good works which make a good man, but a good man who makes good works (Luther). It might seem as though in the strictest Idealistic ethic, that is, in the Kantian ethic, it is precisely this which is meant. Hence for this very reason abstraction is made from the whole material aspect of ethics, for "there is nothing good save a good will." The postulate is right. But is it seriously meant? For if it were so, it would be necessary to ask about the real subject, and not about the Idea. For the Idea of the good will is not the doer. The intelligible self is an idea, not a reality. The real self is a sinner.

Therefore the question should run thus: how can a sinner be made a just man? The answer "through the will" is false, for the will itself is sinful. To put this question seriously means to put the question of faith, that is, the question about that which God alone can do. Only where the question is really asked about what God does is the ethical problem taken seriously. For only here is that taken seriously on which everything depends: how a sinful will may be turned into a good will. That the Reformers took this in such dead earnest shows that the ethical question was asked in greater seriousness than elsewhere. The perception of the *servum arbitrium*—thus the renunciation of Idealism—and the knowledge of justification through grace alone, faith, is the answer to this, the most serious question of ethics, the question of the doer.

This is the significance of justification through faith. In it the new subject of ethics is constituted. If any man be in Christ he is a new creature; for he has been placed in a new sphere. The New Testament and the doctrine of the Church express this with the strongest expressions they can find; they use the simile of birth. The man who is in Christ through faith is the man who has been "born again." This is the new creature, the new subject. This is the good workman, who does good works because he is good, or rather because he is in the Good, because he lives and breathes in the Good. For through faith he is in Christ, and Christ is his righteousness. Indeed, "imputed righteousness" is not a fiction but a divine word, a reality even though it may be a hidden reality. Thus the New Birth is not a postulate, it is not a "thou shalt," but it is a reality. The new man is not an idea, but he is "born," even though secretly, under the veil of the "old man."

From this standpoint then the whole ethic gains a new meaning. It is no longer an ethic of duty but an ethic of being, even if this "being" is highly paradoxical, namely, the *being* in Christ, the *being* through the Word. Hence the characteristic direction of this Ethos is not forwards but backwards, not whither but whence? This is what the Reformers mean by their fundamental distinction between righteousness of works and righteousness of faith. The righteousness of works—and every kind of ethic not based no justification by faith, therefore outside Christ, is work-righteousness—is that which has the good subject as its *goal*; the righteousness of faith is that which has the good subject as its *starting-point*. Life springs from faith. The "good" of man is the Will of God.

Hence, because here the Good is no longer a matter of duty but something which is given as a free gift, there is no longer anything "slavish" about it; it is "childlike," that is, spontaneous and voluntary. It is done not because it is demanded, but because in Christ we can do nothing else.[1] Hence it is no longer law, but love. For love is just the will that of itself does good. Here, and only here, is love founded, because here and here alone is the new subject founded, which does the Good not because he ought—good which we ought

---

[1] Here we are speaking of faith, not of the believer; it will be shown directly that we can never speak of a Christian only in these terms, but that he must also always be regarded as a disobedient child, who must he ordered to do his duty.

to do we cannot do because the sense of compulsion means that we are not good—but because he wills to do it. If what the Gospel says be true, if men are "in Christ," then there is to this extent a really good will, real love, as a possibility which is indeed not possible from the human side, but is a divine possibility. Whoever does not wish to reckon with this does not reckon with the reality of faith.

It was for this very reason that the Reformers cared so supremely that the ethical problem should cease to be a mere problem or a postulate, but that it should become a reality, that they laid stress so one-sidedly on the doctrine of Justification through faith alone. It was not lack of ethical interest, but just because they were in such dead earnest about the whole matter that they took this line. Because they were tired of the ideology of an ethic of duty—of righteousness through works—therefore they preached righteousness through faith alone; because they longed that man should not merely be told to do good, but that he should really *do* it.

Sixthly: Only through faith in Christ, the Mediator, does man gain a really ethical relation to historical reality.

The realistic judgment on history—in the ordinary sense of the word—runs thus: *semper idem*. Historical changes are only transformations of that which is ever the same; they only mean a new camping-place, a shifting of the scene. This is the Idealistic view: history is the realm of progress. For it means Spirit coming to consciousness of itself, the awakening of Spirit, which, like our awakening in the morning, is a continuous process of becoming conscious. Fatalistic Realism must paralyse action at its root. This Idealism of progress must lead to a Utopian over-estimate of the possibilities of human life; hence when contact with reality produces the inevitable reaction, terrible disappointments are the result, which end for their part in the resignation of despair, and complete loss of all faith in the reality of history. It is no accident that the name of the last great German Idealist is Schopenhauer.

The Christian faith knows neither the pessimism of the one nor the optimism of the other. It judges the world more sombrely than Schopenhauer: for it knows of sin, judgment,

and damnation; and it looks at it more optimistically than
Idealism: for it knows not merely of a progress within history,
but of the coming kingdom of eternity, of the resurrection
from the dead and of complete redemption. Because for it, and
for it alone, the Unique exists, is there here alone real decision
and thus real history. Uniqueness (*das Einmalige*), faith in the
Mediator, constitutes the only serious decision. Where the
Unique element, that is, the Mediator, is not known, there
also one knows nothing about real decision—faith—but merely
of that which is relatively decisive, of a relatively serious
decision; hence also only of an indefinite meaning of history.
The perception of the real significance of history, and therefore
the serious view of history, has come into the world through
the Christian faith, faith in the Mediator. History in the
qualified sense exists only through Christ. Hence it is only
since Christ that the historical problem has arisen. No philosopher of the ancient world perceived it. It has only become
visible in the light of the revelation—of the revelation which
is real in Christ.

But the Christian conception of history is certainly very
different from that of faith in "progress." For it is serious, and
faith in progress is superficial. It is serious because it believes
in the decision—thus in the Judgment, therefore not in progress.
For where the Judgment is the conclusion of history, there it
is evident that there is no more talk about progress. Just
because the Christian faith does not believe in progress, it
takes history seriously. For where men believe in progress,
there they know beforehand exactly how all will turn out.
This means there is no sense of serious responsibility in making
decisions. The critical attitude towards history, to see history
under the aspect of the coming Judgment: this is what it
means to take history seriously, as the scene of decisions, which,
by their very nature, are always the same decision—for or
against the decisive fact, the Unique, the Mediator—the
decision of faith. This is what history means: decision for or
against Christ. Because this decision takes place within history,
therefore and to this extent is history of importance.

The sum total of all these decisions faith calls the Church.
From the Christian point of view history is the history of the

Church. Through Christ world history comes to have the quality of Church history. And only through, and since, this qualification does world history exist.

The Christian does not believe in "progress" in the world. But he believes in the victory of the Kingdom of God, which now within history is called the Church. The word "Church" is here used in the sense of the fellowship of those who have made the decision of faith, thus in the sense in which it was used by the Reformers. If, in the strict sense of the word, the ethical question is the question of the "who," the Christian answer can be given in two words only—faith, the Church. For it is of the very essence of faith that it is not a private matter, but that it belongs to the social body of believers. There is no private Christianity, but only a Christianity in fellowship, hence in the Church. For the fellowship of faith is the Church. The Church is thus the ethical subject of fellowship. As there is real Good only in faith, so there is real fellowship only in the fellowship of faith, that is in the Church. Where the empirical Church does not exhibit this spirit of fellowship, it merely shows to how slight an extent it is a real Church.

Every human ethical system is baffled by the question: the individual or the community? For either we fall into a sociological determinism which suppresses the individual, or into an idealistic individualism which weakens the idea of fellowship till it becomes very thin and unsubstantial, either a fellowship of blood relationships or a mere fellowship in a common purpose. The Christian Church is neither of these. We are not born into the Church, yet the Church is not an artificial construction of man. The Church is the fellowship of faith into which we are received.

Thus the Church, the fellowship, is not something which is added to the faith of the individual, as a second thing, which possibly might not be added; the Church is there when faith is there. The individual enters the Church the moment he enters into faith.

Through the Church faith becomes historical. The growth of the Church, of the historical Kingdom of God, of the *ecclesia militans*, is the "hope of progress" of faith. But this hope is limited by the insight that the only kind of progress which can exist is that which is concerned with decision. Hence this growth remains hidden, like the Church itself, since the true Church, although it is an historical reality, is always hidden. There are no statistics for the progress of the Kingdom of Christ. Those statistics are only in the Book of Life into which we human beings cannot look. All that faith knows is this: that no growth in the Kingdom of God is thinkable which weakens the emphasis on decision. If the Good increases, evil also increases. The tares grow with the wheat until the harvest. Then only will the two be separated.

Hence also Christian action in the world is not one of progressive building up. Rather it resembles a sortie from a fortress more than a campaign of conquest, which goes forward from stage to stage. Christian action needs to return to the starting-point continually in order that it may not become something different, or something wrong. For always the one thing that matters is this: that we should live by faith, that God should be honoured; it consists in creating room for God. What is here created has no value of its own; at the best it can only be a pointer towards that which God does and will do. It is not "constitutive," built up bit by bit, from one stage to another. Even when it acts like this—and all creative work must proceed like this—the emphasis is not laid upon this. It is not this which is meant, but all is done for "the glory of God"; all is only good to the extent in which it is a reminder of the Good.

By this very fact it is truly ethical. For everything else means that the Good becomes materialized into the structure of civilization. All Humanist ethics are finally orientated by civilization, and thus make man the means to an impersonal end. The personal meaning of ethics can only be preserved where all that has been attained objectively is valued merely as the means of personal relationships, thus where all finally only serves one purpose: that we live by our faith, that God is allowed to speak His Word. Therefore even in the Christian Ethos the less personal spheres of influence—the State, economics, culture—are subordinated to the more narrow personal spheres, not, as in every kind of ethic of civilization, related to a higher sphere. Here alone the spell of quantitative abstract thought is broken, the idols of civilization are torn down, the personal meaning of life is brought to light: love, or to put it still more simply, the love of our neighbour. For we can only love our neighbour—for he alone is a person addressed by God—and we can only love him personally and directly—not by means of abstract media. But in this unconditionally personal behaviour even the self-determinism of the abstract historical forces is attacked most effectively. We can love our neighbour only "in Christ." This love is the way in which faith expresses itself.

* * *

"Faith, which worketh through love,"—tested by this criterion is not everything which has been said in this book, from the first page to the last, put to shame? If love is the experimental proof of the truth of Christian faith, according to the doctrine of this faith, then is not the lack of this proof absolutely overwhelming? Do not the figures of the lists of the fallen in the war, of the list of the rate of exchange, the statistics of the housing problem and the need of the poor, does not the terrible reality of wrong, violence, lying, and hatred in the midst of a society which for centuries has heard and believed the Christian message speak a language which puts every theological book in the wrong, convicting it of untruth?

In point of fact, all theological, philosophical, or scientific arguments against the Christian faith weigh very lightly in comparison with this inarticulate and sullen, but for this very reason impressive, accusation of non-moral reality. There is only one thing which is still more terrible, and this is one which often almost crushed a hero of faith like Luther: the accusation of our own conscience, which points to the contrast between that which ought to be the result of faith and that which actually takes place in our own lives.

But whence has this accusation its weight? Is it not precisely the truth of this faith, which turns on us, as against those who would like to boast of this faith as their own possession? Can it say anything other than this: why do you not believe better?

617

In the judgment which it passes on us, as "believers," lies the justification of the faith itself, and the region whence it comes. For how could it be made a reproach to the believer that he does not love better, if we did not know that love ought to issue from faith? Indeed, we need now only add: if the world had not experienced—however seldom—that where it is genuine real love springs out of real faith.

Thus the glimpse of our own reality which we can and must gain from the perception of faith becomes a warning, that we also, although we believe, yet never cease to be unbelievers, sinners, that thus faith is for us never merely a gift but also at the same time a demand: Repent, and believe the Gospel! Only in faith can this summons really be heard; but in faith it really is heard, as a demand. Therefore all that we have said about the connection between faith and love, the truth of Christ and the new life, is under one proviso. It is all true— in so far as we believe! Therefore when we, as real men, say that in faith we know that we ought to believe, a second point ought always to be added to the Word of faith, without which the Word would not be true for us: the Word of the Law of God. Faith does not need it, for faith is the fulfilling of the Law; but the man who believes does need it because he is always at the same time also one who does not believe. It is not once, but over and over again, that faith must pass through the discipline of the Law, through repentance, and the believer must as such be reminded and warned over and over again, by the Law, of that which is perfectly natural to faith.

Without this discipline of the Law faith becomes halting and indolent. But this discipline of the Law can only mean the remembrance of that which one knows and possesses in faith. Faith is never a fixed state—*fides non est otiosa*—it means a continual and ever-renewed obedient listening to the First Commandment, which includes within itself all the other commandments. The First Commandment also begins with the indicative: I AM the Lord thy God. But this indicative must be heard: Thou shalt have none other gods but ME. In this commandment *credere et sperare et diligere deum non monemur, hortamur, allicimur tantum, sed sub omnium maxima poena et culpa jubemur (hoc enim est deum habere)* (Luther). It is the Lord who commands—on pain of punishment—that we are to take His grace seriously. Faith would not be the serious decision it is were it not that behind the word of grace stands the whole seriousness of the First Commandment and thus the seriousness of all the other Commandments. Thus faith does not consist in becoming free from the Law, but in pressing through the abstract character of the Law in itself to the personal will which stands behind it, to the personal Will of God who is Love. The Law is not false as a whole, but only when it is set up as an independent impersonal court of appeal; but it is the eternal truth as soon as we see in it the Will of the merciful God who even in giving the law wills to create fellowship.

Christ is also the fulfilling of the Law, in the sense that in Him alone does the meaning of the Law first become revealed. It is not abrogated by Him, but He, the Mediator, has abrogated the impersonal abstract character of the Law and the distorted tendency of legalism, or righteousness through "works." Hence the Mediator can only be trusted by him who earnestly wrestles with the Law and also understands the Atonement in Christ from the point of view of the Law, as the Law can only be rightly understood from the point of view of the Mediator. This is why we said the Word of Christ is simply the First Commandment. The Word of faith is simply the answer to the question of conscience: what then shall we do? The Christ whom we know and recognize in faith is no other than the Lord who seeks for obedient followers. The Christian Faith is not rightly understood if it is not understood as a summons to the Imitation of Christ. For faith is the entrance into the movement of God in Christ, and it must also prove its reality by making sure that this movement actually takes place.

INDEX